Electron Scattering in Gases—From Cross Sections to Plasma Modeling

Electron Scattering in Gases—From Cross Sections to Plasma Modeling

Editor

Grzegorz Piotr Karwasz

MDPI • Basel • Beijing • Wuhan • Barcelona • Belgrade • Manchester • Tokyo • Cluj • Tianjin

Editor
Grzegorz Piotr Karwasz
University Nicolaus Copernicus
Poland

Editorial Office
MDPI
St. Alban-Anlage 66
4052 Basel, Switzerland

This is a reprint of articles from the Special Issue published online in the open access journal *Atoms* (ISSN 2218-2004) (available at: https://www.mdpi.com/journal/atoms/special_issues/ ElectronScatteringGases_PlasmaModeling).

For citation purposes, cite each article independently as indicated on the article page online and as indicated below:

LastName, A.A.; LastName, B.B.; LastName, C.C. Article Title. *Journal Name* **Year**, *Volume Number*, Page Range.

ISBN 978-3-0365-4557-8 (Hbk)
ISBN 978-3-0365-4558-5 (PDF)

© 2022 by the authors. Articles in this book are Open Access and distributed under the Creative Commons Attribution (CC BY) license, which allows users to download, copy and build upon published articles, as long as the author and publisher are properly credited, which ensures maximum dissemination and a wider impact of our publications.

The book as a whole is distributed by MDPI under the terms and conditions of the Creative Commons license CC BY-NC-ND.

Contents

About the Editor vii

Preface to "Electron Scattering in Gases—From Cross Sections to Plasma Modeling" ix

Grzegorz P. Karwasz
"Atoms" Special Issue (Electron Scattering in Gases—From Cross Sections to Plasma Modeling)
Reprinted from: *Atoms* 2022, 10, 54, doi:10.3390/atoms10020054 1

Sebastian Mohr, Maria Tudorovskaya, Martin Hanicinec and Jonathan Tennyson
Targeted Cross-Section Calculations For Plasma Simulations
Reprinted from: *Atoms* 2021, 9, 85, doi:10.3390/atoms9040085 7

Hyun-Kyung Chung, Mi-Young Song, Ji-Won Kwon, Myeong-Geon Lee, Jihoon Park, Namjae Bae, Jeamin Song, Gon-Ho Kim, Dipti and Yuri Ralchenko
Population Kinetics Modeling of Low-Temperature Argon Plasma
Reprinted from: *Atoms* 2021, 9, 100, doi:10.3390/atoms9040100 17

Sylwia Ptasinska
A Missing Puzzle in Dissociative Electron Attachment to Biomolecules: The Detection of Radicals
Reprinted from: *Atoms* 2021, 9, 77, doi:10.3390/atoms9040077 39

Adrián García-Abenza, Ana I. Lozano, Juan C. Oller, Francisco Blanco, Jimena D. Gorfinkiel, Paulo Limão-Vieira and Gustavo García
Evaluation of Recommended Cross Sections for the Simulation of Electron Tracks in Water
Reprinted from: *Atoms* 2021, 9, 98, doi:10.3390/atoms9040098 51

Mehdi Ayouz, Alexandre Faure, Jonathan Tennyson, Maria Tudorovskaya and Viatcheslav Kokoouline
Cross Sections and Rate Coefficients for Vibrational Excitation of H_2O by Electron Impact
Reprinted from: *Atoms* 2021, 9, 62, doi:10.3390/atoms9030062 65

Armando Francesco Borghesani
Accurate Electron Drift Mobility Measurements in Moderately Dense Helium Gas at Several Temperatures
Reprinted from: *Atoms* 2021, 9, 52, doi:10.3390/atoms9030052 77

Felix Laimer, Fabio Zappa, Elisabeth Gruber and Paul Scheier
Electron Ionization of Size-Selected Positively and Negatively Charged Helium Droplets
Reprinted from: *Atoms* 2021, 9, 74, doi:10.3390/atoms9040074 97

Łukasz Kłosowski and Mariusz Piwiński
Magnetic Angle Changer for Studies of Electronically Excited Long-Living Atomic States
Reprinted from: *Atoms* 2021, 9, 71, doi:10.3390/atoms9040071 113

Nafees Uddin, Paresh Modak and Bobby Antony
On the Electron Impact Integral Cross-Sections for Butanol and Pentanol Isomers
Reprinted from: *Atoms* 2021, 9, 43, doi:10.3390/atoms9030043 123

R.I. Campeanu and Colm T. Whelan
Few Body Effects in the Electron and Positron Impact Ionization of Atoms
Reprinted from: *Atoms* 2021, 9, 33, doi:10.3390/atoms9020033 135

Mahmudul H. Khandker, A. K. Fazlul Haque, M. M. Haque, M. Masum Billah, Hiroshi Watabe and M. Alfaz Uddin
Relativistic Study on the Scattering of $e^{\pm}$ from Atoms and Ions of the Rn Isonuclear Series
Reprinted from: *Atoms* **2021**, *9*, 59, doi:10.3390/atoms9030059 . . . . **149**

Luis A. Poveda, Marcio T. do N. Varella and José R. Mohallem
Vibrational Excitation Cross-Section by Positron Impact: A Wave-Packet Dynamics Study
Reprinted from: *Atoms* **2021**, *9*, 64, doi:10.3390/atoms9030064 . . . . **197**

Aloka Kumar Sahoo and Lalita Sharma
Electron Impact Excitation of Extreme Ultra-Violet Transitions in Xe^{7+}–Xe^{10+} Ions
Reprinted from: *Atoms* **2021**, *9*, 76, doi:10.3390/atoms9040076 . . . . **207**

Kamil Fedus
Elastic Scattering of Slow Electrons by Noble Gases—The Effective Range Theory and the Rigid Sphere Model
Reprinted from: *Atoms* **2021**, *9*, 91, doi:10.3390/atoms9040091 . . . . **231**

Rusudan I. Golyatina and Sergey A. Maiorov
Analytical Cross Section Approximation for Electron Impact Ionization of Alkali and Other Metals, Inert Gases and Hydrogen Atoms
Reprinted from: *Atoms* **2021**, *9*, 90, doi:10.3390/atoms9040090 . . . . **251**

Małgorzata Franz, Katarzyna Wiciak-Pawłowska and Jan Franz
Binary-Encounter Model for Direct Ionization of Molecules by Positron-Impact
Reprinted from: *Atoms* **2021**, *9*, 99, doi:10.3390/atoms9040099 . . . . **261**

Annarita Laricchiuta, Roberto Celiberto and Gianpiero Colonna
Electron Impact Ionization of Metastable States of Diatomic Molecules
Reprinted from: *Atoms* **2022**, *10*, 2, doi:10.3390/atoms10010002 . . . . **271**

Fabio Carelli, Kamil Fedus and Grzegorz Karwasz
Total Cross Sections for Electron and Positron Scattering on Molecules: In Search of the Dispersion Relation
Reprinted from: *Atoms* **2021**, *11*, 274, doi:10.3390/coatings11030274 . . . . **279**

About the Editor

Grzegorz Piotr Karwasz

Grzegorz Piotr Karwasz (born 1958) graduated in 1982 from Economics of Foreign Trade (Gdańsk University, Poland) and Technical Physics (Gdańsk Politechnics). PhD in Atomic Physics at Gdańsk University (1991) and habilitation (1997) in Experimental Physics at Nicolaus Copernicus University, Toruń. Employed at Gdańsk Politechnics (1982–1984), Institute of Fluid Flow Machines Polish Academy of Sciences (1984–1996), Pomeranian Pedagogical Academy (1996–2006). Presently heading the Didactics of Physics Division at NCU. In 1985/86 and 1990–2006 at Physics Department, University of Trento, Italy. Mid-term research fellowships at the Czech Academy of Science, Wayne State University in Detroit, Australian National University in Canberra, and the National Fusion Research Institute in Gunsan, Republic of Korea. Working in plasma physics, electron and positron scattering, positron annihilation, didactics of physics, and pedagogy. Awarded (2019) with the prize of Polish Physical Society for divulgation of physics. Scientific expert of the European Union, the Czech Academy of Sciences, and the International Atomic Energy Agency.

Preface to "Electron Scattering in Gases—From Cross Sections to Plasma Modeling"

Experimental studies of electron scattering in gases, at the beginning of the XXth century, contributed to the formulation of modern, wave-like Quantum Mechanics: The minimum of the cross sections in Ar, Kr, Xe, now known as the Ramsauer–Townsend's effect, was a puzzle for the theory, even within the old Quantum. An explosion of interest in atomic processes started with the advent of space flights. Dr Donald Rapp, the author of one of the most accurate sets of cross-sections for electron-impact ionization of molecules wrote me in February 2021: "I didn't realize it at the time, but I had the best possible position one could imagine. I was given a laboratory, a lab assistant, association with several co-workers, and a budget. And I could work on anything I chose, provided it had at least a distant relationship to the ionosphere."

The 1960s also witnessed "the combination of powerful new theoretical techniques together with the availability of electronic computers of increasing capacity", quoting the opera magna *The Theory of Atomic Collisions* by N.F. Mott and H.S.W. Massey. Today, cross-sections for electron (and positron) scattering are needed not only to understand atomic processes in planetary nebula and atmospheres of the Solar System, but first of all to model successfully plasma processes for numerous industrial implementations, starting with semiconductors. In concomitance, the versatility (and the precision) of theoretical methods starts to surpass the experiment.

Here, we present a "cross-section" of different approaches, different applications, different processes: from industrial plasmas [85, 100] to molecules of biological interest [62, 77, 98], from experiments at ultra-low temperatures [52, 74] to processes relevant for thermonuclear synthesis [76]. Thanks to a global response to the invitation, this volume hosts in an equilibrated manner experimental aspects [52, 71, 74, 98], ab-initio theories [33, 43, 59, 64, 76] and semi-empirical approaches [2, 90, 91, 97, 99], both to electron and positron scattering.

We hope that this volume may constitute a short but useful overview of scientific approaches and interests, as portrayed in 2021.

Grzegorz Piotr Karwasz
Editor

Editorial

"Atoms" Special Issue (Electron Scattering in Gases—From Cross Sections to Plasma Modeling)

Grzegorz P. Karwasz

Institute of Physics, Uniwersytet Mikołaja Kopernika w Toruniu, 87 100 Torun, Poland; karwasz@fizyka.umk.pl

Citation: Karwasz, G.P. "Atoms" Special Issue (Electron Scattering in Gases—From Cross Sections to Plasma Modeling). *Atoms* **2022**, *10*, 54. https://doi.org/10.3390/atoms10020054

Received: 5 May 2022
Accepted: 26 May 2022
Published: 27 May 2022

Publisher's Note: MDPI stays neutral with regard to jurisdictional claims in published maps and institutional affiliations.

Copyright: © 2022 by the author. Licensee MDPI, Basel, Switzerland. This article is an open access article distributed under the terms and conditions of the Creative Commons Attribution (CC BY) license (https://creativecommons.org/licenses/by/4.0/).

Experimental studies of electron scattering in gases, under the name of "cathode rays", started before the "official" discovery of the electron by J. J. Thompson (in 1897). At the beginning of the XXth century, experiments on electron scattering contributed to the formulation of modern, wave-like quantum mechanics; the minimum of the cross sections in Ar, Kr, Xe, now known as the Ramsauer–Townsend's effect (see [1] and references therein), cannot be explained even within "old" quantum mechanics. An explosion of the interest in atomic processes started with the advent of space flights. Dr Donald Rapp, the co-author of one of the most accurate measurements of electron-impact ionization of molecules [2], wrote the following in February 2021: "I didn't realize it at the time, but I had the best possible position one could imagine. I was given a laboratory, a lab assistant, association with several co-workers, and a budget. And I could work on anything I chose, provided it had at least a distant relationship to the ionosphere." Today, cross sections for electron (and positron) scattering are needed, not only to understand the atomic processes in planetary nebula and atmospheres of the solar system, but first of all to model plasma processes for numerous implementations, from semiconductor industries to thermonuclear reactors.

In this volume, we present a "cross-section" of different approaches, applications and processes, from industrial plasmas [3,4] to molecules of biological interest [5–7]; from experiments at ultra-low temperatures [8,9] to processes relevant for thermonuclear synthesis [10]. Thanks to a global response to the invitation, this volume hosts in an equilibrated manner the experimental aspects [6,8,9], ab-initio theories [7,10–12] and semi-empirical approaches [13–16], both for electron and positron scattering [11,15–17].

In principle, the more detailed our knowledge is of cross sections, the more precise modeling of plasma parameters can be carried out, but only in principle. Mohr et al. [3] stress that calculations of cross sections, in particular for the formation of neutral fragments and radicals in electron collisions, are time consuming. Therefore, even if the present methods, such as UK R-Matrix codes, are highly versatile, for chemical processes well-targeted modeling must be planned. Mohr et al. present an example of such an approach for the SF_6/O_2 mixtures used in semiconductor etching. The cross sections for the two "input" gases are known, but for the SOF_x species, which may be formed in the plasma, they are not known. The authors evaluate the unknown ionization and dissociation cross sections and then estimate the densities of electrons and radicals. The validity of this approach resides in the economizing computer (and man) power needed to model real situations in plasma reactors.

Chung et al. [4] apply cross sections to optical diagnostics of argon plasma. They assume the corona model, i.e., no collisional interaction between excited states, and no cascading in the de-excitation. The model includes numerous processes, such as stimulated absorption, collisional de-excitation, quenching of metastables on walls etc. More than 20,000 optical transitions are accounted for (primarily from NIST, LXCAT and other databases, and from different theories). Six models, based on alternative datasets, are compared with the authors' experiments with capacitively and inductively coupled plasma. The corona model applies somewhat better to the second type of reactor. Chung et al. show that the present knowledge of cross sections is vast, but other processes, such as quenching and recombination on walls, should be included to obtain more successful modeling.

Three papers discuss "edge-cutting" experiments in electron scattering. Ptasińska [5] presents a review on the role of very-low (below few V) electrons in radiation damage of living cells. The experiments (on molecules in gas phase) showed that low-energy electrons are resonantly captured by DNA constituents (sugars or nucleobases), via a dissociative attachment (DA) process. The experiments detected negatively charged fragments produced in such a dissociation. However, the DA mechanism with DNA does not explain the high lethality of ionizing radiation (electrons from ionization events are the main product of radiation slowing-down processes). In living cells, it is probably the water molecule, which via a resonant electron capture, produces OH and H radicals that together with solvated electrons "kill approximately 70% of cells". Therefore, Ptasińska proposes new experiments aiming to detect "the missing part" of the radiation damage, i.e., neutral radicals.

Collisions of electrons with nano-droplets is the conceptual pathway leading from scattering on single atoms to studies of condensed matter; single scattering events occur in the "bulk-like" environment. Liquid helium droplets are able to capture atoms and molecules, clusters may form inside them and the spectroscopy of cold molecules inside a neutral matrix is possible. Laimer et al. [9] used a tandem mass spectrometer to study the collision of electrically charged He droplets with electrons with variable energy (0–120 eV). By changing the energy of the first electron beam, from 40 eV to 30 eV, positively or negatively charged droplets, with up to 100 million He atoms, can be produced. For positively charged droplets and 22.5 eV collision energy, Laimer et al. observed predominantly a reduction in the charge, while for 120 eV, an increase in the charge was observed (i.e., additional ionization). Laimer et al. discuss several reaction channels, such as Penning ionization in the collision of two metastable He atoms, or electron detachment (combined with the ionization) in the collision of a metastable anion with a metastable He atom. Reactions, probably, undergo via resonant-like processes.

Helium, differently from Ar, Kr and Xe, does not show Ramsauer–Townend minimum in the integral elastic (and momentum transfer) cross sections. Borghesani [8] measured the drift velocities of electrons in moderately dense (up to 10 MPa) helium. Drift conditions (temperature, gas densities and the electric field) have been chosen to evidence the different regimes of scattering, including the low-field region where scattering is well approximated by a rigid-sphere model and the intermediate region where a bubble of solvated electron moves in the electrical field. The paper is an excellent matching between quantum and classical physics.

García-Abenza et al. [6] carried out a critical evaluation using recent data by Song et al. [18] for electron scattering on H_2O. Their methodology, which is "capable of delivering the most accurate datasets", combines both the theory (event-by-event Monte Carlo simulation and Geant4DNA code) and the experiment (the transmission of magnetically confined electrons in gas cell). The independent-atoms model was used to extend differential cross sections for elastic and inelastic scattering into angles that are not measurable in angular-distribution experiments (below 10° and above 130°). The comparison of the simulations with the transmission-current experiment shows that, particularly at high collision energies, more insight is needed into the differential cross sections, especially for inelastic processes with small energy losses.

In this context, the prototype of the so-called magnetic-angle changer spectrometer, projected by Kłosowski and Piwiński [19] to measure differential cross sections in a wide angular range, is particularly interesting. The device consists of as many as 30 pairs of circular wires arranged into coils. The task was to maintain the bending magnetic field low (below 1 mT), in order to avoid the influence of that field on the configurations/populations of metastable atoms in the region of scattering. Numerical simulations show that the spectrometer should allow measurements in the low-angle range, down to 0°. Above 60°, the spectrometer introduces a quite large (of few degrees) angular spread of the incident electron beam, which limits its use.

Total cross sections, which comprise elastic and inelastic processes (rotational, vibrational and electronic excitation, and ionization), are easily measured (see [1]), but are quite difficult to be calculated. Uddin et al. [20] calculated the total cross section for electron scattering (6–5000 eV energy) on butanol and pentanol isomers. They used spherical complex optical potential in which the static (Hartree–Fock), exchange (Hara's) and polarization potentials constitute the real part, and the energy-dependent, imaginary part is responsible for the "absorption" (i.e., electronic excitation and ionization) processes. For butan-1-ol, the comparison with experiments is possible as both the integral elastic and the total cross sections match the measurements well. The cross sections for different isomers (five within the pentanol and four within butanol group) show some differences only in the low energy range (below 20 eV).

The ionization of atoms and molecules, at least in the case of electron collisions, has rather vast experimental coverage. This allows us to test different theoretical and semi-empirical approaches, which, in turn, allow us to predict cross sections for species inaccessible for direct measurements, such as highly charged ions [10], molecular metastables [15] or metals [14].

Campeanu and Whelan [11] calculated triple differential cross sections (TDCS) both for positron and electron scattering on inert gases. The comparison between electrons and positrons allows one to test the exchange effects. Differential cross sections, and particularly those measured in coincidence experiments, bring much more information on the scattering processes than integral values. Campeanu and Whelan concentrated on scattering geometries in which the impinging electron loses more than half its energy, so the recoil effects of the nucleus are significant. Additionally, they modified the kinematics of scattering in order to identify possible role of distortion, post-collision interaction and interference effects. For electron scattering on helium and neon, the theoretical TDCS, different scattering geometries agree very well with the experiments. The paper shows the importance of few-body effects in the ionization process, including the interference effects for non-coplanar geometries and multiple scattering at high energies.

Laricchiuta et al. [21] applied the Binary-Encouter Bethe (BEB) approach to calculate the ionization cross section of the N_2 ($A\ ^3\Sigma_u^+$), CO ($a\ ^3\Pi$) and H_2 ($c\ ^3\Pi_u$) and ($a\ ^3\Sigma_g^+$) metastables. Orbital energies needed as the input data to BEB were obtained from the unrestricted Hartree–Fock approach. The N_2 metastable state is long-lived (2.4 s), so its presence significantly changes the kinetics of nitrogen discharges. Laricchiuta et al.'s results suggest that available experimental determinations may be underestimated by a factor of two. In turn, H_2 metastables show even higher total ionization cross sections, up to about 10×10^{-16} cm^2 at their maxima.

A similar model, derived from the BEB approach, has been applied by Franz et al. [15] for positron ionization of diatomic molecules. In the high energy limit, according to the Born approximation, positron and electron-scattering cross sections should merge. This has been theoretically and experimentally proved for H_2 at energies above 100 eV (see a recent review [22]) but is still uncertain for heavier targets. In particular, in the case of positron scattering and in the energy range between 10–100 eV, a high contribution comes from the formation of the bound electron-positron state (positronium), which leaves the target molecule in the ionized state, making the experimental distinction difficult. The two cases, ionization by electrons and positrons, should show different threshold dependences; after the ionization, the two electrons fly in the opposite directions (in the first case) or in the same direction (for the electron–positron pair). The BEB approach by Franz et al. takes into account these differences. For H_2 and N_2, the results with the "correct" threshold law reproduce the experimental data very well. The agreement is worse for O_2 and CO, but it can be also caused by uncertainties in experiments.

Golyatina and Maiorov [14] discuss integral ionization cross sections. They propose a simple, three-parameter power-like fit, deriving from early (1912) Thomson's formula. The authors make a vast review of experiments for as many as 28 atomic targets, starting from hydrogen to platinum and uranium, including noble gases and transitions metals. For the targets that received somewhat better experimental (and theoretical) coverage, such as alkali metals, the quality of the fit may be judged as good. However, as in the case of positron-impact ionization, more experiments are also needed for the electron ionization of metal vapors.

Two contributions discuss the vibrational excitation. This subject needs new approaches, as the simplified Born approximation works well only in some cases, such as the excitation of infrared-active modes. Ayouz et al. [7] present results for vibrational excitation (and de-excitation) of three modes in H_2O by electron impact, while Poveda et al. [17] demonstrate the excitation of the $\nu = 0 \rightarrow 1$ mode in H_2 by positron impact.

Ayouz et al. [7] used the fixed-nuclei reactace matrix, obtained numerically from the UK molecular R-Matrix code (UKRMol) with the Quantemol-N system. The calculation for the equilibrium geometry predicts the following 4 resonances: 2 narrow at 7.8 eV and 10 eV and 2 wider at 6.7 eV and 11 eV. The calculated excitation cross sections agree well with the recent "recommended" values [18] up to 4 eV. At higher energies, the resonant scattering increases significantly (by a factor of two, as compared to the theory) the vibrational excitation. For the stretching modes, different theories systematically underestimate the experiment. The choice of different orbital basis sets does not improve this discrepancy. Ayouz et al. hypothesized two possible reasons for this discrepancy, one physical, another numerical, including the capturing of the incoming electron into the molecule in the excited vibrational state and/or the underestimation of the polarization interactions in the close-coupling approach.

The vibrational excitation by positron impact, as in CF_4, follows the Born approximation. However, the annihilation rate for positrons colliding with molecules possessing numerous vibrational models, such as complex hydrocarbons, [23] shows sharp resonant enhancements just below the threshold for vibrational modes (we call them "Surko resonances"). Poveda et al. [17] used a wave-packet dynamics for the vibrational $\nu = 0 \rightarrow 1$ excitation of H_2 molecules by positron impact. They used well-established molecular parameters of the molecule (the internuclear distance and the polarizability), and a cut-off polarization. The model reproduces the experimental determination very well in the range from the threshold up to 3 eV. The same model with much higher polariziability values gives a sharp threshold peak, but does not change the cross sections at higher (1–3 eV) energies. This may be a valid indication for the explanation of "Surko" resonances, and links to the discussion of the vibrational excitation in H_2O.

Applications of atomic physics in thermonuclear plasmas require knowledge of cross sections for "exotic" systems, including heavy atoms and highly charged ions, for scattering energies up to tens of keV. The present volume brings two such contributions. Khandker et al. [12] calculated differential, integral elastic, momentum transfer, viscosity, total inelastic and grand total cross sections, together with spin polarization parameters for electron and positron scattering on Rn atoms and ions of radon isonuclear series (up to Rn^{+86}), in the energy range from 1 eV to 1 MeV. A short range complex optical potential has been used; for charged particles, this potential is supplemented by the Coulomb interaction; the Dirac partial wave analysis has been employed. Differential cross sections for electron scattering show phenomena related to the interference between partial waves (i.e., Ramsauer minima) at energies as high as 2000 eV. The absorption potential is particularly important at intermediate energies, up to 500 eV, decreasing elastic scattering by a factor of two. For positron scattering, the influence of the absorption potential persists up to 50 keV. Above 10 keV, the positron and electron scattering cross sections coincide.

Electron-impact excitations of dipole-allowed transitions in the extreme UV range of Xe^{+7}–Xe^{+10} ions were calculated by Sahoo and Sharma [10]. Cross sections for 9, 18, 75 and 57 transitions for Xe^{+7}, Xe^{+8}, Xe^{+9} and Xe^{+10} ions, respectively, have been calculated. The multi-configuration Dirac–Fock method with QED corrections was used for the atomic structure calculations. Cross sections were calculated in the relativistic distorted-wave approach. Generally, the energy levels and transition rates agree well with the available experiments and theories. Transitions that involve the change in the spin have lower cross sections than spin-conserving transitions. Sahoo and Sharma also give the fitting formula for the cross sections, including in the low energy range, a series of powers of energy (somewhat resembling the fit of the ionization cross sections by Golyatina and Mayorov [14]), and the Bethe–Born formula at high energies. Rate coefficients are given for electron temperatures from 5 to 100 eV.

The opposite, i.e., near-to-zero, energy range is "attacked" by Fedus, who re-proposes the modified-effective range theory. This is a semi-empirical approach that allows one to relate the integral elastic, differential elastic and momentum transfer cross sections in the very low energy range. As in this energy range only few partial waves contribute significantly to scattering, the method uses few fitting parameters, such as the zero-energy cross section (i.e., the scattering length) and the effective range. In the MERT fit used in the past both by experimentalists and theoreticians, these were cross section developed into series of power of energy. As a consequence, the applicability of the fit was limited to energies below 1 eV. A modification that consists of the development not of cross sections but of phase shifts [24] allowed one to extend the applicability of MERT up to the threshold for inelastic processes, both for positron and electron scattering. Fedus re-analyses experimental cross sections, both from beam and swarm experiments, in five noble gases (He-Xe). Fedus gives MERT parameters, together with their uncertainties, for single experimental sets of data, as well as for the whole ensemble of data. For He and Ne, Fedus additionally applies the hard-sphere model, similar to the work of Borghesani [8]. The model with radii of the hard spheres obtained from MERT analysis reproduces the phase shift for the s, p, d waves up to 1–3 eV, in pretty good agreement with other theories.

The volume concludes with our contribution [16] that proposes the re-opening of the discussion on some possible "invariance" parameters in electron and positron scattering. All the contributions of this volume relate total and partial cross sections to other atomic/molecular parameters. The question is if all these cross sections are somehow inter-related, i.e., if the rise of the ionization cross section is dependent on the decreasing of the elastic cross section. The absorption model by Khandker et al. [12] would suggest so. However, even this volume shows that the low and high energy ranges are treated separately, both in experiments and in theories. Can we "sew" back the energy ranges, and consider the total (i.e., elastic and inelastic) cross sections in the "whole" energy range, from zero to infinity? Can we further relate such an integral part of the total cross section with other molecular parameters, such as the total number of electrons or polarizability? For our study conducted for electron and positron scattering on molecules that received sufficient experimental coverage, N_2, CO_2, CH_4, CF_4 would suggest some relations, but they are still far from being conclusive.

We hope that this volume may constitute a short but useful overview of the scientific approaches and interests in electron and positron scattering and plasma applications, as portrayed in December 2021.

Funding: This research received no external funding.

Conflicts of Interest: The author declares no conflict of interest.

References

1. Zecca, A.; Karwasz, G.P.; Brusa, R.S. One century of experiments on electron-atom and molecule scattering: A critical review of integral cross-sections. *Rev. Nuovo Cim.* **1996**, *19*, 3. [CrossRef]
2. Rapp, D.; Englander-Golden, P. Total Cross Sections for Ionization and Attachment in Gases by Electron Impact. I. Positive Ionization. *J. Chem. Phys.* **1965**, *43*, 1464. [CrossRef]
3. Mohr, S.; Tudorovskaya, M.; Hanicinec, M.; Tennyson, J. Targeted Cross-Section Calculations for Plasma Simulations. *Atoms* **2021**, *9*, 85. [CrossRef]
4. Chung, H.-K.; Song, M.-Y.; Kwon, J.-W.; Lee, M.-G.; Park, J.; Bae, N.; Song, J.; Kim, G.-H.; Dipti; Ralchenko, Y. Population Kinetics Modeling of Low-Temperature Argon Plasma. *Atoms* **2021**, *9*, 100. [CrossRef]
5. Ptasinska, S. A Missing Puzzle in Dissociative Electron Attachment to Biomolecules: The Detection of Radicals. *Atoms* **2021**, *9*, 77. [CrossRef]

6. García-Abenza, A.; Lozano, A.I.; Oller, J.C.; Blanco, F.; Gorfinkiel, J.D.; Limão-Vieira, P.; García, G. Evaluation of Recommended Cross Sections for the Simulation of Electron Tracks in Water. *Atoms* **2021**, *9*, 98. [CrossRef]
7. Ayouz, M.; Faure, A.; Tennyson, J.; Tudorovskaya, M.; Kokoouline, V. Cross Sections and Rate Coefficients for Vibrational Excitation of H_2O by Electron Impact. *Atoms* **2021**, *9*, 62. [CrossRef]
8. Borghesani, A.F. Accurate Electron Drift Mobility Measurements in Moderately Dense Helium Gas at Several Temperatures. *Atoms* **2021**, *9*, 52. [CrossRef]
9. Laimer, F.; Zappa, F.; Gruber, E.; Scheier, P. Electron Ionization of Size-Selected Positively and Negatively Charged Helium Droplets. *Atoms* **2021**, *9*, 74. [CrossRef]
10. Sahoo, A.K.; Sharma, L. Electron Impact Excitation of Extreme Ultra-Violet Transitions in $Xe7^+$–$Xe10^+$ Ions. *Atoms* **2021**, *9*, 76. [CrossRef]
11. Campeanu, R.I.; Whelan, C.T. Few Body Effects in the Electron and Positron Impact Ionization of Atoms. *Atoms* **2021**, *9*, 33. [CrossRef]
12. Khandker, M.H.; Haque, A.K.F.; Haque, M.M.; Billah, M.M.; Watabe, H.; Uddin, M.A. Relativistic Study on the Scattering of $e\pm$ from Atoms and Ions of the Rn Isonuclear Series. *Atoms* **2021**, *9*, 59. [CrossRef]
13. Fedus, K. Elastic Scattering of Slow Electrons by Noble Gases—The Effective Range Theory and the Rigid Sphere Model. *Atoms* **2021**, *9*, 91. [CrossRef]
14. Golyatina, R.I.; Maiorov, S.A. Analytical Cross Section Approximation for Electron Impact Ionization of Alkali and Other Metals, Inert Gases and Hydrogen Atoms. *Atoms* **2021**, *9*, 90. [CrossRef]
15. Franz, M.; Wiciak-Pawłowska, K.; Franz, J. Binary-Encounter Model for Direct Ionization of Molecules by Positron-Impact. *Atoms* **2021**, *9*, 99. [CrossRef]
16. Carelli, F.; Fedus, K.; Karwasz, G. Total Cross Sections for Electron and Positron Scattering on Molecules: In Search of the Dispersion Relation. *Atoms* **2021**, *9*, 97. [CrossRef]
17. Poveda, L.A.; Varella, M.T.d.N.; Mohallem, J.R. Vibrational Excitation Cross-Section by Positron Impact: A Wave-Packet Dynamics Study. *Atoms* **2021**, *9*, 64. [CrossRef]
18. Song, M.-Y.; Yoon, J.-S.; Cho, H.; Karwasz, G.P.; Kokoouline, V.; Nakamura, Y.; Tennyson, J. "Recommended" cross sections for electron collisions with molecules. *Eur. Phys. J. D* **2020**, *74*, 60. [CrossRef]
19. Kłosowski, Ł.; Piwiński, M. Magnetic Angle Changer for Studies of Electronically Excited Long-Living Atomic States. *Atoms* **2021**, *9*, 71. [CrossRef]
20. Uddin, N.; Modak, P.; Antony, B. On the Electron Impact Integral Cross-Sections for Butanol and Pentanol Isomers. *Atoms* **2021**, *9*, 43. [CrossRef]
21. Laricchiuta, A.; Celiberto, R.; Colonna, G. Electron Impact Ionization of Metastable States of Diatomic Molecules. *Atoms* **2022**, *10*, 2. [CrossRef]
22. Karwasz, G.P.; Karawacki, M.; Carelli, F.; Fedus, K. Hydrogen molecule as seen in electron and positron scattering. *Mol. Phys.* **2022**, e2070087. [CrossRef]
23. Sullivan, J.P.; Gilbert, S.J.; Surko, C.M. Excitation of Molecular Vibrations by Positron Impact. *Phys. Rev. Lett.* **2001**, *86*, 1494. [CrossRef] [PubMed]
24. Idziaszek, Z.; Karwasz, G.P. Applicability of modified effective-range theory to positron-atom and positron-molecule scattering. *Phys. Rev. A* **2006**, *73*, 064701. [CrossRef]

Article

Targeted Cross-Section Calculations For Plasma Simulations

Sebastian Mohr [1,*,†], Maria Tudorovskaya [1,†], Martin Hanicinec [1,2,†] and Jonathan Tennyson [2,†]

1. Quantemol Ltd., 320 Angel, 320 City Road, London EC1V 2NZ, UK; tudorovskaya@gmail.com (M.T.); hanicinecm@quantemol.com (M.H.)
2. Department of Physics and Astronomy, University College, Gower St., London WC1E 6BT, UK; j.tennyson@ucl.ac.uk
* Correspondence: s.mohr@quantemol.com
† These authors contributed equally to this work.

Abstract: Gathering data on electron collisions in plasmas is a vital part of conducting plasma simulations. However, data on neutral radicals and neutrals formed in the plasma by reactions between different radicals are usually not readily available. While these cross-sections can be calculated numerically, this is a time-consuming process and it is not clear from the outset which additional cross-sections are needed for a given plasma process. Hence, identifying species for which additional cross-sections are needed in advance is highly advantageous. Here, we present a structured approach to do this. In this, a chemistry set using estimated data for unknown electron collisions is run in a global plasma model. The results are used to rank the species with regard to their influence on densities of important species such as electrons or neutrals inducing desired surface processes. For this, an algorithm based on graph theory is used. The species ranking helps to make an informed decision on which cross-sections need to be calculated to improve the chemistry set and which can be neglected to save time. The validity of this approach is demonstrated through an example in an SF_6/O_2 plasma.

Keywords: cross-section calculations; R-matrix; plasma simulation

1. Introduction

Plasma simulations are vital tools in both academic and industrial settings to investigate plasma discharges in order to gain a better understanding of the underlying processes and improve plasma applications. In general, plasma simulations consist of two domains: the physical model, such as fluid or particle-based numerical model; and the chemistry set which describes the chemical reactions taking place in the plasma. For a successful simulation, both the physical model and the chemistry need to be chosen carefully so that they take all important effects into account; on the other hand, the investigator does not want to spend time on, for example, gathering data on chemical reactions which ultimately do not have a significant influence on the results or include those in the chemistry set which potentially increases the calculation time significantly without any benefit. One type of data which are regularly missing for a complete chemistry set are cross-sections for electron collisions with neutral particles which are formed in the plasma; especially in gas mixtures with multiple molecular gases, new species are created by chemical reactions between the fragments of electron collision dissociation. Such cross-sections can be calculated, for example, with the UK R-Matrix codes [1,2]. However, this is a time-consuming process and calculating cross-sections for all possible species formed might not be necessary as their impact on important plasma parameters such as the density of electrons or neutrals participating in desired surface reactions is negligible. Therefore, we present a structured approach to identify species which have a significant influence on the discharge before conducting precise cross-section calculations; this allows the investigator to improve the chemistry set without spending time on unnecessary calculations. The paper is structured as follows: First we present the different steps in this approach. It requires running a global plasma model, so a short overview of the model used is given. Then the method, based on the directed relation graph theory [3–6], of identifying key species for which cross-sectional data are missing is presented. This is followed by an overview of the actual cross-section calculations. After the general discussion, an example of using this method for an SF_6/O_2 plasma [7–17] is given, showing the impact of adding new cross-sectional data to a chemistry set using estimated data for electron collisions. Finally, conclusions are drawn.

2. Materials and Methods

In this work, we present a methodical approach to identify species with unknown cross-sections in a plasma chemistry set for which precise cross-section calculations improve the accuracy of the plasma simulation significantly. On the other hand, this also prevents one from performing time-consuming cross-section calculations which ultimately will not have a significant influence. This method consists of three steps:

- Running a plasma simulation;
- Identifying species significantly influencing the densities of specified target species;
- Calculating missing cross-sections.

2.1. Plasma Simulation

In the first step, a plasma simulation is conducted to produce densities and, specifically, production and consumption rates in both the gas phase and via plasma-surface interactions. In general, any kind of plasma simulation from which these rates can be extracted can be used; to keep the calculation time short, a global plasma model is the recommended choice, however. In this work, we use the Quantemol GlobalModel which is available online in Quantemol DataBase (QDB) [18], a plasma chemistry database. Detailed documentation can also be found in QDB, see https://quantemoldb.com as of 20 October 2021. In short, this global model solves the reactor-averaged continuity equations for heavy particles and the electron energy balance equation. The electron density is obtained via charge neutrality. The input parameters are power, pressure, neutral gas temperature, flows, and geometrical factors to determine the power density and diffusive losses. Rates for chemical reactions, for both electrons and ions, are characterised by parameterized rate coefficients; currently the modified Arrhenius form is supported. The values of the parameters can be obtained from Maxwellian electron energy distribution functions (EEDF) or ones obtained from a Boltzmann solver by fitting them to a set of electron temperature–rate coefficient pairs. In this work, Maxwellian EEDFs were used to keep the calculation time short. The result of the global model comprises the densities of all used species and the electron temperature. From these, the rates for both gas phase and plasma–surface interactions can easily be obtained in combination with the reaction set and the geometrical factors. In order to use the model to identify important species with missing cross-sections, electron collisions for these species need to be included. In the absence of precise data, this means that estimated rate coefficients, for example in analogy to the same processes for similar species, must be used. This way, the influence of a specific species can at least be estimated, if not precisely predicted.

2.2. Identifying Key Species

An algorithmic method is used to identify which species have a significant influence on the modelled densities of the set of user-specified species, referred to as species of interest. The set of species of interest is one of the inputs to the method, and needs to be identified by the researcher. The species of interest will generally be tailored to a specific modelling application. As an example, some major etchant species might be appropriately identified as species of interest for a specific etching process model, as well as electrons (as the electron density is a fundamental plasma parameter). The method is loosely based on the directed relation graph (DRG) theory of Lu and Law [3–5], originally developed for the combustion modelling community, but adapted for a plasma environment and expanded to also include the effects of plasma–surface interactions. Only a brief overview of the algorithm is given here, while the reader is referred to the full description of the fast graph–theoretical species ranking method given in [6].

To identify which species significantly influence the densities of some of the specified species of interest, a directed graph is instantiated with all the species present in the modelled system represented by the graph nodes. The directed edges in the graph are weighted by the direct interaction coefficients, which are generally functions of the reaction rates R_j of the volumetric and surface reactions in the chemistry set, and represent a measure of asymmetric coupling between two species (or the edge nodes) that are directly related through some of the reactions. Coupling between two species, however, exists even if they do not share any elementary reactions. The *indirect asymmetric coupling coefficients* W_{AB} between species A and B are therefore defined, reflecting the global (often indirect) effect of the presence of species A (or rather all of its reactions) on the modeled density of the species B. The indirect coupling coefficients are computed by a methodology based on the well-established Dijkstra's search for the "shortest path" in the chemistry graph [19].

Each species X_i is then given a ranking score C, such as

$$C_i = \max_k W_{X_i X_k}, \qquad (1)$$

where the index k runs over all the species of interest specified by the user, while the index i runs over all the remaining species. The input to the method (next to the set of species of interest) are the reaction rates of all the volumetric and surface reactions in the chemistry set (obtained from the plasma simulation, as described in Section 2.1) The output is a listing of all the species (except the species of interest), ranked with regard to how much they influence the densities of the species of interest. This allows one to make an informed decision on what additional rigorous cross-section calculations are required. It should be noted that there is no strict criterion on which ranking score threshold distinguishes significant species, so this still lies within one's discretion. For example, one might first aim to calculate cross-sections for reactions without precise data involving the higher-ranked species, and if that proves not to change the results for the species of interest significantly, one might neglect the lower-ranked species.

2.3. Cross-Section Calculations

In this work, ionization and dissociation cross-sections for SOF_4 are calculated with the QEC (Quantemol-Electron Collisions) software developed by Quantemol Ltd for calculating electron collision properties [2]. The calculations are based on the ab initio R-Matrix theory [20], specifically, it employs the UKRmol+ code suite [1]. In order to ensure good convergence, the cc-pVDZ basis set and configuration interaction level of theory was employed for the calculations allowing for excited electron configurations. There were 52 electrons frozen in 26 orbitals, while the active space was 4 fully occupied and 4 virtual orbitals.

Ionization cross-sections are calculated using the semi-empirical Binary-Encounter-Bethe (BEB) method [21]. The implementation of BEB within QEC uses Hartree–Fock wave functions and Koopman's theorem to provide thresholds to ionization [22] which are obtained from the quantum chemistry code MOLPRO [23].

The total dissociation cross-sections are obtained by adding up the excitation cross-sections to dissociative states of the target molecule. The dissociation limit is calculated by building a potential energy curve. Stretching the S-F bond(s) and the S-O bond and calculating the total energies at these stretched geometries is carried out in order to determine the most likely ionisation channel. We find that S-F bond breaking is more likely to occur. In this approximation, the state is considered dissociative if the excitation energy exceeds the dissociation energy. According to [24], the bond strength is 4.2 eV while the excited state is found at 8.5 eV above the ground state. Therefore, we consider all excited states dissociative. Moreover, the excitation energy is more than twice the bond breaking energy, and we assume that 2 S-F bonds will be broken in the dissociation process.

3. Example SF$_6$/O$_2$ Plasma

SF$_6$/O$_2$ discharges are commonly used, for example, for etching silicon [7–17]. The main chemical etchant is atomic F [10,11,14,16,17]. The addition of oxygen can serve two purposes; they induce reactions of the form

$$SF_x + O \rightarrow SOF_{x-1} + F \qquad (2)$$

which increase the density of atomic F [7,9,16]. On the other hand, oxygen atoms can form a protective layer on the side wall of an etched trench, prohibiting isotropic chemical etching by F [8,11–15,17]. Cross-section sets for SF$_6$ and O$_2$ separately are quite easily obtained. However, no such data exist in ready-to-use form for the SOF$_x$ species generated by reaction (2). It is, however, conceivable that under specific process conditions, the ionization and dissociation of these species can significantly contribute to the respective production processes as well as the collisional electron energy losses. Hence, we present an example of how to use the discussed method to identify significant missing cross-sections and their calculation.

For the first step, the initial plasma simulation, we constructed an SF$_6$/O$_2$ set the following way:

- Electron collision processes for O$_2$ and O species were taken from [25–27];
- Electron collision processes for SF$_x$ were taken from [28–30];
- Electron collision processes for F were taken from [31];
- Neutral–Neutral reactions, specifically the creation of SOF$_x$ species, were taken from [7];
- Ion–Ion recombination and charge exchange, both symmetric and asymmetric, were included for all possible combinations with generic rate coefficients;
- Electron collision ionization and dissociation for SOF$_x$ were included with estimated rate coefficients in analogy to SF$_x$, e.g., SF$_5$ rate coefficients were used for SOF$_4$. We assumed that the neutral dissociation process splits one F and the ionization produces the SOF$_x^+$ ion. One exception is SOF$_4$ which produces SOF$_3^+$ + F on ionization.

For similar reaction sets used in plasma simulations see, for example, [15,16]

The global model was run using this set with the following process parameters:

- Power: 500 W;
- Pressure: 10 Pa;
- Radius: 10 cm;
- Height: 10 cm;
- Total flow: 100 sccm;
- Relative oxygen flow: 10–90%.

It should be noted that these process parameters are not intended to reproduce a specific experiment/process but were chosen to demonstrate the effect of using our proposed method.

The species ranking algorithm was employed with F and electrons as species of interest. Figure 1 shows the 5 highest ranking species for a relative oxygen flow of 50%. Out of the SOF$_x$ species SOF$_4$ and SOF$_3$ are among them, with SOF$_4$ ranking higher. Thus, ionization and dissociation cross-sections for SOF$_4$ were calculated.

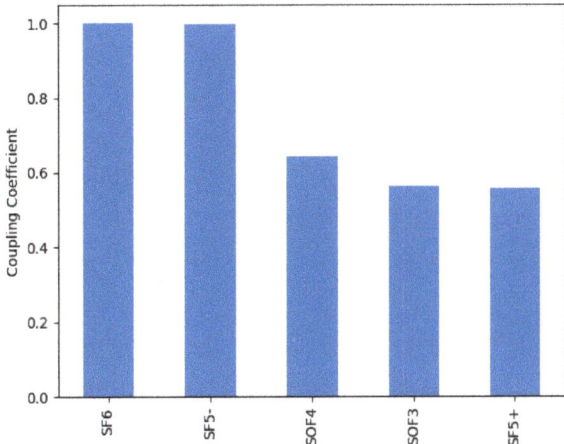

Figure 1. Species ranking with regard to the productions of electrons and F for a relative oxygen flow of 50%. Cross-sections for all SOF_x species are estimated.

Figure 2 shows the calculated ionization cross-section and resulting rate coefficient in comparison with the estimated one; Figure 3 shows the same for the dissociation. We observe some major differences:

- The calculated ionization cross-section is significantly larger than the estimated ones, by about a factor of 4 throughout the entire energy range up to a 1000 eV. However, the threshold energy is also larger, 15.19 eV compared to 11.8 eV for the estimated cross-sections. As a result, the ionization rate coefficient for the calculated cross-section is smaller for low electron temperatures and larger for high electron temperatures. The rate coefficients differ by about a factor of 2 at most.
- While the calculated dissociation cross-section shows significantly smaller values over a large range of energies, it also has a lower threshold energy; concerning the rate coefficients, the larger values of the estimated cross-section has a larger influence than the higher threshold energy. Hence, the estimated rate coefficient is significantly larger than the precisely calculated one over the majority of the investigated electron temperature range.
- The analysis of the neutral dissociation also showed that a breakup into $SOF_2 + 2F$ is more likely than into $SOF_3 + F$ (see the explanation above). Hence, this dissociation reaction was also changed with regard to the reaction products.

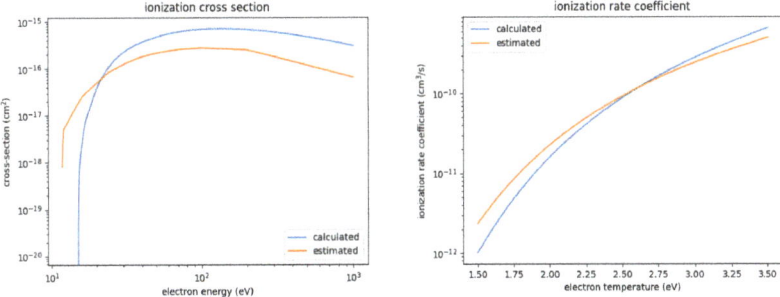

Figure 2. Calculated and estimated ionization cross-section and rate coefficient for SOF_4.

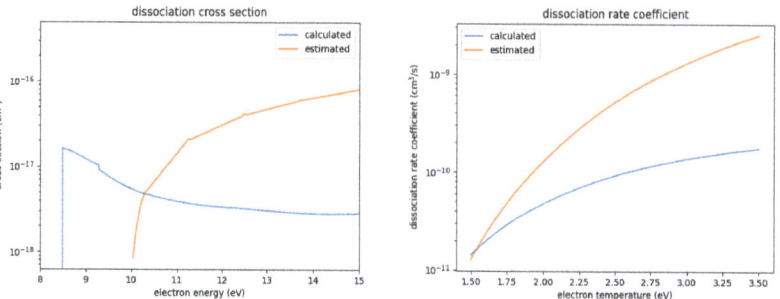

Figure 3. Calculated and estimated dissociation cross-section and rate coefficient for SOF_4.

To illustrate the effect of using calculated cross-sections instead of estimated ones, Figure 4 shows the density for F and electrons for a varied oxygen flow under otherwise the same process conditions. The calculated, precise cross-sections yield consistently higher densities of both F and electrons; only for very small oxygen flows <20% no significant difference is observed.

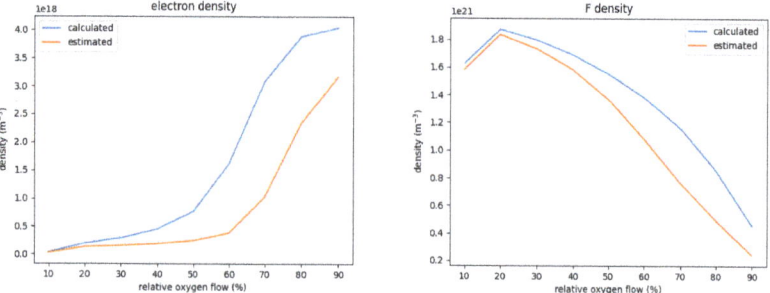

Figure 4. Electron and F density for a variation of the relative oxygen flow. The graphs compare the respective densities between the chemistry set with precisely calculated and the set with estimated cross-sections for the dissociation and ionization of SOF_4.

The higher density of F for the set with the calculated cross-sections can be explained by the significantly higher electron density which increases the production of F from SOF_4 despite the smaller rate coefficient. The higher electron density in turn is a result of differences in the energy necessary to create one electron-ion pair ϵ. This is defined as

$$\epsilon = \epsilon_{ion} + \sum_i \frac{\epsilon_i k_i}{k_{ion}} \qquad (3)$$

with the ionization potential ϵ_{ion}, the characteristic energy loss per collision ϵ_i and the rate coefficients k_{ion} for ionization and k_i for other electron collisions. The sum is taken over all other collision types. This parameter determines the plasma density achieved in a given gas mixture; the lower ϵ, the higher the plasma density. Figure 5 shows this energy for SOF_4 using the estimated and calculated rate coefficients. As can be seen, ϵ is about an order of magnitude smaller for the calculated rate coefficients, mostly as a result of the much smaller rate coefficient for dissociation. For relative oxygen flows above 20%, SOF_4 is one of the most abundant neutrals, only topped by either F or O. Figure 6 shows the ϵ for SOF_4, F, and O weighted by their relative densities for each simulated case. As can be seen, when using the estimated cross-sections, electron collisions with SOF_4 significantly contribute to the collisional energy losses and can even be the major contributors. When using the precisely calculated ones, however, its weighted ϵ is at least one order of magnitude smaller than either the one for F or O both of which do not differ significantly between the different sets. This leads to the significantly increased electron density for the set using calculated cross-sections.

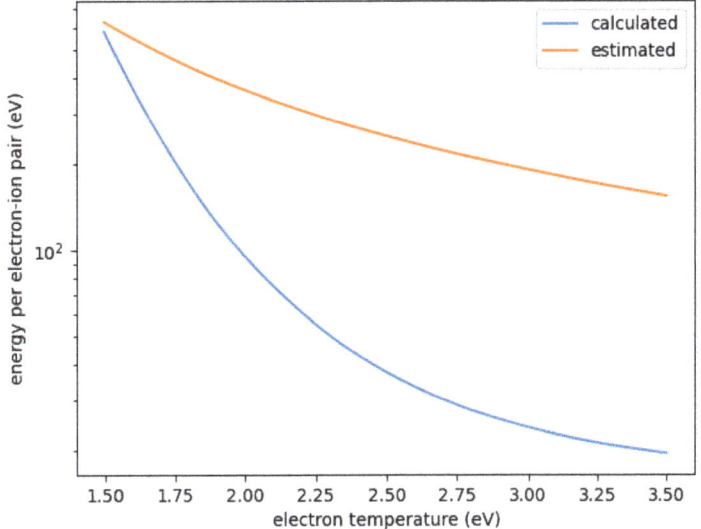

Figure 5. Energy per electron–ion pair for SOF_4 as a function of electron temperature derived from calculated and estimated cross-sections.

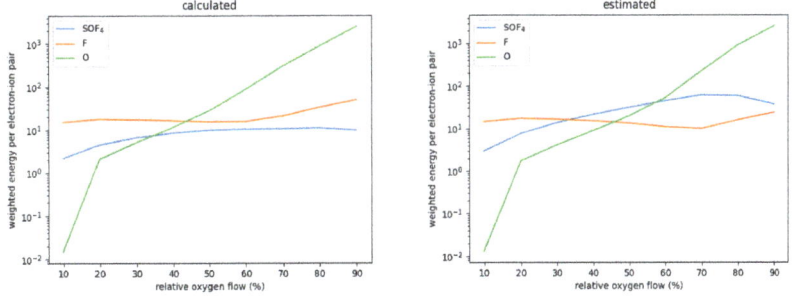

Figure 6. Electron energy per electron–ion pair weighted by their respective relative densities for SOF_4, F, and O as a function of the relative oxygen flows.

Furthermore, if we repeat the ranking on the simulation using the calculated cross-sections, we see in Figure 7 that SOF_3 is now missing from the top-ranked species due to the missing dissociation channel from SOF_4. Other SOF_x also do not appear, so it is unlikely that calculation of cross-sections for these would improve the simulation significantly. Therefore, by doing the analysis via the species ranking we could

- improve the accuracy of our plasma simulation by calculating precise cross-sections which were formerly missing and had to be estimated;
- save time by ruling out species for which precise cross-section calculations will unlikely improve the simulation significantly.

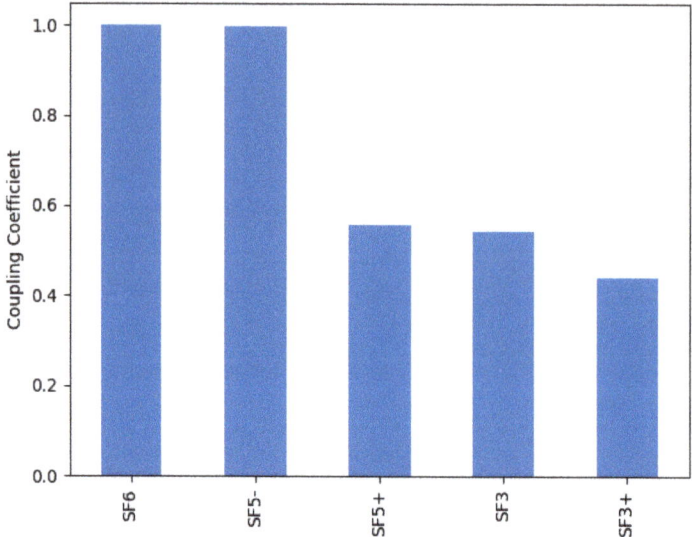

Figure 7. Species ranking with regard to the productions of electrons and F for a relative oxygen flow of 50%. Cross-sections for SOF_4 are precisely calculated.

4. Conclusions

We have presented a method to identify important missing cross-sections in a chemistry set and how adding them to a chemistry set affects the results of plasma simulations. The method consists of three steps:

- Run a plasma simulation such as a global model with a chemistry set containing estimates for missing cross-sections.
- Use the results of the plasma simulation in a species ranking algorithm. This identifies the species with missing cross-sections who potentially influence the densities of target species such as major etchants.
- Calculate precise cross-sections for high-ranking species and substitute these for the estimated ones.

This method gives a fast option to identify for which species precise cross-sections are needed and for which more precise data are not necessary to significantly improve the results of the simulation, preventing wasted time on unnecessary calculations.

This method was demonstrated for an SF_6/O_2 plasma. For a specific set of process conditions, SOF_4 and SOF_3 were identified as potential targets for precise cross-section calculations. As higher-ranking species, first only cross-sections for SOF_4 were calculated. Adding them to the existing set showed major differences in both the density of F and electrons. Furthermore, SOF_3 was not among the highest-ranking species anymore, so the calculation of cross-sections for this species could be skipped. Hence, the suitability of the proposed method to quickly improve plasma simulations via targeted cross-sections calculations was demonstrated.

Author Contributions: S.M. carried out the plasma simulations and analysis of its results. M.T. calculated the cross-sections for SOF_4. M.H. wrote the global model and the ranking algorithm. J.T. advised on the cross-section calculations and ranking algorithm. All authors have read and agreed to the published version of the manuscript.

Funding: Martin Hanicinec thanks EPSRC for a CASE studentship under grant EP/N509577/1.

Data Availability Statement: Reactions data used in this project is available from the QDB database.

Conflicts of Interest: All authors declare an involvement with Quantemol Ltd. who retail both the QEC expert system and the QDB database.

References

1. Mašín, Z.; Benda, J.; Gorfinkiel, J.D.; Harvey, A.G.; Tennyson, J. UKRmol+: A suite for modelling of electronic processes in molecules interacting with electrons, positrons and photons using the R-matrix method. *Comput. Phys. Commun.* **2020**, *249*, 107092. [CrossRef]
2. Cooper, B.; Tudorovskaya, M.; Mohr, S.; O'Hare, A.; Hanicinec, M.; Dzarasova, A.; Gorfinkiel, J.; Benda, J.; Mašín, Z.; Al-Refaie, A.; et al. Quantemol Electron Collision: An expert system for performing UKRmol+ electron molecule collision calculations. *Atoms* **2019**, *7*, 97. [CrossRef]
3. Lu, T.; Law, C.K. A directed relation graph method for mechanism reduction. *Proc. Combust. Inst.* **2005**, *30*, 1333–1341. [CrossRef]
4. Lu, T.; Law, C.K. Linear time reduction of large kinetic mechanisms with directed relation graph: n-Heptane and iso-octane. *Combust. Flame* **2006**, *144*, 24–36. [CrossRef]
5. Lu, T.; Law, C.K. On the applicability of directed relation graphs to the reduction of reaction mechanisms. *Combust. Flame* **2006**, *146*, 472–483. [CrossRef]
6. Hanicinec, M.; Mohr, S.; Tennyson, J. Fast species ranking for iterative species-oriented skeletal reduction of chemistry sets. *Plasma Sources Sci. Technol.* **2021**, *29*, 125024. [CrossRef]
7. Ryan, K.R.; Plumb, I.C. A model for the etching of silicon in SF_6/O_2 plasmas. *Plasma Chem. Plasma Process.* **1990**, *10*, 207–229. [CrossRef]
8. Bartha, J.W.; Greschner, J.; Puech, M.; Maquin, P. Low temperature etching of Si in high density plasma using SF_6/O_2. *Microelectron. Eng.* **1995**, *27*, 453–456. [CrossRef]
9. Pateau, A.; Rhallabi, A.; Fernandez, M.C.; Boufnichel, M.; Roqueta, F. Modeling of inductively coupled plasma SF_6/O_2/Ar plasma discharge: Effect of O_2 on the plasma kinetic properties. *J. Vac. Sci. Technol. A* **2014**, *32*, 021303. [CrossRef]
10. Maruyama, T.; Narukage, T.; Onuki, R.; Fujiwara, N. High-aspect-ratio deep Si etching in SF_6/O_2 plasma. I. Characteristics of radical reactions with high-aspect-ratio patterns. *J. Vac. Sci. Technol. B* **2010**, *28*, 854–861. [CrossRef]
11. Gomez, S.; Jun Belen, R.; Kiehlbauch, M.; Aydil, E.S. Etching of high aspect ratio structures in Si using SF_6/O_2 plasma. *J. Vac. Sci. Technol. A* **2004**, *22*, 606–615. [CrossRef]
12. Aachboun, S.; Ranson, P. Deep anisotropic etching of silicon. *J. Vac. Sci. Technol. A* **1999**, *17*, 2270–2273. [CrossRef]
13. Boufnichel, M.; Aachboun, S.; Grangeon, F.; Lefaucheux, P.; Ranson, P. Profile control of high aspect ratio trenches of silicon. I. Effect of process parameters on local bowing. *J. Vac. Sci. Technol. B Microelectron. Nanometer Struct. Process. Meas. Phenom.* **2002**, *20*, 1508–1513. [CrossRef]
14. Blauw, M.A.; van der Drift, E.; Marcos, G.; Rhallabi, A. Modeling of fluorine-based high-density plasma etching of anisotropic silicon trenches with oxygen sidewall passivation. *J. Appl. Phys.* **2003**, *94*, 6311–6318. [CrossRef]
15. Anderson, H.M.; Merson, J.A.; Light, R.W. A Kinetic Model for Plasma Etching Silicon in a SF_6/O_2 RF Discharge. *IEEE Trans. Plasma Sci.* **1986**, *14*, 156–164. [CrossRef]
16. Rauf, S.; Dauksher, W.J.; Clemens, S.B.; Smith, K.H. Model for a multiple-step deep Si etch process. *J. Vac. Sci. Technol. A* **2002**, *20*, 1177–1190. [CrossRef]
17. Marcos, G.; Rhallabi, A.; Ranson, P. Topographic and kinetic effects of the SF_6/O_2 rate during a cryogenic etching process of silicon. *J. Vac. Sci. Technol. B Microelectron. Nanometer Struct. Process. Meas. Phenom.* **2004**, *22*, 1912–1922. [CrossRef]
18. Tennyson, J.; Rahimi, S.; Hill, C.; Tse, L.; Vibhakar, A.; Akello-Egwel, D.; Brown, D.B.; Dzarasova, A.; Hamilton, J.R.; Jaksch, D.; et al. QDB: A new database of plasma chemistries and reactions. *Plasma Sources Sci. Technol.* **2017**, *26*, 055014. [CrossRef]
19. Dijkstra, E.W. A note on two problems in connexion with graphs. *Numer. Math.* **1959**, *1*, 269–271. [CrossRef]
20. Tennyson, J. Electron-molecule collision calculations using the R-matrix method. *Phys. Rep.* **2010**, *491*, 29–76. [CrossRef]
21. Kim, Y.K.; Rudd, M.E. Binary-encounter-dipole model for electron-impact ionization. *Phys. Rev. A* **1994**, *50*, 3945. [CrossRef]
22. Graves, V.; Cooper, B.; Tennyson, J. The efficient calculation of electron impact ionization cross sections with effective core potential. *J. Chem. Phys.* **2021**, *154*, 114104. [CrossRef]
23. Werner, H.J.; Knowles, P.J.; Knizia, G.; Manby, F.R.; Schütz, M. Molpro: A general-purpose quantum chemistry program package. *WIREs Comput. Mol. Sci.* **2012**, *2*, 242–253. [CrossRef]
24. Herron, J.T. Thermochemical Data on Gas Phase Compounds of Sulfur, Fluorine, Oxygen, and Hydrogen Related to Pyrolysis and Oxidation of Sulfur Hexafluoride. *J. Phys. Chem. Ref. Data* **1987**, *16*, 1. [CrossRef]
25. Phelps, A.V. *Tabulations of Collision Cross Sections and Calculated Transport and Reaction Coefficients for Electron Collisions with O_2*; Technical Report; University of Colorado: Boulder, CO, USA, 1985.
26. Krishnakumar, E.; Srivastava, S.K. Cross-sections for electron impact ionization of O_2. *Int. J. Mass Spectrom. Ion Process.* **1992**, *113*, 1–12. [CrossRef]
27. Itikawa, Y.; Ichimura, A. Cross Sections for Collisions of Electrons and Photons with Atomic Oxygen. *J. Phys. Chem. Ref. Data* **1990**, *19*, 637. [CrossRef]
28. Christophorou, L.G.; Olthoff, J.K. Electron Interactions with SF_6. *J. Phys. Chem. Ref. Data* **2000**, *29*, 267–330. [CrossRef]

29. Tarnovsky, V.; Deutsch, H.; Martus, K.E.; Becker, K. Electron impact ionization of the SF_5 and SF_3 free radicals. *J. Chem. Phys.* **1998**, *109*, 6596–6600. [CrossRef]
30. Phelps, A.V.; Van Brunt, R.J. Electron-transport, ionization, attachment, and dissociation coefficients in SF_6 and its mixtures. *J. Appl. Phys.* **1988**, *64*, 4269–4277. [CrossRef]
31. Morgan, W.L. (Kinema Research and Software). Personal Communication.

Population Kinetics Modeling of Low-Temperature Argon Plasma

Hyun-Kyung Chung [1], Mi-Young Song [1,*], Ji-Won Kwon [2], Myeong-Geon Lee [2], Jihoon Park [2], Namjae Bae [2], Jeamin Song [2], Gon-Ho Kim [2], Dipti [3] and Yuri Ralchenko [4]

1. Korea Institute of Fusion Energy, 169-148 Gwahak-ro, Yuseong-gu, Daejeon 34133, Korea; hkchung@kfe.re.kr
2. Department of Energy Systems Engineering, Seoul National University, Seoul 08826, Korea; anakin1229@snu.ac.kr (J.-W.K.); lmg1142@snu.ac.kr (M.-G.L.); wlgnstlsqkf@snu.ac.kr (J.P.); baenj2002@snu.ac.kr (N.B.); woals356@snu.ac.kr (J.S.); ghkim@snu.ac.kr (G.-H.K.)
3. IAEA Nuclear Data Section Vienna International Centre, P.O. Box 100, 1400 Vienna, Austria; d.dipti@iaea.org
4. Atomic Spectroscopy Group, National Institute of Standards and Technology, Gaithersburg, MD 20899, USA; yuri.ralchenko@nist.gov
* Correspondence: mysong@kfe.re.kr

Abstract: Optical emission spectroscopy has been widely used in low-temperature argon plasma diagnostics. A coronal model is usually used to analyze the measured line ratios for diagnostics with a single temperature and density. However, many plasma processing conditions deviate from single temperature and density, optically thin conditions, or even coronal plasma conditions due to cascades from high-lying states. In this paper, we present a collisional-radiative model to investigate the validity of coronal approximations over a range of plasma conditions of T_e = 1–4 eV and $N_e = 10^8$–10^{13} cm^{-3}. The commonly used line ratios are found to change from a coronal limit where they are independent of N_e to a collisional-radiative regime where they are not. The effects of multiple-temperature plasma, radiation trapping, wall neutralization, and quenching on the line ratios are investigated to identify the plasma conditions under which these effects are significant. This study demonstrates the importance of the completeness of atomic datasets in applying a collisional-radiative model to low-temperature plasma diagnostics.

Keywords: argon optical emission spectroscopy; plasma processing; coronal models; collisional-radiative model; nonlocal thermodynamic equilibrium plasmas; population kinetics; radiation transport; opacity effects; Non-Maxwellian plasmas

1. Introduction

Argon plasmas are widely used for plasma processing applications, and the information on the thermodynamic properties of plasma, such as electron temperature, density, and electron energy distribution function, plays an important role in the control and performance of plasma applications [1–3].

Plasma spectroscopy is a non-intrusive diagnostic technique that provides information on not only the thermodynamic properties of plasma but also the atomic-level population distributions and radiative properties. For many decades, argon optical emission spectroscopy (OES) has been used to obtain electron temperature and density information from the measured line ratios, and more recently, the shape of the electron energy distribution functions [4–7]. For spectroscopic analysis, a population kinetics model should be built to couple the atomic-level population distributions and radiative properties with the plasma thermodynamic properties. For low-electron-density plasmas, a coronal model has been generally adopted to interpret the spectral line intensity distribution [1–3], where an excited atomic state emitting a line of interest is assumed to be populated from the ground state or a metastable state by collisional excitation and depopulated by spontaneous emission to the lower states.

This assumption is valid only if there is no collisional coupling with states other than the ground state, and there are negligible radiative cascades from the upper states. Therefore, the application of the coronal model for spectroscopic analysis is simple, as it requires only collisional excitation rates and spontaneous emission rates of the related atomic transitions. This model has been widely used to explain the emission observed in astrophysical coronal plasmas, tokamak plasmas, and low-density plasmas.

However, the validity of the coronal model may not hold for industrial processing plasmas, even those with relatively low densities. For example, an external electric field is applied in the plasma generation devices of inductively coupled plasma (ICP) and capacitively coupled plasmas (CCP), where electrons tend to have non-Maxwellian energy distributions [8,9]. If high-energy electrons exist as a tail, highly excited states, such as auto-ionizing states and ionized states, may be significantly populated, and the radiative cascades from these states may enhance the population density of the excited states of optical lines. If high-energy electrons are under-populated when compared with the Maxwellian distribution, resulting in the lower-energy electrons being overpopulated, the collisional deexcitation and recombination rates may increase the rate of downward processes.

Radiative self-pumping effects may need to be considered when the plasma size is very large, in the order of centimeters [1–3]. Even if the ion density is low, line opacities can be higher than unity, and the self-pumping effects can reduce the radiative downward processes. In this case, the atomic-level population distribution is a function of the plasma size and, to some degree, the nonlocal plasma conditions. CCP and ICP plasmas may have time dependence in the electron energy distribution function, as some applications use a pulsed-mode operation. Then, the plasma conditions fluctuate over time during the optical measurements, and the observed emission is time integrated. If this is significant, a time-dependent population kinetics model could help test whether the level population distribution converges to a steady-state population within the pulsed operation.

A critical consideration for modeling processing plasmas was found to be the boundary effect, where the atomic state population can be modified by wall contacts. While plasma and material (or wall) interactions are not very well characterized, the diffusion of plasmas near the boundary layer plays a significant role in the population distribution and charge state distribution. It is empirically known that the ground state of a singly ionized argon charge state is neutralized by contact with the wall, and, more importantly, the metastable states of neutral argon atoms are depopulated by contact with the wall. Therefore, the interaction with the wall complicates the analysis, as the population cascades from the high-lying states and the ionized states will be dependent on the wall interaction; moreover, the metastable state population may be quenched [3,10].

A coronal model is a limiting case of a collisional-radiative (CR) model at low density; hence, a general analysis of OES measurements can be performed with a CR model, which includes all relevant atomic processes, beyond a coronal approximation. A well-constructed CR model should provide results consistent with those of a coronal model if the plasma conditions are close to the coronal equilibrium. It has the advantage of allowing the investigation of the validity of coronal approximation for a given plasma condition and identifying the line ratios to provide diagnostic information. Another advantage is that the metastable population distributions are more reliably calculated over a wide range of plasma conditions [11].

In this paper, we present a CR model for near-neutral argon OES and investigate the issues described above for a wide range of plasma conditions. This model is developed based on the principles outlined recently by a nonlocal thermodynamic equilibrium (NLTE) kinetics workshop series [12–18] and a book on the review of NLTE code development over the last 20 years [19]. The atomic datasets and sources used in the model are discussed and evaluated in comparison with the optical measurements. The CR model results are discussed for various non-coronal conditions described above and compared with the existing measurements. This study demonstrates the importance of the completeness of atomic datasets in applying a collisional-radiative model to low-temperature plasma diagnostics.

2. Materials and Methods

2.1. Construction of a Collisional Radiative (CR) Model

To determine the relationship between the observed emission spectra and plasma thermodynamic properties, we need to obtain the atomic-level population distribution as a function of the plasma thermodynamic properties, as the radiative properties of plasmas, such as spectral emission and absorption, are a function of the atomic level population. The emission coefficient is proportional to the upper-level population of radiative transition, and the absorption coefficient is proportional to the lower-level population distribution minus the upper-level population multiplied by the ratio of the statistical weights. The atomic-level population distribution is determined using collisional processes involving mainly electrons and radiative transitions due to spontaneous radiative processes and stimulated radiative processes by the nonlocal radiation field. In this study, we focus on electron-driven collisional processes while ignoring atom–atom or atom–ion collisions, assuming that the atomic density was substantially low. However, Ar_2 molecular emissions have been observed [3], and such processes involving atomic collisions could be important in understanding population kinetics of processing plasma. An atomic-level population distribution is obtained from a set of time-dependent rate equations, including collisional and radiative transitions, as shown in Equation (1):

$$\frac{dn_i}{dt} = -n_i \sum_{j \neq i}^{N_L} W_{ij} + \sum_{j \neq i}^{N_L} n_j W_{ji}, 1 \leq i \leq N_L, \tag{1}$$

where N_L is the number of atomic levels considered in the model. The rates between i and j states, W_{ji}, and W_{ij} are described in Equation (3) in two cases, where the i state is lower than the j state.

$$W_{ij} = B_{ij}\bar{J}_{ij} + N_e C_{ij} + \beta_{ij} + N_e \gamma_{ij} + \sigma_{ij} \tag{2}$$

$$W_{ji} = A_{ji} + B_{ji}\bar{J}_{ij} + N_e D_{ji} + Q_{ji} + N_e \alpha_{ji}^{RR} + N_e \kappa_{ji}^{EC} + N_e^2 \delta_{ji} + \nu_{ji}.$$

The collisional and radiative processes considered in the model are as follows: For bound–bound transitions:

- A_{ji} spontaneous emission,
- B_{ij} stimulated absorption ($i \ll j$) or emission ($i \gg j$),
- C_{ij} collisional excitation,
- D_{ji} collisional deexcitation,
- J_{ij} mean radiation field of a unit of energy per squared area per second per photon frequency, and
- Q_{ji} wall quenching of metastable states.

For bound–free transitions:

- A_{ji} spontaneous emission,
- α_{ij} radiative recombination,
- β_{ij} photoionization plus stimulated recombination,
- γ_{ij} collisional ionization,
- δ_{ij} collisional recombination,
- κ_{ij} electron capture,
- σ_{ij} autoionization, and
- ν_{ij} wall neutralization to the neutral ground state.

Recent advances in CR models have shown that dielectronic recombination (DR) processes play a key role in determining the charge state distribution [17,19]. The process is usually modeled with a substantial number of multiply excited autoionization channels, and a model must include all collisional and radiative processes originating from the autoionization channels. At low densities, the states with a very large principal quantum number contribute to the DR rate coefficients, and the model becomes prohibitively large. Therefore, for coronal and near-coronal plasmas, the DR rate coefficients have been used instead of detailed counting of the autoionization and electron capture processes. This approach is adopted in this work, and only the bound states were included in the CR model of neutral atom and one singly ionized state.

A non-Maxwellian NLTE kinetics code NOMAD is used to solve the rate equations for the atomic-level population distribution and one-dimensional radiative transport equation in a uniform plasma approximation for spectral intensities and power intensities [20]. This code has many useful options for investigating the atomic population kinetics over a wide range of plasma conditions. It is suitable for time-dependent plasmas or two-temperature Maxwellian plasmas and includes radiation trapping effects for a finite plasma size. Wall neutralization effects are included with an enhanced recombination rate to promote recombination processes from singly ionized argon to neutral argon. Similarly, wall quenching is added to the two metastable states to allow decay to the neutral ground state. With regard to the construction of a CR model for near-neutral argon, only a limited number of atomic states have been reported and evaluated; hence, the rest of required atomic datasets that are required should be obtained through code calculations or widely used empirical data. In this section, atomic data are evaluated to ensure tractability of the CR model.

2.2. Atomic Structures

The atomic energy levels of a neutral argon atom are taken from the NIST (National Institute of Standards and Technology atomic spectra database [21]. The highest state included in the NIST database corresponds to the 58d levels that are 15.75558 eV below the continuum limit of 15.7596117 eV. As the most dominant optical emission arises from $3p^5$ 4p, and spectral emissions from the 8s levels or above are hardly observed, a total of 229 bound levels up to $3p^5$ 7h levels of neutral argon atoms, and one level of singly ionized argon ion are included in the model. Because the highest level included in the model is 15.65940 eV, there is an approximately 1 eV gap between the highest level in the model and the continuum limit. It will be interesting to include higher-n Rydberg states and evaluate the effects of collisional cascades through these states. It should be noted that such high-n Rydberg states may no longer be bound because of interactions with ions, electrons, and external electric fields [22], and the highest available bound states could lie much lower than the continuum limit in the plasma with large external electric fields. In this study, the autoionizing states are ignored, and the autoionization and electron capture processes are accounted for by including DR rates in the model. Only bound states are included in this model.

2.3. Spontaneous Emission

Spontaneous emission rates are key atomic data for OES models, especially for plasma conditions at the coronal limit. This is because the population distribution of excited states is determined by collisional excitation from the ground state and the sum of all possible spontaneous emission rates to lower states. Therefore, a complete set of radiative transitions originating from the level of interest is required. However, there are only a few recommended spontaneous emission rates available in the NIST atomic spectroscopy database for strong lines. For this model, 404 transitions are taken from the NIST database, and 51 transitions are taken from the B-spline R-matrix (BSR) calculations [23]. Additional rates are taken from various sources: multiconfiguration Dirac–Hartree–Fock (MCDHF) data for 1048 transitions [24,25], Los Alamos National Laboratory (LANL) data for 1349 transitions [26], and flexible atomic code (FAC) data for 15,265 transitions [27]. Available transitions from the ATBASE code developed at the University of Wisconsin (WISC) are also added [28]. The LANL data are calculated by the LANL group by using the Hartree–Fock method proposed by Cowan [29], and the FAC data are calculated by solving the Dirac equations in the jj coupling scheme by using a parametric potential. The

ATBASE code is also based on the Cowan code. Owing to the lack of electron correlation, the FAC data are known to show poor agreement with other code results or experiments for neutral atom cases. Comparisons among the available datasets show that the accuracy of the FAC data varies over a range.

The oscillator strengths and ratios with the NIST evaluated data, where available, are listed along with the data sources in Tables 1–6 for dominant radiative transitions from Paschen $2p_3$, $2p_1$, $3p_9$, $3p_6$, $3p_1$, and $5p_5$ levels to lower levels. For example, the Paschen notation, the $2p_1$ level refers to $3p_5(2P°_{1/2})4p\,^2[1/2]_0$, and $3p_1$ level refers to $3p_5(2P°_{1/2})5p\,^2[1/2]_0$. The oscillator strengths of the radiative transitions from the Paschen 2p levels to 1s levels are found to be comparable for all sources within a factor of 2. The MCDHF data differ within a factor of two from the NIST or BSR data for most transitions. However, there are a few outliers in the LANL and FAC datasets. For high-lying levels, such as the 3p levels, the agreement is far from reasonable (marked in red) and differs by a factor of at least 10, especially for the transitions of 3d levels. For the $5p_5$ level, the problem is even worse because there are only two published datasets (from NIST and MCDHF), while the remaining datasets contain FAC data for which the accuracy is not guaranteed.

The credibility of the oscillator strength and, therefore, the spontaneous emission rate data is a serious concern not only for collisional radiative models but also for coronal models. In the coronal model, the level population distribution and line ratio analysis are simple functions of the collisional excitation rate from the ground state and the total spontaneous emission rate from the upper level. Denoting the upper-level population as N_u and the ground level population as N_g, N_u is written as a function of the collisional excitation rate C_{gu} and the sum of all spontaneous emission rates to the lower level j A_{uj} as follows:

$$N_u = N_g \frac{C_{gu}}{\sum_j A_{uj}}. \quad (3)$$

The uncertainty in A_{uj} influences the determination of the level population distribution and, therefore, the line ratio analysis. The issue of uncertainties in the spontaneous emission rates is demonstrated in Section 3.1, where the sensitivities of different CR models are discussed.

Table 1. Oscillator strengths of neutral argon levels (2p3). The top row contains the upper level, and the 1st column contains the lower level. The 2nd column shows the oscillator strength, the 3rd column shows the ratio of various sources to the evaluated NIST or BSR values, and the 4th column shows the data source. The ratios deviating substantially from unity are marked in red.

						2p3					
		Ω	Ratio	Data Source		Ω	Ratio	Data Source		Ω	Ratio	Data Source
1s5		0.029		NIST	1s4	0.115		NIST	1s2	0.394		BSR
		0.037	1.31	MCDHF		0.150	1.30	MCDHF		0.494	1.25	MCDHF
		0.021	0.74	LANL		0.109	0.95	LANL		0.528	1.34	LANL
		0.036	0.96	WISC		0.124	0.83	WISC		0.445	0.90	WISC
		0.047	2.21	FAC		0.146	1.34	FAC		0.317	0.60	FAC

Table 2. Oscillator strengths of neutral argon levels (2p1) from various sources. The ratios deviating substantially from unity are marked in red.

	2p1						
	Ω	Ratio	Data Source		Ω	Ratio	Data Source
1s4	0.0005		NIST	1s2	0.1250		NIST
	0.0011	2.10	MCDHF		0.1529	1.22	MCDHF
	0.0052	9.87	LANL		0.1494	1.20	LANL
	0.0030	2.71	WISC		0.1350	0.88	WISC
	0.1088	20.97	FAC		0.0021	0.01	FAC

Table 3. Oscillator strengths of neutral argon levels (3p9) from various sources. The ratios deviating substantially from unity are marked in red.

	3p9										
	Ω	Ratio	Data Source		Ω	Ratio	Data Source		Ω	Ratio	Data Source
1s5	0.004		NIST	3d4'	0.073		NIST	3d1''	0.112		LANL
	0.006	1.75	LANL		0.209	2.87	LANL		0.004	0.04	WISC
	0.005	1.40	WISC		0.180	2.47	WISC		0	0	FAC
	0.007	1.19	FAC		0.029	0.39	FAC	2s5	0.718		MCDHF
3d3	0.007		NIST	3d4	0.083		LANL		0.651	0.91	LANL
	0.000	0.01	LANL		0.060	0.72	WISC		0.715	1.00	WISC
	0.009	1.30	WISC		0.003	0.03	FAC		0.936	1.30	FAC

Table 4. Oscillator strengths of neutral argon levels (3p6) from various sources. The ratios deviating substantially from unity are marked in red.

	3p6										
	Ω	Ratio	Data Source		Ω	Ratio	Data Source		Ω	Ratio	Data Source
1s5	0.004		NIST	3d4	0.092		LANL	3d2	0.000		LANL
	0.006	1.59	LANL		0.088	0.95	WISC		0.001	2.17	WISC
	0.005	1.38	WISC		0.001	0.01	FAC		0.000	0.84	FAC
	0.002	0.43	FAC		0.011		LANL		0.002		LANL
1s4	0.001		NIST	3d1''	0.004	0.35	WISC	3s1''''	0.009	5.74	WISC
	0.001	0.98	LANL		0.015	1.34	FAC		0.000	0.22	FAC
	0.002	1.41	WISC					3s1''	0.008		LANL
	0.003	1.88	FAC		0.416		MCDHF		0.001		WISC
1s2	0.000		NIST	2s5	0.358	0.86	LANL	3s1'''	0.118		LANL
	0.000	1.46	LANL		0.389	0.94	WISC		0.042	0.36	WISC
	0.000	8.03	FAC		0.235	0.66	FAC		0	0	FAC
3d5	0.053		LANL		0.006		MCDHF	2s2	0.201		MCDHF
	0.036	0.68	WISC	2s4	0.008	1.29	LANL		0.173	0.86	LANL
	0.010	0.18	FAC		0.008	1.26	WISC		0.215	1.07	WISC
3d3	0.162		LANL		0.698	85.31	FAC		0.004	0.02	FAC
	0.077		WISC					3s1'	0.019		LANL

Table 5. Oscillator strengths of neutral argon levels (3p1) from various sources. The ratios deviating substantially from unity are marked in red.

					3p1						
		Ω	Ratio	Data Source		Ω	Ratio	Data Source		Ω	Ratio	Data Source
1s4	0.00001		BSR		0.19130		MCDHF		0.0037		MCDHF
	0.00015	13.90	LANL	2s4	0.17222	0.90	LANL	2s2	0.0016	0.43	LANL
	0.00391	358.26	FAC		0.16800	0.88	WISC		0.0080	2.15	WISC
	0.00361		NIST		0.11080	0.64	FAC		0.0761	20.48	FAC
1s2	0.00660	1.83	LANL		2.088e^{-16}		LANL	3s1′	0.2024		LANL
	0.00600	1.66	WISC	3d2	0.01800	8617.39	WISC		0.0340	0.17	WISC
	0.00448	0.68	FAC		0.01256	6013.02	FAC				

Table 6. Oscillator strengths of neutral argon levels (5p5) from various sources. The ratios deviating substantially from unity are marked in red.

					5p5						
	Ω	Ratio	Data Source		Ω	Ratio	Data Source		Ω	Ratio	Data Source
1s4	0.0010		FAC	3s1′	0.0067		FAC	5d5	0.0569		FAC
1s2	0.0003		NIST	3s4	0.0014		FAC	4s4	0.2336		MCDHF
	0.0016	4.98	FAC	4d2	0.0007		FAC		0.0416	0.18	FAC
3d1	0.0002		FAC	4s1′	0.1134		FAC	5d2	0.2246		FAC
2s2	0.0059		FAC	3s1	0.0974		FAC				

2.4. Collisional Excitation

Collisional excitation cross-sections are taken from the following five data sources available at the LXCAT website (https://fr.lxcat.net, accessed on 2 November 2021) in addition to the LANL and FAC data: Biagi [30], BSR [31], IST [32], Puech [33], and NGFS-RDW [34]. Measured optical emission cross-sections [35–37] have been frequently used in OES analyses. Apparent cross-sections or optical emission cross-sections are not appropriate for use in the CR model, as these cross-sections include population cascades from other levels. These can be used under strictly coronal conditions; however, only direct cross-sections should be considered in the CR model. The BSR data are known to be most accurate for neutral and near-neutral systems, and the data for neutral argon have been favorably evaluated through cross-section measurements of metastable and ground state excitation to 4p levels by Boffard et al. [3]. However, the available BSR data [31] are limited to the Paschen 3s ($3p^5$ 5s) levels. Paschen 3p ($3p^5$ 5p) data from the Puech database by Puech and Torchin [33] and the IST data (IST-Lisbon database) [32] are available. A few transitions to $3p^5$ 4d, 5d, and 6d levels from the ground state are available from the Biagi database [30]. NGFSRDW data are calculated by the relativistic distorted wave (RDW) method [34], and either the distorted wave calculations or first-order many body theory are used. The distorted wave method is used for the FAC data. A perturbative approach, such as RDW/DW methods, produces larger direct cross-sections when compared with the BSR cross-sections, even when the BSR includes resonance contributions by cascades through highly excited states.

The cross-sections of a few transitions are compared for eight data sources for the low-lying levels in Figure 1. The comparison shows that the cross-sections differ by a factor of two or more for most transitions in different data sources. A better agreement is found for forbidden transitions, but, for most transitions, the agreement is not good. The BSR data tend to lie below most other data sources, and the NGFSRDW and Boffard data generally lie higher than the other data. Perturbative methods are known to provide slightly higher cross-sections than non-perturbative methods, such as the R-matrix method. The FAC data show fast-decaying cross-sections. At the temperatures of interest, 0.5 eV–3 eV, the threshold values determine the rate coefficients. This is problematic, as transition data involving high-lying levels are only available from the FAC data calculated from the distorted wave method, which is known to be less accurate near threshold values and more accurate at high energies. The FAC data are scaled down by a factor of 10 after comparing them with higher quality datasets for the available transitions. Van Regemorter cross-sections are used if the oscillator strengths are available [38]. In this model, we adopted the BSR dataset as the base dataset and used other data sources for the missing transition data in the order of Biagi, Puech, IST, Boffard, NGFSRDW, LANL, and FAC. Van Regemorter cross-sections were also compared and used for the missing transition data. As demonstrated in Section 3.1, the level population distribution and line ratios are sensitive to the completeness of the collisional transition data, as well as the accuracy of the data.

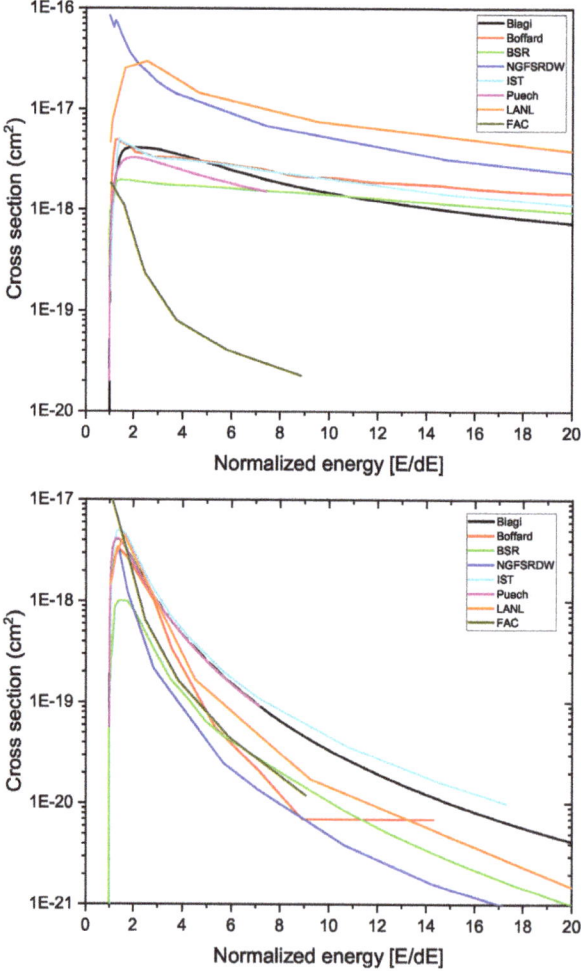

Figure 1. Comparison of collisional excitation cross-sections from the ground state to Paschen levels $2p_1$ (**upper**) and $3d'_4$ (forbidden transition) (**lower**) for various available sources.

2.5. Ionization and Recombination

Bound-free transitions, collisional ionization, radiative recombination, dielectronic recombination (DR), and collisional recombination are considered in the model. The ionization rate coefficient from the ground state is taken from the Biagi database. The BSR and LANL cross-sections are compared with the Lotz formula [39]. The DR rate coefficient is obtained from Mazzotta et al. [40]. FAC datasets are used for the collisional ionization data and radiative recombination data for all excited states.

3. Results

3.1. Sensitivity to Model Completeness

Six CR models, shown in Table 7, are compared to demonstrate the sensitivity of the line ratio analysis to the scope and completeness of the atomic datasets used in the model. Base model A utilizes BSR, Biagi, and Puech collisional data from LXCAT and Van Regemorter cross-sections [38] using NIST oscillator strengths (NIST-VR). LANL and FAC refer to collisional data by LANL code and FAC code. MCDHF-VR/LANL-VR/FAC-VR refers to Van Regemorter collisional data using the MCDHF/LANL/FAC oscillator strengths. MCDHF-GF/LANL-GF/FAC-GF refers to the MCDHF/LANL/FAC oscillator strengths to be used in addition to the NIST oscillator strengths. Model B adds LANL/FAC collisional data in addition to the base model A. Model C adds oscillator strengths from MCDHF and LANL code to model B. Model D adds oscillator strengths from the FAC code to model C. Model E utilizes the base model A and adds only Van Regemorter collisional data using MCDHF/LANL/FAC oscillator strengths. Model F is our final and most complete model, as well as includes the LANL/FAC collisional data and Van Regemorter data using the available oscillator strengths.

Table 7. Total number of transitions included in the 6 models.

A		B		C	
BSR	441	A model	768	B model	17,256
Biagi	11	LANL	846	MCDHF-GF	999
Puech	10	FAC	15,411	LANL-GF	999
NIST-VR	306	Total	17,256	Total	18,255
Total	768				
D		E		F (Complete Model)	
C model	18,255	A model	768	D model	30,787
FAC-GF	12,532	MCDHF-VR	496	MCDHF-VR	496
Total	30,787	LANL-VR	624	LANL-VR	624
		FAC-VR	13,937	FAC-VR	13,937
		Total	15,825	Total	45,844

The calculated line ratios of 425.9 nm/750.4 nm analyzed by Boffard et al. [1] are compared to demonstrate the sensitivities of the CR model to the model completeness. The 425.9 nm line corresponds to the transition between $3p^5(2P^{\circ}_{1/2})4s\ ^2[1/2]^{\circ}_1$ (Paschen 1s$_2$) and $3p^5(^2P^{\circ}_{1/2})5p\ ^2[1/2]_0$ (Paschen 3p$_1$) states. The upper level Paschen 3p$_1$ level is populated from the ground state, and the cross-section is provided by the Puech data. The 750.4 nm line corresponds to the transition between $3p^5(2P^{\circ}_{1/2})4s\ ^2[1/2]^{\circ}_1$ (Paschen 1s$_2$) and $3p^5(^2P^{\circ}_{1/2})4p^2[1/2]_0$ (Paschen 2p$_1$) states. The upper-level Paschen 2p$_1$ level is populated from the ground state, and the cross-section is provided by the BSR data. The cross-sections to the upper levels 3p$_1$ and 2p$_1$ from the ground state stay the same for all 6 models; however, the line ratio of 425.9 nm/750.4 nm changes significantly, as the additional transitions to other levels are included in the model. In Figure 2, the line ratios are plotted as a function of the electron temperature T_e and electron density N_e of 10^8 cm^{-3}. The addition of LANL/FAC collisional data in model B do not change the line ratio of 425.9 nm/750.4 nm significantly. However, when the oscillator strengths (i.e., spontaneous emission rates) of the MCDHF/LANL/FAC data are added to the model, the ratio decreased by more than a factor of 2. As the additional oscillator strengths are included for Van Regemorter rates, the ratio decreased even further, and the results are closer to the measured data [41,42] in Section 4.1 and to the calculations performed using the measured optical emission cross-sections by Boffard et al. [1].

The comparison in Figure 2 shows the importance of including all relevant spontaneous emission rates when calculating the line ratios at the coronal conditions, such as $N_e = 10^8$ cm^{-3} considered here. Figure 3 shows quite different trends in the line ratio comparisons at N_e of 10^{13} cm^{-3}, the highest density case of this investigation. The line ratio is much closer among different models, as collisions make the level population distributions deviate from the coronal limit by increasing the collisional depopulation to be comparable with the spontaneous emission rates. All five models (model B–model F) are closer to the measured data [41,42] in Section 4.1, slightly below the coronal calculations of Boffard et al. [1].

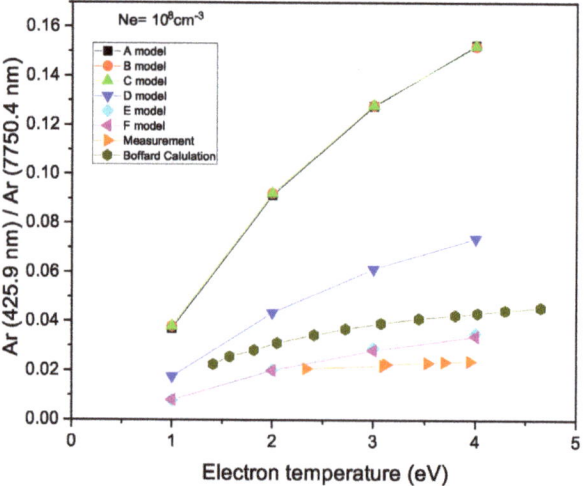

Figure 2. Line ratios of Ar 425.9 nm and 750.4 nm as a function of T_e at $N_e = 10^8$ cm^{-3} for six models considered in this work. Simulation results were compared with the calculations by Boffard et al. [1] and the measured data [41,42].

A CR model should converge to a coronal limit if N_e is sufficiently low and the line ratio is independent of N_e. However, as N_e increases, the line ratio deviates from the ratio at the coronal limit, as demonstrated for the line ratio of Ar 357.2 nm/Ar 425.9 nm in Figure 4. The transition at Ar 357.2 nm corresponds to the transition between the $3p^5(2P^{\circ}_{1/2})4s$ $^2[1/2]^{\circ}_1$ (Paschen 1s$_2$) and $p^5(2P^{\circ}_{3/2})7p$ $^2[1/2]_0$ (Paschen 5p$_5$) states. Unfortunately, there is no reliable collisional data from the ground state to the 5p$_5$ level, except for the measured optical emission cross-section for the transition from the 5p$_5$ level to the 1s$_2$ level. The optical emission cross-section is 4.6×10^{-20} cm^2 at 25 eV [35]. The direct excitation cross-section is related to the sum of all optical emission cross-sections of transitions originating from the 5p$_5$ level, as follows. The branching ratio of the 357.2 nm transition is roughly 1/3; hence, a factor of 3 may be chosen as the apparent cross-section of the 5p$_5$ level. Then, the apparent cross-section is the sum of the direct cross-section and cascade contribution, and the direct cross-section should be greater than 4.6×10^{-20} cm^2 but smaller than 3 times 4.6×10^{-20} cm^2. Hence, the BSR cross-section was scaled to be approximately 8.5×10^{-20} cm^2 at 25 eV was used. The line ratios are compared with the measurements and calculations by Boffard et al. [1] in Figure 4 as a function of N_e. All 6 models showed very large differences in the results of the line ratio of Ar 357.2 nm/Ar 425.9 nm at T_e = 2 eV. The decreasing trend of the line ratio with N_e agrees with the Boffard data.

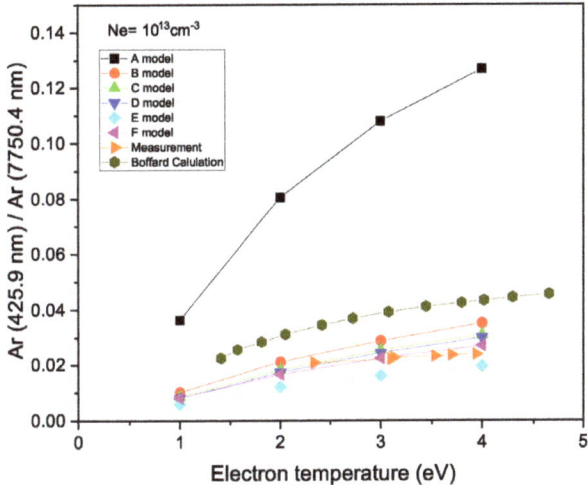

Figure 3. Line ratios of Ar 425.9 nm and 750.4 nm as a function of T_e at $N_e = 10^{13}$ cm^{-3} for the six models considered in this work. Simulations were compared with calculations by Boffard et al. [1] and the measured data [41,42].

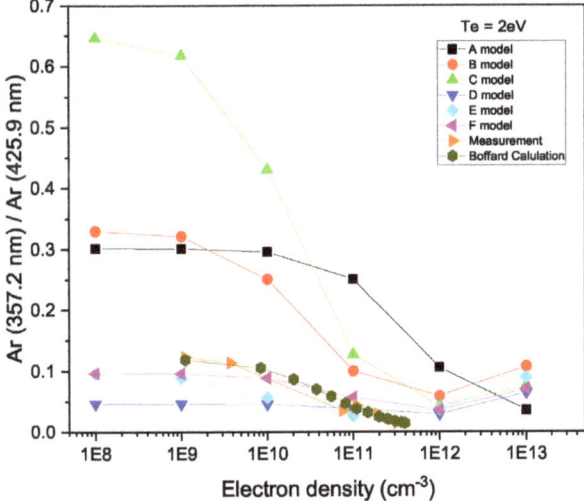

Figure 4. Comparison of line ratios of Ar 357.2 nm and 425.9 nm between simulations and values reported by Boffard et al. [1] at T_e = 2 eV.

The most complete model F agrees best with the Boffard data, although the absolute value differs by approximately 20–30%. This is likely to be attributed to the uncertainties in the spontaneous emission rates, as well as collisional rates involving the 5p$_5$ level, as most transition data involving this level are from the FAC code. Although quite sensitive to N_e, the line ratios are found to be insensitive to T_e under 4 eV, the maximum temperature considered in the simulations. In the following results, we use the most complete model F as our model for discussion.

3.2. Radiation Trapping Effects

The effects of radiation trapping on the line intensities and ratios are discussed in the context of the measured pressure dependence of optical emission cross-sections for the selected levels of Ar by Boffard et al. [1]. Radiation trapping for Paschen $2p_x - 1s_y$ ($x = 1 - 10, y = 2 - 5$) lines is attributed to the large number of atoms in the 1s metastable and resonance levels, direct trapping from the ground state, or indirect contributions due to cascades from the higher resonance levels. It was suggested to use Ar np_1 and np_5 levels (both J = 0) to avoid the radiation trapping effects because the optical excitation from the metastable state is weak.

The radiation trapping effects are functions of parameters, such as atomic density, thermodynamic conditions, plasma size, line shapes, etc. To investigate the radiation trapping effects, we assume the following: First, the atomic density or gas pressure is the most important parameter influencing the trapping effects, and it is fixed at 10^{13} cm^{-3} in our comparison. Second, different N_e and T_e will produce different lower level population distributions; therefore, we compares the lines for the same density and temperature to maintain the lower-level population the same for comparison. Third, the length of the line of sight increases the optical depth and, hence, the radiation trapping effect linearly, which allows the comparison of the radiation trapping effect in a straightforward manner. Finally, different line shape profiles can modify the optical depths and, hence, the radiation trapping effect. In this investigation, the line shape is calculated for the Doppler profile and is, therefore, fixed.

Figures 5 and 6 compare the ratios of the line intensities of 451.1 nm and 750.4 nm with (10 cm plasma size) and without the radiation trapping effect as a function of T_e for the electron densities of 10^8 - 10^{13} cm^{-3}. If the radiation trapping effects are insignificant, the ratios of line intensity for the 10 cm case and the optically thick case will be close to unity. The ratios deviate from 1 more significantly for 451.1 nm emitted from the $2p_5$ level than for 750.4 nm emitted from the $2p_1$ level for N_e below 10^{12} cm^{-3}. A slight T_e dependence on the radiation trapping effects was observed in the case of 451.1 nm, and the lower T_e ratios deviated further away from unity. As N_e increases further, collisions change the ground and metastable level population significantly, and the combined effects drive the line intensities away from the coronal limit and the optically thin case.

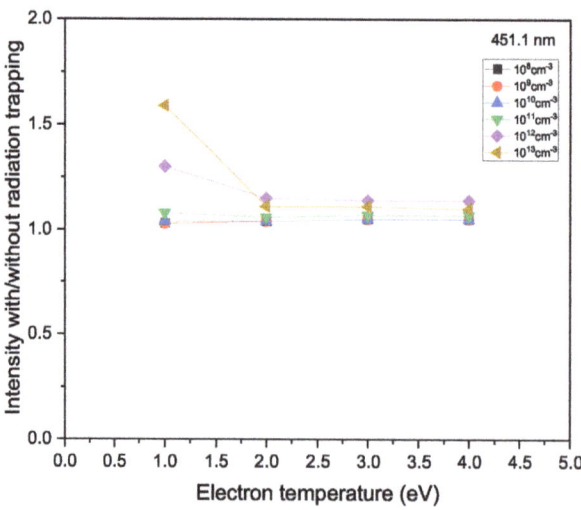

Figure 5. Comparison of intensity ratios of 451.1 nm with (10 cm plasma size) and without radiation trapping effect (optically thin case) for different electron densities and temperatures.

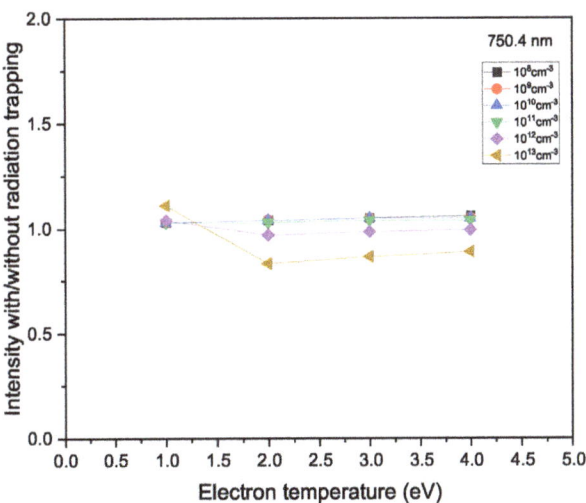

Figure 6. Comparison of intensity ratios of 750.4 nm with (10 cm plasma size) and without radiation trapping effect (optically thin case) for different electron densities and temperatures.

In OES analysis, the radiation trapping effects are usually considered with the gas pressure. It is a dominant factor, but the radiation trapping effects should be considered with all factors that influence the population kinetics, for example, gas density, N_e, and T_e, as well as the length of the line of sight. In addition, if wall recombination and quenching, or two-temperature distribution effects are combined, the radiation trapping effects may be even more dramatic because these effects modify the lower-level population distribution significantly.

3.3. Non-Maxwellian Electron Energy Distributions

Plasmas are frequently found to deviate from a single temperature Maxwellian electron energy distribution. It is useful to understand how line intensities change with non-thermal electron energy distribution functions. We compares two cases: (1) 99% bulk T_e of 1–4 eV and 1% of 10 eV non-thermal electrons and (2) 60% bulk T_e of 1–4 eV and 40 % of 0.1 eV cold electrons for different electron densities. Radiation trapping was not considered. The first example involves the observation of the effects of 1% 10 eV non-thermal electrons on line ratios of 99% 1–4 eV electron plasmas for a range of electron densities.

Figure 7 shows the ratios of the enhancement due to hot electrons. The ratios of the two lines in the analysis can remain the same if the two line intensities are enhanced by the same factor. In this case, the ratio of the enhancement is close to unity; therefore, the line ratios can be used as a robust diagnostic of the bulk plasma conditions regardless of the existence of small fractions of Non-Maxwellian electrons. Comparing the two line ratios, 357.2 nm/425.9 nm and 425.9 nm/750.4 nm, we find that the former is rather insensitive to the addition of 1% hot electrons, whereas the latter is modified significantly at 1–2 eV. The changes in the ratio become smaller as N_e becomes higher.

In summary, if N_e is high and T_e is high, the effect of 1% 10 eV electrons will be negligible, and the line ratios can be used as a bulk temperature diagnostic. The commonly used line ratios of 425.9 nm/750.4 nm are shown to be more sensitive to the addition of hot electrons; hence, one should be cautious when using this line ratio as a bulk temperature diagnostics. Investigation of the population mechanisms revealed that the cascades from high-lying states are significant for low-lying states, such as $2p_1$, the upper level of 750.4 nm. The population cascades increase the enhancement significantly at low temperatures, leading to a large enhancement in the line intensity and deviation from the single T_e line ratio of 425.9 nm/750.4 nm.

Figure 8 shows that the ratios of line intensity ratios are rather insensitive to the 40% cold electrons when N_e is sufficiently low. Contrary to the expectation that the line intensities will be reduced due to lower collisionalities, the line intensities are enhanced in the case of 2–4 eV. The ground state population is found to have significantly changed by adding 40% cold electrons in the case of 2–4 eV, where the ground state of neutral atoms is mostly ionized (without wall effects). With the cold electrons, the collisional ionization rate is 40% smaller while radiative recombination and dielectric recombination are higher, which leads to a lower charge state distribution and, hence, higher ground-state population of neutral atoms. Therefore, reduced high-lying and ionized state populations result in reduced cascades from those states and increase the validity of the coronal models for line ratio analysis. The modified line ratios with 40% cold electrons are lower than that in the single temperature case, whereas those with 1% 10 eV non-thermal electrons are generally higher than that in the single temperature case.

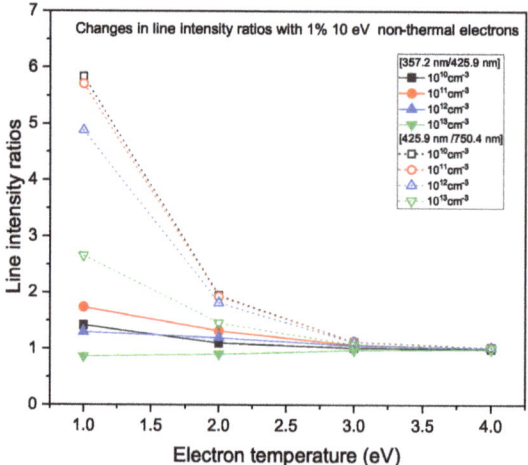

Figure 7. Comparison of the ratios of line ratios of 357.2 nm/425.9 nm and 425.9 nm/750.4 nm with 1% 10 eV non-thermal electrons to those of lines with single-temperature electrons under various plasma conditions.

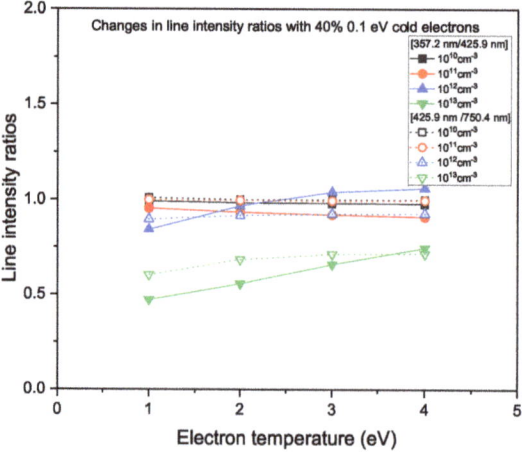

Figure 8. Comparison of the ratios of line intensity ratios of 357.2 nm/425.9 nm and 425.9 nm/750.4 nm when 40% 0.1 eV cold electrons exist to the line ratios with only thermal electrons.

3.4. Wall Recombination and Quenching Effects

All the investigations in the previous subsections are performed without considering the boundaries, that is, the wall effects. However, processing plasmas is unique in the sense that the steady-state operation of the plasma is sustained by externally applied fields compensatory energy and particle losses by the wall or boundaries. The main function of the wall in terms of population kinetics is to provide a substantial amount of recombination to the plasma. In general, argon plasmas at 2 eV and N_e of 10^{13} cm^{-3} should ionize substantially to the singly ionized system considering the atomic ionization and recombination rate coefficients. However, Langmuir probe measurements show that the degree of ionization is as low as 1%.

This introduces a difficulty in building a general CR model because the charge balance should be coupled with the diffusion of atoms to the wall and the spatial distribution of plasma conditions established by wall contact [7,10]. Because the diffusion and spatial behavior of plasmas is out of the scope of this work, we focus on the effect of wall recombination on the line ratio analysis. The main influence is the reduction in the charge state population; consequently, the cascades from the ionized states through Rydberg or high-lying states are significantly reduced, as well. To investigate the effect of wall recombination on the line ratios, we added an ad-hoc wall recombination rate to the total recombination rate to make the charge states comparable to those from the Langmuir probe measurements.

As expected from the fact that the wall recombination reduces the ionization, which in turn increases the ground state population, the modified line ratios have similar trends to those in the case of 40% cold electrons, as shown in Figure 9. There is a slight difference in that the enhancement is similar for all lines because only the ground state population changes, whereas, with the 40% cold electrons, the collisional rates change according to the bulk electron temperatures. The ratio of line intensity ratios will be close to unity if the wall effects are negligible. As shown in Figure 9, the commonly used line ratios of 357.2 nm/425.9 nm and 425.9 nm/750.4 nm are not significantly affected by wall recombination for low N_e cases, where the coronal approximation is relatively good.

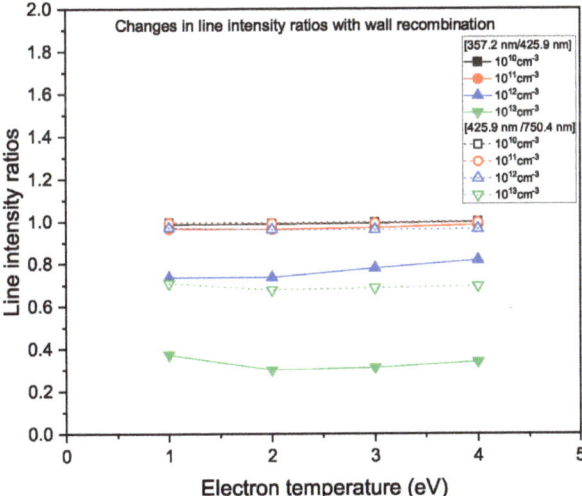

Figure 9. Comparison of the ratios of line intensity ratios for 357.2 nm/425.9 nm and 425.9 nm/750.4 nm with wall recombination to the line ratios without wall recombination.

Additionally, it is noted that the wall contact changes the metastable population distributions. Metastable state populations play an important role in stepwise excitation and ionization as N_e increases. Therefore, the quenching of the metastable population distribution could be very important in line ratio analysis. The wall quenching rate is assumed to be the same as the wall recombination rate, assuming that the wall recombination and quenching rates are a function of the diffusion velocity of particles regardless of their quantum state in this comparison. The results show that the quenching of metastable states did not result in any significantly greater difference than the wall recombination. The line ratios were modified in the same way as that in the case of wall recombination for 357.2 nm, 425.9 nm, and 750.4 nm. It is cautioned that lines sensitive to metastable populations are likely to be affected to a greater extent by wall quenching.

4. Discussion

We use the CR model to analyze OES measurements and discuss spectroscopic diagnostic of low temperature plasmas in this section. The CR models are built using several combinations of atomic datasets described in the previous section. Unfortunately, the uncertainties of the atomic datasets are large, and most transition data beyond the $3p^5\,5s$ levels are not evaluated as discussed in the previous section. Therefore, it is difficult to evaluate the accuracy of the CR model applied to the line-ratio analysis. One may be tempted to choose a set of atomic data to best reproduce the experimental dataset. However, because spectroscopic measurements are influenced by many factors, such as non-thermal electron energy distributions, radiation trapping, wall neutralization and quenching, and collisions with atoms and other impurities in the plasmas, determining the quality of atomic datasets based on plasma spectroscopic measurements is not appropriate. Instead, we investigated the model sensitivities due to different atomic datasets and model completeness and examined the effects of these factors on the line ratio analysis to establish the uncertainties of spectroscopic diagnostics. In this section, we compare our CR model with measurements where the electron density N_e and temperature T_e are measured by Langmuir method. This comparison will help identify robust diagnostic line ratios that can be used to collect plasma information. For the simulations discussed below, the plasma conditions are fixed at a gas density of 10^{13} cm^{-3}, and the electron density N_e and temperature T_e are varied in the range of 10^8–10^{13} cm^{-3} and 1–4 eV, respectively. The size of the plasma is zero in all the results, except for the comparisons of the radiation trapping effects, which used a 10 cm plasma size.

4.1. Comparisons with Optical Emission Spectroscopy Measurements

The final and the complete CR model (F model) is compared with the measured line ratios of the spectra from inductively coupled plasma (ICP) and capacitively coupled plasmas (CCP). The capacitively coupled plasmas (CCP) had an argon gas pressure of 20 mTorr and RF power of 200–700 W. The Langmuir probe measurements indicate that the electron densities change from 1×10^{10} cm^{-3} to 2.5×10^{10} cm^{-3} and electron temperatures stay constant at ~3.2 eV over the RF power variation assuming Maxwellian distribution. The inductively coupled plasma (ICP) conditions measured by the Langmuir probe vary from 5×10^{10} cm^{-3} to 2×10^{11} cm^{-3}. and 1.5 to 2.5 eV, depending on the change in gas pressure from 6 mTorr to 20 mTorr. The Langmuir probe measurements for inductively coupled plasma (ICP) and capacitively coupled plasmas (CCP) are shown in Figures 10 and 11, respectively.

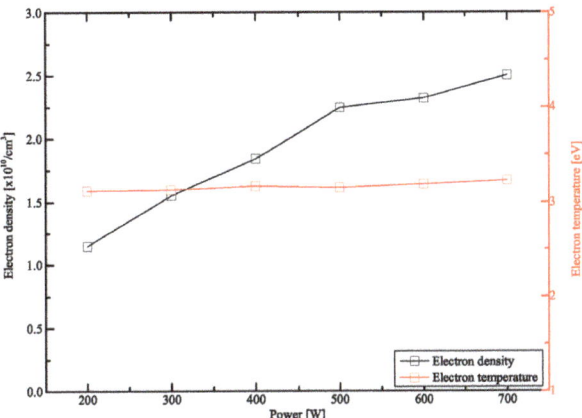

Figure 10. Langmuir probe measurements of electron density and temperature as a function of RF power in the CCP plasma. The gas pressure was fixed at 20 mTorr.

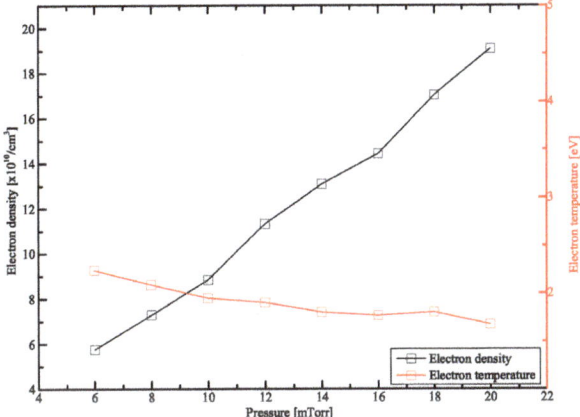

Figure 11. Langmuir probe measurements of electron density and temperature as a function of gas pressure in the ICP plasma. The input power was fixed at 500 W.

The CR calculations are performed for the experimental conditions of density and temperature. The plasma size is assumed to be 1.7 cm from the D-gap of 3.4 cm for CCP plasmas, and the wall recombination is added to make the degree of ionization very low, as observed. A single T_e was assumed. The CR results are compared with the CCP OES data measured from the experimental features in Figure 12. The CR results are compared with the ICP OES data for the 425.9 nm and 750.4 nm line ratios. It is noted that N_e changes from 5×10^{10} cm^{-3} to 2×10^{11} cm^{-3}. The line ratio of 425.9 nm and 750.4 nm is sensitive to N_e above 1×10^{11} cm^{-3}. Figure 13 shows the comparison between the CR results and ICP data for $N_e = 1 \times 10^{10}$ to 1×10^{12} cm^{-3} with and without radiation trapping effects. This shows that the dependence of the line ratio on N_e is different with and without radiation trapping. With radiation trapping, the line ratio increases with N_e. In contrast, the optically thin cases show that the line ratios decrease with increasing N_e. The measured line ratios are slightly lower than the CR results. The trend with increasing N_e (decreasing T_e) agrees with the optically thin case.

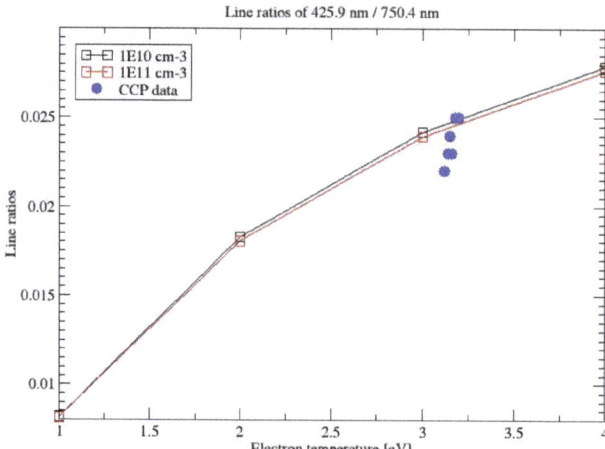

Figure 12. Comparison of line ratio of 425.9 nm/750.4 nm between CR results and CCP data for $N_e = 5 \times 10^{10}$ cm^{-3} to 2×10^{11} cm^{-3}. A slightly lower T_e corresponds to a lower N_e and lower RF power. The measured line ratios have some dependence on N_e, whereas the simulations do not.

Comparisons with the CCP and ICP data show that the single-temperature CR model predicts the electron density and temperature ranges from the measured line ratios comparable to the Langmuir measurements. The experimental conditions may be included in the CR model as a refinement, such as the multi-temperature cases, different radiation trapping conditions, or wall quenching ratios. However, the calculated line ratios do not change dramatically from the single temperature values. The source of discrepancies between CR results and ICP plasma data below 2 eV needs more investigation.

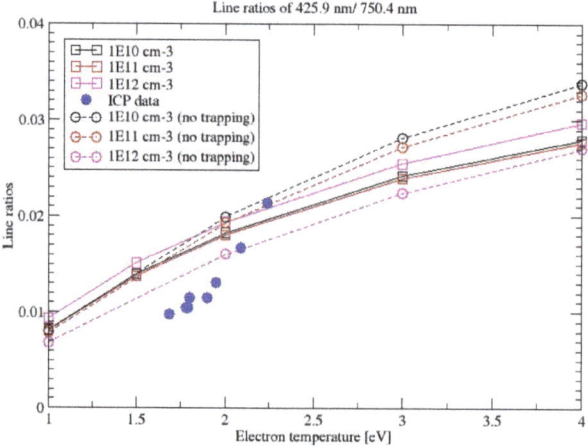

Figure 13. Comparison of line ratio of 425.9 nm/750.4 nm between CR results and ICP data for $N_e = 1 \times 10^{10}$ to 1×10^{12} cm^{-3} with and without radiation trapping effects. A lower T_e corresponds to a higher Ne value. The optically thin case reproduces the measured line ratios better by producing lower line ratios for higher N_e values, i.e., above 1×10^{11} cm^{-3}.

5. Conclusions and Future Work

A CR model employing a complete set of atomic data is constructed to verify the coronal approximation for the OES analysis in plasma processing. Atomic datasets consist of data from various sources, mainly from NIST atomic spectroscopy databases and LXCAT databases. Low-lying states have relatively reliable atomic data from the evaluated NIST data and BSR collisional data. The data for the high-lying state are provided by the LANL and FAC code data, which introduce uncertainties in the analysis of lines originating from those levels. Comparisons of six models with different atomic datasets show that it is critical to have a complete set of atomic data to ensure reasonable and credible line intensities and, hence, line ratios for application in OES.

A non-LTE kinetics code, NOMAD, is used to solve the rate equations for the level population distributions. The code contains time-dependent population kinetics options, radiation trapping effects, and multi-temperature options. The line ratios change when the radiation trapping effects are included and non-thermal electrons are considered. Wall recombination and quenching do not affect the line ratios if the coronal approximation is valid for the plasma conditions. It is found that, for electron densities $>10^{12}$ cm^{-3}, the plasma is in the CR regime, and the coronal approximation is not valid; therefore, line ratio analysis should consider plasma conditions, such as multi-temperature effects, radiation trapping, wall recombination, and quenching. Comparisons with the CCP and ICP OES measurement show that our CR model yields comparable result with the Langmuir probe measurements of the plasma conditions. In this study, we focus on only a few line ratios analyzed by Boffard et al. [1] and others [2]. In the future, additional line ratios will be studied to provide electron temperature and density diagnostics over a wide range of plasma conditions, particularly with greater focus on wall recombination and quenching rates.

Author Contributions: Conceptualization, H.-K.C. and M.-Y.S.; methodology, H.-K.C. and D.; software, H.-K.C.; validation, H.-K.C., M.-Y.S. and G.-H.K.; formal analysis, H.-K.C.; investigation, J.-W.K., M.-G.L., J.P., N.B., J.S.; resources, Y.R.; data curation, J.-W.K., M.-G.L., J.P., N.B., J.S.; writing—original draft preparation, H.-K.C.; writing—review and editing, G.-H.K., M.-Y.S.; visualization, supervision, M.-Y.S.; project administration, M.-Y.S.; funding acquisition, M.-Y.S. All authors have read and agreed to the published version of the manuscript.

Funding: This research was supported by the R&D Program of "Plasma BigData ICT Convergence Technology Research Project (code No. 1711124799)" through the Korea Institute of Fusion Energy (KFE) funded by the Government funds, Republic of Korea.

Institutional Review Board Statement: Not applicable.

Informed Consent Statement: Not applicable.

Data Availability Statement: Numerical data for cross sections can be obtained from the authors upon request.

Acknowledgments: Not applicable.

Conflicts of Interest: The authors declare no conflicts of interest.

References

1. Boffard, J.B.; Lin, C.C.; DeJoseph, C.A., Jr. Application of excitation cross sections to optical plasma diagnostics. *J. Phys. Appl. Phys.* **2004**, *37*, R143–R161. [CrossRef]
2. Zhu, X.M.; Pu, Y.K. Optical emission spectroscopy in low-temperature plasmas containing argon and nitrogen: Determination of the electron temperature and density by the line-ratio method. *J. Phys. Appl. Phys.* **2010**, *43*, 403001. [CrossRef]
3. Donnelly, V.M. Plasma electron temperatures and electron energy distributions measured by trace rare gases optical emission spectroscopy. *J. Phys. Appl. Phys.* **2004**, *37*, R217–R236. [CrossRef]
4. Boffard, J.B.; Jung, R.O.; Lin, C.C.; Aneskavich, L.E.; Wendt, A.E. Argon 420.1–419.8 nm emission line ratio for measuring plasma effective electron temperatures. *J. Phys. Appl. Phys.* **2012**, *45*, 045201. [CrossRef]
5. Boffard, J.B.; Jung, R.O.; Lin, C.C.; Aneskavich, L.E.; Wendt, A.E. Optical diagnostics for characterization of electron energy distributions: argon inductively coupled plasmas. *Plasma Sources Sci. Technol.* **2011**, *20*, 055006. [CrossRef]
6. Dipti.; Gangwar, R.K.; Srivastava, R.; Stauffer, A.D. Collisional-radiative model for non-Maxwellian inductively coupled argon plasmas using detailed fine-structure relativistic distorted-wave cross sections. *Eur. Phys. J.* **2013**, *67*, 203. [CrossRef]

7. Huh, S.R.; Kim, N.K.; Jung, B.K.; Chung, K.J.; Hwang, Y.S.; Kim, G.H. Global model analysis of negative ion generation in low-pressure inductively coupled hydrogen plasmas with bi-Maxwellian electron energy distributions. *Phys. Plasmas* **2015**, *22*, 033506. [CrossRef]
8. Godyak, V.A. Nonequilibrium EEDF in gas discharge plasmas. *IEEE Trans. Plasma Sci.* **2006**, *34*, 755–766. [CrossRef]
9. Godyak, V.A.; Piejak, R.B. Abnormally low electron energy and heating-mode transition in a low-pressure argon rf discharge at 13.56 MHz. *Phys. Rev. Lett.* **1990**, *65*, 996–999. [CrossRef]
10. Bogaerts, A.; Gijbels, R.; Vlcek, J. Collisional-radiative model for an argon glow discharge. *J. Appl. Phys.* **1998**, *84*, 121–136. [CrossRef]
11. Gangwar, R.K.; Sharma, L.; Srivastava, R.; Stauffer, A.D. Argon plasma modeling with detailed fine-structure cross sections. *J. Appl. Phys.* **2012**, *111*, 053307. [CrossRef]
12. Lee, R.W.; Nash, J.; Ralchenko, Y. Review of the NLTE kinetics code workshop. *J. Quant. Spectrosc. Radiat. Transf.* **1997**, *58*, 737–742. [CrossRef]
13. Bowen, C.; Decoster, A.; Fontes, C.J.; Fournier, K.; Peyrusse, O.; Ralchenko, Y. Review of the NLTE emissivities code comparison virtual workshop. *J. Quant. Spectrosc. Radiat. Transf.* **2003**, *81*, 71–84. [CrossRef]
14. Bowen, C.; Lee, R.; Ralchenko, Y. Comparing plasma population kinetics codes: Review of the NLTE-3 Kinetics Workshop. *J. Quant. Spectrosc. Radiat. Transf.* **2006**, *99*, 102–119. [CrossRef]
15. Rubiano, J.; Florido, R.; Bowen, C.; Lee, R.; Ralchenko, Y. Review of the 4th NLTE Code Comparison Workshop. *High Energy Density Phys.* **2007**, *3*, 225–232. [CrossRef]
16. Fontes, C.; Abdallah, J.; Bowen, C.; Lee, R.; Ralchenko, Y. Review of the NLTE-5 kinetics workshop. *High Energy Density Phys.* **2009**, *5*, 15–22. [CrossRef]
17. Chung, H.K.; Bowen, C.; Fontes, C.; Hansen, S.; Ralchenko, Y. Comparison and analysis of collisional-radiative models at the NLTE-7 workshop. *High Energy Density Phys.* **2013**, *9*, 645–652. [CrossRef]
18. Piron, R.; Gilleron, F.; Aglitskiy, Y.; Chung, H.K.; Fontes, C.; Hansen, S.; Marchuk, O.; Scott, H.; Stambulchik, E.; Ralchenko, Y. Review of the 9th NLTE code comparison workshop. *High Energy Density Phys.* **2017**, *23*, 38–47. [CrossRef] [PubMed]
19. Ralchenko, Y. *Modern Methods in Collisional-Radiative Modeling of Plasmas*; Springer Series on Atomic, Optical, and Plasma Physics; Springer: Berlin/Heidelberg, Germany, 2016. [CrossRef]
20. Ralchenko, Y.; Maron, Y. Accelerated recombination due to resonant deexcitation of metastable states. *J. Quant. Spectrosc. Radiat. Transf.* **2001**, *71*, 609–621. [CrossRef]
21. Kramida, A.; Ralchenko, Y.; Reader, J. NIST Atomic Spectra Database (Ver. 5.5.6). 2018. Available online: https://www.nist.gov/pml/atomic-spectra-database (accessed on 2 November 2021).
22. Inglis, D.R.; Teller, E. Ionic Depression of Series Limits in One-Electron Spectra. *Astrophys. J.* **1939**, *90*, 439. [CrossRef]
23. Zatsarinny, O.; Bartschat, K. B-spline calculations of oscillator strengths in neutral argon. *J. Phys. At. Mol. Opt. Phys.* **2006**, *39*, 2145–2158. [CrossRef]
24. Hassouneh, O.; Salah, W. Atomic data of intermediate autoionzing Rydberg series nf[K]J (n = 4, 5), nd[K]J (n = 5, 6), np[K]J (n = 6, 7) and ns[K]J (n = 7, 8) of neutral argon atom in the multiconfiguration Dirac-Hartree-Fock framework. *Eur. Phys. J. Plus* **2017**, *132*, 312. [CrossRef]
25. Salah, W.; Hassouneh, O. Multiconfiguration Dirac-Hartree-Fock energy levels, oscillator strengths, transition probabilities, hyperfine constants and Landé g-factor of intermediate Rydberg series in neutral argon atom. *Eur. Phys. J. Plus* **2017**, *132*, 160. [CrossRef]
26. LANL. LANL Database. 2018. Available online: https://www.lanl.gov/collaboration/pathogen-database/index.php (accessed on 2 November 2021).
27. Gu, M.F. The flexible atomic code. *Can. J. Phys.* **2008**, *86*, 675–689. [CrossRef]
28. Wang, P. *ATBASE User's Guide*; Report No. UWFDM-942; University of Wisconsin Fusion Technology Institute: Madison, WI, USA, 1993.
29. Cowan, R.D. *The Theory of Atomic Structure and Spectra*; University of California Press: Berkeley, CA, USA; Los Angeles, CA, USA; London, UK, 1981.
30. BIAGI, S.F. Biagi Database, 2018. Available online: www.lxcat.net/Biagi (accessed on 2 November 2021).
31. Zatsarinny, O.; Bartschat, K. BSR Database. 2018. Availableonline:www.lxcat.net/BSR (accessed on 2 November 2021).
32. Alves, L.L.; Guerra, V. IST-Lisbon Database. 2018. Available online: www.lxcat.net/IST-Lisbon (accessed on 2 November 2021).
33. Puech, V. Puech Database. 2018. Available online: www.lxcat.net/Puech (accessed on 2 November 2021).
34. Stauffer, A. NGFSRDW Database. 2018. Available online: www.lxcat.net/NGFSRDW (accessed on 2 November 2021).
35. Boffard, J.B.; Chiaro, B.; Weber, T.; Lin, C.C. Electron-impact excitation of argon: Optical emission cross sections in the range of 300–2500nm. *At. Data Nucl. Data Tables* **2007**, *93*, 831–863. [CrossRef]
36. Chilton, J.E.; Lin, C.C. Measurement of electron-impact excitation into the $3p^53d$ and $3p^55s$ levels of argon using Fourier-transform spectroscopy. *Phys. Rev. A* **1999**, *60*, 3712–3721. [CrossRef]
37. Stewart, M.D.; Chilton, J.E.; Boffard, J.B.; Lin, C.C. Use of radiation trapping for measuring electron-impact excitation cross sections for higher resonance levels of rare-gas atoms. *Phys. Rev. A* **2002**, *65*, 032704. [CrossRef]
38. van Regemorter, H. Rate of Collisional Excitation in Stellar Atmospheres. *Astrophys. J.* **1962**, *136*, 906. [CrossRef]

39. Lotz, W. Electron-Impact Ionization Cross-Sections and Ionization Rate Coefficients for Atoms and Ions. *Astrophys. J. Suppl.* **1967**, *14*, 207. [CrossRef]
40. Mazzotta, P.; Mazzitelli, G.; Colafrancesco, S.; Vittorio, N. Ionization balance for optically thin plasmas: Rate coefficients for all atoms and ions of the elements H to Ni*. *Astron. Astrophys. Suppl. Ser.* **1998**, *133*, 403–409. [CrossRef]
41. Lee, M.-G.; Kwon, J.-W.; Park, J.; Bae, N.; Kim, G.-H.; Chung, H.K. Modeling of Optical Emission Spectroscopy for low temperature Argon plasma. In Proceedings of the 7th International Conference on Microelectronics and Plasma Technology, Incheon, Korea, 25–28 July 2018.
42. Kwon, J.-W.; Lee, M.-G.; Ryu, S.; Jang, Y.; Chung, H.-K.; Song, M.-Y.; Kim, G.H. Effect of High Energy Electron on OES Line Intensity Ratio in Non-Maxwellian Argon Plasmas. In Proceedings of the XXXIV International Conference on Phenomena in Ionized GasesM, Sapporo, Japan, 14–19 July 2019.

Review

A Missing Puzzle in Dissociative Electron Attachment to Biomolecules: The Detection of Radicals

Sylwia Ptasinska [1,2]

[1] Radiation Laboratory, University of Notre Dame, Notre Dame, IN 46556, USA; sptasins@nd.edu
[2] Department of Physics, University of Notre Dame, Notre Dame, IN 46556, USA

Abstract: Ionizing radiation releases a flood of low-energy electrons that often causes the fragmentation of the molecular species it encounters. Special attention has been paid to the electrons' contribution to DNA damage via the dissociative electron attachment (DEA) process. Although numerous research groups worldwide have probed these processes in the past, and many significant achievements have been made, some technical challenges have hindered researchers from obtaining a complete picture of DEA. Therefore, this research perspective calls urgently for the implementation of advanced techniques to identify non-charged radicals that form from such a decomposition of gas-phase molecules. Having well-described DEA products offers a promise to benefit society by straddling the boundary between physics, chemistry, and biology, and it brings the tools of atomic and molecular physics to bear on relevant issues of radiation research and medicine.

Keywords: ionizing radiation; electron scattering; dissociative electron attachment; mass spectrometry; DNA damage

Citation: Ptasinska, S. A Missing Puzzle in Dissociative Electron Attachment to Biomolecules: The Detection of Radicals. *Atoms* **2021**, *9*, 77. https://doi.org/10.3390/atoms9040077

Academic Editor: Grzegorz Piotr Karwasz

Received: 30 August 2021
Accepted: 3 October 2021
Published: 7 October 2021

Publisher's Note: MDPI stays neutral with regard to jurisdictional claims in published maps and institutional affiliations.

Copyright: © 2021 by the author. Licensee MDPI, Basel, Switzerland. This article is an open access article distributed under the terms and conditions of the Creative Commons Attribution (CC BY) license (https://creativecommons.org/licenses/by/4.0/).

1. Background and Knowledge Gap

Over the past several decades, significant resources in the atomic and molecular physics community have been directed towards the understanding of collisional processes with biomolecular targets. They are of great importance in radiation research and provide a breadth of potential interests to the life sciences and their applications. However, to translate the outcomes of these molecular processes into a cellular environment, it is necessary to advance our knowledge of scattering processes. A comprehensive understanding of the physical and chemical processes involved at the molecular level remains elusive, even in terms of a single collision between a particle and a target molecule. To achieve a better picture of such physical events, one of the areas that has shown a significant increase in interest, particularly in the electron-scattering community, is a fundamental understanding of electron–biomolecule interactions.

In general, electron–molecule interactions occur in a plethora of physicochemical processes in all types of matter, including living matter, because electrons, together with generated ions and excited molecules, are the most abundant products of ionizing radiation [1]. If the electrons are produced in the condensed phase, they are often referred to as "secondary electrons." These secondary electrons are created as a result of high-energy photon absorption or during the passage of impinging particles and are due to further inelastic collisions with electrons bound in matter [1]. Moreover, it is commonly accepted that secondary electrons with a lesser amount of energy than the ionization energy of water (~12.5 eV) are "low-energy electrons (LEEs)." A single LEE that interacts with atoms or molecules can determine physical and chemical transformations. For example, it can induce the cleavage of a chemical bond, thus damaging molecules and generating a population of reactive species such as ions and radicals. Subsequently, these reactive species may interact within the medium and lead to form new products or induce further damage.

The pioneering work of Sanche and coworkers in 2000 demonstrated that LEEs can induce severe DNA damage [2]. Since then, a "boom in scientific interest" has emerged and has led to the exploration of the effects of electron scattering from molecules of biological relevance in the gas and condensed phases. During collisions at energies below the molecular target's ionization threshold, LEEs can be scattered elastically or can lead to rotational, vibrational, and electronic excitation or electron attachment to the target. The excitation can then lead to a neutral dissociation process and the attachment to a dissociative electron attachment (DEA) process (Figure 1). Both quantum processes occur at specific energies, which are referred to as resonances; they correspond to the various energy levels of the transient state and can result in the formation of at least one or more radicals if molecular bond breakage occurs [3].

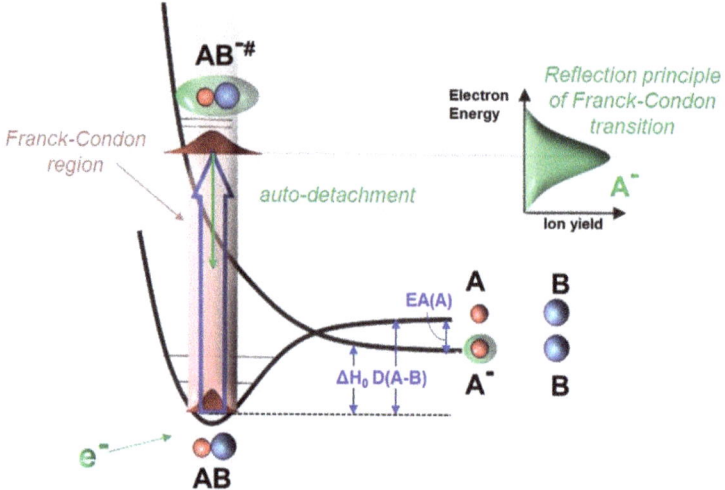

Figure 1. Schematic diagram for the DEA process: $e^- + AB \rightarrow AB^{-\#} \rightarrow A^- + B$ in which AB is a molecular target, $AB^{-\#}$ is a vibrationally excited transient negative ion (TNI), A^- is a negative ion product, B is a neutral radical formed, ΔH_0 is the reaction enthalpy, EA(A) is the electron affinity of neutral fragment A, and D(A-B) is the bond (A-B) dissociation energy. First, the TNI is formed through a vertical transition from the electronic ground state of the neutral molecule to the potential energy surface of the negative ion within the Franck–Condon region. Then, primarily, the TNI will decay into the neutral molecule by electron auto-detachment. If the lifetime of TNI is long enough that the doorway of dissociation becomes accessible, the system stabilizes by breaking down into an anion fragment (A^-) and a neutral fragment (B) or multiple neutral fragments. Experimentally, the ion yield of A^- is monitored by scanning the electron energy and is shown as a resonant peak that reflects the initial Franck–Condon transition.

In Sanche's pioneering work, resonant structures were also observed in the quantum yields measured in the formation of strand breaks in DNA caused by LEEs as a function of incident electron energy. They were compared to the DEA yields for the two condensed-phase analogues of the DNA constituents, thymine and tetrahydrofurfuryl alcohol, and for water [2]. In the experiments with the DNA analogues, the dissociation patterns observed were the ones in which the molecule lost a hydrogen anion, which is the anion that is then detected with mass spectrometry. The resemblance of both yields, that is, for electron-induced single-strand breaks (SSBs) and double-strand breaks (DSBs) in DNA, and the dissociation of the condensed-phase compounds, prompted the authors to conclude that DNA damage can be initiated by resonant electron attachment to different locations in DNA that is followed by bond dissociation. Already at that time, the DEA process had been intensively studied for a few decades because of ready access to mass-spectrometric tools. Then, the DEA studies have been even more extensive for molecules with a wide range of complexity, from simple diatomic molecules to more complex biomolecular systems in the gas and condensed phases, as well as in clusters [4]. Furthermore, the current state of the art in research on LEE collisions with biomolecules, including DEA studies, was reviewed recently [5]. The authors collected and summarized the main findings in this field, showing the way they are relevant to fundamental and applied studies, highlighting recent experimental and theoretical developments, and attempting to indicate further needs to advance the field. One of the needs in technical development they indicated is the necessity to detect radicals formed during DEA. In the past, only a handful of studies had been published that attempted to investigate radicals attributable to LEE impact, particularly in the condensed phase. Researchers have realized that radical detection would provide a complete description of the dissociation processes that must be employed to determine the mechanism of radiation damage in any biological system, including DNA.

2. Radiation Damage to DNA

Generally, radiation damage to DNA in an aqueous solution can be subdivided into direct damage and indirect damage [6]. The term "direct damage" refers to the ionization of DNA itself or the electron/hole transfer to DNA from its immediate solvent shell. The term "indirect damage" refers to DNA's attack by the highly reactive species produced by radiation, including free radicals. Free radicals are atomic or molecular species that contain at least one unpaired electron in their structure, and they are stable in vacuo. All reactive species, both radicals and non-radicals (which, contrary to radicals, are closed-shell species), are products of the dissociative excitation and ionization of water and other cellular components present in the surrounding medium, and their possible reaction mechanisms have been studied extensively [6]. However, despite this effort, there remains controversy over the importance and contribution of both direct and indirect effects to DNA damage in vivo. In addition to the complexity of the cellular environment and radiation quality (particle type and energy), there are many factors that contribute to this challenge, such as the different model systems used or different theoretical and experimental approaches taken. Typical radiation chemistry experiments have shown that the doses that are used to damage genetic compounds in the solution are at least one order or even four orders of magnitude greater in these experiments than those that are used to kill mammalian cells [7]. This discrepancy in the level of doses raises a major concern about the precise estimation of radiation effects. Informal estimates of indirect damage to DNA derive from the fact that water, which constitutes 70% to 80% of the cellular mass, absorbs most of the energy of the impinging ionization radiation (~99%) and leads to the production of three types of radicals, the hydroxyl radical (OH), hydrogen (H), and solvated electrons that can attack DNA within a picosecond of diffusion time [6]. Indeed, the early studies on OH formed because of the radiolysis of water showed that indirect effects were responsible for killing approximately 70% of cells [7]. For more than half a century, a vast number of experimental studies had been dedicated to acquiring an understanding of radiation-induced DNA damage by radiolytic species, both radicals and non-radicals, including reactive oxygen and nitrogen species, and providing detailed pathways of their reaction mechanisms [8]. Simultaneously, theoretical attempts were made to describe the action of radiation on DNA through modeling along with the rapid increase in the development of programming languages and computer coding in recent decades attributable to the access to faster and higher-performing technology [1]. Thus, water is the main source of reactive species in an aqueous solution; however, other compounds in a cell located in close proximity to DNA can also provide reactive species, which then induce damage to DNA. For example, proteins wrapped around DNA can play the role of a double-edged sword. On the one hand, they provide physical shielding from ionizing radiation, which protects DNA and decreases damage to it [9]. However, on the other hand, the constituents of a protein can release free radicals upon exposure to ionizing radiation [10], and some model studies have shown that amino acids can increase DNA damage [11].

In addition to studies on radical-induced DNA damage, there have been wide discussions on the role of secondary electrons that are precursors of solvated electrons [12]. The quanta of radiation can generate up to several thousand secondary electrons per event, with kinetic energies as high as half of the energy of the primary quanta down to 0 eV, which includes the formation of LEEs (see Figure 2). LEEs also dominate the secondary electron emission distribution from biomolecular targets exposed to different energies of primary radiation [13,14].

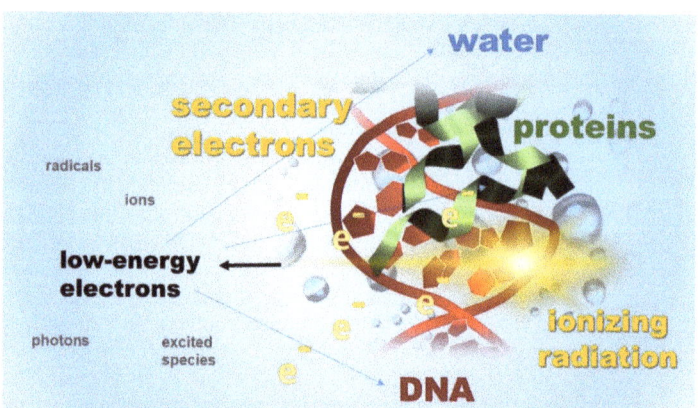

Figure 2. An illustrative representation of LEEs produced from interactions between high-energy radiation and cellular constituents. The inelastic collisions of these LEEs with surrounding molecules cause their damage, e.g., DNA damage, and produce distinct energetic species, i.e., excited species, ions, and radicals that are further driving forces in a wide variety of radiation-induced chemical reactions.

Another physical process, i.e., intermolecular Coulomb decay (ICD) [15], which is one of the well-established mechanisms involved in biological systems, can also produce free electrons [16]. This process can be initiated by photon absorption by a molecule with a higher ionization potential than that of a neighboring molecule in a weakly coupled system. The excitation energy of the molecule is released by energy exchange with the neighboring molecule, which leads to the emission of an electron from the neighboring molecule rather than from the molecule excited initially. The kinetic energy of the emitted electron is typically on the order of several electron volts (<15 eV) [17]. For example, a recent study of the impact of slow, highly-charged ions (Xe^{40+} ion with 0.6 keV) on graphene reported that up to 80 electrons per ion can be produced in a single event [17]. Moreover, because of the Coulomb explosion of two cationic radicals that are formed during this process, the system decomposes. Therefore, ICD has been proposed to be another important factor in base-pair fragmentation [18] and DNA-strand breaks [19,20]. For example, it has been estimated that the ICD that produces radicals and LEEs may contribute up to 50% of the SSBs at the DNA–water interface during low-energy ionization events.

Undoubtedly, the complexity of the radiation-induced processes in the cellular environment, and the secondary electrons' contribution to the damage of living matter, including the process of DEA [21–23], remains the subject of vigorous debate among physicists and chemists. Beyond the physical and chemical changes induced by ionizing radiation, ionizing radiation has also two general types of adverse biological effects: deterministic and stochastic [24,25]. Deterministic effects cause immediate changes in a cell (e.g., cell death), and their severity occurs only above a certain threshold of radiation dose. Stochastic effects cause long-term changes, and although their probability of occurrence increases with the radiation dose, their severity is the same regardless of how low the dose of radiation was to which the cell was exposed. Hence, any single stochastic event even with a low cross section for its appearance but leading to DNA damage attributable to ionizing radiation can ultimately lead to fatal results in the cell [25]. Thus, all processes that involve LEEs play essential roles in radiation damage to biomolecules and contribute to the alteration and/or fragmentation of biomolecules; they therefore need to be understood and clearly identified [26,27].

3. The State of the Art of Detection Techniques for Neutrals Formed due to LEE Impacts

Generally, the electron attachment to any molecule triggers several dissociation pathways of a transient negative ion (TNI) (see Figure 1). In the DEA process, the resulting fragments are a negative ion and its counterpart. The counterpart can be a single radical that has no charge or several radical fragments, which are neutrals. Most DEA experimental studies employ mass spectrometric instrumentation to detect negative fragments from gas-phase molecules or those desorbed from films [5]. Only a few studies have reported the detection of non-charged fragments because such detections require certain techniques to be incorporated into existing DEA experimental setups or the modification of these setups (which increases the costs of such apparatus significantly). In some cases, changes to these very sensitive set-ups are impossible to make. Despite these challenging technical issues, some results have been reported for neutral desorbed from thin films of nitromethane [28], thymine, bromo-uracil-substituted oligonucleotides [29], modified forms of 11-mercaptoundecanoic acid [30], and DNA [31]. In these cases, electron or photon ionization mass spectrometry was used. In addition, to obtain more information about any species remaining on the irradiated films that could not be desorbed, other in vacuo or ex vacuo analysis techniques were used [27]. However, there has been only one report on detecting radicals that were non-charged species formed from the DEA process of molecules in the gas phase [32]. This study used a double-step ionization technique to identify the neutrals from the dissociation of carbon tetrachloride (CCl_4) at close to a 0 eV electron impact. Previously, a similar approach was taken at much higher electron energies than those at which DEA occurs for many plasma-related compounds [33–40]. In these plasma studies, appearance mass spectrometry was used, which is based on the difference between the appearance potential for the ionization of radicals and that for the dissociative ionization of precursor molecules [40]. It has been used widely in the diagnostics of neutral species in plasmas [41]. This technique has been applied successfully in cross-sectional measurements of electron-impact neutral dissociation of gas-phase methane (CH_4) into CH_3 and CH_2 radicals [33,34]; carbon tetrafluoride (CF_4) into CF_3, CF_2, and CF [35]; silicon tetrafluoride (SiF_4) into SiF_3, SiF, and Si [36]; trifluoromethane (CHF_3) into CF_3, CF_2, C_F, CHF_2, and CHF [37]; and sulfur hexafluoride (SF_6) into SF_3, SF_2, and SF [38,39]. To date, no studies of biomolecules in the gas phase have been performed, while the neutral products have been studied only for halogenated compounds [32–40] or small molecules, particularly hydrocarbons [41]. However, the neutrals formed from these compounds were not produced at energies corresponding to DEA, which occurs below 12 eV, but at much higher energies, above 14 eV and most often at approximately 70 eV, an electron energy region with the highest cross-section for ionization.

In all of these gas-phase studies, neutrals were detected indirectly by ionizing them, and charged products were seen with mass spectrometry. To achieve this, either one electron source or two ionization sources were used. In a study published on DEA to CCl_4, the experimental setup was the same as for the conventional gas-phase DEA experiments with one electron source, which was pulsed [32]. In this study, a target molecule was subjected to an electron beam of alternating energies to induce different types of interactions at each step. In each step, the electron beam's desired combination of energy and pulse frequency was applied. Moreover, the ionic fragments acquired in each step could also be specified with respect to their mass and charge (Figure 3). Thus, in the first step, the electron energy was set at the known resonance peak for the DEA processes and was kept the same throughout the measurement. In contrast, while the electron energy of the second step was scanned, the electron energy was changed at a fixed increment in each iteration of the two steps to determine the energy at which the signal from the expected radical fragment occurred. This energy corresponded to the ionization threshold of the species that was needed to form a cation. The iteration of both steps was repeated until the cation signal appeared. However, rather than repeating these steps using only one electron source, another electron source could be used in the second step to ionize radicals. The choice to use one or two sources would depend on accessible resources, the electron sources' electronic properties, such as electron beam frequency and energy range, and the experimental set-up's geometry.

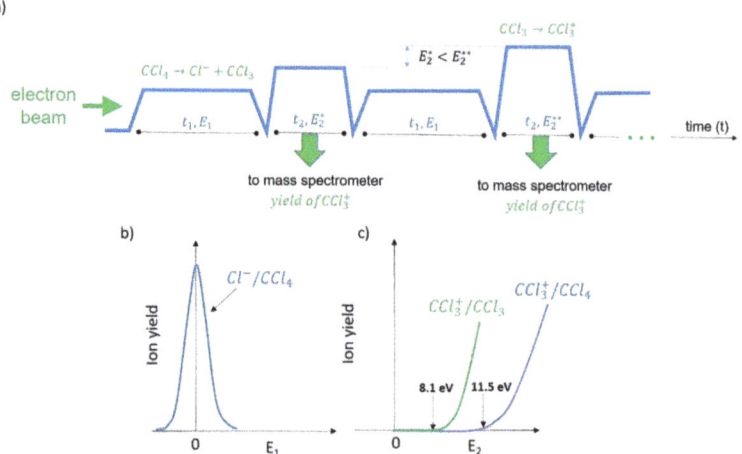

Figure 3. (a) A time flow of the experiment for the neutral products from DEA to CCl_4 using a stepwise electron spectroscopy technique [32]; (b) the Cl^- ion formation by DEA to CCl_4; (c) the ionization threshold for the CCl_3^+ ion from the CCl_3 radical and the appearance energy of the CCl_3^+ fragment due to the dissociation of CCl_4 upon the electron impact. In the first step of the acquisition scheme (a), the electron beam energy E_1 was set at approximately 0 eV, and the electrons interact with the molecular beam in the collision region during time t_1. The Cl^- ions (formed by DEA to CCl_4 (b)) were acquired during the same period t_1. Then, the electron energy was increased to E_2, which was slightly below the ionization energy of CCl_3. The energy E_2 continued to be increased in each iteration until the ion signal for CCl_3^+ was clearly detectable. During the second step (t_2), the electron beam of energy E_2 interacts with the mix of CCl_4 and the products that resulted from the interaction in the first step, i.e., Cl^- and CCl_3. The mass spectrometer was set to detect the ion yield of CCl_3^+ during the second step t_2. Because there was a mix of CCl_4, Cl^-, and CCl_3 during the second step inside the electron–molecule interaction region, the CCl_3^+ acquired could be produced by both the electron impact fragmentation of CCl_4 molecules (from the target beam) and the electron impact ionization of the CCl_3 fragment formed during time t_1. However, there was a difference between the appearance energy of CCl_3^+ from CCl_4 and the ionization energy of the CCl_3 (c). In other words, the appearance energy of CCl_3^+ was over 3 eV higher than the ionization energy of CCl_3. During the experiment, the electron energies in the steps, E_1 and E_2, were controllable. The same procedure can be applied to detect or exclude other possible neutrals, e.g., CCl, CCl_2, and so on, produced in the DEA process by properly adjusting the E_2 value. In addition, the period of t_1 and t_2 is controllable as well. For example, it was set such that t_1 and t_2 were equal to 1 s and 0.1 s, respectively, in the experiment published for the CCl_3 detection from DEA to CCl_4 [32].

Regardless of the experimental arrangements, the general idea is that the neutral precursor can be identified by comparing the threshold energies necessary to ionize a given species. Typically, the appearance energy (i.e., the minimum energy required for the molecule to dissociate and for its ionization to provide a cationic fragment simultaneously) is much higher than the ionization energy (i.e., the minimum energy required to remove the valence electron) (see Figure 3). Another way to detect radicals using mass spectrometry is by electron attachment that leads to the formation of an anion. In some cases, identifying neutrals by the electron attachment method is preferable when the electron affinity is high for a given radical, as will be mentioned below for the nucleobase moieties [42].

Other ionization techniques can be used to detect radicals, as in the case of desorbed species produced via DEA in the condensed phase, where the photon beam was used to ionize the products [28,31]. In addition to these two ionization methods, i.e., electron ionization and photoionization, technical approaches can be adopted by detecting the emission light from the excited neutral species, such as using Fourier transform infrared spectroscopy or laser-induced fluorescence. These techniques can be complementary to those in which mass spectrometry is involved.

4. Molecular Targets of Opportunity

Because no experimental studies have described all of the products formed by DEA, many possibilities are open for the advancement of our understanding of this process and are necessary to provide its complete picture. Thus far, in attempts to provide detailed fragmentation channels, neutral species are deduced based upon anionic species formed in the experiment and predicted by computational quantum modeling methods, which calculate the most energetically favorable fragmentation channels. This is determined by the reaction enthalpies of possible products; however, this approach disregards the formation of TNI as a precursor species before dissociation.

4.1. Nucleobabses

Beyond the fundamental description of DEA processes, detecting neutral radicals is essential from the perspective of DNA radiation damage, particularly in the case of DSBs by LEEs. It has been shown that the formation of a TNI can lead to SSBs in DNA attributable to the direct interaction of an LEE with the DNA's sugar–phosphate backbone or due to electron capture by a nucleobase and charge transfer to the DNA backbone [2]. However, it is still unclear how a single LEE with an energy of between 5 and 15 eV can cause a DSB. The molecular description of the mechanism for DSBs can support more complex decomposition pathways [43] that involve direct and indirect effects of LEEs [44,45], and it still requires further investigation. One of the possible pathways is radical formation via DEA in close proximity to the sugar–phosphate backbone. Thus, these neutral radicals can be produced from the DNA itself or the surrounding molecules. For example, one of the most abundant anionic species for all nucleobases (NB) is the anion fragment formed via H loss in the following reaction:

$$e^- + NB \rightarrow NB^{-\#} \rightarrow H + NB^-_{-H} \qquad (1)$$

in which $NB^{-\#}$ is the TNI, H is the hydrogen radical, and NB^-_{-H} is a closed-shell anion of the nucleobase with H loss. Like nucleobases, all studied amino acids also yield H loss upon electron impact as the most abundant dissociation channel [5]. The resulting hydrogen radicals can interact with the DNA strand and cause damage [11], because the H radical is an electrophilic species with a strong preference for attacking electron-rich sites, although at a lower rate than the OH radical [6].

Interestingly, the detection of neutral products of the channel complementary to Reaction 1, in which the hydrogen anion is formed (Reaction 2), can be of great significance in severe damage to DNA.

$$e^- + NB \rightarrow NB^{-\#} \rightarrow NB_{-H} + H^- \qquad (2)$$

in which $NB^{-\#}$ is the TNI, H^- is the closed-shell hydrogen anion, and NB_{-H} is a neutral radical of the nucleobase without hydrogen. The resulting radical is an excellent electron acceptor and can receive electrons from the neighboring constituents to form the closed-shell species. The values of adiabatic electron affinity of the neutral radicals of the nucleobases

(U—uracil, T—thymine, A—adenine, C—cytosine, G—guanine) without hydrogen follow the order ($U_{-H} > T_{-H} > A_{-H} > C_{-H} > G_{-H}$), which differs somewhat from the order of electron affinity for the closed-shell nucleobases [42]. The formation of these radicals and their further interaction with DNA can potentially lead to a strand break or dimer formation (e.g., the thymine dimer). Although the formation of H^- from nucleobases is well established, no measurements have been performed to detect the neutral NB_{-H} in a DEA process.

Therefore, one of the important groups of molecules that would shed light on LEE effects on DNA damage are the nucleobases. Radicals created via DEA to nucleobases can have severe consequences, because the pyrimidine dimer, particularly thymine dimer, is a common result of ultraviolet radiation damage to DNA [6]. DEA to thymine has been studied extensively, and their anionic fragments have been identified and characterized well with respect to their resonant structures [46–53]. Therefore, the initial effort could focus on detecting radicals of nucleobases without hydrogen (Reaction 2). To identify NB_{-H} formation, the electron energy should be set at one of the resonant energies, i.e., above 4 eV, where H^- is observed for nucleobases (first-step ionization). A mass spectrum in the positive mode could be recorded at an electron ionization energy of 70 eV (second-step ionization), which for most molecular species has the highest cross-section for ionization. The presence of NB_{-H}^+ indicates solely the formation of NB_{-H} in Reaction 2, as in earlier electron ionization studies, no NB_{-H}^+ was formed from NB. To confirm these assignments, the complementary negative ion mode can also be performed, in which the electron energy can be scanned at the fixed mass corresponding to NB_{-H}. This allows observation of the resonant formation of anions from NB_{-H} (second-step ionization). Because the electron affinity for NB_{-H} and the probability of the closed-shell anion formation are high [54], the resonant structure in ion yields is expected. A similar methodology can be used to detect other neutral fragments from nucleobases.

4.2. Water

As mentioned above, OH radicals from surrounding water molecules can also cause indirect DNA damage, and it has been suggested that an electron energy above 5 eV causes DSBs that are correlated with the presence of H_2O–DNA complexes [45].

Therefore, it is of great importance to detect neutral radicals from DEA to water, which is a simple, yet vital, system for understanding the chemical reactivity that leads to DSBs in DNA. An early attempt to study free radicals from water dissociation was performed at an electron impact of 100 eV [55]. DEA to gas-phase water has been studied extensively and remeasured frequently by several groups, and cross sections for DEA have been compiled recently [56]. Three anionic fragments, i.e., H^-, OH^-, and O^-, produced from intact water molecules were observed experimentally:

$$e^- + H_2O \rightarrow H_2O^{-\#} \rightarrow H^- + (OH) \text{ or } (O + H) \quad (3)$$

$$e^- + H_2O \rightarrow H_2O^{-\#} \rightarrow OH^- + (H) \quad (4)$$

$$e^- + H_2O \rightarrow H_2O^{-\#} \rightarrow O^- + (H + H) \text{ or } (H_2) \quad (5)$$

To study neutral fragments (stated in parentheses in Reactions 3–5) formed through DEA to water, the electron energy should be set at the resonance energy where a specific negative ion was observed (first-step ionization), as shown in Figure 4. Then, the mass spectrometer should be set at the mass corresponding to the counterpart neutral fragment of the anion observed while the electron energy is scanned either in the positive or negative modes of the mass spectrometer (second-step ionization). The positive mode (cation detection) can determine the threshold energy for the neutral fragments' ionization. One must keep in mind that the energy scans can include the contribution from water molecules present in the chamber (hereafter denoted as background H_2O) while performing the second-step ionization. However, the appearance energies and anionic resonances of cations and anions produced from background H_2O, respectively, have been documented well [56,57], and they differ from those expected from neutral fragments. Therefore, the signals obtained from background H_2O can be subtracted. The scheme of the experimental procedure is presented in Figure 4 for Reaction 3. For example, the appearance energy for OH^+ from gas-phase water is 18.2 eV, whereas the ionization of the OH fragment is approximately 5 eV lower [57]. Therefore, by scanning the ion yield for mass 17 as a function of electron energy, one can deduce whether the cation observed derives from an intact water molecule or the counter-product of the DEA process. The negative mode (anion detection) can be used to observe the resonant formation of an anion from neutral fragments. It is also expected that the anion yield features formed from gas-phase water differ from those fragments, because the electron affinity for an intact molecule differs from that of neutral fragments. It is important to note that there are reports of radical detection from water dissociation attributable to LEE-induced neutral dissociation, but not via DEA [56].

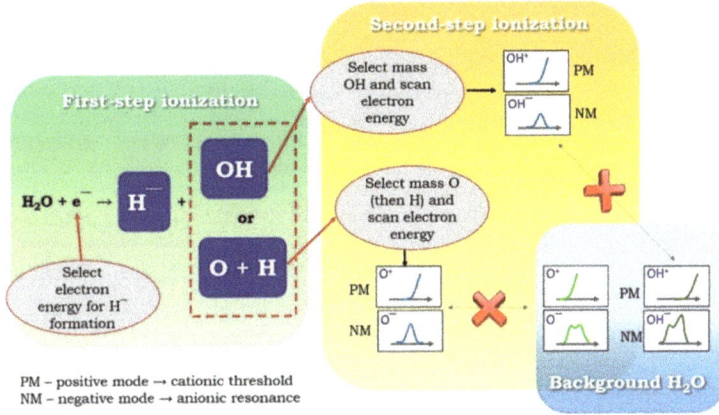

Figure 4. Experimental procedure for neutral fragment identification from water using the two-step ionization method (see the description in the text). The cross mark indicates that the ionization threshold for a neutral fragment differs from the appearance energy of the same fragment formed directly from water and that the resonance structure for anion formation will show different spectra.

5. Conclusions

A continuing quest to understand fundamental phenomena induced by ionizing radiation, particularly LEEs, which are invariable primary products in any irradiated matter, is still the ongoing focus of the radiation research community. Although these free or quasi-free electrons do not travel very far because of their many inelastic collisions, and because they become thermalized within approximately 1 picosecond, they play an essential role in the dissociation of molecules along their way and in the production of longer-lived species such as radicals [22,58,59].

Despite the extensive research by atomic and molecular physics groups on LEE interactions with gas-phase and condensed-phased biomolecules, some fundamental aspects remain unexamined at the molecular level. One of these is detecting radicals from the DEA process, which is a missing puzzle for obtaining a complete picture of this process. Because stable radicals formed in this process are non-charged species, it is not possible to detect them directly by mass spectrometry, which is used commonly to study DEA. Therefore, modified mass spectrometric techniques or other currently available technical advances need to be used to reveal detailed fragmentation patterns. Obtaining fully described patterns can be incorporated into the database of electronic properties of biomolecules, which are invaluable to build accurate theoretical and computational models of radiation effects [5,60]. This can reveal new mechanistic information on DNA damage during irradiation and can be used to plan radiotherapy treatment. The discovery of all products formed via DEA will transform our fundamental understanding of LEE interactions with biomolecular systems and has the great potential to yield physical information on the chemistry and biology of radiation-induced damage of living cells. Thus, a thorough understanding of this basic and significant collisional process may lead more broadly to enhanced medical applications in the fields of radiotherapy, radiodiagnostics, and radiation protection.

Funding: The work was supported by the U.S. Department of Energy Office of Science, Office of Basic Energy Sciences under Award Number DE-FC02-04ER15533. This is contribution number NDRL 5335 from the Notre Dame Radiation Laboratory.

Institutional Review Board Statement: Not applicable.

Informed Consent Statement: Not applicable.

Conflicts of Interest: The author declares no conflict of interest.

References

1. Plante, I. A review of simulation codes and approaches for radiation chemistry. *Phys. Med. Biol.* **2021**, *66*, 03TR02. [CrossRef]
2. Boudaïffa, B.; Cloutier, P.; Hunting, D.; Huels, M.A.; Sanche, L. Resonant Formation of DNA Strand Breaks by Low-Energy (3 to 20 eV) Electrons. *Science* **2000**, *287*, 1658–1660. [CrossRef] [PubMed]
3. Slaughter, D.S.; Rescigno, T.N. Breaking up is hard to do. *Nat. Phys.* **2018**, *14*, 109–110. [CrossRef]
4. Fabrikant, I.I.; Eden, S.; Mason, N.J.; Fedor, J. Chapter Nine—Recent Progress in Dissociative Electron Attachment: From Diatomics to Biomolecules. In *Advances in Atomic, Molecular, and Optical Physics*; Arimondo, E., Lin, C.C., Yelin, S.F., Eds.; Academic Press: Cambridge, MA, USA, 2017; Volume 66, pp. 545–657.
5. Gorfinkiel, J.D.; Ptasinska, S. Electron scattering from molecules and molecular aggregates of biological relevance. *J. Phys. B At. Mol. Opt. Phys.* **2017**, *50*, 182001. [CrossRef]
6. Sonntage, C.V. *Free-Radical-Induced DNA Damage and Its Repair*, 1st ed.; Springer: Berlin, Germany, 2006; p. 523.
7. Ward, J.F. Radiolytic damage to genetic material. *J. Chem. Educ.* **1981**, *58*, 135–139. [CrossRef]
8. Dizdaroglu, M.; Jaruga, P. Mechanisms of free radical-induced damage to DNA. *Free Radic. Res.* **2012**, *46*, 382–419. [CrossRef] [PubMed]
9. Spotheim-Maurizot, M.; Davídková, M. Radiation damage to DNA in DNA–protein complexes. *Mutat. Res./Fundam. Mol. Mech. Mutagenesis* **2011**, *711*, 41–48. [CrossRef]
10. Sagstuen, E.; Sanderud, A.; Hole, E.O. The Solid-State Radiation Chemistry of Simple Amino Acids, Revisited. *Radiat. Res.* **2004**, *162*, 112–119. [CrossRef]
11. Ptasińska, S.; Li, Z.; Mason, N.J.; Sanche, L. Damage to amino acid–nucleotide pairs induced by 1 eV electrons. *Phys. Chem. Chem. Phys.* **2010**, *12*, 9367–9372. [CrossRef]
12. Alizadeh, E.; Sanche, L. Precursors of solvated electrons in radiobiological physics and chemistry. *Chem. Rev.* **2012**, *112*, 5578–5602. [CrossRef]
13. Moretto-Capelle, P.; Le Padellec, A. Electron spectroscopy in proton collisions with dry gas-phase uracil base. *Phys. Rev. A* **2006**, *74*, 062705. [CrossRef]
14. Padellec, A.L.; Moretto-Capelle, P.; Richard-Viard, M.; Champeaux, J.; Cafarelli, P. Ionization and fragmentation of DNA, RNA bases induced by proton impact. *J. Phys. Conf. Ser.* **2008**, *101*, 012007. [CrossRef]
15. Jahnke, T.; Hergenhahn, U.; Winter, B.; Dörner, R.; Frühling, U.; Demekhin, P.V.; Gokhberg, K.; Cederbaum, L.S.; Ehresmann, A.; Knie, A.; et al. Interatomic and Intermolecular Coulombic Decay. *Chem. Rev.* **2020**, *120*, 11295–11369. [CrossRef] [PubMed]
16. Harbach, P.H.P.; Schneider, M.; Faraji, S.; Dreuw, A. Intermolecular Coulombic Decay in Biology: The Initial Electron Detachment from FADH$^-$ in DNA Photolyases. *J. Phys. Chem. Lett.* **2013**, *4*, 943–949. [CrossRef] [PubMed]
17. Schwestka, J.; Niggas, A.; Creutzburg, S.; Kozubek, R.; Heller, R.; Schleberger, M.; Wilhelm, R.A.; Aumayr, F. Charge-Exchange-Driven Low-Energy Electron Splash Induced by Heavy Ion Impact on Condensed Matter. *J. Phys. Chem. Lett.* **2019**, *10*, 4805–4811. [CrossRef] [PubMed]
18. Xu, S.; Guo, D.; Ma, X.; Zhu, X.; Feng, W.; Yan, S.; Zhao, D.; Gao, Y.; Zhang, S.; Ren, X.; et al. Damaging Intermolecular Energy and Proton Transfer Processes in Alpha-Particle-Irradiated Hydrogen-Bonded Systems. *Angew. Chem. Int. Ed.* **2018**, *57*, 17023–17027. [CrossRef] [PubMed]
19. Grieves, G.A.; Orlando, T.M. Intermolecular Coulomb Decay at Weakly Coupled Heterogeneous Interfaces. *Phys. Rev. Lett.* **2011**, *107*, 016104. [CrossRef]
20. Gokhberg, K.; Kolorenč, P.; Kuleff, A.I.; Cederbaum, L.S. Site- and energy-selective slow-electron production through intermolecular Coulombic decay. *Nature* **2014**, *505*, 661–663. [CrossRef]
21. Kohanoff, J.; McAllister, M.; Tribello, G.A.; Gu, B. Interactions between low energy electrons and DNA: A perspective from first-principles simulations. *J. Phys. Condens. Matter* **2017**, *29*, 383001. [CrossRef]

22. Ma, J.; Kumar, A.; Muroya, Y.; Yamashita, S.; Sakurai, T.; Denisov, S.A.; Sevilla, M.D.; Adhikary, A.; Seki, S.; Mostafavi, M. Observation of dissociative quasi-free electron attachment to nucleoside via excited anion radical in solution. *Nat. Commun.* **2019**, *10*, 102. [CrossRef]
23. Dong, Y.; Liao, H.; Gao, Y.; Cloutier, P.; Zheng, Y.; Sanche, L. Early Events in Radiobiology: Isolated and Cluster DNA Damage Induced by Initial Cations and Nonionizing Secondary Electrons. *J. Phys. Chem. Lett.* **2021**, *12*, 717–723. [CrossRef] [PubMed]
24. Desouky, O.; Ding, N.; Zhou, G. Targeted and non-targeted effects of ionizing radiation. *J. Radiat. Res. Appl. Sci.* **2015**, *8*, 247–254. [CrossRef]
25. Jenkins, N.W.; Parrish, J.M.; Sheha, E.D.; Singh, K. Intraoperative risks of radiation exposure for the surgeon and patient. *Ann. Transl. Med.* **2021**, *9*, 84. [CrossRef]
26. Gauduel, Y.; Glinec, Y.; Malka, V. Femtoradical events in aqueous molecular environments: The tenuous borderline between direct and indirect radiation damages. *J. Phys. Conf. Ser.* **2008**, *101*, 012004. [CrossRef]
27. Gao, Y.; Zheng, Y.; Sanche, L. Low-Energy Electron Damage to Condensed-Phase DNA and Its Constituents. *Int. J. Mol. Sci.* **2021**, *22*, 7879. [CrossRef]
28. Bazin, M.; Ptasinska, S.; Bass, A.D.; Sanche, L.; Burean, E.; Swiderek, P. Electron induced dissociation in the condensed-phase nitromethane: II. Desorption of neutral fragments. *J. Phys. Condens. Matter* **2010**, *22*, 084003. [CrossRef]
29. Abdoul-Carime, H.; Dugal, P.C.; Sanche, L. Damage induced by 1-30 eV electrons on thymine- and bromouracil-substituted oligonucleotides. *Radiat. Res.* **2000**, *153*, 23–28. [CrossRef]
30. Houplin, J.; Amiaud, L.; Humblot, V.; Martin, I.; Matar, E.; Azria, R.; Pradier, C.-M.; Lafosse, A. Selective terminal function modification of SAMs driven by low-energy electrons (0–15 eV). *Phys. Chem. Chem. Phys.* **2013**, *15*, 7220–7227. [CrossRef] [PubMed]
31. Chen, Y.; Aleksandrov, A.; Orlando, T.M. Probing low-energy electron induced DNA damage using single photon ionization mass spectrometry. *Int. J. Mass Spectrom.* **2008**, *277*, 314–320. [CrossRef]
32. Li, Z.; Milosavljević, A.R.; Carmichael, I.; Ptasinska, S. Characterization of Neutral Radicals from a Dissociative Electron Attachment Process. *Phys. Rev. Lett.* **2017**, *119*, 053402. [CrossRef] [PubMed]
33. Nakano, T.; Toyoda, H.; Sugai, H. Electron-Impact Dissociation of Methane into CH_3 and CH_2 Radicals I. Relative Cross Sections. *Jpn. J. Appl. Phys.* **1991**, *30*, 2908. [CrossRef]
34. Nakano, T.; Toyoda, H.; Sugai, H. Electron-Impact Dissociation of Methane into CH_3 and CH_2 Radicals II. Absolute Cross Sections. *Jpn. J. Appl. Phys.* **1991**, *30*, 2912. [CrossRef]
35. Nakano, T.; Sugai, H. Partial Cross Sections for Electron Impact Dissociation of CF_4 into Neutral Radicals. *Jpn. J. Appl. Phys.* **1992**, *31*, 2919. [CrossRef]
36. Nakano, T.; Sugai, H. Cross section measurements for electron-impact dissociation of SiF_4 into neutral radicals. *J. Phys. D Appl. Phys.* **1993**, *26*, 1909. [CrossRef]
37. Fisher, E.R.; Kickel, B.L.; Armentrout, P.B. Collision-induced dissociation and charge transfer reactions of SF^+_x ($x = 1 - 5$): Thermochemistry of sulfur fluoride ions and neutrals. *J. Chem. Phys.* **1992**, *97*, 4859. [CrossRef]
38. Iio, M.; Goto, M.; Sugai, H. Relative Cross Sections for Electron—Impact Dissociation of SF_6 into SF_x ($x = 1 - 3$) Neutral Radicals. *Contrib. Plasma Phys.* **1995**, *35*, 405–413. [CrossRef]
39. Christophorou, L.G.; Olthoff, J.K. Electron Interactions With SF_6. *J. Phys. Chem. Ref. Data* **2000**, *29*, 267. [CrossRef]
40. Sugai, H.; Toyoda, H. Appearance mass spectrometry of neutral radicals in radio frequency plasmas. *J. Vac. Sci. Technol. A* **1992**, *10*, 1193. [CrossRef]
41. Benedikt, J.; Kersten, H.; Piel, A. Foundations of measurement of electrons, ions and species fluxes toward surfaces in low-temperature plasmas. *Plasma Sources Sci. Technol.* **2021**, *30*, 033001. [CrossRef]
42. Berdys, J.; Anusiewicz, I.; Skurski, P.; Simons, J. Damage to Model DNA Fragments from Very Low-Energy (<1 eV) Electrons. *J. Am. Chem. Soc.* **2004**, *126*, 6441–6447. [CrossRef]
43. Hahn, M.B.; Meyer, S.; Schröter, M.-A.; Seitz, H.; Kunte, H.-J.; Solomun, T.; Sturm, H. Direct electron irradiation of DNA in a fully aqueous environment. Damage determination in combination with Monte Carlo simulations. *Phys. Chem. Chem. Phys.* **2017**, *19*, 1798–1805. [CrossRef] [PubMed]
44. Alizadeh, E.; Orlando, T.M.; Sanche, L. Biomolecular Damage Induced by Ionizing Radiation: The Direct and Indirect Effects of Low-Energy Electrons on DNA. *Annu. Rev. Phys. Chem.* **2015**, *66*, 379–398. [CrossRef] [PubMed]
45. Orlando, T.M.; Oh, D.; Chen, Y.; Aleksandrov, A.B. Low-energy electron diffraction and induced damage in hydrated DNA. *J. Chem. Phys.* **2008**, *128*, 195102. [CrossRef] [PubMed]
46. Denifl, S.; Sulzer, P.; Zappa, F.; Moser, S.; Kräutler, B.; Echt, O.; Bohme, D.K.; Märk, T.D.; Scheier, P. Isotope effects in dissociative electron attachment to the DNA base thymine. *Int. J. Mass Spectrom.* **2008**, *277*, 296–299. [CrossRef]
47. Kopyra, J.; Koenig-Lehmann, C.; Illenberger, E. On the absolute value for the cross-section of dissociative electron attachment (DEA) to the DNA base thymine. *Int. J. Mass Spectrom.* **2009**, *281*, 89–91. [CrossRef]
48. Ptasinska, S.; Denifl, S.; Scheier, P.; Illenberger, E.; Märk, T.D. Bond- and Site-Selective Loss of H Atoms from Nucleobases by Very-Low-Energy Electrons (<3 eV). *Angew. Chem. Int. Ed.* **2005**, *44*, 6941–6943. [CrossRef]
49. Ptasińska, S.; Denifl, S.; Grill, V.; Märk, T.D.; Scheier, P.; Gohlke, S.; Huels, M.A.; Illenberger, E. Bond-Selective H^- Ion Abstraction from Thymine. *Angew. Chem. Int. Ed.* **2005**, *44*, 1647–1650. [CrossRef]

50. Chernyshova, I.V.; Kontrosh, E.E.; Shpenik, O.B. Collisions of Slow Electrons with Thymine Molecules. *Opt. Spectrosc.* **2018**, *125*, 845–852. [CrossRef]
51. Ptasińska, S.; Denifl, S.; Grill, V.; Märk, T.D.; Illenberger, E.; Scheier, P. Bond- and Site-Selective Loss of H$^-$ from Pyrimidine Bases. *Phys. Rev. Lett.* **2005**, *95*, 093201. [CrossRef]
52. Ptasińska, S.; Denifl, S.; Mróz, B.; Probst, M.; Grill, V.; Illenberger, E.; Scheier, P.; Märk, T.D. Bond selective dissociative electron attachment to thymine. *J. Chem. Phys.* **2005**, *123*, 124302. [CrossRef]
53. Burrow, P.D.; Gallup, G.A.; Scheer, A.M.; Denifl, S.; Ptasinska, S.; Märk, T.; Scheier, P. Vibrational Feshbach resonances in uracil and thymine. *J. Chem. Phys.* **2006**, *124*, 124310. [CrossRef] [PubMed]
54. Gu, J.; Leszczynski, J.; Schaefer, H.F. Interactions of Electrons with Bare and Hydrated Biomolecules: From Nucleic Acid Bases to DNA Segments. *Chem. Rev.* **2012**, *112*, 5603–5640. [CrossRef] [PubMed]
55. Melton, C.E. Radiolysis of water vapor in a wide range radiolysis source of a mass spectrometer. I. Individual and total cross sections for the production of positive ions, negative ions, and free radicals by electrons. *J. Phys. Chem.* **1970**, *74*, 582–587. [CrossRef]
56. Song, M.-Y.; Cho, H.; Karwasz, G.P.; Kokoouline, V.; Nakamura, Y.; Tennyson, J.; Faure, A.; Mason, N.J.; Itikawa, Y. Cross Sections for Electron Collisions with H_2O. *J. Phys. Chem. Ref. Data* **2021**, *50*, 023103. [CrossRef]
57. NIST Chemistry WebBook. Available online: http://webbook.nist.gov (accessed on 30 August 2021).
58. Arumainayagam, C.R.; Lee, H.L.; Nelson, R.B.; Haines, D.R.; Gunawardane, R.P. Low-energy electron-induced reactions in condensed matter. *Surf. Sci. Rep.* **2010**, *65*, 1–44. [CrossRef]
59. Tsuchida, H.; Kai, T.; Kitajima, K.; Matsuya, Y.; Majima, T.; Saito, M. Relation between biomolecular dissociation and energy of secondary electrons generated in liquid water by fast heavy ions. *Eur. Phys. J. D* **2020**, *74*, 212. [CrossRef]
60. Mason, N.J. Electron Induced Processing; Applications and Data Needs. *AIP Conf. Proc.* **2007**, *901*, 74–84. [CrossRef]

Article

Evaluation of Recommended Cross Sections for the Simulation of Electron Tracks in Water

Adrián García-Abenza [1], Ana I. Lozano [1,2], Juan C. Oller [3], Francisco Blanco [4], Jimena D. Gorfinkiel [5], Paulo Limão-Vieira [2] and Gustavo García [1,6,*]

1. Instituto de Física Fundamental, Consejo Superior de Investigaciones Científicas, 28006 Madrid, Spain; adrian.garcia.abenza@csic.es (A.G.-A.); ai.lozano@fct.unl.pt (A.I.L.)
2. Atomic and Molecular Collisions Laboratory, CEFITEC, Department of Physics, Universidade NOVA de Lisboa, 2829-516 Caparica, Portugal; plimaovieira@fct.unl.pt
3. Centro de Investigaciones Energéticas Medioambientales y Tecnológicas-CIEMAT, 28040 Madrid, Spain; jc.oller@ciemat.es
4. Departamento de Estructura de la Materia, Física Térmica y Electrónica e IPARCOS, Universidad Complutense de Madrid, 28040 Madrid, Spain; pacobr@fis.ucm.es
5. School of Physical Sciences, The Open University, Milton Keynes MK7 6AA, UK; jimena.gorfinkiel@open.ac.uk
6. Centre for Medical Radiation Physics, University of Wollongong, Wollongong, NSW 2522, Australia
* Correspondence: g.garcia@csic.es

Abstract: The accuracy of the most recent recommended cross sections dataset for electron scattering from gaseous H_2O (*J. Phys. Chem. Ref. Data* **2021**, *50*, 023103) is probed in a joint experimental and computational study. Simulations of the magnetically confined electron transport through a gas cell containing H_2O for different beam energies (3, 10 and 70 eV) and pressures (2.5 to 20.0 mTorr) have been performed by using a specifically designed Monte Carlo code. The simulated results have been compared with the corresponding experimental data as well as with simulations performed with Geant4DNA. The comparison made between the experiment and simulation provides insight into possible improvement of the recommended dataset.

Keywords: electron scattering cross sections; electron transport in gases; electron track simulation

1. Introduction

Water (H_2O) is the main constituent of all living organisms, it is a key molecular compound in the interaction of primary radiation with biological systems, where radiolysis (photoelectric and Compton effects) dictates the type of prevalent local chemistry at the molecular level. Additionally, the outcome provided by event-by-event Monte Carlo simulations, which require reliable and consistent sets of cross sections as input data [1–3], has been widely used in modelling radiation protocols in hospitals and/or clinical units devoted to radiotherapy treatment planning. Water has been attracting the attention of the international scientific community for several decades. In particular, in the last 20 years, we note widespread interest across the globe in cross sections for electron scattering from water at both the experimental and theoretical levels [4–17] (see also references therein). However, there is still no consensus on a recommended set of cross sections for electron scattering from H_2O, particularly regarding dipole driven cross sections where important discrepancies are found. In fact, rotational excitations play a significant role in those discrepancies, as they are either not properly accounted or even not resolved in experimental setups at electron scattering angles close to 0 degrees, making the computation of the total cross section (TCS) [18] or the momentum transfer cross sections (MTCSs) required for deriving swarm transport coefficients [7,11] more difficult. Therefore, it is of major interest to evaluate the reliability of the proposed datasets.

In the Madrid laboratory, we have successfully implemented a well-proven methodology capable of delivering the most accurate dataset [19–21] through a procedure combining experimental and simulation methods. In this study we aim at evaluating the reliability and applicability of the most recent recommended cross sections dataset for electron scattering from gaseous H_2O [22]. For this purpose, we have used those cross sections as input data for our novel event-by-event Monte Carlo code. The simulated results are then compared with the experimental data for the transmitted intensity of magnetically confined electrons [23] at different energies in the range of 3 to 70 eV, through a gas cell at different sample pressures (2.5 to 20.0 mTorr). Finally, we compare those results with simulations performed with the Geant4DNA [24–27] code for the same conditions.

2. Results and Discussion

In this section we present the cross sections for electron scattering from H_2O recommended by Song et al. [22], together with a brief description of their origin. Next, we probe these cross sections as input data for our Monte Carlo simulation. A comparison with the results obtained using Geant4DNA relative to the experimental data is then thoroughly discussed.

2.1. Recommended Cross Sections

The most recent compilation from the literature (up to the end of 2019) on electron scattering cross sections data from water has been reported by Song and collaborators [22]. Their recommended TCSs are based on the elastic + rotational excitation R-matrix calculations of Tennyson and co-workers from 0.01 up to 7 eV [28–30], the experimental data of Szmytkowski and Mozejko [31] together with those from Kadokura et al. [32] between 7 and 50 eV, and those from Muñoz et al. [18] from 1 up to 10,000 eV. For the elastic integral cross sections (ICSs), Song et al. [22] followed the previously recommendation of Itikawa and Mason [10] adding the theoretical values of Faure et al. [29] for energies between 0.1 and 7 eV. For the electron energy range between 7 and 50 eV, Song et al. interpolated the theoretical values of Faure et al. [29] and used the experimental data recommended by Itikawa and Mason [10] above 50 eV. As far as elastic differential cross sections (DCSs) are concerned, the most recent measurements of Matsui et al. [33] were recommended in the incident energy range of 2−100 eV [22].

Regarding inelastic processes, the vibrational excitation integral cross sections recommended are those from Khakoo et al. [34] for incident energies of 10–100 eV, whereas the data of Seng and Linder [35] is used from threshold up to 10 eV. Concerning $\tilde{A}^1B_1$ electronic excitation cross section, Song et al. [22] recommend Ralphs et al. [36] for energies below 17 eV and the BE f-scaled data for energies above 17 eV [37,38]. For the excitation of the $\tilde{a}^3B_1$ state, the data of Matsui et al. [33] for energies above 12 eV and Ralphs's for energies below 12 eV are recommended. It is relevant to note that excitation cross sections for $^3A_2$, $^1A_2$, $^3A_1$, and $^1A_1$ electronic states were also reported by Ralphs et al. [36], yet these were not recommended by Song et al. [22] based on the disagreement found between that data and the previous experimental results of Thorn et al. [37], the latter thoroughly discussed in ref. [39]. For rotational excitations, Song et al. [22] recommend the previous cross sections from $J''(0_{00})$ to $J' = 0–3$, [10], together with the calculated data of Machado et al. [40] up to 100 eV electron impact energy. The recommended data for water neutral dissociation yielding •OH radical formation in the ground and first excited states and O (^1S), are from Harb et al. [41] and Kedzierski et al. [42], respectively. Finally, the recommended electron-impact ionization cross sections are those from Lindsay and Mangan [43] based on previous measurements of Straub et al. [44].

2.2. Input Data for Our Simulation

The required input data for electron transport simulation based on event-by-event Monte Carlo methods are the total cross sections, the partial integral cross sections, the angular distribution functions, and the energy loss distribution functions of all the relevant physical processes (both elastic and inelastic). For the present simulations we have used those cross sections, with complementary data for both elastic and inelastic DCSs.

We note that Song et al. [22] recommended elastic ICSs and DCSs, which are rotationally unresolved. Therefore, in our simulation we have not explicitly included rotational excitations but rather considered both elastic and rotational excitation processes as a single rotationally unresolved elastic process (see Section 3.2 for further details). Moreover, Song et al. [22] recommended DCSs values are reported between 10–20° and 130° scattering angles, based on the R-matrix calculation of Faure et al. [29] to complement the experimental DCSs from Matsui et al. [33]. However, not all of the data required to either extend the available DCS values to all the scattering angles or to interpolate to all the required energies are available from ref. [29]. For this reason, we have repeated the calculation of elastic electron scattering cross sections for a larger number of scattering energies employing exactly the same model used by Faure et al. (see Section 3.3).

With these additional results (available online[1]), we have extrapolated, after appropriate scaling, the recommended DCSs to 0° and 180° covering thus the whole angular range for electron impact energies below 15 eV. Above this energy, we followed a similar procedure by using the sum of our elastic IAM-SCAR+I [45–47] calculation and the rotational excitation cross sections calculated within the first Born approximation [48,49]. In Figure 1 we show the results of our calculated DCSs and the recommended experimental values for some selected incident energies.

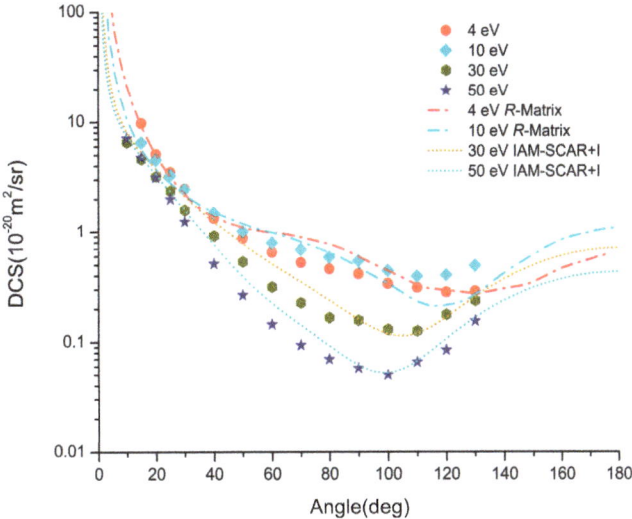

Figure 1. Rotationally summed differential cross sections calculated with the R-matrix method for energies below 15 eV and differential elastic IAM-SCAR+I plus rotational (Born) cross sections for higher energies, compared to the recommended experimental values at 4, 10, 30, and 50 eV [33].

A very important input dataset which was not considered at all in the recent review [22] pertains to DCSs for the inelastic processes, from which the inelastic angular distribution function can be derived. As it is required for our simulations, and in order to show the relevance of these data for the shape and magnitude of the transmission spectra, we have considered two different cases. In case A, we assumed that all inelastic processes lead to isotropic scattering, whereas in case B, the inelastic angular distribution is assumed to be the same as that of the elastic scattering. In the latter case, we have used the 'uncorrected' (see Section 3.3 R-matrix DCSs for electron energies below 15 eV and the IAM-SCAR+I (pure elastic) DCSs for energies above 15 eV (see Figure 2).

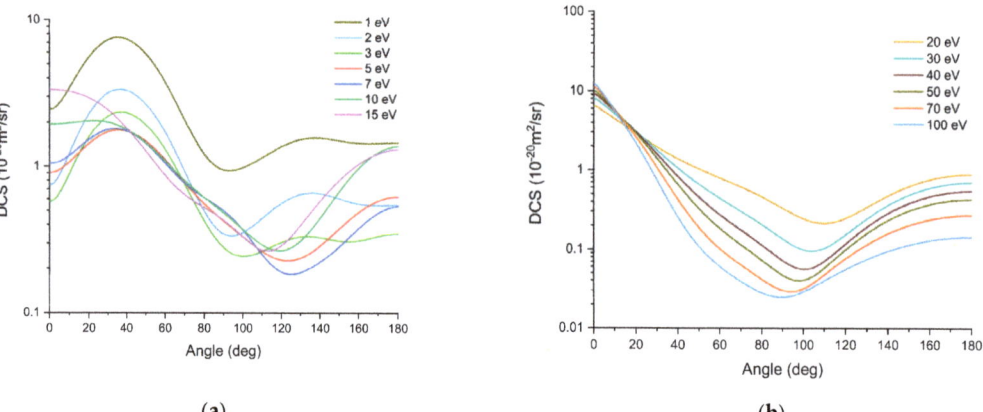

Figure 2. Theoretical elastic differential cross sections for H_2O. (**a**) Uncorrected (see text) R-matrix results in the electron energy range 1–15 eV. (**b**) IAM-SCAR+I results in the electron energy range 20–100 eV.

Another requirement for the input of our simulation code is an energy loss distribution function for each inelastic process considered (see Figure 3). We have used the experimental averaged energy loss spectrum from Muñoz et al. [18] for the ionization energy loss distribution, as well as for the electronic excitation and neutral dissociation processes. For vibrational excitations, we have used the electron energy loss spectrum from El-Zein et al. [50] following the same procedure as noted by Blanco and co-workers [51].

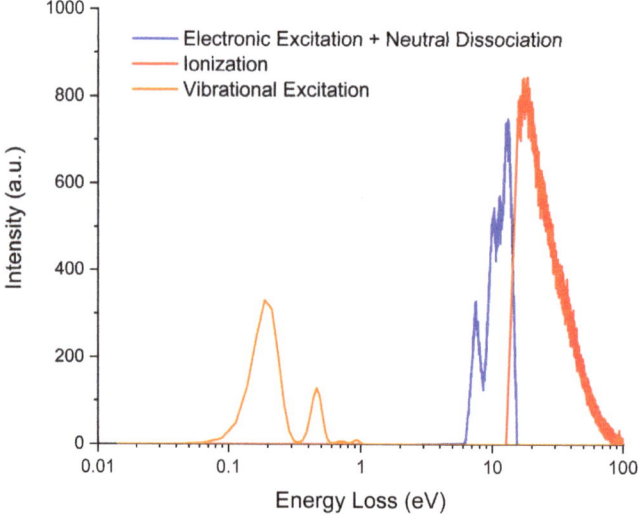

Figure 3. Proposed electron energy loss distribution function associated to each inelastic process in the energy range 1–100 eV. See legend for the different processes depicted.

Finally, it is also important to note that the present TCSs are given by the sum of the partial ICS for each of the physical processes considered in the simulation. Therefore, our TCSs do not exactly match those recommended by Song et al. [22], although these values lie in the 7% range of reasonable uncertainty which can be generally attributed to obtaining TCS data. Table 1 summarizes the ICS and TCS used as input data for our simulation.

Table 1. Integral cross sections (ICS) for each considered physical process and total cross section (TCS), used as input data for the present Monte Carlo simulation of electron transport through gaseous H_2O together with TCS recommended values of ref. [22]. Energy in eV and cross sections in units of 10^{-20} m^2.

Energy	Elastic + Rotational	Electron Attachment	Ionization	Vibrational Excitation	Electronic Excitation	Neutral Dissociation	TCS ^{a}	TCS ^{b}
0.1	987.8	0	0	0	0	0	987.8	987.8
0.2	533.1	0	0	0.096	0	0	533.2	533.1
0.3	368.1	0	0	2.764	0	0	370.9	368.1
0.4	282.1	0	0	2.509	0	0	284.6	282.1
0.5	229.0	0	0	1.446	0	0	230.4	229
0.6	193.0	0	0	0.945	0	0	193.9	193
0.7	166.9	0	0	0.948	0	0	167.8	166.9
0.8	147.2	0	0	0.951	0	0	148.15	147.2
0.9	131.7	0	0	0.861	0	0	132.6	131.7
1	119.3	0	0	0.830	0	0	120.13	119.3
1.2	101.8	0	0	0.826	0	0	102.7	100.6
1.5	81.6	0	0	0.826	0	0	82.4	81.8
2	63.1	0	0	0.489	0	0	63.6	63.1
3	43.6	0	0	0.674	0	0	44.3	43.6
4	36.2	0	0	0.598	0	0	36.8	36.2
5	31.5	8.2×10^{-4}	0	0.760	0	0	32.3	31.5
6	28.6	0.0328	0	1.005	0	0	29.6	28.6
7	25.5	0.0331	0	1.122	0.01	0	26.6	25.5
8	22.8	0.0128	0	1.112	0.10	0	24.0	22.8
9	21.2	0.0144	0	1.047	0.180	0.034	22.5	21.2
10	20.8	0.0054	0	0.955	0.268	0.103	22.13	20.9
12	19.0	0.0054	0	0.738	0.225	0.213	20.17	19.5
15	16.5	3.6×10^{-4}	0.126	0.438	0.193	0.330	17.6	17.2
17	15.1	1.0×10^{-4}	0.245	0.316	0.175	0.390	16.3	16.5
20	13.6	0	0.428	0.225	0.155	0.481	14.9	15.7
25	11.7	0	0.761	0.15309	0.129	0.681	13.4	14.1
30	10.1	0	1.02	0.1217	0.148	0.893	12.3	12.9
35	8.9	0	1.26	0.10089	0.133	1.056	11.4	12.2
40	7.9	0	1.43	0.08432	0.131	1.169	10.7	11.5
45	7.3	0	1.59	0.07144	0.129	1.245	10.3	10.9
50	6.6	0	1.72	0.0617	0.126	1.30	9.8	10.2
75	4.4	0	2.04	0.04101	0.112	1.44	8.10	8.6
100	3.4	0	2.16	0.0168	0.098	1.41	7.11	7.4

^{a} Sum of the partial ICSs used in the present simulation. ^{b} Recommended TCS values from Song et al. [22].

2.3. Experiment vs. Simulation

The main goal of this study is to evaluate the reliability of a recently recommended dataset of cross sections for electron scattering from H_2O to be used for modelling purposes. A well-proven procedure to validate the accuracy of a given cross sections dataset is via event-by-event Monte Carlo simulations of the magnetically confined electron transport through a gas cell, as proven in previous studies [19–21]. As described in Section 3.1, under these conditions, after any collision event the expected scattering angle is transformed into an energy loss in the axial direction. Therefore, the results given by the simulations are very sensitive to both the integral and the differential cross sections used as input data. As the cross sections for elastic processes have only been recommended up to 100 eV [22], we focused our analysis in the low-energy range to make a comparison between the results from the simulation and the experiment for three different electron energies (viz. 3, 10, and 70 eV). Moreover, for each incident energy, we considered two different cases for the pressure in the gas cell, except for the lowest energy (see below). This methodology provides some insight into the effect of increasing the number of multiple collisions, which is relevant for the accuracy and reliability of the input data dependent simulation results.

In Figures 4–6 we depict the integrated transmission curves obtained from our simulations and from Geant4DNA for electron beam incident energies of 3, 10, and 70 eV, respectively. The experimental distributions obtained with the magnetically confined electron beam system are also plotted in these figures for comparison. For 3 eV, we restrict the transmitted spectrum to a gas pressure of 2.5 mTorr given that at higher pressures we have encountered reasonable instabilities; for 10 eV, the electron transmission was obtained at 5.0 and 10.0 mTorr; and for 70 eV, at 10.0 and 20.0 mTorr.

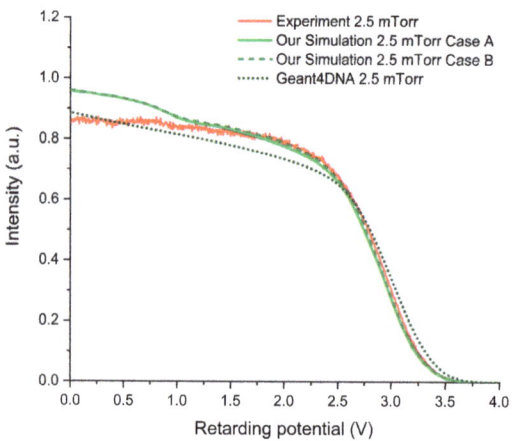

Figure 4. Experimental and simulated transmission spectra (i.e., the intensity of the electrons with a corresponding axial kinetic energy above the retarding potential barrier) of a 3 eV electron beam through 2.5 mTorr of gaseous H_2O.

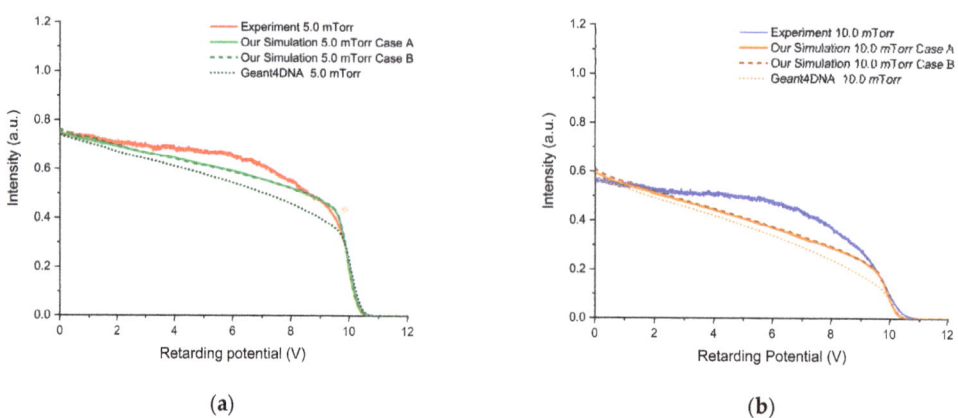

Figure 5. Experimental and simulated transmission spectra (i.e., the intensity of the electrons with a corresponding axial kinetic energy above the retarding potential barrier) of a 10 eV electron beam through (**a**) 5.0 and (**b**) 10.0 mTorr of gaseous H_2O.

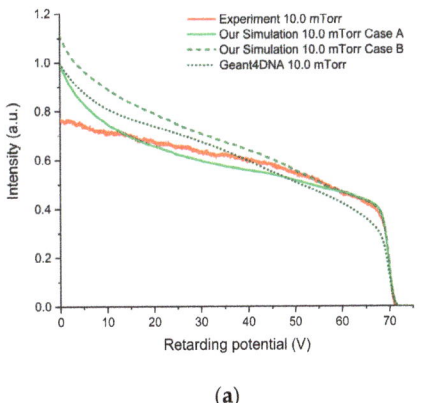
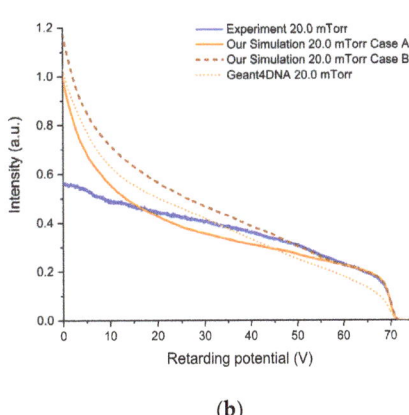

Figure 6. Experimental and simulated transmission spectra (i.e., the intensity of the electrons with a corresponding axial kinetic energy above the retarding potential barrier) of a 70 eV electron beam through (**a**) 10.0 and (**b**) 20.0 mTorr of gaseous H_2O.

For each incident energy we obtained, in general, a good agreement between the simulations and the experimental results for the lowest pressure values considered, while significant discrepancies were found for the highest-pressure values. The results obtained from the simulations performed with Geant4DNA are qualitatively similar to ours but with some systematic discrepancies, which can be attributed to the differences between our input cross sections and those derived from the models considered by Geant4DNA at low energies (see Section 3.2 for further details).

With respect to the results at 3 eV, the main discrepancy appears in the low retarding potential region of the spectra, particularly below 1 V (i.e., where electrons with axial kinetic energies below 1 eV are incorporated to the integral transmission curve), where our simulation shows a significant enhancement which is not visible in the Geant4DNA results and is just slightly appreciable in the experimental data. This suggests that the recommended rotationally unresolved DCSs are overestimating the high angle contribution. However, as we mentioned in a previous study dealing with a larger polyatomic molecule, *para*-benzoquinone [20], a lower probability of the low-energy electrons reaching the detector would also contribute to such discrepancy.

At 10 eV we notice that both our simulation and the Geant4DNA results remain systematically below the experimental transmission curve. At this energy, elastic processes are still predominant, such that the observed systematic underestimation suggests a substantial overestimation of the recommended integral elastic cross sections. In addition, at this energy both electronic excitation and neutral dissociation channels are becoming more significant, so perhaps the overestimation of the elastic cross section at 10 eV is accompanied by an underestimation of the cross section of one of these inelastic processes. Hence, a more accurate cross sections dataset of these processes might significantly improve the agreement between simulations and experiment.

For an incident energy of 70 eV, all inelastic channels are now open, and their influence in the transmission spectra becomes at least as important as that of the elastic one. Our simulations reproduce the experimental results with excellent agreement for retarding potentials above 60 V, suggesting reasonably accurate integral cross sections. However, some discrepancies appear below that energy, which can be attributed to the contribution of the DCSs. As we mentioned in Section 2.1, a set of DCSs for the inelastic processes was absent from the recommended dataset [22], which we are using as input for our simulation. When comparing the present simulations using the two limit assumptions for the inelastic angular distributions (Case A, isotropic; and Case B, the same as that for pure elastic processes) with the experimental results, we observe a significant discrepancy in the slope of the transmission spectrum in the 20–60 V retarding potential range for both cases. In fact, the experimental results seem to lie somewhere in-between these two cases. Moreover, the results obtained with Geant4DNA, in no better agreement with the experimental data than ours, also show a transmission slope which lies in-between our two simulation cases. The discrepancies below 20 V (i.e., where electrons with axial kinetic energies below 20 eV are incorporated to the integral transmission curve) can again be mainly explained by the lower probability of low-energy electrons reaching the detector. Therefore, the results at this incident energy suggest that the inelastic angular distributions play a major role in shaping the transmission spectra. Taking this into account, the incorporation of inelastic DCSs to the cross section compilation of H_2O should lead to a major improvement in the simulation of electron tracks through gaseous water.

Finally, in order to better illustrate the magnitude of the discrepancies found between the present simulated and experimental results as a function of pressure, Table 2 shows the number of processes and the total deposited energy per incident electron for different electron energies and gas pressures. A close inspection of this table reveals that the number of total interactions notably increase with pressure (by a factor of 3 or 4, at 10 and 70 eV, respectively). As the number of total interactions per incident electron increases, the discrepancies between the simulation and experiment are magnified due to the higher number of times that the cross sections data, with their respective uncertainties, are used. At 70 eV incident energy, ionization processes are significant and, accordingly, a high number of secondary electrons are produced, thus making the simulation more challenging. In addition, at the highest pressure considered (20.0 mTorr), the formation of water clusters, which are not considered in our simulations, might be playing a non-negligible role. It is important to note that despite the simulation including all inelastic processes, electronic excitations and electron attachment have such a low rate in the considered experimental conditions that their influence in the shape of the transmission curve is too small to enable evaluation of the accuracy of the associated recommended cross sections from this study.

Table 2. Average number of interactions for each physical process and total energy deposited (bottom row) per initial electron at different incident energy and gas pressure conditions. Simulations were performed for case A (isotropic inelastic scattering assumption).

Process	3 eV 2.5 mTorr	10 eV 5.0 mTorr	10 eV 10.0 mTorr	70 eV 10.0 mTorr	70 eV 20.0 mTorr
Elastic + Rotational	1.99	2.41	6.07	3.77	14.43
Ionization	0.0	0.0	0.0	0.36	0.70
Electronic Exc.	0.0	0.03	0.06	0.03	0.09
Vibrational Exc.	0.03	0.10	0.23	0.07	0.32
Attachment	0.0	0.001	0.002	0.001	0.002
Neutral Dissociation	0.0	0.01	0.02	0.27	0.55
Total Interactions	2.02	2.54	6.38	4.50	16.09
Deposited Energy	0.009 eV	0.271 eV	0.620 eV	5.002 eV	9.902 eV

3. Materials and Methods

In this study we have combined the use of experimental and computational methods in a powerful procedure to validate the accuracy of a given cross sections dataset for electron scattering from gaseous water molecules. Such procedure has previously been applied with success to other molecules of biological interest, such as furfural [19], para-benzoquinone [20], and pyridine [21]. In the following subsections, we briefly describe the experimental setup used, as well as the simulation and computational procedures.

3.1. Magnetically Confined Electron Beam Experiment

The experimental results of the transmitted electron intensity spectra through gaseous H_2O have been performed in a state-of the art magnetically confined electron beam experiment (see Figure 7) which has been described in detail elsewhere [23]. Some recent improvements in the performance of this experimental setup have been achieved after introducing small modifications consisting mainly on the replacement of the grids by collimators with apertures of 1.5 mm in diameter, which are depicted in Figure 7 as C_i (i = 1–7). This modification allows one to apply the potentials along the electrons' path avoiding the formation of secondary electrons and it does not affect the working principle of this setup, which consists of the axial magnetic confinement of the electron beam (around 0.1 T) inside both the nitrogen gas trap and the scattering chamber (see Figure 7). As reported before [23], under these conditions, any collision event converts the expected scattering angle into an energy loss in the axial direction. A hairpin filament generates the electron beam which is guided through a nitrogen gas trap where it can be cooled, thereby reducing its initial energy spread of 500 meV down to about 100–200 meV in the optimal working conditions. Subsequently, before entering the scattering chamber, where a constant pressure of gaseous H_2O is introduced through a leak valve, the electron beam is pulsed. Using a retarding potential analyzer (RPA), at the exit of the scattering chamber, the integrated transmission for electrons up to a given axial kinetic energy is recorded and, by performing an energy scan, the integrated transmission curves can be obtained.

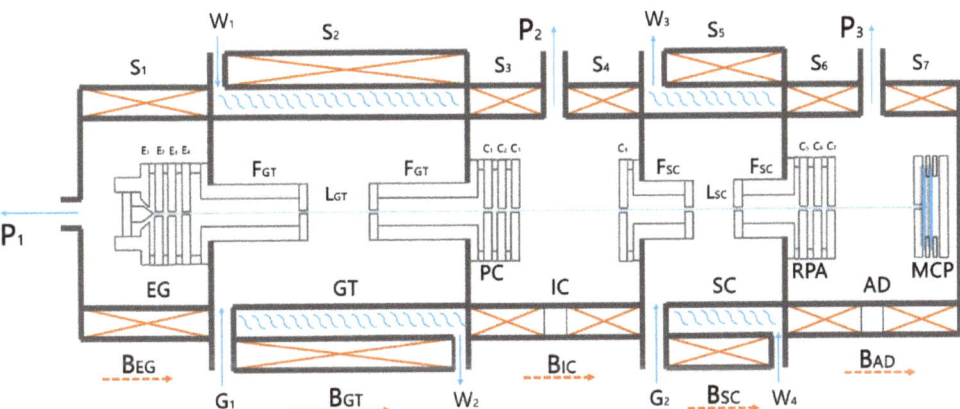

Figure 7. Schematic representation of the magnetically confined electron beam experiment: EG, electron gun; GT, gas trap; IC, interphase chamber; PC, pulse-controlling system; SC, scattering chamber; RPA, retarding potential analyzer; AD, detection area; MCP, microchannel plate detector; C_1–C_7 various transmission collimators; P1, P2, P3, differential pumping system; B_{EG}, B_{GT}, B_{IC}, B_{SC}, B_{AD}, axial magnetic fields of the different chambers generated by the corresponding solenoids (S_1–S_7); W_1–W_4, water cooling system; G1, G2, gas inlet to the GT and SC, respectively. (See also text and ref. [23] for further explanation).

3.2. Simulation Procedure

A specifically designed and developed event-by-event Monte Carlo code, fully built and implemented in Python, has been used to simulate the transmitted intensity of magnetically confined electrons through gaseous H_2O.

This code has a modular structure that allows one to easily implement, revise, and modify each of the physical processes involved in a specific simulation. When simulating charged particles tracks, the code considers the different physical processes by sampling the step length between collisions, the interaction type, the energy loss, and the angular deflection of the scattered particles. This sampling procedure is performed from the probability distributions derived from the input dataset consisting of the total cross sections, the partial integral cross sections, the energy loss spectra, and the differential cross sections. Special attention is needed for sampling the scattering angle of the rotational excitations as their DCS are very strongly peaked in the forward scattering direction and a double logarithmic fitting for the interpolation at low angles is required in order to perform an accurate sampling. This is especially important in the present simulations, where rotational excitations and pure elastic collisions are merged into one single quasi-elastic process.

In the present study, we generated 10^4 incident electrons with an initial energy distribution obtained from the experimental transmission measurements with no gas (0 mTorr) in the collision chamber for each specific condition (incident energy and gas pressure) investigated. Although we could have achieved an electron beam energy resolution of around 100–200 meV, for the present study we have worked with suboptimal conditions (see Supplementary Information in Supplementary Materials for the precise energy resolution determination) in order to make even more challenging for the simulation to reproduc the transmitted energy spectra. This number of electrons was found to be enough to ensure that statistical uncertainties on the simulated transmitted intensities are less than 1%. It is also important to note that the RPA only affects the axial component of the emerging electrons' momentum. Therefore, the simulated transmitted intensity is obtained by measuring only the kinetic energy associated with such component.

We have also performed simulations using the Geant4DNA [2,26] code, which is an extension of the well-known multipurpose Monte Carlo simulation toolkit Geant4 [52]. This extension includes models for processes relevant to the simulation of biological damage induced by ionizing radiation at the DNA scale. These processes mainly account for low-energy electron collisions with water and other DNA analogue molecules such as tetrahydrofuran (THF) and pyrimidine. The Geant4DNA simulation procedure has been thoroughly described by the Geant4DNA collaboration [2,3] so no further details will be given here. Among the available models for low-energy electron transport through water, we have selected those which have the lowest energy limit in their applicability. For elastic processes, we have used the Screened Rutherford model; for electronic excitations and ionizations we have selected the Emfietzoglou model; and for vibrational excitations and electron attachment we have applied the Sanche Excitation model and the Melton Attachment model, respectively.

3.3. Theoretical Calculation of Elastic and Rotational Cross Sections

The electronically elastic cross sections below 15 eV were calculated using the R-matrix method, as implemented in the UKRmol[1] suite [53], within the fixed-nuclei approximation. As mentioned above, the model used in these calculations is identical to that employed by Faure et al. [29]. The model can be briefly summarized as follows (see [54] for more details): the molecular geometry corresponds to $r_{OH} = 1.81 a_0$ and an angle between the OH bonds $\alpha = 104.5°$. The Dunning DZP basis set was used for O and the TZP for H, this latter augmented with one diffuse s and two p functions, to generate pseudonatural orbitals that best describe (within this basis) the ground state and lowest six excited states of H_2O. Seven target states were included in the close-coupling expansion: a complete active space configuration interaction model was used to expand the electronic state wavefunctions, in which the 1s orbitals of O were kept frozen and the eight remaining electrons were allowed to occupy the orbitals in the active space ($2a_1$, $3a_1$, $4a_1$, $5a_1$, $1b_1$, $2b_1$, $1b_2$). This model produces a good description of the target states [54]: the ground state dipole moment (a critical quantity when describing electron scattering from a polar molecule) obtained is $\mu = 0.7334$ a.u. (the experimental value is $\mu = 0.7295$ a.u.). An R-matrix radius of 10 a_0 was sufficient to ensure the electronic density associated to these states was negligible outside the R-matrix sphere. Gaussian type orbitals with angular momentum $l \leq 4$ were used to describe the continuum. Using this model, K- and T-matrices were generated and used as input to a modified version of POLYDCS [55]. This modification enables the use of T-matrices and therefore the accurate calculation of elastic DCS above the first electronic excitation threshold. K-matrices were used to calculate DCS below the first excitation threshold (as done by Faure et al.) and T-matrices were employed to perform the calculations above it.

The DCS are determined (by POLYDCS) using a closure formula which compensates for the truncation of the partial wave expansion of the continuum and, at the same time, removes the divergence of this expansion in the fixed-nuclei approximation [56]. The dipolar Born approximation is used to calculate the contribution of partial waves not included in the R-matrix calculation: the cross sections thus determined are said to be 'Born-corrected'. The cross sections thus obtained are not rotationally elastic: they are rotationally summed over a number of final states (the initial rotational state was assumed to be the one corresponding to J = 0 in our calculations). The 'uncorrected' cross sections for energies ≤ 7 eV presented in Figure 2. Correspond to performing a POLYDCS calculation assuming the molecule is non-polar, i.e., no Born-approximation based terms are added to the differential cross sections, but the frame transformation is performed. The uncorrected results for 7 eV < E $\leq$ 15 eV were calculated using the T-matrices and a different program that implements a similar approach, DCS [57].

4. Conclusions

The accuracy of the cross sections dataset for electron collisions with H_2O recommended by Song et al. [22] has been critically evaluated by simulating the transmission of magnetically confined electrons with 3, 10, and 70 eV kinetic energy through different pressures of water vapor using their data as input. Also, simulations using Geant4DNA have been performed and compared with the experimental results and those from our own Monte Carlo simulation code.

The recommended dataset from ref. [22] presents two main deficiencies to serve as input for our simulation code: (a) the elastic DCSs recommended are experimental values and do not extend either to angles below 10–20° or above 130°. Thus, we had to extrapolate these by using an extended R-matrix dataset for incident energies up to 15 eV and a dataset calculated with the IAM-SCAR+I method for electron energies in the range of 15–100 eV; (b) angular DCSs for the inelastic processes are absent in the recommended dataset, so we have performed simulations considering two limit cases (A and B) in order to gain a better understanding of the role played by the inelastic angular distributions in shaping the transmission curves. Case A considered that all inelastic processes yielded an isotropic scattering distribution, while case B assumed that the inelastic angular distribution contributes equally as the pure elastic scattering.

In general, a good agreement in the transmission spectra, although with some discrepancies, has been obtained for all incident energies at the lowest pressures considered here. Nonetheless, some insight as to how to improve the cross section dataset has been gained by considering the observed discrepancies. Some inaccuracy in the rotationally unresolved elastic DCSs at 3 eV is suggested by the disagreement found in the low energy region of the transmission spectra. At 10 eV, the results suggest an overestimation of the integral elastic cross sections. The results obtained at 70 eV with our two simulations assuming different angular distributions for the inelastic processes revealed the importance of these DCSs for an accurate simulation of the electron transport process. Therefore, the present results clearly show the need to incorporate recommended data for those inelastic DCSs in order to improve the simulations of electron transport through gaseous H_2O.

Supplementary Materials: The following are available online at https://www.mdpi.com/article/10.3390/atoms9040098/s1. Table S1: IAM-SCAR+I elastic DCS H2O; Table S2: FBA rotational DCS H2O; Table S3: Simulation input elastic+rotational DCS H2O, SI: Transmitted Spectra No Gas. The elastic DCS and integral cross section calculated with the R-matrix method are available for download here: https://doi.org/10.5281/zenodo.5566537.

Author Contributions: Formal analysis, A.G.-A., A.I.L. and J.D.G.; investigation, A.G.-A. and A.I.L.; methodology, J.C.O., F.B., J.D.G., P.L.-V. and G.G.; software, A.G.-A., J.C.O., F.B. and J.D.G.; writing—original draft, A.G.-A. and A.I.L.; writing—review and editing, J.D.G., P.L.-V. and G.G. All authors have read and agreed to the published version of the manuscript.

Funding: This study has been partially funded by the Spanish Ministerio de Ciencia e Innovación (Project PID2019-104727RB-C21) and CSIC (Project LINKA20085).

Institutional Review Board Statement: Not applicable.

Informed Consent Statement: Not applicable.

Data Availability Statement: The data presented in this study are available in the Supplementary Materials section and in https://doi.org/10.5281/zenodo.5566537.

Acknowledgments: A.G.-A. thank MICIU for his grant within the "Garantía Juvenil" programme. A.I.L., P.L.-V. acknowledge the Portuguese National Funding Agency (FCT) through research grants CEFITEC (UIDB/00068/2020) and PTDC/FIS-AQM/31281/2017. J.D.G. acknowledges support of the UK-AMOR consortium funded by EPSRC (EP/R029342/1).

Conflicts of Interest: The authors declare no conflict of interest.

Note

[1] The suite can be downloaded from: https://doi.org/10.5281/zenodo.2630454 and https://doi.org/10.5281/zenodo.2630474 (accessed on 1 November 2021).

References

1. Verkhovtsev, A.; Traore, A.; Muñoz, A.; Blanco, F.; García, G. Modeling secondary particle tracks generated by intermediate- and low-energy protons in water with the Low-Energy Particle Track Simulation code. *Radiat. Phys. Chem.* **2017**, *130*, 371–378. [CrossRef]
2. Incerti, S.; Baldacchino, G.; Bernal, M.; Capra, R.; Champion, C.; Francis, Z.; Guèye, P.; Mantero, A.; Mascialino, B.; Moretto, P.; et al. THE GEANT4-DNA PROJECT. *Int. J. Model. Simul. Sci. Comput.* **2010**, *01*, 157–178. [CrossRef]
3. Bernal, M.A.; Bordage, M.C.; Brown, J.M.C.; Davídková, M.; Delage, E.; El Bitar, Z.; Enger, S.A.; Francis, Z.; Guatelli, S.; Ivanchenko, V.N.; et al. Track structure modeling in liquid water: A review of the Geant4-DNA very low energy extension of the Geant4 Monte Carlo simulation toolkit. *Phys. Med.* **2015**, *31*, 861–874. [CrossRef]
4. Yousfi, M.; Benabdessadok, M.D. Boltzmann equation analysis of electron-molecule collision cross sections in water vapor and ammonia. *J. Appl. Phys.* **1998**, *80*, 6619. [CrossRef]
5. Karwasz, G.P.; Brusa, R.S.; Zecca, A. One century of experiments on electron-atom and molecule scattering: A critical review of integral cross-sections. *La Riv. del Nuovo Cim.* **2001**, *24*, 1–101. [CrossRef]
6. Robson, R.E.; White, R.D.; Ness, K.F. Transport coefficients for electrons in water vapor: Definition, measurement, and calculation. *J. Chem. Phys.* **2011**, *134*, 064319. [CrossRef]
7. Ness, K.F.; Robson, R.E.; Brunger, M.J.; White, R.D. Transport coefficients and cross sections for electrons in water vapour: Comparison of cross section sets using an improved Boltzmann equation solution. *J. Chem. Phys.* **2012**, *136*, 024318. [CrossRef] [PubMed]
8. Shirai, T.; Tabata, T.; Tawara, H. Analytic cross sections for electron collisions with CO, CO_2, and H_2O relevant to edge plasma impurities. *At. Data Nucl. Data Tables* **2001**, *79*, 143–184. [CrossRef]
9. Blanco, F.; Muñoz, A.; Almeida, D.; Ferreira da Silva, F.; Limão-Vieira, P.; Fuss, M.C.; Sanz, A.G.; García, G. Modelling low energy electron and positron tracks in biologically relevant media. *Eur. Phys. J. D* **2013**, *67*, 199. [CrossRef]
10. Itikawa, Y.; Mason, N. Cross Sections for Electron Collisions with Water Molecules. *J. Phys. Chem. Ref. Data* **2005**, *34*, 1–22. [CrossRef]
11. Song, M.-Y.; Yoon, J.-S.; Cho, H.; Karwasz, G.P.; Kokoouline, V.; Nakamura, Y.; Tennyson, J. "Recommended" cross sections for electron collisions with molecules. *Eur. Phys. J. D* **2020**, *74*, 60. [CrossRef]
12. De Urquijo, J.; Basurto, E.; Juárez, A.M.; Ness, K.F.; Robson, R.E.; Brunger, M.J.; White, R.D. Electron drift velocities in He and water mixtures: Measurements and an assessment of the water vapour cross-section sets. *J. Chem. Phys.* **2014**, *141*, 014308. [CrossRef]
13. Fuss, M.C.; Ellis-Gibbings, L.; Jones, D.B.; Brunger, M.J.; Blanco, F.; Muñoz, A.; Limão-Vieira, P.; García, G. The role of pyrimidine and water as underlying molecular constituents for describing radiation damage in living tissue: A comparative study. *J. Appl. Phys.* **2015**, *117*, 214701. [CrossRef]
14. Muñoz, A.; Blanco, F.; Garcia, G.; Thorn, P.A.; Brunger, M.J.; Sullivan, J.P.; Buckman, S.J. Single electron tracks in water vapour for energies below 100 eV. *Int. J. Mass Spectrom.* **2008**, *277*, 175–179. [CrossRef]
15. Anzai, K.; Kato, H.; Hoshino, M.; Tanaka, H.; Itikawa, Y.; Campbell, L.; Brunger, M.J.; Buckman, S.J.; Cho, H.; Blanco, F.; et al. Cross section data sets for electron collisions with H_2, O_2, CO, CO_2, N_2O and H_2O. *Eur. Phys. J. D* **2012**, *66*, 36. [CrossRef]
16. Ruíz-Vargas, G.; Yousfi, M.; Urquijo, J. de Electron transport coefficients in the mixtures of H_2O with N_2, O_2, CO_2 and dry air for the optimization of non-thermal atmospheric pressure plasmas. *J. Phys. D. Appl. Phys.* **2010**, *43*, 455201. [CrossRef]

17. White, R.D.; Cocks, D.; Boyle, G.; Casey, M.; Garland, N.; Konovalov, D.; Philippa, B.; Stokes, P.; De Urquijo, J.; González-Magaña, O.; et al. Electron transport in biomolecular gaseous and liquid systems: Theory, experiment and self-consistent cross-sections. *Plasma Sources Sci. Technol.* **2018**, 053001. [CrossRef]
18. Muñoz, A.; Oller, J.C.; Blanco, F.; Gorfinkiel, J.D.; Limão-Vieira, P.; García, G. Electron-scattering cross sections and stopping powers in H2O. *Phys. Rev. A* **2007**, *76*, 052707. [CrossRef]
19. Lozano, A.I.; Krupa, K.; Ferreira da Silva, F.; Limão-Vieira, P.; Blanco, F.; Muñoz, A.; Jones, D.B.; Brunger, M.J.; García, G. Low energy electron transport in furfural. *Eur. Phys. J. D* **2017**, *71*, 226. [CrossRef]
20. Lozano, A.I.; Oller, J.C.; Jones, D.B.; da Costa, R.F.; Varella, M.T.d.N.; Bettega, M.H.F.; Ferreira da Silva, F.; Limão-Vieira, P.; Lima, M.A.P.; White, R.D.; et al. Total electron scattering cross sections from para-benzoquinone in the energy range 1–200 eV. *Phys. Chem. Chem. Phys.* **2018**, *20*, 22368–22378. [CrossRef] [PubMed]
21. Costa, F.; Traoré-Dubuis, A.; Álvarez, L.; Lozano, A.I.; Ren, X.; Dorn, A.; Limão-Vieira, P.; Blanco, F.; Oller, J.C.; Muñoz, A.; et al. A Complete Cross Section Data Set for Electron Scattering by Pyridine: Modelling Electron Transport in the Energy Range 0–100 eV. *Int. J. Mol. Sci.* **2020**, *21*, 6947. [CrossRef]
22. Song, M.-Y.; Cho, H.; Karwasz, G.P.; Kokoouline, V.; Nakamura, Y.; Tennyson, J.; Faure, A.; Mason, N.J.; Itikawa, Y. Cross Sections for Electron Collisions with H2O. *J. Phys. Chem. Ref. Data* **2021**, *50*, 023103. [CrossRef]
23. Lozano, A.I.; Oller, J.C.; Krupa, K.; Ferreira da Silva, F.; Limão-Vieira, P.; Blanco, F.; Muñoz, A.; Colmenares, R.; García, G. Magnetically confined electron beam system for high resolution electron transmission-beam experiments. *Rev. Sci. Instrum.* **2018**, *89*, 063105. [CrossRef]
24. Incerti, S.; Ivanchenko, A.; Karamitros, M.; Mantero, A.; Moretto, P.; Tran, H.N.; Mascialino, B.; Champion, C.; Ivanchenko, V.N.; Bernal, M.A.; et al. Comparison of GEANT4 very low energy cross section models with experimental data in water. *Med. Phys.* **2010**, *37*, 4692–4708. [CrossRef]
25. Allison, J.; Amako, K.; Apostolakis, J.; Arce, P.; Asai, M.; Aso, T.; Bagli, E.; Bagulya, A.; Banerjee, S.; Barrand, G.; et al. Recent developments in GEANT4. *Nucl. Instrum. Methods Phys. Res. Sect. A Accel. Spectrometers Detect. Assoc. Equip.* **2016**, *835*, 186–225. [CrossRef]
26. Incerti, S.; Kyriakou, I.; Bernal, M.A.; Bordage, M.C.; Francis, Z.; Guatelli, S.; Ivanchenko, V.; Karamitros, M.; Lampe, N.; Lee, S.B.; et al. Geant4-DNA example applications for track structure simulations in liquid water: A report from the Geant4-DNA Project. *Med. Phys.* **2018**, *45*, e722–e739. [CrossRef] [PubMed]
27. Incerti, S.; Douglass, M.; Penfold, S.; Guatelli, S.; Bezak, E. Review of Geant4-DNA applications for micro and nanoscale simulations. *Phys. Med.* **2016**, *32*, 1187–1200. [CrossRef]
28. Zhang, R.; Faure, A.; Tennyson, J. Electron and positron collisions with polar molecules: Studies with the benchmark water molecule. *Phys. Scr.* **2009**, *80*, 015301. [CrossRef]
29. Faure, A.; Gorfinkiel, J.D.; Tennyson, J. Low-energy electron collisions with water: Elastic and rotationally inelastic scattering. *J. Phys. B At. Mol. Opt. Phys.* **2004**, *37*, 801. [CrossRef]
30. Faure, A.; Gorfinkiel, J.D.; Tennyson, J. Electron-impact rotational excitation of water. *Mon. Not. R. Astron. Soc.* **2004**, *347*, 323–333. [CrossRef]
31. Szmytkowski, C.; Możejko, P. Electron-scattering total cross sections for triatomic molecules: NO2 and H2O. *Opt. Appl.* **2006**, *36*, 543–550.
32. Kadokura, R.; Loreti, A.; Kövér, Á.; Faure, A.; Tennyson, J.; Laricchia, G. Angle-Resolved Electron Scattering from H2O near 0°. *Phys. Rev. Lett.* **2019**, *123*. [CrossRef]
33. Matsui, M.; Hoshino, M.; Kato, H.; da Silva, F.F.; Limão-Vieira, P.; Tanaka, H. Measuring electron-impact cross sections of water: Elastic scattering and electronic excitation of the ã3B1 and Ã1B1 states. *Eur. Phys. J. D* **2016**, *70*, 77. [CrossRef]
34. Khakoo, M.A.; Winstead, C.; McKoy, V. Vibrational excitation of water by electron impact. *Phys. Rev. A* **2009**, *79*, 052711. [CrossRef]
35. Seng, G.; Linder, F. Vibrational excitation of polar molecules by electron impact. II. Direct and resonant excitation in H2O. *J. Phys. B At. Mol. Phys.* **1976**, *9*, 2539. [CrossRef]
36. Ralphs, K.; Serna, G.; Hargreaves, L.R.; Khakoo, M.A.; Winstead, C.; McKoy, V. Excitation of the six lowest electronic transitions in water by 9–20 eV electrons. *J. Phys. B At. Mol. Opt. Phys.* **2013**, *46*, 125201. [CrossRef]
37. Thorn, P.A.; Brunger, M.J.; Teubner, P.J.O.; Diakomichalis, N.; Maddern, T.; Bolorizadeh, M.A.; Newell, W.R.; Kato, H.; Hoshino, M.; Tanaka, H.; et al. Cross sections and oscillator strengths for electron-impact excitation of the ÃB11 electronic state of water. *J. Chem. Phys.* **2007**, *126*, 064306. [CrossRef]
38. Kim, Y.-K. Scaled Born cross sections for excitations of H2 by electron impact. *J. Chem. Phys.* **2007**, *126*, 064305. [CrossRef]
39. Brunger, M.J. Electron scattering and transport in biofuels, biomolecules and biomass fragments. *Int. Rev. Phys. Chem.* **2017**, *36*, 333–376. [CrossRef]
40. Machado, L.E.; Brescansin, L.M.; Iga, I.; Lee, M.-T. Elastic and rotational excitation cross-sections for electron-water collisions in the low- and intermediate-energy ranges. *Eur. Phys. J. D-At. Mol. Opt. Plasma Phys.* **2005**, *33*, 193–199. [CrossRef]
41. Harb, T.; Kedzierski, W.; McConkey, J.W. Production of ground state OH following electron impact on H2O. *J. Chem. Phys.* **2001**, *115*, 5507. [CrossRef]
42. Kedzierski, W.; Derbyshire, J.; Malone, C.; McConkey, J.W. Isotope effects in the electron impact break-up of water. *J. Phys. B At. Mol. Opt. Phys.* **1998**, *31*, 5361. [CrossRef]
43. Lindsay, B.G.; Mangan, M.A. 5.1 Ionization. *Interact. Photons Electrons Mol.* **2005**, 5001–5077. [CrossRef]
44. Straub, H.C.; Lindsay, B.G.; Smith, K.A.; Stebbings, R.F. Absolute partial cross sections for electron-impact ionization of H2O and D2O from threshold to 1000 eV. *J. Chem. Phys.* **1998**, *108*, 109–116. [CrossRef]

45. Blanco, F.; García, G. Screening corrections for calculation of electron scattering from polyatomic molecules. *Phys. Lett. A* **2003**, *317*, 458–462. [CrossRef]
46. Blanco, F.; Ellis-Gibbings, L.; García, G. Screening corrections for the interference contributions to the electron and positron scattering cross sections from polyatomic molecules. *Chem. Phys. Lett.* **2016**, *645*, 71–75. [CrossRef]
47. Dubuis, A.T.; Costa, F.; da Silva, F.F.; Limão-Vieira, P.; Oller, J.C.; Blanco, F.; García, G. Total electron scattering cross section from pyridine molecules in the energy range 10–1000 eV. *Chem. Phys. Lett.* **2018**, *699*, 182–187. [CrossRef]
48. Jain, A. Theoretical study of the total (elastic+inelastic) cross sections for electron -H_2O (NH_3) scattering at 10-3000 eV. *J. Phys. B At. Mol. Opt. Phys.* **1988**, *21*, 905–924. [CrossRef]
49. Álvarez, L.; Costa, F.; Lozano, A.I.; Oller, J.C.; Muñoz, A.; Blanco, F.; Limão-Vieira, P.; White, R.D.; Brunger, M.J.; García, G. Electron scattering cross sections from nitrobenzene in the energy range 0.4–1000 eV: The role of dipole interactions in measurements and calculations. *Phys. Chem. Chem. Phys.* **2020**, *22*, 13505–13515. [CrossRef]
50. El-Zein, A.A.A.; Brunger, M.J.; Newell, W.R. Excitation of vibrational quanta in water by electron impact. *J. Phys. B At. Mol. Opt. Phys.* **2000**, *33*, 5033. [CrossRef]
51. Blanco, F.; Roldán, A.M.; Krupa, K.; McEachran, R.P.; White, R.D.; Marjanović, S.; Petrović, Z.L.; Brunger, M.J.; Machacek, J.R.; Buckman, S.J.; et al. Scattering data for modelling positron tracks in gaseous and liquid water. *J. Phys. B At. Mol. Opt. Phys.* **2016**, *49*, 145001. [CrossRef]
52. Agostinelli, S.; Allison, J.; Amako, K.; Apostolakis, J.; Araujo, H.; Arce, P.; Asai, M.; Axen, D.; Banerjee, S.; Barrand, G.; et al. Geant4—A simulation toolkit. *Nucl. Instrum. Methods Phys. Res. Sect. A Accel. Spectrometers Detect. Assoc. Equip.* **2003**, *506*, 250–303. [CrossRef]
53. Carr, J.M.; Galiatsatos, P.G.; Gorfinkiel, J.D.; Harvey, A.G.; Lysaght, M.A.; Madden, D.; Mašín, Z.; Plummer, M.; Tennyson, J.; Varambhia, H.N. UKRmol: A low-energy electron-and positron-molecule scattering suite. *Eur. Phys. J. D* **2012**, *66*, 58. [CrossRef]
54. Gorfinkiel, J.D.; Morgan, L.A.; Tennyson, J. Electron impact dissociative excitation of water within the adiabatic nuclei approximation. *J. Phys. B At. Mol. Opt. Phys.* **2002**, *35*, 543–555. [CrossRef]
55. Sanna, N.; Gianturco, F.A. Differential cross sections for electron/positron scattering from polyatomic molecules. *Comput. Phys. Commun.* **1998**, *114*, 142–167. [CrossRef]
56. Gianturco, F.A.; Jain, A. The theory of electron scattering from polyatomic molecules. *Phys. Rep.* **1986**, *143*, 347–425. [CrossRef]
57. Mašín, Z. DCS: A Program to Generate Orientation-Averaged DCS for Electronically Elastic and Inelastic Collsions. Available online: https://gitlab.com/Masin/DCS (accessed on 1 May 2021).

 *atoms*

Article

Cross Sections and Rate Coefficients for Vibrational Excitation of H_2O by Electron Impact

Mehdi Ayouz [1,*], Alexandre Faure [2], Jonathan Tennyson [3], Maria Tudorovskaya [4] and Viatcheslav Kokoouline [5,*]

[1] LGPM, CentraleSupélec, Université Paris-Saclay, 8-10 rue Joliot-Curie, F-91190 Gif-sur-Yvette, France
[2] IPAG, CNRS, Université Grenoble Alpes, F-38000 Grenoble, France; alexandre.faure@univ-grenoble-alpes.fr
[3] Department of Physics and Astronomy, University College London, Gower Street, London WC1E 6BT, UK; j.tennyson@ucl.ac.uk
[4] Quantemol Ltd., 320 City Rd., The Angel, London EC1V 2NZ, UK; tudorovskaya@gmail.com
[5] Department of Physics, University of Central Florida, Orlando, FL 32816, USA
* Correspondence: mehdi.ayouz@centralesupelec.fr (M.A.); slavako@ucf.edu (V.K.)

Abstract: Cross-sections and thermally averaged rate coefficients for vibration (de-)excitation of a water molecule by electron impact are computed; one and two quanta excitations are considered for all three normal modes. The calculations use a theoretical approach that combines the normal mode approximation for vibrational states of water, a vibrational frame transformation employed to evaluate the scattering matrix for vibrational transitions and the UK molecular R-matrix code. The interval of applicability of the rate coefficients is from 10 to 10,000 K. A comprehensive set of calculations is performed to assess uncertainty of the obtained data. The results should help in modelling non-LTE spectra of water in various astrophysical environments.

Keywords: water; vibrational excitation; R-matrix; electron-molecule collisions; interstellar medium

1. Introduction

The water molecule is fundamental in a variety of research fields, such as biochemistry, meteorology and astrophysics. On Earth, water exists in all three phases (gas, liquid and solid), and life as we know it would not be possible without liquid water. Water is also ubiquitous in astronomical environments, from the Solar System to distant galaxies, where it is observed in both gaseous and solid forms (see ref. [1] for a review). Collisions between free electrons and water molecules thus play an important role in molecular environments as diverse as biological systems, cometary atmospheres and stellar envelopes.

Electron-H_2O collisions have been extensively studied for many years, both theoretically and experimentally (for a recent review see ref. [2]). Vibrationally elastic and inelastic cross-sections have been measured and computed, and the agreement between experiment and theory is generally good. Rotational and vibrational excitation is dominated by dipole-allowed $\Delta j = 1$ and $\Delta v = 1$ transitions, respectively, except possibly in the presence of resonances. We note, however, that cross-sections for individual rotational transitions (vibrationally elastic or inelastic) have not been measured so far. As a result, the best available cross-sections for rotational excitation are those computed by Machado et al. [3] for energies above 7 eV and those of Faure et al. [4] for lower energies, as recommended by refs. [2,5]. Because experiments can hardly distinguish between the two stretching excitations (symmetric and asymmetric) of water, vibrational measurements usually provide cross-sections for bending excitation (010) and for the sum of the two stretching excitations (100) and (001) (in normal mode notations). From their compilation of literature data, Song et al. [2] recommend the experimental vibrational cross-sections obtained by Khakoo et al. [6] for energies above 3 eV and those of Send and Linder [7] for lower energies. The most accurate theoretical data are the cross-sections of ref. [8] obtained by combining the vibrational coupled-channel theory with an interaction potential described as a sum of electrostatic, electron exchange and polarization contributions. The agreement with measurements is generally good for the bending mode but the combined stretching-mode cross-section is about a factor of two smaller than the experimental data for energies below 10 eV. We note that the theoretical data of refs. [4,8] were used by Faure and Josselin [9] to derive rate coefficients in the temperature range of 200–5000 K for use in astrophysical models.

In all previous experimental and theoretical studies, only dipole-allowed vibrational transitions $\Delta \nu = 1$ were reported. In the envelopes of giant stars, however, water has been observed in high-energy rotational transitions within several vibrational states, i.e., (010), (100), (001) and (020) [10]. Such environments are not in local thermodynamic equilibrium (LTE), and the observed spectra contain precious information about local physical conditions. For example, one strong maser (microwave amplification by stimulated emission of radiation) transition at 268.149 GHz, arising from $j_{k_a k_c} = 6_{52} \to 7_{43}$ in the (020) vibrational state, was detected towards the evolved star VY CMa [11]. In order to extract information from such non-LTE spectra, cross-sections for one-quantum but also two-quantum transitions ($\Delta \nu = 1$ and 2) need to be computed. In addition, rovibrational state-to-state data are required. In all previous works for electron collisions with water, however, vibrational cross-sections were computed for one-quantum transitions only and without considering specific initial and final rotational states. It should be noted, in this context, that Stoecklin and co-workers have recently performed rovibrational state-to-state close-coupling calculations for the quenching of the bending mode (010) of water by (spherical) H_2 [12] and helium atoms [13].

In the present work, new theoretical calculations for the vibrational (de-)excitation of water by electron-impact are performed using the R-matrix theory combined with the vibrational frame transformation. Similar preliminary calculations were presented in ref. [2]. Here, we provide, for the first time, cross-sections for two-quantum transitions and for all three vibrational modes. Rate coefficients are deduced, and simple fits are provided in the temperature range from 10 to 10,000 K for use in models. The theoretical approach is briefly introduced in the next section. The results are presented and discussed in Section 3. Conclusions are summarized in Section 4.

2. Theoretical Approach

The theoretical approach employed in this study is presented in detail in refs. [14–17]. Here, we sketch below only the main ideas.

2.1. Ab Initio Calculations

Our model employs the fixed-nuclei reactance matrix (K-matrix) obtained numerically using the UK molecular R-Matrix code (UKRMol) [18,19] with the Quantemol-N expert system [20]. The K-matrix for the $e^- - H_2O$ collisions is computed for each geometry configuration of the molecule. It is labelled by the irreducible representations of the molecular point group. The ground-state electronic configuration of H_2O at its equilibrium geometry of the C_{2v} point group is

$$X^1 A_1 : 1a_1^2 \, 2a_1^2 \, 1b_2^2 \, 3a_1^2 \, 1b_1^2.$$

Performing the R-matrix calculations, we freeze the 2 core electrons $1a_1^2$ and keep 8 electrons free in the active space of $2a_1, 3a_1, 4a_1, 5a_1, 1b_1, 1b_2, 2b_2, 3b_2$ molecular orbitals. A total number of 508 configuration state functions (CSFs) are used for the above-ground state. All the generated states up to 10 eV were retained in the final close-coupling calculation. We employed an R-matrix sphere of radius 10 bohrs and a partial-wave expansion with continuum Gaussian-type orbitals up to $l \leq 4$.

Several basis sets, including DZP (double zeta-polarization contracted [21]) and cc-pVTZ (correlation-consistent polarized valence triple-zeta [22]) types, were tested to investigate the stability of the target properties, such as the dipole moment and ground state energy. Finally, we chose the cc-pVTZ basis set with the above complete active space (CAS) to perform the scattering calculations. In the following, this calculation will be referred as Model 1.

One of the important features of the present theoretical approach is the use of an energy-independent S-matrix. A convenient way to identify a weak or a strong energy dependence of the matrices is the eigenphase sum. Figure 1 displays the eigenphase sum of different irreducible representations at equilibrium and at displacements away from the equilibrium along each normal mode coordinate. Here and below, all normal coordinates are dimensionless. At equilibrium, the lowest resonance is found at 7.8 eV and has the $^2B_1$ symmetry.

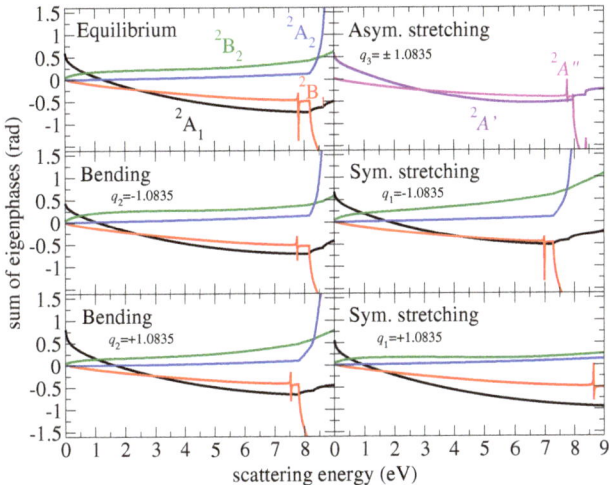

Figure 1. The sum of eigenphases as a function of the electron scattering energy for equilibrium geometry and displacements $q_i = \pm 1.0835$ along each normal mode. The eigenphase sums for $q_3 = +1.0835$ and $q_3 = -1.0835$ of the asymmetric stretching mode are identical. The curves are color coded according the different symmetries of the $e^- + H_2O$ system (see the left upper panel).

To construct elements of the scattering matrix for transitions from one vibrational level v to another v', which are then used to compute the cross−section, one needs the vibrational wave functions of the target molecule. At low collisional energies, the molecule can be characterized by three normal modes of vibration: bending, symmetric stretching and asymmetric stretching with respective frequencies ω_2, ω_1 and ω_3 and corresponding coordinates $q = \{q_2, q_1, q_3\}$. In this study, for the vibrational motion of H_2O, we use the normal mode coordinates and vibrational wave functions in the normal-mode approximation.

The electronic structure and normal mode frequencies are determined by the complete active space self-consistent field (CASSCF) method using the ab initio quantum chemistry package MOLPRO [23]. The cc-pVTZ basis set is employed for all the atoms. Table 1 gives the optimized geometry and vibrational frequencies, obtained in the present calculation, and compares the results with available experimental data. Figure 2 shows how inter-particle distances r_1, r_2 and the bond angle θ change as functions of normal mode coordinates: bond lengths. Note that displacements along the bending and symmetric stretching modes do not break the C_{2v} molecular symmetry, while the asymmetric stretching mode reduces the symmetry to the C_s group.

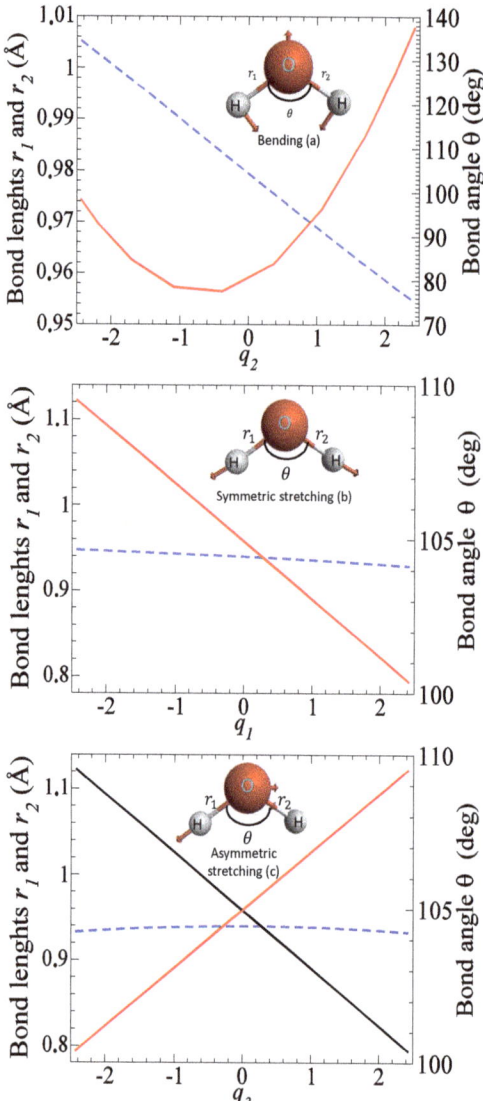

Figure 2. Normal modes of H_2O. The figure shows the dependence of inter-particle distances r_1, r_2 and the bond angle θ as functions of normal mode coordinates: (**a**) bending, (**b**) symmetric stretching and (**c**) asymmetric stretching. The arrows indicate the direction and magnitude of displacements for each mode. Bond lengths are given with solid lines with values on the left axis, while the bond angle is given with a dashed line with values on the right axis of each panel. Note that the curves of the bond lengths r_1 (black) and r_2 (red) are indistinguishable for the bending and symmetric stretching modes.

Table 1. The structure and vibrational frequencies (in eV) of H_2O obtained in this study and compared with experimental data from ref. [24].

Mode	This Study	Exp. [24,25]
Bending (010)	0.207	0.198
Symmetric stretching (100)	0.472	0.453
Asymmetric stretching (001)	0.488	0.466
Bond lengths r_1, r_2 (Å)	0.958	0.958
Bond angle θ (Degrees)	104.44	104.50

2.2. Cross-Sections for Vibrational Excitation

The fixed-geometry reactance matrix $K(q)$ is transformed to the fixed-geometry scattering matrix $S(q)$. The channels (indexes) of two matrices correspond to different states of target, which could be excited at a given scattering energy, and different partial-wave quantum numbers of the incident electron. For water, the first excited electronic state is at 7.14 eV above the ground vibronic level [2,26]. Here, we consider energies below the excitation of the lowest excited states. Therefore, each channel in the scattering matrix is labeled with the partial-wave indexes only, which are the angular momentum l of the incident electron and its projection λ on the molecular axis of symmetry.

The scattering matrix $S(R)$ is then converted by the vibrational frame transformation

$$S_{v'v} = \sum_{l'\lambda'l\lambda} \int dq \chi_{v'}(q) S_{l'\lambda',l\lambda}(q) \chi_v(q) \quad (1)$$

to the matrix $S_{v'v}$ in the representation of vibrational channels. Functions χ_v are vibrational wave functions of the target molecule.

In this study, we consider excitation of one mode at a time with one or two quanta, while the two other modes are kept in their ground state. Although the integral in the above expression is formally over the three normal-mode coordinates, in practice, we integrate only over one coordinate, which is the one corresponding to the mode that is being excited. For the example, the excitation of the mode i from state v_i to v'_i is given with the integral

$$S_{v'_i v_i} \approx \sum_{l'\lambda'l\lambda} \int dq_i \chi_{v'_i}(q_i) S_{l'\lambda',l\lambda}(q) \chi_{v'_i}(q_i) \quad (2)$$

evaluated over the coordinate q_i, with values of the two other normal-mode coordinates (the matrix $S_{l'\lambda',l\lambda}(q)$ depends on all three coordinates) fixed at the equilibrium values, i.e., 0. The integral is evaluated using the Gaussian–Legendre quadrature with 10 points. Functions χ_{v_i} are eigenfunctions of one-dimensional harmonic oscillator in the dimensionless coordinate q_i, i.e., solutions of the equation

$$\left(-\frac{d^2}{dq_i^2} + q_i^2\right) \chi_{v_i} = (2v_i + 1)\chi_{v_i}. \quad (3)$$

Having the scattering matrix in the vibrational representation, the cross-section for the $v'_i \leftarrow v_i$ process is given

$$\sigma_{v'_i \leftarrow v_i} = \frac{\pi \hbar^2}{2mE_{el}} |S_{v'_i v_i} - \delta_{v'_i v_i}|^2, \quad (4)$$

where m and E_{el} are the mass and energy of the incident electron.

3. Results

3.1. Cross Sections

Figure 3 gives the computed cross-sections for transitions between the three lowest vibrational levels for the three modes. Both excitation and de-excitation cross-sections were calculated. There have been several experiments measuring cross-sections for excitation of the ground vibrational level by one quantum. In the experiments, contributions from the two stretching modes were not resolved. Figures 4 and 5 compare the present results with the experimental [6,7,27,28], theoretical [8,29] and previously evaluated and recommended [2,30] data available in the literature. See the review of ref. [2] for details about the data.

For the bending mode and energies below 3 eV, the present cross-section agrees well with the experiment by Seng and Linder [7] but is somewhat below the data obtained from a swarm analysis by Yousfi and Benabdessadok [30]. At energies above 4 eV, the present values are below by about 30% than the swarm data and by a factor of two than the recent experiment by Khakoo et al. [6]. For the stretching mode (Figure 5), all available experimental data generally agree with each other, while the present results and other previous theoretical cross-sections are all systematically below the experimental values.

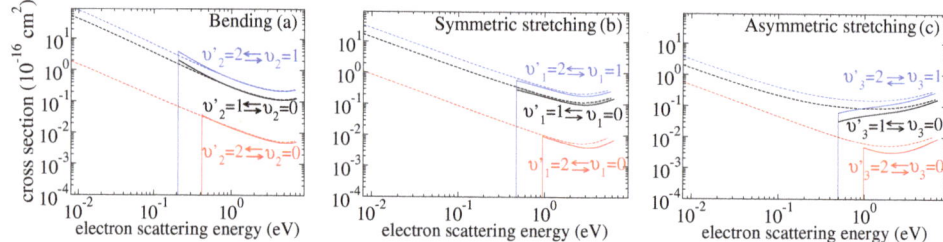

Figure 3. The calculated cross sections as functions of the electron scattering energy for the vibrational excitation of H_2O for different vibrational states $v_i = 0, 1, 2$ of the three normal modes i (see the text for detailed discussion): (**a**) cross−sections for the bending mode, (**b**) for symmetric stretching mode and (**c**) for asymmetric stretching mode.

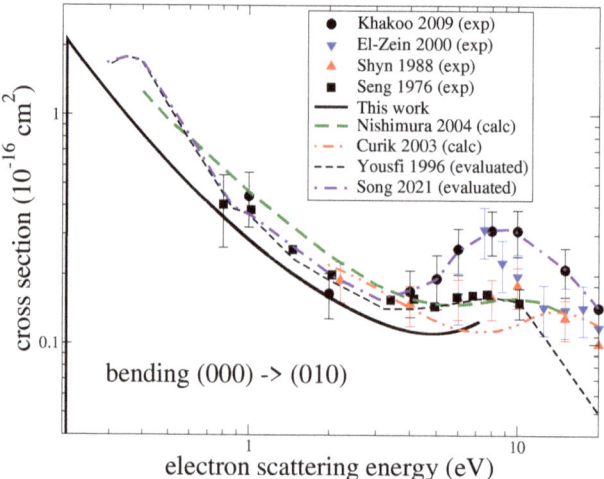

Figure 4. A comparison of cross sections available in the literature for the excitation of the bending mode $(000) \to (010)$. The black solid line is the theoretical result obtained in this study.

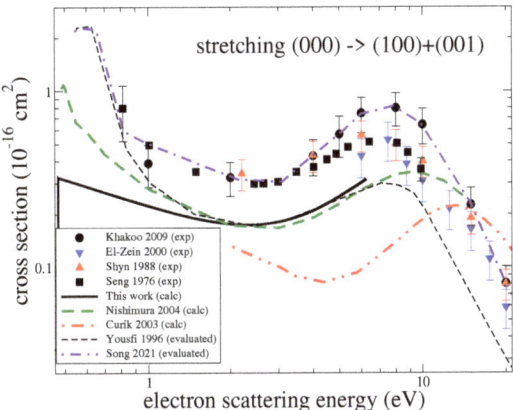

Figure 5. A comparison of cross sections available in the literature for the excitation of the stretching modes $(000) \rightarrow (100) + (001)$. The black solid line is the theoretical result obtained in this study.

It is worth mentioning that in the beam experiments, a wide resonant structure near 8 eV is observed. It is especially pronounced in the experiment by Khakoo et al. [6] and less pronounced, manifested rather as a shoulder, in the swarm data by Yousfi and Benabdessadok [30]. In our calculations, we observe four resonances near that energy: two narrow resonances of $^2B_1$ symmetry at 7.8 eV and of $^2A_1$ symmetry at 10 eV, and two wider resonances: a $^2A_2$ resonance at 6.7 eV and a $^2B_2$ resonance at 11 eV with a width of about 1 eV. Therefore, the resonant structure observed in the experiments (with unresolved rotational structure) can be explained well by the presence of these four resonances. However, it is clear that the theory is unable to reproduce the magnitude of the excitation cross-section correctly, as observed in the experiments. Therefore, it is likely that in the present and previous theoretical calculations, an effect, responsible for a larger vibrational excitation at energies above 3 eV, is not accounted for. One possibility is that in this region of energies, the resonant states, mentioned above, can capture the electron into their vibrational states, which would significantly enhance the excitation cross-section. A similar resonant mechanism was observed in electron-impact vibrational excitation CO [31]. Another consideration is that close-coupling calculations, such as the ones performed here, do not provide a converged treatment of polarization interactions [32]. It is, therefore, possible that the underestimation of polarization effects contributes to the under prediction of the vibrational excitation cross-section.

3.2. Rate Coefficients

The excitation cross-sections were used to compute the thermally averaged rate coefficients (see, for example, Equation (13) of ref. [14]). The coefficients are shown in Figure 6.

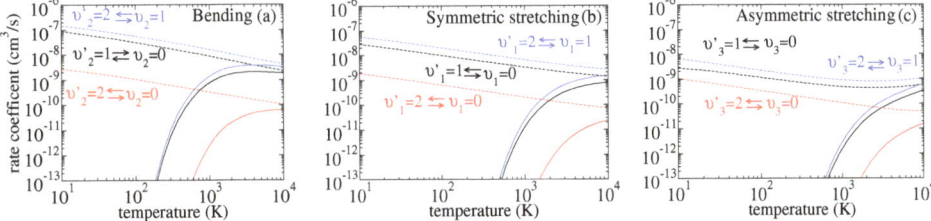

Figure 6. Same as Figure 3 for the calculated rate coefficients. Dashed lines represent de-excitation transitions, while the solid lines of the same colour refer to opposite processes.

Similarly to the previous studies [14,33,34], for a more convenient use in models, the numerical rate coefficients are fitted to the following analytical formula

$$\alpha^{fit}_{v_i' \leftarrow v_i}(T) = \frac{1}{\sqrt{T}} e^{-\frac{\Delta_{v_i' \leftarrow v_i}}{T}} P^{fit}_{v_i' v_i}(x), \tag{5}$$

where

$$P^{fit}_{v_i' v_i}(x) = a_0 + a_1 x + a_2 x^2 \quad \text{and} \quad x = \ln(T). \tag{6}$$

The coefficients a_j ($j = 0, 1, 2$) are fitting parameters. The quantity $P^{fit}_{v_i' v_i}(x)$ is the (de-)excitation probability. It weakly depends on the scattering energy. In Equation (5), $\Delta_{v_i' \leftarrow v_i}$ is the threshold energy defined as

$$\Delta_{v_i' v_i} = \begin{cases} E_{v_{i'}} - E_{v_i} > 0 & \text{for excitation,} \\ 0 & \text{for de-excitation.} \end{cases} \tag{7}$$

The coefficients a_j are obtained for each pair of transitions $v' \leftrightarrow v$ from a numerical fit. The numerical parameters of a_j listed in Tables 2–4. To use the fit, temperature T in Equation (6) should be in kelvins.

Table 2. Parameters a_0, a_1 and a_2 of the polynomial $P^{fit}_{v_i' v_i}(x)$ of Equations (5) and (6) between the three lowest vibrational states for the bending mode of H_2O. The pairs of the final and initial vibrational levels for each normal mode are at the second line in each header of the tables. The third line in each header gives the threshold energies $\Delta_{v_i' \leftarrow v_i}$ in Equation (7).

$v_i' \leftarrow v_i$	$1 \leftarrow 0$	$2 \leftarrow 0$	$0 \leftarrow 1$	$2 \leftarrow 1$	$0 \leftarrow 2$	$1 \leftarrow 2$
Δ_{v_i', v_i} (K)	2403	4807	0	2403	0	0
a_0	5.76×10^{-7}	2.23×10^{-8}	2.63×10^{-7}	1.08×10^{-6}	8.33×10^{-9}	3.99×10^{-7}
a_1	-6.32×10^{-8}	-3.05×10^{-9}	2.24×10^{-8}	-1.19×10^{-7}	7.07×10^{-10}	6.83×10^{-8}
a_2	2.76×10^{-9}	1.95×10^{-10}	-2.97×10^{-9}	5.30×10^{-9}	-5.27×10^{-11}	-7.34×10^{-9}

Table 3. Same as Table 2 for the symmetric stretching mode of H_2O.

$v_i' \leftarrow v_i$	$1 \leftarrow 0$	$2 \leftarrow 0$	$0 \leftarrow 1$	$2 \leftarrow 1$	$0 \leftarrow 2$	$1 \leftarrow 2$
Δ_{v_i', v_i} (K)	5489	10978	0	5488	0	0
a_0	2.92×10^{-7}	1.01×10^{-8}	1.10×10^{-7}	5.69×10^{-7}	6.62×10^{-9}	2.32×10^{-7}
a_1	-5.68×10^{-8}	-1.06×10^{-9}	-8.08×10^{-9}	-1.07×10^{-7}	-1.82×10^{-10}	-1.79×10^{-8}
a_2	4.29×10^{-9}	7.76×10^{-11}	1.09×10^{-9}	8.00×10^{-9}	2.39×10^{-11}	2.16×10^{-9}

Table 4. Same as Table 2 for the asymmetric stretching mode of H_2O.

$v_i' \leftarrow v_i$	$1 \leftarrow 0$	$2 \leftarrow 0$	$0 \leftarrow 1$	$2 \leftarrow 1$	$0 \leftarrow 2$	$1 \leftarrow 2$
Δ_{v_i', v_i} (K)	5673	11345	0	5672	0	0
a_0	3.56×10^{-7}	1.66×10^{-8}	4.27×10^{-8}	6.64×10^{-7}	4.49×10^{-9}	8.57×10^{-8}
a_1	-9.80×10^{-8}	-3.59×10^{-9}	-1.51×10^{-8}	-1.82×10^{-7}	-5.01×10^{-10}	-2.94×10^{-8}
a_2	7.05×10^{-9}	2.45×10^{-10}	1.66×10^{-9}	1.31×10^{-8}	5.15×10^{-11}	3.15×10^{-9}

3.3. Assessment of Uncertainties

The main source of uncertainty of the present results is due to electron scattering calculations. To assess the uncertainty, we computed the cross-section-varying parameters of the scattering model. The main scattering model (Model 1) is described above. In the second set of calculations (Model 2), the electronic basis was reduced from cc-pVTZ to DZP, and the same CAS (CAS$_1$) was employed. In Model 3, we freeze the $2a_1$ and $1b_2$ molecular orbitals, which leads to a reduced complete active space (CAS$_2$) in the configuration interaction calculations with respect to Model 1 by two orbitals. In Model 4, a larger basis cc-pVQZ (correlation-consistent polarized valence quadruple-zeta) and CAS$_1$ were used. Figure 7 demonstrates a comparison of cross-sections obtained using the models. As evident from the figure, reducing the basis set from cc-pVTZ to DZP (Model 1 vs. Model 2) changes the results by about 30% (stretching) and 50% (bending), while increasing the basis set from cc-pVTZ to cc-pVQZ (Model 1 vs. Model 4) changes the result less, by about 5–15%. Therefore, the convergence of Model 1 with respect to the basis set is about 5% (stretching) and 15% (bending). Changing the CAS (Model 1 vs. Model 3) changes the cross-sections by about 5–10%. Therefore, we estimate the uncertainty of Model 1 to be about 20% for the bending mode and about 10% for the stretching mode.

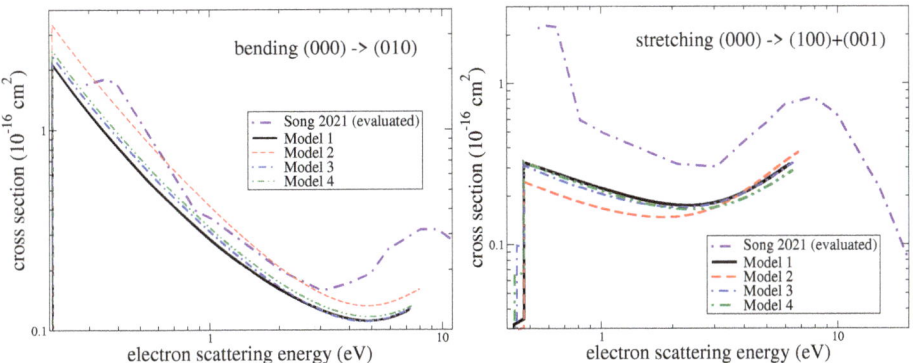

Figure 7. Cross sections for the excitation of the bending (**left panel**) and stretching (**right panel**) modes obtained using the four different models (see the text). Model 1 is used to produce final results of the study. The three other models, in which the basis set and the CAS were changed compared to Model 1, are used to assess the uncertainty of the results: Model 1—the cc-pVTZ basis and CAS$_1$; Model 2—the DZP basis and CAS$_1$; Model 3—the cc-pVTZ basis and CAS$_2$; Model 4—the cc-pVQZ basis and CAS$_1$.

4. Conclusions

Summarizing the results of the present study, we computed cross-sections for the vibrational excitation of the water molecule by electron impact using a purely ab initio approach. We would like to stress that cross-sections for excitation by two quanta in one collision were obtained and reported for the first time. The uncertainty of the obtained cross-sections is estimated to be 20% for the excitation of the bending mode and 10% for the stretching modes. The resonant structure observed in experimental data near 6–10 eV was characterized using the ab initio calculations. The overall agreement of the present cross-sections with the experiment is within experimental uncertainties (including different experiments) for the bending mode. For the stretching modes, the present theory gives cross-sections somewhat smaller than in the experiment: The difference is slightly larger than the combined uncertainties of the experiment and the theory. Finally, thermally averaged rate coefficients were derived from the obtained cross-sections. The coefficients were fitted to an analytical formula for a convenient use by modellers.

Rotationally resolved vibrational cross-sections are currently being computed and will be reported later.

Finally, we note that the methodology for computing non-resonant vibrational excitation cross-sections employed here has recently been incorporated, with some simplifications, into the QEC (Quantemol Electron Collisions) expert system [35] used to run the new (UKRmol+) UK Molecule R-matrix code [36]. The main simplifications are: (1) The integral of Equation (2) is evaluated using the linear approximation for the scattering matrix near the equilibrium geometry [37–40]. (2) The electron-scattering calculation for all geometries are performed without taking into account any symmetry of the molecule, i.e., the C_1 group of molecular symmetry is used. As here, MOLPRO is used to automatically generate the normal modes.

Author Contributions: Conceptualization, M.A., A.F., J.T., M.T. and V.K.; methodology, M.A., J.T., M.T. and V.K.; software, M.A., A.F., J.T., M.T. and V.K.; validation, M.A., A.F., J.T., M.T. and V.K.; formal analysis, M.A., A.F., J.T., M.T. and V.K.; investigation, M.A., A.F., J.T., M.T. and V.K.; resources, M.A., A.F., J.T. and V.K.; data curation, M.A., J.T., M.T. and V.K.; writing—original draft preparation, M.A., A.F., J.T., M.T. and V.K.; writing—review and editing, M.A., A.F., J.T., M.T. and V.K.; project administration, M.A., A.F., J.T., M.T. and V.K.; funding acquisition, M.A., A.F., J.T. and V.K. All authors have read and agreed to the published version of the manuscript.

Funding: This research was funded by the Thomas Jefferson Fund of the Office for Science and Technology of the Embassy of France in the United States, the National Science Foundation, Grant No. PHY-1806915, and by the program "Accueil des chercheurs étrangers" of CentraleSupélec. A.F. was funded by ANR 'WATERSTARS', project ANR-20-CE31-0011.

Data Availability Statement: The rate coefficients obtained in this study can immediately be obtained from the tables provided above. Numerical data for cross sections reported in Figures 3–5 can be obtained from the authors upon request.

Conflicts of Interest: The authors declare no conflict of interest.

References

1. Van Dishoeck, E.F.; Herbst, E.; Neufeld, D.A. Interstellar Water Chemistry: From Laboratory to Observations. *Chem. Rev.* **2013**, *113*, 9043–9085. [CrossRef]
2. Song, M.Y.; Cho, H.; Karwasz, G.P.; Kokoouline, V.; Nakamura, Y.; Tennyson, J.; Faure, A.; Mason, N.J.; Itikawa, Y. Cross Sections for Electron Collisions with H_2O. *J. Phys. Chem. Ref. Data* **2021**, *50*, 023103. [CrossRef]
3. Machado, L.E.; Brescansin, L.M.; Iga, I.; Lee, M.T. Elastic and rotational excitation cross-sections for electron-water collisions in the low- and intermediate-energy ranges. *Eur. Phys. J. D* **2005**, *33*, 193–199. [CrossRef]
4. Faure, A.; Gorfinkiel, J.D.; Tennyson, J. Low-energy electron collisions with water: Elastic and rotationally inelastic scattering. *J. Phys. B At. Mol. Phys.* **2004**, *37*, 801–807. [CrossRef]
5. Itikawa, Y.; Mason, N. Cross Sections for Electron Collisions with Water Molecules. *J. Phys. Chem. Ref. Data* **2005**, *34*, 1–22. [CrossRef]
6. Khakoo, M.; Winstead, C.; McKoy, V. Vibrational excitation of water by electron impact. *Phys. Rev. A* **2009**, *79*, 052711. [CrossRef]
7. Seng, G.; Linder, F. Vibrational excitation of polar molecules by electron impact. II. Direct and resonant excitation in H_2O. *J. Phys. B At. Mol. Phys.* **1976**, *9*, 2539–2551. [CrossRef]
8. Nishimura, T.; Gianturco, F. Vibrational excitation of water by low-energy electron scattering: Calculations and experiments. *Europhys. Lett.* **2004**, *65*, 179. [CrossRef]
9. Faure, A.; Josselin, E. Collisional excitation of water in warm astrophysical media. I. Rate coefficients for rovibrationally excited states. *Astron. Astrophys.* **2008**, *492*, 257–264. [CrossRef]
10. Baudry, A.; Humphreys, E.M.L.; Herpin, F.; Torstensson, K.; Vlemmings, W.H.T.; Richards, A.M.S.; Gray, M.D.; De Breuck, C.; Olberg, M. Vibrationally excited water emission at 658 GHz from evolved stars. *Astron. Astrophys.* **2018**, *609*, A25. [CrossRef]
11. Tenenbaum, E.D.; Dodd, J.L.; Milam, S.N.; Woolf, N.J.; Ziurys, L.M. Comparative Spectra of Oxygen-rich Versus Carbon-rich Circumstellar Shells: VY Canis Majoris and IRC +10216 at 215–285 GHz. *Astrophys. J. Lett.* **2010**, *720*, L102–L107. [CrossRef]
12. Stoecklin, T.; Denis-Alpizar, O.; Clergerie, A.; Halvick, P.; Faure, A.; Scribano, Y. Rigid-Bender Close-Coupling Treatment of the Inelastic Collisions of H_2O with para-H_2. *J. Phys. Chem. A* **2019**, *123*, 5704–5712. [CrossRef] [PubMed]
13. Stoecklin, T.; Cabrera-González, L.D.; Denis-Alpizar, O.; Páez-Hernández, D. A close coupling study of the bending relaxation of H_2O by collision with He. *J. Chem. Phys.* **2021**, *154*, 144307. [CrossRef]
14. Ayouz, M.; Kokoouline, V. Cross Sections and Rate Coefficients for Vibrational Excitation of HeH^+ Molecule by Electron Impact. *Atoms* **2016**, *4*, 30. [CrossRef]
15. Ayouz, M.; Kokoouline, V. Cross Sections and Rate Coefficients for Rovibrational Excitation of HeH^+ Isotopologues by Electron Impact. *Atoms* **2019**, *7*, 67. [CrossRef]
16. Liu, H.; dos Santos, S.F.; Yuen, C.H.; Cortona, P.; Kokoouline, V.; Ayouz, M. Theoretical study of electron-induced vibrational excitation of NO_2. *Plasma Sources Sci. Technol.* **2019**, *28*, 105017. [CrossRef]
17. Liu, H.; Santos, S.F.d.; Yuen, C.H.; Cortona, P.; Ayouz, M.; Kokoouline, V. Vibrational excitation of N_2O by an electron impact and the role of the Renner-Teller effect in the process. *Phys. Rev. A* **2020**, *102*, 032808. [CrossRef]
18. Tennyson, J. Electron–molecule collision calculations using the R-matrix method. *Phys. Rep.* **2010**, *491*, 29–76. [CrossRef]
19. Carr, J.; Galiatsatos, P.; Gorfinkiel, J.; Harvey, A.; Lysaght, M.; Madden, D.; Mašín, Z.; Plummer, M.; Tennyson, J.; Varambhia, H. UKRmol: A low-energy electron- and positron-molecule scattering suite. *Eur. Phys. J. D* **2012**, *66*, 58. [CrossRef]

20. Tennyson, J.; Brown, D.B.; Munro, J.J.; Rozum, I.; Varambhia, H.N.; Vinci, N. Quantemol-N: An expert system for performing electron molecule collision calculations using the R-matrix method. *J. Phys. Conf. Ser.* **2007**, *86*, 012001. [CrossRef]
21. Dunning, T.H. Gaussian Basis Functions for Use in Molecular Calculations. I. Contraction of (9s5p) Atomic Basis Sets for the First-Row Atoms. *J. Chem. Phys.* **1970**, *53*, 2823–2833. [CrossRef]
22. Dunning, T.H. Gaussian basis sets for use in correlated molecular calculations. I. The atoms boron through neon and hydrogen. *J. Chem. Phys.* **1989**, *90*, 1007–1023. [CrossRef]
23. Werner, H.J.; Knowles, P.J.; Knizia, G.; Manby, F.R.; Schütz, M. Molpro: A general-purpose quantum chemistry program package. *WIREs Comput. Mol. Sci.* **2012**, *2*, 242–253. [CrossRef]
24. Johnson, R.D., III. *NIST Computational Chemistry Comparison and Benchmark Database*; NIST Standard Reference Database Number 101; NIST: Gaithersburg, MD, USA, 2010.
25. Császár, A.G.; Czako, G.; Furtenbacher, T.; Tennyson, J.; Szalay, V.; Shirin, S.V.; Zobov, N.F.; Polyansky, O.L. On equilibrium structures of the water molecule. *J. Chem. Phys.* **2005**, *122*, 214305. [CrossRef] [PubMed]
26. Thorn, P.; Campbell, L.; Brunger, M. Electron excitation and energy transfer rates for H_2O in the upper atmosphere. *PMC Phys. B* **2009**, *2*, 1. [CrossRef]
27. El-Zein, A.; Brunger, M.; Newell, W. Excitation of vibrational quanta in water by electron impact. *J. Phys. B At. Mol. Opt. Phys.* **2000**, *33*, 5033. [CrossRef]
28. Shyn, T.; Cho, S.; Cravens, T. Vibrational-excitation cross sections of water molecules by electron impact. *Phys. Rev. A* **1988**, *38*, 678. [CrossRef] [PubMed]
29. Curik, R.; Carsky, P. Vibrationally inelastic electron scattering on polyatomic molecules by the discrete momentum representation (DMR) method. *J. Phys. B At. Mol. Opt. Phys.* **2003**, *36*, 2165. [CrossRef]
30. Yousfi, M.; Benabdessadok, M.D. Boltzmann equation analysis of electron-molecule collision cross sections in water vapor and ammonia. *J. Appl. Phys.* **1996**, *80*, 6619–6630. [CrossRef]
31. Laporta, V.; Cassidy, C.; Tennyson, J.; Celiberto, R. Electron-impact resonant vibration excitation cross sections and rate coefficients for carbon monoxide. *Plasma Sources Sci. Technol.* **2012**, *21*, 045005. [CrossRef]
32. Jones, M.; Tennyson, J. On the use of pseudostates to calculate molecular polarizabilities. *J. Phys. B* **2010**, *43*, 045101. [CrossRef]
33. Kokoouline, V.; Faure, A.; Tennyson, J.; Greene, C.H. Calculation of rate constants for vibrational and rotational excitation of the H_3^+ ion by electron impact. *Mon. Not. R. Astron. Soc.* **2010**, *405*, 1195–1202.
34. Jiang, X.; Yuen, C.H.; Cortona, P.; Ayouz, M.; Kokoouline, V. Cross sections for vibronic excitation of CH^+ by low-energy electron impact. *Phys. Rev. A* **2019**, *100*, 062711. [CrossRef]
35. Cooper, B.; Tudorovskaya, M.; Mohr, S.; O'Hare, A.; Hanicinec, M.; Dzarasova, A.; Gorfinkiel, J.; Benda, J.; Mašín, Z.; Al-Refaie, A.; et al. Quantemol Electron Collision: An expert system for performing UKRmol+ electron molecule collision calculations. *Atoms* **2019**, *7*, 97. [CrossRef]
36. Mašín, Z.; Benda, J.; Gorfinkiel, J.D.; Harvey, A.G.; Tennyson, J. UKRmol+: A suite for modelling of electronic processes in molecules interacting with electrons, positrons and photons using the R-matrix method. *Comput. Phys. Comms.* **2020**, *249*, 107092. [CrossRef]
37. Fonseca dos Santos, S.; Douguet, N.; Kokoouline, V.; Orel, A. Scattering matrix approach to the dissociative recombination of HCO^+ and N_2H^+. *J. Chem. Phys.* **2014**, *140*, 164308. [CrossRef]
38. Douguet, N.; Fonseca dos Santos, S.; Kokoouline, V.; Orel, A. Simplified model to describe the dissociative recombination of linear polyatomic ions of astrophysical interest. *EPJ Web Conf.* **2015**, *84*, 07003. [CrossRef]
39. Kokoouline, V.; Ayouz, M.; Mezei, J.Z.; Hassouni, K.; Schneider, I.F. Theoretical study of dissociative recombination and vibrational excitation of the BF_2^+ ion by an electron impact. *Plasma Sources Sci. Technol.* **2018**, *27*, 115007. [CrossRef]
40. Ayouz, M.A.; Yuen, C.H.; Balucani, N.; Ceccarelli, C.; Schneider, I.F.; Kokoouline, V. Dissociative electron recombination of NH_2CHOH^+ and implications for interstellar formamide abundance. *Mon. Not. R. Astron. Soc.* **2019**, *490*, 1325–1331. [CrossRef]

Article

Accurate Electron Drift Mobility Measurements in Moderately Dense Helium Gas at Several Temperatures

Armando Francesco Borghesani

Dipartimento di Fisica & Astronomia "Galileo Galilei" and CNISM, University of Padua, I-35131 Padua, Italy; armandofrancesco.borghesani@unipd.it; Tel.: +39-049-827-7019

Abstract: We report new accurate measurements of the drift mobility µ of quasifree electrons in moderately dense helium gas in the temperature range $26\,\text{K} \leq T \leq 300\,\text{K}$ for densities lower than those at which states of electrons localized in bubbles appear. By heuristically including multiple-scattering effects into classical kinetic formulas, as previously done for neon and argon, an excellent description of the field E, density N, and temperature T dependence of µ is obtained. Moreover, the experimental evidence suggests that the strong decrease of the zero-field density-normalized mobility $\mu_0 N$ with increasing N from the low up to intermediate density regime is mainly due to weak localization of electrons caused by the intrinsic disorder of the system, whereas the further decrease of $\mu_0 N$ for even larger N is due to electron self-trapping in cavities. We suggest that a distinction between weakly localized and electron bubble states can be done by inspecting the behavior of $\mu_0 N$ as a function of N at intermediate densities.

Keywords: electron mobility; multiple-scattering effects; disordered systems; weak localization

Citation: Borghesani, A.F. Accurate Electron Drift Mobility Measurements in Moderately Dense Helium Gas at Several Temperatures. *Atoms* **2021**, *9*, 52. https://doi.org/10.3390/atoms9030052

Academic Editor: Grzegorz Piotr Karwasz

Received: 14 July 2021
Accepted: 2 August 2021
Published: 4 August 2021

Publisher's Note: MDPI stays neutral with regard to jurisdictional claims in published maps and institutional affiliations.

Copyright: © 2021 by the authors. Licensee MDPI, Basel, Switzerland. This article is an open access article distributed under the terms and conditions of the Creative Commons Attribution (CC BY) license (https://creativecommons.org/licenses/by/4.0/).

1. Introduction

The study of the transport properties of excess electrons in dielectric gases or liquids may shape detailed knowledge of the dynamics and energetics of electron states in disordered media and of the relationship between the electron-host atom interactions and the thermodynamic properties of the system. In particular, the negative density effect, i.e., the decline of the electron drift mobility µ with increasing gas number density N, initially observed in dense helium [1–7], has attracted a great deal of theoretical work [8–15] because of the possible connection between multiple-scattering effects at a high density and the electron localization induced by the intrinsic disorder of the medium [16,17].

Several multiple-scattering theories have been developed for the thermal electrons mobility μ_0, i.e., in the limit of vanishingly small density-reduced electric field $E/N \to 0$, where E is the drift electric field. All these theories are based on a complex shift of the electron kinetic energy in a dense medium [18,19] and on quantum corrections to the electron-atom scattering rate when the electron mean free path ℓ and the thermal electron wavelength λ_T become comparable [11,20]. They are proved quite successful at the description of the density dependence of the zero-field limit of the density-normalized electron mobility $\mu_0 N$ in helium.

Unfortunately, the theoretical prediction for $\mu_0 N$ in dense neon was proven wrong or, at best, incomplete [21], mainly because it was based on the assumption of a nearly energy-independent momentum-transfer scattering cross section σ_{mt}. Moreover, these theories explained the different density effects (negative in helium and neon but positive in argon, i.e., $\mu_0 N$ increasing with N [22,23]) by invoking different physical mechanisms according to the sign of the scattering length a.

In order to give a unique description of the electron-atom scattering process in a dense gas, independent of the sign of a, we have developed a model [24] that heuristically incorporates the multiple-scattering effects introduced by previous theories [25,26].

We briefly recall here the main three multiple-scattering effects that are taken into account in the heuristic model. The first one is the density-dependent energy shift $E_k(N)$ of the electron kinetic energy ϵ. E_K is the zero-point kinetic energy arising from the exclusion of the electron from the hard-core volume of the atoms [27]. It can explicitly be obtained by replacing the fluid structure with a locally ordered array of hard-sphere scatterers and by matching the electron wave function with its asymptotic expression at the surface of the Wigner–Seitz sphere [28] of volume $4\pi r_{ws}^3/3 = 1/N$ centered on each atom, thereby getting [29]

$$E_k(N) = \frac{\hbar^2}{2m} k_0^2. \tag{1}$$

m is the electron mass, $\hbar = h/2\pi$, and h is the Planck's constant. The wave vector k_0 is determined by the eigenvalue equation

$$\tan[k_0 r_{ws} + \eta_0(k_0)] = k_0 r_{ws}, \tag{2}$$

in which $\eta_0(k)$ is the s-wave phaseshift [30]. In order to account for the superposition of the tails of the atomic potentials, $-\eta_0(k_0)/k_0$ is replaced by the hard-core radius of the Hartree-Fock potential $\tilde{a} = \sqrt{\sigma_T(k_0)/4\pi}$, in which σ_T is the total scattering cross section [27]. This energy shift produces a large effect if the momentum-transfer scattering cross section is a rapidly varying function of the electron energy.

The second effect is due to correlations among scatterers. The electron wave packet encompasses a volume of the gas whose linear dimension is of the order of the electron wavelength $\lambda = \hbar/\sqrt{2m\epsilon}$. This volume contains many atoms, and the electron is scattered off all of them simultaneously. The total amplitude of the scattered wave is obtained by summing up coherently all partial scattering amplitudes contributed by each atom. The net result is that the scattering cross section is weighted by the static structure factor of the gas $S(0) = N k_B T \chi_T$ [31]. Here, k_B is the Boltzmann's constant, and χ_T is the gas isothermal compressibility.

Finally, the third multiple-scattering effect is the enhancement of the electron backscattering rate due to quantum self-interference of the electron wave function scattered off atoms located along paths connected by time-reversal symmetry [32]. The strength of this effect depends on the ratio of the electron thermal wavelength λ_T to the electron mean free path $\ell = 1/N\sigma_{mt}$. For $\lambda_T/\ell \leq 1$, a perturbative treatment is adequate yielding for the scattering rate ν the linearized expression [10]

$$\nu(\epsilon) = \nu_0 \left(1 + f\frac{\lambda}{\ell}\right) = \nu_0 \left(1 + f\frac{\hbar\nu_0}{\epsilon}\right), \tag{3}$$

in which $\nu_0 = \sqrt{2\epsilon/m} N \sigma_{mt}$ is the scattering rate in the dilute gas limit, and f is a number of order unity [10]. This perturbative treatment is adequate for argon [23] and neon [21] because their cross sections are relatively small at thermal and shifted energies.

However, for helium, σ_{mt} is so large and the experimental N so high that $\lambda/\ell \gtrsim 1$. In this case, we are in presence of the so-called *weak localization* regime in the jargon of the theory of disordered systems [33,34]. If disorder is enhanced by increasing N, electrons become completely localized with exponentially decaying wave functions (known also as *Anderson localized states*) [16], and a mobility edge appears at the finite energy ϵ_c [35,36].

At the mobility edge the scattering rate diverges. Polischuk obtains the mobility edge with a sophisticated diagrammatic technique [12]. The same result can be obtained by following a more simple, intuitive approach. The correction term enhancing the scattering rate in Equation (3) must be proportional to the actual scattering rate $\nu(\epsilon)$ rather than to the unperturbed scattering rate ν_0. It is then easy to get

$$\nu(\epsilon) = \frac{\nu_0}{1 - f\hbar\nu_0/2\epsilon} = \frac{\nu_0}{1 - f\lambda/\ell} \tag{4}$$

that perfectly agrees with the result of Polischuk [12]. The location of the mobility edge corresponds to the Ioffe-Regel criterion for localization $\lambda \simeq \ell$ [25], and the mobility edge energy is obtained as

$$\epsilon_c = \frac{2}{m}\left[\frac{f}{2}\hbar N S(0) \sigma_{\text{mt}}(\epsilon_c)\right]^2. \tag{5}$$

in which the cross section enhancement due to correlation among scatterers is included. We note that there is some disagreement in the literature about the value of f. Its value is $f = 2\pi/3 \approx 2.09$ for Polischuk [12] and $f = 2$ for Atrazhev [10]. The difference is quite small ($\approx 4\%$) and does not significantly affect the results.

The heuristic model [23] is obtained by including the above-mentioned multiple-scattering effects into the equation for the mobility of the classical kinetic theory [26]. Its advantage is that it also predicts the electric field dependence of μ in addition to the N dependence of μ_0. Moreover, it does not entail adjustable parameters and can be applied to all noble gases independently of the sign of the electron–atom scattering length.

The density-normalized mobility is given by [26]

$$\mu N = -\frac{e}{3}\left(\frac{2}{m}\right)^{1/2} \int_{\epsilon_c}^{\infty} \left[\frac{\epsilon}{\sigma_{\text{mt}}^\star(\epsilon)}\right] \frac{dg(\epsilon)}{d\epsilon} d\epsilon. \tag{6}$$

$g(\epsilon)$ is the Davydov–Pidduck energy distribution function [26,37]

$$g(\epsilon) = A \exp\left\{-\int_0^{\epsilon}\left[k_B T + \frac{Me^2}{6mz}\left(\frac{E}{N\sigma_{\text{mt}}^\star(z)}\right)^2\right]^{-1} dz\right\} \tag{7}$$

Here, M is the atom mass, and A is the normalization constant given by enforcing the condition $\int_0^{\infty} \epsilon^{1/2} g(\epsilon) d\epsilon = 1$. $\sigma_{\text{mt}}^\star$ is the effective momentum-transfer scattering cross section that takes into account the three multiple-scattering effects, and it is expressed by

$$\sigma_{\text{mt}}^\star(\epsilon) = \mathcal{F}(w)\sigma_{\text{mt}}(w)\left[1 - f\hbar\frac{\mathcal{F}(w)\sigma_{\text{mt}}(w)}{(2mw)^{1/2}}\right]^{-1}, \tag{8}$$

in which $w = \epsilon + E_k$ is the shifted energy. $\mathcal{F}(w)$ is given by

$$\mathcal{F}(w) = \frac{1}{4w^2}\int_0^{2w} q^3 S(q)\, dq. \tag{9}$$

For not too large values of the exchanged momentum q, the Ornstein–Zernike approximation [38] can be used, yielding a Lorentzian form of the structure factor

$$S(q) = \frac{S(0) + (qL)^2}{1 + (qL)^2}, \tag{10}$$

in which $L^2 = 0.1l^2[S(0) - 1]$, and $l \approx 0.1$ nm is the short-range correlation length [39].

The previous formulas do not have any adjustable parameters and allow the researchers to compute μN as a function of E, N, and T for any gas whose cross sections and thermodynamic equation of state are known. In particular, the density dependence of $\mu_0 N$ can simply be obtained by setting $E/N = 0$ in Equation (7).

The model we have outlined is developed to describe the mobility of quasifree electrons by possibly taking into account the existence of weakly localized, non-propagating states. It has proven extremely successful when applied to argon [23,40] and neon [21,24].

However, in this latter case, sufficiently high-density and low-temperature electrons get self-trapped in (partially) empty cavities giving birth to low-mobility electron bubbles for which the use of the heuristic model is no longer applicable. In cold, dense helium gas, the formation of electron bubbles is also a well-known phenomenon [1–3,6,7,41,42]. The comparison of the theoretical predictions for the quasifree electrons has, thus, to be made only for such N and T ranges, in which electron bubbles are not significantly present. It is interesting to note, however, that the previous multiple-scattering theories for $\mu_0 N$ were applied to an extended N range, thereby leading, in our opinion, to some confusion about the relationship between Anderson-localized and bubble states.

Therefore, we have carried out new, accurate measurements in broad T and N ranges in order to gain insight both in the process of electron bubble formation at high densities and at higher temperatures and in the behavior of quasifree electrons up to intermediate densities. The results on bubble formation have already been published [42]. In this paper, we will present mobility data from low up to intermediate density in the range $26\,\text{K} \leq T \leq 300\,\text{K}$ in order to investigate the behavior of quasifree electrons, compare the previous multiple-scattering theories with the present heuristic model, and shed some light on the relationship between disorder-induced non-propagating states and self-trapped states in bubbles.

The paper is organized as follows: In Section 2, the details of the experiments are briefly described. In Section 3, the experimental results are presented and discussed. In Section 4, we will discuss if experimental data allow the distinction between Anderson-localized states and electron bubbles with the aid of the prediction of the heuristic model.

Following the Conclusions in Section 5, in Appendix A, we will give some details on the different effects on the mobility of the two relevant energy scales, E_K and ϵ_c, which are necessary for the description of the experimental electron mobility.

2. Experimental Details

The measurements are carried out using the pulsed photoemission technique and apparatus exploited in previous measurements of electron mobility, O_2^- mobility, and resonant electron attachment in dense helium, neon, and argon gases and have already been thoroughly described [21,40,42–47]. We recall here only the main technical features of the experiment.

A high-pressure cell is mounted on the cold head of a cryocooler inside a triple-shield thermostat. The cell can withstand pressure up to $P \approx 10\,\text{MPa}$ and can be cooled down to $T \approx 25\,\text{K}$. The cell temperature is stabilized within $\pm 0.01\,\text{K}$, and the pressure is measured with an accuracy of $\pm 1\,\text{kPa}$. The gas used is ultra-high purity helium with nominal O_2 content of 1 ppm. However, in order to make accurate mobility measurements, the impurity content must be lowered by recirculating the gas in a closed loop through a LN_2-cooled activated-charcoal trap and a commercial Oxisorb cartridge [48]. The final impurity content is estimated to be a fraction of one ppb. The gas density N is computed from the measured values of T and P by means of an accurate equation of state [49,50].

The parallel plate drift capacitor is located in the cell and is energized by a d.c. high-voltage generator [51]. A thin slice of electrons is photoinjected from the cathode by a short pulse ($\approx 4\,\mu\text{s}$) of VUV light produced by a Xe flashlamp [52] and is drifted towards the anode. The injected charge amounts to 4 through 400 fC, depending on the gas pressure in the cell and on the applied electric field strength, and is low enough to avoid space-charge effects.

The current induced at the anode by the drifting electrons is passively integrated to improve the signal-to-noise ratio. The voltage signal is acquired by a digital oscilloscope and fetched by a personal computer for offline analysis. Several signals are acquired for any experimental conditions and are software-averaged to improve the signal quality.

The drift time τ is obtained by analyzing the time evolution of the voltage signal at the anode [53]. The drift velocity is obtained as $v_D = \tau/d$, where d is the drift distance, and the mobility is obtained as $\mu = v_D/E$, where E is the applied electric field. The estimated accuracy on μ is much better than 5%.

3. Experimental Results and Discussion

In this section, the experimental data will be presented and discussed.

3.1. The Need for Accurate Measurements

The present measurements in helium are aimed at validating the heuristic model developed for the description of the mobility of quasifree electrons in dense noble gases [23]. This goal justifies the need for new accurate measurements of the mobility. Actually, the main attention in the past was focused onto the negative density effect shown by $\mu_0 N$ that eventually leads to the formation of electron bubbles. As $\mu_0 N$ decreases by nearly five orders of magnitude in a restricted density range at low temperature [2–4,6,7,41], the mobility at low and medium density, where no localization takes yet place, was not investigated with the necessary accuracy in the past. In order to clarify this point, the present $\mu_0 N$ data for $T = 77.2$ K are compared in Figure 1, with one of the most accurate experiments at nearly the same temperature [4].

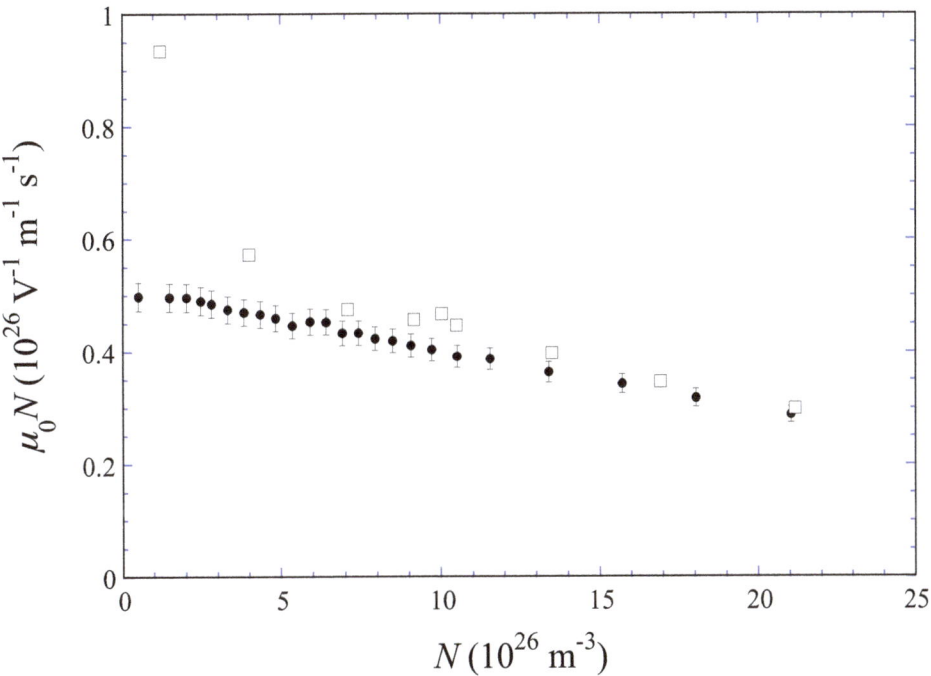

Figure 1. $\mu_0 N$ vs. N at $T \approx 77$ K. Comparison of the present measurements accuracy at $T = 77.2$ K (closed points) with literature data at $T = 77.6$ K (open squares) [4].

Literature data are more scattered than the present ones, especially at low density, where they strongly disagree with the classical kinetic theory prediction based on the commonly accepted momentum-transfer scattering cross section [30]. On the contrary, it will be shown in the following that the present data agree very well with this prediction. At lower temperatures, the accuracy of literature data in the low density range is even worse [2,3,41].

3.2. Choice of the Correct Density Range to Explore

Another important point to be discussed before proceeding is the determination of the density range in which the quasifree electron mobility is not affected by the presence of electrons localized in cavities. As the mobility of the electron bubbles is roughly four to five orders of magnitude smaller than that of quasifree electrons, any significant presence of them would spoil the comparison of the experimental outcome with the theory for quasifree electrons.

Actually, the present measurements were carried out in very broad N and T ranges because of the great interest in ascertaining whether the phenomenon of electron self-trapping in cavities also occurs at higher temperatures than previously observed. The high-density $\mu_0 N$ data [42] have shown that localization takes place at any T, indeed, provided that N is large enough to yield an excess Helmoltz free energy of the localized state with respect to the quasifree one $\Delta\mathcal{A}(N,T) \lesssim 0$ with $|\Delta\mathcal{A}(N,T)| \gtrsim k_B T$, in which k_B is the Boltzmann constant. The excess free energy $\Delta\mathcal{A}(N,T)$ was computed by adopting a simple electron bubble model [54], taking into account that the gas has no surface tension and that the helium atoms have non-negligible thermal energy at the temperatures of the experiment. The threshold density $N^\star$ at which quasifree electrons and electron bubbles are equiprobable is obtained by solving the equation

$$\Delta\mathcal{A}(N^\star, T) = 0, \tag{11}$$

yielding a quite satisfactory agreement with the data [42]. However, at $N^\star$, the fraction of electron bubble states is 50%, and its contribution to the mobility is far from negligible. Thus, the threshold density, above which they cannot actually be neglected any longer, must experimentally be determined by inspecting the electric field dependence of μ for different N. A typical example is shown in Figure 2 for $T = 26.1$ K.

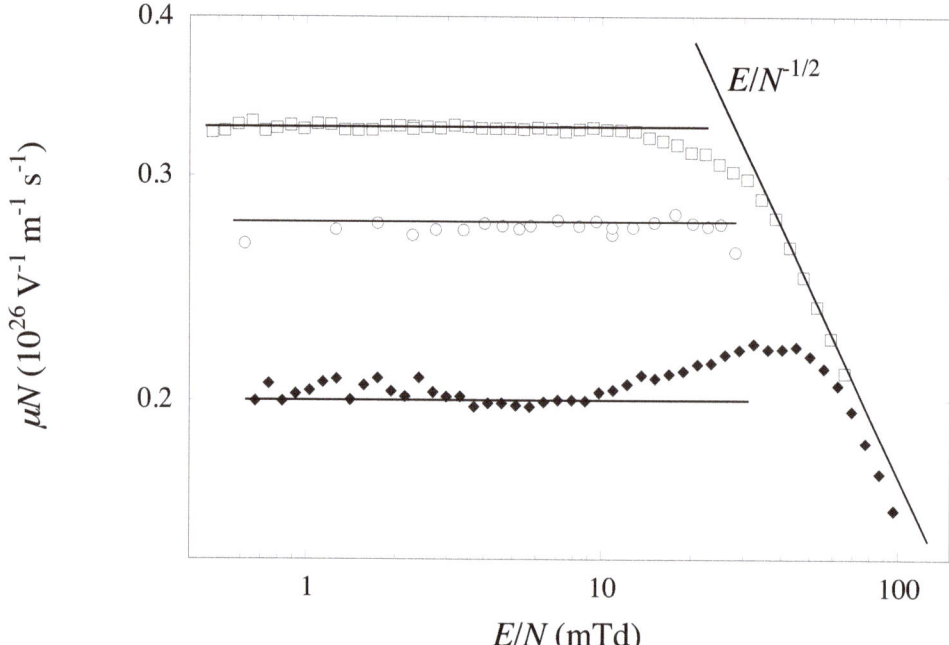

Figure 2. μN vs. E/N at $T = 26.1$ K for densities close to the onset of the electron self-trapping in bubbles. From top: $N = 17.33$, 19.47, and 22.76 in units of 10^{26} m^{-3}. 1 mTd $= 10^{-24}$ V m^2. The line $\propto (E/N)^{-1/2}$ is the prediction of the classical kinetic theory for scattering of quasifree, epithermal electrons off hard spheres [26]. The presence of electron bubble states for the highest N is proven by the rise of μN above its zero-field limit (shown as a constant line) before joining the high-field behavior.

Helium can be considered a hard-sphere scatterer to a good approximation as its momentum-transfer scattering cross section σ_{mt} is roughly independent of energy (it varies from 4.87 Å^2 at energy $\epsilon = 0$ to 6.8 Å^2 at $\epsilon = 1$ eV) [30]. For such a system, the classical kinetic theory predicts that, at constant T, μN is constant at weak electric field and is proportional to $(E/N)^{-1/2}$ at a high field. By inspecting Figure 2, in which the electric field dependence of μN is shown for $T = 26.1$ K for some N, we note that μN at the lower N follows the classically expected behavior. If N is further increased, the behavior of μN changes even qualitatively. At weak fields, μN is constant but, upon a further increase of the field strength, μN increases with E/N and shows a maximum before joining the density-independent, high-field region. This specific behavior, observed for N large enough even at very low temperature [6,7], was previously reported also in dense neon gas [44] and is intepreted as the field-assisted hindrance to self-trapping or field-assisted release of electrons from the bubbles [55]. This interpretation is also supported by experimental evidence in liquid neon [56].

The logical consequence drawn from the observed field dependence of μN is that a temperature-dependent threshold N_{th} density exists for electron bubble states of low mobility to be experimentally detected. In Figure 3, N_{th} is reported along with the computed density $N^\star$.

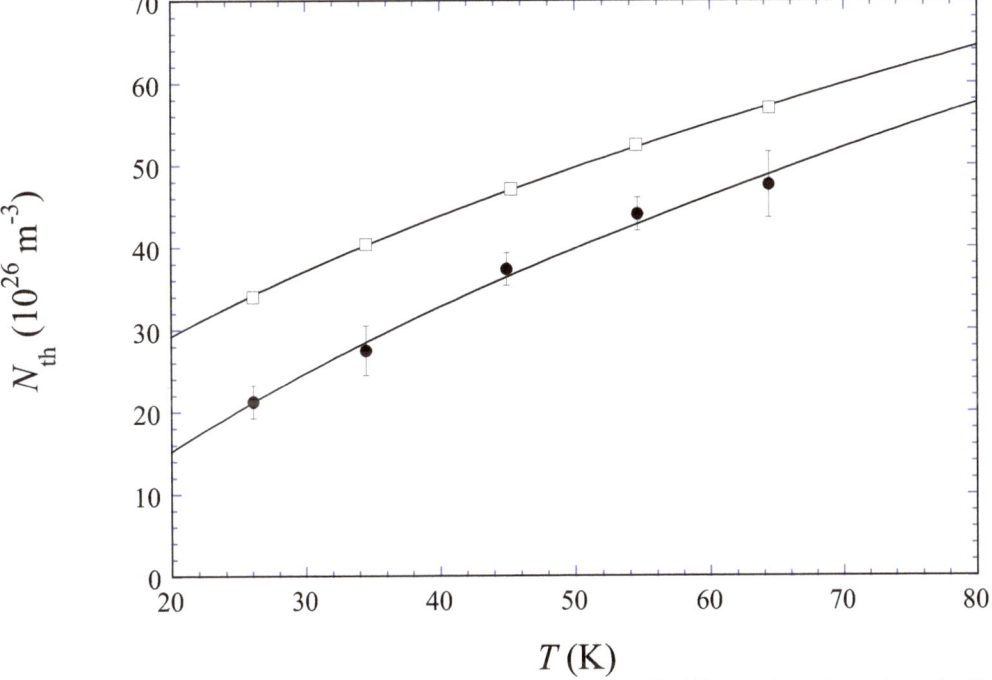

Figure 3. Temperature dependence of the threshold density N_{th} for the onset of bubble state formation as determined by the inspection of the field dependence of μN (closed points). Open squares: temperature dependence of the density $N^\star$ at which quasifree electrons and electron bubbles are equiprobable according to the bubble model [42]. The lines are only a guide for the eye.

As a result, the analysis of the mobility of quasifree electrons will be restricted to $N \leq N_{th}(T)$.

3.3. Density Dependence of the Zero-Field Limit of the Density Normalized Mobility

In Figure 4, $\mu_0 N$ is shown as a function of N for several T. As previously discussed, the data are shown only for $N < N_{th}$ to be sure that only quasifree electrons contribute to the mobility. At the highest temperatures, the pressure necessary to reach N_{th} exceeds the experimental cell capability, and thus, the measurements are restricted to not too high density values. At all temperatures, $\mu_0 N$ shows the well-known negative density effect that is extremely well described by the heuristic model, represented by the solid lines through the data in the figure.

According to the model, three density-dependent processes combined to determine the behavior of the mobility: the quantum density-dependent shift of the kinetic energy of the electron $E_k(N)$, the correlation among scatterers, and the quantum self-interference of the electron wave packet scattered by atoms located along paths connected by time-reversal symmetry. In the case of helium, the first one is not very effective because σ_{mt} does not depend very much on the electron energy. On the contrary, this effect is very important in neon [21,43] and argon [22,24,40,57–59], whose cross sections are strongly energy dependent [13,60].

The correlation among scatterers is a second process that increases the scattering cross section by the long-wavelegth limit of the static structure factor $S(0) = Nk_B T \chi_T$. The effect of $S(0)$ is very important close to the critical point, which, for helium, occurs for $T_c = 5.2 \, \text{K}$ and $N_c = 104.8 \times 10^{26} \, \text{m}^{-3}$ [49,50]. As the present experiment is carried out for $T \gg T_c$, $S(0) \approx 1$ always, its effect is quite negligible.

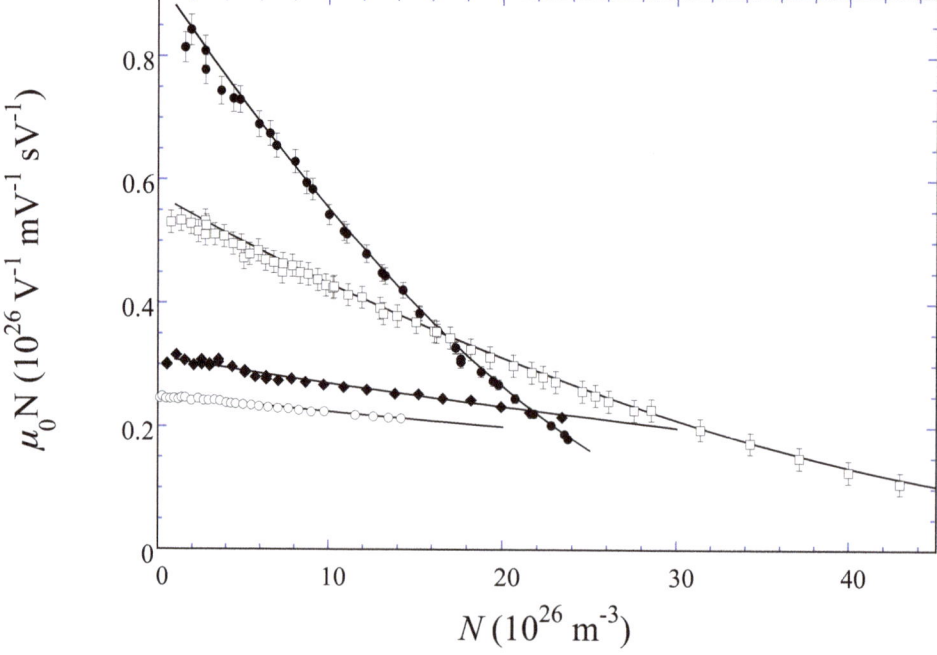

Figure 4. $\mu_0 N$ vs. N. $T = 26.1 \, \text{K}$ (closed points), $T = 64.4 \, \text{K}$ (open squares), $T = 199.5 \, \text{K}$ (closed diamonds), and $T = 295.5 \, \text{K}$ (open points). Lines: heuristic model prediction. The data are only presented for $N \leq N_{th}$, at which electron bubbles are still either absent or present in a negligible proportion. The error bars for the highest T are of the same size of the dots and are not shown.

The last process is the quantum self-interference of the electron wave packet scattered off atoms located along paths connected by time-reversal symmetry. As discussed in the

Introduction, this process leads to an increase of the scattering rate, which is $\propto \lambda/\ell$, i.e., proportional to the ratio of the electron quantum wavelength λ to its mean free path ℓ. However, if the scattering cross section is large, i.e., if the mean free path is short, and the temperature is low, i.e., the electron thermal wavelength is large, the quantum self-interference process is so strong to lead to the weak electron localization via the appearance of the mobility edge [11,12,17]. Electrons in the low-energy tail of the distribution function below the mobility edge energy ϵ_c do not propagate. In helium, this is the dominant process that produces most of the observed negative density effect of the mobility.

The mobility edge introduces an infrared cutoff in the electron energy distribution function, which gives rise to a strong exponential decrease in $\mu_0 N$ with increasing N. On one hand, the quite fair agreement with experiments of the older theories, all of which are based on a complex shift of the electron energy in a dense disordered medium due to multiple-scattering effects [13–15], is explained by various additional assumptions (not all fully correct) invoked by the authors, as discussed in the literature [8,9,20]. Their apparent success is due to the fact that they predict an exponential decrease of the mobility with increasing N. It has also to be noted that these theories invoke different phenomena to explain the different density effects observed in repulsive gases (such as helium and neon) and in attractive gases (such as argon) [10,12,14].

On the other hand, the heuristic model takes into account all the three multiple-scattering effects in a natural way. Their relative weight is automatically accounted for by the strength and energy dependence of the scattering cross section and by the thermodynamic state of the gas through which electrons are drifted. As a further benefit, the heuristic model treats the scattering of low energy electrons in noble gases in a unified way independently of the sign of the scattering length.

The heuristic model shares with the theories of Atrazhev [10] and of Polischuk [12] the concept of enhancement of the scattering rate due quantum self-interference (that eventually leads to the appearance of the mobility edge) but accounts for the two additional multiple-scattering effects (quantum density-dependent shift of the electron kinetic energy in the dense disordered medium and correlation among scatterers), although their influence only marginally affects the electron mobility in helium in the particular thermodynamic conditions of the experiment.

3.4. Validation of the Accuracy of the Present Experiment and of Its Outcome

A way to validate the accuracy of the results of the present experiment is to show that the present data agree well with the prediction of the classical kinetic theory in the limit of low density [26]. If $N \to 0$, all multiple-scattering effects vanish. Both the mobility edge ϵ_c and the energy shift $E_k(N)$ tend to 0 and the long wavelength limit of the structure factor $S(0) \to 1$. In this limit, the classical formula predicts

$$\mu_0 N \to (\mu_0 N)_0 = \frac{4e}{3\sqrt{2\pi m (k_B T)^5}} \int_0^\infty \frac{\epsilon}{\sigma_{mt}(\epsilon)} e^{-\epsilon/k_B T} \, d\epsilon. \tag{12}$$

The zero-density extrapolation of the mobility obtained from the investigated isotherms (some of which are reported in Figure 4) are compared in Figure 5 with the theoretical prediction, Equation (12), based on O'Malley's low-energy electron-helium cross section [30]. The data are in excellent agreement with the classical prediction, thereby lending credibility to the accuracy of the experiment. It has to be noted that both the data as well as the theoretical line are extremely well fitted to an inverse power law of the temperature, namely $(\mu_0 N)_0 \propto T^{-0.536}$. The exponent differs from the value $-1/2$, which is typical of gas of hard-sphere scatterers, because of the weak energy dependence of the electron-helium momentum-transfer scattering cross section.

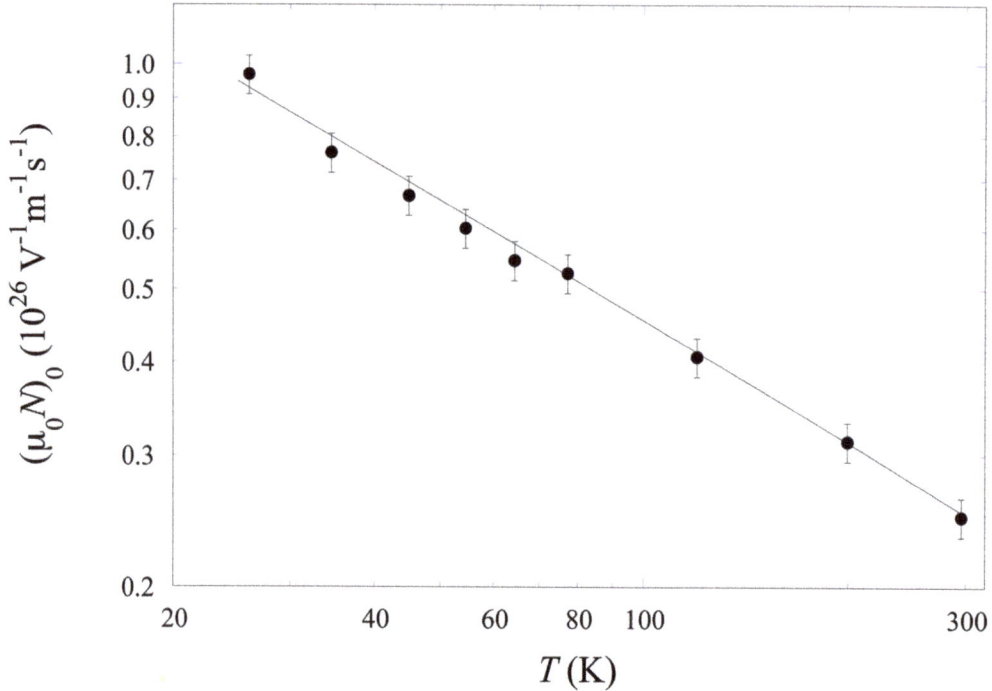

Figure 5. $(\mu_0 N)_0$ vs. T. The solid line is the prediction of the heuristic model which, for $N \to 0$, must coincide with the classical kinetic prediction [26]. Data and theory are well fitted to the inverse power law $T^{-0.536}$ close to the $T^{-1/2}$ behavior of a gas of hard-sphere scatterers.

An additional confirmation of the validity of the heuristic model is obtained by inspecting how it is able to reproduce the electric field dependence of the experimental data. In Figure 6, we show typical μN vs. E/N data for $T = 64.4$ K for several $N < N_{th}$, i.e., for densities below the onset of electron bubble formation. The heuristic model is able to accurately describe the field dependence of μN for well over a decade in N and nearly three decades in E/N. Similar results are obtained at all temperatures.

A small discrepancy between the experiment and model can still be spotted in the transition region between thermal and epi-thermal behavior. On one hand, this discrepancy could be ascribed to imperfect knowledge of the scattering cross section at energies higher than thermal. On the other hand, it has to be noted that, for any given N, the same energy shift $E_K(N)$ is used for all fields and energies in Equation (6), although it is obtained by a solving Equation (2), which is only valid for s-wave scattering.

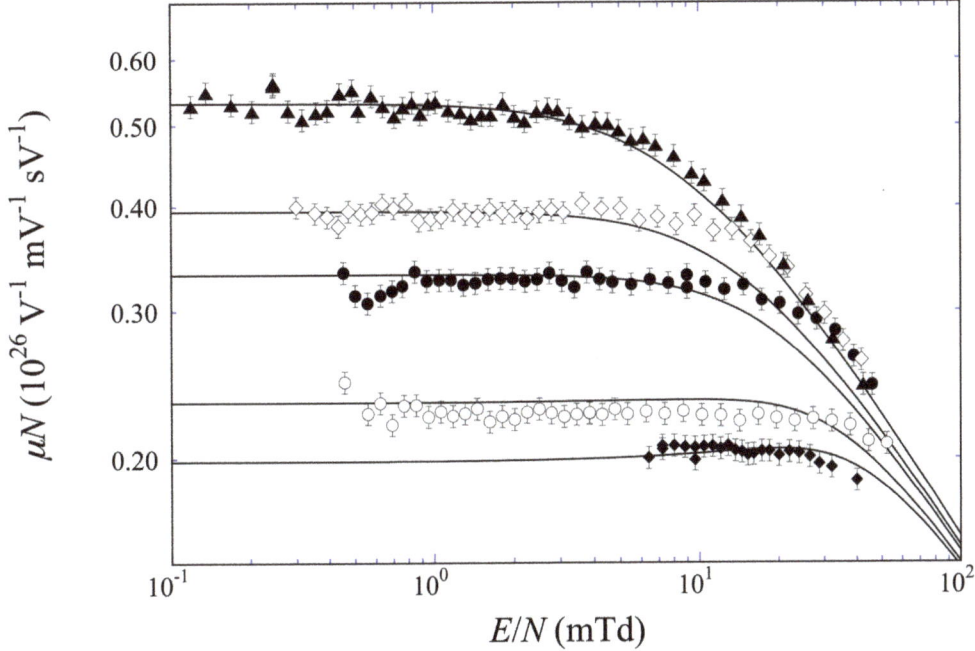

Figure 6. μN vs. E/N for $T = 64.4$ K. Densities (from top, in units of 10^{26} m^{-3}): $N = 2.79, 12.95, 18.20, 27.54, 31.38$. The solid lines are the predictions of the heuristic model.

4. Weakly Localized States vs. Electron Bubble States

It is well known that electrons in cold dense helium, either liquid or gas, do give origin to states localized in cavities (for a review, see Ref. [61]). The cavities form as a consequence of the delicate balance between the free energies of the quasifree and the localized electrons and because the medium is compliant enough not to withstand the quantum pressure exerted by the wavefunction of the localized electron that pushes away the nearby atoms, thereby digging out the cavity.

On the other hand, it is also well known that a static structural disorder can lead to the vanishing of electron diffusion because of the formation of Anderson-localized states [12,16,17,35]. In this case, the electron wave function exponentially decays with distance owing to multiple-scattering effects induced by the disorder. Under this respect, helium is a school case of a dense, disordered system consisting of (nearly) hard-sphere scatterers.

It still unclear, however, if Anderson-localized states might be precursors of electron bubbles. Actually, non-propagating states might remain for a time long enough to favor the enhancement and stabilization of the cavity because of the medium compliance.

We believe that the actual measurements might give some hints to solve this issue. As an argument, we will investigate the experimental behavior of μN as a function of E/N for densities at which electron bubbles definitely exist [42].

In Figure 7, the field dependence of μN is reported for $T = 26.1$ K and for $N = 32.36 \times 10^{26}$ m^{-3} and $N = 34.31 \times 10^{26}$ m^{-3}. μN is constant at weak fields and shows a rapid enhancement towards the electron epithermal behavior $\sim E/N^{-1/2}$ for stronger fields.

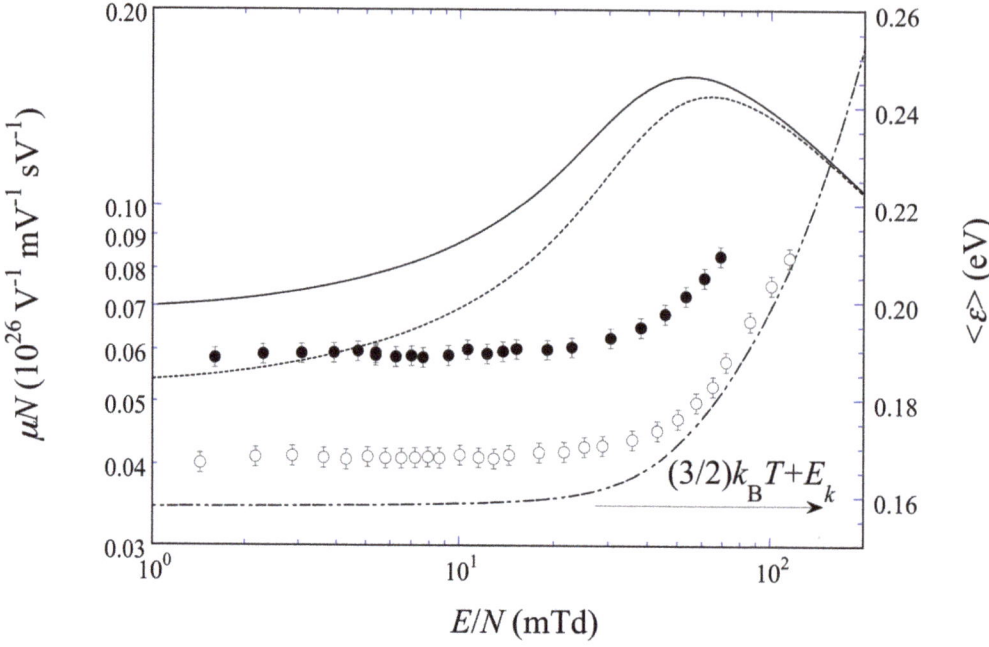

Figure 7. Left scale: μN vs. E/N for $T = 26.1$ K for $N = 32.36$ (closed points) and $N = 34.31$ (open points). The solid and dotted lines are the predictions of the heuristic model. N is in units of 10^{26} m^{-3}. Right scale: the average electron energy for $N = 34.31 \times 10^{26}$ m^{-3} (dash-dotted line), which includes the contribution of $E_k(N)$.

For these densities, the heuristic model fails at reproducing the low-field mobility predicting far too large values. The rationale for this failure might be that, for these densities, there is coexistence of both weakly localized electrons and self-trapped electrons in bubbles. The heuristic model obviously accounts for the Anderson-localized states through the infrared cutoff in the electron energy distribution function due to the mobility edge. On the contrary, the measured mobility is a weighted sum of the contributions of the quasifree states, which are very mobile, and of the electron bubbles, which, though very slowly, do still propagate.

The heuristic model predicts that μN increases upon increasing E/N before reaching the epithermal behavior. This increase takes place at much weaker E/N values than experimentally observed. The transition between the low- and high-field behavior experimentally occurs in the same field region in which the average electron energy (dashed–dotted line in Figure 7) starts increasing above its thermal value $\langle \epsilon \rangle \geq (3/2)k_B T + E_k(N)$. We note that, in this field range, the electron drift velocity becomes comparable with the sound speed ≈ 300 m/s [50,62].

We, thus, draw the conclusion that Anderson-localized states cannot be precursors of electron bubbles. Actually, if they were such precursors, the decrease of their number upon increasing field should lead to an increase of the measured mobility that, by contrast, remains constant. The mobility only increases at stronger fields where the average electron energy and the drift velocity are large enough to hinder the electron self-trapping process in cavities.

Such point of view is further confirmed, in our opinion, if the fraction of quasifree electrons is compared with the mobility behavior as a function of the reduced field.

The fraction f_{free} of quasifree states with energy in excess of the mobility edge energy ϵ_c is given by

$$f_{\text{free}} = \int_{\epsilon_c}^{\infty} \epsilon^{1/2} g(\epsilon)\, d\epsilon. \tag{13}$$

In Figure 8, we plot the experimental mobility (closed points) and the model prediction (solid line) for $T = 34.5\,\text{K}$ and $N = 41.74 \times 10^{26}\,\text{m}^{-3}$ and compare their behavior with f_{free} (dashed line, right scale).

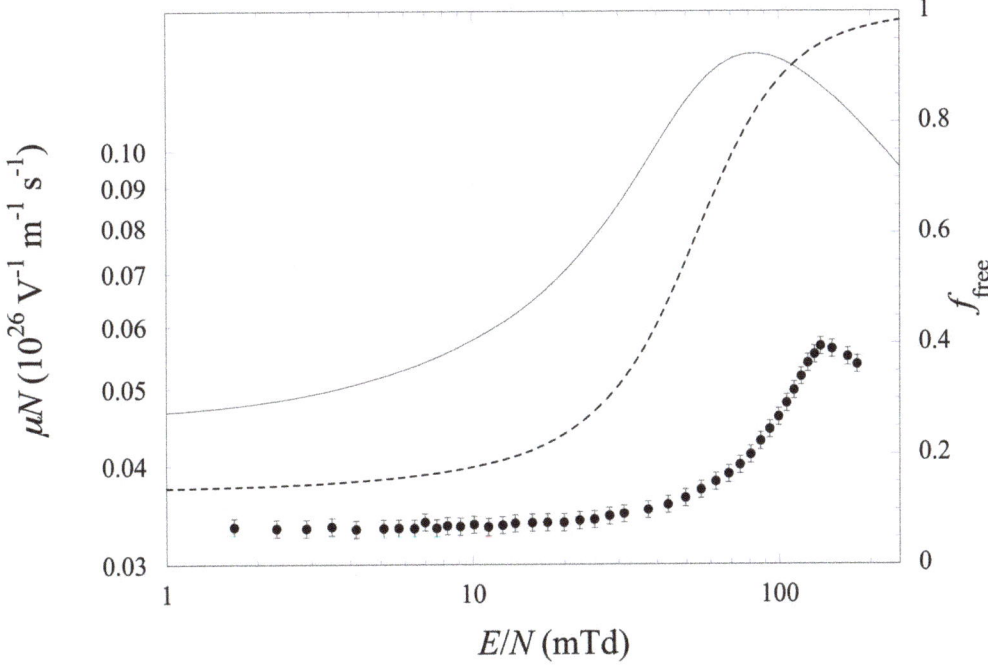

Figure 8. Left scale: μN vs. E/N for $T = 34.5\,\text{K}$ for $N = 41.74 \times 10^{26}\,\text{m}^{-3}$ (closed points) and prediction of the heuristic model (solid line). Dashed line: the fraction of quasifree electrons f_{free} (right scale).

At such high a density, $\mu_0 N$ is well below the predicted value by the heuristic model and by all other theoretical models [10,12–14] because a non-negligible fraction of electrons are localized in bubbles and significantly contributes to the mobility decline with density. By inspecting Figure 8, it can be noted that the quasifree electron fraction is $f_{\text{free}} \approx 10\,\%$ at low fields and rapidly increases towards $f_{\text{free}} = 100\,\%$ at high fields. However, its rise begins at much weaker field strength than the mobility rise. Therefore, we can conclude that the reduction of the fraction of non-propagating states below the mobility edge is not the principal mechanism of the mobility increase with electric field at high densities and that these weakly localized states are probably not the precursors of the electron states self-trapped in cavities.

5. Conclusions

In this paper, we have presented new and accurate experimental measurements of electron mobility in helium gas in a wide temperature range for low to intermediate densities. The experimental ranges have been selected in a way to exclude the presence of electron bubbles that might spoil the theoretical analysis.

We have shown that the heuristic model, originally developed for neon and argon, also works very well for helium. On one hand, it encompasses the multiple-scattering effects taken into account also by previous theories. It supersedes them because all the multiple-scattering effects are included at once in a unified picture. In particular, for helium, the main effect is produced by the presence of a disorder-induced mobility-edge that leads to a nearly exponential decrease of the zero-field limit of the density-normalized mobility $\mu_0 N$ by shrinking the phase space available to freely propagating electrons.

On the other hand, at least for the noble gases, the heuristic model treats the electron-atom scattering process in a dense, disordered medium as a unique phenomenon that does not depend if the electron-atom interaction potential is mainly attractive or repulsive. The different density effect shown by different gases is only a manifestation of the energy dependence of the scattering cross sections.

Moreover, in comparison with the previous theories, the present heuristic model is also able to describe the electric field dependence of the quasifree electron mobility with great accuracy.

In helium, owing to the near energy independence of the scattering cross section and to the distance from the criticality of the present measurements, the most important multiple-scattering process affecting the electron mobility is the existence of a disorder-produced mobility edge at which the scattering cross section diverges. States with energy below the mobility-edge energy do not propagate and are weakly-localized, and thus, the phase space of propagating electrons shrink. The resulting infrared cutoff in the electron energy distribution function leads to a strong, nearly exponential decrease in $\mu_0 N$ with increasing density that explains the approximate success of previous theories.

The availability of an accurate theoretical model and experimental measurements has allowed us to suggest a clear distinction between disorder-induced, non-propagating, Anderson-localized states and electron bubbles. From the theoretical analysis of the experimental data in a thermodynamic state in which electron bubbles are present, the conclusion can be drawn that Anderson-localized states may coexist with electron bubbles.

It would be interesting if an analysis similar to the present one could be carried out on measurements of electron mobility in dense carbon dioxide [63,64], ammonia [65], and methanol [66] that show a significant negative density effect and even self-trapping in cavities.

Funding: This research received no external funding.

Institutional Review Board Statement: Not applicable.

Informed Consent Statement: Not applicable.

Data Availability Statement: The data presented in this study are only available on request from the corresponding author because they are still under consideration for further analysis.

Acknowledgments: The author acknowledges useful discussions with M. Santini , A.M. De Riva, D. Neri, and P. Lamp. Thanks are due to G. Delfitto for technical assistance.

Conflicts of Interest: The author declares no conflict of interest.

Appendix A. Influence of $E_k(N)$ and of ϵ_c on the Mobility of Quasifree Electrons

Two characteristic energies have to be considered in the heuristic model to produce an accurate description of the mobility data without any adjustable parameters, namely the density-dependent energy shift $E_k(N)$ and the mobility edge energy ϵ_c. ϵ_c slightly depends on T because of $S(0)$. However, for all T and N of the present experiment, $S(0) \approx 1$ within less than 10%, and ϵ_c turns out to practically be temperature independent.

The two energies are very different values, as shown in Figure A1. Roughly speaking, E_k is more than ≈ 20 times larger than ϵ_c at all densities.

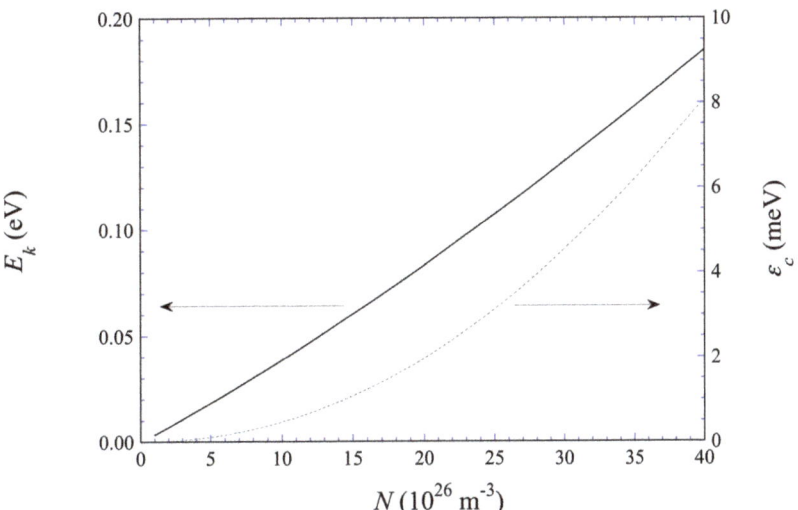

Figure A1. The density dependence of the energy shift E_k (left scale) and of the mobility edge energy ϵ_c (right scale).

Despite this big difference between the two quantities, in the case of helium gas, the smaller one produces the bigger effect on the mobility. Actually, $E_k(N)$ produces a rigid shift of the electron energy distribution function whose zero is shifted from $\epsilon = 0$ to $\epsilon = E_k(N)$. By a suitable change of variables in the integrals for the mobility [23], it can be shown that the effect of E_k is to force the evaluation of the energy-dependent electron-atom scattering cross section at the shifted energy, as demonstrated by Equation (8). If the cross section is nearly independent of energy, as is the case of helium, its evaluation at a shifted energy gives nearly the same value, and the effect on the mobility is small. On the contrary, the action of E_k produces the dominant effect in neon [21,43,44] and argon [22,23,40,58], whose cross sections very rapidly vary with energy.

The action of the mobility edge energy is more subtle. It introduces an infrared cutoff in the mobility integrals. Electron states with energies below ϵ_c do not propagate. Thus, the cutoff actually shrinks the phase space available to the freely propagating states. For thermal electrons and (nearly) energy-independent cross sections, the zero-field density normalized mobility is given by

$$\mu_0 N \propto \int_{\epsilon_c}^{\infty} \epsilon e^{-\epsilon/k_B T}\, d\epsilon = e^{-\epsilon_c/k_B T} \int_0^{\infty} (z+\epsilon_c) e^{-z/k_B T}\, dz \sim e^{-\epsilon_c/k_B T} (\mu_0 N)_0. \tag{A1}$$

Loosely speaking, the classical mobility $(\mu_0 N)_0$ is thus multiplied by an exponential factor of the form $\exp(-\epsilon_c/k_B T)$. Actually, the exact integral weakens the quadratic density dependence of ϵ_c in the argument of the exponential. In any case, the strong density dependence of the exponential leads to the observed negative density effect of the electron mobility in helium. Furthermore, in neon and argon, the quantum self-interference effect leads to the appearance of a mobility edge. However, in these gases, the cross section at thermal energies is so small that $\epsilon_c \approx 0$ and can safely be neglected, thus allowing the other multiple-scattering effects to fully manifest.

As mentioned before, the infrared cutoff ϵ_c leads to a reduction of the fraction f_{free} of freely propagating electron states. It is interesting to investigate how f_{free} depends on T, N, and E/N as a consequence of the presence of ϵ_c.

In Figure A2, we show the influence of N on the field dependence of f_{free} at constant T. For all N, the action of the electric field is to broaden the electron energy distribution function so that the fraction of states with energy $\epsilon > \epsilon_c$ always increases with the increasing E/N.

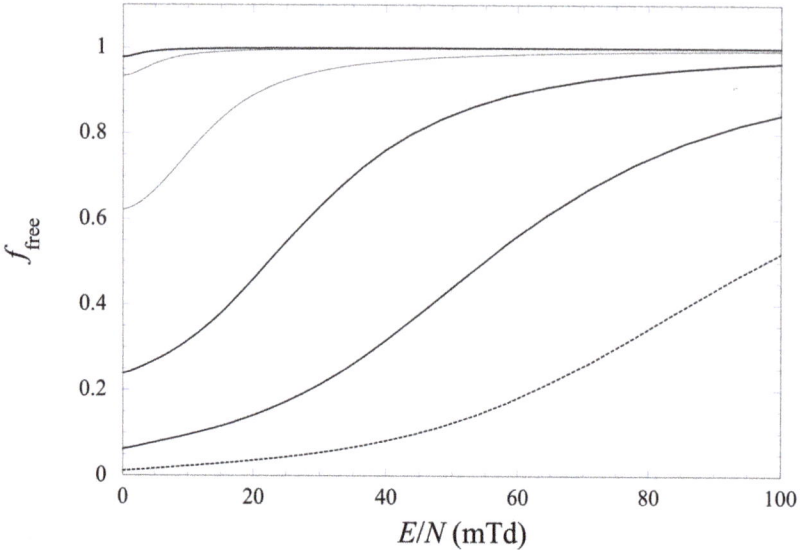

Figure A2. f_{free} as a function of E/N at $T = 26.1$ K. From top: N : 5, 10, 20, 30, 40, 50 (in units of 10^{26} m^{-3}). Note that for $T = 26.1$ K, the threshold density is $N_{\text{th}} \gtrsim 20$.

At a low density, f_{free} is practically always equal to 1. Upon increasing N, f_{free} steadily decreases. The higher the density is, the larger the field strength required to produce larger proportions of quasifree electrons is.

Similar considerations can be made about the effect of temperature on f_{free} at constant density, as shown in Figure A3.

At constant N and T, the action of the field is the same as discussed for the previous figure. At constant E/N and N, the action of T is clear. Upon increasing T, the electron energy distribution gets broader, and the average electron energy increases, thereby increasing the fraction of electrons with energy in excess of ϵ_c. It has to be once more noted that, at the density of Figure A3 for $T \lesssim 50$ K, a large number of electrons are self-trapped in bubbles.

It is finally interesting to note that fraction of quasifree states at $E/N = 0$ is a universal function of $y_c = \sqrt{\epsilon_c / k_B T} \propto N/\sqrt{T}$

$$\lim_{E/N \to 0} f_{\text{free}} = \frac{2}{\sqrt{\pi}} y_c e^{-y_c^2} + \text{erfc}(y_c), \tag{A2}$$

in which erfc(x) is the error function [12].

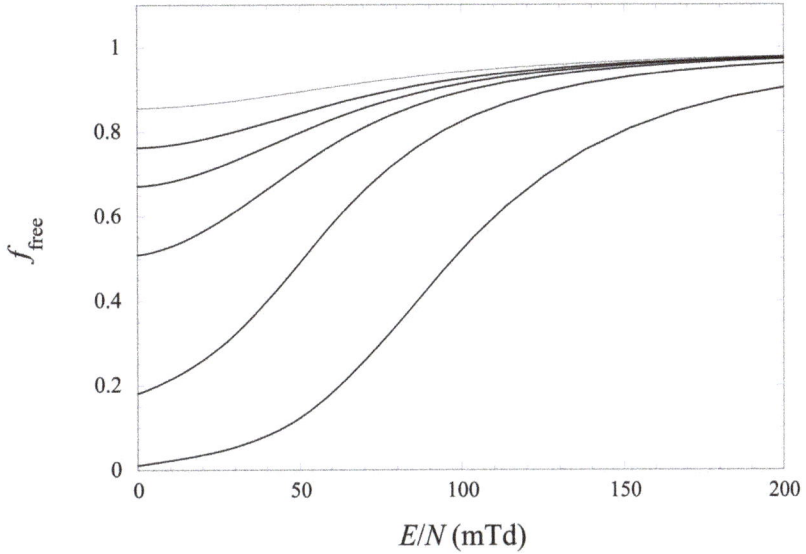

Figure A3. f_{free} vs. E/N at $N = 50 \times 10^{26}$ m^{-3} for several T. From top: T (K) = 300, 200, 150, 100, 50, 26.1.

References

1. Levine, J.; Sanders, T.M. Anomalous electron mobility and complex negative ion formation in low-temperature helium vapor. *Phys. Rev. Lett.* **1962**, *8*, 159–161. [CrossRef]
2. Levine, J.L.; Sanders, T.M. Mobility of electrons in low-temperature helium gas. *Phys. Rev.* **1967**, *154*, 138–149. [CrossRef]
3. Harrison, H.R.; Sander, L.M.; Springett, B.E. Electron mobility and localization in dense He$_4$ gas. *J. Phys. B At. Mol. Phys.* **1973**, *6*, 908–917. [CrossRef]
4. Bartels, A. Density dependence of electron drift velocities in helium and hydrogen at 77.6 K. *Appl. Phys.* **1975**, *8*, 59–64. [CrossRef]
5. Schwarz, K.W.; Prasad, B. Dynamics of electron localization in dense helium gas. *Phys. Rev. Lett.* **1976**, *36*, 878–881. [CrossRef]
6. Schwarz, K.W. Anomalous electron mobilities in dense helium gas. *Phys. Rev. Lett.* **1978**, *41*, 239–242. [CrossRef]
7. Schwarz, K.W. Electron localization in dense helium gas: New experimental results. *Phys. Rev. B* **1980**, *21*, 5125–5136. [CrossRef]
8. Iakubov, I.T.; Polischuk, A.Y. Influence of multiple scattering processes on the electron mobility in moderately dense gases. *Phys. Lett. A* **1982**, *91*, 67–69. [CrossRef]
9. Iakubov, I.T.; Polischuk, A.Y. Quantum density corrections to mobility and dispersion law for electrons in a medium of disordered scatterers. *J. Phys. B At. Mol. Phys.* **1982**, *15*, 4029–4041. [CrossRef]
10. Atrazhev, V.M.; Iakubov, I.T. The electron drift velocity in dense gases. *J. Phys. D Appl. Phys.* **1977**, *10*, 2155–2163. [CrossRef]
11. Ya Polischuk, A. Quantum corrections to electron conductivity in a disordered medium of anisotropic scatterers. *J. Phys. B At. Mol. Phys.* **1983**, *16*, 3853–3858. [CrossRef]
12. Polischuk, A.Y. Theory of electron mobility in dense gases with small polarizability. *Phys. B+C* **1984**, *124*, 91–95. [CrossRef]
13. O'Malley, T.F. Multiple scattering effect on electron mobilities in dense gases. *J. Phys. B At. Mol. Phys.* **1980**, *13*, 1491–1504. [CrossRef]
14. Braglia, G.L.; Dallacasa, V. Theory of electron mobility in dense gases. *Phys. Rev. A* **1982**, *26*, 902–914. [CrossRef]
15. O'Malley, T.F. General Model For Electron Drift and Diffusion in a Dense Gas. *J. Phys. B At. Mol. Opt. Phys.* **1992**, *25*, 163–180. [CrossRef]
16. Anderson, P.W. Absence of diffusion in certain random lattices. *Phys. Rev.* **1958**, *109*, 1492–1505. [CrossRef]
17. Cutler, M.; Mott, N.F. Observation of Anderson localization in an electron gas. *Phys. Rev.* **1969**, *181*, 1336–1340. [CrossRef]
18. Foldy, L.L. The multiple scattering of waves. I. General theory of isotropic scattering by randomly distributed scatterers. *Phys. Rev.* **1945**, *67*, 107–119. [CrossRef]
19. Lax, M. Multiple scattering of waves. *Rev. Mod. Phys.* **1951**, *23*, 287–310. [CrossRef]
20. Ya Polischuk, A. Quantum corrections to the Boltzmann equation for electrons in a disordered medium. *J. Phys. B At. Mol. Phys.* **1983**, *16*, 3845–3851. [CrossRef]
21. Borghesani, A.F.; Bruschi, L.; Santini, M.; Torzo, G. Electron mobility in neon at high densities. *Phys. Rev. A* **1988**, *37*, 4828–4835. [CrossRef]

22. Bartels, A. Density dependence of the electron drift velocity in argon. *Phys. Lett. A* **1973**, *44*, 403–404. [CrossRef]
23. Borghesani, A.F.; Santini, M.; Lamp, P. Excess electron mobility in high-density argon gas. *Phys. Rev. A* **1992**, *46*, 7902–7909. [CrossRef]
24. Borghesani, A.F.; Santini, M. Electron localization-delocalization transition in high-density neon gas. *Phys. Rev. A* **1992**, *45*, 8803–8810. [CrossRef]
25. Ioffe, A.F.; Regel, A.R. Non-crystalline, amorphous and liquid electronic semiconductors. In *Progress in Semiconductors*; Gibson, A.F., Ed.; Wiley: Hoboken, NJ, USA, 1960; Volume 4, pp. 237–291.
26. Huxley, L.G.; Crompton, R.W. *The Diffusion and Drift of Electrons in Gases*; Wiley: New York, NY, USA, 1974.
27. Springett, B.E.; Jortner, J.; Cohen, M.H. Stability criterion for the localization of an excess electron in a nonpolar fluid. *J. Chem. Phys.* **1968**, *48*, 2720–2731. [CrossRef]
28. Wigner, E.; Seitz, F. On the constitution of metallic sodium. *Phys. Rev.* **1933**, *43*, 804–810. [CrossRef]
29. Hernandez, J.P.; Martin, L.W. Analysis of excess electron states in neon gas. *Phys. Rev. A* **1991**, *43*, 4568–4571. [CrossRef] [PubMed]
30. O'Malley, T.F. Extrapolation of electron-rare gas atom cross sections to zero energy. *Phys. Rev.* **1963**, *130*, 1020–1029. [CrossRef]
31. Lekner, J. Scattering of waves by an ensemble of fluctuating potentials. *Philos. Mag.* **1968**, *18*, 1281–1286. [CrossRef]
32. Ascarelli, G. Hall mobility of electrons in liquid xenon. *J. Phys. Condens. Matter* **1992**, *4*, 6055–6072. [CrossRef]
33. Adams, P.W.; Paalanen, M.A. Localization in a Nondegenerate Two-Dimensional Electron Gas. *Phys. Rev. Lett.* **1987**, *58*, 2106, [CrossRef] [PubMed]
34. Adams, P.W.; Paalanen, M.A. Anderson Localization of Electrons in Dense He^4 Gas. *Phys. Rev. Lett.* **1988**, *61*, 451, [CrossRef] [PubMed]
35. Mott, N.F. Electrons in disordered structures. *Adv. Phys.* **1967**, *16*, 49–144. [CrossRef]
36. Mott, N. *Metal-Insulator Transitions*; Taylor & Francis: Abingdon, UK, 1974.
37. Cohen, M.H.; Lekner, J. Theory of hot electrons in gases, liquids, and solids. *Phys. Rev.* **1967**, *158*, 305–309. [CrossRef]
38. Stanley, H.E. *Introduction to Phase Transitions and Critical Phenomena*; International Series of Monographs on Physics; Oxford University Press: Oxford, UK, 1971; Volume 46.
39. Thomas, J.E.; Schmidt, P.W. X-ray study of critical opalescence in argon. *J. Chem. Phys.* **1963**, *39*, 2506–2516. [CrossRef]
40. Borghesani, A.F. Electron mobility maximum in dense argon gas at low temperature. *J. Electrostat.* **2001**, *53*, 89–106. [CrossRef]
41. Jahnke, J.A.; Silver, M.; Hernandez, J.P. Mobility of excess electrons and O2- formation in dense fluid helium. *Phys. Rev. B* **1975**, *12*, 3420–3427. [CrossRef]
42. Borghesani, A.F.; Santini, M. High-temperature electron localization in dense He gas. *Phys. Rev. E* **2002**, *65*, 8, [CrossRef] [PubMed]
43. Borghesani, A.; Bruschi, L.; Santini, M.; Torzo, G. Density dependence of the electronic mobility in high density neon gas. *Phys. Lett. A* **1985**, *108*, 255–258. [CrossRef]
44. Borghesani, A.F.; Santini, M. Electron mobility and localization effects in high-density Ne gas. *Phys. Rev. A* **1990**, *42*, 7377–7388. [CrossRef]
45. Borghesani, A.F.; Neri, D.; Santini, M. Low-temperature O_2^- mobility in high-density neon gas. *Phys. Rev. E* **1993**, *48*, 1379–1389. [CrossRef]
46. Neri, D.; Borghesani, A.F.; Santini, M. Electron attachment to O_2 molecules in dense helium and argon gases. *Phys. Rev. E* **1997**, *56*, 2137–2142. [CrossRef]
47. Borghesani, A.F. Resonant low-energy electron attachment to O_2 impurities in dense neon gas. *Plasma Sources Sci. Technol.* **2020**, *29*, 35024, [CrossRef]
48. Torzo, G. A simple recirculating pump for high-pressure high-purity gas. *Rev. Sci. Instrum.* **1990**, *61*, 1162–1163. [CrossRef]
49. Angus, S.; Reuck, K.M.D.; McCarty, R.D. *International Thermodynamic Tables of the Fluid State—4 Helium*; Pergamon: New York, NY, USA, 1977.
50. Sychev, V.V.; Vasserman, A.A.; Kozlov, A.D.; Spiridonov, G.A.; Tsymarny, V.A. *Thermodynamic Properties of Helium*; Hemisphere: Washington, DC, USA, 1987.
51. Borghesani, A.F.; Delfitto, G. A low-cost, continuously adjustable, high-voltage, regulated DC power supply. *Meas. Sci. Technol.* **1990**, *1*, 825–827. [CrossRef]
52. Borghesani, A.F.; Bruschi, L.; Santini, M.; Torzo, G. Simple photoelectronic source for swarm experiments in high-density gases. *Rev. Sci. Instrum.* **1986**, *57*, 2234–2237. [CrossRef]
53. Borghesani, A.F.; Santini, M. Electron swarm experiments in fluids-signal waveform analysis. *Meas. Sci. Technol.* **1990**, *1*, 939–947. [CrossRef]
54. Miyakawa, T.; Dexter, D.L. Stability of electronic bubbles in liquid neon and hydrogen. *Phys. Rev.* **1969**, *184*, 166–172. [CrossRef]
55. Atrazhev, V.M. Delocalisation of electrons in dense helium gas by external electric field. *J. Phys. D: Appl. Phys.* **1984**, *17*, 889–902. [CrossRef]
56. Sakai, Y.; Schmidt, W.F.; Khrapak, A. High- and low-mobility electrons in liquid neon. *Chem. Phys.* **1992**, *164*, 139–152. [CrossRef]
57. Bartels, A.K. Messungen der Elektronendriftgeschwindigkeit in He, Ar, H2 und N2 bei Sehr Hohen Gasdichten (zur Frage der kollektiven WechselWirkung von Elektronen mit dem Gas). Ph.D. Thesis, Hamburg University, Hamburg, Germany, 1974.

58. Borghesani, A.F.; Santini, M. Electron mobility maximum in near-critical argon gas. *Int. J. Thermophys.* **2001**, *22*, 1109–1121. [CrossRef]
59. Borghesani, A.F.; Lamp, P. Injection of photoelectrons into dense argon gas. *Plasma Sources Sci. Technol.* **2011**, *20*, 34001, [CrossRef]
60. Weyhreter, M.; Barzick, B.; Mann, A.; Linder, F. Measurements of differential cross sections for e-Ar, Kr, Xe scattering at E = 0.05 - 2 eV. *Zeitschrift Phys. D Atoms Mol. Clust.* **1988**, *7*, 333–347. [CrossRef]
61. Borghesani, A.F. *Ions and Electrons in Liquid Helium*; International Series of Monographs on Physics; Oxford University Press: Oxford, UK, 2007; Volume 137.
62. McCarty, R.D.; Arp, V.D. A New Wide Range Equation of State for Helium. In *Advances in Cryogenic Engineering*; ACRE; Springer: Boston, MA, USA,1990; Volume 35, pp. 1465–1475. [CrossRef]
63. Haddad, G.N.; Elford, M.T. Low-energy electron scattering cross sections in carbon dioxide. *J. Phys. B At. Mol. Phys.* **1979**, *12*, [CrossRef]
64. Elford, M.; Haddad, G. The Drift Velocity of Electrons in Carbon Dioxide at Temperatures between 193 and 573 K. *Aust. J. Phys.* **1980**, *33*, 517–530. [CrossRef]
65. Krebs, P.; Giraud, V.; Wantschik, M. Electron Localization in Dense Ammonia Vapor. *Phys. Rev. Lett.* **1980**, *44*, 211, [CrossRef]
66. Krebs, P.; Lang, U. Electron Mobility and Multiple Scattering Effects in Dense Methanol Gas. *J. Phys. Chem.* **1996**, *100*, 10482–10489. [CrossRef]

Article

Electron Ionization of Size-Selected Positively and Negatively Charged Helium Droplets

Felix Laimer *, Fabio Zappa, Elisabeth Gruber and Paul Scheier *

Institut für Ionenphysik und Angewandte Physik, Universität Innsbruck, Technikerstr. 25,
A-6020 Innsbruck, Austria; fabio.zappa@uibk.ac.at (F.Z.); e.gruber@uibk.ac.at (E.G.)
* Correspondence: felix.laimer@uibk.ac.at (F.L.); paul.scheier@uibk.ac.at (P.S.); Tel.: +43-512-507-52660 (P.S.)

Abstract: A beam of size-selected charged helium droplets was crossed with an electron beam, and the ion efficiency curves for the product droplets in all different charge states were recorded. We estimate that the selected helium droplets on their passage through the electron beam are hit by several hundred electrons which can interact with the individual He atoms of the droplets. Reaction channels corresponding to the removal or capture of up to eight electrons were identified, and in all cases, inelastic scattering and the formation of metastable helium played a significant role.

Keywords: electron ionization; electron capture; helium droplets; cross section

Citation: Laimer, F.; Zappa, F.; Gruber, E.; Scheier, P. Electron Ionization of Size-Selected Positively and Negatively Charged Helium Droplets. *Atoms* **2021**, *9*, 74. https://doi.org/10.3390/atoms9040074

Academic Editor: Grzegorz Piotr Karwasz

Received: 31 August 2021
Accepted: 30 September 2021
Published: 5 October 2021

Publisher's Note: MDPI stays neutral with regard to jurisdictional claims in published maps and institutional affiliations.

Copyright: © 2021 by the authors. Licensee MDPI, Basel, Switzerland. This article is an open access article distributed under the terms and conditions of the Creative Commons Attribution (CC BY) license (https://creativecommons.org/licenses/by/4.0/).

1. Introduction

Ionization, neutralization, and fragmentation of ions upon electron impact are fundamental processes in natural and technical plasmas [1,2]. Cross sections can be calculated, for instance, by utilizing the semiclassical Deutsch–Märk formalism [3] or the binary-encounter-dipole theory [4,5]. For H_2^+, the electron ionization cross sections were determined by full quantum calculations [6], and excellent agreement was found with the experimental values [7]. The experimental determination of cross sections of ionic targets is a challenging task, and only very few instruments have been designed for this purpose. The groups of Defrance and Salzborn independently developed a method to obtain absolute cross sections by determining the overlap geometry between the ion beam and the electron beam by scanning the electron beam through the ion beam either mechanically [8] or with a pair of deflector plates [9,10]. Dolder and Peart obtained the overlap by moving an aperture through the region where the ion and electron beam overlap [11]. The electron impact on large molecular target ions was investigated for fullerene cations by Matt et al. [12], who reported an increase in the charge state with and without fragmentation. The group of Salzborn extended these studies and determined the absolute cross sections for positively and negatively charged fullerene ions [13,14]. To our knowledge, no data are available for larger clusters.

Helium droplets have been investigated since their first production by Becker and coworkers in 1961 [15], but it took almost 30 years until the scientific community became aware of their full potential. With the discovery that helium droplets are able to capture atoms [16] and molecules [17], the formation of clusters and complexes [16,18] and the spectroscopy of cold molecules in the most inert matrix were achieved [17,19]. Aside from optical spectroscopy of neutral dopants [20–23], mass spectrometry of charged products formed via various ionization techniques is a commonly utilized method [24–27]. The high excitation and ionization energy of helium requires rather advanced light sources and makes electron guns simple alternatives that are frequently utilized. Mass spectra obtained upon electron ionization of undoped helium droplets are dominated by small helium cluster ions of the form He_n^+. According to the literature, these cluster ions are predominantly formed via electron ionization of a He atom and subsequent resonant hole hopping toward the center of the droplet [28–30]. After typically 11 hops, vibrationally excited He_2^+ is formed that is either ejected from the droplet or becomes solvated by polarized neighboring He atoms and thereby forming a so-called Atkins snowball [31]. Mateo and Eloranta determined from electronic structure calculations a linear He_3^+ ionic core of such snowballs [32]. However, since positively charged ions are strongly heliophilic, the mass spectrometric observation of small helium cluster ions implies that these have to be ejected from large droplets or are the residue from the evaporation of small, charged helium droplets. Based on the binding energy of He_2^+, the internal energy of vibrationally excited He_2^+ is able to vaporize only 3500 He atoms at most. Thus, a different mechanism such as Coulomb repulsion between more than one charged species is required to explain the ejection of low-mass ions from larger He droplets.

Recently, Laimer et al. discovered that both the positive [33] and negative ionization [34] of helium droplets, aside from the low-mass ions often recorded in mass spectrometers, also leads to the formation of a massive, charged residual droplet that contains the majority of the mass of the neutral precursor. In fact, the mass loss due to evaporation of neutral He atoms and ejection of low-mass ions is negligible for droplets containing several million He atoms. In both studies, neutral helium droplets were ionized via electron bombardment. Then, a first spherical sector electrostatic energy analyzer selected a narrow slice from the charged droplet distribution, and these droplets were bombarded by a second electron beam. A second energy analyzer was used to analyze the mass per charge values of the final product droplets and investigate the arrangement of charge centers. Furthermore, these droplets can become highly charged, with appearance sizes for multiply charged droplets being more than an order of magnitude larger for anionic droplets [34].

In the present paper, we investigate in detail the processes that lead to a change in the charged state of large differently charged helium droplets upon electron bombardment. Ion efficiency curves are measured in the electron energy range between 0 eV and 120 eV for all possible charged product ions formed upon electron bombardment of the mass per charge of selected helium droplets, utilizing a tandem set-up consisting of an electron ionization source followed by an electrostatic energy analyzer. The underlying mechanisms that are involved in changes in the charge state are identified by analyzing the positions of the resonances and the thresholds of the corresponding processes for individual charge states. In the case of positively charged helium droplets, an increase in the charge state preferentially proceeds at electron energies higher than 25 eV, whereas a reduction in the charge state happens at two narrow resonances of 2 eV and 22 eV, which can be assigned to electron attachment and the formation of intermediate He^{*-}, respectively.

2. Materials and Methods

Neutral He droplets were formed via expansion of He gas (99.9999% purity, Messer Austria GmbH, Gumpoldskirchen, Austria) with a stagnation pressure of 2 MPa through a pinhole nozzle with a diameter of 5 μm (A0200P, Plano GmbH, Wezlar, Germany) attached to an oxygen-free copper block (MB-OF101 with a residual-resistance ratio, RRR > 200, Montanwerke Brixlegg, Brixlegg, Austria) that was mounted to the second stage of a closed-circuit cryocooler (RDK-408D2, Sumitomo Heavy Industries Ltd., Tokyo, Japan). Through a combination of the cooling by the cryocooler and resistive heating, we were able to control the temperature of the compressed He down to 4.2 K. In the present investigation, temperatures of 7 K and 9 K were selected, and 11.7 mm downstream from the nozzle, the droplets passed through a skimmer with an aperture of 0.8 mm on their way into the first ionization source. Here, the droplets were ionized by the impact of electrons with a kinetic energy of 40 eV and an electron current of 300 μA for promoting the formation of positively charged droplets and 30 eV and 430 μA for negatively charged droplets. The ionizer design was based on a Nier-type electron source using a tungsten coil filament. Charged droplets were then mass-per-charge selected by a spherical sector electrostatic 90° energy analyzer with a central radius of 7 cm and a distance between the plates of 2 cm. The resolving power of the two energy analyzers was limited by the apertures and was determined from the width and position of the precursor peaks to E/ΔE~63. The m/z-selected charged droplets could then be ionized further by a second electron ionization source of the same type as the first one. A second electrostatic analyzer identical to the first one was then employed to analyze the final mass-per-charge ratio of the droplets, which were detected with a Channeltron-type secondary electron multiplier (Dr. Sjuts, KBL 510). The energy resolution when measuring electron energy-dependent ion efficiency curves was estimated by analyzing the signal decrease for the cationic precursor peak signal around 22 eV. A Gaussian fit on the derivative of the slope gave an upper limit of ±0.65 eV for the spread in electron energy. A residual gas pressure of about 10^{-6} Pa was achieved with turbomolecular pumps (one HiPace 2300, two HiPace 700 and one TMU 521, Pfeiffer Vacuum Technology AG, Aßlar, Germany) backed by two oil-free roughing pumps (ACP 40, Pfeiffer Vacuum Technology AG, Aßlar, Germany). A schematic diagram of the apparatus is shown in Figure 1.

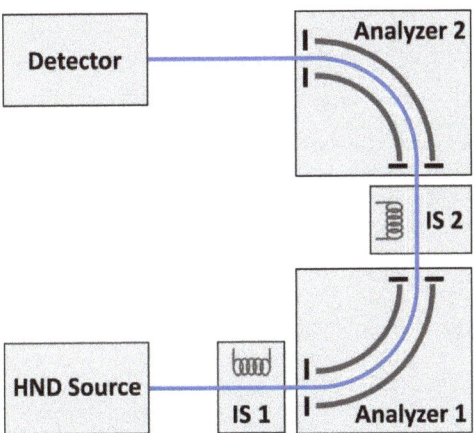

Figure 1. Schematic of the experimental set-up.

The velocity distributions at different nozzle temperatures of the droplet beam were measured recently by Laimer et al. via a time-of-flight method by pulsing the electron energy [35]. The velocities of the singly charged He droplets of the selected precursor mass-per charge-values at 7 K and 9 K ranged from v = 155 to 169 m/s and 196 m/s, respectively. The kinetic energy of a charged droplet passing the electrostatic energy analyzer could be determined from the electric field E applied and its central radius, with the mass-per-charge value of the droplet being equivalent to $2E/v^2$.

3. Results and Discussion

3.1. Penetration Depth of the Electrons in the He Droplets

The high density and large size of He droplets lead to non-uniform ionization and excitation probability of the He atoms inside. Using Beer's law, the density of liquid helium (0.02 Å^{-3} [36]) and the cross sections for electron ionization and excitation of helium atoms [37], the penetration depth of electrons can be determined as a function of their kinetic energy. Figure 2 shows the distance at which the electron current is attenuated to 1/e = 37%. The horizontal line indicates the diameter of a He droplet containing 5.7 million He atoms. The vertical line corresponds to the ionization energy of He. For droplets of this size, metastable He formation at collision energies around 22 eV can be expected to happen throughout the volume of the droplet, whereas electron ionization is preferentially happening close to the surface and facing the impinging electron beam.

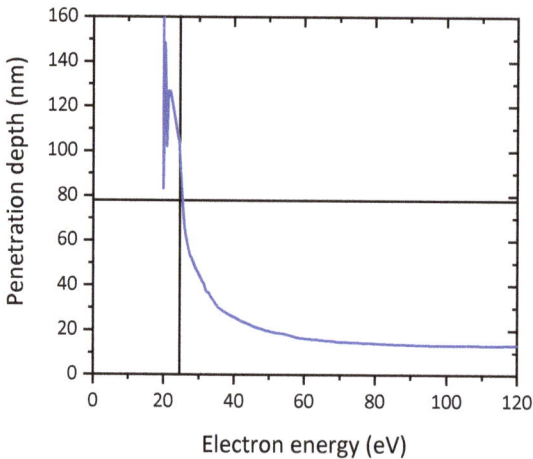

Figure 2. Penetration depth of electrons in liquid helium, determined from Beer's law using the bulk density of He and the cross sections for electron excitation and ionization. The horizontal line indicates the diameter of a He droplet containing 5.7 million He atoms, and the vertical line indicates the ionization energy of He.

3.2. Cations to Cations

Positively charged He droplets were formed upon electron bombardment of neutral He droplets (expansion conditions of 7 K and 2 MPa, average neutral droplet size of 1.1×10^7 [38]) with an electron energy of 40 eV and an electron current of 300 µA. This results in a log-normal-shaped m/z distribution with an average value of about 7 million He atoms per charge [35]. The first energy filter (Analyzer 1 in Figure 1) selected a narrow slice of this distribution at a relative m/z of 2.7×10^6 He atoms per charge (corresponding to a relative m/z value of 1 in Figure 3). In the second ion source (IS 2 in Figure 1), the selected droplets were crossed with a 210-µA electron beam, and depending on the electron energy, differently charged product droplets were formed. At 22 eV (blue line in Figure 3), most product droplets had higher m/z values than the selected precursor, thus indicating a reduction of the charge state. Peaks at the exact fractional numbers demonstrated negligible mass loss due to evaporation of neutral He atoms, as was already observed previously [33]. At 120 eV, an increase in the charge state resulted in lower m/z values (purple line in Figure 3). The presence of differently charged precursor droplets and a relatively poor energy resolution of the energy analyzer resulted in a curve where only the most intense product channels could be seen as narrow peaks at fractional number m/z values, such as $1/4$, $1/3$, $1/2$, $2/3$ and $3/4$. By setting the second ion source to 80 eV and 100 µA, the formation of very highly charged droplets was strongly reduced, which enabled a better assignment of individual reaction channels (red line).

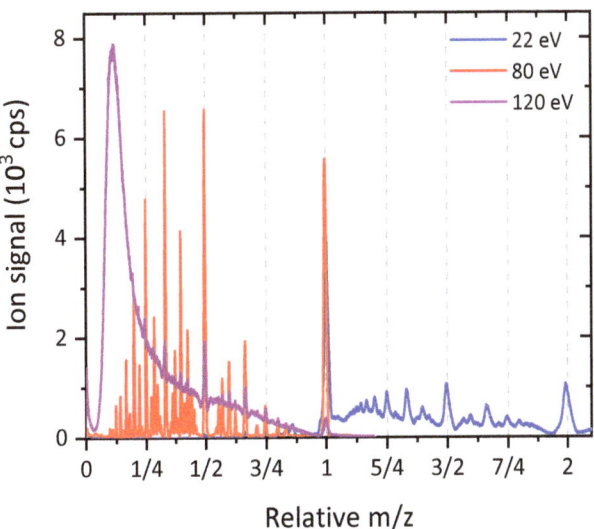

Figure 3. Charge distributions of positively charged He droplets resulting from electron bombardment of mass-per-charge selected positively charged He droplets containing 2.7×10^6 He atoms per charge. Electron energy of 22.5 eV resulted predominantly in a reduction in the charge state (blue line), whereas 120 eV (purple line) increased the charge state and led to a pile-up of peaks at a relative m/z value of 0.11 or 3×10^5 He atoms per charge. The red line was measured with the second ion source set to 80 eV and a reduced current of 100 µA.

3.2.1. Ion Efficiency Curves

The ion efficiency curves of all major product charge states were measured, recording the ion yield at the corresponding relative m/z values as a function of the electron energy of the second ion source from 0 eV to 120 eV. For a selected mass-per-charge value of 5.7 million He atoms per charge, most reaction channels that led to an increase in the charge state are plotted in Figure 4. The corresponding reaction channels found at relative m/z values lower than one are plotted in Figure 3. The curve labels are ordered according to the ratio of the initial and final charge states of the droplets. Reactions with z_i/z_f close to one (yellow to red lines) exhibited an asymmetric peak structure with a maximum at around 30 eV, followed by a minimum at 10 eV and a gentle increase up to 120 eV. Additionally, reaction channels with much lower z_i/z_f values (blue to purple lines) exhibited a relatively narrow peak-like shape quite different to typical electron ionization cross sections of atoms and small molecules. A similar resonance-like behavior was previously observed for the partial cross sections of fragment ions of fullerenes [39]. In that case, with increasing electron energy, neutral C_2 loss transforms larger product ions into smaller ones, resulting in narrow, peak-like cross section curves. In the present case, the removal of an additional electron at higher electron energies became more likely and thereby led to a decrease in the ion yield of lower-charged species and, at the same time, an increase in the signal of higher-charged product droplets.

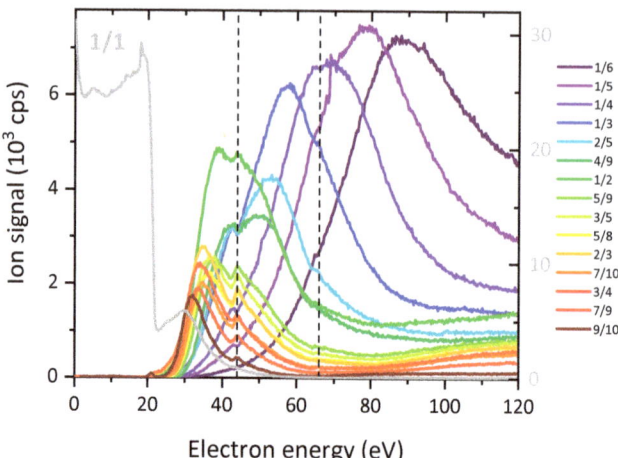

Figure 4. Ion efficiency curves for electron ionization of positively charged He droplets with a mass-per-charge ratio of 5.7 million He atoms per charge. The curves' labels are sorted according to the ratio of the precursor to final charge state, which is equivalent to the relative m/z values of the corresponding peaks in Figure 3. Note the two pronounced anomalies in the ion signal of several curves around 44 eV and 66 eV, designated by vertical dashed lines.

Since the first energy analyzer only selected the mass per charge, the peak at a relative m/z = 1/2 corresponded to singly charged He droplets containing 5.7 million He atoms that became doubly charged. However, it would also contain the signal from reactions where multiply charged droplets with an initial charge state z_i containing z_i times 5.7 million He atoms were ionized into a final charge state of $z_f = 2z_i$. The reaction channel that did not lead to a change in the charge state (designated as 1/1, the light gray line) is plotted with its corresponding y-axis drawn at the right side of the diagram. Both the maxima and threshold energies of the curves shifted to higher electron energies with decreasing z_i/z_f values. In addition, several curves exhibit pronounced peaks and wiggles at around 44 eV and 66 eV. These peaks match the resonances reported by Mauracher et al. [40], where He^{*-} and He$_2$$^{*-}$ were efficiently formed and ejected from undoped He droplets. Ion efficiency curves for two other initial m/z values are shown in the Supplementary Materials (Figures S1 and S2). Droplet formation at 9 K resulted in neutral droplets that contained on average 4 million He atoms [38]. Thus, the contribution of multiply charged droplets at a selected m/z value of 4×10^6, for instance, was substantially lower than in the case of the same selected m/z values when the He source was operated at a temperature of 7 K. This led to better separation of the peaks at lower relative m/z values. The appearance energy values for three different mass-per-charge values selected by the first analyzer (the ion efficiency curves for two data sets obtained for 2.7 and 4 million He atoms per charge are shown in the Supplementary Materials in Figures S1 and S2) were obtained by utilizing the vanishing current method for all curves where a well-defined final charge state was distinguishable. All appearance energies obtained by this method possessed an error of ±1 eV introduced by a background signal. The results are listed in the Supplementary Materials in Table S1 and plotted in Figure 5 as a function of the difference of the final and initial charge states $z_f - z_i$. Despite the significant uncertainty in the determination of threshold values, it is apparent that all reaction channels followed the same trend, and it is remarkable that the threshold values for the reactions +1 → +5 and +5 → +9 were almost identical, albeit with a five times higher initial charge state for the latter process. The linear fit to the data in Figure 5 gave a value of 19.83 eV for $z_f - z_i = 0$, which is almost exactly the excitation energy of a He atom into the metastable 2^3S state. The slope of the linear fit in Figure 5 is 1.66 eV. The cross section of a He droplet containing N > 10^4 He atoms was $4\pi r^2$, with $r = 0.22 \times N^{1/3}$. Thus, a droplet containing 5.7 million He atoms had a geometric cross section of 19,400 nm^2. The electron beam had a diameter of about 1 mm and a current of 300 µA. During the passage of such a droplet through the electron beam, which took about 6.5 µs (1 mm/155 m/s), we could estimate that this droplet would be hit by 234 electrons. The threshold energy required for multiple ionization would be determined by the most energetic process that one of these electrons had to drive. The energy of 19.83 eV indicates a mechanism that requires two metastable He atoms for the formation of a cation, as proposed by Renzler et al. [41]. Thereby, at least $2 \times (z_f - z_i)$ metastable He atoms have to be formed to increase the charge state of a He droplet from z_i to z_f. The electrons emitted by the processes were as follows:

$$He^* + He^* \rightarrow He^+ + He + e^- \text{ and}$$

$$He^{*-} + He^* \rightarrow He^+ + He + e^-$$

These electrons had kinetic energies in the order of 15 eV and thus were easily ejected from the droplets. Both the electrostatic interaction of electrons with multiply charged He droplets and the Coulomb energy required to accommodate additional charges in He droplets containing millions of He atoms were in the range of 0.1 eV and could not account for a slope of 1.66 eV.

At a hypothetical threshold energy, all projectile electrons have to escape after inelastic scattering and He* formation with essentially no excess kinetic energy, which becomes less probable for an increasing number of electrons. Thus, we propose that the unexpected increase of the appearance energy with increasing charging of He droplets (as seen in Figure 5) is simply related to the diminishing probability for the escape of large numbers of low-energy electrons.

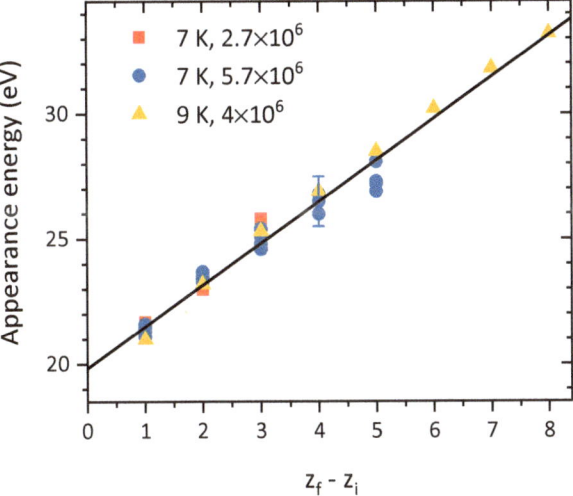

Figure 5. Appearance energies of the ion efficiency curves for electron ionization of positively charged He droplets, plotted as a function of the difference of the final and initial charge states $z_f - z_i$. Different symbols designate different expansion conditions and selected mass-per-charge values by the first energy analyzer. The black line is a linear fit to the data with a slope of 1.66 eV per removed electron. A general uncertainty of ±1 eV for every threshold, determined by the vanishing current method, is plotted as a single error bar symbolically.

Figure 6a shows the ion efficiency curves for reactions that led to a reduction in the charge state of positively charged He droplets, having an initial mass-per-charge value of

5.7 million He atoms per charge. The corresponding reaction channels are found at relative m/z values larger than 1 in Figure 3. The color-coded curves are labeled with the ratio of the initial and final charge state z_i/z_f of the corresponding reaction channels in ascending values. In addition, the reaction channel that did not lead to a change in the charge state (designated as 1/1, the light gray line) is plotted with its corresponding y-axis at the right side of the diagram.

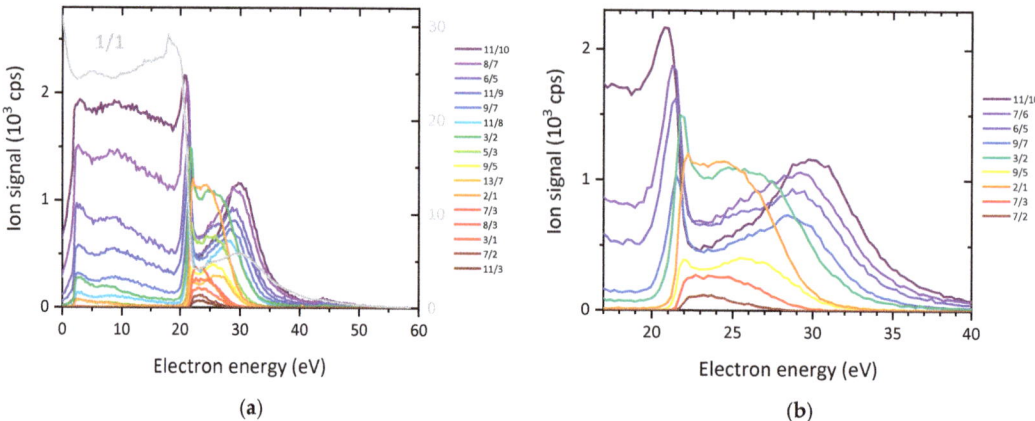

Figure 6. (a) Ion efficiency curves for electron capture of positively charged He droplets with a mass-per-charge ratio of 5.7 million He atoms per charge upon electron bombardment. The curves labels are sorted according to the ratio of the precursor to the final charge state. (b) Selection of every second data from (a), shown in more detail in the energy range around the 22 eV and 30 eV resonances.

The reduction of the charge state (i.e., the capture of the projectile electron) requires a minimum energy of about 2 eV, where a more- or less-pronounced resonance can be seen, followed by a second broad feature at around 10 eV and a narrow peak at around 22 eV, again followed by a broad peak at around 30 eV and a very weak resonance at around 44 eV. Table S2 in the Supplementary Materials lists the positions of these resonances for all ion efficiency curves measured for two different mass-per-charge values of the initially selected positively charged droplets. The ion efficiency curves for m/z = 2.7 million He atoms per charge are shown in the Supplementary Materials in Figure S3. Figure 6b shows the energy range between 17 eV and 40 eV in more detail.

According to Figure 7, the actual positions of the features around 22 eV and 30 eV seemed to depend on the ratio of the final and initial charge states. For both initially selected mass-per-charge values (designated by solid symbols for 2.7 and open symbols for 5.7 million He atoms per charge), the data followed the same nonlinear trend. The lines were allometric fits to the data of the form of

$$y = a + b \cdot x^c,$$

The fitting parameters were a = 22.42 (25.28), b = −2.14 (6.79) and c = 3.25 (3.28) for the two resonances, respectively.

Both resonance positions exhibited a smooth monotonic behavior. The low-energy resonance started at low z_f/z_i values of 22.5 eV and dropped with increasing z_f/z_i to less than 21 eV. In contrast, the high-energy resonance increased from 25 eV at z_f/z_i = 0.2 to 30 eV at z_f/z_i = 0.9. Both curves followed a similar power dependence with fit parameters c = 3.25 and 3.28 for the low- and high-energy resonances, respectively. Large z_f/z_i values corresponded to the single-electron capture of a highly charged He droplet, whereas small values were obtained when a highly charged droplet captured $z_i - 1$ electrons or a positively charged droplet was neutralized (i.e., z_f = 0). The values of 22.42 eV and 25.28 eV for $z_f/z_i = 0$ indicate electronic excitation and threshold ionization of He atoms as potential underlying processes, respectively. The formation of He* as well as the formation of He$^+$ additionally generated one or two low-energy electrons, respectively, which if trapped inside the droplet would reduce its charge state.

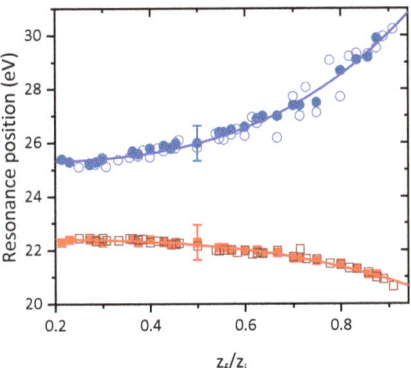

Figure 7. Positions of the resonances for charge reduction as a function of the ratio of the final and initial charge states, determined from the ion efficiency curves shown in Figure 6a,b. Bold symbols designate mass-per-charge values of the selected precursor droplets of 2.7 million He atoms per charge, and open symbols represent those of 5.7 million He atoms per charge. A general uncertainty of ±0.65 eV for all resonance positions considering the spread in electron energy of the set-up is plotted as a single error bar for both resonances.

The charge centers of the multiply charged He droplets were located close to their surface [33], quite different from the highly charged water droplets [42,43]. The mass of a droplet scales with the cube of its radius, whereas the surface is only proportional to the square of the radius. Droplets with the same mass-per-charge values were selected by the energy analyzers. However, with the increasing charge state z, their surface charge densities rose with $z^{1/3}$. Thus, the energy gain of an electron due to the Coulomb attraction from charged droplets having the same mass-per-charge ratio was larger for droplets having a high initial charge state z_i, albeit with a larger radius. This explains qualitatively the lowering of the low-energy resonance to a value of 20.3 at $z_f/z_i = 1$, which was close to 19.8 eV for the formation of He in the 2^3S state. The high-energy resonance reached a value of 32 eV at $z_f/z_i = 1$, and a tentative explanation for this resonance is dissociative electron attachment to impurities, such as H_2O from the residual gas captured by large He droplets or H_2 impurities in the He gas used for the droplet formation. Both H_2O and H_2 exhibit resonances for dissociative electron attachment at about 10 eV when embedded in He droplets [44,45] and subsequent resonances upshifted by the energy required to form metastable He in droplets (i.e., 19.8 + 1.66 = 21.46 eV). The probability for both impurities to be found in a droplet increased with the size of the droplet; in the case of water, it scaled with the geometric cross section that was proportional to the number of He atoms in the droplet to the power of 2/3, and for hydrogen, it was proportional to the number of He atoms. Thus, highly charged droplets are inevitably prone to more impurities and exhibit more intense peaks at these electron energy ranges. However, as the droplets were already initially charged, we expect that these impurities are preferentially localized at the charge centers.

3.2.2. Total Cross Sections

For ionization (increase in the charge state, red line) and electron capture (decrease in charge state, blue line), we summed up all measured ion efficiency curves and plotted them in Figure 8 together with the channel that did not lead to a change in the charge state (light gray line). With the second ion source turned off, we recorded a signal of 40,000 cps. If only cationic droplets were formed, the sum of all cationic product ions (black solid line in Figure 8) should have been a constant line at 40,000 cps. Two narrow resonances at 2 eV and 22 eV as well as a weaker feature at 44 eV could be assigned to neutralization or the formation of negatively charged droplets via electron capture and He*$^-$ formation. At electron energies higher than 60 eV, a monotonic decrease of the sum of the cationic droplets was observed, which resulted from droplets having either a final charge state $z_f < 1$ (anions or neutral) or being very large (unresolved reaction channels to high charge states in Figure 3). Only reaction channels with $z_f/z_i \leq 6$ were recorded in the present study. Thus, a substantial part of the cationic products was missing which, according to Figure 4, was expected to have a maximum ion yield at electron energies larger than 80 eV. This readily explains the gradual loss of cationic product droplets at electron energies higher than 60 eV.

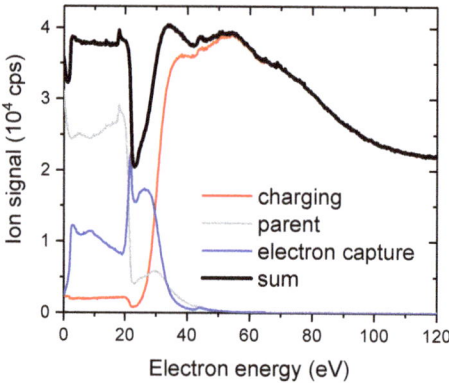

Figure 8. The sum of all ion efficiency curves measured for charging ($z_f > z_i$, red line) and electron capture ($z_f < z_i$, blue line) of positively charged He droplets with an initial mass-per-charge ratio of 5.7 million He atoms per charge. The light gray line represents the ion efficiency curve of the selected charged precursor droplets, and the bold black line is the sum of these three channels (i.e., the yield of all positively charged product ions).

In Figure 9, the loss of positively charged He droplets (40,000 cps minus the sum of all positively charged product ions, the black line in Figure 8) is plotted (black bold line) together with the anion efficiency curve for the formation of negatively charged He droplets upon electron irradiation of neutral droplets with an average size of 1.8 million He atoms [38] (blue line).

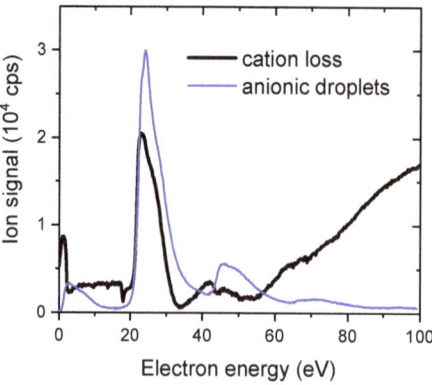

Figure 9. The loss of positively charged He droplets upon electron irradiation (black bold line) in comparison with the formation of negatively charged He droplets upon electron capture into neutral He droplets.

3.3. Anions to Cations

In this section, we will focus on the interaction of electrons with negatively charged He droplets that are formed upon electron bombardment of neutral He droplets at the same expansion conditions (7 K and 2 MPa, average droplet size of 11 million He atoms [38]) with an electron energy of 30 eV and an electron current of 430 µA. The first energy filter (Analyzer 1 in Figure 1) selected a narrow slice of a log-normal-shaped distribution at a relative m/z of 3.2×10^7 He atoms per charge (corresponding to a relative m/z value of 1 in Figure 10a). In the second ion source (IS 2 in Figure 1), the selected droplets were crossed with a 175-µA electron beam and an electron energy of 60 eV. The contribution of multiply charged precursor droplets was very low, although only 4 million He atoms were sufficient to stabilize two negatively charged ionic centers [34]. Plotting the curve versus the reciprocal of the relative m/z value led to peaks centered at the corresponding charge state of the product ions (Figure 10b). Individual peaks could be resolved in this figure up to z = 27.

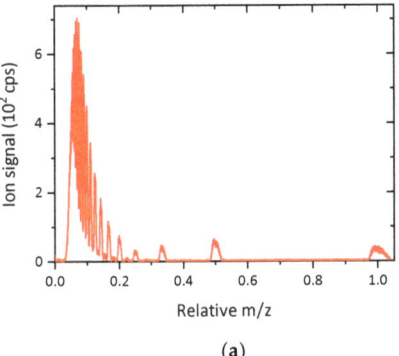
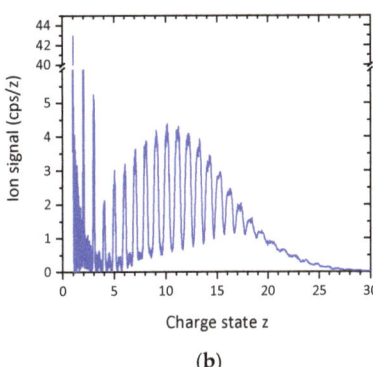

Figure 10. (a) Charge distributions of positively charged He droplets resulting from electron bombardment of mass-per-charge selected, negatively charged He droplets containing 32 million He atoms per charge. The electron energy of the second ion source (IS 2 in Figure 1) was set to 60 eV at an electron current of 175 µA. (b) The same data plotted as a function of the reciprocal of m/z, exhibiting pronounced peaks at integer values of z up to z = 27.

3.3.1. Ion Efficiency Curves

Ion efficiency curves for the formation of cationic He droplets upon electron ionization of negatively charged precursors containing 12 million He atoms per charge are plotted in Figure 11. The left diagram (a) contains data upon electron ionization of a singly charged anionic helium droplet, and the right diagram (b) shows data of a doubly charged anionic helium droplet. The conversion of anions into cations requires a certain amount of energy to remove at least two electrons from a large droplet. Penning ionization of He^{*-}, as described by Renzler et al. [41], would be a possible mechanism, as well as direct ionization of a He atom of the droplets. In both cases, the electrons require enough kinetic energy to escape the Coulomb attraction by the now positively charged droplets.

3.3.2. Appearance Energies

Via the vanishing current method, the threshold energies were determined with an uncertainty of ±1 eV for all reaction channels measured at two initial mass-per-charge values of −12 and −32 million (shown in the Supplementary Materials, Figure S4) He atoms per charge, and the values are summarized in Table S3 and plotted in Figure 12 as a function of the final charge state z_f of the resulting cationic droplets. In contrast to the cations shown in Figure 5, the x-axis corresponds to the final charge state and not the difference $z_f - z_i$. Again, we assigned a slope of the fit of 1.34 eV to the decreasing probability of the ejection of an increasing number of low-energy electrons. The only difference with the initially positively charged droplets (shown in Figure 5) was the fact that the appearance energies did not seem to depend on the initial charge state. The repulsive Coulomb interaction between the electrons and the initially negatively charged He droplets supported the escape of low-energy electrons. However, we were only able to obtain data for $z_i = -1$ and -2.

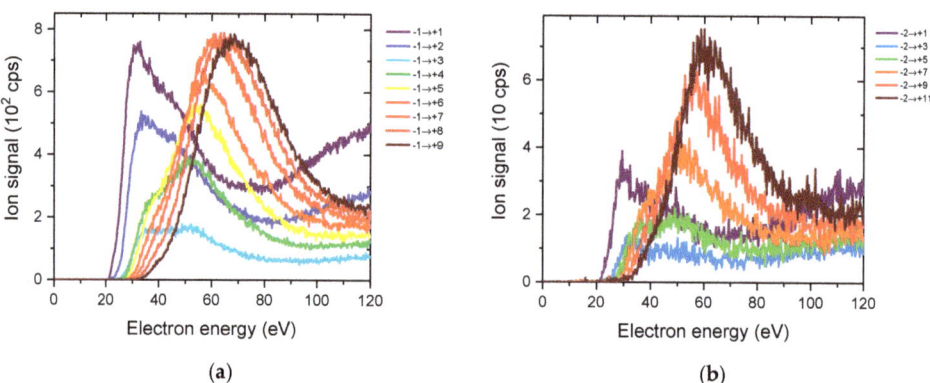

Figure 11. (a) Ion efficiency curves for electron ionization of negative singly charged He droplets with a mass-per-charge ratio of 12 million He atoms per charge. The curves are sorted according to the final charge states of the resulting positively charged droplets. (b) Ion efficiency curves for the formation of positively charged He droplets upon electron ionization doubly charged anionic He droplets containing 24 million He atoms.

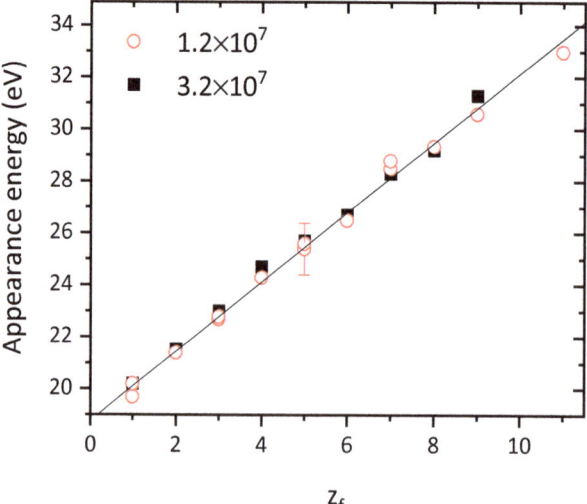

Figure 12. Appearance energies of the ion efficiency curves for electron ionization of negatively charged He droplets and the formation of cations, plotted as a function of the final charge states z_f of the positively charged product droplet for two He droplet source temperatures (12 and 32 million He atoms per charge, designated as open circles and filled squares, respectively). The black line is a linear fit to the data with a slope of 1.34 eV per removed electron. A general uncertainty of ±1 eV that applies to every threshold, determined by the vanishing current method, is represented by a single error bar.

3.4. Anions to Anions

The ion efficiency curve for the attachment of an electron to an already negatively charged droplet is shown exemplarily for a triply charged anionic He droplet containing 120 million He atoms in Figure 13. This process proceeded via two narrow resonances located at 3 eV and 22 eV, and above 30 eV, an almost linear rise of the ion efficiency curve is observed. At these energies, He$^+$ was likely formed, and the net charge would be reduced if both the projectile and secondary electron were trapped in the large He droplet having a diameter of 220 nm. This increase of negative charging at electron energies higher than 30 eV was expected to be one of the loss channels for cationic He droplets mentioned in Section 3.2.2.

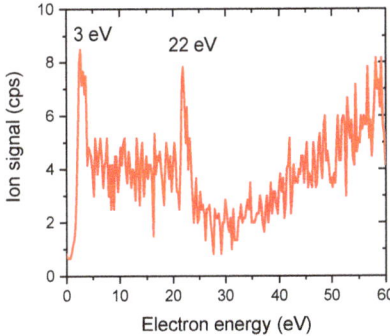

Figure 13. Anion efficiency curve for the single electron capture of a triply charged anionic He droplet containing 120 million He atoms. The process is preferentially operational at two narrow resonances of 3 eV and 22 eV.

4. Conclusions

The interaction of electrons with mass-per-charge-selected He droplets containing millions of He atoms was studied in detail. Ion efficiency curves were determined for individual reaction channels that could be assigned to the removal or addition of electrons. In contrast to the single-collision conditions typically used for electron scattering experiments with molecular or atomic targets, the huge geometric cross section of the investigated helium droplets and the high electron currents chosen in the present study ensured multi-collision conditions, with up to several hundred electron hits per droplet. As was already reported previously [33,34], the mass loss due to neutral He evaporation or asymmetric Coulomb explosion was negligible, and so the interaction of electrons with large He droplets essentially only changed their charge states. Individual relative cross section curves for charging positively charged He droplets clearly showed that with increasing electron energy product, the droplets were preferentially ending up in higher charge states. Threshold energies at 22 eV and intensity anomalies in several ion efficiency curves demonstrate that metastable He formation is an important mechanism at all electron energies, since the cross section for electron ionization of He* is almost 20 times larger than that of ground state helium [37]. The total cross section for ionization exhibited a steep increase from 25 eV to 35 eV, followed by a gentle rise up to 70 eV and an exponential decrease at higher electron energies. The latter we explained with ionization into highly charged droplets that could not be assigned in the present experiments. In the case of electron capture, low-energy electrons can be directly trapped, preferentially with kinetic energies around 2 eV or after inelastic scattering and He* formation at 22 eV and, to a less extent, at 44 eV. At these electron energies, we observed the loss of positively charged He droplets into neutral or negatively charged products.

Some results obtained in the present study for He droplets may also hold for droplets and nanoparticles made of other atoms and molecules, such as water. In that case, similar experiments could provide valuable insight into the radiation physics and chemistry of water as well as the initial processes happening in electrospray ionization.

Supplementary Materials: The Supplementary Materials containing tables and additional figures referenced in the results and discussion section is available online at https://www.mdpi.com/article/10.3390/atoms9040074/s1.

Author Contributions: Conceptualization, F.L. and P.S.; methodology, formal analysis, and data curation, F.L.; writing—original draft preparation, P.S.; writing—review and editing, F.Z., E.G., F.L. and P.S.; funding acquisition, E.G. and P.S. All authors have read and agreed to the published version of the manuscript.

Funding: Open Access Funding by the European Region Fund, Project No EFRE 2016-4, and Open Access Funding by the Austrian Science Fund (FWF), grant number T1181.

Data Availability Statement: The data presented in this work are available from the corresponding author upon reasonable request.

Conflicts of Interest: The authors declare no conflict of interest.

References

1. Janev, R.K.; Reiter, D. Collision processes of CHy and CHy+ hydrocarbons with plasma electrons and protons. *Phys. Plasmas* **2002**, *9*, 4071–4081. [CrossRef]
2. McCall, B.J.; Huneycutt, A.J.; Saykally, R.; Geballe, T.R.; Djuric, N.; Dunn, G.H.; Semaniak, J.; Novotny, O.; Al-Khalili, A.; Ehlerding, A.; et al. An enhanced cosmic-ray flux towards ζ Persei inferred from a laboratory study of the H3+–e- recombination rate. *Nature* **2003**, *422*, 500–502. [CrossRef] [PubMed]
3. Deutsch, H.; Becker, K.; Probst, M.; Märk, T.D. The Semiempirical Deutsch-Märk Formalism: A Versatile Approach for the Calculation of Electron-Impact Ionization Cross Sections of Atoms, Molecules, Ions, and Clusters. In *Advances in Atomic, Molecular, and Optical Physics*; Arimondo, E., Berman, P.R., Lin, C.C., Eds.; Elsevier: Amsterdam, The Netherlands, 2009; Volume 57, pp. 87–155.
4. Kim, Y.; Irikura, K.; Ali, M. Electron-impact total ionization cross sections of molecular ions. *J. Res. Natl. Inst. Stand. Technol.* **2000**, *105*, 285–291. [CrossRef] [PubMed]
5. Uddin, M.; Basak, A.K.; Islam, A.K.M.; Malik, F.B. Electron impact single ionization of light ionic targets with charge $q > 2$. *J. Phys. B* **2004**, *37*, 1909–1922. [CrossRef]
6. Pindzola, M.S.; Robicheaux, F.; Colgan, J. Electron-impact ionization of H+2 using a time-dependent close-coupling method. *J. Phys. B* **2005**, *38*, L285–L290. [CrossRef]
7. Peart, B.; Dolder, K.T. Collisions between electrons and H2+ions. IV. Measurements of cross sections for dissociative ionization. *J. Phys. B* **1973**, *6*, 2409–2414. [CrossRef]
8. Müller, A.; Tinschert, K.; Achenbach, C.; Salzborn, E.; Becker, R. A new technique for the measurement of ionization cross sections with crossed electron and ion beams. *Nucl. Instrum. Methods Phys. Res. Sect. B* **1985**, *10-11*, 204–206. [CrossRef]
9. Defrance, P.; Brouillard, F.; Claeys, W.; Van Wassenhove, G. Crossed beam measurement of absolute cross sections: An alternative method and its application to the electron impact ionisation of He+. *J. Phys. B* **1981**, *14*, 103–110. [CrossRef]
10. Belic, D.S.; Ristic, M.M.; Cherkani-Hassani, H.; Urbain, X.; Defrance, P. Electron-impact dissociation of N2D+ cations to D+ fragments. *Eur. Phys. J. D* **2020**, *74*, 1–8. [CrossRef]
11. Dolder, K.T.; Peart, B. Collisions between electrons and ions. *Rep. Prog. Phys.* **1976**, *39*, 693–749. [CrossRef]
12. Matt, S.; Echt, O.; Rauth, T.; Dünser, B.; Lezius, M.; Stamatovic, A.; Scheier, P.; Märk, T.D. Electron impact ionization and dissociation of neutral and charged fullerenes. *Z. Phys. D* **1997**, *40*, 389–394. [CrossRef]
13. Scheier, P.; Hathiramani, D.; Arnold, W.; Huber, K.; Salzborn, E. Multiple Ionization and Fragmentation of Negatively Charged Fullerene Ions by Electron Impact. *Phys. Rev. Lett.* **2000**, *84*, 55–58. [CrossRef]
14. Hathiramani, D.; Aichele, K.; Arnold, W.; Huber, K.; Salzborn, E.; Scheier, P. Electron-Impact Induced Fragmentation of Fullerene Ions. *Phys. Rev. Lett.* **2000**, *85*, 3604–3607. [CrossRef]
15. Becker, E.W.; Klingelhöfer, R.; Lohse, P. Notizen: Strahlen aus kondensiertem Helium im Hochvakuum. *Z. Nat. A* **1961**, *16*, 1259. [CrossRef]
16. Scheidemann, A.; Toennies, J.P.; Northby, J.A. Capture of neon atoms by He4 clusters. *Phys. Rev. Lett.* **1990**, *64*, 1899–1902. [CrossRef]
17. Goyal, S.; Schutt, D.L.; Scoles, G. Vibrational spectroscopy of sulfur hexafluoride attached to helium clusters. *Phys. Rev. Lett.* **1992**, *69*, 933–936. [CrossRef]
18. Goyal, S.; Schutt, D.L.; Scoles, G. Infrared spectroscopy in highly quantum matrixes: Vibrational spectrum of sulfur hexafluoride ((SF6)n=1,2) attached to helium clusters. *J. Phys. Chem.* **1993**, *97*, 2236–2245. [CrossRef]
19. Hartmann, M.; Miller, R.E.; Toennies, J.P.; Vilesov, A. Rotationally Resolved Spectroscopy of SF6in Liquid Helium Clusters: A Molecular Probe of Cluster Temperature. *Phys. Rev. Lett.* **1995**, *75*, 1566–1569. [CrossRef]

20. Callegari, C.; Lehmann, K.K.; Schmied, R.; Scoles, G. Helium nanodroplet isolation rovibrational spectroscopy: Methods and recent results. *J. Chem. Phys.* **2001**, *115*, 10090. [CrossRef]
21. Toennies, J.P.; Vilesov, A.F. Superfluid Helium Droplets: A Uniquely Cold Nanomatrix for Molecules and Molecular Complexes. *Angew. Chem. Int. Ed.* **2004**, *43*, 2622–2648. [CrossRef]
22. Choi, M.Y.; Douberly, G.E.; Falconer, T.M.; Lewis, W.K.; Lindsay, C.; Merritt, J.M.; Stiles, P.L.; Miller, R.E. Infrared spectroscopy of helium nanodroplets: Novel methods for physics and chemistry. *Int. Rev. Phys. Chem.* **2006**, *25*, 15–75. [CrossRef]
23. Stienkemeier, F.; Lehmann, K. Spectroscopy and dynamics in helium nanodroplets. *J. Phys. B* **2006**, *39*, R127–R166. [CrossRef]
24. Northby, J.A. Experimental studies of helium droplets. *J. Chem. Phys.* **2001**, *115*, 10065. [CrossRef]
25. Callicoatt, B.E.; Förde, K.; Ruchti, T.; Jung, L.; Janda, K.C.; Halberstadt, N. Capture and ionization of argon within liquid helium droplets. *J. Chem. Phys.* **1998**, *108*, 9371–9382. [CrossRef]
26. Mauracher, A.; Echt, O.; Ellis, A.; Yang, S.; Bohme, D.; Postler, J.; Kaiser, A.; Denifl, S.; Scheier, P. Cold physics and chemistry: Collisions, ionization and reactions inside helium nanodroplets close to zero K. *Phys. Rep.* **2018**, *751*, 1–90. [CrossRef]
27. Tiggesbäumker, J.; Stienkemeier, F. Formation and properties of metal clusters isolated in helium droplets. *Phys. Chem. Chem. Phys.* **2007**, *9*, 4748–4770. [CrossRef] [PubMed]
28. Atkins, K.R. *Course XXI on Liquid Helium, Proceedings of International School of Physics Enrico Fermi, New York*; Careri, G., Ed.; Academic Press: New York, NY, USA, 1963; pp. 403–413.
29. Halberstadt, N.; Janda, K.C. The resonant charge hopping rate in positively charged helium clusters. *Chem. Phys. Lett.* **1998**, *282*, 409–412. [CrossRef]
30. Ellis, A.M.; Yang, S. Model for the charge-transfer probability in helium nanodroplets following electron-impact ionization. *Phys. Rev. A* **2007**, *76*, 032714. [CrossRef]
31. Atkins, K.R. Ions in Liquid Helium. *Phys. Rev.* **1959**, *116*, 1339–1343. [CrossRef]
32. Mateo, D.; Eloranta, J. Solvation of Intrinsic Positive Charge in Superfluid Helium. *J. Phys. Chem. A* **2014**, *118*, 6407–6415. [CrossRef]
33. Laimer, F.; Kranabetter, L.; Tiefenthaler, L.; Albertini, S.; Zappa, F.; Ellis, A.M.; Gatchell, M.; Scheier, P. Highly Charged Droplets of Superfluid Helium. *Phys. Rev. Lett.* **2019**, *123*, 165301. [CrossRef]
34. Laimer, F.; Zappa, F.; Scheier, P.; Gatchell, M. Multiply Charged Helium Droplet Anions. *Chem.—A Eur. J.* **2021**, *27*, 7283–7287. [CrossRef]
35. Laimer, F.; Zappa, F.; Scheier, P. Size and Velocity Distribution of Negatively Charged Helium Nanodroplets. *J. Phys. Chem. A* **2021**, *125*, 7662–7669. [CrossRef]
36. Krishna, M.V.R.; Whaley, K.B. Wave functions of helium clusters. *J. Chem. Phys.* **1990**, *93*, 6738–6751. [CrossRef]
37. Bogdanov, E.; Demidov, V.; Kaganovich, I.D.; Koepke, M.E.; Kudryavtsev, A. Modeling a short dc discharge with thermionic cathode and auxiliary anode. *Phys. Plasmas* **2013**, *20*, 101605. [CrossRef]
38. Gomez, L.F.; Loginov, E.; Sliter, R.; Vilesov, A.F. Sizes of large He droplets. *J. Chem. Phys.* **2011**, *135*, 154201. [CrossRef]
39. Matt, S.; Dünser, B.; Lezius, M.; Deutsch, H.; Becker, K.; Stamatovic, A.; Scheier, P.; Märk, T.D. Absolute partial and total cross-section functions for the electron impact ionization of C60 and C70. *J. Chem. Phys.* **1996**, *105*, 1880–1896. [CrossRef]
40. Mauracher, A.; Daxner, M.; Postler, J.; Huber, S.E.; Denifl, S.; Scheier, P.; Toennies, J.P. Detection of Negative Charge Carriers in Superfluid Helium Droplets: The Metastable Anions He*– and He2*–. *J. Phys. Chem. Lett.* **2014**, *5*, 2444–2449. [CrossRef]
41. Renzler, M.; Daxner, M.; Weinberger, N.; Denifl, S.; Scheier, P.; Echt, O. On subthreshold ionization of helium droplets, ejection of He+, and the role of anions. *Phys. Chem. Chem. Phys.* **2014**, *16*, 22466–22470. [CrossRef]
42. Kwan, V.; Consta, S. Molecular Characterization of the Surface Excess Charge Layer in Droplets. *J. Am. Soc. Mass Spectrom.* **2020**, *32*, 33–45. [CrossRef]
43. Kwan, V.; Malevanets, A.; Consta, S. Where Do the Ions Reside in a Highly Charged Droplet? *J. Phys. Chem. A* **2019**, *123*, 9298–9310. [CrossRef]
44. Zappa, F.; Denifl, S.; Mähr, I.; Bacher, A.; Echt, O.; Märk, T.D.; Scheier, P. Ultracold Water Cluster Anions. *J. Am. Chem. Soc.* **2008**, *130*, 5573–5578. [CrossRef]
45. Renzler, M.; Kuhn, M.; Mauracher, A.; Lindinger, A.; Scheier, P.; Ellis, A.M. Anionic Hydrogen Cluster Ions as a New Form of Condensed Hydrogen. *Phys. Rev. Lett.* **2016**, *117*, 273001. [CrossRef]

Article

Magnetic Angle Changer for Studies of Electronically Excited Long-Living Atomic States

Łukasz Kłosowski * and Mariusz Piwiński

Institute of Physics, Faculty of Physics, Astronomy and Informatics, Nicolaus Copernicus University in Toruń, Grudziądzka 5, 87-100 Toruń, Poland
* Correspondence: lklos@fizyka.umk.pl

Abstract: A new geometry of a magnetic angle changer (MAC) device is proposed, which allows experiments to be run on electron impact excitation of long-lived states of target atoms. The details of the device's design are presented and discussed together with a numerical analysis of its magnetic field.

Keywords: backscattering; electron optics; inelastic collisions; numerical simulations

Citation: Kłosowski, Ł.; Piwiński, M. Magnetic Angle Changer for Studies of Electronically Excited Long-Living Atomic States. *Atoms* **2021**, *9*, 71. https://doi.org/10.3390/atoms9040071

Academic Editors: Jean-Christophe Pain and Grzegorz Piotr Karwasz

Received: 16 August 2021
Accepted: 23 September 2021
Published: 28 September 2021

Publisher's Note: MDPI stays neutral with regard to jurisdictional claims in published maps and institutional affiliations.

Copyright: © 2021 by the authors. Licensee MDPI, Basel, Switzerland. This article is an open access article distributed under the terms and conditions of the Creative Commons Attribution (CC BY) license (https://creativecommons.org/licenses/by/4.0/).

1. Introduction

A magnetic angle changer (MAC) [1,2] was invented two decades ago as a device which allows the running of low-energy (below 100 eV) electron collisional experiments in the full range of scattering angles when a crossed-beam geometry is applied. Several various types of such devices have been used since then, allowing differential cross sections (DCS) and electron impact coherence parameters (EICP) to be obtained for numerous targets at various electron impact energies. A summary of such devices can be found in a review by G. King [3]. The most interesting devices worth mentioning are the MAC of M. Allan, using a single power supply [4], the MAC of B. Mielewska, providing zero magnetic field in the central part of the device [5], and the MAC of I. Linert providing a broad region of the homogeneous field [6].

Briefly, a MAC is a set of coaxial magnetic coils. Its total magnetic dipole moment is usually zero, providing negligible magnetic fields outside the device, which does not disturb electron beam sources or detectors of scattered particles. The device is symmetric, with a symmetry plane perpendicular to the main axis. The symmetry plane is transparent to electrons (no coils), identical to the experiment's scattering plane. The electron–target interaction region is placed in the central point of the MAC device.

The magnetic field of the MAC bends the electrons' trajectories in a way where the final direction is shifted by an angle defined by the electron's kinetic energy, the device's geometry, and electric currents flowing through its coils. This is very useful in experiments conducted at very large scattering angles, around 180°. Without a MAC, this would require placing an electron beam source (electron gun) and electron detector at the same angular position. If the MAC is used, electrons scattered at such large angles are deflected to a region where detectors can be physically placed.

Additionally, for inelastic scattering, the device can separate electrons scattered at 0° from the primary beam, allowing experiments to be run at very small scattering angles.

The magnetic field in the central region of the MAC (identical with the scattering region) is usually of the order of millitesla. Such a relatively weak field does not influence scattering processes significantly. It may, however, cause some issues in the interpretation of experimental results, especially in the EICP measurement.

The EICP can be defined as various sets of parameters describing the shape, orientation, and alignment of the electron charge cloud of collisionally excited atoms. More details can be found in the review by Andersen et al. [7]. In the case of P states of two-valence-electron atoms, the most convenient EICPs are Andersen parameters P_l, γ and $L_\perp$ [8], defined as follows. An atom in its P state can be described as a superposition of three possible magnetic substates:

$$|P\rangle = a_{-1}|m=-1\rangle + a_0|m=0\rangle + a_{+1}|m=+1\rangle, \quad (1)$$

where a_{-1}, a_0, and a_{+1} are complex coefficients. Due to the planar symmetry of the scattering system, additional conditions for the coefficients appear. The mathematical form of these conditions depends on the choice of axes used to describe the atom. If a so-called natural reference frame is used, then such a condition is simply $a_0 = 0$. In such a frame, the quantization axis is perpendicular to the scattering plane defined by the momentum vectors of incoming and outgoing electrons. Equation (1) is then simplified to:

$$|P\rangle = a_{-1}|m=-1\rangle + a_{+1}|m=+1\rangle. \quad (2)$$

Then the angular part of electron cloud density in spherical coordinates (θ, ϕ) can be described using the expression:

$$|\Psi(\theta,\phi)|^2 = \frac{3}{8\pi}\sin^2\theta(1 + P_l\cos(2\phi - 2\gamma)), \quad (3)$$

where P_l is the shape parameter and γ is the alignment angle. They are related to the a coefficients (assuming normalization) with the expressions:

$$P_l = 2|a_{-1}a_{+1}| \quad (4)$$

$$\gamma = \frac{1}{2}\arg(-a^*_{-1}a_{+1}) \quad (5)$$

The third parameter $L_\perp$ is angular momentum transfer, and it is given with the expression:

$$L_\perp = |a_{+1}|^2 - |a_{-1}|^2. \quad (6)$$

Moreover, it is related to the shape parameter with the equation:

$$L_\perp^2 + P_l^2 = 1. \quad (7)$$

The geometrical interpretation of the parameters is presented in Figure 1.

In experiments on the EICP measurements in a weak magnetic field, an additional effect analogous to a well-known Hanle effect [9] is present, which was described in detail in the past [10,11]. The phenomenon was initially observed as a modification of the polarization state of light resonantly scattered by atoms placed in a magnetic field [12]. The effect finds numerous applications in atomic physics and astrophysics [13], and is used for example, to determine magnetic fields in laboratory plasmas [14] or in astronomical objects [15].

The Hanle-like effect we intend to avoid here is caused by the same mechanism in terms of quantum mechanics. The difference is that the atoms are excited not by resonant light, but by electron impact.

The presence of the magnetic field causes slight energy shifting in the atom's state, depending on the atom's magnetic dipole moment orientation and the magnitude of the field. For simplicity, we may assume that the magnetic field is parallel to the quantization axis in the considered reference frame. The energy shifts have opposite signs for both substates in Equation (2), causing a time-evolving phase shift between $|m=-1\rangle$ and $|m=+1\rangle$. This way, the charge cloud from Equation (3) will precess with Larmour frequency:

$$\omega = \frac{Be}{2m}, \quad (8)$$

where B is the magnetic field, e is the elementary charge, and m is the electron mass.

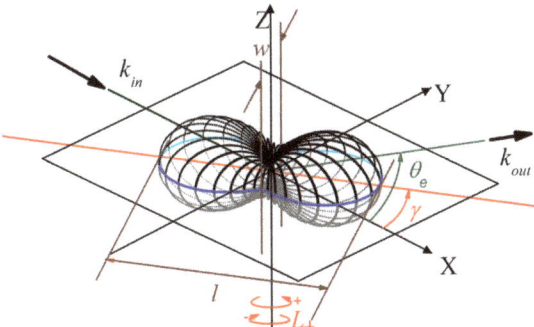

Figure 1. Geometrical interpretation of EICP. The 3-dimensional plot represents the angular part of the electron charge cloud in an atom's P state described with Equation (3). The value of $|\Psi|^2$ corresponds to the distance of the particular point of the surface from the center of the reference frame. The scattering plane is defined by the electron's initial and final wave vectors $\vec{k}_{in}$ and $\vec{k}_{out}$. The axes' orientation is chosen to form a so-called natural frame, where the quantization axis Z is perpendicular to the scattering plane. The electron is scattered at the angle θ_e. The alignment angle is denoted with γ. The shape parameter is given by the expression: $P_l = \frac{l-w}{l+w}$, where l and w are the length and width of the charge cloud, respectively.

Such a precession affects the measurement readout. The EICPs are usually studied using the electron-photon coincidence technique [16,17]. In such experiments, photons emitted from electron-impact excited atoms are detected. The information on EICP of the atom is written in the polarization state of the photon and in angular distribution of its emission probability. Such polarization or distribution can be determined experimentally.

There is a finite time interval between the collision act and photon emission, given by an exponential distribution described with the excited state's lifetime τ. This way, the precession of the charge cloud in the finite time leads to blurring the measurement results to $\tilde{P}_l$ and $\tilde{\gamma}$ values given with the expressions obtained by convolution of cloud rotation and exponential decay [10]:

$$\tilde{\gamma} = \gamma + \frac{1}{2}\arctan\frac{Be\tau}{m}, \tag{9}$$

$$\tilde{P}_l = \frac{P_l}{\sqrt{1 + \left(\frac{Be\tau}{m}\right)^2}}. \tag{10}$$

It is worth noting that the magnetic field does not influence the angular momentum transfer $L_\perp$.

There are two ways of dealing with the problem of the MAC's field effect: One is to predict the effect's magnitude and include corrections in experimental data analysis, as was done in the e-Ca superelastic scattering experiment by the Manchester group [18]. Since Ca's 4^1P_1 state has a lifetime of 4.5 ns [19], then at 1 mT, the corrections are about 23° for γ and 0.69 for P_l, which are acceptable values.

The other way is to provide a near-zero magnetic field in the scattering region, allowing the Hanle-like effect to be reduced, as presented in our angular-correlation coincidence experiment on e-He scattering [10,20,21].

Both approaches are sufficient if the lifetime of the atomic state excited during the collision is short, of the order of a nanosecond. The situation becomes more complicated if the lifetime is longer, such as He 2^3P state's 98 ns [22]. In such a case, the corrections cannot be used, as the 1 mT field would blur the results of the shape parameter to 6% of its actual value, where the alignment angle cannot be determined well. On the other hand, excitation to the triplet state is very interesting as one of few examples where we can observe purely spin-exchange collisions. The EICP for such scattering were measured only in a limited range of energies and scattering angles [23] and analyzed theoretically in only a few approaches [24,25].

Additionally, in the case of He's 2^3P state, a central-zero-field MAC would be useless, as the scattering region has finite dimensions, approximately 1 mm in diameter. The zero magnetic field is available only at the center of the MAC, but the field reaches up to 0.1 mT in outer parts of the finite region. This way, the Hanle-like effect of up to 30° would be observed in the outer layers of the scattering area. The experimental results would then include the magnetic field's effect averaged over the interaction region, which would be very difficult to deconvolve.

2. New Magnetic Angle Changer Geometry

To bypass the issues described above, a MAC of improved geometry can be used. It combines the features of three devices mentioned above (Allan's, Mielewska's and Linert's). Besides assuring zero magnetic dipole moment and zero magnetic field in the central region, it should also provide zero magnetic field in the center's vicinity. In other words, the magnetic field should be a homogeneous zero value in the whole scattering region.

To describe such a MAC, it is convenient to use cylindrical coordinates. The center of the device is the origin of the coordinate system, and the main axis is the system's Z axis. The position of each coil, denoted with index i, is then given with its radius r_i and distance from the symmetry plane z_i. Each coil transmits an electric current I_i (positive value for counterclockwise currents and negative for clockwise). For simplicity, one can assume the MAC is made of non-magnetic material with negligible magnetic susceptibility (copper in the experiment).

The zero magnetic moment condition is then fulfilled by the equation:

$$\sum_{i=1}^{N} I_i r_i^2 = 0, \tag{11}$$

where N is the total number of wire coils used in the MAC ($N = 30$ in the proposed design). The zero-field condition is fulfilled by the equation:

$$\sum_{i=1}^{N} \frac{I_i r_i^2}{(r_i^2 + z_i^2)^{\frac{3}{2}}} = 0. \tag{12}$$

To provide the homogeneity of the field, the second derivative of the magnetic field along the Z coordinate should be zero:

$$\frac{\partial^2}{\partial Z^2} \sum_{i=1}^{N} \frac{I_i r_i^2}{(r_i^2 + (z_i - Z)^2)^{\frac{3}{2}}} \bigg|_{Z=0} = 0, \tag{13}$$

which leads to a condition, which is a generalization of a Helmholtz coil:

$$\sum_{i=1}^{N} \frac{I_i r_i^2 (r_i^2 - 4z_i^2)}{(r_i^2 + z_i^2)^{\frac{7}{2}}} = 0. \tag{14}$$

For simplicity of operation, it was assumed at the design stage that all the wires would be supplied with an electric current of the same value. Various geometries satisfy these conditions (11), (12), and (14). One of them was chosen for practical realization. The choice was made based on further numerical simulations of the electron beam's behavior. The selected MAC, among all the geometries we found, provided the best efficiency of bending the electron's trajectories and the lowest angular spread of the beam (see Section 2.2).

2.1. The Device Used in the Experiment

The cross section of the proposed MAC is presented in Figure 2, together with the produced field.

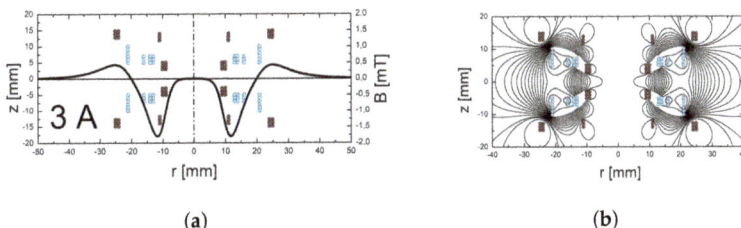

Figure 2. The geometry of the proposed MAC coil. Panel (**a**) represents the cross-section through the wires. For clarity, the cores used to wind the coil are not shown. The colors of the wires indicate the direction of the electric current. Additionally, the magnetic field function at 3 A of the driving current is presented to show the wide field-free area in the central part of the device. The magnetic field was calculated numerically by integration of field contribution from all conductors using the Biot–Savart law. Panel (**b**) represents magnetic field lines in the cross-section of the MAC, also obtained from Biot–Savart.

The device consists of 30 pairs of circular wires arranged into coils. Details of their geometry are collected in Table 1.

Table 1. Collected information on the geometry of the MAC's coils. r_i refers to the radius of i-th coil, and z_i is its distance from the device's symmetry plane.

i	r_i [mm]	z_i [mm]	Current Direction
1	9	3	+
2	9	4	+
3	9	5	+
4	10	3	+
5	10	4	+
6	10	5	+
7	11	11.9	+
8	11	12.9	+
9	11	13.9	+
10	13	5	−
11	13	6	−
12	13	7	−
13	14	5	−
14	14	6	−
15	14	7	−
16	16	5	−
17	16	6	−
18	16	7	−
19	21	5	−
20	21	6	−
21	21	7	−
22	21	8	−
23	21	9	−
24	21	10	−
25	24	12.8	+
26	24	13.8	+
27	24	14.8	+
28	25	12.8	+
29	25	13.8	+
30	25	14.8	+

The device was set up using copper cores and 0.9 mm insulated copper wires. Such choice enables good heat transmission, essential for cooling at several amperes of operating current. Additional cooling was provided using a tap water system analogous to the one used with the previous MAC [10]. Photographs of the ready-to-use device are presented in Figure 3.

Figure 3. Photographs of the MAC constructed based on the proposed design. Panel (**a**) shows the device's overview, with a ruler to indicate the size. Panel (**b**) shows the gap in the MAC's symmetry plane (scattering plane in the experiment). Some material is left in the gap to provide mechanical support of the upper part.

2.2. Numerical Analysis of the MAC's Performance

To prove the efficiency of the MAC, a set of numerical simulations was performed. Trajectories of electrons traveling through the device's field were calculated by integrating classical equations of motion using well-known Runge–Kutta methods with Lorentz forces and magnetic fields calculated from the Biot–Savart law, analogous to the method described ure 4.

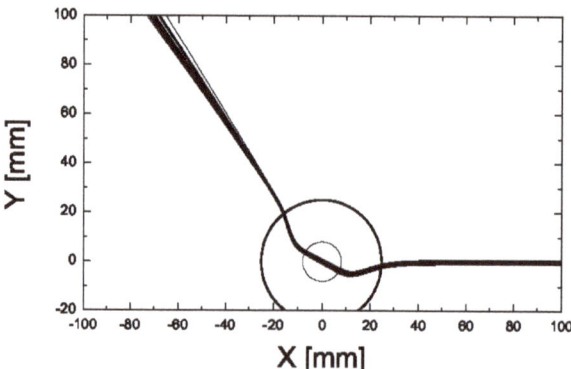

Figure 4. Example trajectories of electrons in the MAC's field obtained numerically at a 4 A coil current and 100 eV electron energy (projection in device's symmetry plane). The circle denotes the MAC's contour. The electrons are incoming from the right and are deflected up at about 50 degrees.

Similar simulations were repeated in various current and energy conditions for electron beams of 1 mm in diameter. This allowed us to determine the MAC's deflection efficiency and estimate the angular spread of the electron beam introduced by the magnetic field. The deflection angle ϑ of the electron's trajectory can be calculated numerically in simulations, providing its nonlinear dependence from an expression $\frac{I_{MAC}}{\sqrt{E}}$, where I_{MAC} is the MAC's electric current, and E is the electron's kinetic energy. At low scattering angles, where the function is close to linear, such calculations can be simplified by using the approximate expression [10]:

$$\vartheta \approx \frac{2e}{\sqrt{2mE}} \int_0^\infty B(r)dr \qquad (15)$$

where e and m are the electron's charge and mass, and $B(r)$ is the magnetic field function, proportional to I_{MAC} (example presented in Figure 2a). Numerically obtained deflection

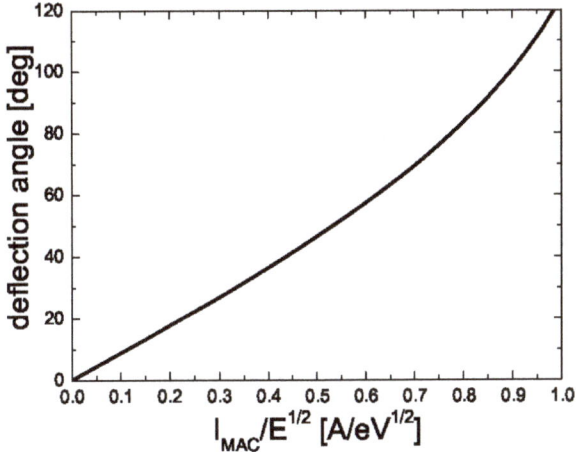

Figure 5. The deflection angle of electron trajectories obtained numerically. It is clear that at lower deflection angles, the linear function from Equation (15) provides a good approximation.

Additionally, since the magnetic field can cause some angular spread of the deflection angles, some additional simulations were performed for electron beams of finite width (1 mm in diameter). The estimated spread is presented in Figure 6.

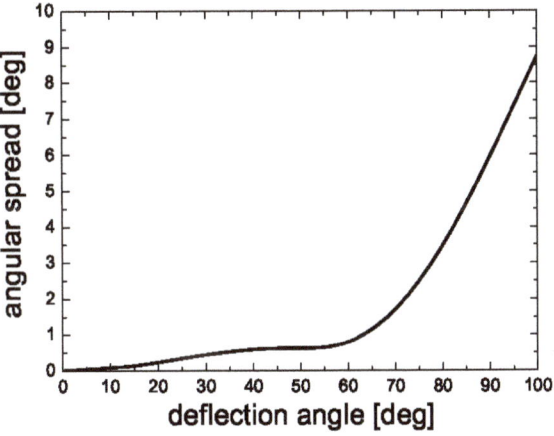

Figure 6. Numerically obtained angular spread of the electron beam introduced by the presence of the MAC's magnetic field.

It is clear that for deflection angles below 60 degrees, the angular spread is low and can be neglected for most electron scattering experiments, where beam divergences are usually greater than 1 degree. At deflection angles above 80 degrees, the spread grows rapidly, limiting the range of the MAC's use. On the other hand, the deflection of an electron beam of 60° is sufficient for most experiments involving backward scattering.

3. Summary

To summarize, a new, efficient magnetic angle changer was designed and built. Numerical analysis shows its efficiency for electron beams typically used in electron scattering experiments. The device can provide a near-zero, homogeneous magnetic field in its central part. It may allow experiments on electron impact coherence parameters to be run in the full range of scattering angles for atomic states with lifetimes close to 100 nanoseconds (such as the 2^3P state of the helium atom, as mentioned above), which will be the topic of further research of our group.

Author Contributions: Conceptualization, Ł.K. and M.P.; design of the device, Ł.K.; production of the device, Ł.K. and M.P.; numerical analysis, Ł.K.; preparation of the manuscript Ł.K. and M.P. All authors have read and agreed to the published version of the manuscript.

Funding: This research received no external funding.

Institutional Review Board Statement: Not applicable.

Informed Consent Statement: Not applicable.

Conflicts of Interest: The authors declare no conflict of interest.

References

1. Read, F.H.; Channing, J.M. Production and optical properties of an unscreened but localized magnetic field. *Rev. Sci. Instrum.* **1996**, *67*, 2372–2377. [CrossRef]
2. Zubek, M.; Gulley, N.; King, G.C.; Read, F.H. Measurements of elastic electron scattering in the backward hemisphere. *J. Phys. B At. Mol. Opt. Phys.* **1996**, *29*, L239–L244. [CrossRef]
3. King, G.C. Chapter 1-the use of the magnetic angle changer in atomic and molecular physics. In *Advances in Atomic, Molecular, and Optical Physics*; Arimondo, E., Berman, P.R., Lin, C.C., Eds.; Academic Press: Cambridge, MA, USA, 2011; Volume 60, pp. 1–64.
4. Allan, M. Excitation of the 2^3S state of helium by electron impact from threshold to 24 eV: measurements with the 'magnetic angle changer'. *J. Phys. At. Mol. Opt. Phys.* **2000**, *33*, L215–L220. [CrossRef]
5. Mielewska, B.; Linert, I.; King, G.C.; Zubek, M. Differential cross sections for elastic electron scattering in argon over the angular range 130°–180°. *Phys. Rev. A* **2004**, *69*, 062716. [CrossRef]
6. Linert, I.; King, G.C.; Zubek, M. A study of electron impact excitation of molecular oxygen at a scattering angle of 180°. *J. Electron Spectrosc. Relat. Phenom.* **2004**, *134*, 1–8. [CrossRef]
7. Andersen, N.; Gallagher, J.W.; Hertel, I.V. Collisional alignment and orientation of atomic outer shells I. Direct excitation by electron and atom impact. *Phys. Rep.* **1988**, *165*, 1–188. [CrossRef]
8. Andersen, N.; Hertel, I.V.; Kleinpoppen, H. Shape and dynamics of states excited in electron-atom collisions: A comment on orientation and alignment parameters by consideration of attractive and repulsive forces. *J. Phys. B At. Mol. Phys.* **1984**, *17*, L901–L908. [CrossRef]
9. Hanle, W. Zuschriften und vorläufige Mitteilungen. *Naturwissenschaften* **1923**, *11*, 690–691. [CrossRef]
10. Kłosowski, Ł.; Piwiński, M.; Dziczek, D.; Wiśniewska, K.; Chwirot, S. Magnetic angle changer—New device allowing extension of electron–photon coincidence measurements to arbitrarily large electron scattering angles. *Meas. Sci. Technol.* **2007**, *18*, 3801–3810. [CrossRef]
11. Murray, A.J.; MacGillivray, W.; Hussey, M. Theoretical modeling of resonant laser excitation of atoms in a magnetic field. *Phys. Rev. A* **2008**, *77*, 013409. [CrossRef]
12. Wood, R.W.; Ellett, A. On the influence of magnetic fields on the polarisation of resonance radiation. *Proc. R. Soc. London. Ser. Contain. Pap. Math. Phys. Character* **1923**, *103*, 396–403.
13. Moruzzi, G.; Strumia, F. (Eds.) *The Hanle Effect and Level-Crossing Spectroscopy*; Atomic, Molecular, Optical and Plasma Physics; Springer: Berlin/Heidelberg, Germany, 2012.
14. Presura, R. Hanle effect as candidate for measuring magnetic fields in laboratory plasmas. *Rev. Sci. Instrum.* **2012**, *83*, 10D528. [CrossRef]
15. Raouafi, N.E.; Riley, P.; Gibson, S.; Fineschi, S.; Solanki, S.K. Diagnostics of coronal magnetic fields through the hanle effect in uv and ir lines. *Front. Astron. Space Sci.* **2016**, *3*, L215. [CrossRef]
16. Bederson, B. The "perfect" scattering experiment. II. *Comments At. Mol. Phys.* **1969**, *1*, 65–69.

17. Macek, J.; Jaecks, D.H. Theory of atomic photon–particle coincidence measurements. *Phys. Rev. A* **1971**, *4*, 2288–2300. [CrossRef]
18. Hussey, M.; Murray, A.; MacGillivray, W.; King, G.C. Low energy super-elastic scattering studies of calcium over the complete angular range using a magnetic angle changing device. *J. Phys. B At. Mol. Opt. Phys.* **2008**, *41*, 055202. [CrossRef]
19. Available online: https://physics.nist.gov/PhysRefData/Handbook/Tables/calciumtable3.htm (accessed on 15 August 2021).
20. Kłosowski, Ł.; Piwiński, M.; Dziczek, D.; Wiśniewska, K.; Zubek, M.; Chwirot, S. Coincidence investigation of inelastic electron-atom collisions with magnetic selection of scattering angle—Feasibility study. *Eur. Phys. J. Spec. Top.* **2007**, *144*, 173–177. [CrossRef]
21. Kłosowski, Ł.; Piwiński, M.; Dziczek, D.; Pleskacz, K.; Chwirot, S. Coincidence measurements of electron-impact coherence parameters for e-he scattering in the full range of scattering angles. *Phys. Rev. A* **2009**, *80*, 062709. [CrossRef]
22. Available online: https://physics.nist.gov/PhysRefData/Handbook/Tables/heliumtable3.htm (accessed on 15 August 2021).
23. Humphrey, I.; Williams, J.F.; Heck, E.L. A feasibility study of the measurement of the stokes parameters of the 33p, 31d and 33d states of helium. *J. Phys. At. Mol. Phys.* **1987**, *20*, 367–391. [CrossRef]
24. Fon, W.C.; Berrington, K.A.; Burke, P.G.; Kingston, A.E. The 11s to 23s and 11s to 23p excitation of helium by electron impact. *J. Phys. At. Mol. Phys.* **1979**, *12*, 1861–1872. [CrossRef]
25. Cartwright, D.C.; Csanak, G. Electron-photon coincidence parameters for the excitation of the n3P (n = 2–8) states of helium *J. Phys. B* **1986**, *19*, L485–L491. [CrossRef]

Article

On the Electron Impact Integral Cross-Sections for Butanol and Pentanol Isomers

Nafees Uddin [1,2], Paresh Modak [1] and Bobby Antony [1,*]

[1] Atomic and Molecular Physics Laboratory, Department of Physics, Indian Institute of Technology (Indian School of Mines) Dhanbad, Jharkhand 826004, India; nafeesuddin27@gmail.com (N.U.); paresh@ap.ism.ac.in (P.M.)
[2] JIMS Engineering Management Technical Campus, 48/4 Knowledge Park III, Greater Noida 201306, India
* Correspondence: bobby@iitism.ac.in; Tel.: +91-947-019-4795

Abstract: The need for a reliable and comprehensive database of cross-sections for many atomic and molecular species is immense due to its key role in R&D domains such as plasma modelling, bio-chemical processes, medicine and many other natural and technological environments. Elastic, momentum transfer and total cross-sections of butanol and pentanol isomers by the impact of 6–5000 eV electrons are presented in this work. The calculations were performed by employing the spherical complex optical potential formalism along with single-centre expansion and group additivity rule. The investigations into the presence of isomeric variations reveal that they are more pronounced at low and intermediate energies. Elastic, total cross-sections (with the exception of n-pentanol) and momentum transfer cross-sections for all pentanol isomers are reported here for the first time, to the best of our knowledge. Our momentum transfer cross-sections for butanol isomers are in very good agreement with the experimental and theoretical values available, and in reasonable consensus for other cross-sections.

Keywords: electron scattering; integral cross sections; alcohols; isomeric effect; butanol; pentanol

1. Introduction

Recently, there has been a heightened interest in the study of higher alcohols for their significant role in industrial applications and research. Species such as butanol and pentanol are axial to the development of bio-fuels [1] and are the mainstay of all major proposed solutions to the looming world energy crisis. To understand the processes that follow the ignition of plasma and to model the spark ignition behaviour of such bio-fuels, many fundamental data are required that can be sourced from electron-scattering studies of these molecules [2]. Moreover, there is a pressing need for a reliable and comprehensive database of cross-sections for these species, as they play a key role in R&D domains such as plasma modelling [3], bio-chemical processes [4], health [5], environment [6], etc.

In the present times, the isomers of higher alcohols have also been seen as viable alternatives of their n-structure counterparts as bio-fuels [7]. Electron-scattering data, however, are scarcely available for such molecules. These data are also critical for the accurate modelling of planetary atmospheres [8]. In order to facilitate a complete dataset of cross-sections [9], we report the data for elastic (Q_{el}), momentum transfer (Q_{mtcs}) and total cross-sections (Q_t) for butanol and pentanol isomers under the present theoretical study. This is in continuation to the theoretical calculations of total ionisation cross-sections (Q_{ion}) for the same species, reported in our earlier work [10].

Our calculations were performed using the spherical complex optical potential (SCOP) [11,12] methodology and the group additivity rule (GAR) [13], along with single-centre expansion applied to model the charge density of each group, efficiently. A visual approach to the selection of groups on the basis of the electrostatic potential surface of the target molecule was employed, the details of which are provided in ref. [10]. The input parameters such as polarizability, ionisation energies, etc., for pentanol isomers were also calculated in our earlier work [10], though the first excited states of the targets were calculated in this work, the data being unavailable for the same in the literature. The next section describes our theoretical methodology followed by results and discussions with conclusions presented in the final section of this article.

2. Theoretical Methodology

We used the SCOP [14] formalism for the calculation of cross-sections that employ a model optical potential to represent the scattering dynamics, expressed as:

$$V_{opt} = V_{real}(r, E_i) + iV_{im}(r, E_i) \tag{1}$$

The Schrödinger equation for the system was then solved by the partial wave analysis using the potential in Equation (1), yielding the solutions as complex phase shifts that are used to obtain cross-sections. The potential represented by the first term on the right-hand side of Equation (1) is the sum of static potential (V_{st}), exchange potential (V_{ex}) and polarization potential (V_{pol}).

$$V_{real} = V_{st} + V_{ex} + V_{pol} \tag{2}$$

The static potential was derived from the charge density (ρ) of the atomic constituents of the target molecule where ρ is expanded about the scattering centre, which is the atom in case of atomic targets. In our case, however, the targets are molecules with hydrogen atoms attached to either a carbon atom or an oxygen atom, which are much heavier than the hydrogen itself. Consequently, the charge density of the hydrogen atom is expanded about the heavier atom, i.e., the carbon or the oxygen atom. This is called single-centre expansion. Due to the large size of our targets, it is fair to assume that they are composed of multiple independent scattering centres, comprising groups of atoms. The contributions of single-electron collisions from these groups may be added linearly to obtain the cross-section for the whole molecule, a process that is known as the group additivity rule. To remove any ambiguity in the identification of these groups, we devised a selection mechanism based on the electrostatic potential surface of the molecule, described in our earlier work [10].

The static potential was obtained from the parameterized Hartree–Fock wave equation by Cox and Bonham [15], while the exchange potential was calculated using Hara's [16] non-parametric, free-electron gas model. The parameter-free, correlation polarization potential by Zhang et al. [17] was used to account for the polarization effects.

The second term on the right-hand side of Equation (1) corresponds to the loss of scattered flux due to electronic excitation and ionization channels. The absorption potential is a quasi-free Pauli-blocking type and its expression as given by Staszewska et al. [18] is:

$$V_{abs}(r, E_i) = -\rho(r)\sqrt{\frac{T_{loc}}{2}}\left(\frac{8\pi}{10k_F^3 E_i}\right)\theta(p^2 - k_f^2 - 2\Delta)(A_1 + A_2 + A_3) \tag{3}$$

Here, the local kinetic energy is:

$$T_{loc} = E_i - (V_{st} + V_{ex} + V_{pol}) \tag{4}$$

where k_f is the Fermi wave vector given by $k_f = \sqrt[3]{3\pi^2\rho(r)}$ and p is the momentum of the incident electron computed as $p^2 = 2E_i$. The dynamic functions A_1, A_2 and A_3 are dependent on the ionisation potential (IP), the Heaviside unit step function $\theta(x)$ and the Δ parameter, the value of which is such that it limits the value of the total inelastic cross-section. As approximated by Staszewska, the value of Δ is equal to IP, which is a constant. The inelastic channels are closed for incident energies lower than Δ, but below the ionization threshold, however, there is a finite probability of excitation to discrete states.

An energy dependent form of Δ checks the excessive loss of flux into the inelastic channels at intermediate energies, which is represented as:

$$\Delta(E_i) = 0.8I + \beta(E_i - I) \tag{5}$$

The constant β is calculated by setting $\Delta = I$ (ionization energy) for $E_i = E_p$, E_p being the incident energy where the inelastic cross-section is maximum. It is fair to consider the inelastic channels to be opened at the first excitation energy requiring energy dependency of Δ. For energies higher than E_p, however, Δ is fixed at ionization energy.

The optical potential constructed in Equation (1) for the target molecular system was incorporated in the Schrödinger equation, which was solved numerically using Numerov's method under partial wave analysis. The solutions yielded complex phase shifts, which carry information about scattering dynamics and were employed to calculate relevant cross-sections. The elastic cross-section for l partial waves is calculated as:

$$Q_{el}(E_i) = \frac{\pi}{k^2} \sum_{l=0}^{\infty} (2l+1) |\eta_l exp(Re\delta_l) - 1|^2 \tag{6}$$

and the inelastic cross-section is given by:

$$Q_{inel}(E_i) = \frac{\pi}{k^2} \sum_{l=0}^{\infty} (2l+1) \left(1 - \eta_l^2\right) \tag{7}$$

where, $\eta_l = exp(-2Im\delta_l)$ is the absorption factor for each partial wave with the number of partial waves, in our case being capped at 61, satisfying convergence of the results in our calculations. The sum of Equations (6) and (7) gives the total cross-section (Q_t), i.e.:

$$Q_t = Q_{el} + Q_{inel} \tag{8}$$

The complex phase shifts obtained as the solutions of Schrödinger equation were also used to calculate the momentum transfer cross-section using:

$$Q_{mtcs}(E_i) = \frac{4\pi}{k^2} \sum_{l=0}^{\infty} (l+1) \sin^2[\delta_{l+1}(k) - \delta_l(k)] \tag{9}$$

We used the same data for target parameters, calculated by us or otherwise, as in our earlier work [10] and is displayed in Tables 1 and 2. This includes ionisation energies (IP) and molecular polarizabilities.

The excitation energies listed in Tables 1 and 2 were calculated using Gaussian software [19]. The geometry of the molecules was optimized using the hybrid functional (B3LYP) along with 6-311++G (d,) basis set within density functional theory [20,21]. Excited states calculations [22] were performed by implementing time dependent density functional theory on these optimized structures.

Table 1. Target properties (butanol isomers).

Target Species	IP (eV) [23]	Polarizability α (Å^3)	First Excited State (eV)
Butan-1-ol	9.99 ± 0.05	8.57 [24]	6.23
Butan-2-ol	9.88 ± 0.03	8.57 [24]	6.29
2-methylpropan-1-ol	10.02 ± 0.03	8.92 [25]	6.24
2-methypropan-2-ol	9.90 ± 0.03	8.92 [25]	6.23

Table 2. Target properties (pentanol isomers).

Target Species	IP (eV) [10]	Polarizability α (Å³) [10]	First Excited State (eV)
Pentan-1-ol	10.00	10.118	6.25
Pentan-2-ol	9.78	10.112	6.30
Pentan-3-ol	9.78	10.056	6.30
2-methylbutan-1-ol	9.86	10.000	6.20
3-methylbutan-2-ol	9.88	10.014	6.19

3. Results and Discussion

The calculated cross-sections of molecules are represented graphically (Figures 1–13). Atomic units were used for calculations with the cross-section values in the units of Å² on the Y-axis and energy of the projectile in eV on the X-axis (logarithmic scale on both axes). Comparison data for the molecules are plotted in separate figures and, wherever it is not available, calculated data of all isomers of the target molecule are plotted in the same graph.

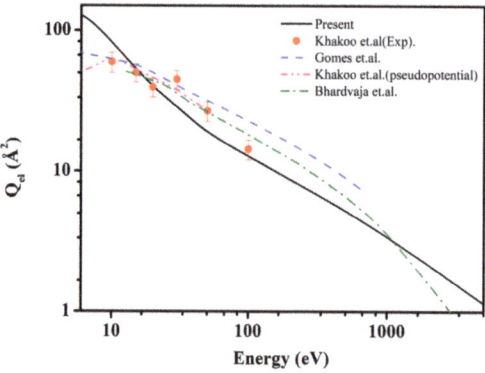

Figure 1. Elastic cross-section of butan-1-ol: solid black line represents present result, solid circles (red) depict experimental data from Khakoo et al., dashed (blue) line is ICS from Gomes et al., dash-dot line (green) is from Bhardvaja et al. and pink dash-dot-dot line represents pseudopotential calculations from Khakoo et al.

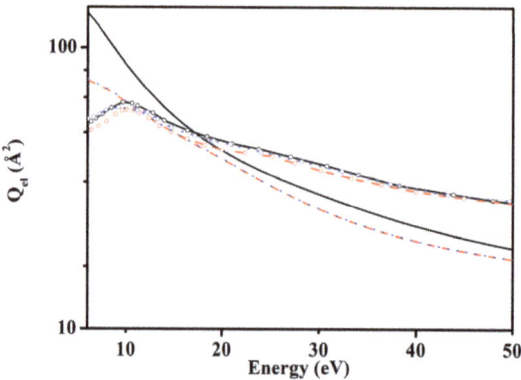

Figure 2. Solid lines (black) represent butan-2-ol, dashed lines (red) represent 2-methylpropan-1-ol and dotted lines (blue) represent 2-methylpropan-2-ol results. Lines (only) show present results and lines with open circles are results from Bettega et al.

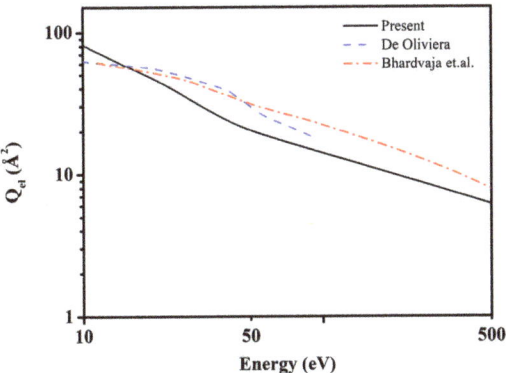

Figure 3. Elastic cross-section of pentan-1-ol: solid black line shows present results, dashed blue line displays results by de Oliviera et al. and dash-dot red line represents results by Bhardvaja et al.

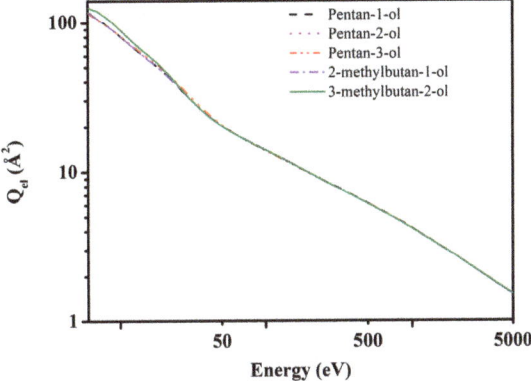

Figure 4. Elastic cross-section of pentanol isomers (present): black dashed line is for pentan-1-ol, purple dotted line represents pentan-2-ol, red dash-dot-dot line represents pentan-3-ol, violet dash-dot line represents 2-methylbutan-1-ol and green solid line represents 3-methylpropan-2-ol.

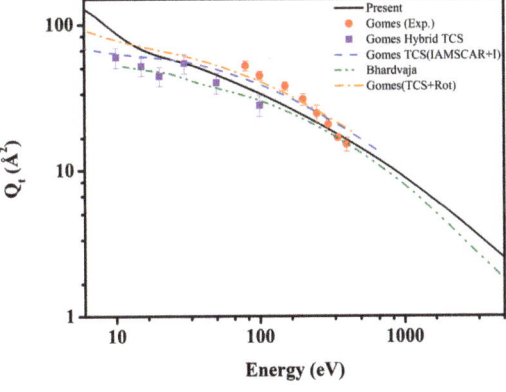

Figure 5. Total cross-section butan-1-ol: black solid line shows present results, red circles are experimental results by Gomes et al., purple squares are 'hybrid TCS' by Gomes et al., blue dashed lines are calculated values by Gomes et al., green dash-dot-dot line is from Bhardvaja et al. and orange dash-dot-dash line shows TCS + rotational from Gomes et al.

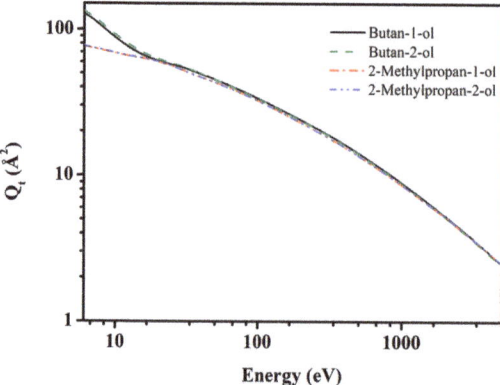

Figure 6. Total cross-section of butanol isomers (present): solid (black) line represents butan-1-ol, dashed (olive) line is for butan-2-ol, dash-dot (red) line is for 2-methylpropan-1-ol and dash-dot-dot (blue) line represents 2-methylpropan-2-ol.

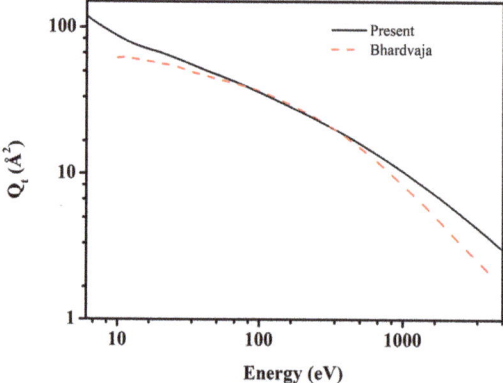

Figure 7. Total cross-section pentan-1-ol: solid (black) line represents present results and dashed (red) line represents results by Bhardvaja et al.

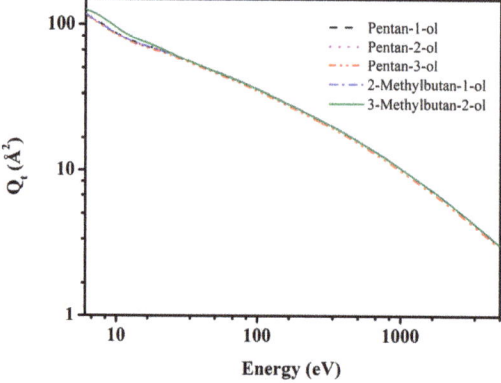

Figure 8. Total cross-section of pentanol isomers (present): dashed (black) line represents penta-1-ol, dotted (purple) is for pentan-2-ol, dash-dot-dot (red) line is for pentan-3-ol, dash-dot (blue) line represents 2-methylbutan-1-ol and solid (olive) line represents 3-methylbutan-2-ol results.

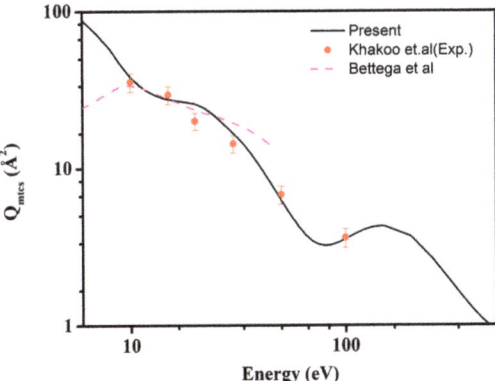

Figure 9. Momentum transfer cross-section of butan-1-ol: solid (black) line shows present results, circles (red) represent experimental results of Khakoo et al. and dashed (pink) line shows calculated results of Bettega et al.

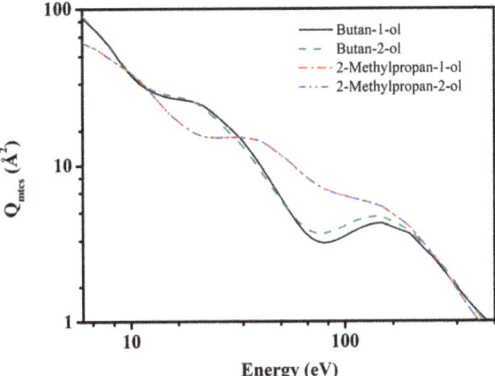

Figure 10. Momentum transfer cross-section of butanol isomers (present): solid (black) line represents butan-1-ol, dashed (olive) line is for butan-2-ol, dash-dot (red) line is for 2-methylpropan-1-ol and dash-dot-dot (blue) line represents 2-methylpropan-2-ol.

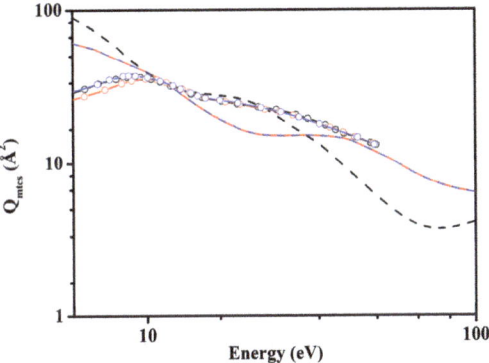

Figure 11. Momentum transfer cross-section for butanol isomers: present results are depicted as lines and results from Bettega et al. are shown as lines with open circles. Butan-2-ol results are shown in black, 2-methylpropan-1-ol in red and 2-methypropan-2-ol results in blue colour.

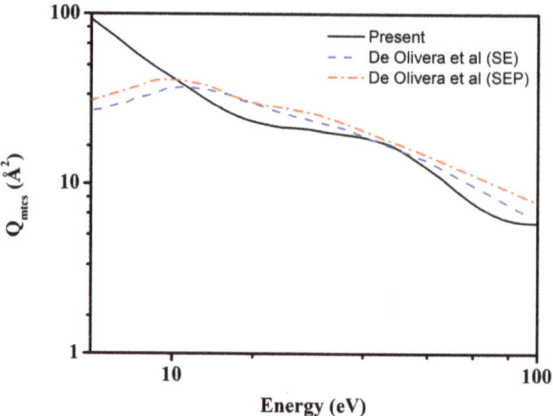

Figure 12. Momentum transfer cross-section of pentan-1-ol: solid (black) line shows present results, dashed (blue) lines show calculated (SE) results of de Oliviera et al. and dash-dot (red) line represents calculated (SEP) results of de Oliviera et al.

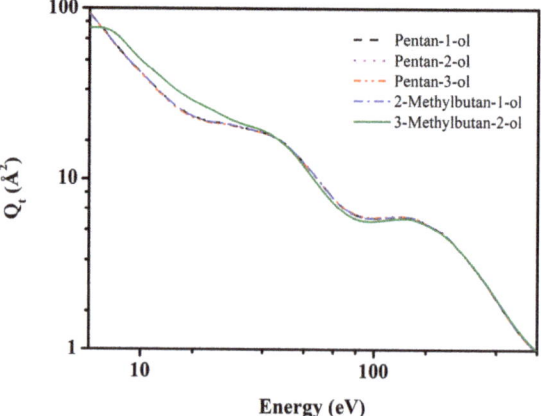

Figure 13. Momentum transfer cross-section of pentanol isomers: dashed (black) line represents penta-1-ol, dotted (purple) is for pentan-2-ol, dash-dot-dot (red) line is for pentan-3-ol, dash-dot (blue) line represents 2-methylbutan-1-ol and solid (olive) line represents 3-methylbutan-2-ol results.

3.1. Elastic Cross-Section

Our elastic cross-section values for butan-1-ol (Figure 1) were on the higher side for lower energies (<10 eV) as compared to the experimental data of Khakoo et al. [26], their calculated results and that of Gomes et al. [27]. This may be inherent to our methodology and can be attributed to the fact that we considered inelastic channels open at the first excitation energy albeit there being no distinction between the various open channels. The number of scattering centres in straight chain isomers was larger than the branched ones in our implementation of group additivity rule [10], to which their higher cross-section values below the ionization threshold can be attributed. This, however, improved the overall results, especially in the context of contribution to energies above the ionisation threshold. The agreement with experimental results at intermediate energies, therefore, was reasonable within the given stated range of uncertainties. Just above the ionization threshold, present data points overestimate the reported results since the inner excitations were not included in the present case. These inner excitations were dominating inelastic channels besides the ionization above the ionization threshold. Therefore, elastic cross-section reduces significantly just above the ionization threshold. Our results (Figure 2) show a distinct difference in the elastic cross-sections of straight chain isomers as compared to the branched ones, and the same can be observed in the results of Bettega et al. [28] too, although the difference in their case is marginal. It is noteworthy here, that the branched isomers of alcohols are polar molecules due to the presence of hydroxyl group. This effect is mitigated for straight chain isomers.

The integral elastic cross-sections of pentan-1-ol reported by de Oliviera et al. [29] have higher values at intermediate energies than calculated elastic cross-sections of Bhardvaja et al. [30] and our results (Figure 3), though the trends appear similar. The effect of the isomeric structure on the elastic cross-section of pentanol isomers, however, appears to be of minor significance in our results (Figure 4) except for 3-methylbutan-2-ol. This deviation from the trend in comparison with butanol isomers needs more investigation, as this secondary amyl alcohol has a methyl group as well as a hydroxyl group attached to the inner carbon atoms.

3.2. Total Cross-Section

The experimental total cross-section (TCS) for butan-1-ol reported by Gomes et al. [27] in the energy range 80–400 eV starts off higher than all theoretically calculated cross-sections, including their own and falls of more rapidly approaching 400 eV. All theoretical calculations, more or less, show an identical trend in results, though differing in magnitude. Our results are in excellent agreement with experimental data between 250 and 400 eV. Gomes et al. [27] derived a 'hybrid TCS' from the elastic integral cross-section of Khakoo et al. and the calculated total ionization cross-section of Ghosh et al. [31] by adding Binary-Encounter-Bethe (BEB) with an implementation of outer valence Green's function (OVGF), which is shown in (Figure 5). Given the fact that there is a difference in magnitude of the 'hybrid TCS' and experimental TCS of Gomes et al. [27], it is noteworthy that our results at the lower end of intermediate energies are in good agreement with the former and at the higher end with the latter. A comparison of total cross-sections of butanol isomers (Figure 6) continues to display the trend observed in the case of our results for their elastic cross-sections.

Our calculated TCS of pentan-1-ol (Figure 7) is in very good agreement with the calculated results of Bhardvaja et al. [30], except for very low and very high energies. There are no experimental results available for the same to the best of our knowledge for comparison with our data. Interestingly, the TCS results of pentanol isomers (Figure 8) inherited the same features from their elastic cross-sections and here again, 3-methylbutan-2-ol displays a deviation from the trend observed in butanol isomers.

3.3. Momentum Transfer Cross-Section

The Q_{mtcs} results of butan-1-ol from our calculations (Figure 9) are in excellent agreement with experimental results of Khakoo et al. [26] and the theoretical results of Bettega et al. [28]. Here again our results below 10 eV were quite high as compared to the other two. The reason is same as for the elastic curve.

As far as a comparison of our Q_{mtcs} results for butanol isomers (Figure 10) is concerned, they showed a similar trend as Q_{el} and Q_t, i.e., the values were higher in magnitude for straight chain isomers than the branched ones. The agreement, when compared with calculated results (Figure 11) of Bettega et al. [28], is in parts and is better for butan-2-ol.

There are no experimental data available for pentan-1-ol to the best of our knowledge, hence, we compared the present results (Figure 12) with static-exchange and static-exchange plus polarization calculations of de Oliviera et al. [29], which are in very good agreement with our results except for energies lower than the ionisation threshold. Since there is no experimental or theoretical data available for Q_{mtcs} of isomers except for pentan-1-ol, a comparison of our results (Figure 13) shows that they are in line with the observations for our elastic and total cross-sections. The isomer effect here again is not significant for the ones other than 3-methylbutan-2-ol, which has values higher in magnitude in low to intermediate energy range as compared to others. The trend shown by all isomers, however, is consistent and along expected lines.

4. Conclusions

Electron-scattering elastic, total and momentum transfer cross-sections for butanol and pentanol isomers were calculated and presented in this study. The SCOP method was employed for the calculations. Taking into consideration the large size of the molecules, the group additivity rule was used with scattering centres identified based on the electrostatic potential surface generated for each target. The first excited states were calculated for all the target species and cross-sections are reported for incident electron energies ranging from 6 to 5000 eV. With this dataset, the cross-section database is complete for both butanol and pentanol isomers. While our elastic and total cross-sections for most target isomers are in good agreement with available measured and/or calculated results, our momentum transfer cross-section calculations are in excellent agreement with available data for butan-1-ol. There was a small but significant difference observed in the cross-sections of straight chain and branched isomers, although the trends are contrary for butanol and pentanol, which is not appreciable at higher energies.

Author Contributions: N.U. and B.A. conceived of the presented idea. N.U. performed the computations. P.M. assisted with calculations. B.A. supervised the work. All authors discussed the results and contributed to the final manuscript. All authors have read and agreed to the published version of the manuscript.

Funding: This research received no external funding.

Data Availability Statement: Data available on request from the authors.

Conflicts of Interest: The authors declare no conflict of interest.

References

1. Erdiwansyah; Mamat, R.; Sani, M.; Sudhakar, K.; Kadarohman, A.; Sardjono, R. An overview of higher alcohol and biodiesel as alternative fuels in engines. *Energy Rep.* **2019**, *5*, 467–479. [CrossRef]
2. Lopes, M.C.A.; Silva, D.G.M.; Bettega, M.H.F.; da Costa, R.F.; Lima, M.A.P.; Khakoo, M.A.; Winstead, C.; McKoy, V. Low Energy Electron Scattering from Fuels. *J. Phys. Conf. Ser.* **2012**, *388*, 012014. [CrossRef]
3. Ridenti, M.; Filho, J.; Brunger, M.; Lima, M.P. Electron scattering by biomass molecular fragments: Useful data for plasma applications? *Eur. Phys. J. D* **2016**, *70*, 16. [CrossRef]
4. Boudaïffa, B.; Cloutier, P.; Hunting, D.; Huels, M.A.; Sanche, L. Resonant formation of DNA strand breaks by low-energy (3 to 20 eV) electrons. *Science* **2000**, *287*, 1658–1660.
5. Sanz, A.G.; Fuss, M.C.; Muñoz, A.; Blanco, F.; Limão-Vieira, P.; Brunger, M.J.; Buckman, S.J.; Garcia, G. Modelling low energy electron and positron tracks for biomedical applications. *Int. J. Radiat. Biol. Inf. UK Ltd.* **2011**, *88*, 71–76. [CrossRef]
6. Joshipura, K.N.; Antony, B.; Vinodkumar, M. Electron scattering and ionization of ozone, O2 and O4 molecules. *J. Phys. B At. Mol. Opt. Phys.* **2002**, *35*, 4211–4221. [CrossRef]
7. Sarathy, S.M.; Park, S.; Weber, B.; Wang, W.; Veloo, P.S.; Davis, A.C.; Togbe, C.; Westbrook, C.K.; Park, O.; Dayma, G.; et al. A comprehensive experimental and modeling study of iso-pentanol combustion. *Combust. Flame* **2013**, *160*, 2712–2728. [CrossRef]
8. Campbell, L.; Brunger, M. Electron collisions in atmospheres. *Int. Rev. Phys. Chem.* **2016**, *35*, 297–351. [CrossRef]
9. Tanaka, H.; Brunger, M.J.; Campbell, L.; Kato, H.; Hoshino, M.; Rau, A.R.P. Scaled plane-wave Born cross sections for atoms and molecules. *Rev. Mod. Phys.* **2016**, *88*, 025004. [CrossRef]
10. Uddin, N.; Verma, P.; Alam, M.J.; Ahmad, S.; Antony, B. Electron impact total ionization cross section for C4 and C5 isomeric alcohols. *Int. J. Mass Spectrom.* **2018**, *431*, 37–42. [CrossRef]
11. Jain, A. Electron scattering with methane molecules at 20–500 eV. *J. Chem. Phys.* **1984**, *81*, 724–728. [CrossRef]
12. Joshipura, K.N.; Patel, P.M. Total electron scattering cross sections for NO, CO, and eV). *J. Phys. B At. Mol. Opt. Phys.* **1996**, *29*, 3925–3932. [CrossRef]
13. Joshipura, K.N.; Vinodkumar, M. Various total cross-sections for electron impact on. *Eur. Phys. J. D* **1999**, *5*, 229.
14. Antony, B.; Joshipura, K.; Mason, N. Electron impact ionization studies with aeronomic molecules. *Int. J. Mass Spectrom.* **2004**, *233*, 207–214. [CrossRef]
15. Cox, H.L.; Bonham, R.A. Elastic Electron Scattering Amplitudes for Neutral Atoms Calculated Using the Partial Wave Method at 10, 40, 70, and 100 kV for Z = 1 to Z = 54. *J. Chem. Phys.* **1967**, *47*, 2599–2608. [CrossRef]
16. Hara, S. The Scattering of Slow Electrons by Hydrogen Molecules. *J. Phys. Soc. Jpn.* **1967**, *22*, 710–718.

17. Zhang, X.; Sun, J.; Liu, Y. A new approach to the correlation polarization potential-low-energy electron elastic scattering by the atoms. *J. Phys. B At. Mol. Opt. Phys.* **1992**, *25*, 1893–1897. [CrossRef]
18. Staszewska, G.; Schwenke, D.W.; Thirumalai, D.; Truhlar, D.G. Quasifree-scattering model for the imaginary part of the optical potential for electron scattering. *Phys. Rev. A.* **1983**, *28*, 2740–2751. [CrossRef]
19. Frisch, M.J.; Trucks, G.W.; Schlegel, H.B.; Scuseria, G.E.; Robb, M.A.; Cheeseman, J.R.; Scalmani, G.; Barone, V.; Petersson, G.A.; Nakatsuji, H.; et al. Gaussian~09 Revision, C.01. Available online: https://gaussian.com/g09citation/ (accessed on 1 August 2020).
20. Becke, A.D. Density-functional exchange-energy approximation with correct asymptotic behavior. *Phys. Rev. A* **1988**, *38*, 3098–3100. [CrossRef]
21. Lee, C.; Yang, W.; Parr, R.G. Development of the Colle-Salvetti correlation-energy formula into a functional of the electron density. *Phys. Rev. B* **1988**, *37*, 785–789. [CrossRef]
22. Faizan, M.; Afroz, Z.; Alam, M.J.; Rodrigues, V.; Ahmad, S.; Ahmad, A. Structural, vibrational and electronic absorption characteristics of the monohydrate organic salt of 2-amino-5-bromo-6-methyl-4-pyrimidinol and 2,3-pyrazinedicarboxylic acid: A combined experimental and computational study. *J. Mol. Struct.* **2019**, *1177*, 229–241. [CrossRef]
23. Computational Chemistry Comparison and Benchmark DataBase Release 21 (August 2020) Standard Reference Database 101 National Institute of Standards and Technology. Available online: http://cccbdb.nist.gov/ (accessed on 1 August 2020).
24. Gussoni, M.; Rui, M.; Zerbi, G. Electronic and relaxation contribution to linear molecular polarizability. An analysis of the experimental values. *J. Mol. Struct.* **1998**, *447*, 163–215. [CrossRef]
25. Haynes, W.M. *CRC Handbook of Chemistry and Physics*, 95th ed.; Haynes, W.M., Ed.; CRC Press: Boca Raton, FL, USA, 2014.
26. Khakoo, M.A.; Muse, J.; Silva, H.; Lopes, M.C.A.; Winstead, C.; McKoy, V.; De Oliveira, E.M.; Da Costa, R.F.; Varella, M.; Bettega, M.; et al. Elastic scattering of slow electrons by n-propanol and n-butanol. *Phys. Rev. A* **2008**, *78*, 062714. [CrossRef]
27. Gomes, M.; da Silva, D.G.M.; Fernandes, A.C.P.; Ghosh, S.; Pires, W.A.D.; Jones, D.B.; Blanco, F.; García, G.; Brunger, M.J.; Lopes, M.C.A. Electron scattering from 1-butanol at intermediate impact energies: Total cross sections. *J. Chem. Phys.* **2019**, *150*, 194307. [CrossRef] [PubMed]
28. Bettega, M.; Winstead, C.; McKoy, V. Low-energy electron scattering from C_4H_9OH isomers. *Phys. Rev. A* **2010**, *82*, 062709. [CrossRef]
29. De Oliveira, E.M.; do N Varella, M.T.; Bettega, M.H.F.; Lima, M.A.P. Elastic scattering of slow electrons by n-pentanol alcohol. *Eur. Phys. J. D* **2014**, *68*, 65. [CrossRef]
30. Bharadvaja, A.; Kaur, S.; Baluja, K.L. Study of electron collision from bioalcohols from 10 to 5000 eV. *Eur. Phys. J. D* **2019**, *73*, 251. [CrossRef]
31. Ghosh, S.; Nixon, K.; Pires, W.; Amorim, R.; Neves, R.; Duque, H.; da Silva, D.; Jones, D.; Blanco, F.; Garcia, G.; et al. Electron impact ionization of 1-butanol: II. Total ionization cross sections and appearance energies. *Int. J. Mass Spectrom.* **2018**, *430*, 44–51. [CrossRef]

Few Body Effects in the Electron and Positron Impact Ionization of Atoms

R.I. Campeanu [1,*] and Colm T. Whelan [2]

1. Department of Physics and Astronomy, York University, Toronto, ON M3J 1P3, Canada
2. Physics Department, Old Dominion University, Norfolk, VA 23529, USA; cwhelan@odu.edu
* Correspondence: campeanu@yorku.ca

Abstract: Triple differential cross sections (TDCS) are presented for the electron and positron impact ionization of inert gas atoms in a range of energy sharing geometries where a number of significant few body effects compete to define the shape of the TDCS. Using both positrons and electrons as projectiles has opened up the possibility of performing complementary studies which could effectively isolate competing interactions that cannot be separately detected in an experiment with a single projectile. Results will be presented in kinematics where the electron impact ionization appears to be well understood and using the same kinematics positron cross sections will be presented. The kinematics are then varied in order to focus on the role of distortion, post collision interaction (pci), and interference effects.

Keywords: ionization; electron; positron; few body

1. Introduction

In a coincidence experiment, a projectile of momentum k_0, energy E_0 impinges on a target atom and ionizes it. The ejected electron and scattered projectile are detected with their angles and energies resolved. The momentum vectors of the scattered projectile, k_1 and the ejected electron, k_2, form a plane and thus we can define all possible kinematics by the set $(k_0, k_1, k_2, \Phi, \theta_1, \theta_2)$, where Φ defines the angle k_0 makes to the plane of detection, the "gun angle", see Figure 1.

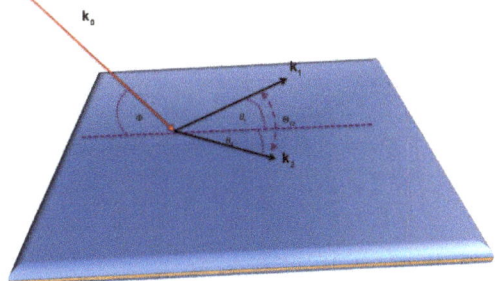

Figure 1. The incoming projectile has momentum $\mathbf{k}_0$ and energy E_0, and it comes in at an angle Φ with respect to the plane in which the two final state particles are detected at angles θ_1, θ_2 with respect to the projection of the incoming direction on their plane. $\Phi = 0°$ corresponds to coplanar geometry, $\Phi = 90°$ to perpendicular plane geometry. Θ_{12} is the angle between the two detected particles.

The great advantage of the coincidence approach is that it allows us to focus on particular geometries and kinematics where three subtle body effects can be observed. In less differential measurements, these effects will be swamped by the gross features of the interactions. Thus far, complementary studies of electron and positron impact ionization have been restricted to asymmetric geometries [1–3] with $E_1 \gg E_2$, and θ_1 small where the triple differential cross section tends to have the same character as the first Born approximation, being symmetric about the direction of momentum transfer with the only significant structures coming from target wave function effects [4]. In these kinematics, it is particularly difficult to disentangle the different few body contributions [5,6]; this problem is enhanced because what few differences there are tend to be in the absolute size of the cross section which is extremely demanding to measure accurately [7]. In this paper, we focus on energy sharing geometries and explore the possibility of observing differences in the shape of the cross section. In energy sharing geometries, we are dealing with a "hard collision" where the incident electron loses more than half its energy; conservation of momentum then requires the lost projectile momentum to be carried off by the recoiling ion and we would, therefore, expect the nucleus to play an important role. The conventional second Born approximation struggles to include the $e^{\pm}$ interaction with the nucleus [8] and is not best suited for these geometries. A full close coupling calculation would be ideal that is very computationally demanding, and it is not readily applicable to multi-electron targets [5,9,10]. Our ambition here is to focus on mechanisms and to give direction to the ongoing coincidence studies of electron and positron impact ionization. The distorted wave Born approximation (DWBA) [11–13] is only the first order in the projectile—target electron interaction; however, it allows for the elastic scattering of the incoming projectiles and outgoing particles in the field of the atom/ion. Furthermore, the DWBA has provided excellent agreement with electron impact ionization in energy sharing kinematics and, because of its relative simplicity and flexibility, is an ideal vehicle to explore positron scattering and the different few body mechanisms.

2. Scattering Approximations

2.1. Electron Impact

In the DWBA, the TDCS for ionization of the nl orbital of an inert gas atom is given by:

$$\frac{d^3\sigma}{d\Omega_1 d\Omega_2 dE} = 2(2\pi)^4 \frac{k_1 k_2}{k_0} \sum_{m=-l}^{l} [|f_{nlm}|^2 + |g_{nlm}|^2 - Re(f^*_{nlm} g_{nlm})] \quad (1)$$

where f is the direct amplitude and g the exchange amplitude. In the DWBA, the direct and exchange amplitudes are given by

$$\begin{aligned} f_{nlm}(\mathbf{k}_1, \mathbf{k}_2) &= \langle \chi^-(\mathbf{k}_1, \mathbf{r}_1) \chi^-(\mathbf{k}_2, \mathbf{r}_2) | \tfrac{1}{\|\mathbf{r}_1 - \mathbf{r}_2\|} | \chi_0^+(\mathbf{k}_0, \mathbf{r}_1) \psi_{nlm}(\mathbf{r}_2) \rangle \\ g_{nlm}(\mathbf{k}_1, \mathbf{k}_2) &= \langle \chi^-(\mathbf{k}_1, \mathbf{r}_2) \chi^-(\mathbf{k}_2, \mathbf{r}_1) | \tfrac{1}{\|\mathbf{r}_1 - \mathbf{r}_2\|} | \chi_0^+(\mathbf{k}_0, \mathbf{r}_1) \psi_{nlm}(\mathbf{r}_2) \rangle \end{aligned} \quad (2)$$

In (2), $\chi_0^+(\mathbf{k}_0, \mathbf{r}_1)$ is the distorted-wave representing the incident electron and is calculated in the static-exchange potential of the neutral atom. The χ^-'s are the distorted waves that are calculated in the static-exchange potentials of the ion and then orthogonalized to ψ_{nlm}. These are normalized to a delta function i.e.,

$$\langle \chi^{\pm}(\mathbf{k}, \mathbf{r}) | \chi^{\pm}(\mathbf{k}', \mathbf{r}) \rangle = \delta(\mathbf{k} - \mathbf{k}') \quad (3)$$

For the target wave functions, we use the Hartree–Fock orbitals given in [14]. The electron–electron interaction occurs exactly once, and no account is taken of post collisional interaction (pci) between the two final state electrons. In our calculations below, the full non-local exchange potential is not used and rather a localized version [13,15–18] is employed. Its use greatly simplifies the static exchange calculations in that one only needs to solve differential rather than integro-differential equations. Because we treat each of the exiting electrons as moving in the field of a spin $\frac{1}{2}$ ion, there is an inherent ambiguity in the choice of exchange potential in the final channels, and we could choose it to be singlet or triplet [9,13]. For most energies, there is little or no difference between results calculated with the singlet or triplet potentials [13,18], but, at low energies, there is a weakness in the singlet form in that, for some energies, it can become complex. A method has been proposed in [16] to make the potential real again if this happens, but this method results in a discontinuous singlet potential and generally gives results in poorer agreement with experiments than the equivalent triplet calculation, see [4,13]. In addition, we orthogonalize both outgoing waves to the bound orbital ψ_{nlm} so that the direct amplitude f_{nlm} has the correct behavior as the momentum transfer $\mathbf{q} \equiv \mathbf{k}_0 - \mathbf{k}_1$ tends to zero.

We can explore the effect of elastic scattering by the atom/ion by "switching" these interactions on and off in (2). This can lead to some interesting insights into what is happening and is a way of investigating multiple scattering mechanisms [12,19]. For example, by replacing the distorted wave $\chi_0^+(\mathbf{k}_0, \mathbf{r}_1)$ with a plane wave $(2\pi)^{-3/2} e^{i\mathbf{k}_0}$, we effectively "switch-off" the interaction between the incoming projectile and the atom.

The neglect of pci will be important at low energies [12,20]. To take some account of it, a Gamow factor N_{e-e-} [12,21] has been employed:

$$\frac{d^3\sigma^{DWBApci}}{d\Omega_1 d\Omega_2 dE} = N_{e-e-} \frac{d^3\sigma^{DWBA}}{d\Omega_1 d\Omega_2 dE} \qquad (4)$$

where

$$N_{e-e-} = \frac{\gamma}{e^\gamma - 1} \qquad (5)$$

with

$$\gamma = \frac{2\pi}{\|\mathbf{k}_1 - \mathbf{k}_2\|} \qquad (6)$$

The N_{e-e-} factor tends to give the dominant angular behavior of the TDCS at low energies, and it does correctly force the cross section to go to zero when $\mathbf{k}_1 = \mathbf{k}_2$. However, the overall normalization is lost. To ameliorate this, it is has been proposed [4,17] to normalize N_{e-e-} so that it is fixed to 1 when the angle between $\mathbf{k}_1$ and $\mathbf{k}_2$ is 180°, i.e., when we have a colinear arrangement. A modified version of the N_{e-e-} factor has been suggested by Ward and Macek [22]. These authors suggested replacing N_{e-e-} with

$$M_{e-e-} = N_{e-e-} |{}_1F_1(-i\nu_3, 1, -2ik_3 r_{3av})|^2 \qquad (7)$$

where

$$\begin{aligned} k_3 &= \tfrac{1}{2}\|\mathbf{k}_1 - \mathbf{k}_2\| \\ \nu_3 &= -\frac{1}{\|\mathbf{k}_1 - \mathbf{k}_2\|} \\ r_{3av} &= \tfrac{3}{\epsilon}[\tfrac{\pi}{4\sqrt{(3)}}(1 + \tfrac{0.627}{\pi}\sqrt{\epsilon}\ln\epsilon)]^2 \end{aligned} \qquad (8)$$

with ϵ being the total energy of the two emerging electrons. The factor r_{3av} was chosen by the requirement that the M_{e-e-} factor reproduces the correct Wannier threshold law. In this way, it is hoped that M_{e-e-} should be able to stand on its own without renormalization. Certainly at low energies, this hope was not realized in the case of helium or hydrogen [4].

2.2. Positron Scattering

The DWBA TDCS equations look similar to (1) and (2), except that, in this case, there is no exchange amplitude g_{nlm} and the distorted-waves $\chi_0^+(\mathbf{k}_0, \mathbf{r}_1)$ and $\chi^-(\mathbf{k}_1, \mathbf{r}_1)$ for the positron are generated in the static potential, which is the minus of the static potential for electron impact. The distorted-wave $\chi^-(\mathbf{k}_2, \mathbf{r}_2)$ for the slow ejected electron is orthogonalized to the bound state. There is now no longer any ambiguity in the choice of exchange potential. The ground state of our targets is spin singlet ($S = 0$) and therefore the ejected electron wave function must be calculated in the singlet static-exchange potential.

To estimate pci, we now change the sign of γ in (5).

$$N_{e+e-} = \frac{\Gamma}{e^\Gamma - 1} \qquad (9)$$

with

$$\Gamma = -\frac{2\pi}{\|\mathbf{k}_1 - \mathbf{k}_2\|} \qquad (10)$$

We still have the problem of choosing a normalization. Once again, we could assume that, when the three particles are colinear ($\theta_{12} = 180°$), the pci effects are minimal and normalize $N_{e^+e^-} = 1$ at the point. This is not ideal but is probably the best we can do. An undesirable feature is that, while $N_{e^-e^-} \to 0$ as $\Theta_{12} \to 0$, $N_{e^+e^-}$ goes to infinity in this limit, see Figure 2.

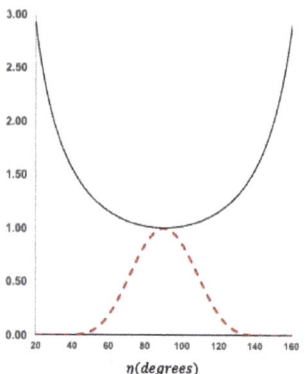

Figure 2. Plot of the Gamov factors for electron, dashed red and positron, solid black, with $\theta_1 = \theta_2, E_1 = E_2 = 1$ eV.

3. Results

3.1. Coplanar Symmetric Geometry

In these geometries, both outgoing particles have equal energies $E_1 = E_2$ and are detected with the same angle,

$$\eta = \theta_1 = \theta_2 = \frac{\Theta_{12}}{2} \qquad (11)$$

The incoming projectile loses more than half its kinetic energy in the interaction; in such a "hard" collision, one expects collisions with the nucleus to play an important role and, as such, they are ideal testing grounds for the DWBA. There are a number of interesting experiments in coplanar symmetric geometry (i.e., $\Phi = 0°$) [23–25]. For impact energies between 500 eV and 100 eV, the DWBA does well. We illustrate this in Figure 3a. The physics underlying the form of the TDCS are easily understood in terms of a simple model [26] in which the target electron is assumed to be at rest relative to its nucleus, and the ionization process is viewed as a free collision between the incident and target electron. Two mechanisms leading to a coplanar symmetric final state may be distinguished. In the first, the incident electron collides with a target electron; conservation of energy and momentum would suggest that the electrons would emerge at 90° to each other. Of course, this is an over simplification since we should also take into account the fact that the target electron is not free but is in an atom with a definite binding energy and momentum distribution. Nevertheless, we would expect this mechanism to be responsible for the main peak near $\eta = 45°$. The second mechanism involves a double collision in which the incident electron is first elastically backscattered from the nucleus, and then the ionization process is, as before, a nearly free electron–electron collision with the electrons emerging at right angles to each other but now in the backward directions, i.e., at $\eta = 135°$. The DWBA contains both mechanisms, and we do as expected see two peaks at approximately the correct angles. It is instructive to perform a model calculation where the incident electron is replaced with a plane wave, and we designate this approximation as DWD-WPW. Intuitively, in DWDWPW, the second mechanism is effectively "switched off". In Figure 3b, we show a comparison between the DWBA and the DWDWPW. As expected, the large angle peak has disappeared. In addition, in Figure 3b, we show the DWBA calculation for positron impact ionization. There is no large peak in the positron case but rather an intimation of a suppressed structure where the peak should be. We interpret this as a reflection of the weaker backward scattering of positrons as compared to electrons.

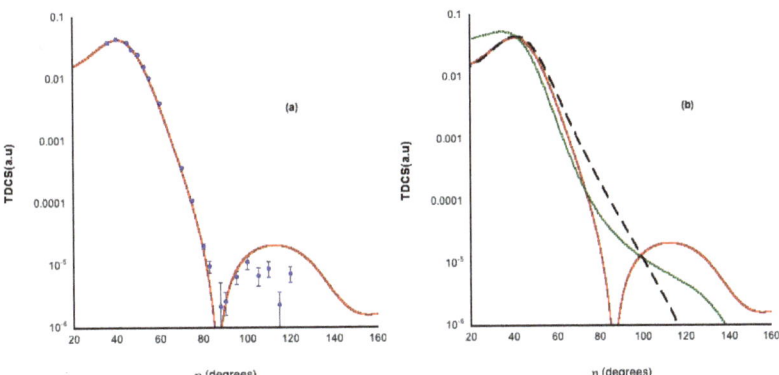

Figure 3. TDCS for the ionization of helium in coplanar symmetric geometry (i.e., $\Phi = 0°$) for $E_0 = 200$ eV. (**a**) Electron impact: experiment [25], theory DWBA (singlet exchange potential), no polarization no pci, experiment was relative and has been normalized to give the best visual fit to the DWBA; (**b**) Comparison of the TDCS calculated in the DWBA for positron: dotted green line, for electron: DWBA, solid red and the model calculation, DWDWPW, dashed black.

As the impact energy is lowered, the DWBA, as given by (1) and (2), performs less well. Experiment [24,27] finds a large angle peak that grows relative to the binary as the impact energy is decreased until it is approximately equal to the binary for $E_0 = 50$ eV [24]. On the other hand, the large angle peak in the DWBA remains orders of magnitude smaller. The DWBA takes no account of polarization or capture of the incoming electron into the final ion state, nor of electron–electron repulsion in the final state—all of which could be quite important not only as effects in themselves but also as they interfere with each other. In [12], an attempt was made to take these effects in a simple model: pci was included via the Gamov factor and an "ad-hock" polarization potential added in the initial and final channel, i.e.,

$$V_{pol} = \begin{cases} -\frac{\alpha}{2r^4} & r \geq r_0 \\ -\frac{\alpha}{2r_0^4} & r < r_0 \end{cases} \quad (12)$$

where $\alpha = 1.39$ was the polarizability of neutral helium $He(1s^2)$ in the incident channel and the polarizability of $He^+(1s)$ ($\alpha = 0.28125$) for the outgoing channels and $r_0 = 0.7565$. It was only with the combination of both pci and polarization for which shape agreement could be found with experiment. The polarization potential used in [12] was essentially chosen to give good agreement with the experiments of [24], but it worked well for a range of low energies. We show an example in Figure 4. Whelan et al. [28] extended the model to hydrogen where the incident channel polarization potential defined by analogy to He, i.e., α was taken to be the polarizability of H and

$$r_0^H = r_0^{He} \frac{<r>_H}{<r>_{He}} \quad (13)$$

where $<r>$ denotes the expectation value of r in the ground state of the atom. Whelan et al. [28] predicted that a double peak structure would be seen in coplanar symmetric geometry for H at an impact energy of 20 eV, a prediction that was immediately confirmed by experiment [29,30]. The positron results in Figure 4c show nothing of the structure found in the electron case.

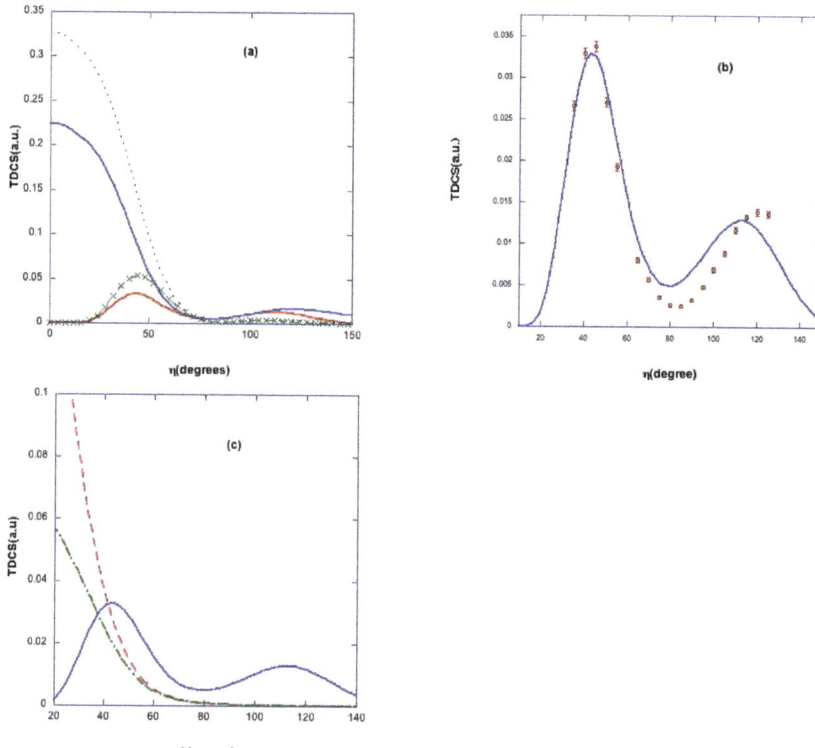

Figure 4. TDCS for the ionization of helium in coplanar symmetric geometry (i.e., $\Phi = 0°$) for $E_0 = 54.6$ eV. (**a**) Various theoretical curves for electron impact, dotted black: DWBA (singlet exchange potential); solid blue: DWBA (singlet exchange potential) with polarization but no pci, green dashed line with crosses: DWBA (singlet exchange potential) with pci but no polarization; red solid line, DWBA with polarization and pci; (**b**) Electron impact; experiment [27], theory DWBA (singlet exchange potential) with polarization and pci; (**c**) Solid blue curve DWBA (singlet exchange potential) for electron impact with polarization and pci, dashed red curve DWBA for positron impact with polarization and pci, green dashed-double dotted DWBA for positron impact with polarization but no pci.

3.2. Non Coplanar Energy Sharing Geometries

In the electron experiments of [31] on helium, the angle Φ was varied and a deep minimum in the TDCS observed for $\Phi = 67.5°$ (see Figure 5). In [20,32], DWBA calculations were presented, and the deep minimum reproduced. In the same paper, it was shown that the minimum existed even in the simplest calculation of this type where neither polarization nor post collisional electron–electron interaction was included. Rasch et al. explored the possibility of such distinct interference effects being observed in other targets, and they found that such a structure would be observed in other closed shell atoms but only for s states. They **predicted** such that it would be evident in $Ne(2s)$ at an impact energy of 110.5 eV for $\Phi \approx 42°$. This predication was subsequently confirmed [33]; see Figure 6. In addition, shown in this figure is the DWBA with $N_{e^-e^-}$ and the deep minimum is still visible, but, as would be expected, the cross section is reduced for smaller values of Θ_{12}. The equivalent positron impact calculation is also shown. The deep minimum has been replaced by a shallower and wider one, and the minimum value shifted towards smaller η values. The inclusion of $N_{e^+e^-}$ enhances the cross section for smaller Θ_{12} values.

In Figure 5, we show the experimental TDCS for the electron impact ionization of He [31] compared with our DWBA calculation, with and without pci. The minimum persists if shifted by a few degrees once polarization is added. Recently, in [34], this geometry was reexamined in a number of approximations. Their time dependent close coupling calculation (TDCC) is reasonably close to the DWBA, but their 3DW approximation only gives a shallow indentation at the critical angle, and, while both the Coulomb Born calculations (with and without M_{e-e-}) produce a deep minimum it has been shifted to larger angles away from the experiment and is four orders of magnitude too deep. In Figure 5b, we show the positron impact TDCS, in the DWBA, for the same kinematics. A deep minimum is no longer seen.

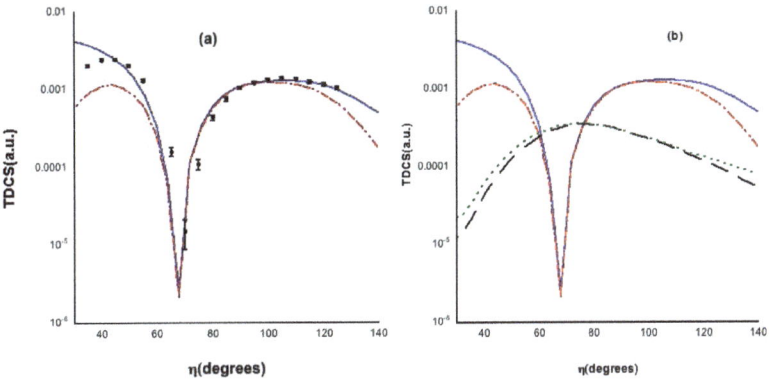

Figure 5. TDCS for ionization of helium with a projectile impact energy of $E_0 = 64.6$ eV, and "gun angle" of $\Phi = 67.5°$: (**a**) comparison of theory and experiment for electron impact, experiment [31]: solid blue curve DWBA (using singlet exchange) with no pci; red dashed double dotted DWBA (singlet exchange potential) with pci; (**b**) electron impact as in subfigure (**a**), positron impact black dashed DWBA (singlet exchange potential), no pci, dotted green, DWBA (singlet exchange potential) with pci.

In order to produce the sharp features seen in Figure 5, we undertook a series of model calculations, shown in Figure 7.

First, we considered a first Born approximation type calculation, i.e., a non exchange calculation with a plane wave for the incoming and scattered electron and the wavefunction of the ejected electron calculated in the static potential of the ion and no pci. Next, we added the N_{e-e-} factor "switched on" the singlet static exchange potential distortion for the scattered electron; this we designate as PWDWPW. Then, we "switched on" distortion for the ejected electron, and this is our DWDWPW model. Finally, we replaced the scattered electron plane wave with a distorted wave to give us the regular DWBA. It is only when we have distorted waves in both the incident and final channels do we see the sharp minimum. The minimum is to be seen with and without pci and the inclusion of polarization makes no difference. It is found only when we include distortion for all the electrons. It is entirely absent from the positron calculation. Our model calculations indicate that it is not a result of pci nor of target polarization and is only present when we allow for the elastic scattering for both the incoming and outgoing electrons. The evaluation of the TDCS involves computing a six-dimensional integral over a highly oscillatory argument, and, as such, destructive interference effects may yield very small values for certain cases. This is the only explanation that is consistent with all the model calculations. Thus, we can interpret the structure as the result of a purely quantum mechanical interference effect. This is in agreement with the predictions of [20] for neon.

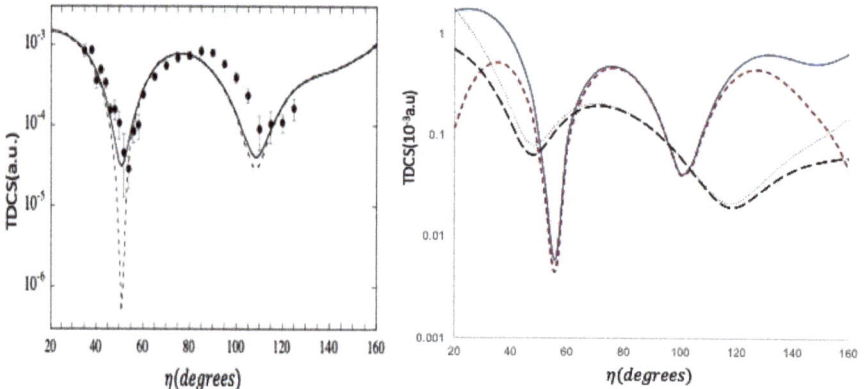

Figure 6. Left panel: TDCS for the electron impact ionization of $Ne(2s)$, $E_0 = 110.5$ eV, $\Phi = 42°$, experimental points [33]; solid line DWBA calculation of [20], dashed line theory convoluted over the experimental angular uncertainty. **Right panel**: TDCS for the electron and positron impact ionization of $Ne(2s)$, $E = 37$ eV, $\Phi = 40°$, electron impact DWBA (singlet exchange potential), solid blue, DWBA (singlet exchange potential)+$N_{e^-e^-}$ short dashed red, positron impact: DWBA, long dashed black, DWBA+$N_{e^+e^-}$, green dotted.

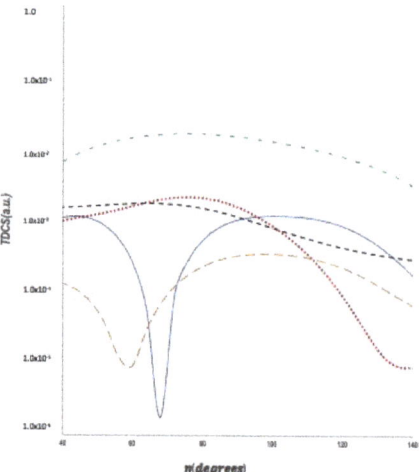

Figure 7. TDCS for the electron impact ionization of helium, $E_0 = 64.6$ eV, $\Phi = 67.5°$ comparison of different model calculations: 1st Born, as described in the text dotted black line; PWDWPW: purple dashed line; DWDWPW green dashed dotted line; DWBA solid blue line.

It is of interest to see if the same type of structure can be observed in open shell systems. In [13], a similar deep minimum was observed in the TDCS for the electron impact of hydrogen in coplanar symmetric geometry for an impact energy of 29 eV in a pure DWBA calculation with no pci or polarization. However, when pci and polarization are added, this deep minimum disappears, and this is probably a refection of the very strong polarization potential used. A recent paper [35] predicts, using a Coulomb Born (CB1) approximation, that there will be a deep minimum in the TDCS for the positron impact ionization of hydrogen at an impact energy of 100 eV and a gun angle of 56.13°. We have repeated their calculation using the DWBA, (see Figure 8) and while there is something of the same feature in our DWBA calculations, our dip is seven orders of magnitude shallower, and it is wider. This not altogether surprising since interference effects are very delicate, and it is likely that the position and magnitude of this effect in the Coulomb Born calculations of [35] will depend on their choice of effective charge, which is somewhat arbitrary.

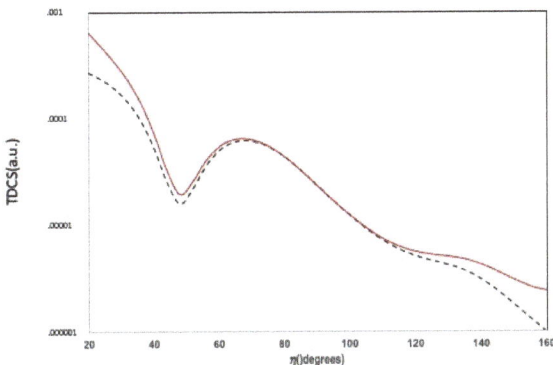

Figure 8. TDCS for the positron impact ionization of hydrogen in energy sharing geometry, $E_0 = 100$ eV, $\Phi = 56.13°$. DWBA:solid red DWBA $+N_{e^+e^-}$: dashed black

3.3. Energy Sharing Perpendicular Plane Geometry

There are experiments in the perpendicular plane [27,36], i.e., $\Phi = 90°$. These experiments were analyzed in [12,19] with a simple multiple scattering argument to explain the general behavior of the cross section and obtained very good agreement with the experiment using a DWBA approach. Within the DWBA, there are only two paths to the perpendicular plane:

1. Single scattering: For a free collision between an incident and a stationary electron resulting in two outgoing electrons of equal energy, conservation of energy and momentum requires all three vectors $\mathbf{k}_0, \mathbf{k}_1, \mathbf{k}_2$ to lie in the same plane with $\Theta_{12} = 90°$. Now, the atomic electron is not free but rather in a bound state with a momentum distribution, for both electrons to end up in the perpendicular plane as the result of a single collision, the incoming electron would have to collide with a bound electron that had momentum

$$\mathbf{k} = \boldsymbol{\kappa} - \mathbf{k}_0 \qquad (14)$$

where $\boldsymbol{\kappa} \cdot \mathbf{k}_0 = 0$, thus both electrons will emerge in the perpendicular plane with momentum $\boldsymbol{\kappa} = \mathbf{k}_1 + \mathbf{k}_2$. Since the electron distribution in the helium atom is sharply peaked to zero, the most probable value will be

$$\begin{aligned} \kappa &= 0 \\ &= \mathbf{k}_1 + \mathbf{k}_2 \\ \Rightarrow \mathbf{k}_1 &= -\mathbf{k}_2 \\ \Rightarrow \Theta_{12} &= 180° \end{aligned} \qquad (15)$$

Thus, for single scattering, one would expect a single peak at $\eta = 90°$. This is purely a wavefunction effect, and it would be misleading to interpret the back to back emission as being in some way related to the Wannier mechanism [37], since the peak is seen in the DWBA without pci.

2. Double scattering: here, the incoming electron is first elastically scattered into the plane perpendicular to the incoming beam and then in a second collision ionizes the atom with both final state electrons coming out at roughly 90° to each other.

As $\|\mathbf{k}_0\|$ increases, it becomes more difficult for the electron to ionize via the single scattering mechanism and thus the double scattering mechanism will dominate at higher energies, and the most favorable condition for single scattering will be $\mathbf{k}_0 \approx 0$. This interpretation was is in qualitative accordance with the experiment of [27,36]. At the lowest energy, a single peak at $\eta = \frac{\Theta_{12}}{2} = 90°$ is observed. As the impact energy is increased, secondary peaks are observed in the vicinity of $\eta = 45°$ and $135°$.

The DWBA calculations [12] reproduce these features and are generally in good agreement with the relative experiments. At low energies, Ehrhardt and collaborators [38,39] measured the cross sections for a fixed angle of $\Theta_{12} = 180°$, and a common point to all the planes was obtained by rotating the gun angle. In Figure 9 (left panel), we show a comparison between this absolute measurement and the distorted wave approximation scaled by the $M_{e^-e^-}$ and $N_{e^-e^-}$, with the latter normalized to 1 when $\Theta_{12} = 180°$. The DWBA +$N_{e^-e^-}$ is in remarkably good agreement with the absolute experimental value while the DWBA+$M_{e^-e^-}$ is significantly too small. The DWBA with $N_{e^-e^-}$ also gives a better fit to the relative measurements of [40] (middle panel). In Figure 9 (right panel), we also show a comparison between the $(e^-,2e^-)$ and (e^+,e^+e^-) cross sections, for the small energy E values. In both the electron and positron cases, there is no indication of a double scattering peak, and the positron cross section is much smaller.

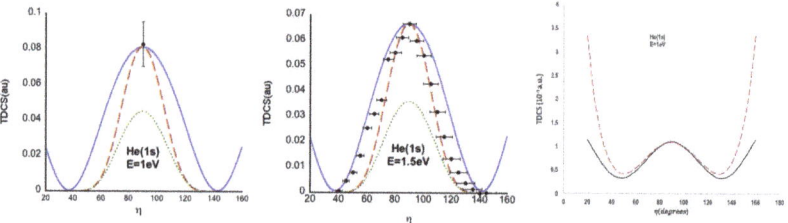

Figure 9. TDCS for the ionization of helium with $\Phi = 90°, \theta_1 = \theta_2 = \eta, E_1 = E_2 = E$ eV. Electron impact: The absolute measurement of [38] (**left panel**) is shown, and the relative measurements of [40] (**middle panel**) the DWBA (triplet exchange) without pci, solid blue line; DWBA with $N_{e^-e^-}$ factor normalized to 1 at $\Theta = 180°$, dashed red line, DWBA with $M_{e^-e^-}$ dotted green line; Positron impact (**right panel**): DWBA without pci, solid black line, DWBA +$N_{e^+e^-}$, dashed red.

In Figure 10, we show a comparison between theory and experiment for $E_0 = 64.6$, $E = 20$ eV. The "double scattering" peaks are visible in the electron case for DWBA without pci, and its addition tends to suppress the peaks at $45°$ and $135°$, even though they are still clearly visible in the measurement. It would appear that, in this case, the use of $N_{e^-e^-}$ is too strong. We also show the DWBA for positron impact which is now almost structureless and much smaller in size.

In the positron case, the cross section is greatly reduced in absolute size, and the double scattering peaks at $\eta \approx 45°$ and $\eta \approx 13°$ are missing for all impact energies. For our lowest energy $E_1 = E_2 = 1$ eV, in Figure 9, we do see a peak in the positron case for $\eta = 90°$, but the maximum value is much smaller than in the electron case. For $E_1 = E_2 = 20$ eV, this peak completely disappears.

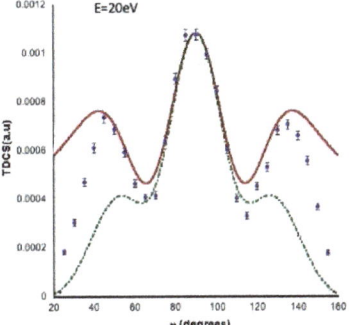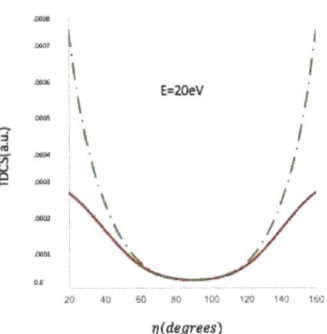

Figure 10. TDCS for electron (**left panel**) and positron impact (**right panel**) ionization of helium in the perpendicular plane ($\Phi = 90°$), $E_0 = 64.6$ eV, experimental points [31]. The theoretical curves are: solid red curve: DWBA with no pci; green dashed dotted DWBA with pci.

4. Conclusions

Our electron scattering calculations show many interesting structures that highlight different and sometimes competing few body effects. In coplanar symmetric geometry, we find that, for high impact energies, the DWBA theory correctly reproduces the experimental results. However, for low impact energies, the agreement with the experiment is obtained only by adding corrections for both polarization and post-collisional electron–electron interaction. For non-coplanar symmetric geometries, a deep minimum in the TDCS is seen experimentally for certain gun angles. The DWBA theory reproduces this minimum even without polarization and pci. We interpret these structures in terms of interference effects, and it is necessary to allow for both the elastic scattering of the incoming electron and the exiting electrons if these structures are to appear. The experimental data in the perpendicular plane are well reproduced by the DWBA approximation that allows for two different pathways into the perpendicular plane, a single scattering mechanism at low impact energies, and a multiple scattering mechanism at elevated energies. The equivalent structures in the positron case are much less pronounced. Indeed, we find little evidence for the strong interference effects that are seen in the TDCS for e^+ on atomic hydrogen in the Coulomb Born calculations of [35]. The particular structures predicted in the Coulomb Born calculations are probably an artifact of the choice of effective charge.

Author Contributions: Both authors worked closely together during the entire project including the writing of this paper. All authors have read and agreed to the published version of the manuscript.

Funding: The research received financial support from the Natural Science and Engineering Research Council of Canada.

Acknowledgments: We thank Andrew Murray for supplying us with his data.

Conflicts of Interest: The authors declare no conflict of interest.

References

1. Du Bois, R.D.; Gavin, J.; de Lucio, O.G. Differential cross sections for ionization of argon by 1 keV positron and electron impact. *J. Phys. Conf. Ser.* **2014**, *488*, 072004. [CrossRef]
2. Gavin, J.; de Lucio, O.G.; DuBois, R.D. Triply differential measurements of single ionization of argon by 1-keV positron and electron impact. *Phys. Rev. A* **2017**, *95*, 062703. [CrossRef]
3. Campeanu, R.I.; Walters, H.R.J.; Whelan, C.T. The electron and positron impact ionization of inert gases. *Phys. Rev. A* **2018**, *97*, 062702. [CrossRef]
4. Miller, F.K.; Whelan, C.T.; Walters, H.R.J. Energy sharing (e,2e) collisions-ionization of the inert gases in the perpendicular plane. *Phys. Rev. A* **2015**, *91*, 012706. [CrossRef]

5. Curran, E.P.; Whelan, C.T.; Walters, H.R.J. On the electron impact ionisation of H(1s) in coplanar asymmetric geometry. *J. Phys. B At. Mol. Opt. Phys.* **1991**, *24*, L19. [CrossRef]
6. Lucey, S.P.; Rasch, J.; Whelan, C.T. On the use of analytic ansatz wavefunctions in the study of (e,2e) processes. *Proc. R. Soc. A* **1999**, *455*, 349. [CrossRef]
7. Rasch, J.; Whelan, C.T.; Allan, R.J.; Walters, H.R.J. The normalization of the experimental triple differential cross section of noble gas atoms in extreme asymmetric geometry. In *Electron and Photon Impact Ionization*; Whelan, C.T., Walters, H.R.J., Eds.; Plenum: New York, NY, USA, 1997; pp. 305–318.
8. Walters, H.R.J. Perturbative methods in electron- and positron-atom scattering. *Phys. Rep.* **1984**, *116*, 1. [CrossRef]
9. Curran, E.P.; Walters, H.R.J. Triple differential cross sections for electron impact ionisation of atomic hydrogen—A coupled pseudostate calculation. *J. Phys. B At. Mol. Opt. Phys.* **1987**, *20*, 333. [CrossRef]
10. Bartlett, P.L.; Stelbovics, A.T. The application of propagating exterior complex scaling in atomic collisions. In *Fragmentation Processes: Topics in Atomic and Molecular Physics*; Whelan, C.T., Ed.; Cambridge University Press: Cambridge, UK, 2013; pp. 48–71.
11. Madison, D.H.; Calhoun, R.V.; Shelton, W.N. Triple-differential cross sections for electron-impact ionization of helium. *Phys. Rev. A* **1977**, *16*, 552. [CrossRef]
12. Whelan, C.T.; Allan, R.J.; Walters, H.R.J.; Zhang, X. (e,2e), effective charges, distorted waves and all that ! In $(e,2e)$ & *Related Processes*; Whelan, C.T., Walters, H.R.J., Lahmam-Bennani, A., Ehrhardt, H., Eds.; Kluwer: Dordrecht, The Netherlands, 1993; pp. 33–74.
13. Rasch, J. (e,2e) Processes with Neutral Atom Targets. Ph.D. Thesis, University of Cambridge, Cambridge, UK, 1996.
14. Clementi, E.; Roetti, C. Roothan-Hartree-Fock atomic wavefunctions. *At. Data Nucl. Data Tables* **1974**, *14*, 177. [CrossRef]
15. Furness, J.B.; Carthy, I.E.M. Semi phenomenological optical model for electron scattering. *J. Phys. B At. Mol. Opt. Phys.* **1973**, *6*, 2280. [CrossRef]
16. Riley, M.E.; Truhlar, D.G. Approximations for exchange potentials in electron scattering. *J. Chem. Phys.* **1975**, *63*, 2182. [CrossRef]
17. Martinez, J.M.; Walters, H.R.J.; Whelan, C.T. The electron impact ionization of one and two electron atoms and ions close to the ionization threshold. *J. Phys. B At. Mol. Opt. Phys.* **2008**, *41*, 065202. [CrossRef]
18. Bransden, B.H.; McDowell, M.R.C.; Noble, C.J.; Scott, T. Equivalent exchange potentials in electron scattering. *J. Phys. B At. Mol. Opt. Phys.* **1976**, *9*, 1301. [CrossRef]
19. Zhang, X.; Whelan, C.T.; Walters, H.R.J. (e,2e) cross sections for the ionisation of helium in coplanar symmetric geometry. *J. Phys. B At. Mol. Opt. Phys.* **1990**, *23*, L509. [CrossRef]
20. Rasch, J.; Whelan, C.T.; Allan, R.J.; Lucey, S.P.; Walters, H.R.J. Strong interference effects in the triple differential cross section of neutral atom targets. *Phys. Rev. A* **1997**, *56*, 1379. [CrossRef]
21. Botero, J.; Macek, J.H. Threshold angular distributions of(e,2e) cross sections of helium atoms. *Phys. Rev. Lett.* **1992**, *68*, 576. [CrossRef]
22. Ward, S.J.; Macek, J.H. Wave functions for continuum states of charged fragments. *Phys. Rev. A* **1994**, *49*, 1049. [CrossRef]
23. Pochat, A.; Tweed, R.J.; Peresses, J.; Joachain, J.; Piraux, C.B.; Byron, F.W., Jr. Second-order effects in large-angle coplanar symmetric (e, 2e) processes. *J. Phys. B At. Mol. Opt. Phys.* **1983**, *16*, L755. [CrossRef]
24. Rösel, T.; Dupré, C.; Röder, J.; Duguet, A.; Jung, K.; Lahmam-Bennani, A.; Ehrhardt, H. Coplanar symmetric(e,2e) cross sections on helium and neon. *J. Phys. B At. Mol. Opt. Phys.* **1991**, *24*, 3059. [CrossRef]
25. Frost, L.; Freienstein, P.; Wagner, M. 200 eV coplanar symmetric (e,2e) on helium: A sensitive test of reaction models. *J. Phys. B At. Mol. Opt. Phys.* **1990**, *23*, L715. [CrossRef]
26. Zhang, X.; Whelan, C.T.; Walters, H.R.J. Energy sharing (e,2e) collisions-ionisation of Helium in the perpendicular plane. *J. Phys. B At. Mol. Opt. Phys.* **1990**, *23*, L173. [CrossRef]
27. Murray, A.J. Electron impact ionization using (e,2e) coincidence techniques from threshold to intermediate energies. In *Fragmentation Processes: Topics in Atomic and Molecular Physics*; Whelan, C.T., Ed.; Cambridge University Press: Cambridge, UK, 2013; pp. 164–206.
28. Whelan, C.T.; Allan, R.J.; Walters, H.R.J. PCI, polarisation and exchange effects in (e,2e) collisions *J. Phys. IV* **1993**, *3*, C6. [CrossRef]
29. Röder, J.; Rasch, J.; Jung, K.; Whelan, C.T.; Ehrhardt, H.; Allan, J.R.; Walters, H.R.J. Coulomb 3 body effects in low energy electron impact ionization of H(1s). *Phys. Rev. A* **1994**, *53*, 225. [CrossRef]
30. Whelan, C.T.; Allan, R.J.; Rasch, J.; Walters, H.R.J.; Zhang X.; Röder, J.; Jung, K.; Walters, H.R.J.; Ehrhardt, H. Coulomb 3-body effects in (e,2e) Collisions: The ionisation of H in coplanar symmetric geometry. *Phys. Rev. A* **1994**, *50*, 4394. [CrossRef]
31. Murray, A.J. Electron impact ionization using (e,2e) coincidence techniques from threshold to intermediate energies. In $(e,2e)$ & *Related Processes*; Whelan, C.T., Walters, H.R.J., Lahmam-Bennani, A., Ehrhardt, H., Eds.; Kluwer: Dordrecht, The Netherlands, 1993; pp. 327–340.
32. Rasch, J.; Whelan, C.T.; Allan, R.J.; Walters, H.R.J. An explanation of the structure observed in out of plane symmetric measurements on helium. In *Electron and Photon Impact Ionization*; Whelan, C.T., Walters, H.R.J., Eds.; Plenum: New York, NY, USA, 1997; pp. 185–193.
33. Murray, A.J.; Read, F.H. Deep interference minima in experimental ionization differential cross sections. *Phys. Rev. A* **2000**, *63*, 012714. [CrossRef]

34. DeMars, C.M.; Kent, J.B.; Ward, S.J. Deep minima in the Coulomb-Born triply differential cross sections for ionization of helium by electron and positron impact. *Eur. Phys. J. D* **2020**, *74*, 48. [CrossRef]
35. DeMars, C.M.; Ward, S.J.; Colgan, J.; Amari, S.; Madison, D.H. Deep Minima in the Triply Differential Cross Section for Ionization of Atomic Hydrogen by Electron and Positron Impact. *Atoms* **2020**, *8*, 26. [CrossRef]
36. Woolf, M.B.J. (e,2e) Measurements in the Perpendicular Plane. Ph.D. Thesis, University of Manchester, Manchester, UK, 1996.
37. Wannier, G.H. The threshold law for single ionization of atoms or ions by electrons. *Phys. Rev.* **1953**, *90*, 817. [CrossRef]
38. Ehrhardt, H.; Rösel, T. Near threshold (e,2e) ionisation of helium and atomic hydrogen. In *(e, 2e) & Related Processes*; Whelan, C.T., Walters, H.R.J., Lahmam-Bennani, A., Ehrhardt, H., Eds.; Kluwer: Dordrecht, The Netherlands, 1993; pp. 76–82.
39. Rösel, T.; Röder, J.; Frost, L.; Jung, K.; Ehrhardt, H.; Jones, S.; Madison, D.H. Absolute triple differential cross section for ionization of helium near threshold. *Phys. Rev. A* **1992**, *46*, 2539. [CrossRef] [PubMed]
40. Nixon, K.L.; Murray, A.J.; Kaiser, C. Low energy (e,2e) studies of the noble gases in the perpendicular plane. *J. Phys. B At. Mol. Opt. Phys.* **2010**, *43*, 085202. [CrossRef]

Article

Relativistic Study on the Scattering of e$^{\pm}$ from Atoms and Ions of the Rn Isonuclear Series

Mahmudul H. Khandker [1], A. K. Fazlul Haque [1], M. M. Haque [1,*], M. Masum Billah [1], Hiroshi Watabe [2] and M. Alfaz Uddin [3]

1. Atomic and Molecular Physics Lab, Department of Physics, University of Rajshahi, Rajshahi 6205, Bangladesh; kmhasan_phy@yahoo.com (M.H.K.); fhaque@ru.ac.bd (A.K.F.H.); masumphy@ru.ac.bd (M.M.B.)
2. Cyclotron and Radioisotope Center, Division of Radiation Protection and Safety Control, Tohoku University, 6-3 Aoba, Aramaki, Aoba, Sendai 980-8578, Japan; watabe@cyric.tohoku.ac.jp
3. Department of Physics, Pabna University of Science and Technology, Pabna 6600, Bangladesh; uddinmda@yahoo.com
* Correspondence: mhpdru@gmail.com; Tel.: +880-171-634-6268

Abstract: Calculations are presented for differential, integrated elastic, momentum transfer, viscosity, inelastic, total cross sections and spin polarization parameters S, T and U for electrons and positrons scattering from atoms and ions of radon isonuclear series in the energy range from 1 eV–1 MeV. In addition, we analyze systematically the details of the critical minima in the elastic differential cross sections along with the positions of the corresponding maximum polarization points in the Sherman function for the aforesaid scattering systems. Coulomb glory is investigated across the ionic series. A short range complex optical potential, comprising static, polarization and exchange (for electron projectile) potentials, is used to describe the scattering from neutral atom. This potential is supplemented by the Coulomb potential for the same purpose for a charged atom. The Dirac partial wave analysis, employing the aforesaid potential, is carried out to calculate the aforesaid scattering observables. A comparison of our results with other theoretical findings shows a reasonable agreement over the studied energy range.

Keywords: electron and positron scattering; spin asymmetry; critical minima; total polarization; coulomb glory

Citation: Khandker, M.H.; Haque, A.K.F.; Haque, M.M.; Billah, M.M.; Watabe, H.; Uddin, M.A. Relativistic Study on the Scattering of e$^{\pm}$ from Atoms and Ions of the Rn Isonuclear Series. *Atoms* **2021**, *9*, 59. https://doi.org/10.3390/atoms9030059

Academic Editor: Grzegorz Piotr Karwasz

Received: 6 August 2021
Accepted: 23 August 2021
Published: 27 August 2021

Publisher's Note: MDPI stays neutral with regard to jurisdictional claims in published maps and institutional affiliations.

Copyright: © 2021 by the authors. Licensee MDPI, Basel, Switzerland. This article is an open access article distributed under the terms and conditions of the Creative Commons Attribution (CC BY) license (https://creativecommons.org/licenses/by/4.0/).

1. Introduction

Lepton scattering from atoms and ions is of immense importance in both experimental and theoretical studies. Electron (e$^-$) scattering from neutral atomic targets is an efficient tool to glean projectile-target interaction [1], the structure of atoms or molecules and matter in bulk. The electrons passing through matter are not only scattered, but also produce ions of different charges. Explicit interpretation of the spectroscopic observations and theoretical modeling of the formation and time evolution of artificial, terrestrial, space and astrophysical plasmas require the electron-ion scattering cross section data [2]. On the other hand, positron-ion scattering is important for understanding the dynamics of the collisions of positrons with ions, atoms and molecules in interstellar medium [3]. For the positron (e$^+$) projectile, phaseshifts are very sensitive to the polarization as the repulsive static potential partially cancels the attractive polarization potential [4]. Therefore, e$^+$-atom collision can furnish a useful, and sometimes more sensitive test of the techniques used for studying the lepton scattering processes.

The elastic differential cross section (DCS) data can provide detailed information on collision dynamics and the optical potential. The total cross section (TCS) as well as its integrated elastic cross section (IECS) and inelastic cross section (INCS) determine the mean free path between two elastic collisions. The momentum-transfer cross section

(MTCS) is used to compute the average momentum transferred by the projectile to the target on collision. The viscosity cross section (VCS) is needed for expansion of the multiple scattering formula used as an input to the Monte Carlo simulation of the electron transport in solids. Regarding collision dynamics, more detailed information can be unfolded by studying spin asymmetry parameters S, T and U. The S parameter, the so called Sherman function, associated with leptons spin-polarized perpendicular to the scattering plane, serves to measure the beam polarization [5]. The angle of rotation of the component of the polarization vector in polarized projectiles can be obtained by other two parameters T and U. The determination of critical minima (CM) points in the DCS is useful as a complete spin polarization of the scattered projectile occurs in the vicinity of these CMs [6,7]. All aforesaid observables of lepton scattering from neutral atoms, ions, and molecules have many applications in various pure and applied sciences.

To date, a considerable number of attempts, both experimentally [8–11] and theoretically [12–17], have been made to study the collisions of electrons with rare-gas atoms. Due to the inertness and availability, rare-gas atoms are often used as targets in experimental studies of scattering in a goal to understand lepton-atom interaction and test collision dynamics. The recent development of rare-gas halide high-power lasers has increased interest in studies the electrons scattering from inert gases. In physical sciences radon is used as a tracer because of its short half-life (3.8 days). Despite such applications, studies on $e^{\pm}$–radon scattering, particularly across the isonuclear series, are limited. To date, as we are aware, there is no experiment on e^-/e^+–radon scattering available in the literature. The high cost and radioactivity of radon stand as barrier to a experimental research with it.

On the theoretical side, Kapil and Vats [18] performed relativistic calculations of the DCS, IECS and MTCS as well as S, T and U for positrons scattering by radon and radium atoms in the energy range 2–500 eV. The same observables in the same energy range for electrons scattering from Yb, Rn and Ra were calculated by Neerja et al. [19]. At energies E_i = 20–1000 eV, the TCS for positron scattering from all the rare gases were reported by Baluja and Jain [12]. IECS, MTCS and VCS for the neutral atomic targets (Z_T = 1–92) were tabulated by Mayol and Salvat [20] for 100 eV to 1 GeV electrons, and by Dapor and Miotello [21] for 500–4000 eV positrons. Sin Fai Lam [13] predicted DCS, TCS and S for low energy ($E_i \leq 30$ eV) electrons from krypton, xenon and radon atoms. It is worth mentioning that all of these cross sections were calculated only for neutral atomic targets. This fact underscores the necessity for the study of lepton-ion scattering from the perspectives of fundamental and practical importance. Furthermore, this situation motivates us to undertake the study of scatterings of electrons and positrons from radon atoms and ions up to charge state q^{86+}.

In this study, we have investigated elastic DCS, IECS, MTCS, VCS, INCS, TCS, S, T and U for both electrons and positrons scattering from radon isonuclear series including neutral atoms as well as ions over a wider energy range of 1 eV $\leq E_i \leq$ 1 MeV. In DCSs of the e^--Rn system, we have investigated CM and determined maximum spin polarization (MSP) points in the vicinity of these CMs. Coulomb glory, the amplification of elastic backscattering of electrons from positive ions owing to the electrostatic screening of nuclear potential by atomic electrons, has been investigated throughout the ionic series of radon. The aforesaid scattering observables are obtained by solving Dirac relativistic equation within the framework of partial wave analysis using a modified Coulomb potential (MCP) [15] in the form

$$V(r) = V_{\text{mc}}(r) = \frac{zqe^2}{r} + V_{\text{sr}}(r). \tag{1}$$

The first term on the right-hand side of the above equation is the long-range Coulomb potential due to the Coulomb interaction between primary electron or positron with the target with the ionic charge q. e is magnitude of the electron charge, and $z = -1$ for electron and +1 for positron. The short-range part, $V_{sr}(r)$ is given by a local complex optical potential [22–25] in the form

$$V_{sr}(r) = V_{op}(r) = V_R(r) - iW_{abs}(r), \qquad (2)$$

where, $V_R(r)$ and $iW_{abs}(r)$ denote, respectively, the real and imaginary parts of the potential. The real part consists of static, exchange and correlation–polarization potentials. The electron number density of the target, required for the generation of these components, is obtained numerically from the multiconfiguration Dirac–Fock wavefunctions [26]. In case of $e^{\pm}$-atom scattering, the long-range part of Equation (1) is absent and, therefore, the interaction potential becomes pure short ranged optical potential given in Equation (2). For unscreened nuclear targets, on the other hand, the short-range part of Equation (1) vanishes, and the scattering reduces to pure Coulomb scattering.

Our results are compared with other calculations available in the literature. The rest of this paper is organized as follows. Section 2 gives the outline of the theory. In Section 3, we present potential details and numerics. Results of our theory and comparison with existing calculations are given in Section 4. In Section 5, we draw our conclusions. Atomic units ($\hbar = m_e = e = 1$) are used throughout unless otherwise indicated.

2. Theory

2.1. Optical Potential

In our MCP approach, the Coulomb potential is complemented by a short-range complex optical potential given in the following form

$$V_{sr}(r) = V_{st}(r) + V_{ex}(r) + V_{cp}(r) - iW_{abs}(r). \qquad (3)$$

Here, the real components $V_{st}(r)$, $V_{ex}(r)$, $V_{cp}(r)$ are, respectively, the static, the exchange and the correlation polarization potentials. Furthermore, the imaginary component $W_{abs}(r)$ represents the absorption potential. The static potential $V_{st}(r)$ arises from the electrostatic interactions of the projectile with the target electrons and protons. The exchange potential $V_{ex}(r)$ is used to handle the non-local rearrangement collisions between primary and bound electrons arising due to their indistinguishability. For positron scattering, $V_{ex}(r) = 0$ as there is no exchange probability between the projectile and bound electrons. The correlation polarization potential $V_{cp}(r)$ describes the distortion of the target charge distribution by the projectile electron or positron. The absorption potential $W_{abs}(r)$ incorporates the loss of beam intensity to various inelastic channels during the collision.

2.1.1. Static Potential

The electrostatic potential $V_{st}(r)$ in Equation (3), at a distance r from the nucleus of the target, is given by

$$V_{st}(r) = ze[\phi_n(r) + \phi_e(r)], \qquad (4)$$

where, $\phi_n(r)$ and $\phi_e(r)$ are, respectively, potentials due to nuclear and electronic charge distributions. Under static-field approximation, the interaction potential is completely determined by the nuclear and electronic charge distributions. In the present study, we consider a Fermi nuclear charge distribution [27] and the Dirac–Fock electron density, generated from relativistic Hartree–Fock wavefunctions by Desclaux [26]. The static potential can, therefore, be presented as [28]

$$\phi_n(r) = e \int d\mathbf{r}' \frac{\varrho_n(r')}{|\mathbf{r} - \mathbf{r}'|} \quad \text{and} \quad \phi_e(r) = -e \int d\mathbf{r}' \frac{\varrho_e(r')}{|\mathbf{r} - \mathbf{r}'|}. \qquad (5)$$

Here, ϱ_n and ϱ_e, the number densities of protons and orbital electrons, respectively, are normalized as

$$\int \varrho(r)4\pi r^2 dr = \begin{cases} Z - q, & \text{for } \varrho_e \\ Z, & \text{for } \varrho_n \end{cases} \quad (6)$$

with $Z - q$ being the number of dressing electrons of the target and Z, the atomic number of the target.

2.1.2. Exchange Potential

The exchange potential $V_{ex}(r)$ in Equation (3), a type of semi-classical exchange potential [29], is obtained from the non-local exchange interaction with the help of a WKB-like approximation for the wave functions. It is expressed as

$$V_{ex}(r) = \frac{1}{2}[E_i - V_{st}(r)] - \frac{1}{2}\{[E_i - V_{st}(r)]^2 + 4\pi a_0 e^4 \varrho_e(r)\}^{1/2}. \quad (7)$$

Here, E_i and a_0 are the incident electron energy and the Bohr radius, respectively.

2.1.3. Polarization Potential

The correlation polarization potential $V_{cp}(r)$ in Equation (3) is a combination of long range Buckingham potential $V_{cp,B}(r)$ and a short-range correlation potential $V_{co}(r)$. This global type correlation-polarization potential is expressed as [30]

$$V_{cp}^{\pm}(r) \equiv \begin{cases} \max\{V_{co}^{\pm}(r), V_{cp,B}(r)\} & \text{if } r < r_c \\ V_{cp,B}(r) & \text{if } r \geq r_c, \end{cases} \quad (8)$$

where r_c is the outer radius at which the above two contributions intersect for the first time.

The long-range part, independent of the charge of the incoming projectile, has the following asymptotic form

$$V_{cp,B}(r) = -\frac{\alpha_d e^2}{2(r^2 + d^2)^2}, \quad (9)$$

with α_d is the dipole polarizability of the target. The phenomenological cut off parameter d is given by [31]

$$d^4 = \frac{1}{2}\alpha_d a_0 (Z - q)^{-1/3} b_p^2, \quad (10)$$

where, b_p is an adjustable parameter that decreases as the projectile energy increases and is expressed by the following empirical formula [30]

$$b_p^2 = \max\{(E - 50 \text{ eV})/(16 \text{ eV}), 1\}. \quad (11)$$

At $r < r_c$, the asymptotic expansion completely breaks down, and the interaction potential for the correlation between the projectile and electron cloud can be described by the following analytic expression given by Perdew and Zunger [32]

$$V_{co}^{(-)}(r) = -\frac{e^2}{a_0}(0.0311 \ln(r_s) - 0.0584 + 0.00133 r_s \ln(r_s) \\ -0.0084 r_s), \quad \text{for } r_s < 1 \quad (12)$$

and

$$V_{co}(r) = -\frac{e^2}{a_0}\beta_0 \frac{1 + (7/6)\beta_1 r_s^{\frac{1}{2}} + (4/3)\beta_2 r_s}{(1 + \beta_1 r_s^{\frac{1}{2}} + \beta_2 r_s)^2}, \quad \text{for } r_s \geq 1 \quad (13)$$

where, $\beta_0 = 0.1423$, $\beta_1 = 1.0529$ and $\beta_2 = 0.3334$.

For positron impact scattering, the present study uses the correlation potential of Jain [33] as given by

$$V_{co}^{(+)}(r) = \frac{e^2}{2a_0}\{-1.82r_s^{-1/2} + [0.051\ln(r_s) - 0.115]\ln(r_s) + 1.167\}, \quad \text{for } r_s < 0.302, \qquad (14)$$

$$V_{co}^{(+)}(r) = \frac{e^2}{2a_0}\left[-0.92305 - 0.09098r_s^{-2}\right], \quad \text{for } 0.302 \leq r_s < 0.56, \qquad (15)$$

and

$$V_{co}^{(+)}(r) = \frac{e^2}{2a_0}\left[-\frac{8.7674}{(r_s+2.5)^3} + \frac{-13.151+0.9552r_s}{(r_s+2.5)^2} + \frac{2.8655}{(r_s+2.5)} - 0.6298\right], \quad \text{for } 0.56 \leq r_s < 8.0. \qquad (16)$$

For $8.0 \leq r_s \leq \infty$ (i.e., at the asymptotic region), the polarization potential is accurately given by Equation (9). The parameter r_s is given by the following equation

$$r_s \equiv \frac{1}{a_0}\left[\frac{3}{4\pi\varrho_e(r)}\right]^{\frac{1}{3}}. \qquad (17)$$

2.1.4. Absorption Potential

The absorption potential $W_{abs}(r)$ in Equation (3) is a semi-relativistic imaginary potential proposed by Salvat et al. [34]. This negative imaginary term is included in the optical potential to account for the loss of incident flux from elastic channel to inelastic channels above the inelastic threshold. This absorption potential depends on the cross section for binary collisions between the projectile and target electron. Within the framework of Born–Lindhard formulation a non-relativistic formulation of the absorption potential for electron scattering can be obtained under local density approximation (LDA) as by Salvat [30]

$$W_{abs}^{nr} = A_{abs}\frac{\hbar}{2}[v_L^{nr}\varrho_e(r)\sigma_{bc}(E_L,\varrho_e,\Delta)]. \qquad (18)$$

Here, v_L^{nr} is the non-relativistic velocity with which the projectile interacts as if it were moving within a homogeneous gas of density ϱ_e. This velocity is given by

$$v_L^{nr} = \sqrt{2E_L/m_e} \qquad (19)$$

corresponding to the local kinetic energy

$$E_L(r) = \begin{cases} E - V_{st}(r) - V_{ex}(r) & \text{for electron} \\ \max\{E - V_{st}(r), 0\} & \text{for positron.} \end{cases} \qquad (20)$$

The term $\sigma_{bc}(E_L,\varrho_e,\Delta)$ in Equation (18) represents the non-relativistic Born approximated cross section for collisions involving energy transfer greater than a certain energy gap Δ. This energy gap is the threshold energy for the inelastic channel and accounts for the minimum energy lost by the projectile. The energy gap adopted for the present computation is given by

$$\Delta = \begin{cases} \epsilon_1 & \text{for electron} \\ I - 6.8 & \text{for positron} \end{cases} \qquad (21)$$

with ϵ_1 is the first excitation energy, I is the ionization potential and 6.8 eV is positronium binding energy.

The relativistic effects are accounted by Salvat [30] in the expression (18) by introducing the relativistic velocity

$$v_L^r = c\sqrt{\frac{E_L(E_L + 2m_ec^2)}{(E_L + m_ec^2)^2}} \qquad (22)$$

The semi-relativistic form for W_{abs} is

$$W_{\text{abs}} = \frac{v_L^{\text{nr}}}{v_L} W_{\text{abs}}^{\text{nr}} = \sqrt{\frac{2(E_{rmL} + m_e c^2)^2}{m_e c^2 (E_L + 2m_e c^2)}} \times A_{\text{abs}} \frac{\hbar}{2} [v_L^n \varrho_e(r) \sigma_{\text{bc}}(E_L, \varrho_e, \Delta)], \quad (23)$$

where, c is the velocity of light in vacuum. The value of the empirical parameter A_{abs} depends on the projectile-target combination and can be determined by fitting the available data. In the present calculations, $A_{\text{abs}} = 2$ for electron and 1 for positron scattering.

2.2. Dirac Partial Wave Analysis

The relativistic Dirac equation for a projectile moving with a velocity v in a central field $V_{mC}(r)$ is given as

$$\left[c\boldsymbol{\alpha} \cdot \mathbf{p} + \beta m_0 c^2 + V_{mC}(r) \right] \psi(\mathbf{r}) = (E + m_0 c^2) \psi(\mathbf{r}), \quad (24)$$

with $E + m_0 c^2$ being the total energy of the projectile and the operators $\boldsymbol{\alpha}$ and β, the usual 4×4 Dirac matrices. Solutions of the Dirac equation are the spherical waves and are given by [35]

$$\psi_{E\kappa m}(\mathbf{r}) = \frac{1}{r} \begin{pmatrix} P_{E\kappa}(r) \Omega_{\kappa,m}(\hat{\mathbf{r}}) \\ i Q_{E\kappa}(r) \Omega_{-\kappa,m}(\hat{\mathbf{r}}) \end{pmatrix}, \quad (25)$$

where $P_{E\kappa}(r)$ and $Q_{E\kappa}(r)$ are the upper- and lower-component radial functions and $\Omega_{\kappa,m}(\hat{\mathbf{r}})$ are the spherical spinors. $\kappa = (\ell - j)(2j + 1)$ is the relativistic quantum number with j and ℓ being the total and orbital angular momentum quantum numbers. The radial functions $P_{E\kappa}(r)$ and $Q_{E\kappa}(r)$ of Dirac spherical waves are the solutions of the coupled system of differential equations [35]

$$\frac{dP_{E\kappa}}{dr} = -\frac{\kappa}{r} P_{E\kappa}(r) + \frac{E - V + 2m_0 c^2}{c} Q_{E\kappa}(r) \quad (26)$$

and

$$\frac{dQ_{E\kappa}}{dr} = -\frac{E - V}{c} P_{E\kappa}(r) + \frac{\kappa}{r} Q_{E\kappa}(r). \quad (27)$$

The spherical waves in Equation (25) are normalized so that the large-component radial function $P_{E\kappa}(r)$ oscillates asymptotically with unit amplitude and takes the following form

$$P_{E\kappa}(r) \sim \sin\left(kr - \ell\frac{\pi}{2} - \eta \ln 2kr + \delta_\kappa\right). \quad (28)$$

Here, $k = \frac{p}{\hbar} = \frac{\sqrt{E(E + 2m_e c^2)}}{\hbar c}$ is the relativistic wave number of the projectile and $\eta = \frac{q e^2 m_e}{\hbar k}$ is the Sommerfeld parameter. The global phase shift δ_κ, describing the large r behavior of the spherical wave solutions, is given by the following equation

$$\delta_\kappa = \Delta_\kappa + \mathring{\delta}_\kappa, \quad (29)$$

with Δ_κ being the Dirac-Coulomb phase shift of the potential tail and $\mathring{\delta}_\kappa$, the complex inner phase shift caused by the complex short-range potential. Dirac-Coulomb phase shift Δ_κ is given by [36]

$$\Delta_\kappa = \arg[\zeta(E + 2m_e c^2) - i(\kappa + \lambda)c\hbar k] - (\lambda - \ell - 1)\frac{\pi}{2} \\ + \arg \Gamma(\lambda + i\eta) - S(\zeta, \kappa)\pi, \quad (30)$$

where, $\zeta = \frac{qe^2}{\hbar c} \approx q\alpha = q/137$, $\lambda = \sqrt{\kappa^2 - \zeta^2}$, and $S(\zeta, \kappa) = 1$ if $\zeta < 0$ and $\kappa < 0$, and $= 0$ otherwise. The phase shift Δ_κ can now be used to obtain the direct and spin flip scattering amplitudes for the scattering of $e^\pm$ from Coulomb potential $V_{coul} = \frac{zqe^2}{r}$ as

$$f^{(C)}(\theta) = \frac{1}{2ik}\sum_{\ell=0}^{\infty}\{(\ell+1)[\exp(2i\Delta_{-\ell-1}) - 1] + \ell[\exp(2i\Delta_\ell) - 1]\}P_\ell(\cos\theta) \quad (31)$$

and

$$g^{(C)}(\theta) = \frac{1}{2ik}\sum_{\ell=0}^{\infty}\{\exp(2i\Delta_\ell) - \exp(2i\Delta_{-\ell-1})\}P_\ell^1(\cos\theta). \quad (32)$$

To calculate the inner phase shifts $\hat{\delta}_\kappa$, the integration of radial equations is started at $r = 0$ and extended outwards up to a distance r_m beyond the effective range of the interaction potential. For $r > r_m$ the potential takes asymptotic Coulombian form and the normalized upper-component radial Dirac function can be written as

$$P_{E\kappa}(r) = \cos\hat{\delta}_\kappa f_{E\kappa}^{(u)}(r) + \sin\hat{\delta}_\kappa g_{E\kappa}^{(u)}(r). \quad (33)$$

$f_{E\kappa}^u(r)$ and $g_{E\kappa}^u(r)$ regular and irregular Dirac–Coulomb functions, respectively. The phase shifts $\hat{\delta}_\kappa$ can now be obtained by matching the outer analytical form to the inner numerical solution at r_m. The continuity of the radial function $P_{E\kappa}(r)$ and its derivative is required for this boundary condition. This procedure gives

$$\exp(2i\hat{\delta}_\kappa) = \frac{D_{out}[f_{E\kappa}^{(u)}(r_m) + ig_{E\kappa}^{(u)}(r_m)] - [(f_{E\kappa}^{(u)})'(r_m) + i(g_{E\kappa}^{(u)})'(r_m)]}{[(f_{E\kappa}^{(u)})'(r_m) - i(g_{E\kappa}^{(u)})'(r_m)] - D_{out}[f_{E\kappa}^{(u)}(r_m) - ig_{E\kappa}^{(u)}(r_m)]}, \quad (34)$$

where the primes indicate the derivatives with respect to r and D_{out}, the logarithmic derivative of the outgoing numerical radial function at the matching point. The complex form of the phase shift $\hat{\delta}_\kappa$ is due to the complex short-range potential $V_{sr}(r)$ in Equation (3). The scattering amplitudes $f^{sr}(\theta)$ and $g^{sr}(\theta)$, for the short-range potential, are given as

$$f^{sr}(\theta) = \frac{1}{2ik}\sum_{\ell=0}^{\infty}\{(\ell+1)\exp(2i\Delta_{-\ell-1})[\exp(2i\hat{\delta}_{-\ell-1}) - 1] + \ell \exp(2i\Delta_\ell)[\exp(2i\hat{\delta}_\ell) - 1]\}P_\ell(\cos\theta) \quad (35)$$

and

$$g^{sr}(\theta) = \frac{1}{2ik}\sum_{l=0}^{\infty}\{\exp(2i\Delta_\ell)[\exp(2i\hat{\delta}_\ell) - 1] - \exp(2i\Delta_{-\ell-1})[\exp(2i\hat{\delta}_{-\ell-1}) - 1]\}P_l^1(cos\theta). \quad (36)$$

Here, $P_l(\cos\theta)$ and $P_l^1(\cos\theta)$ are, respectively, the Legendre polynomials and associated Legendre functions. θ is the scattering angle.

For the scattering of electrons and positrons from neutral atoms, Equation (29) reduces as $\delta_\kappa = \hat{\delta}_\kappa$. Therefore, the direct and spin flip scattering amplitudes can be written as

$$f(\theta) = f^{at}(\theta) = \frac{1}{2ik}\sum_{l=0}^{\infty}[(l+1)\{\exp(2i\delta_{\kappa=-l-1}) - 1\} + l\{\exp(2i\delta_{\kappa=l}) - 1\}]P_l(\cos\theta) \quad (37)$$

and

$$g(\theta) = g^{at}(\theta) = \frac{1}{2ik}\sum_{l=1}^{\infty}[\exp(2i\delta_{\kappa=l}) - \exp(2i\delta_{\kappa=-l-1})] \times P_l^1(\cos\theta). \quad (38)$$

In the present MCP approach, to describe $e^\pm$-ion scattering, the scattering amplitudes, $f(\theta)$ and $g(\theta)$, are employed as

$$f(\theta) = f^{sr}(\theta) + f^C(\theta), \quad g(\theta) = g^{sr}(\theta) + g^C(\theta). \quad (39)$$

2.3. Scattering Cross Sections

Once the phase shifts and the scattering amplitudes are determined, the elastic DCS per unit solid angle for unpolarized $e^\pm$ are obtained by the following equation

$$\frac{d\sigma}{d\Omega} = |f(\theta)|^2 + |g(\theta)|^2. \tag{40}$$

In case of bare nucleus, the contributions to scattering amplitudes from short-range potential become zero and, therefore, the DCS per unit solid angle for the elastic scattering of $e^\pm$ by the bare radon is calculated using

$$\frac{d\sigma}{d\Omega} = |f^C(\theta)|^2 + |g^C(\theta)|^2. \tag{41}$$

The initially unpolarized $e^\pm$ beam becomes polarized after being scattered in the direction θ. The degree of this spin polarization is given by Sherman function [37]

$$S(\theta) \equiv i\frac{f(\theta)g^*(\theta) - f^*(\theta)g(\theta)}{|f(\theta)|^2 + |g(\theta)|^2}. \tag{42}$$

The integrated elastic, momentum transfer, viscosity, total and inelastic cross sections are defined by the following respective expressions

$$\sigma_{\text{el}} = \int \frac{d\sigma}{d\Omega}d\Omega = 2\pi \int_0^\pi (|f(\theta)|^2 + |g(\theta)|^2)\sin(\theta)d\theta, \tag{43}$$

$$\sigma_{\text{m}} = 2\pi \int_0^\pi (1 - \cos\theta)\left(\frac{d\sigma}{d\Omega}\right)\sin(\theta)d\theta, \tag{44}$$

$$\sigma_{\text{v}} = 3\pi \int_0^\pi \left[1 - (\cos\theta)^2\right]\left(\frac{d\sigma}{d\Omega}\right)\sin(\theta)d\theta, \tag{45}$$

$$\sigma_{\text{tot}} = \frac{4\pi}{k}\text{Im}f(0) \tag{46}$$

and

$$\sigma_{\text{ine}} = \sigma_{\text{tot}} - \sigma_{\text{el}} \tag{47}$$

Here, Im$f(0)$ denotes the imaginary part of the direct scattering amplitude in the forward direction at $\theta = 0$.

The Coulomb glory effect is estimated by scaling DCS in Equation (40) as [38]

$$\frac{d\tilde{\sigma}}{d\Omega} = \left(\frac{4E}{q}\right)^2 \frac{d\sigma}{d\Omega} \tag{48}$$

The scaled Rutherford differential cross section (SRCS), independent of energy and ionic charge, is given as

$$\frac{d\tilde{\sigma}^c}{d\Omega} = \frac{1}{\sin^4\theta/2}. \tag{49}$$

The value of SRCS is unity at 180° and hence the scaled differential cross section (SDCS), $\frac{d\tilde{\sigma}}{d\Omega}$ in Equation (48) represents the ratio of e^--ion DCS and corresponding Rutherford DCS at $\theta = 180°$.

3. Numerical Analysis

In Figure 1a,b, we present r-dependence real part of the short-range potential V_{sr} as well as the Coulomb potential V_c both for electron and positron projectiles. We present separately the contribution of static potential $V_{\text{st}}(r)$, because it dominates the optical potential. All of these potentials are plotted as a function of distance r from the nucleus. The

Bohr radius $a_0 = \frac{\hbar^2}{me^2} = 1$ a.u., and the location of the nth electronic shell is approximated as

$$r = a_0 \frac{n^2}{Z}. \tag{50}$$

It is worth mentioning that, due to the presence of the exchange and the absorption part in optical potential, there are some dependence on the collision energy, and the potentials shown in Figure 1 are calculated for 1 keV. The nuclear radius of radon is $\simeq 1.4 \times 10^{-4}$ a.u. At $r < 10^{-4}$ a.u., the nuclear potential accounts for the finite nuclear size and is derived from the Fermi charge distribution. As in Figure 1a, the electronic potential coincides with the Coulomb field in the region $r \lesssim 10^{-3}$ a.u., i.e., outside the nucleus, but well inside the K-shell. The respective potentials for positron scattering are shown in Figure 1b. Due to opposite charge of the projectile the optical potential for positron scattering has basically a sign reversal as compared to the electronic potential.

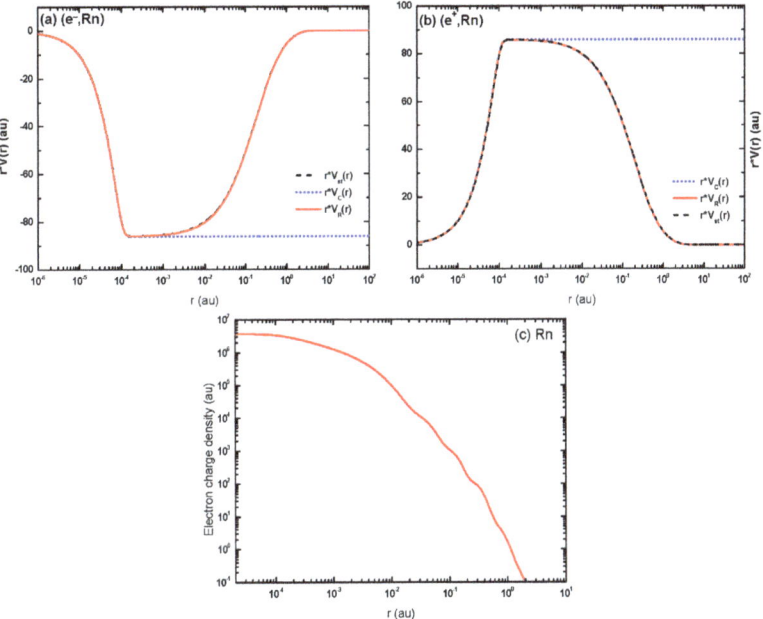

Figure 1. Potentials (multiplied by r) for electrons (**a**) and positrons (**b**) as a function of distance r from the nucleus. Shown are the real part V_R (——, red) and its static part V_{st} (– – – –, black) of the short range OPM potential. The Coulomb field $V_c = -Z/r$ is also included ($\cdots\cdots$, blue). In (**c**) shown is the r dependence of electron charge density.

Figure 1c displays the r-dependence of electronic number density ϱ_e for the radon atom. This figure demonstrates clearly the electronic shell structure as well as the positions of hump appearing in the density distribution. From Equation (50), one gets $r \approx 0.016$, 0.065, 0.147 and 2.344 a.u., respectively, for the K-, L-. M- and N-shells, which agree nicely with the humps in the corresponding density. Two more humps are present in ϱ_e, the positions of which are, however, underpredicted by the above formula since there are only 18 and 8 electrons in the O and P-shells, respectively.

Figure 2 demonstrates the sensitivity of different constituents of the real part of V_{sr} used in the present study to predict DCS and $S(\theta)$ both for electrons and positrons scattering from ^{222}Rn atoms. For a sample case the energy dependence of the DCS and of the $S(\theta)$ are given at the scattering angle $\theta = 90°$, proceeding from V_{st} to V_{opt} by successively including V_{ex}, V_{cp} and W_{abs}. It is evident from this figure that the static potential V_{st} is the dominant contributor to both DCS and $S(\theta)$ over the entire energy range. The remaining components (i.e., the exchange V_{ex}, the polarization V_{cp} and the absorption W_{abs}) have very small contribution except at lower energies. For electron impact scattering, in Figure 2a,b, the inclusion of the V_{ex} leads to a considerable modification of the structures both in DCS and $S(\theta)$. Furthermore, this influence of V_{ex} remains important up to 100 eV for the DCS and 50 eV for the $S(\theta)$. Due to the absence of V_{ex}, the DCS and $S(\theta)$ for positron scattering, in Figure 2c,d, show monotonous behavior. This behavior indicates that the atomic electrons just screen the nuclear field in the case of positron impact, while they act as individual scattering centers for electron scattering.

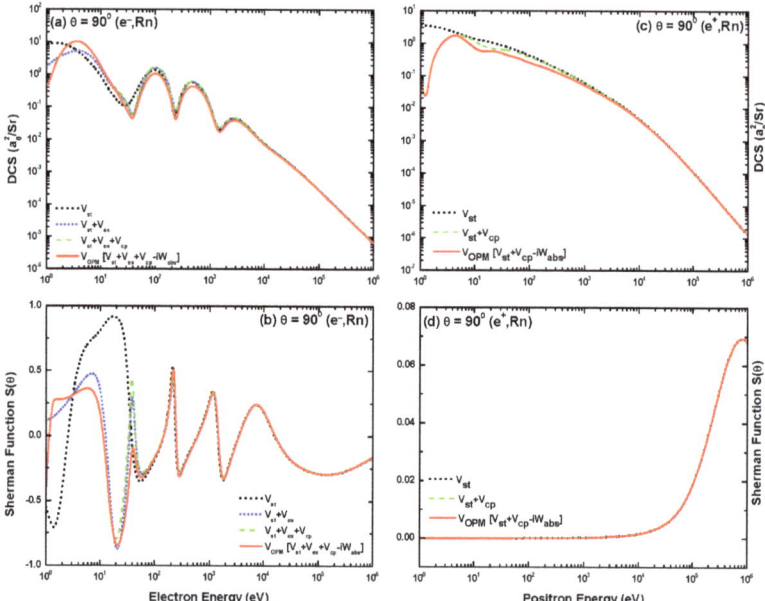

Figure 2. Energy dependence of (**a,c**) the DCS and (**b,d**) the Sherman function $S(\theta)$ for electron (**a,b**) and positron (**c,d**) impact on ^{222}Rn at a scattering angle of 90°. Shown are the results ($\cdots\cdots$, black) from V_{st}; ($\cdots\cdots$, blue) from $V_{st} + V_{ex}$; ($----$, green) from $V_R = V_{st} + V_{ex} + V_{cp}$ and $V_R = V_{st} + V_{cp}$, respectively, for electron and positron projectiles; and (———, red) from $V_{opt} = V_{st} + V_{ex} + V_{cp} - iW_{abs}$ for electron scattering and $V_{opt} = V_{st} + V_{cp} - iW_{abs}$ for positron scattering, respectively.

The polarization potential V_{cp} contributes significantly only at energies below 10 eV and its contribution decreases rapidly at higher energies. At this lower energies, the V_{cp} counteracts V_{ex} by reducing the excursions in the DCS and in S. However, for positron scattering, the V_{cp} induces some minor modulations into the monotonous DCS and $S(\theta)$ at $E_i = 10$–100 eV. The absorption potential W_{abs} diminishes the contribution of V_{st} starting from the ionization threshold (~ 10 eV) and continues up to 5 keV for the DCS, but up to 100 eV for the $S(\theta)$. It is worth mentioning that the magnitudes of both the DCS and $S(\theta)$ are several fold lower for positron projectile signifying that the positron scattering is rather weaker as compared to its electron counterpart.

In Figure 3, we present DCS and Sherman function for 50–5000 eV electrons impact on ^{222}Rn to demonstrate the effect of different contributions to the V_{sr}. One can notice, from Figure 3a at 50 eV, a significant difference between the DCS results from V_{st} and V_{opt}, particularly in the forward hemisphere. This is due to the greater influence of the other potential constituents on the cross section at lower energies than so at higher energies. The absorption potential remains important at energies up to about 500 eV, decreasing the DCS by up to a factor of 2. Even at 5 keV, its influence is still visible. Comparison is also made with the result for a pure Coulomb field V_c, for which the DCS diverges at zero angle. It is seen that the V_{sr} results gradually approach the Coulombic behavior with increasing energy. This happens due to the deeper penetration of the projectile at higher energies and thereby making the effect of the screening of the nucleus by the surrounding electrons lesser and lesser.

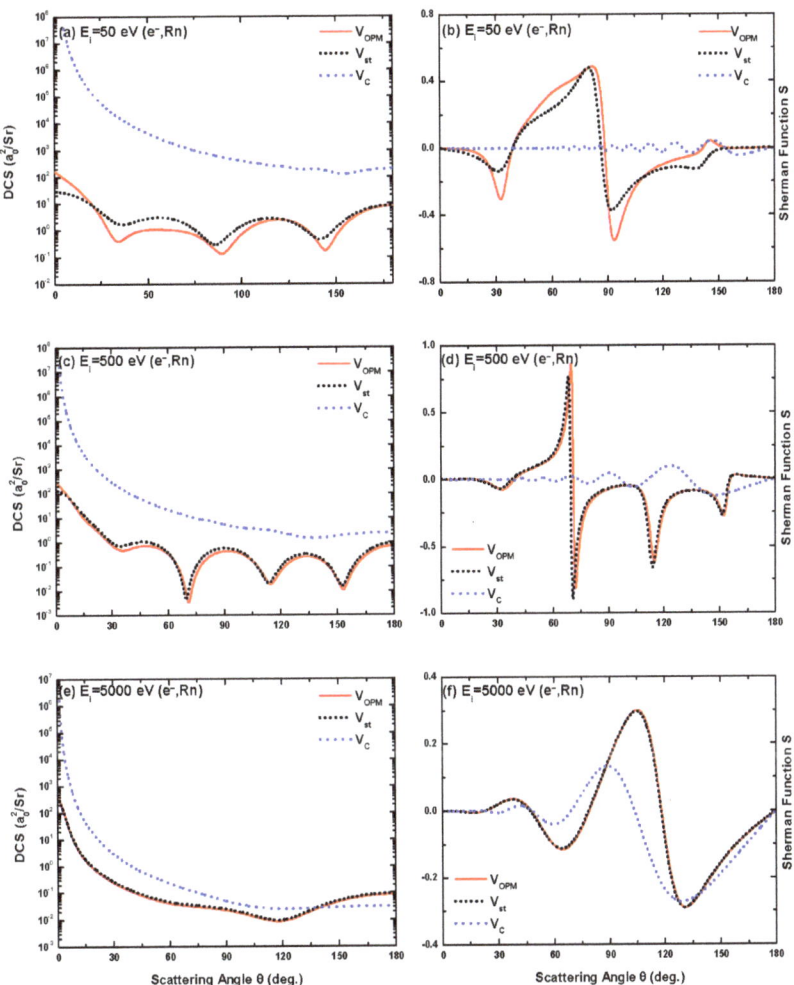

Figure 3. Angular dependence of (**a**,**c**,**e**) the DCS and (**b**,**d**,**f**) the Sherman function for electrons at 50 eV (**a**,**b**), 500 eV (**c**,**d**) and 5000 eV (**e**,**f**) colliding with ^{222}Rn. Shown are the results from V_{st} (· · ·, black) and V_{opt} (——, red). Included also are the results for the Coulomb field V_c (· · ·, blue).

As concerns the Sherman function with its three resonance structures at the DCS minima, the sign of the excursion is conserved at the first two structures, but reversed at the third one when other contributions are added to V_{st}. With increasing energy, oscillatory behavior of the Sherman function from the Coulomb field gradually matches the respective behavior induced by the full V_{sr} potential. Figure 4 displays the respective results for positron impact. The correlation-polarization potential induces oscillations both in the DCS and in $S(\theta)$ at small energies. The influence of the absorption potential is even stronger than for electrons, particularly for the spin asymmetry. Furthermore, the Coulombic behavior is not yet approached at 5 keV.

Figure 5 displays energy dependence of the DCS and the Sherman function for $e^{\pm}$-^{222}Rn scattering comparing the predictions of the V_{st} and V_{sr} with those of the Coulomb field V_c. For electron impact scattering, as seen in Figure 5a, the differences between the DCS results predicted by V_{sr} and those by V_c gradually decrease with increasing energy, and almost vanish at energies beyond 10 keV. In the case of $S(\theta)$, in Figure 5b, the oscillatory behavior induced by these two potentials gradually matches with increasing incident energies. Same features are observed for the positron impact scattering as evident in Figure 5c,d. However, the differences between the DCS results predicted by these two potentials persist in more higher energies (50 keV) indicating that the influence of the absorption potential is even stronger than for electrons.

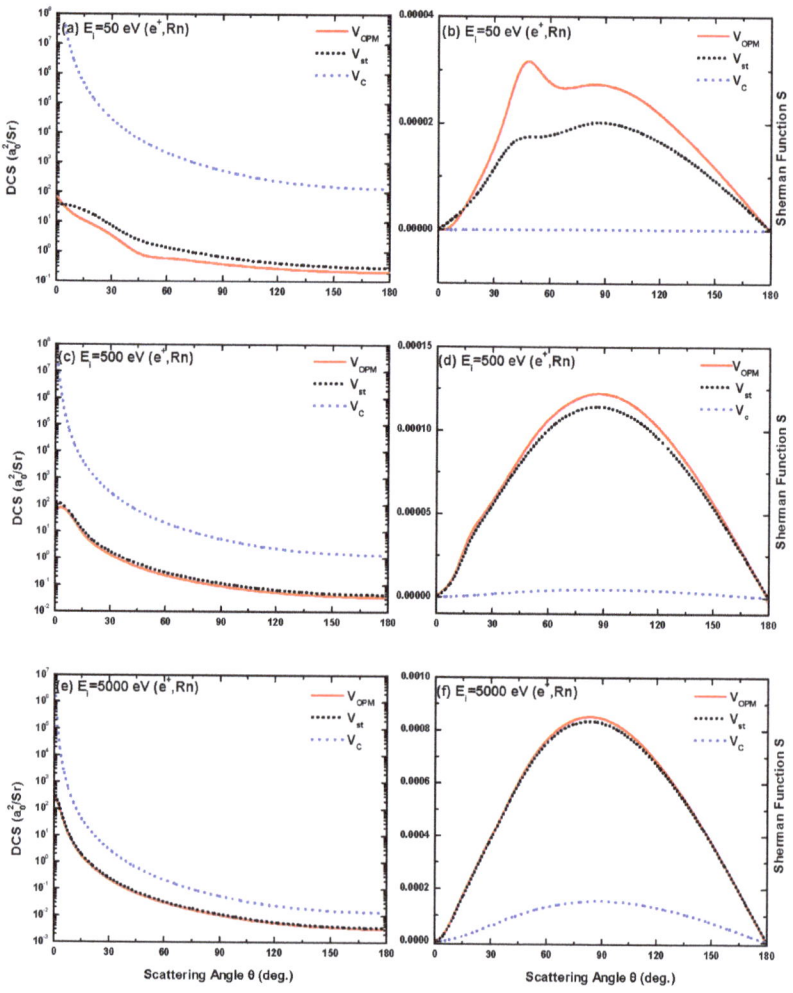

Figure 4. Same as Figure 3, but for the positron impact scattering.

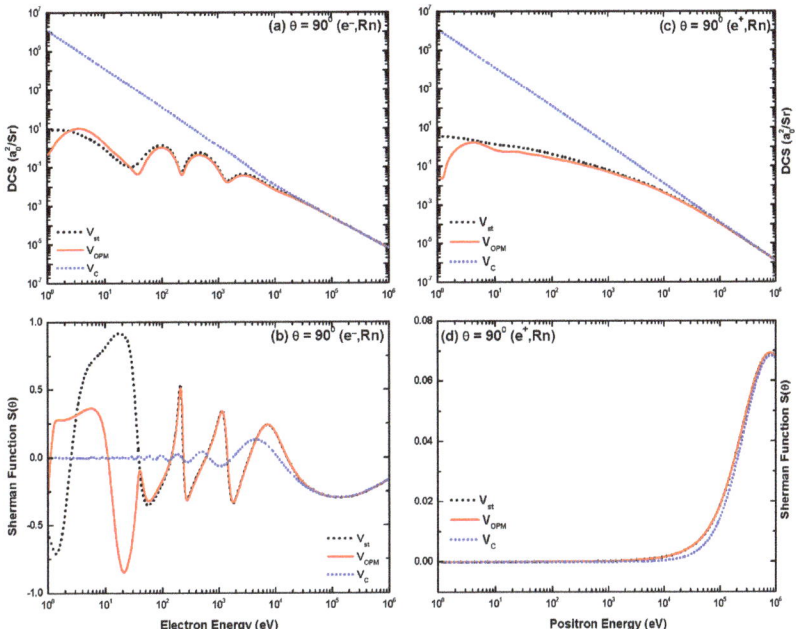

Figure 5. Energy dependence of (**a,c**) the DCS and (**b,d**) the Sherman function $S(\theta)$ for electron (**a,b**) and positron (**c,d**) impact scattering from ^{222}Rn at a scattering angle of 90°. Shown are the results from V_{st} (······, black), V_{opt} (———, red) and V_c (······, blue).

4. Results and Discussion

4.1. Electron Scattering from Neutral Radon

The DCS for electrons elastically scattered from neutral radon calculated using our modified Coulomb potential over a wide range of energies 10 eV $\leq E_i \leq$ 10 keV are presented in Figures 6–9. As seen in these figures, the number of minima in the present DCS distributions varies with energy from 1 at $E_i = 10$ eV to 3 at $20 \leq E_i \leq 200$ eV and to 4 at $300 \leq E_i \leq 700$ eV. The DCS again reveals 3 minima at $900 \leq E_i \leq 1000$ eV and 2 at $1500 \leq E_i \leq 5000$ eV. With a further increase in the collision energy to $E_i \geq 6000$ eV, the number of minima reduces to 1. These minima in the cross sections, the so-called Ramsauer–Townsend (R-T) structures [39], are due to diffraction effects arising from the quantum-mechanical nature of matter. The R-T structures disappear when the collision becomes so energetic that the lepton-atom interactions occur inside the K-shell. These structures are, therefore, of great interest to study collision dynamics.

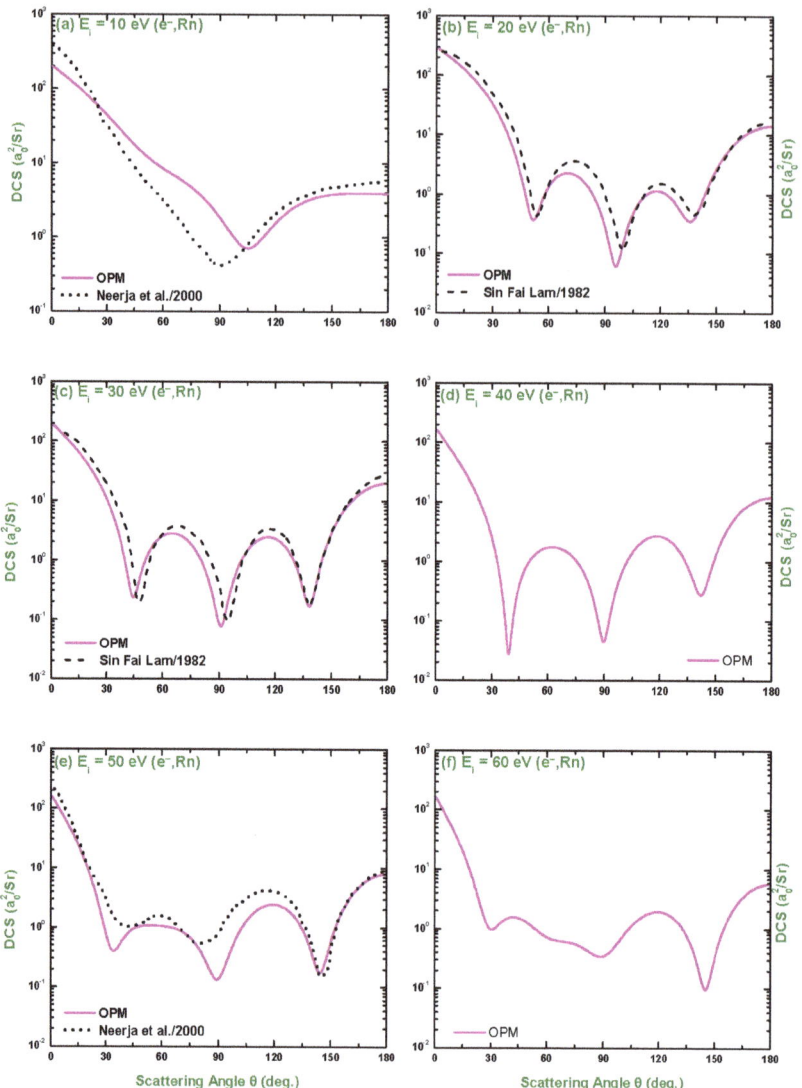

Figure 6. Angular dependence of the differential cross section of electrons scattering from ^{222}Rn at impact energies E_i = 10, 20, 30, 40, 50 and 60 eV. Shown are the results from our MCP (———), Neerja et al. [19] (······) and Sin Fai Lam [13] (– – –).

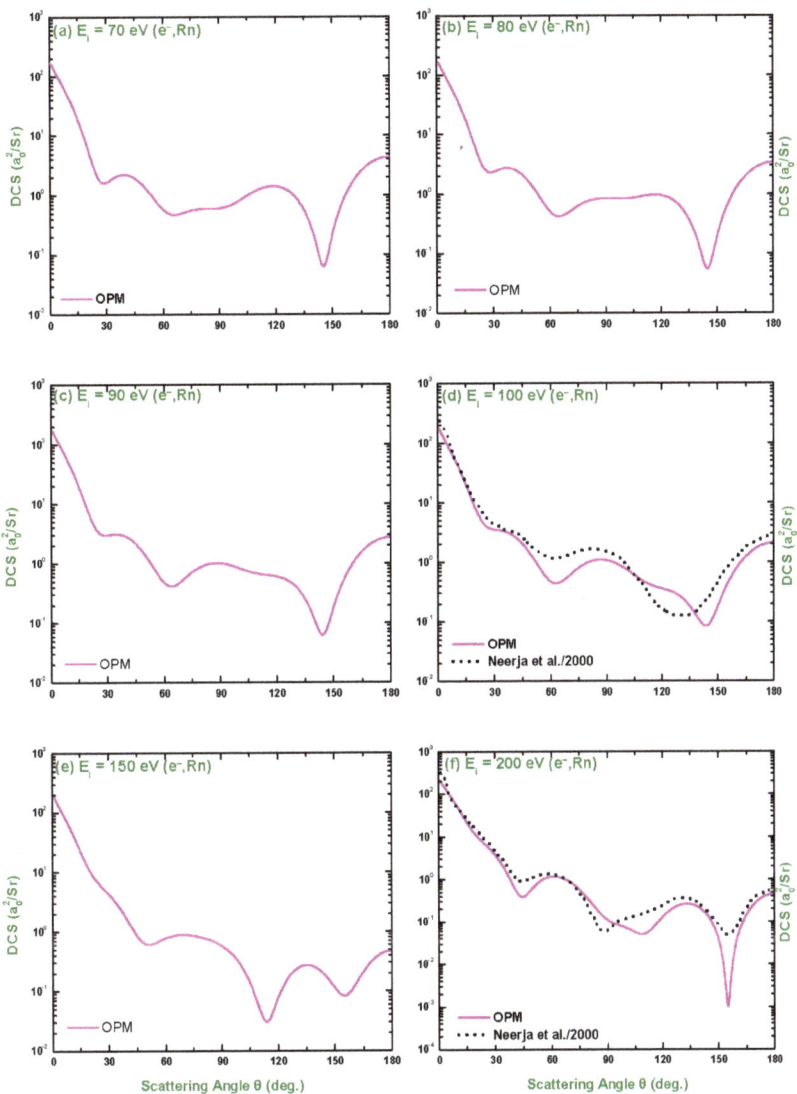

Figure 7. Angular dependence of the differential cross section of electrons scattering from ^{222}Rn at E_i = 70, 80, 90, 100, 150 and 200 eV. Included are the results from Neerja et al. [19] ($\cdots\cdots$) at 100 and 200 eV.

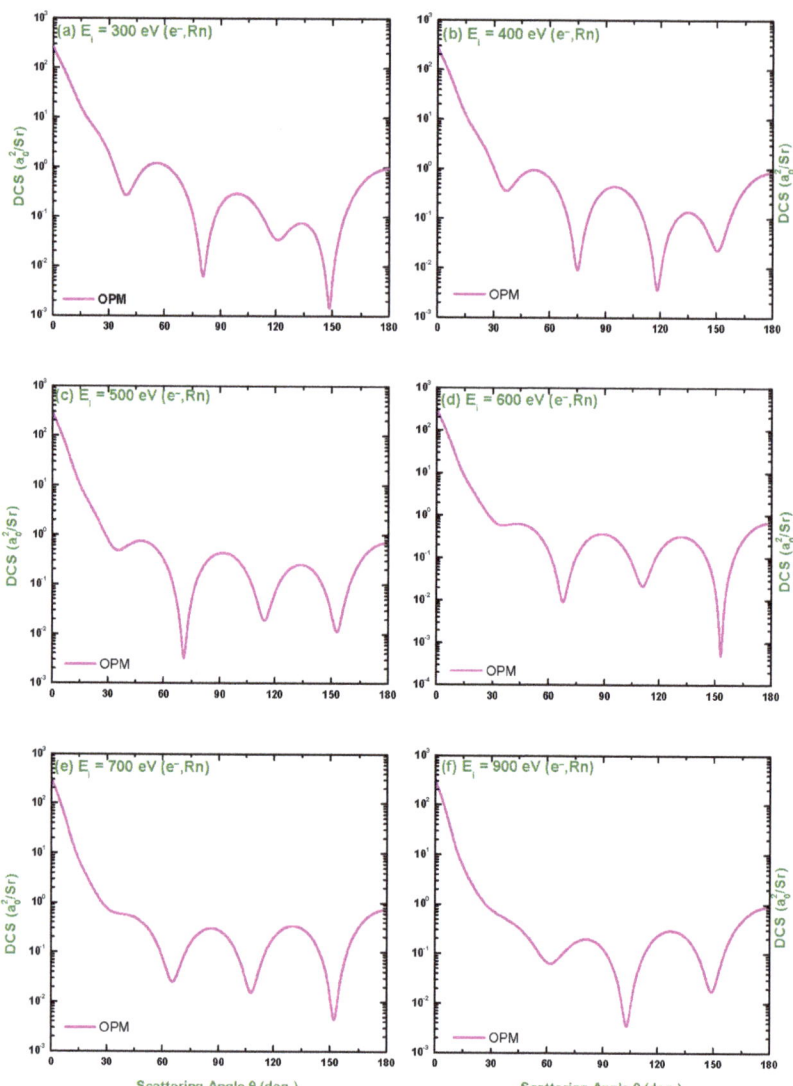

Figure 8. Angular dependence of the differential cross section of electrons scattering from ^{222}Rn at E_i = 300, 400, 500, 600, 700 and 900 eV.

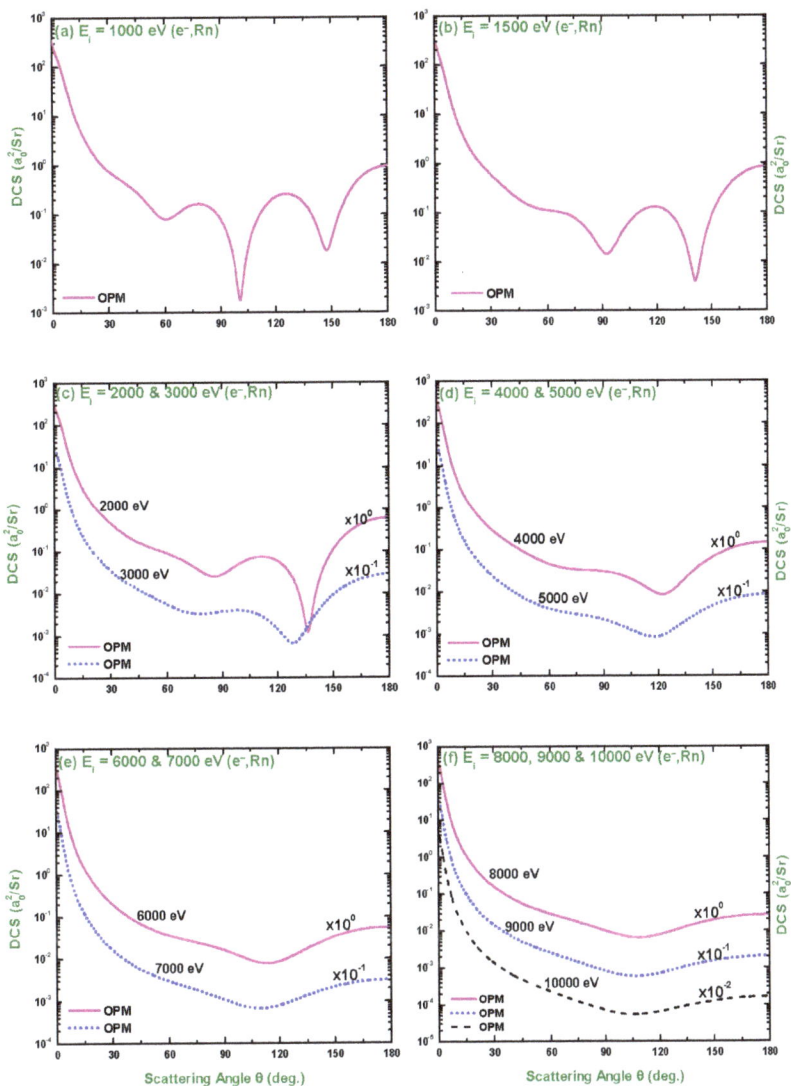

Figure 9. Angular dependence of the differential cross section of electrons scattering from ^{222}Rn at $1 \leq E_i \leq 10$ keV.

As there is no experimental data for this scattering system, we compare our DCS results with the optical model calculations of Neerja et al. [19] available at 10–200 eV and semi-relativistic calculations of Sin Fai Lam [13] at 20–30 eV. For $E_i \geq 300$ eV, we have found neither any experimental nor other theoretical results to compare with. We anticipate that the present results might be useful for applications and comparisons for future experimental as well as theoretical studies. The comparison, where possible, revealed that the three methods exhibit oscillations at about the same scattering angles but with little differences in the magnitude. These differences signify the sensitivity of the theoretical models involving different interaction potentials. It is worth mentioning that Neerja et al. [19] used optical potential but without the long-range Coulomb potential. The poor agreement of our results with those of [19], at 10 eV in Figure 6a, may be due to the onset of the inelastic threshold that interplay between the real and imaginary components of the optical potential due to dispersion.

In Figures 10–12, we present our MCP results of the Sherman function S for e^--^{222}Rn scattering at incident energies $10 \leq E_i \leq 1000$ eV. One can see in these figures that the minima in $S(\theta)$ are strongly related to the minima in the DCS distributions. However, the structures in $S(\theta)$ are much more pronounced than those in the DCS. This is expected because the spin asymmetry is more sensitive to the choice of potentials and methods of calculations. It is also evident that, at low energies ($E_i \leq 100$ eV), the magnitudes of $|S|$ are higher at forward scattering angles than at backward angles. This is due to the effect of the exchange potential that deepens the minima, but is less important at backward angles. In contrast, at higher energies (≥ 150 eV), the magnitude of $|S|$ gets larger with increasing scattering angle. This is the effect of the stronger nuclear field on the spin polarization at the smaller projectile-nucleus distance.

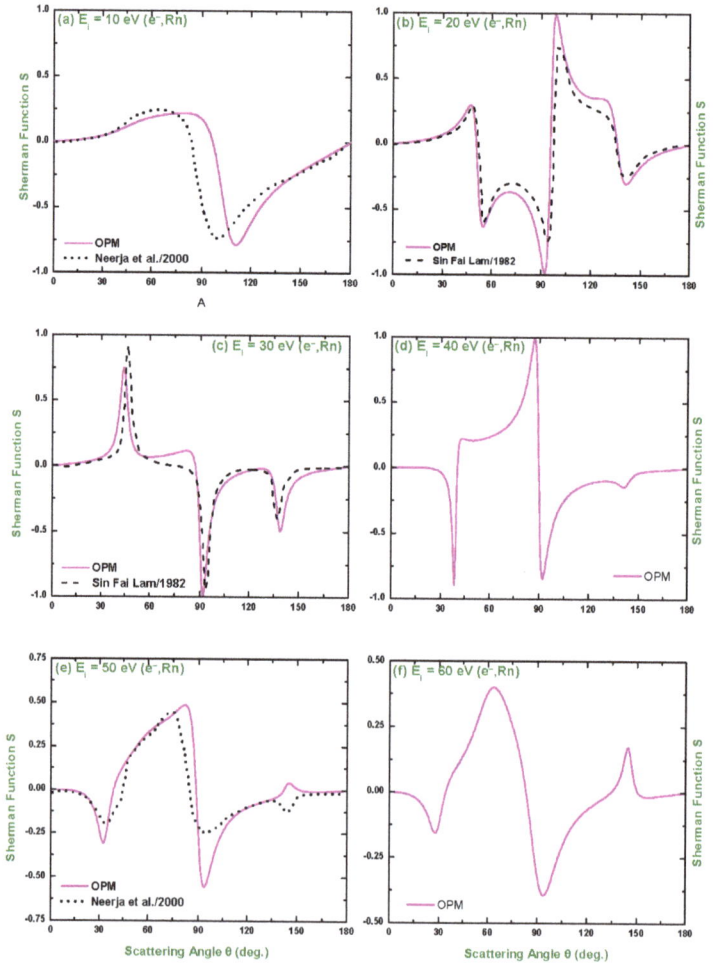

Figure 10. Angle dependent Sherman function S for elastic scattering of 10, 20, 30, 40, 50 and 60 eV electrons from neutral radon atoms: —— curves, present calculations (MCP); ······ curves, ref. [19] and − − − curves, Ref. [13].

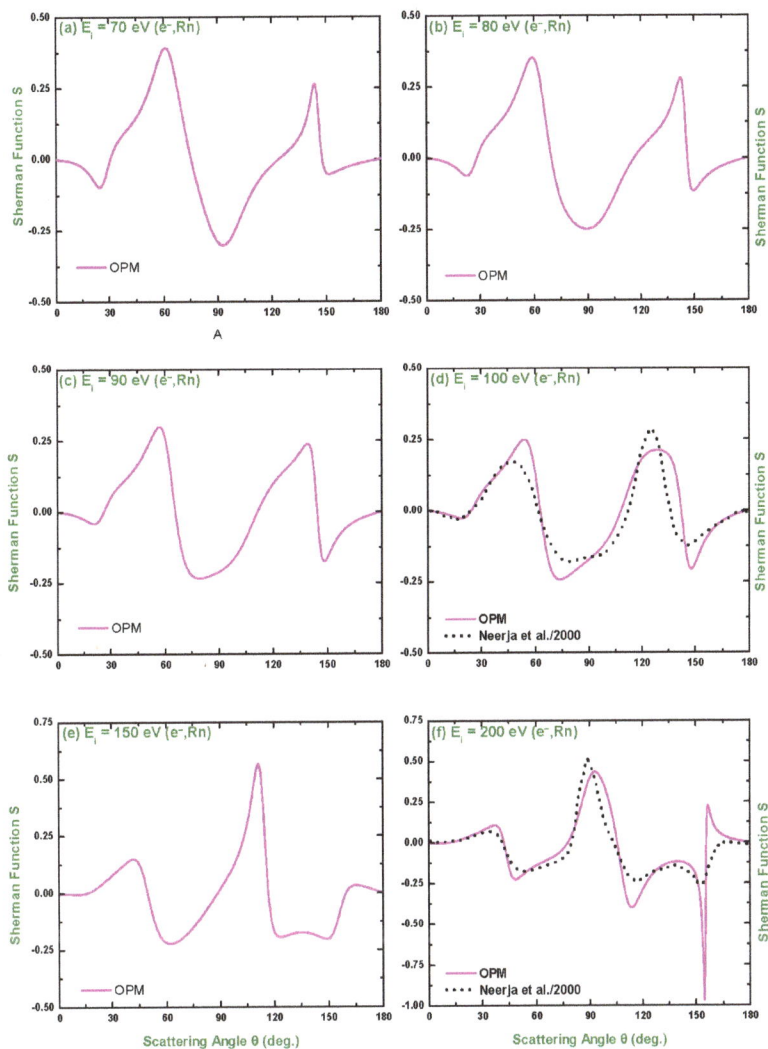

Figure 11. Same as Figure 10, but at impact energies of 70, 80, 90, 100, 150 and 200 eV.

Because of the absence of any experimental data we compare our S results again with the calculations of Neerja et al. [19], available at 10, 50, 100 and 200 eV, and of Sin Fai Lam [13], available at 20 and 30 eV. Similar to the DCS comparison, one can observe that these three calculations of Sherman function agree closely with one another with the deviations as follows: (i) a tiny differences in magnitude of $|S|$ at the minima or maxima positions, (ii) at 10 eV, present method predicts a minimum at 110°, while that from [19] is observed at 100°, (iii) at 50 eV, the third extremum predicted by the present method and that of Neerja et al. [19] are opposite in sign. All of these differences might be attributed due to the different components of optical potentials used in these two methods as already mentioned earlier. More data and calculations might be helpful to shed light on the presence of these discrepancies.

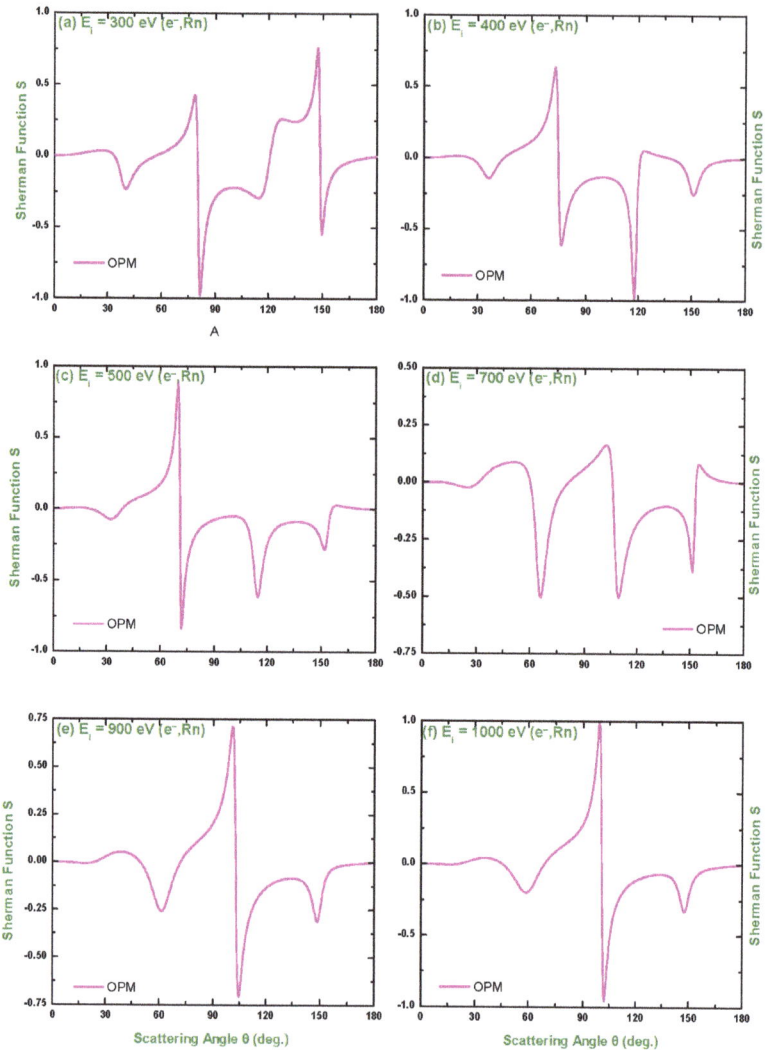

Figure 12. Same as Figure 10, but at impact energies of 300, 400, 500, 700, 900 and 1000 eV.

Figure 13 displays the energy dependence of the DCS and Sherman function of the elastic e$^-$-^{222}Rn scattering over the energy range 1 eV $\leq E_i \leq$ 1 MeV at two forward scattering angles ($\theta = 30°$ and $90°$) and one backward angle ($\theta = 150°$). This figure (panels a, c and e) clearly demonstrates that strong R-T structures are present in the DCSs at all scattering angles for kinetic energies $E_i <$ 3 keV. It is also revealed that the R-T structures gradually fade out as E_i approaches towards the M-subshells binding energies (3–4.6 keV [40]). Beyond 3 keV, the DCS declines monotonously with E_i. This is expected because the pure Coulomb field of the nucleus dominates in this energy regime.

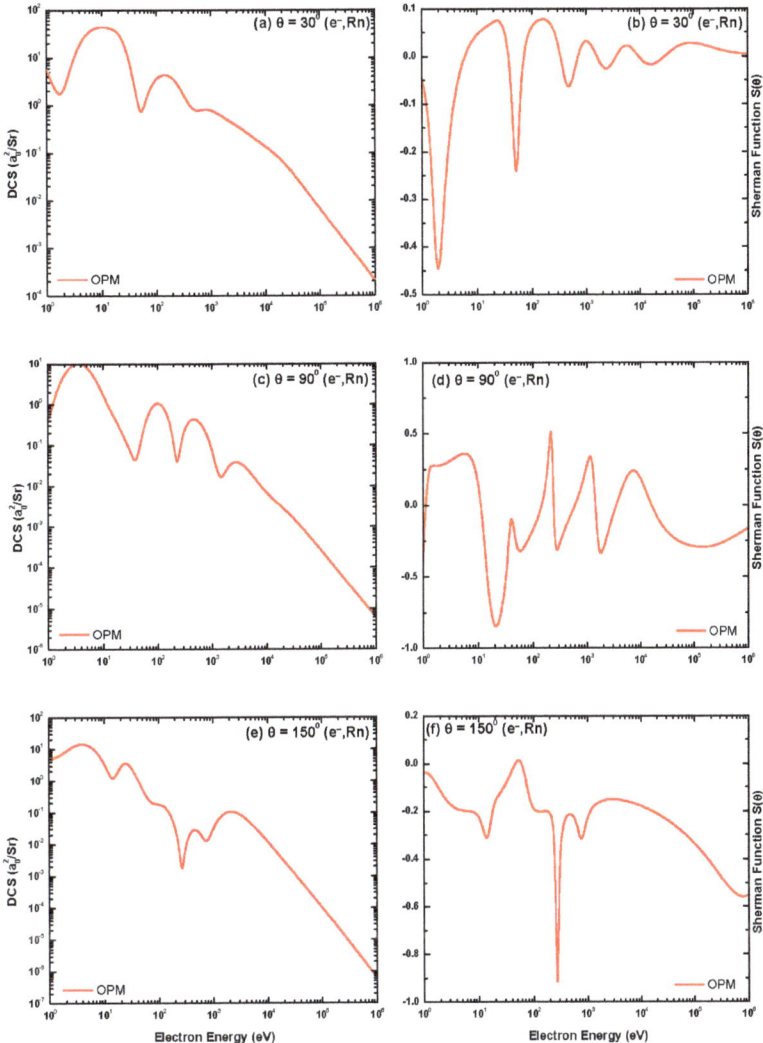

Figure 13. Energy dependence of the DCS and the Sherman function for elastic scattering of electrons from neutral radon atoms at scattering angles (**a**,**b**): 30°, (**c**,**d**): 90° and (**e**,**f**): 150°.

The energy variation of the corresponding Sherman function (panels b, d and f in Figure 13) shows that the magnitude of $|S|$ increases with the increase of scattering angles θ. The appearance of the structure continues up to more energies at lower scattering angles than at higher one. However, the position of the highest extremum is shifted to higher energies with increasing the scattering angles. All of these features might be explained as the fact that the exchange potential, which significantly affects the minima, has less influence in the backward direction. For high energies, on the other hand, due to the smaller projectile-nucleus distance, the stronger nuclear field has a significant effect on the spin polarization implying that the magnitude of $|S|$ increases with increasing scattering angle.

Figure 14 depicts the energy variation of additional polarization parameters $U(\theta)$ and $T(\theta)$ at few selected angles ($\theta = 30°, 90°$ and $150°$). The complete dependence of the scattering process on the spin variables can be obtained from these parameters, where

$$U = \frac{2\mathrm{Im} f(\theta) g^*(\theta)}{|f(\theta)|^2 + |g(\theta)|^2} \tag{51}$$

and

$$T = \frac{|f(\theta)|^2 - |g(\theta)|^2}{|f(\theta)|^2 + |g(\theta)|^2} \tag{52}$$

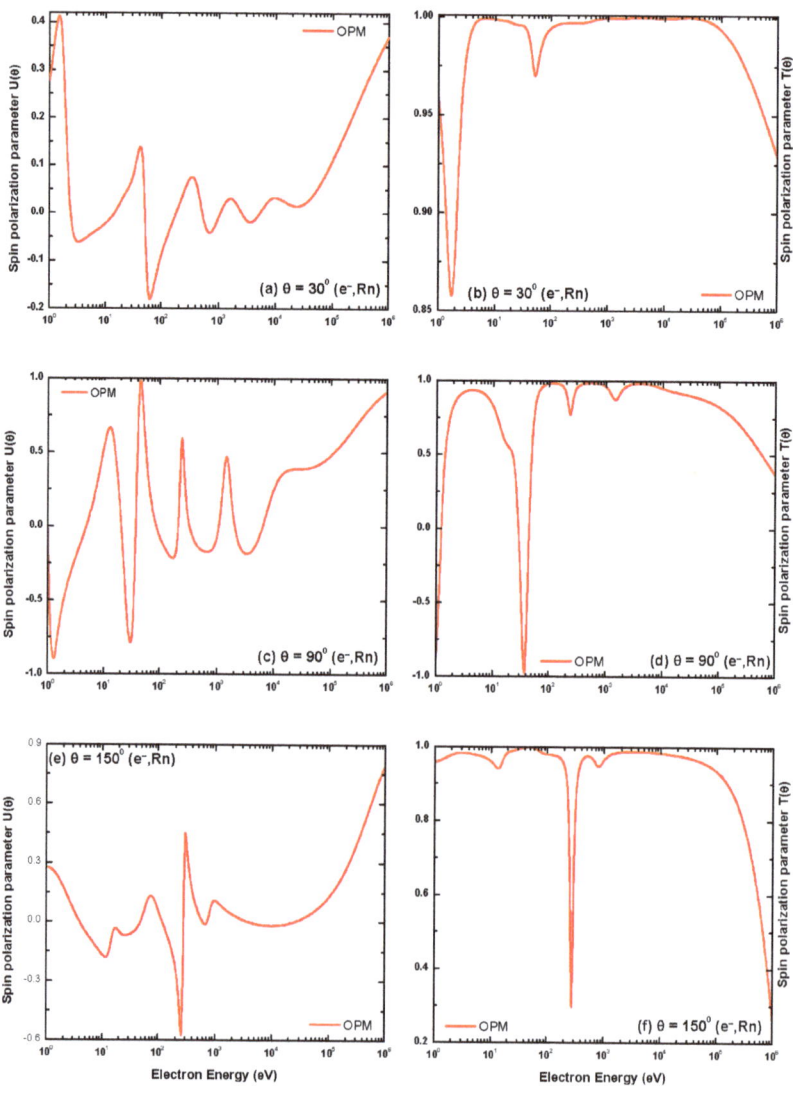

Figure 14. Energy dependence of the spin polarization parameters U and T for elastic scattering of electrons from neutral radon atoms at scattering angles (**a**,**b**): $30°$, (**c**,**d**): $90°$ and (**e**,**f**): $150°$.

As no experimental data and other theoretical studies of U and T parameters are available in the literature, we display only our present results providing further impetus for experimental data for anticipated applications. The spin asymmetry parameters $S(\theta)$, $U(\theta)$ and $T(\theta)$ arise from the interference effect of the direct and spin-flip amplitudes and they are sensitive to both the spin-dependent and correlation interactions. The values of U and T depend on S by the conservation relation: $S^2 + U^2 + T^2 = 1$, and are useful indicators of the total polarization, $S(\theta) = \pm 1$.

In Figure 15a, we display the energy dependence of the angular distribution of the DCS minima obtained for electrons elastically scattered from neutral radon atoms. As seen in this figure, the low-angle minima, corresponding to curves 1 and 2, are not found in the DCSs below 11 eV, but maintain their appearance up to 1200 eV. The angular positions of these minima vary from 28° at 75 eV to 83° at 300 eV. The intermediate-angle minima (curve 3), on the other hand, are present at all energies below 2000 eV with the angular positions varying between 88° and 120°. The high-angle minima (curve 4) in the DCS are seen to appear for collision energies $10.8 \leq E_i \leq 2500$ eV.

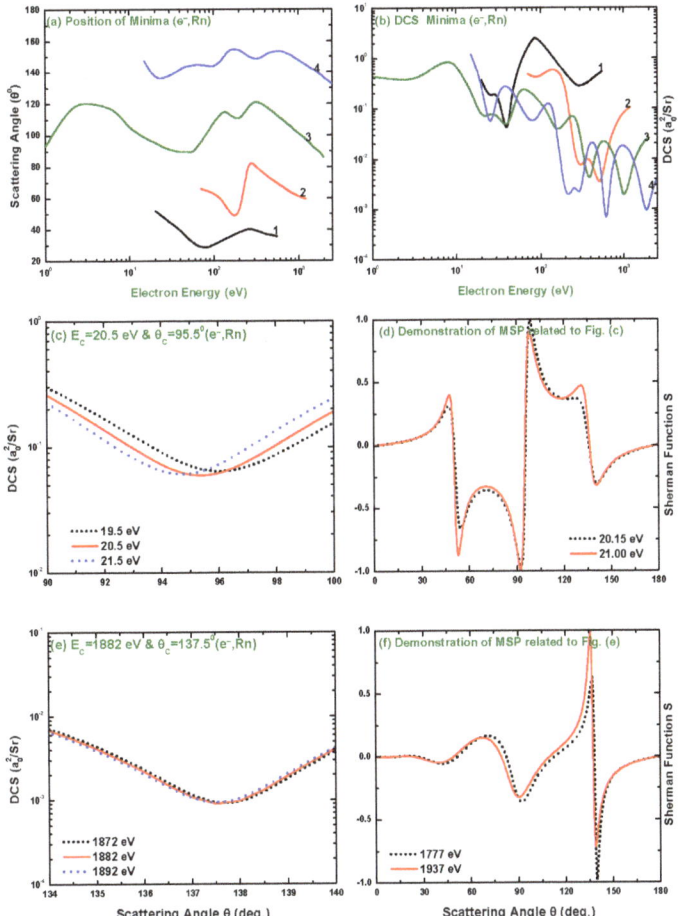

Figure 15. Energy dependence of the angular positions (**a**) and the DCS values (**b**) of the deep minima for electrons elastically scattered from neutral radon atoms. Furthermore, are presented the angular dependence of the DCS and $S(\theta)$ for some incident energies in the vicinity of the critical minimum at (E_c=20.5 eV, $\theta_c = 95.5°$) (**c**,**d**) and (E_c=1882 eV, $\theta_c = 137.5°$) (**e**,**f**).

There are some deep minima which remain conspicuous among the minimal DCS values. Furthermore, these deepest minima can be traced by plotting the energy dependent angular distribution of the DCS minima, shown in Figure 15a. The present study predict a total of 18 deep minima in the DCS, those are depicted in Figure 15b. There are 6 such deep minima from each of the low-angle (curves 1 and 2), intermediate-angle (curve 3) and high-angle (curve 4) regions. The low-angle minima are visible at 22.8, 39.2, 100, 284.0, 300 and 502.75 eV; the intermediate-angle minimum are at 2.5, 20.5, 38.6, 180, 381.0 and 1004.5 eV; and the high-angle minimum are at 24.8, 80, 199.0, 289.5, 608.0 and 1882.0 eV. For these energy-dependent DCS deep minima to be a critical minimum (CM), there are three important criteria: (i) the magnitude of the spin-flip amplitude must be larger than that of the direct amplitude, i.e., $\mid g(\theta) \mid > \mid f(\theta) \mid$, (ii) the DCS at a CM attains a local minimum, and (iii) in the vicinity of a CM, the scattered electrons acquires total polarization ($S = \pm 1$).

In view of criterion (i), among the 18 deep minima, shown in Figure 15b, 14 deep minima qualify to be CM. The remaining 4 minima, located at 80, 100, 180 and 300 eV, are not CM as $\mid g(\theta) \mid < \mid f(\theta) \mid$ for them. The energy and angular positions of the 14 CMs, denoted, respectively, by the critical energies E_c and the critical angles θ_c, are listed in Table 1. The positions of these CMs in terms of impact energy as well as scattering angle are clearly shown in 3D-plot of the DCS in Figure 16. The highest critical energy ($E_c = 1882.0$ eV) occurs at $\theta_c = 137.5°$ whereas the highest critical angle ($\theta_c = 155.0°$) shows up at E_c=199.0 eV.

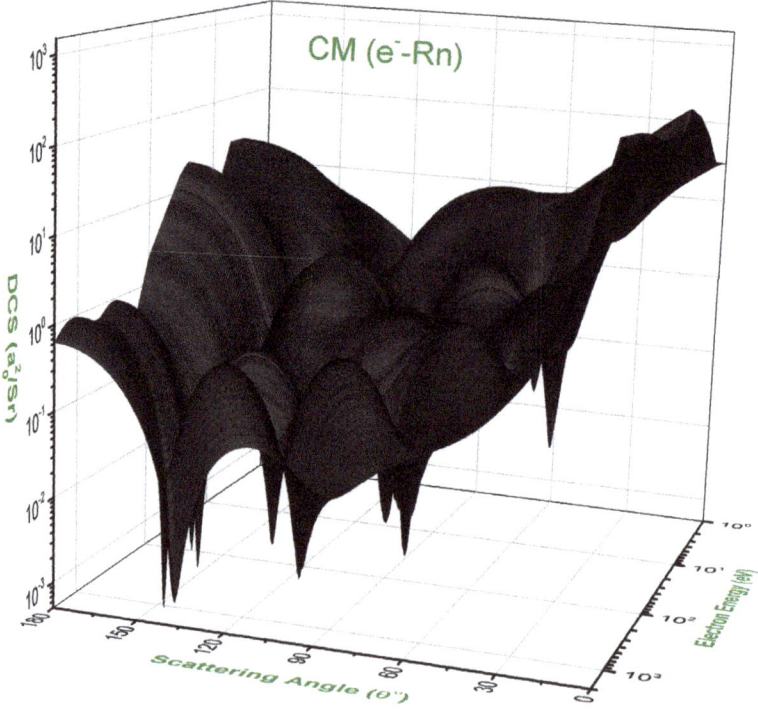

Figure 16. A three dimensional plot of the present DCS for electrons elastically scattered from neutral radon atoms.

Table 1. The positions of the DCS CM predicted by the present theory for electrons elastically scattered from neutral radon atoms.

E_c $|(eV)|$	θ_c (deg.)	$|f(\theta)|$ (cm)	$|g(\theta)|$ (cm)
2.5	120.5	1.92×10^{-9}	3.90×10^{-9}
20.5	95.5	3.73×10^{-10}	1.46×10^{-9}
22.8	49.5	1.66×10^{-10}	2.06×10^{-9}
24.8	136.5	1.89×10^{-10}	9.11×10^{-10}
38.6	90.0	2.04×10^{-10}	1.10×10^{-9}
39.2	39.5	2.59×10^{-10}	8.38×10^{-10}
199.0	155.0	7.92×10^{-11}	1.90×10^{-10}
284.0	82.0	6.46×10^{-11}	3.76×10^{-10}
289.5	149.0	1.42×10^{-11}	1.73×10^{-10}
381.0	119.5	8.37×10^{-11}	3.05×10^{-10}
502.75	71.0	1.30×10^{-11}	3.35×10^{-10}
608.0	153.5	6.49×10^{-11}	9.92×10^{-11}
1004.5	101.0	1.44×10^{-11}	3.05×10^{-10}
1882.0	137.5	3.45×10^{-11}	1.94×10^{-10}

In Figure 15c–f, also we consider our predicted CMs for criteria by presenting angular variations of DCS and Sherman function for some incident energies in the vicinity of two CMs at ($E_c = 20.5$ eV; $\theta_c = 95.5°$) and (1882.0 eV, 137.5°). As evident in Figure 15c, the DCS attains its lowest value exactly at $E_c = 20.5$ eV. A slight increase in energy to 21.5 eV or decrease to 19.5 eV, the DCS gets higher value. Similar result is also observed in Figure 15e, where the DCS value is lowest at $E_c = 1882.0$ eV than the values at 1892.0 and 1872.0 eV in the proximity. Again, from Figure 15d, it follows that, in the vicinity of the CM at ($E_c = 20.5$ eV; $\theta_c = 95.5°$), the maximum spin polarization (MSP) varies from -0.990 at ($E_i = 21$ eV; $\theta = 92.0°$) to $+0.999$ at ($E_i = 20.15$ eV; $\theta = 98.5°$). A similar behavior is also observed in Figure 15f for the CM at ($E_c = 1882.0$ eV; $\theta_c = 137.5°$). Here, the MSP attains to $+0.989$ and -0.982 at ($E_c = 1937.0$ eV; $\theta_c = 136.0°$) and ($E_c = 1777.0$ eV; $\theta_c = 139.5°$), respectively, from positive and negative excursion. In the vicinity of each of 14 CMs, we have calculated MSP points at which the polarization reaches extremal values of both signs. A total of 28 such points are found and are listed in Table 2 with their energy E_d and angular θ_d positions. One can see in Table 2 that a large polarization is achieved at all of these points that can be considered as total polarization points [41]. Figure 17 displays a 3D plot of the positions of these MSP points. All these results demonstrate the efficacy of the present theory in determining the CM positions precisely.

Table 2 also presents the energy widths ΔE, the difference between E_c and E_d, and the angular widths $\Delta \theta$, the difference between θ_c and θ_d, for each MSP point. The evaluation of these energy and angular widths are important to know the sharpness of the DCS and corresponding S distribution at a CM. For an example, if we consider the high-angle CM at ($E_c = 608.0$ eV, $\theta_c = 153.5°$), the corresponding MSP $= +0.98937$ at $E_d = 612.7$ eV with $+\Delta E = |608.0 - 612.7| = 4.7$ eV and $+\Delta \theta = |153.5 - 153.0| = 0.0°$, while MSP$= -0.91133$ at $E_d = 610.7$ eV with $-\Delta E = |608.0 - 610.7| = 2.7$ eV and $-\Delta \theta = |153.5 - 153.0| = 0.5°$. Therefore, the widths of the DCS valley are $4.7 + 2.7 = 7.4$ eV along the energy axis and $0.0° + 0.5° = 0.5°$ along the angular axis. These widths indicate that the angular DCS distribution at the CM and the corresponding S distribution near the MSP points are both very sharp.

Table 2. Maximum spin polarization (MSP) with their positions (E_d, θ_d) and deviations in energy ΔE and angle $\Delta \theta$ from the respective CM positions for e^--^{222}Rn elastic scattering.

MSP	E_d (eV)	θ_d (deg)	$\pm \Delta E$ (eV)	$\pm \Delta \theta$ (deg)
+0.99912	2.90	116.5	0.40	4.0
−0.83577	4.95	124.0	2.45	3.5
+0.99897	20.15	98.5	0.35	3.0
−0.98950	21.00	92.0	0.50	3.5
+0.99888	24.10	47.5	1.30	2.0
−0.99728	21.70	52.0	1.10	2.5
+0.99172	23.70	134.5	1.10	2.0
−0.99993	25.60	137.5	0.80	1.0
+0.99863	40.60	87.0	2.00	3.0
−0.97013	34.00	92.0	4.60	2.0
+0.99630	36.70	41.0	2.50	1.5
−0.99872	40.70	38.5	1.50	1.0
+0.97862	192.00	156.0	7.00	1.0
−0.99858	201.50	154.5	2.50	0.5
+0.91586	266.00	82.5	18.00	0.5
−0.99647	299.00	82.0	15.00	0.0
+0.99018	291.50	148.0	2.00	1.0
−0.96734	276.20	150.0	13.30	1.0
+0.99993	360.00	121.0	21.00	1.5
−0.99981	401.00	118.0	20.00	1.5
+0.97688	486.00	70.5	16.75	0.5
−0.93089	517.50	71.5	14.75	0.5
+0.98937	612.70	153.5	4.70	0.0
−0.91133	610.70	153.0	2.70	0.5
+0.99497	1002.00	99.5	2.50	1.5
−0.95727	1004.00	102.5	0.50	1.5
+0.98881	1937.0	136.0	55.00	1.5
−0.98166	1777.0	139.5	105.0	2.0

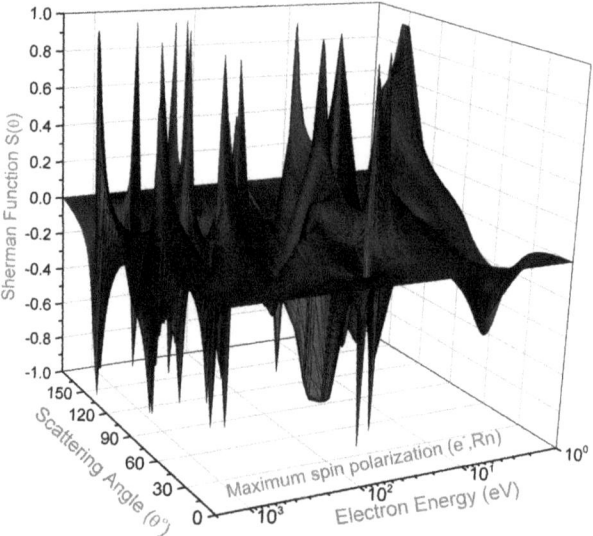

Figure 17. A 3D-plot of the present Sherman function for electrons elastically scattered from neutral radon atoms.

In Figure 18, we resent our results of the integrated elastic (IECS), momentum-transfer (MTCS), viscosity (VCS), inelastic (INCS) and total (TCS) cross sections for 1 eV$\leq E_i \leq$ 100 keV electrons scattering from neutral radon atoms. We are not aware of any experimental data of these observables available in the literature. Therefore, we compare our results of IECS, MTCS, INCS and TCS with theoretical predictions of Neerja et al. [19] available at E_i = 2.0–500.00 eV and IECS, MTCS and VCS of Mayol and Salvat [20] at E_i = 100 eV–100 keV. The comparison shows that our results agree well with those of Mayol and Salvat [20]. At $E_i <$ 100 eV, our results disagree significantly with those of Neerja et al. [19] specially in the vicinity of minima positions. In this energy domain, the present theory predicts deep minima whereas the predictions from [19] show very shallow minima. One can see that, beyond 5 eV (the first excitation energy of radon),the TCS is greater than IECS. This expected because of the absorption of some particles into the inelastic channels.

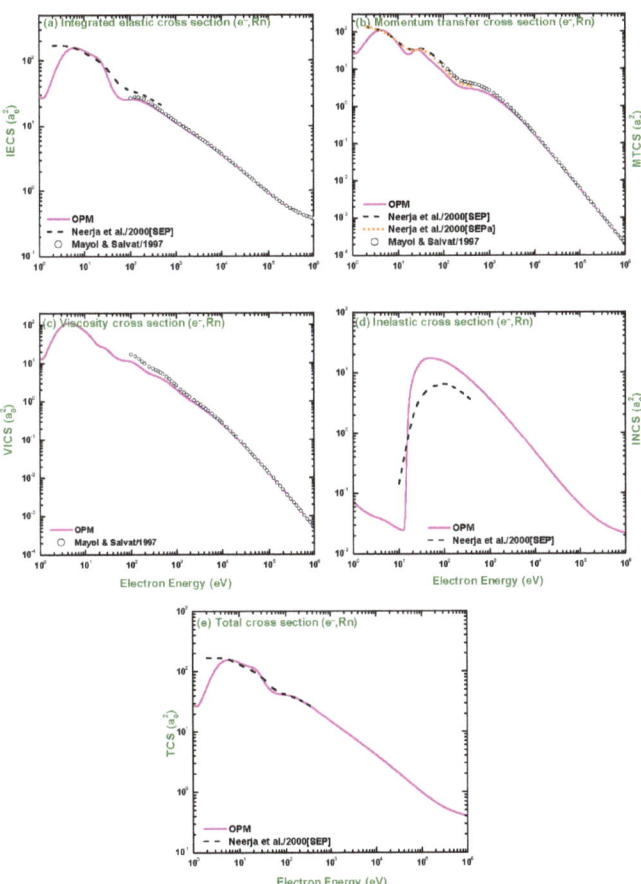

Figure 18. Energy dependence of the (a) integrated elastic, (b) momentum-transfer, (c) viscosity, (d) inelastic and (e) total cross sections for electron impact scattering from neutral radon atoms. Presented are the theoretical calculations — for the present results, – – – for Neerja et al. [19], ... for Neerja et al. [19] and ○ ○ ○ for Mayol and Salvat. SEP and SEPa, respectively, denote the static-exchange-polarization potentials and SEP with absorption potential.

4.2. Positron Scattering from Neutral Radon

Figures 19–22 present angular dependent DCS for the elastic scattering of positrons from neutral radon at impact energies 10 eV $\leq E_i \leq$ 10 keV. As evident in these figures, unlike electron DCSs the positron counterparts show relatively fewer number of maxima and minima. Two significant minima are seen at E_i = 10 eV and only one at 10 < $E_i \leq$ 30 eV. After that few very shallow minima are obtained within the energy domain of 40 eV $\leq E_i \leq$ 150 eV confined to lower scattering angles. At 200 eV and beyond, the DCS values decrease monotonously with increasing incident energies.

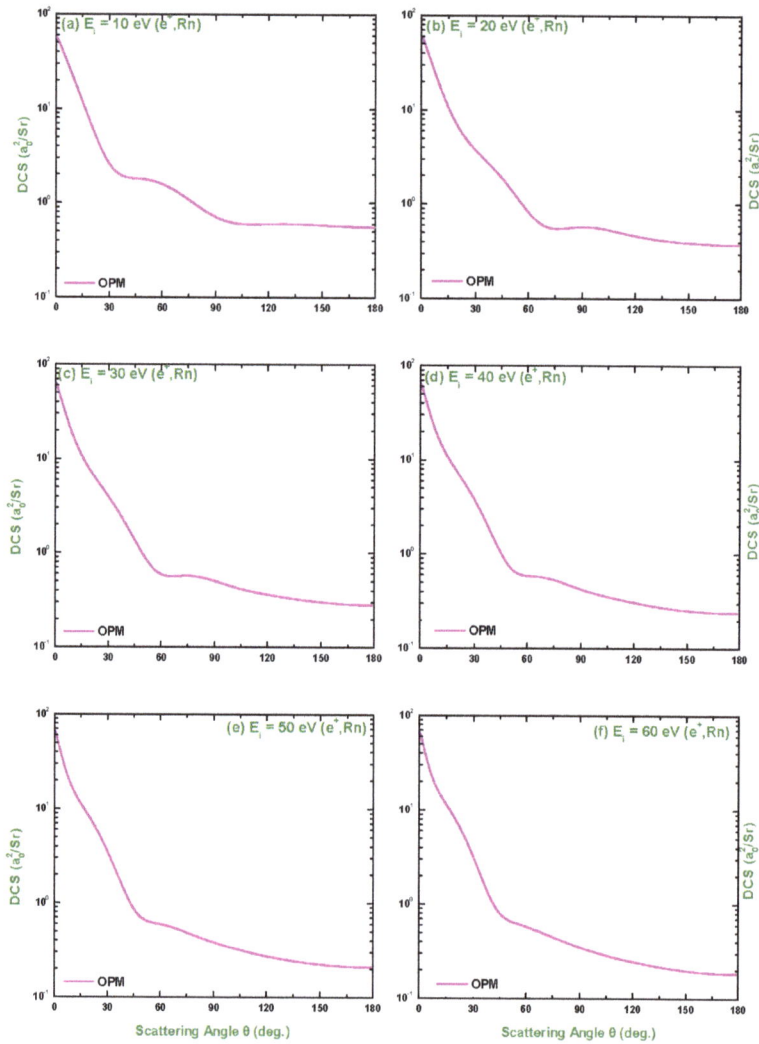

Figure 19. Differential cross sections for 10, 20, 30, 40, 50 and 60 eV positrons elastically scattered from neutral radon atoms as a function of scattering angle.

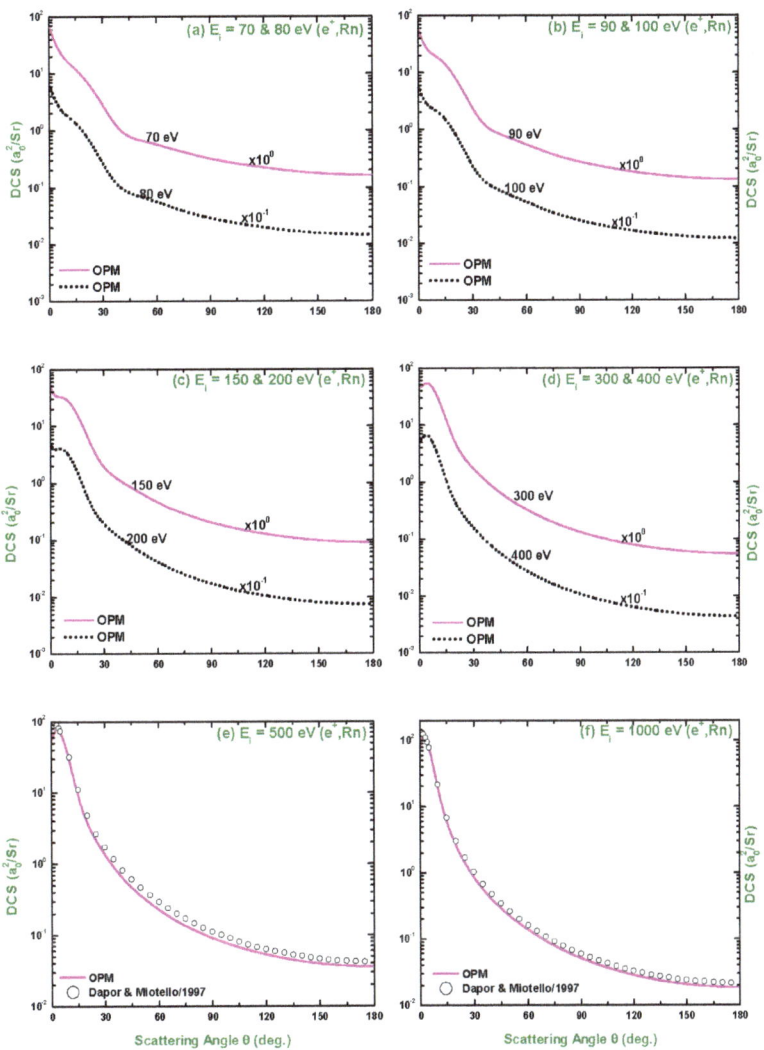

Figure 20. Same as Figure 19, but at impact energies of (**a**) 70 and 80 eV, (**b**) 90 and 100 eV, (**c**) 150 and 200 eV, (**d**) 300 and 400 eV, (**e**) 500 eV, and (**f**) 1000 eV. In addition, the calculations of Dapor and Miotello [21] at 500 and 1000 eV are presented.

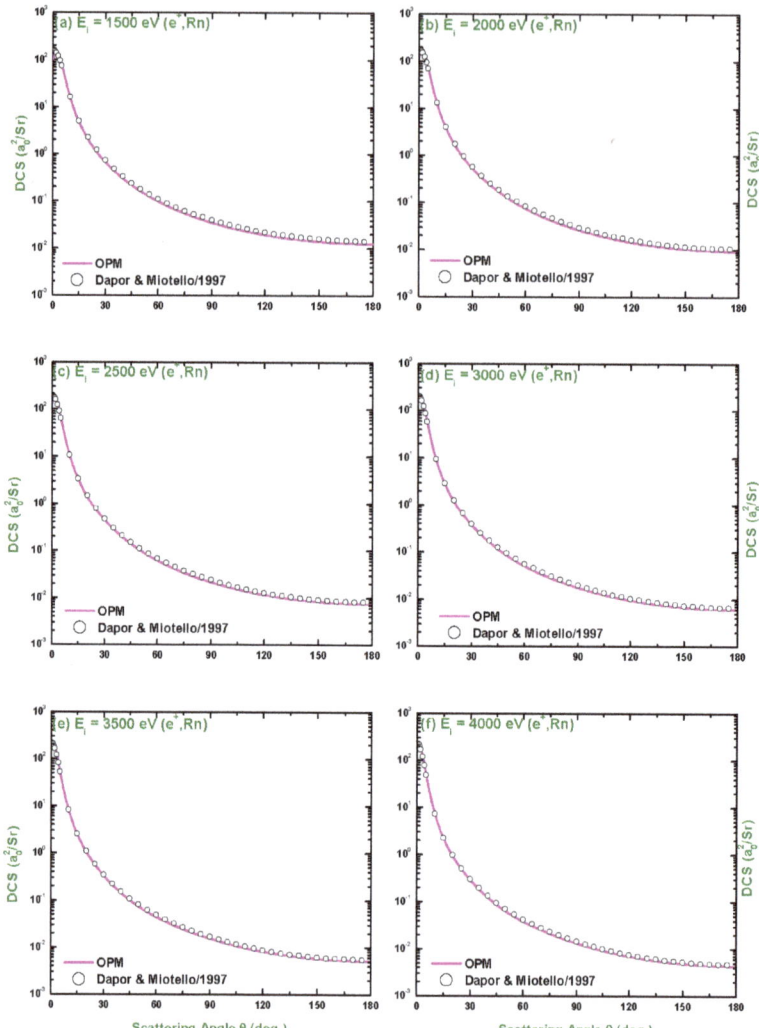

Figure 21. Same as Figure 19, but at impact energies of 1500, 2000, 2500, 3000, 3500 and 4000 eV. ∘ ∘ ∘ curves are the calculations of Dapor and Miotello [21].

We have not found any experimental measurements for positron impact on radon targets. The present DCS results for positron impact scattering are, therefore, compared with the only calculations of Dapor and Miotello [21] available for E_i = 500–4000 eV. The comparison shows that the two calculations agree very well with each other except a slight differences in magnitude at 500 eV for higher scattering angles.

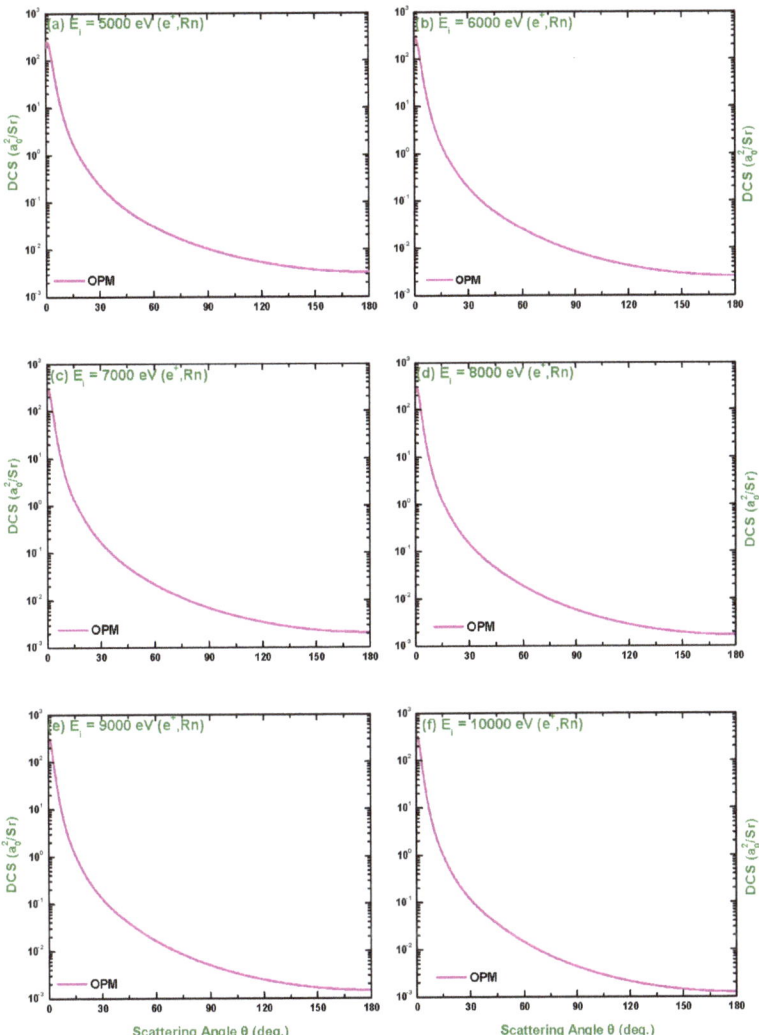

Figure 22. Same as Figure 19, but at impact energies of 5, 6, 7, 8, 9 and 10 keV.

In Figure 23, we display energy dependence of the DCS and of the corresponding Sherman function for positron scattering from neutral radon atoms at three scattering angles 30°, 90° and 150°. As seen in this figure, minor structures appear in the DCS distributions at lower scattering angles, and they fade with the increase of energy. The present DCSs are again compared with those of Dapor and Miotello [21]. Similar to the case of electron scattering, the Sherman function increases with increasing scattering angles. However, the positron spin polarization is considerably smaller than that of its electron counterpart. This might be due to the Coulomb-dominated behavior of the positron potential [42].

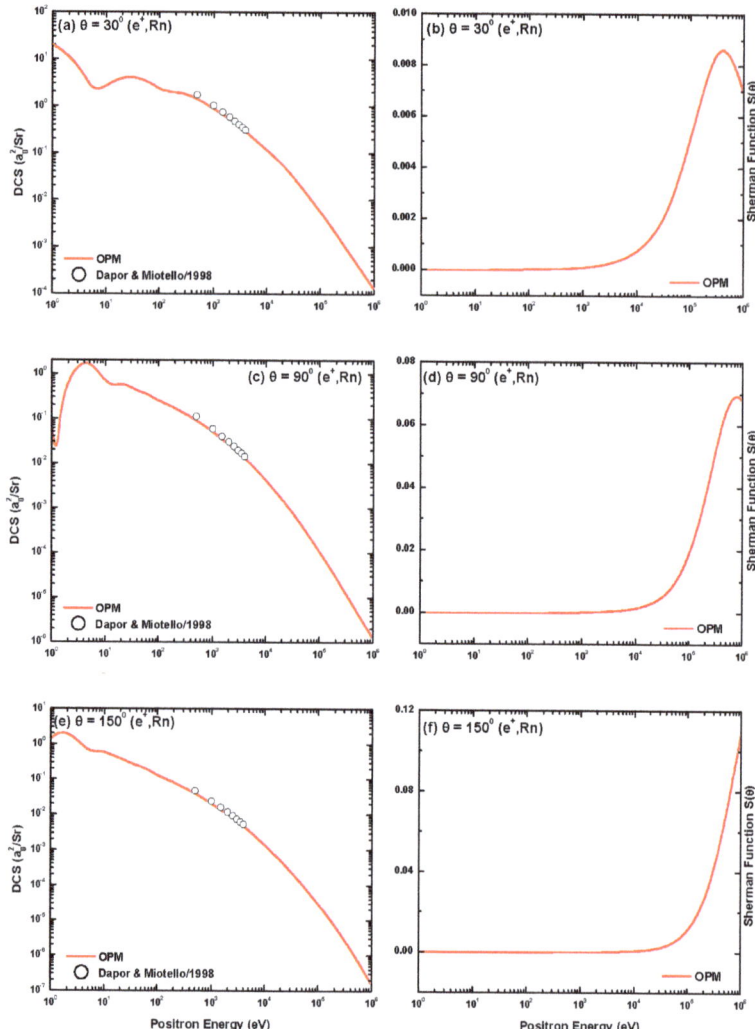

Figure 23. Energy dependence of the DCS and the Sherman function for positrons elastically scattered from neutral radon atoms at scattering angles (**a**,**b**): 30°, (**c**,**d**): 90° and (**e**,**f**): 150°.

Energy dependence of the spin polarization parameters U and T for positrons elastically scattered from neutral radon atoms are depicted in Figure 24 at $\theta = 30°, 90°$ and 150°. It is observed in this figure that, as expected, the variation of U and T with energy are opposite to each other. Starting from zero, the magnitude of $|U(\theta)|$ increases very slowly up to $E_i = 10$ keV, and beyond that it increases rapidly and reaches its maximum value. The maximum value of $|U(\theta)|$ is obtained at $\theta = 90°$. Below and beyond this scattering angle, the $|U(\theta)|$ values decrease. The parameter T, on the other hand, starts at its maximum and slowly decreases with energies. Beyond $E_i = 10$ keV, the values of $|T(\theta)|$ sharply fall to its minimum, which is the lowest at $\theta = 90°$. We are not aware of any experimental or any other theoretical studies regarding these parameter for $e^\pm -$ Rn scattering. We expect that the present study will encourage both experimental and theoretical groups to pay their attention to this scattering system.

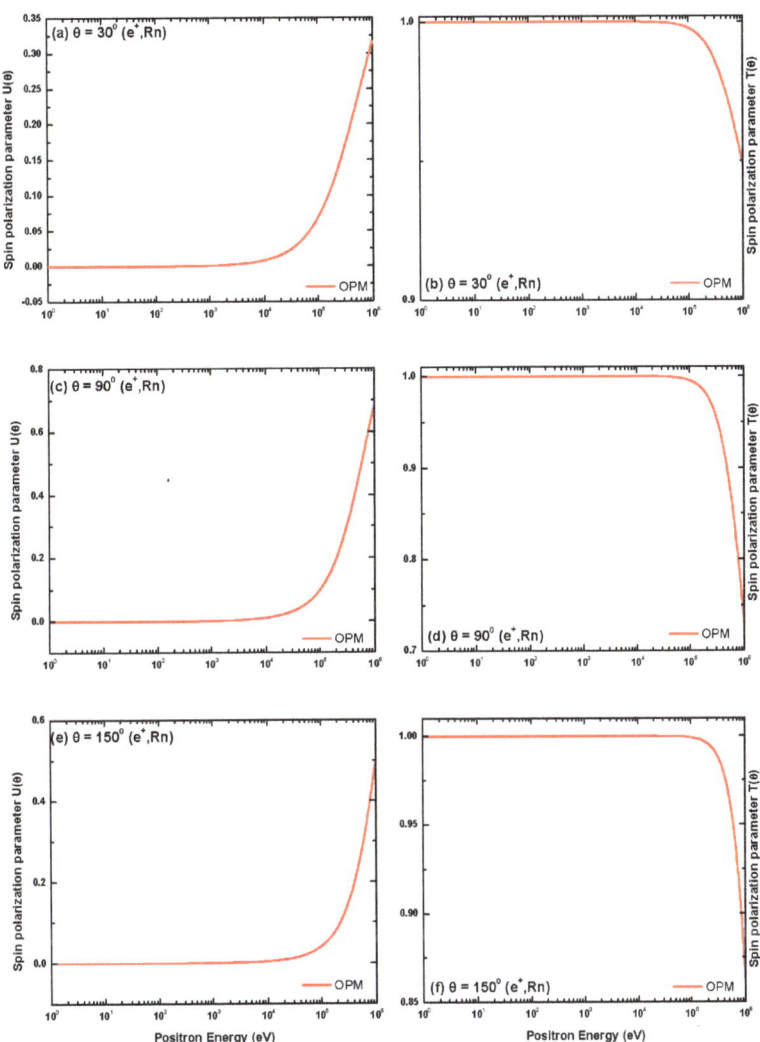

Figure 24. Energy dependence of the spin polarization parameters U and T for positrons elastically scattered from neutral radon atoms at scattering angles (**a**,**b**): 30°, (**c**,**d**): 90° and (**e**,**f**): 150°.

For e^+-^{222}Rn scattering, the present results of IECS, MTCS, VCS, INCS and TCS calculated for 1 eV $\leq E_i \leq$ 1 MeV are presented in Figure 25. It is noticeable that all these results are considerably different in values and shape from their electron counterparts. The magnitude of these cross sections is two to three times smaller than those due to electron scattering. Regarding the shape, on the other hand, some structures are clearly visible in IECS, MTCS and VCS curves for electron scattering, whereas they are very shallow in the case of positron scattering. These variations certainly support the fact that the e^+-^{222}Rn interaction is rather weaker as compared to its electron counterpart. It is worth mentioning that the interaction potentials involved in these two projectiles are drastically different. In the case of positron projectile, the static potential (V_{st}) is repulsive and the exchange potential (V_{ex}) is absent as opposed to the electron projectile. Moreover, the polarization potential of the short range parts also different for both the projectiles.

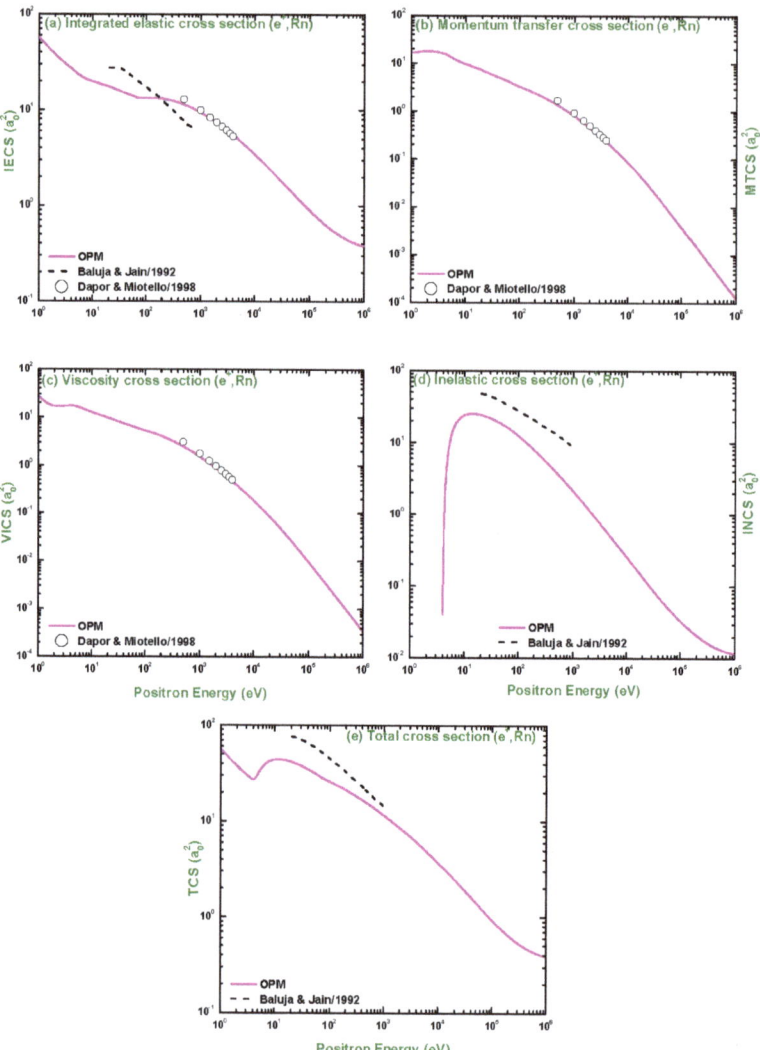

Figure 25. Energy dependence of the (**a**) integrated elastic, (**b**) momentum-transfer, (**c**) viscosity, (**d**) inelastic and (**e**) total cross sections for positron impact scattering from neutral radon atoms. Presented are the theoretical calculations —— for the present results, – – – for Baluja and Jain [12] and ○ ○ ○ for Dapor and Miotello [21].

Because of the absence of any experimental data of the above scattering observables we compare our IECS, INCS and TCS results with the theoretical calculations of Baluja and Jain [12] available for 20 eV $\leq E_i \leq$ 1 keV and our IECS, MTCS and VCS results with those of Dapor and Miotello [21] available for 0.5 keV $\leq E_i \leq$ 4 keV. The comparison shows that the present results produce a nice agreement with those of Dapor and Miotello [21]. However, a noticeable disagreement is seen between our results and those of Baluja and Jain [12], especially in the case of IECS. This difference again might be due to the different procedures of calculations used by these two methods.

4.3. $e^{\pm}$ Scattering from Radon Ions

In Figures 26 and 27, the energy dependent DCS and the corresponding Sherman function for e^{-}-Rn^{q+} scattering are displayed, where q = 1, 10, 30, 50, 70 and 86 indicates the ionic states, at a fixed scattering angle of 90°. To the best of our knowledge, there are neither any experimental nor any other theoretical studies on theses scattering systems available in the literature.

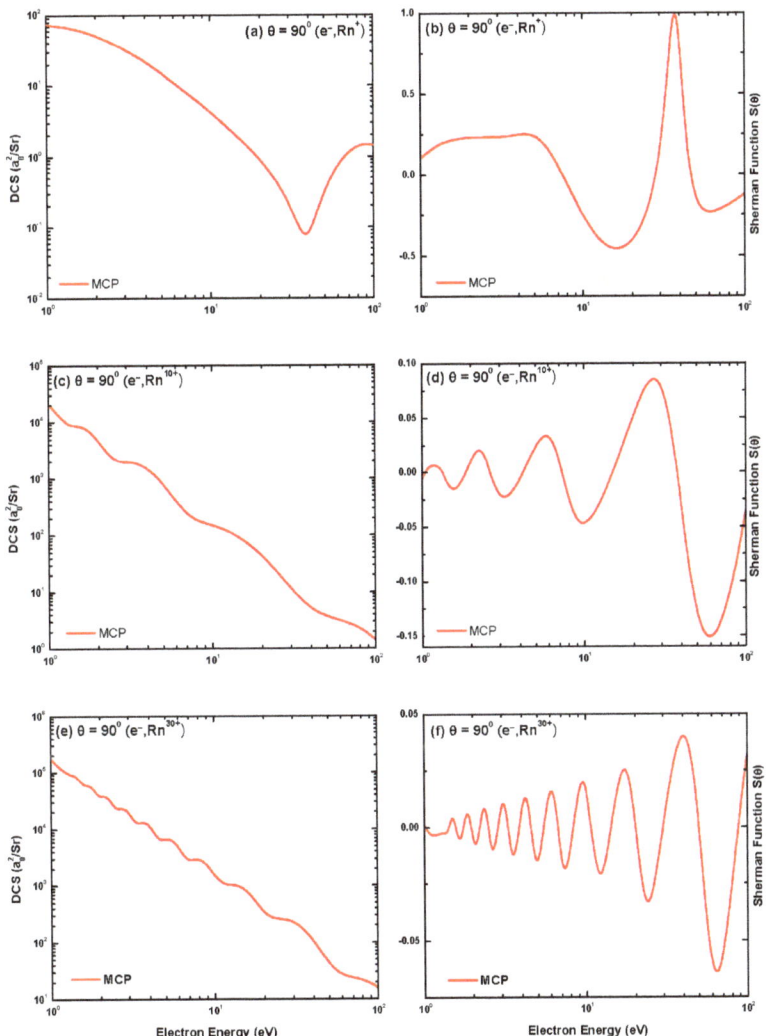

Figure 26. Energy dependent DCS and corresponding Sherman function for the elastic scattering of electrons from (**a,b**): Rn$^+$, (**c,d**): Rn^{10+} and (**e,f**): Rn^{30+} at fixed scattering angle $\theta = 90°$.

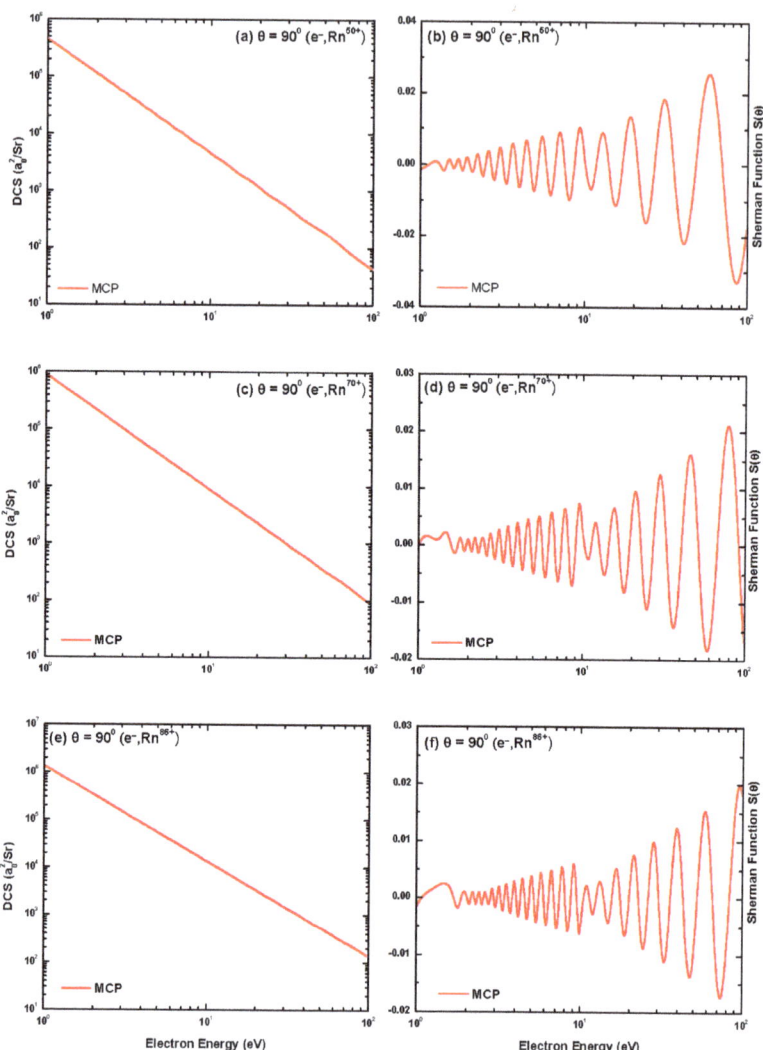

Figure 27. Energy dependent DCS and corresponding Sherman function for the elastic scattering of electrons from (**a**,**b**): Rn^{50+}, (**c**,**d**): Rn^{70+} and (**e**,**f**): Rn^{86+} at fixed scattering angle $\theta = 90°$.

As seen in Figures 26 and 27, the DCS values, at a particular energy, increase with increasing ionic charge of the target. This is expected according to the Rutherford scattering formula. The number of structures in DCSs increases with increasing ionic charge. However, increasing charge state weakens the interference pattern. This might be due to the decreasing contributions of short range potential of the bound electrons. Sharp structures in DCS are observed at low energies. This could be explained as the interference effect between the scattered waves due to the short range and Coulombic forces. At such low energies, velocity of the incident electron is comparable to the velocities of the bound electrons of the ion. Furthermore, the short range potential becomes important due to the enhanced electron-electron correlations. The structures in the Sherman function are related to those in the DCSs, but they are more pronounced in Sherman function distributions.

Figures 28 and 29 display the DCS and the corresponding Sherman function results for positron projectiles elastically scattered from various ionic states of radon. It is seen that the variation of the cross section and the corresponding Sherman function with the ionic charge is similar to their electron counterpart. However, the spin asymmetry for positrons is extremely small signifying that the positron scattering is rather weaker than the electron scattering.

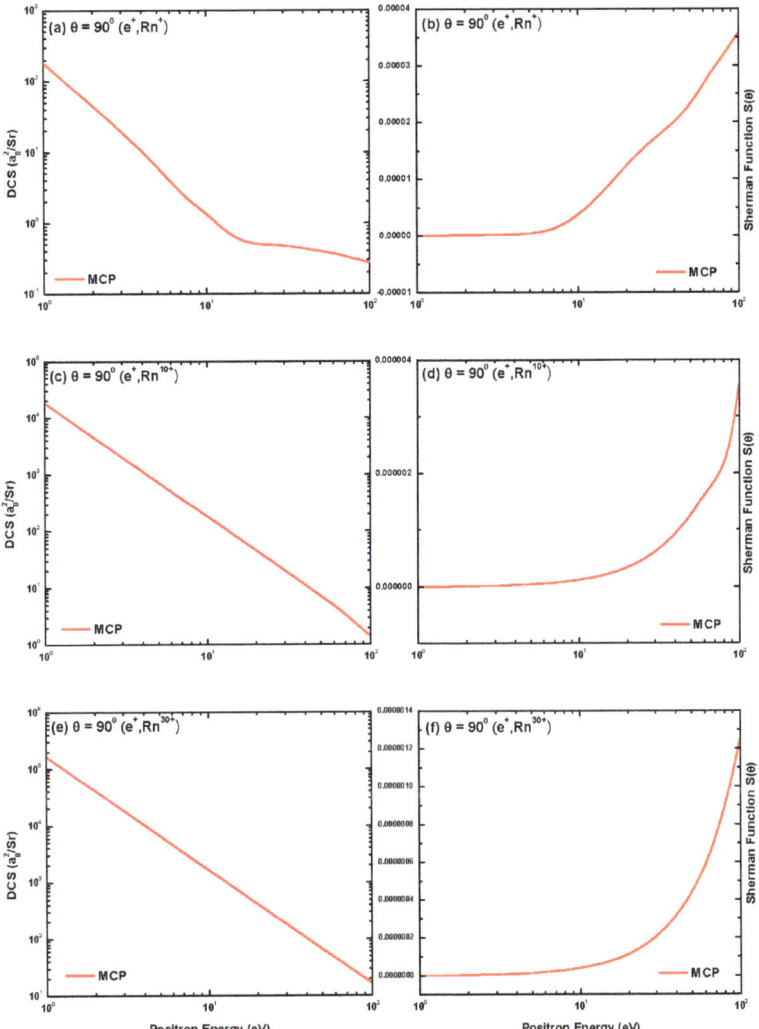

Figure 28. Energy dependent DCS and corresponding Sherman function for positrons elastically scattered from (**a**,**b**): Rn^+, (**c**,**d**): Rn^{10+} and (**e**,**f**): Rn^{30+} at fixed scattering angle $\theta = 90°$.

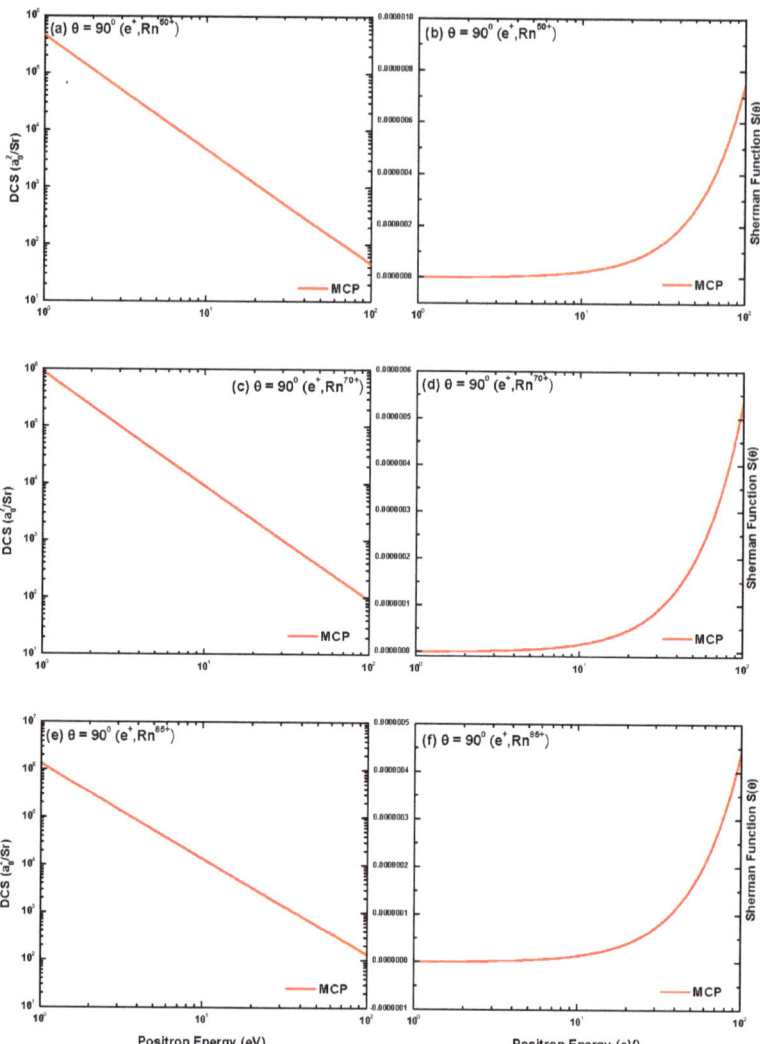

Figure 29. Energy dependent DCS and corresponding Sherman function for positrons elastically scattered from (**a**,**b**): Rn^{50+}, (**c**,**d**): Rn^{70+} and (**e**,**f**): Rn^{86+} at fixed scattering angle $\theta = 90°$.

Figure 30 displays the energy variation of the IECS, MTCS and VCS of electrons elastically scattered from different charge states of radon ions. As seen in this figure, for ions with lower q (< 30), the IECS increases with increasing the charge. This is expected because of the screening effect of the surrounding electron cloud. The interaction potential energy of the projectile electron with bound electron cloud is opposite in sign to that of the nucleus charge. Furthermore, the screening effect of the surrounding electron cloud is, therefore, strong for the ions of lower charge. The cross section increases as the increase of q diminishes the screening effect. It is also evident that, for ($q \geq 30$), the IECS is almost independent of q and varies in conformity with the Rutherford scattering formula corresponding to the nuclear charge Z. For ions with higher q, the cross section is almost solely determined by the nuclear charge of the ion. From Figure 28, one can see the similar trend in the energy dependent MTCS and VCS with the ion charge q.

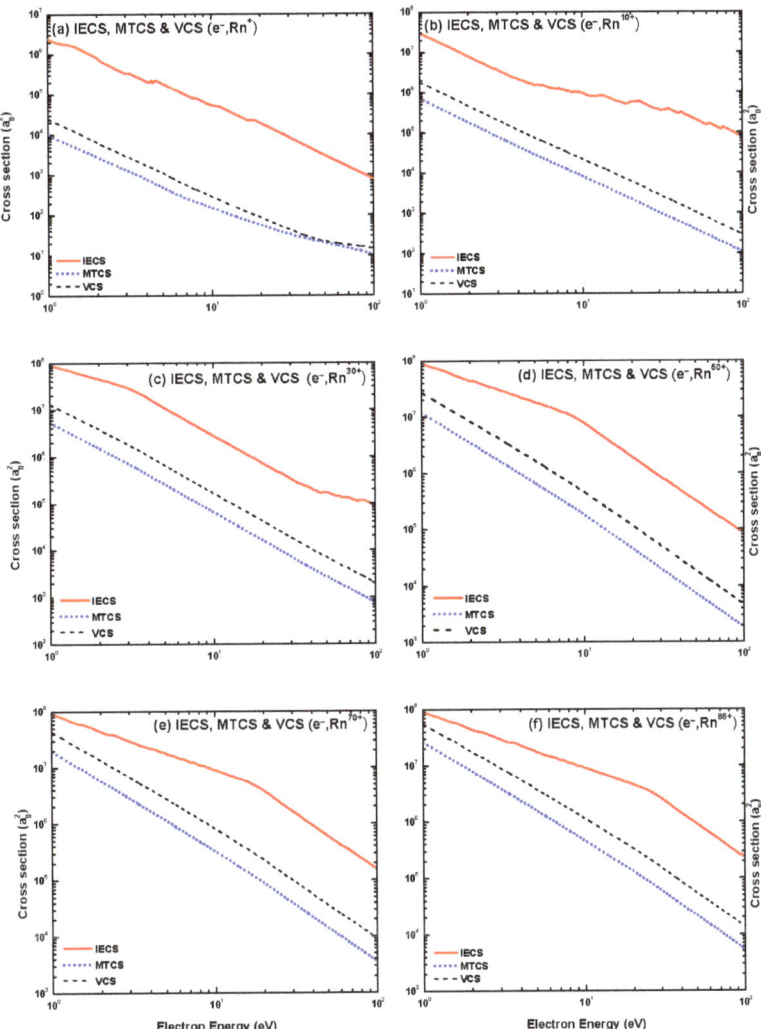

Figure 30. Energy dependence of the IECS, MTCS and VCS for the elastic scattering of electrons from (**a**) Rn^+, (**b**) Rn^{10+}, (**c**) Rn^{30+}, (**d**) Rn^{50+}, (**e**) Rn^{70+} and (**f**) Rn^{86+}.

Figure 31 presents the Coulomb glory at three different ionic states (q = 40, 55 and 70) of radon. This Coulomb glory arises due to the electrostatic screening of nuclear potential by atomic electrons. Because of the presence of Coulomb glory the scaled differential cross section (SDCS) becomes maximum at $\theta = 180°$. An important feature of the Coulomb glory is that for a particular ion charge, there is a critical energy at which the SDCS gets its maximum value. In the vicinity of that critical energy the cross sections become smaller. As seen in Figure 31a, for q = 40, the maximum SDCS is observed at E_i = 850 eV. Furthermore, SDCS gets lower values both for increasing energy to 1200 eV or decreasing to 300 eV. Similar results are also observed for the ionicities q = 55, in Figure 31b, and for q = 70, in Figure 31c. The maximum SDCSs, for later two ionicities, are observed at E_i = 450 and 225 eV, respectively.

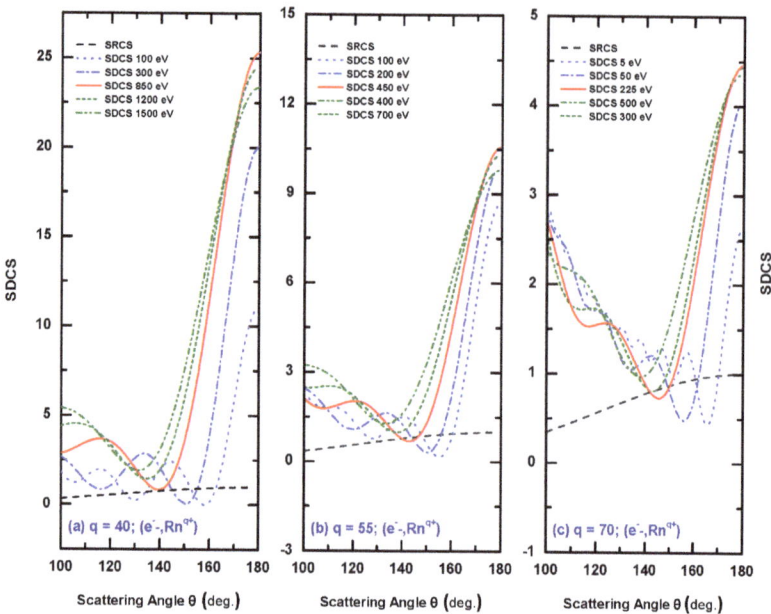

Figure 31. Angular variation of the scaled differential cross section for e^--Rn^{q+} scattering at different energies for the ionicities q = (**a**) 40, (**b**) 55 and (**c**) 70. Furthermore, are present the scaled Rutherford cross sections for the same scattering systems.

Figure 31 also revealed that, for a particular ion charge, the width of the maximum increases with increasing energy, the ratio of ion DCS to Rutherford DCS decreases with the increase of ion charge. One can also observed that, with the increase of ion charge, the strongest Coulomb glory shifts toward low incident energy. This is expected because the strength of the potential of the electronic cloud at the origin is stronger for lower degree of ionicities than higher ones. It means that ion-target of high ion charge can cause low energy electron to get backscattered and vice versa. This causes strongest Coulomb glory to be observed at low incident energy for higher ion charge and at comparatively high incident energy for low ion charge.

4.4. Comparison of the Electron and Positron Impact Results

In Figure 32, we compare the energy dependent DCS and the corresponding Sherman function results at 90° for the scattering of electrons and positrons from neutral radon atoms. The basic features of the DCS in the energy region above some tens of eV up to a few keV are oscillations originated due to the diffraction of the projectile beam by the atomic target electrons. The structures disappear when the collision becomes energetic enough so that the beam has passed even the innermost K-shell electrons before the scattering events take place. As seen in Figure 32a, for electron impact scattering, three DCS minima appear within E_i = 30 eV to 3 keV, and beyond that the DCS decreases monotonously with increasing energy. For positron impact scattering, on the other hand, the number of DCS minima reduces to 2 and confined to low energies: the first minimum is at 2 eV and the second one at 20 eV. The reduced number of DCS minima for positron projectile is due to the absence of exchange potential, and low energy structure is the influence of the correlation polarization potential. One can also see from Figure 32a that the values of positron DCS at all energies are smaller than those of electron DCS. This feature supports the fact that the target electrons do not serve as scattering centers for the positrons. Instead, they screen the central field, thereby lowering the DCS as compared to its electron counterpart.

Figure 32b displays the Sherman function results comparing between the electron and positron impact scattering. For the case of electron scattering, pronounced structures are observed in the Sherman function, the positions of which strongly correlate to those in the DCS. For positron projectile, on the other hand, no structure appears up to 100 keV, and the value of spin asymmetry is extremely low. This fact can be related to the repulsive potential which prevents the positron to penetrate the nucleus in contrast to its electron counterpart.

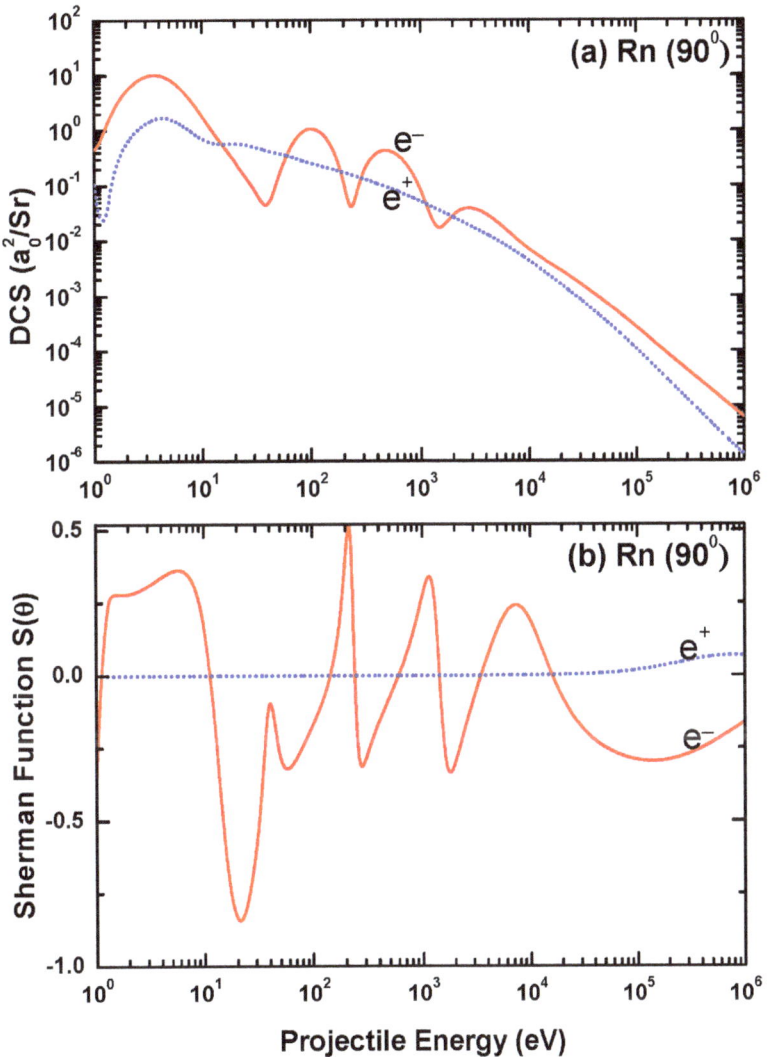

Figure 32. Comparison of (**a**) the differential cross section and (**b**) the corresponding Sherman function for the collisions of electrons and positrons from neutral radon targets at the scattering angle of 90°.

In Figure 33, we compare our spin polarization parameters U and T results, respectively, in Figure 33a,b, between electron and positron impact scatterings at fixed angle $\theta = 90°$. It is revealed that, for electron scattering, multiple structures appear in both U and T up to several hundred keV. However, the structures are more stronger at lower energy and become less pronounced with increasing energy. For positron scattering, on the other hand, no structures are observed in U and T. Starting from zero the U parameter increases very slowly with energy up to 300 keV and then increases rapidly. The same feature is also observed in the case of T parameter but with opposite sign.

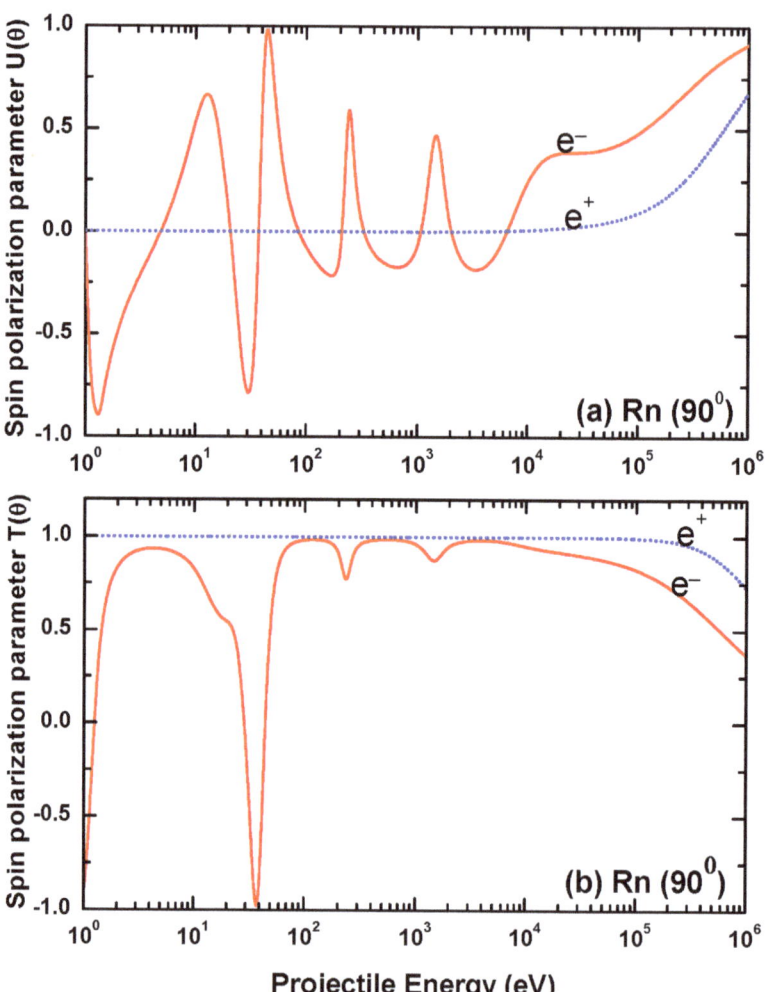

Figure 33. Comparison of (**a**) the differential cross section and (**b**) the corresponding Sherman function for the collisions of electrons and positrons from Rn^{50+} ion targets at the scattering angle of 90°.

Figure 34 compares the DCS and the Sherman functions of the electron and positron impact scattering from Rn^{50+} ion targets. There is no significant difference between electron and positron DCSs except a shallow minimum observed at 200 eV in electron DCS. In electron impact Sherman function shows multiple structures with higher excursion with increasing energy, whereas the Sherman function, for positron impact scattering, is almost zero all through the displayed energy domain.

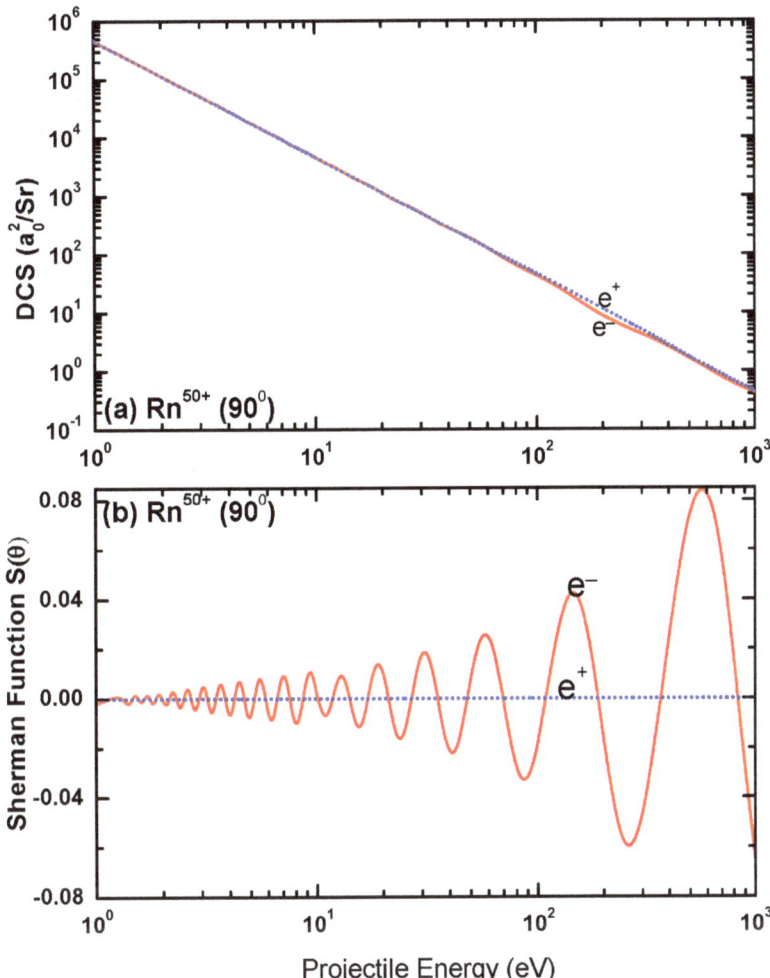

Figure 34. Comparison of (**a**) the differential cross section and (**b**) the corresponding Sherman function for the collisions of electrons and positrons from Rn^{50+} ion targets at the scattering angle of 90°.

In Figure 35, we depict energy variation of the IECS, MTCS, VCS, INCS and TCS results for electron scattering from neutral radon atoms in comparison with those for positron impact scattering. The comparison shows, at higher energy region (well above 1 keV), no significant difference in the above mentioned observables between the two collision systems. However, at lower energy region ($E_i < 1$ keV), the cross sections produce a remarkable change with changing the projectile. The R-T structures, for electron projectile, are stronger both in number and intensity than those for positron counterpart. This result indicates that the exchange, the polarization and the absorption potentials almost vanish at energies beyond 1 keV. Furthermore, the static part, opposite in sign for the two projectiles, is the sole contributor to the scattering and the potentials, with the same magnitude but opposite in sign, make the same contribution to the scattering.

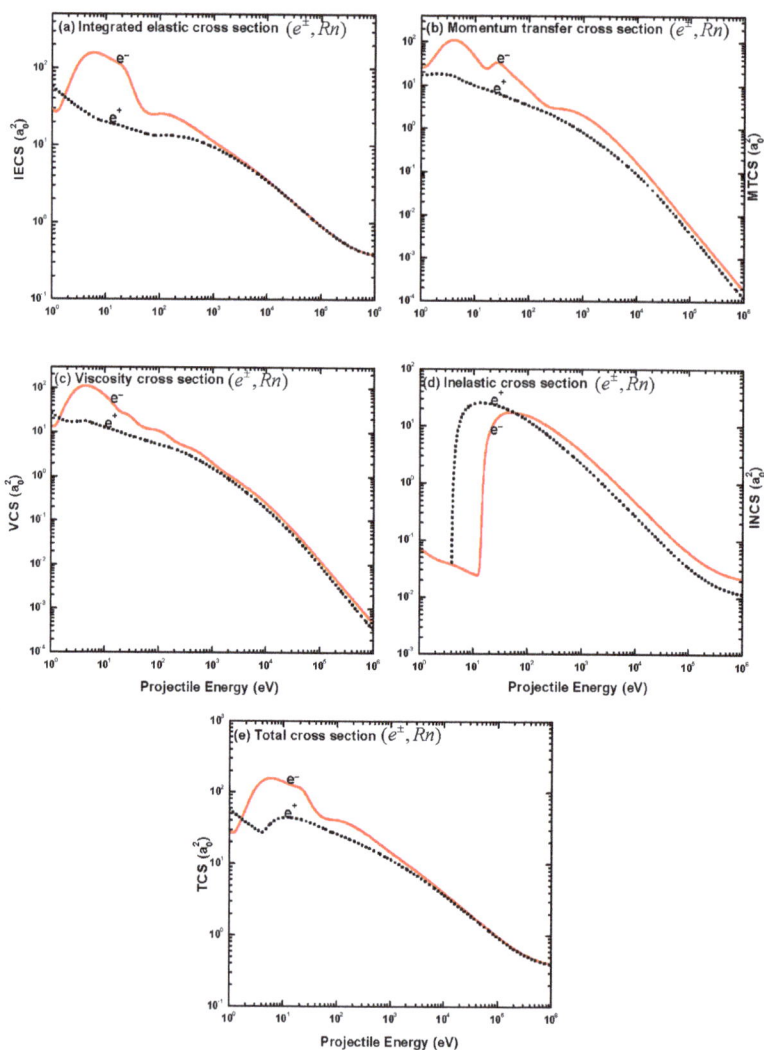

Figure 35. Comparison of IECS, MTCS, VCS, INCS and TCS results for the collisions of electrons and positrons from neutral radon at the scattering angle of 90°.

5. Conclusions

In this paper, we report on the calculations of DCS, IECS, MTCS, VCS, INCS, TCS and spin asymmetry parameters S, U and T for both the electrons and positrons impact scattering from radon isonuclear series over a wide collision energy $1\,\text{eV} \leq E_i \leq 1\,\text{MeV}$. The aforesaid scattering observables have been calculated within Dirac relativistic partial wave analysis employing a modified Coulomb potential. For the first time, the present study furnishes the detailed analysis of the CM in the DCS distributions and the total spin-polarization in the elastic scattering of electrons from neutral radon atoms. We also present SDCS and RDCS, and demonstrate the Coulomb glory effects. We have not found any experimental results, available in the literature, of these scattering observables for these scattering systems. However, a comparison of our evaluated cross sections shows a reasonable agreement with the available theoretical results.

As expected, in the low energy DCSs, the present study observes interference structures for electron scattering and structureless behavior in the case of positron scattering, whereas high energy DCSs for these two projectiles are similar in pattern. This indicates that the exchange potential, present in e$^-$-atom interaction, is responsible for the production of maxima-minima. The same effect causes greater number of maxima- minima in the angular distributions of DCS and S , at different energies, for the former scattering system than the latter. Furthermore, this effect is negligible at high energies, thereby leading to the almost parallel behavior of the DCS for both the projectiles. This study also reveals the effect of the short-range potential , originating from the screening bound electrons, on the cross section up to to charge state Rn^{30+}. Beyond this charge state, the cross section is almost independent of the charge state, due to the dominance of nuclear potential and diminution of screening effect. The energy dependence of the IECS, MTCS, VCS, INCS and TCS shows a non-monotonous pattern of the minimum-maximum type up to the collision energy of 1 keV. At all energies and for both the aforesaid projectiles, the DCS maximum occurs at the scattering angle $\theta = 0$ and it gradually falls off with the increase of the scattering angle in region of small angles. This arises due to the property of the Legendre polynomial factor in the expression for $f(\theta)$ in the Equation (30).

For the present electron impact scattering, we obtain 18 deep DCS minima including 14 CMs, where the DCS attains its smallest value. In the proximity of these CMs, we determine 28 MSP points where the spin polarization varies from +0.92 to +1.00 and from -0.84 to -1.00, respectively, in positive and negative excursions. All of these MSP points can be termed as the total polarization points. These results demonstrate the efficacy of the present modified Coulomb potential in determining accurately the deepest DCS valley and CM positions. Pronounced Coulomb glory effect, an amplification of elastic backscattering due to the attractive screened Coulomb potential, is observed in the angular distribution of elastically scattered electrons. Because of the strength of the potential of electronic cloud to scatter electron through $\theta = 180°$, the strongest Coulomb glory effect is seen to shift towards lower charge state. All of these analyses for e$^\pm$-Rn scattering systems still await verification by future experimental as well as theoretical studies.

Author Contributions: M.H.K.: investigation, writing and review; A.K.F.H.: methodology and supervision; M.M.H.: writing original draft preparation and Editing; M.M.B.: data curation and editing. H.W.: review and resources; M.A.U.: software, review and conceptualization. All authors have read and agreed to the published version of the manuscript.

Funding: This research received no external funding.

Conflicts of Interest: The authors declare no conflict of interest.

References

1. Andersen, N.; Gallagher, J.W.; Hertel, I.V. Collisional alignment and orientation of atomic outer shells I. Direct excitation by electron and atom impact. *Phys. Rep.* **1988**, *165*, 1–188. [CrossRef]
2. Müller, A. Fundamentals of electron-ion interaction. *Hyperfine Interact.* **1996**, *99*, 31–45. [CrossRef]
3. Jean, P.; Gillard, W.; Marcowith, A.; Ferrière, K. Positron transport in the interstellar medium. *Astron. Astrophys.* **2009**, *508*, 1099–1116. [CrossRef]
4. Massey, H.S.W., Lawson, J. Thompson, D.G. Quantum theory of atoms, molecules and the solid state. In *A tribute to John C. Slater*; Academic Press: New York, NY, USA, 1966.
5. Tioukine, V.; Aulenbacher, K.; Riehn, E. A Mott polarimeter operating at MeV electron beam energies. *Rev. Sci. Instr.* **2011**, *82*, 033303. [CrossRef]
6. Afroz, S.; Haque, M.M.; Haque, A.F.; Jakubassa-Amundsen, D.H.; Patoary, M.A.R.; Shorifuddoza, M.; Khandker, M.H.; Uddin, M.A. Elastic scattering of electrons and positrons from ^{115}In atoms over the energy range 1 eV–0.5 GeV. *Results Phys.* **2020**, *18*, 103179. [CrossRef]
7. Hassan, R.; Haque, M.M.; Haque, A.K.F.; Shorifuddoza, M.; Khandker, M.H.; Patoary, M.A.R.; Basak, A.K.; Maaza, M.; Saha, B.C.; Uddin, M.A. Relativistic study on the scattering of electrons and positrons from atomic iron at energies 1 eV–10 keV. *Mol. Phys.* **2020**, *119*, 1849838 . [CrossRef]
8. McKenna, P.; Williams, I.D. Differential cross section measurements for elastic scattering of electrons from Ar^{2+} and Xe^{2+}. *Phys. Scr.* **2001**, *T92*, 370-372. [CrossRef]

9. Brotton, S.J.; McKenna, P.; Gribakin, G.; Williams, I.D. Angular distribution for the elastic scattering of electrons from $Ar^+(3s^23p^{52}P)$ above the first inelastic threshold. *Phys. Rev. A* **2002**, *66*, 062706. [CrossRef]
10. Kauppila, W.E.; Kwan, C.K.; Przybyla, D.; Smith, S.J.; Stein, T.S. Positron–inert-gas-atom elastic DCS measurements. *Can. J. Phys.* **1996**, *74*, 474–482. [CrossRef]
11. Gulley, R.J.; Alle, D.T.; Brennan, M.J.; Brunger, M.J.; Buckman, S.J. Differential and total electron scattering from neon at low incident energies. *J. Phys. B* **1994**, *27*, 2593. [CrossRef]
12. Baluja, K.L.; Jain, A. Positron scattering from rare gases (He, Ne, Ar, Kr, Xe, and Rn): Total cross sections at intermediate and high energies. *Phys. Rev. A* **1992**, *46*, 1279. [CrossRef]
13. Lam, L.S.F. Relativistic effects in electron scattering by atoms. III. Elastic scattering by krypton, xenon and radon. *J. Phys. B At. Mol. Phy.* **1982**, *15*, 119. [CrossRef]
14. Khandker, M.H.; Billah, M.M.; Watabe, H.; Haque, A.K.F.; Uddin, M.A. Theoretical studies on the elastic scattering of $e\pm$off the ions of xenon isonuclear series. *Phys. Scr.* **2020**, *96*, 025402. [CrossRef]
15. Khandker, M.H.; Haque, A.K.F.; Maaza, M.; Uddin, M.A. Scattering of $e\pm$from the neon isonuclear series over the energy range 1 eV–0.5 GeV. *Jap. J. Appl. Phys.* **2020**, *59*, SHHA05. [CrossRef]
16. Khandker, M.H.; Haque, A.K.F.; Maaza, M.; Uddin, M.A. Elastic scattering of electrons from the ions of argon isonuclear series. *Phys. Scr.* **2019**, *94*, 075402. [CrossRef]
17. Haque, M.M.; Haque, A.K.F.; Jakubassa-Amundsen, D.H.; Patoary, M.A.R.; Basak, A.K.; Maaza, M.; Saha, B.C.; Uddin, M.A. $e^\pm$Ar scattering in the energy range 1 eV$\leq E_i \leq$ 0.5 GeV. *J. Phys. Commun.* **2019**, *3*, 045011. [CrossRef]
18. Kapil, K.S.; Vats, R.P. Elastic positron scattering by radon and radium atoms. *Phys. Scr.* **2012**, *85*, 045304. [CrossRef]
19. Tripathi, A.N.; Jain, A.K. Spin polarization and cross sections in elastic scattering of electrons from Yb, Rn, and Ra atoms. *Phys. Rev. A* **2000**, *61*, 032713.
20. Mayol, R.; Salvat, F. Total and transport cross sections for elastic scattering of electrons by atoms. *At. Data Nucl. Data Tables* **1997**, *65*, 55–154. [CrossRef]
21. Dapor, M.; Miotello, A. Differential, total, and transport cross sections for elastic scattering of low energy positrons by neutral atoms (Z= 1–92. E= 500–4000 eV). *At. Data Nucl. Data Tables* **1998**, *69*, 1–100. [CrossRef]
22. Haque, M.M.; Haque, A.K.F.; Bhattacharjee, P.P.; Uddin, M.A.; Patoary, M.A.R.; Basak, A.K.; Maaza, M.; Saha, B.C. Relativistic treatment of scattering of electrons and positrons by mercury atoms. *Mol. Phys.* **2019**, *117*, 2303–2319. [CrossRef]
23. Haque, A.K.F.; Haque, M.M.; Bhattacharjee, P.P.; Uddin, M.A.; Patoary, M.A.R.; Hossain, M.I.; Basak, A.K.; Mahbub, M.S.; Maaza, M.; Saha, B.C. Relativistic calculations for spin-polarization of elastic electron—mercury scattering. *J. Phys. Commun.* **2017**, *1*, 035014. [CrossRef]
24. Hassan, R.; Abdullah, M.N.A.; Shorifuddoza, M.; Khandker, M.H.; Patoary, M.A.R.; Haque, M.M.; Das, P.K.; Maaza, M.; Billah, M.M.; Haque, A.K.F.; Uddin, M.A. Scattering of $e^\pm$ off silver atom over the energy range 1 eV–1 MeV. *Eur. Phys. J. D* **2021**, *75*, 1–23. [CrossRef]
25. Kumar, A.; Abdullah, M.N.A.; Haque, A.K.F.; Singh, I.; Uddin, M.A. Elastic scattering of electrons by Sr atom: a study of critical minima and spin polarization. *J. Phys. Commun.* **2019**, *3*, 065001. [CrossRef]
26. Desclaux, J. P. A multiconfiguration relativistic Dirac-Fock program. *Comp. Phys. Commun.* **1975**, *9*, 31–45. [CrossRef]
27. Hahn, B. Ravenhall, D.G. Hofstadter, R. High-energy electron scattering and the charge distributions of selected nuclei. *Phys. Rev.* **1956**, *101*, 1131. [CrossRef]
28. Jakubassa-Amundsen, D.H.; Barday, R. The Sherman function in highly relativistic elastic electron–atom scattering. *J. Phys. G Nucl. Part. Phys.* **2012**, *39*, 025102. [CrossRef]
29. Furness, J.B.; McCarthy, I.E. Semiphenomenological optical model for electron scattering on atoms. *J. Phys. B At. Mol. Phys.* **1973**, *6*, 2280. [CrossRef]
30. Salvat, F. Optical-model potential for electron and positron elastic scattering by atoms. *Phys. Rev. A* **2003**, *68*, 012708. [CrossRef]
31. Mittleman, M.H.; Watson, K.M. Effects of the Pauli principle on the scattering of high-energy electrons by atoms. *Ann. Phys.* **1960**, *10*, 268. [CrossRef]
32. Perdew, J.P.; Zunger, A. Self-interaction correction to density-functional approximations for many-electron systems. *Phys. Rev. B* **1981**, *23*, 5048. [CrossRef]
33. Jain, A. Low-energy positron-argon collisions by using parameter-free positron correlation polarization potentials. *Phys. Rev. A* **1990**, *41*, 2437. [CrossRef]
34. Salvat, F.; Jablonski, A.; Powell, C.J. ELSEPA—Dirac partial-wave calculation of elastic scattering of electrons and positrons by atoms, positive ions and molecules. *Comput. Phys. Commun.* **2005**, *165*, 157–190. [CrossRef]
35. Rose, M.E. *Relativistic Electron Theory*; Wiley: New York, NY, USA, 1961.
36. Salvat, F.; Fernandez-Varea, J.M.; Williamson, W. Accurate numerical solution of the radial Schrödinger and Dirac wave equations. *Comput. Phys. Commun.* **1995**, *90*, 151. [CrossRef]
37. Kessler, J. Electron spin polarization by low-energy scattering from unpolarized targets. *Rev. Mod. Phys.* **1969**, *41*, 3. [CrossRef]
38. Maiorova, A.V.; Telnov, D.A.; Shabaev, V. M.; Tupitsyn, I.I.; Plunien, G.; Stöhlker, T. Backward scattering of low-energy antiprotons by highly charged and neutral uranium: Coulomb glory. *Phys. Rev. A* **2007**, *76*, 032709 [CrossRef]
39. Lucas, M.W.; Jakubassa-Amundsen, D.H.; Kuzel, M.; Groeneveld, K.O. Quasifree electron scattering in atomic collisions: The Ramsauer–Townsend effect revisited. *Int. J. Mod. Phys. A* **1997**, *12*, 305–78. [CrossRef]

40. Carlsson, T.A. *Photoelectron and Auger Spectroscopy*; Springer Science & Business Media: New York, NY, USA, 1975
41. Walker, D.W. Relativistic effects in low energy electron scattering from atoms. *Adv. Phys.* **1971**, *20*, 257–323. [CrossRef]
42. Haque, A.K.F.; Uddin, M.A.; Jakubassa-Amundsen, D.H.; Saha, B.C. Comparative study of eV to GeV electrons and positrons scattering elastically from neutral atoms. *J. Phys. B* **2018**, *51*, 175202. [CrossRef]

Article

Vibrational Excitation Cross-Section by Positron Impact: A Wave-Packet Dynamics Study

Luis A. Poveda [1,*], Marcio T. do N. Varella [2] and José R. Mohallem [3]

1. Departamento de Física, Centro Federal de Educação Tecnológica de Minas Gerais, Belo Horizonte 30421-169, MG, Brazil
2. Intituto de Fisica, Universidade de São Paulo, São Paulo 05315-970, SP, Brazil; mvarella@if.usp.br
3. Departamento de Física, Universidade Federal de Minas Gerais, Belo Horizonte 30123-970, MG, Brazil; rachid@fisica.ufmg.br
* Correspondence: poveda@cefetmg.br

Abstract: The vibrational excitation cross-section of a diatomic molecule by positron impact is obtained using wave-packet propagation techniques. The dynamics study was carried on a two-dimensional potential energy surface, which couples a hydrogenlike harmonic oscillator to a positron via a spherically symmetric correlation polarization potential. The cross-section for the excitation of the first vibrational mode is in good agreement with previous reports. Our model suggests that a positron couples to the target vibration by responding instantly to an interaction potential, which depends on the target vibrational coordinate.

Keywords: positron; model potential; wave-packet propagation; vibrational cross-section

1. Introduction

A fundamental question in positron–matter interaction is how a positron couples to the vibrational modes of molecules, after experimental measurements [1–3] and theoretical models [4–11] agree appreciably for vibrational excitation cross-sections for low-energy positron–molecule scattering. The observation of this phenomenon in great detail follows the development of high-intensity, monoenergetic positron beams [12,13], which, in turn, cool the source of positron via inelastic collisions, presumably involving vibrational modes [11,14] with a buffer gas of molecules.

The prominent consequence of the strong coupling between the positron and the nuclear degrees of freedom refers to the abnormally large positron annihilation rates observed in polyatomic targets [15–17]. The resonant features of the annihilation spectra have been described using a Breit–Wigner amplitude, which relies on the existence of a positron–molecule bound state or vibrational Feshbach resonance (VFR) [18], mainly populated by the infrared active modes of the molecule [17,18]. The VFRs are further enhanced by intramolecular vibrational energy redistribution [18]. On the other hand, the multimodal nature of positron annihilation on molecules was uncovered within a projection operator approach [19,20]. This model suggests that resonances in the annihilation phenomenon arise from the formation of a transient positron–molecule complex, with a lifetime long enough to give rise to narrow vibrational resonances via constructive interference [19,20]. This model attributes an important role to the correlation-polarization forces, as the mechanism that triggers the positron–molecule attachment, not only involving bound states but virtual states as well [19,20]. The coupling of the positron to molecular vibrations appeared to be more intriguing after experimental measurements of annihilation rates revealed that the positron can couple directly to a quasi-continuum of multimode vibrational states [21]. In order to describe the observed data, it was necessary to average the annihilation parameter over all the energetically allowed multimode vibrational excitations, also assuming that the positron couples to the quasi-continuum of states with the same strength [21].

The richness of the positron–molecule physics is closely related to the ability of the molecule to bind a positron. As the positron is a light positive particle, the formation of a positron–molecule complex results from the compromise between a flexible attractive electron cloud and a quasi-rigid repulsive nuclei structure. This picture is supported by a collection of experimental [22,23] and theoretical results [24–28] that indicate an strong correlation between positron–molecule binding energies and molecular properties such as dipole moment, polarizability, ionization potential, and number of π-electrons. However, for a quantitative description of the bonding between a molecule and a positron, a subtle effect should be taken into account, e.g., the nonzero probability amplitude that a target electron tunnels to the positron-attractive well. This effect, which appears as a virtual positronium formation in the many-body positron–molecule self energy, is responsible for a dramatic increase in the positron–molecule attachment [29].

In this work, the interaction of a positron with a diatomic molecule is studied using a potential energy surface (PES) that couples a correlation-polarization potential curve, for the positron–target interaction, with a hydrogenlike harmonic oscillator. On this PES, a time-dependent wave-packet propagation is performed and the cross-section for the excitation of the first vibrational mode of the oscillator is computed, a procedure somewhat similar to that of the reference [30]. In seeking comparison, the mass and natural frequency of the harmonic oscillator were chosen with values close to those known for a hydrogen molecule. The coupling between the molecular vibrational and positron translational modes was described using a linear representation of the H_2 polarizabilities as a function of the H–H internuclear separation, reported by Kołos and Wolniewicsz [31]. The computed $0 \to 1$ vibrational excitation cross-section then displays good agreement with previously reported experimental and theoretical results, suggesting that the oscillator embedded in the positron continuum couples to it through a correlation polarization force, which depends on the target oscillatory coordinate. Since the present model employs harmonic approximation, only the $0 \to 1$ vibrational excitation is accounted for. While more sophisticated positron–vibration couplings could in principle be considered, the available experimental data for H_2 are limited to the fundamental vibrational transition.

In the next section, the model potential is described in detail. The wave-packet propagation method is presented in Section 3. The results and discussion are given in Section 4 and some conclusions given in Section 5. Atomic units are assumed throughout the text, unless otherwise stated.

2. The Model Potential

The model potential is written as the sum of oscillator (OSC) and positron (POS) components as follows:

$$V(r, R) = V_{osc}(R) + V_{pos}(r, R) \quad (1)$$

where r is the scattering coordinate for the projectile–target distance relative to the center of mass of the system and R is the internal coordinate of the target vibrational mode.

The OSC term in the above equation is the potential energy of a harmonic oscillator

$$V_{osc}(R) = \frac{1}{2}\mu\omega^2 R^2 \quad (2)$$

where the reduced mass is set to $\mu = 1000$, corresponding to a homonuclear diatom with atomic mass $M = 2000$. The natural frequency $\omega = 0.02$ (4389.5 cm^{-1}) provides a harmonic oscillator with parameters close to those of the hydrogen molecule.

The POS term includes the static (V_{st}) and the correlation-polarization (V_{cp}) potentials. The former is represented in the form

$$V_{st}(r) = \left(\frac{a_1}{r}\right)^{a_2} \exp\left(-a_3 r^{a_4}\right) \quad (3)$$

which reproduces the spherically symmetric static potential energy of H_2, at the Hartee–Fock level, where $\{a_i\} = \{1.1973, 2.6633, 0.6179, 1.2003\}$.

The V_{cp} term, in turn, is written as

$$V_{cp}(r,R) = -\frac{\alpha(R)}{2r^4} f_\rho(r) \quad (4)$$

where

$$\alpha(R) = aR + \alpha_0 \quad (5)$$

with $a = 4.35$ and $\alpha_0 = 5.18$ is a linear approximation (referred to as $1.4\,a_0$) to the dipole polarizability for H_2 from Kołos and Wolniewitz [31].

In Equation (4),

$$f_\rho(r) = 1 - \exp\left(-\frac{r^6}{\rho^6}\right) \quad (6)$$

is the cut-off function proposed by Mitroy and Ivanov [32] in order to damp the $-1/r^4$ term at short distances. The cut-off parameter ρ is chosen to reproduce the desirable result [26,32]. In this case, $\rho = 5$ leads to a cross-section close to the experimental values.

Figure 1 shows one-dimensional cuts of the different components of the two-dimensional PES in the function of r, for $R = 0$ and $\rho = 5$. The inset shows the ab initio values of the H_2 polarizability and the straight line from Equation (5). We observed that with this simple representation, the cross-section was almost indistinguishable from those of a model that fits all the data to a higher degree polynomial. This is so because the average position of the wave-packet in the R coordinate oscillates very close to the origin of the quadratic well.

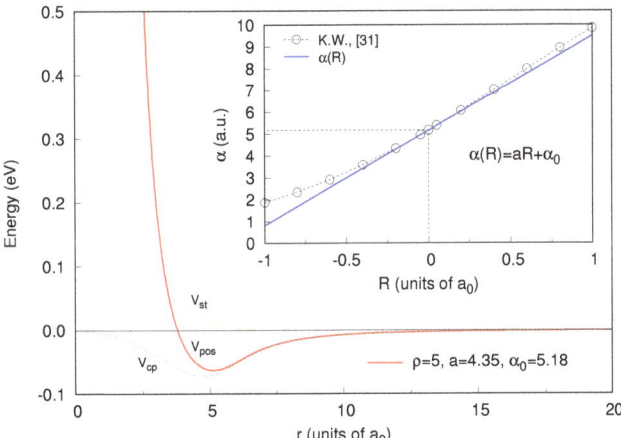

Figure 1. Cuts of the different components of the model potential. The empty dots in the inset are the data from ref. [31]. See text for details.

This model potential assumes a very simple *anzatz* for the coupling of a low-energy positron to a harmonic vibrational mode. The coupling is included as a parametric dependence of the positron–target correlation-polarization potential V_{cp} on the oscillator coordinate R. Note that, here, the target potential remains unchanged under the action of the positron field, a plausible assumption for a small, weakly polarizable molecule as H_2.

3. Wave-Packet Dynamics

The time propagation of the wave packet (WP) was performed using a split evolution operator in the form

$$\Psi(r, R, t + \Delta t) = e^{-iK\frac{\Delta t}{2}} e^{-iV\Delta t} e^{-iK\frac{\Delta t}{2}} \Psi(r, R, t) \qquad (7)$$

where V is the PES from Equation (1) and

$$K = \frac{p^2}{2m} + \frac{P^2}{2\mu} \qquad (8)$$

is the total kinetic energy operators involving the momenta p and P—conjugates of r and R, respectively.

In Equation (8), m is the reduced mass of the system defined as

$$m = \frac{m_p M}{m_p + M} \qquad (9)$$

where $M = 2000$ is the total mass of the oscillator and $m_p = 1$ is the positron mass.

The initial WP was prepared as the normalized product

$$\Psi_i(r, R, t = 0) = g(r)\chi_i(R) \qquad (10)$$

where $\chi_i(R)$ is the wave function of the i-th state of a harmonic oscillator with energy ε_i. In the present study, the oscillator is initially in its ground state, $i = 0$.

In Equation (10), $g(r)$ represents an incoming Gaussian wave packet

$$g(r) = \left(\frac{1}{2\pi\delta r_0^2}\right)^{1/4} e^{-(r-r_0)^2/4\delta r_0^2} e^{ik_0 r} \qquad (11)$$

with initial average position r_0, initial average momentum k_0 toward the interaction region, and full width at half maximum (FWHM) $\Delta r_0 = 2\sqrt{\ln 2}\delta r_0$.

Equations (7)–(11) were represented in a discretized grid of the $r \times R$ space with $N_r \times N_R$ points. At every instant, the WP was propagated using Equation (7) by doing a sequence of forward-backward-forward fast Fourier transforms (FFTs) between the coordinate and momentum spaces.

The cross-section (CS) for the vibrational excitation from state i to state j is obtained by applying a method commonly used for reactive and nonreactive scattering [33,34]. The method consists in expanding the outgoing wave function $\Psi(r_\infty, R, t)$ evaluated at large separations $r = r_\infty$ in the eigenstates of the oscillator,

$$\Psi_i(r = r_\infty, R, t) = \sum_f C_{if}(t)\chi_f(R) \qquad (12)$$

such that the coefficients of the expansion, computed as

$$C_{if}(t) = \int_{R_{min}}^{R_{max}} \chi_f^*(R)\Psi_i(r_\infty, R, t)dR \qquad (13)$$

represent the flux of the initial WP into the f-th vibrational channel after the scattering event.

Hence, the probability of a transition from the vibrational state i to state j of the oscillator will be proportional to the squared modulus of the Fourier transform of the coefficient $C_{if}(t)$. The $i \to f$ vibrational excitation CS as a function of the initial positron momentum k is computed as

$$\sigma_{if}(k) = \frac{\pi}{m}\frac{k_f}{k_i}\left|\frac{\tilde{C}_{if}(E)}{\tilde{g}(k)}\right|^2 \qquad (14)$$

where $\tilde{C}_{if}(E)$ and $\tilde{g}(k)$ are the FFTs of Equations (11) and (13), respectively. In Equation (14), $k_{i(j)} = \sqrt{2m\left[E - \varepsilon_{i(j)}\right]}$, where E is the total energy, which is conserved during the propagation.

The total propagation time was 131,072 atomic units (3.17 ps), large enough for $|C(t)|^2$ to fall below 10^{-7}, thus guaranteeing that the initial WP is completely dissociated. At this point, a problem arises if the WP is partly reflected back into the interaction region at the edges of the grid. Considering that it is impractical to prevent the WP from reaching the grid's edge during the whole time propagation, by using sufficiently large grids, the usual solutions involve the use of a complex absorbing potential in the dissociation regions [35]. In the present case, we choose a more straightforward solution [36], which consists in multiplying the WP, in the last Δr_{damp} dissociation region of the grid, by a damping function

$$\exp\left(-b_{damp}\Delta r_{damp}^3\right) \quad (15)$$

which smoothly decreases from 1 to zero near the grid edge. Due to the quadratic increase in the potential with the R coordinate, it was not necessary to apply a similar damping along the R-edge of the rectangular grid. Note further, that the damping should be applied at time intervals Δt_{damp} larger than the propagation time step to avoid nonphysical reflections of the WP.

Table 1 collects the parameters employed in the propagation. The center of the WP was initially placed at $r_0 = 100$ a.u., with an initial kinetic energy of 0.82 eV. To ensure that only the outgoing WP is involved in the computation of the coefficient from Equation (13), r_∞ was set to 200 a.u. This point is twice as far as the initial WP, which has an initial FWHM of 20 a.u. After going through r_∞, the WP was damped with Equation (15) over the region Δr_{damp}, which represents almost 80% of the total size of the grid along the r coordinate. Such a large damping region was necessary to counteract the rapid spreading of the WP, due to the small mass of the projectile. In turn, the values for Δt_{damp} and b_{damp} were chosen by trial-and-error, until it was verified that a negligible amount of the dissociated WP reached the edge of the grid.

Table 1. Parameters of the dynamics (in a.u.).

Parameter	Value
Grid parameters	
r_{min}	0.0
r_{max}	1200
N_r	1024
R_{min}	−1.0
R_{max}	1.0
N_R	32
r_∞	200
Δt	0.01
Δr_{damp}	950
Δt_{damp}	1000
b_{damp}	10^{-7}
Initial WP parameters	
r_0	100
Δr_0	20
k_0	−0.245
Δk_0	0.14

Note that we used a FFT power-of-two algorithm, implying that the number of grid points must be a power of two along the r and R coordinates. Hence, considering that the the cost of a propagation is very sensitive to the grid size, we first performed a convergence test. Thus, we found that for $N_r = 2^{10}$ and $N_R = 2^5$, the computed cross-section was indistinguishable from those obtained if the grid size was twice as large for either coordinate. Further, as a simple test, it was verified that by representing the quadratic well of Equation (2) with a grid of 32 points in the interval from -1 to 1, the energy spectra of the oscillator was accurately reproduced by applying a screening technique on the time-dependent propagation [37].

The initial WP was chosen narrow enough in position so that an energy interval wide enough around 0.54 eV, the threshold for the first vibrational mode of the oscillator, is well covered. However, note that the narrower the WP in position, the faster it will spread; then, a good compromise was found by setting the FWHM $\Delta r_0 = 20$ a.u. The bandwidth in energy of the initial WP can be estimated as

$$\Delta E = \frac{(k_0 + \Delta k_0/2)^2}{2m} - \frac{(k_0 - \Delta k_0/2)^2}{2m} \tag{16}$$

where Δk_0 is the FWHM of the initial WP in the momentum space.

From Equation (16), $\Delta E \approx 1$ eV, such that around the average initial incident energy $k_0^2/2m = 0.82$ eV, the cross-section can be reliably described. This can be seen in the red curve of Figure 2, which represents the $0 \to 1$ vibrational excitation CS, computed with the present method. Notice that the curve is smooth between the threshold energy and 2 eV, after which it begins to show a slightly oscillatory behavior, increasing in amplitude with energy. For a good description of the CS for energies above 2 eV, The WP should have a FWHM less than 20 a.u., but it would be necessary to choose a new set of damping parameters in order to remove WP reflections at the edge of the grid.

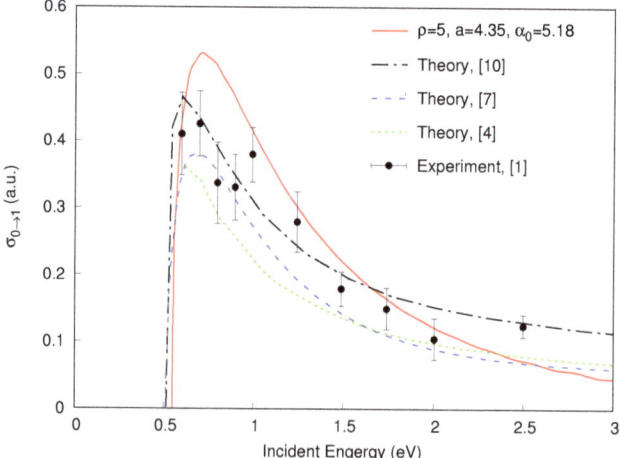

Figure 2. Comparison of the $0 \to 1$ vibrational excitation CSs, in function of the incident positron energy. The solid red line is the present result.

4. Results and Discussion

Figure 2 shows a comparison of the presently computed $0 \to 1$ vibrational excitation CS, as a function of the initial positron energy, with previous results obtained with other methods [4–6,10]. Our results show the typical behavior of the cross-section with a sharp onset at threshold, followed by a peak with maximum around 0.5 a.u. height, falling down to zero as the energy increases. The good agreement with reported theories [4–6,10] and one experiment [1] suggests that the present model potential is appropriate to describe the $0 \to 1$ excitation CS of the oscillator. In this sense, it becomes arguable that the coupling between the positron and the first vibrational mode of the target can be accounted for by the instantaneous response of the molecule to the positron through the R-dependent attractive correlation polarization potential.

Figure 3 shows the $0 \to 1$ vibrational excitation CSs from different PESs obtained by changing, one at a time, the values of the cut-off parameter ρ and the slope a of the $\alpha(R)$ function, given by Equation (5). From the figure, it is clear that a decrease (increase) in the value of a leads to a decrease (increase) in the cross-section as a whole, as expected from the fact that a is a measure of the coupling strength between the translational and vibrational degrees of freedom. In turn, an increase (decrease) of ρ around 5 gives rise to an decrease (increase) in the cross-section, leaving its characteristic shape unchanged.

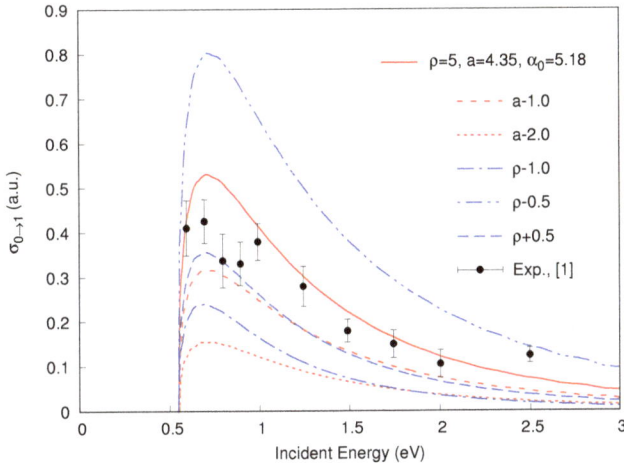

Figure 3. Vibrational excitation CSs in function of the incident energy for different values of the ρ and a parameters in Equations (5) and (6), respectively.

The influence of the parameter α_0 on the cross-section was also investigated. Figure 4 shows cuts of the PES along the r coordinate for $R = 0$, with increasing values of the target polarizability at equilibrium, α_0. The other parameters of the V_{cp} terms, ρ and a, were fixed at 5 and 4.35, respectively. This trend describes the situation for a positron, which couples with the same strength ($a = $ const.) to an increasingly polarizable target. The deepest well corresponds to a target eight times more polarizable than that of the hydrogen molecule. Using this family of PESs, propagations were carried out with the same parameters of Table 1. The resulting $0 \to 1$ vibrational excitation CSs are shown in Figure 5. From the figure, it is clear that the cross-section tends to depict a threshold resonance as the target polarizability increases, presumably due to the emergence of a bound state as the potential well becomes deeper.

The above discussion suggests that for the hydrogen molecule, the typical behavior of the $0 \to 1$ vibrational excitation CS arises from a weak coupling between the positron and the molecular vibration, mainly dominated by the dependence of the positron–target correlation-polarization potential on the vibrational coordinate. In the present model, this is represented by the dependence of the polarizability on the R coordinate. Moreover, as the target becomes more polarizable, the coupling between the positron and the vibrational modes may be enhanced by the emergence of resonances or even bound states. In such a scenario, commonly observed in large polyatomics, the nucleus skeleton of the molecule would be appreciably perturbed by the presence of the positron field; thus, increasing the coupling between the positron and the molecular vibration.

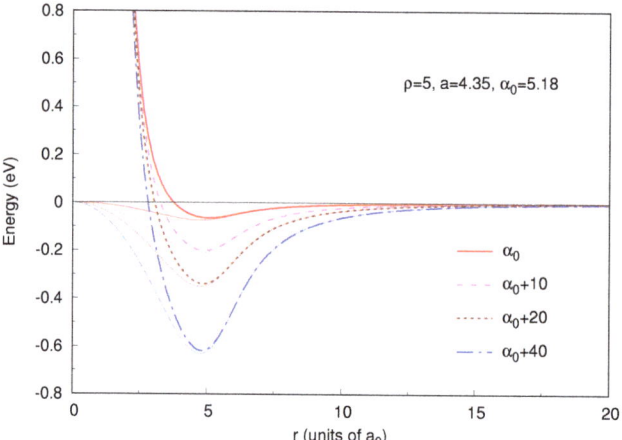

Figure 4. Cuts of the PES for increasing values of α_0.

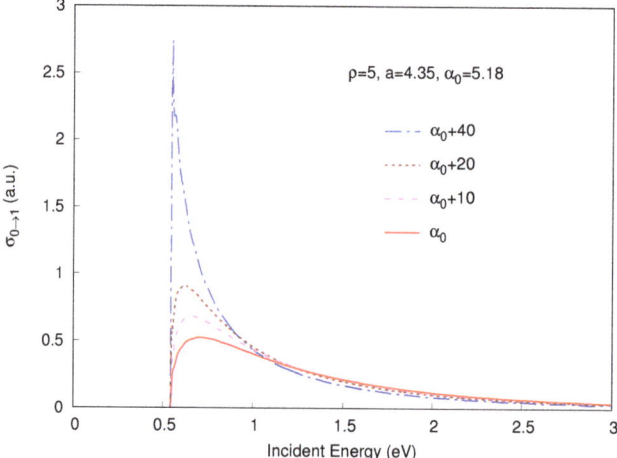

Figure 5. $0 \rightarrow 1$ vibrational excitation CSs obtained with the different PESs from the Figure 4.

5. Conclusions

In this work, we show that a simple model that couples a harmonic oscillator to a positron through a correlation-polarization potential can capture the main physics involved in a single-mode vibrational excitation by positron impact. Here, this phenomenon was studied using a time-dependent wave-packet propagation. The $0 \rightarrow 1$ vibrational excitation cross-section was computed by projecting, at every time step, the dissociated wave-packet with the first excited state of the oscillator. The cross-section shows good agreement with reported values and suggests that the target vibration can be coupled to the positron continuum by the dependence of the target polarizability on the vibrational coordinate. On the other hand, the $0 \rightarrow 1$ vibrational excitation cross-section tends to depict a threshold resonance for an increasingly polarizable target. Future work will be devoted to studying positron coupling with higher vibrational modes, in which case, a more realistic description of the oscillator beyond the harmonic approximation would be required.

Author Contributions: Conceptualization, L.A.P., M.T.d.N.V. and J.R.M.; Data curation, L.A.P.; Funding acquisition, J.R.M.; Investigation, L.A.P., M.T.d.N.V. and J.R.M.; Methodology, L.A.P. and M.T.d.N.V.; Project administration, J.R.M.; Resources, J.R.M.; Software, M.T.d.N.V.; Supervision, J.R.M.; Writing—original draft, L.A.P.; Writing—review & editing, L.A.P., M.T.d.N.V. and J.R.M. All authors have read and agreed to the published version of the manuscript.

Funding: This research was funded by Conselho Nacional de Desenvolvimento Científico e Tecnológico grant numbers 304571/2018-0 and 307125/2019-0.

Institutional Review Board Statement: Not applicable.

Informed Consent Statement: Not applicable.

Acknowledgments: Luis Poveda thanks Carlos Magno and Luis d'Fonseca for helpful discussions. Marcio Varella and José Mohallem acknowledge support from the Brazilian agency Conselho Nacional de Desenvolvimento Científico e Tecnológico (CNPq), Grants: 304571/2018-0 and 307125/2019-0, respectively.

Conflicts of Interest: The authors declare no conflict of interest.

References

1. Sullivan, J.P.; Gilbert, S.J.; Surko, C.M. Excitation of Molecular Vibrations by Positron Impact. *Phys. Rev. Lett.* **2001**, *86*, 1494. [CrossRef]
2. Gilbert, S.J.; Greaves, R.G.; Surko, C.M. Positron Scattering from Atoms and Molecules at Low Energies. *Phys. Rev. Lett.* **1999**, *82*, 5032–5035. [CrossRef]
3. Marler, J.P.; Surko, C.M. Systematic comparison of positron- and electron-impact excitation of the ν_3 vibrational mode of CF_4. *Phys. Rev. A* **2005**, *72*, 062702. [CrossRef]
4. Gianturco, F.A.; Mukherjee, T. Dynamical coupling effects in the vibrational excitation of H_2 and N_2 colliding with positrons. *Phys. Rev. A* **1997**, *55*, 1044–1055. [CrossRef]
5. Mukherjee, T.; Ghosh, A.S.; Jain, A. Low-energy positron collisions with H_2 and N_2 molecules by using a parameter-free positron-correlation-polarization potential. *Phys. Rev. A* **1991**, *43*, 2538–2543. [CrossRef] [PubMed]
6. Varella, M.T.D.N.; Lima, M.A.P. Near-threshold vibrational excitation of H_2 by positron impact: A projection-operator approach. *Phys. Rev. A* **2007**, *76*, 052701. [CrossRef]
7. Varella, M.T.D.N.; de Oliveira, E.M.; Lima, M.A. Near threshold vibrational excitation of molecules by positron impact: A projection operator approach. *Nucl. Instr. Meth. B* **2008**, *266*, 435–440. [CrossRef]
8. Mazon, K.T.; Tenfen, W.; Michelin, S.E.; Arretche, F.; Lee, M.T.; Fujimoto, M.M. Vibrational cross sections for positron scattering by nitrogen molecules. *Phys. Rev. A* **2010**, *82*, 032704. [CrossRef]
9. Mukherjee, T.; Mukherjee, M. Low-energy positron–nitrogen-molecule scattering: A rovibrational close-coupling study. *Phys. Rev. A* **2015**, *91*, 062706. [CrossRef]
10. Zammit, M.C.; Fursa, D.V.; Savage, J.S.; Bray, I.; Chiari, L.; Zecca, A.; Brunger, M.J. Adiabatic-nuclei calculations of positron scattering from molecular hydrogen. *Phys. Rev. A* **2017**, *95*, 022707. [CrossRef]
11. Poveda, L.A.; Assafrão, D.; Pinheiro, J.G.; Mohallem, J.R. Close-coupling scattering cross sections and a model for positron cooling in a buffer gas of molecular nitrogen. *Phys. Rev. A* **2019**, *100*, 062706. [CrossRef]
12. Gilbert, S.J.; Kurz, C.; Greaves, R.G.; Surko, C.M. Creation of a monoenergetic pulsed positron beam. *App. Phys. Lett.* **1997**, *70*, 1944–1946. [CrossRef]
13. Danielson, J.R.; Dubin, D.H.E.; Greaves, R.G.; Surko, C.M. Plasma and trap-based techniques for science with positrons. *Rev. Mod. Phys.* **2015**, *87*, 247–306. [CrossRef]
14. Natisin, M.R.; Danielson, J.R.; Surko, C.M. Positron cooling by vibrational and rotational excitation of molecular gases. *J. Phys. B At. Mol. Opt. Phys.* **2014**, *47*, 225209. [CrossRef]
15. Young, J.A.; Surko, C.M. Feshbach-resonance-mediated positron annihilation in small molecules. *Phys. Rev. A* **2008**, *78*, 032702. [CrossRef]
16. Young, J.A.; Surko, C.M. Feshbach-resonance-mediated annihilation in positron interactions with large molecules. *Phys. Rev. A* **2008**, *77*, 052704. [CrossRef]
17. Gribakin, G.F.; Young, J.A.; Surko, C.M. Positron-molecule interactions: Resonant attachment, annihilation, and bound states. *Rev. Mod. Phys.* **2010**, *82*, 2557–2607. [CrossRef]
18. Gribakin, G.F.; Lee, C.M.R. Positron Annihilation in Molecules by Capture into Vibrational Feshbach Resonances of Infrared-Active Modes. *Phys. Rev. Lett.* **2006**, *97*, 193201. [CrossRef]
19. d'A Sanchez, S.; Lima, M.A.P.; Varella, M.T.D.N. Feshbach projection operator approach to positron annihilation. *Phys. Rev. A* **2009**, *80*, 052710. [CrossRef]
20. d'A Sanchez, S.; Lima, M.A.; Varella, M.T.D.N. Multimode vibrational couplings in resonant positron annihilation. *Phys. Rev. Lett.* **2011**, *107*, 103201. [CrossRef]

21. Jones, A.C.L.; Danielson, J.R.; Natisin, M.R.; Surko, C.M.; Gribakin, G.F. Ubiquitous Nature of Multimode Vibrational Resonances in Positron-Molecule Annihilation. *Phys. Rev. Lett.* **2012**, *108*, 093201. [CrossRef]
22. Danielson, J.R.; Young, J.A.; Surko, C.M. Analysis of experimental positron-molecule binding energies. *J. Phys. Conf. Ser.* **2010**, *199*, 012012. [CrossRef]
23. Danielson, J.R.; Jones, A.C.L.; Gosselin, J.J.; Natisin, M.R.; Surko, C.M. Interplay between permanent dipole moments and polarizability in positron-molecule binding. *Phys. Rev. A* **2012**, *85*, 022709. [CrossRef]
24. Amaral, P.H.R.; Mohallem, J.R. Positron binding to atoms and apolar molecules: A convergence of theory and experiment. *Phys. Rev. A* **2012**, *86*, 042708. [CrossRef]
25. Romero, J.; Charry, J.A.; Flores-Moreno, R.; Varella, M.T.D.N.; Reyes, A. Calculation of positron binding energies using the generalized any particle propagator theory. *J. Chem. Phys.* **2014**, *141*, 114103. [CrossRef] [PubMed]
26. Swann, A.R.; Gribakin, G.F. Positron Binding and Annihilation in Alkane Molecules. *Phys. Rev. Lett.* **2019**, *123*, 113402. [CrossRef]
27. Suzuki, H.; Otomo, T.; Iida, R.; Sugiura, Y.; Takayanagi, T.; Tachikawa, M. Positron binding in chloroethenes: Modeling positron-electron correlation-polarization potentials for molecular calculations. *Phys. Rev. A* **2020**, *102*, 052830. [CrossRef]
28. Amaral, P.H.R.; Mohallem, J.R. Machine-learning predictions of positron binding to molecules. *Phys. Rev. A* **2020**, *102*, 052808. [CrossRef]
29. Hofierka, J.; Cunningham, B.; Rawlins, C.M.; Patterson, C.H.; Green, D.G. Many-body theory of positron binding in polyatomic molecules. *arXiv* **2021**, arXiv:2105.06929.
30. Sugiura, Y.; Suzuki, K.; Koido, S.; Takayanagi, T.; Kita, Y.; Tachikawa, M. Quantum dynamics calculation of the annihilation spectrum for positron–proline scattering. *Comp. Theor. Chem.* **2019**, *1147*, 1–7. [CrossRef]
31. Kołos, W.; Wolniewicz, L. Polarizability of the Hydrogen Molecule. *J. Chem. Phys.* **1967**, *46*, 1426–1432. [CrossRef]
32. Mitroy, J.; Ivanov, I.A. Semiempirical model of positron scattering and annihilation. *Phys. Rev. A* **2002**, *65*, 042705. [CrossRef]
33. Marston, C.; Balint-Kurti, G.; Dixon, R. Time dependent quantum dynamics of reactive scattering and the calculation of product quantum state distributions—A study of the collinear F + H_2(v = 0)->HF(v') + H reaction. *Theor. Chim. Acta* **1991**, *79*, 313–322. [CrossRef]
34. Bradley, K.S.; Schatz, G.C.; Balint-Kurti, G.G. Wave Packet Methods for the Direct Calculation of Energy-Transfer Moments in Molecular Collisions. *J. Phys. Chem. A* **1999**, *103*, 947–952. [CrossRef]
35. Vibók, Á.; Halász, G.J. Parametrization of complex absorbing potentials for time-dependent quantum dynamics using multi-step potentials. *Phys. Chem. Chem. Phys.* **2001**, *3*, 3048–3051. [CrossRef]
36. Dixon, R.N.; Marston, C.C.; Balint-Kurti, G.G. Photodissociation dynamics and emission spectroscopy of H_2S in its first absorption band: A time dependent quantum mechanical study. *J. Chem. Phys.* **1990**, *93*, 6520–6534. [CrossRef]
37. Takatsuka, K.; Hashimoto, N. A novel method to calculate eigenfunctions and eigenvalues in a given energy range. *J. Chem. Phys.* **1995**, *103*, 6057–6067. [CrossRef]

Article

Electron Impact Excitation of Extreme Ultra-Violet Transitions in Xe^{7+}–Xe^{10+} Ions

Aloka Kumar Sahoo [†] and Lalita Sharma [*,†]

Department of Physics, Indian Institute of Technology, Roorkee 247667, India; aloka_s@ph.iitr.ac.in
* Correspondence: lalita.sharma@ph.iitr.ac.in; Tel.: +91-1332-28-5729
† These authors contributed equally to this work.

Abstract: In the present work, a detailed study on the electron impact excitation of Xe^{7+}, Xe^{8+}, Xe^{9+} and Xe^{10+} ions for the dipole allowed (E1) transitions in the EUV range of 8–19 nm is presented. The multi-configuration Dirac–Fock method is used for the atomic structure calculation including the Breit and QED corrections along with the relativistic configuration interaction approach. We have compared our calculated energy levels, wavelengths and transition rates with other reported experimental and theoretical results. Further, the relativistic distorted wave method is used to calculate the cross sections from the excitation threshold to 3000 eV electron energy. For plasma physics applications, we have reported the fitting parameters of these cross sections using two different formulae for low and high energy ranges. The rate coefficients are also obtained using our calculated cross sections and considering the Maxwellian electron energy distribution function in the electron temperature range from 5 eV to 100 eV.

Keywords: MCDF wavefunctions; wavelengths; transition rates; relativistic distorted wave method; cross sections; rate coefficients

1. Introduction

Spectroscopic and collisional data of highly charged xenon ions in the extreme ultra-violet (EUV) spectral range play a vital role in several research areas. For example, laser produced xenon plasma exhibits [1] the possibility to become an EUV source for the next generation lithography. Xenon ions are detected in the UV spectrum of the astrophysical objects viz., hot DO-type white dwarf [2] and planetary nebula [3]. In the next generation fusion reactor ITER, xenon is expected to be used as edge plasma coolant. Xenon ions being used in ion thruster for electric propulsion [4] plays key role in making the modern space exploration cheaper. Since emissions from various charged species of xenon ions carry information about the plasma parameters and impurities, their atomic structure and dynamical properties in the EUV range are essential for the accurate diagnostics of the aforementioned plasmas. Therefore, in this work we have focused on the electron impact excitation of the electric dipole (E1) transitions in Xe^{7+}, Xe^{8+}, Xe^{9+} and Xe^{10+} ions in the EUV region 8–19 nm. We consider excitation of E1 transitions that are responsible for the most intense lines of the spectra.

To determine the emission properties of xenon ions, experiments have been performed with either laser or gas discharge-produced plasmas. Churilov and Joshi [5] recorded xenon spectra in the 7–17 nm region on a 10.7 m grazing incidence spectrograph and analyzed the $4p^6 4d^9$–($4p^6 4d^8 5p$ + $4p^6 4d^8 4f$ + $4p^5 4d^{10}$) transition array of Rh-like Xe^{9+}. They also identified the resonance transitions arising from the excited $4d^9(6p + 5f + 7p + 6f)$ states of Pd-like Xe^{8+} and $4d^{10}5s$ ^2S–$4d^9 5s 4f$ ^2P transitions for Ag-like Xe^{7+}. Churilov et al. [6] observed the transition array $4d^8$–($4d^7 5p + 4d^7 4f + 4p^5 4d^9$) of Xe^{10+} using a low inductance vacuum spark and a 10.7 m grazing incidence photograph in the EUV region 10.5–15.7 nm. These lines were analyzed using Hartree–Fock (HFR) calculations in relativistic mode with the help of the Cowan suite of codes [7]. Fahy et al. [8] reported the EUV spectra of

Xe^{6+} to Xe^{41+} in the wavelength region of 4.5 to 20 nm using the electron beam ion trap (EBIT) facility at NIST while varying electron beam energy from 180 eV to 8 keV. They also calculated the transition probabilities and wavelengths using the HF approximation with the Cowan code [7]. Ali and Nakamura [9] observed the EUV spectra of Rh-like Xe^{9+}–Cd-like Xe^{6+} and Cu-like Xe^{25+}–Se-like Xe^{20+} using a compact electron beam ion trap (CoBIT) and a flat-field grazing incidence spectrometer in the wavelength range of 15–20 nm with an uncertainty of 0.05 Å. The electron beam energy was varied between 200–890 eV during these measurements. Ali and Nakamura [10] also used their experimental facilities to record EUV spectra of highly charged Xe^{8+}–Xe^{11+} and Ba^{18+}–Ba^{21+} ions in the wavelength range 9–13 nm. Merabet et al. [11] studied spectra of various xenon ions (Xe^{2+}–Xe^{10+}) in the EUV region 10–16 nm using a compact electron cyclotron resonance ion source (CECRIS) equipped with a grazing monochromator operating in 4–90 nm.

Various theoretical studies have been carried out to report energy levels, wavelengths, oscillator strengths and transition probabilities of xenon ions. Safronova et al. [12] calculated the atomic properties of Pd-like ions Xe^{8+} with nuclear charge ranging from Z = 47 to 100 using relativistic many-body perturbation theory (RMBPT) with Breit correction. Ivanova [13] used the relativistic perturbation theory with a model potential to calculate the energy levels of Ag-, Pd- and Rh-like ions with Z = 52–86. Motoumba et al. [14] reported transition probabilities and oscillator strengths for the transition array 4d^8 – (4p^{5}4d^9 + 4d^{7}5p + 4d^{7}4f) of Xe^{10+} in the EUV spectral range of 10.2–15.7 nm. These results were obtained using two different methods viz., the semi-empirical pseudo-relativistic Hartree–Fock (HFR) method and the relativistic multiconfiguration Dirac–Hartree–Fock (MCDHF) theory within the relativistic configuration interaction (RCI) approximation. Motoumba et al. [15] also employed the above two methods to report transition probabilities and oscillator strengths for 92 spectral lines of Xe^{9+} ion in the range of 11–16.4 nm. Shen et al. [16] used Flexible Atomic Code (FAC), based on a fully relativistic approach, to calculate the energy levels, oscillator strengths, electron impact collision strengths as well as effective collision strengths for Xe^{10+}.

It is clear from the above discussion that most of the previous experimental or theoretical studies on Xe^{7+}–Xe^{10+} ions have focused on their spectroscopic properties, while the electron impact cross section data are scarcely reported. However, various studies in the past have clearly demonstrated that using accurate cross section results in a collisional radiative model provides a better agreement with the measurements on the plasma parameters, *viz.*, electron temperature and density [17–20]. Therefore, reliable cross sections are essential for the success of any plasma model. In general, suitable theoretical methods are employed to carry out cross section calculations due to limitations, such as accurate identification of the fine-structure levels for open shell ions, in performing the scattering experiments.

In the present work, we have studied electron impact excitation of Xe^{7+}, Xe^{8+}, Xe^{9+} and Xe^{10+} ions. The core shell configuration (1s^2 2s^2 2p^6 3s^2 3p^6 3d^{10} 4s^2 4p^6) is removed in the representation of the ground and excited state configurations of these four ions. We have considered the transition arrays 4d^{10}5s ^{2}S$_{1/2}$–(4d^{9}5s4f + 4d^{9}5s5p) for Xe^{7+}, 4d^{10} ^{1}S$_0$–(4d^{9}5p + 4d^{9}4f + 4d^{9}6p + 4d^{9}5f + 4d^{9}7p + 4d^{9}6f) for Xe^{8+}, 4p^{6}4d^9–(4p^{6}4d^{8}5p + 4p^{6}4d^{8}4f + 4p^{5}4d^{10}) for Xe^{9+} and 4d^8–(4d^{7}5p + 4d^{7}4f + 4p^{5}4d^9) for Xe^{10+}. These arrays result into 9, 18, 75 and 57 E1 transitions in Xe^{7+} through Xe^{10+} in EUV range. We have used multiconfiguration Dirac–Fock method within RCI approximation to calculate the energy levels, wavelengths and transition rates. These results are compared in detail with the previously reported measurements and theoretical calculations. The target ion wavefunctions are further implemented in the evaluation of the transition (T–) matrix amplitude using relativistic distorted wave (RDW) approximation and excitation cross sections are obtained up to 3000 eV electron energy. The analytical fitting of the electron excitation cross sections is also performed as it is more convenient to feed the analytical expression with fitting parameters for plasma modeling. Further, assuming electron energy distribution to be

Maxwellian, we have also calculated excitation rate coefficients using our cross sections for electron temperature range 5–100 eV.

2. Theory

In order to calculate the energy levels, wavelengths and transition probabilities, we have obtained MCDF wavefunctions of Xe^{7+}–Xe^{10+} ions using GRASP2K code [21]. In the MCDF method, the atomic state functions (ASFs) are written as linear combination of configuration state functions (CSFs) having same parity P and angular momentum quantum number J, as follows:

$$\Psi(PJM) = \sum_{i=1}^{n} a_i \Phi_i(PJM). \qquad (1)$$

Here a_i refers to the mixing coefficient of the CSF $\Phi_i(PJM)$ which are anti-symmetrized products of a common set of orthonormal orbitals. In our calculations, we take as many CSFs as are having at least 0.001% value of the mixing coefficient. The configurations that are included in the atomic-structure calculations of xenon ions are listed in Table 1. These configurations are shown here in their non-relativistic notations. The MCDF method implements a self-consistent field procedure for obtaining the radial functions and the mixing coefficients. Further, we performed RCI calculations by considering the Breit and quantum electrodynamic (QED) corrections in the Dirac–Coulomb Hamiltonian. The transition probabilities are computed from the matrix element of dipole operator of the electromagnetic field.

Table 1. Configurations of the initial and final states and the CSFs in non-relativistic notations.

Ions	Initial State	Final State		CSFs
Xe^{7+}	$4d^{10}5s$	$4d^9(5s5p, 4f5s)$	even	$4d^{10}(5s, 5d, 6s, 6d)$, $4d^9(5s5d, 5s6s, 5s7s, 5s^2, 5p^2)$
			odd	$4d^{10}(4f, 5p, 6p)$, $4d^9(4f5s, 5s5p, 5s5f, 5s6f, 5p5d)$
Xe^{8+}	$4d^{10}$	$4d^9(4f, 5p, 5f, 6p, 6f, 7p)$	even	$4d^{10}$, $4d^9(5s, 5d, 6s, 6d, 7s, 7d)$, $4d^8(5s^2, 5p^2, 5d^2)$
			odd	$4d^9(4f, 5p, 5f, 6p, 6f, 7p, 7f)$
Xe^{9+}	$4d^9$	$4d^8(4f, 5p), 4p^54d^{10}$	even	$4d^9$, $4d^8(5s, 5d, 6s, 6d, 7s, 7d)$, $4p^54d^9(5p, 5f)$, $4d^7(5s^2, 5p^2, 5d^2, 5f^2, 5s5d, 5s6s, 5s6d, 5p5f)$
			odd	$4d^8(4f, 5p, 5f, 6p, 6f, 7p)$, $4d^7(5s5p, 5s5f, 5s6p)$, $4p^54d^{10}$, $4d^64f^3$
Xe^{10+}	$4d^8$	$4d^7(4f, 5p), 4p^54d^9$	even	$4d^8, 4d^75d, 4p^54d^8(5p, 5f), 4d^6(5s^2 + 5p^2)$
			odd	$4d^7(4f, 5p, 5f, 6f)$, $4p^54d^9, 4p^54d^85d$, $4d^54f^3$

We further use the bound state wavefunctions of the ion in the relativistic distorted wave theory to determine the electron impact excitation parameters. The T-matrix in the

RDW approximation for excitation of an N electron ion from an initial state a to a final state b can be written as [22]:

$$T_{a \to b}^{RDW}(\gamma_b, J_b, M_b, \mu_b; \gamma_a, J_a, M_a, \mu_a) = \langle \chi_b^- | V - U_b(N+1) | A \chi_a^+ \rangle. \quad (2)$$

Here, $J_{a(b)}$, $M_{a(b)}$ denote the total angular momentum quantum number and its associated magnetic quantum number in the initial(final) state, whereas, $\gamma_{a(b)}$ represents additional quantum numbers required for unique identification of the state. $\mu_{a(b)}$ refers to the spin projection of the incident(scattered) electron. A is the anti-symmetrization operator to consider the exchange of the projectile electron with the target electrons and U_b is the distortion potential which is taken to be a function of the radial co-ordinates of the projectile electron only. In our calculations, we choose U_b to be a spherically averaged static potential of the excited state of ion. In the above Equation (2), V is the Coulomb interaction potential between the incident electron and the target ion. The wave function $\chi_{a(b)}^{+(-)}$ represents the product of the N-electron target wave functions $\Psi_{a(b)}$ and a projectile electron distorted wave function $F_{a(b)}^{+(-)}$ in the initial 'a' and final 'b', states, that is:

$$\chi_{a(b)}^{+(-)} = \Psi_{a(b)}(1, 2, ..., N)) F_{a(b)}^{+(-)}(k_{a(b)}, N+1). \quad (3)$$

Here, '+(−)' sign denotes an outgoing(incoming) wave, while $k_{a(b)}$ is the linear momentum of the projectile electron in the initial(final) state. Equation (2) contains entire information about the excitation process. We, however, are interested in computing only the integrated cross section which is obtained by taking square of the mode value of the complex T-matrix with appropriate normalization, as expressed below:

$$\sigma_{a \to b} = (2\pi)^4 \frac{k_b}{k_a} \frac{1}{2(2J_a+1)} \sum_{M_b \mu_b M_a \mu_a} \int |T_{a \to b}^{RDW}(\gamma_b, J_b, M_b, \mu_b; \gamma_a, J_a, M_a, \mu_a)|^2 d\Omega. \quad (4)$$

3. Results and Discussion

3.1. Atomic-Structure Calculations

We have used GRASP2K code [21] to perform MCDF and RCI calculations to obtain energy levels, wavelengths and transition rates of Xe^{7+}–Xe^{10+} ions. Our energy values are presented and compared with other theoretical and experimental results through Tables 2–5 for the four ions. The fine-structure states are represented in the relativistic $j - j$ coupling scheme in which all shells, excluding s, split into two subshells with $j = l \pm 1/2$. For example, a p shell will be broken as $\bar{p}$ with $j = 1/2$ and p with $j = 3/2$. In order to identify the levels, their indices are assigned in each table. This will help to clearly recognise the states for which wavelengths, transition rates, electron impact cross sections and excitation rate coefficients will be presented.

Table 2. Comparison of our calculated energy levels (in eV) with other results for Xe^{7+}. A fully filled subshell is omitted in the relativistic representation of the configurations.

Index	State *	J	State	Present	NIST [23]
1	$4d^{10}5s\ ^2S_{1/2}$	1/2	$5s_{1/2}$	0.0000	0.0000
2	$4d^95s5p\ (5/2, ^3P_1)$	3/2	$(4d_{5/2}^5 5s_{1/2})_2 5\bar{p}_{1/2}$	66.2099	67.1436
3	$4d^95s5p\ (3/2, ^3P_0)$	3/2	$(4d_{3/2}^3 5s_{1/2})_1 5\bar{p}_{1/2}$	67.1423	68.2470
4	$4d^95s5p\ (3/2, ^3P_0)$	3/2	$(4d_{3/2}^3 5s_{1/2})_2 5\bar{p}_{1/2}$	68.1925	69.0120
5	$4d^95s5p\ (3/2, ^3P_1)$	1/2	$(4d_{3/2}^3 5s_{1/2})_1 5\bar{p}_{1/2}$	69.1417	69.9456
6	$4d^95s5p\ (3/2, ^3P_2)$	1/2	$(4d_{3/2}^3 5s_{1/2})_1 5p_{3/2}$	69.5680	70.4968
7	$4d^95s5p\ (5/2, ^1P_1)$	3/2	$(4d_{5/2}^5 5s_{1/2})_3 5p_{3/2}$	72.9254	72.5665
8	$4d^95s5p\ (3/2, ^1P_1)$	1/2	$(4d_{3/2}^3 5s_{1/2})_2 5p_{3/2}$	74.7061	74.3872
9	$4d^95s4f\ ^2P_{1/2}$	1/2	$(4d_{5/2}^5 4f_{7/2})_1 5s_{1/2}$	103.5676	100.5830
10	$4d^95s4f\ ^2P_{3/2}$	3/2	$(4d_{5/2}^5 4f_{7/2})_1 5s_{1/2}$	103.6716	100.6000

* Notation as per the NIST [23] database.

Table 3. Same as Table 2 but for Xe^{8+}.

Index	State *	J	State	Present	Other Reported
1	$4d^{10}\,^1S_0$	0	$4d_0^6$	0.0000	0.0000 [a]
2	$4d^9 5p\,^3P_2$	2	$4d_{5/2}^5 5\tilde{p}_{1/2}$	71.0998	71.3452 [b]
3	$4d^9 5p\,^3P_1$	1	$4d_{3/2}^3 5\tilde{p}_{1/2}$	73.4043	73.7114 [a]
4	$4d^9 5p\,^3P_0$	0	$4d_{3/2}^3 5p_{3/2}$	74.9525	75.3707 [b]
5	$4d^9 5p\,^1P_1$	1	$4d_{3/2}^3 5\tilde{p}_{1/2}$	75.0407	74.9951 [a]
6	$4d^9 5p\,^3D_3$	3	$4d_{5/2}^5 5p_{3/2}$	74.9691	75.0613 [b]
7	$4d^9 5p\,^3D_1$	1	$4d_{3/2}^3 5p_{3/2}$	76.5287	76.6556 [a]
8	$4d^9 5p\,^3D_2$	2	$4d_{3/2}^3 5p_{3/2}$	76.8981	77.0124 [b]
9	$4d^9 4f\,^3P_0$	0	$4d_{5/2}^5 4\tilde{f}_{5/2}$	81.5153	
10	$4d^9 4f\,^3P_1$	1	$4d_{5/2}^5 4\tilde{f}_{5/2}$	81.8543	82.5053 [a]
11	$4d^9 4f\,^3P_2$	2	$4d_{5/2}^5 4f_{7/2}$	82.5160	
12	$4d^9 4f\,^3D_3$	3	$4d_{5/2}^5 4\tilde{f}_{5/2}$	85.4793	
13	$4d^9 4f\,^3D_1$	1	$4d_{3/2}^3 4\tilde{f}_{5/2}$	86.1987	86.3315 [a]
14	$4d^9 4f\,^3D_2$	2	$4d_{3/2}^3 4f_{7/2}$	86.4396	
15	$4d^9 4f\,^1P_1$	1	$4d_{5/2}^5 4f_{7/2}$	106.6396	103.2057 [a]
16	$4d^9 6p\,^3P_2$	2	$4d_{5/2}^5 6\tilde{p}_{1/2}$	117.0829	
17	$4d^9 6p\,^3P_1$	1	$4d_{5/2}^5 6p_{3/2}$	118.2765	119.4365 [a]
18	$4d^9 6p\,^3P_0$	0	$4d_{3/2}^3 6p_{3/2}$	119.8886	
19	$4d^9 6p\,^1P_1$	1	$4d_{3/2}^3 6\tilde{p}_{1/2}$	119.4555	120.5896 [a]
20	$4d^9 6p\,^3D_3$	3	$4d_{5/2}^5 6p_{3/2}$	118.5929	
21	$4d^9 6p\,^3D_1$	1	$4d_{3/2}^3 6p_{3/2}$	120.3813	121.4157 [a]
22	$4d^9 6p\,^3D_2$	2	$4d_{3/2}^3 6p_{3/2}$	120.5895	
23	$4d^9 5f\,^3P_0$	0	$4d_{5/2}^5 5\tilde{f}_{5/2}$	122.3364	
24	$4d^9 5f\,^3P_1$	1	$4d_{5/2}^5 5\tilde{f}_{5/2}$	122.5205	123.0839 [a]
25	$4d^9 5f\,^3P_2$	2	$4d_{5/2}^5 5f_{7/2}$	122.7973	
26	$4d^9 5f\,^3D_1$	1	$4d_{5/2}^5 5f_{7/2}$	124.0985	124.5409 [a]
27	$4d^9 5f\,^3D_3$	3	$4d_{5/2}^5 5\tilde{f}_{5/2}$	123.3075	125.8984 [b]
28	$4d^9 5f\,^3D_2$	2	$4d_{3/2}^3 5f_{7/2}$	124.8695	
29	$4d^9 5f\,^1P_1$	1	$4d_{3/2}^3 5\tilde{f}_{5/2}$	129.4696	128.5494 [a]
30	$4d^9 7p\,^3P_2$	2	$4d_{5/2}^5 7\tilde{p}_{1/2}$	138.0878	
31	$4d^9 7p\,^3P_1$	1	$4d_{3/2}^3 7\tilde{p}_{1/2}$	140.2617	140.1840 [a]
32	$4d^9 7p\,^3P_0$	0	$4d_{3/2}^3 7p_{3/2}$	140.5323	
33	$4d^9 7p\,^1P_1$	1	$4d_{5/2}^5 7p_{3/2}$	138.7018	141.6688 [a]
34	$4d^9 7p\,^3D_3$	3	$4d_{5/2}^5 7p_{3/2}$	138.8464	
35	$4d^9 7p\,^3D_1$	1	$4d_{3/2}^3 7p_{3/2}$	140.7750	142.2001 [a]
36	$4d^9 7p\,^3D_2$	2	$4d_{3/2}^3 7p_{3/2}$	140.8804	
37	$4d^9 6f\,^3P_0$	0	$4d_{5/2}^5 6\tilde{f}_{5/2}$	140.6424	
38	$4d^9 6f\,^3P_1$	1	$4d_{5/2}^5 6\tilde{f}_{5/2}$	140.7218	142.0305 [a]
39	$4d^9 6f\,^3P_2$	2	$4d_{5/2}^5 6f_{7/2}$	140.8523	
40	$4d^9 6f\,^3D_3$	3	$4d_{5/2}^5 6\tilde{f}_{5/2}$	141.0695	
41	$4d^9 6f\,^3D_1$	1	$4d_{5/2}^5 6f_{7/2}$	141.7116	142.9743 [a]
42	$4d^9 6f\,^3D_2$	2	$4d_{3/2}^3 6f_{7/2}$	142.8798	
43	$4d^9 6f\,^1P_1$	1	$4d_{3/2}^3 6\tilde{f}_{5/2}$	144.2122	145.1465 [a]

* LS Coupling notation, a—Churilov and Joshi [5], b—NIST [23].

Table 4. Same as Table 2 but for Xe^{9+}.

Index	Configuration	J	Level†	State	Present	Exp [5]	HFR [15]	MCDHF [15]
1	4d^9	5/2	0	$4d^5_{5/2}$	0.0000	0.0000	0.0000	0.0000
2	4d^9	3/2	16725	$4d^3_{3/2}$	2.0213	2.0736	2.0736	2.0485
3	4d^{8}5p	7/2	629040	$4d^4_2 5\bar{p}_{1/2}$	77.7037	77.9911	78.0033	77.0501
4	4p^{5}4d^{10}	3/2	629234	$4p^3_{3/2}$	80.4530	78.0151	77.9893	79.0030
5	4d^{8}5p	3/2	644130	$4d^4_2 5\bar{p}_{1/2}$	79.8222	79.8620	79.8418	80.1652
6	4d^{8}5p	5/2	646494	$(4\bar{d}^3_{3/2}4d^5_{5/2})_3 5\bar{p}_{1/2}$	79.9613	80.1551	80.1541	79.2899
7	4d^{8}5p	7/2	646880	$(4\bar{d}^3_{3/2}4d^5_{5/2})_3 5\bar{p}_{1/2}$	79.9342	80.2029	80.1946	79.3275
8	4d^{8}5p	3/2	654245	$(4\bar{d}^3_{3/2}4d^5_{5/2})_2 5\bar{p}_{1/2}$	80.9040	81.1161	81.1284	80.2543
9	4d^{8}5p	1/2	656520	$4d^4_0 5\bar{p}_{1/2}$	81.2487	81.3981	81.3843	80.5229
10	4d^{8}5p	5/2	657645	$(4\bar{d}^3_{3/2}4d^5_{5/2})_2 5\bar{p}_{1/2}$	81.4372	81.5376	81.5389	80.7503
11	4d^{8}5p	7/2	658993	$4d^4_4 5p_{3/2}$	81.5424	81.7048	81.7286	80.8887
12	4d^{8}5p	3/2	662160	$(4\bar{d}^3_{3/2}4d^5_{5/2})_2 5\bar{p}_{1/2}$	82.0310	82.0974	82.1027	81.3059
13	4d^{8}5p	5/2	664256	$4d^4_4 5p_{3/2}$	82.4106	82.3573	82.3841	81.7013
14	4d^{8}5p	5/2	668525	$(4\bar{d}^3_{3/2}4d^5_{5/2})_3 5p_{3/2}$	82.6723	82.8866	82.8941	82.0430
15	4d^{8}5p	7/2	669531	$4d^4_2 5p_{3/2}$	82.9641	83.0113	83.0269	82.2869
16	4d^{8}5p	5/2	671045	$4d^4_2 5p_{3/2}$	83.2829	83.1990	83.2350	82.5064
17	4d^{8}5p	7/2	672762	$(4\bar{d}^3_{3/2}4d^5_{5/2})_3 5p_{3/2}$	83.2202	83.4119	83.4178	82.5993
18	4d^{8}5p	3/2	674159	$4d^2_2 5\bar{p}_{1/2}$	83.5709	83.5851	83.5608	82.8836
19	4d^{8}5p	5/2	675652	$4d^2_2 5\bar{p}_{1/2}$	83.7487	83.7702	83.7698	83.0561
20	4d^{8}4f	7/2	676893	$4d^4_4 \bar{f}_{5/2}$	83.7547	83.9241	83.9372	84.1222
21	4d^{8}5p	3/2	677421	$(4\bar{d}^3_{3/2}4d^5_{5/2})_1 5\bar{p}_{1/2}$	84.1519	83.9895	83.9671	83.4135
22	4d^{8}5p	1/2	677704	$4d^4_2 5p_{3/2}$	84.2510	84.0246	84.0003	83.5000
23	4d^{8}4f	5/2	678351	$4d^4_4 \bar{f}_{5/2}$	83.9360	84.1048	84.0633	84.2632
24	4d^{8}5p	1/2	681425	$4d^2_2 5p_{3/2}$	84.3833	84.4860	84.4868	83.7512
25	4d^{8}4f	3/2	682437	$4d^4_4 \bar{f}_{5/2}$	84.4992	84.6114	84.7406	84.8364
26	4d^{8}5p	5/2	682838	$(4\bar{d}^3_{3/2}4d^5_{5/2})_2 5p_{3/2}$	84.7124	84.6612	84.6886	83.9971
27	4d^{8}5p	3/2	682998	$(4\bar{d}^3_{3/2}4d^5_{5/2})_3 5p_{3/2}$	84.8127	84.6810	84.6763	84.1210
28	4d^{8}5p	7/2	684240	$(4\bar{d}^3_{3/2}4d^5_{5/2})_2 5p_{3/2}$	84.8282	84.8350	84.8315	84.2146
29	4d^{8}4f	1/2	684807	$4d^4_4 f_{7/2}$	84.7890	84.9053	84.9555	84.9699
30	4d^{8}4f	7/2	687770	$4d^4_4 f_{7/2}$	85.1100	85.2727	85.2648	85.3875
31	4d^{8}5p	3/2	688121	$4d^4_2 5p_{3/2}$	85.5112	85.3162	85.3159	84.7514
32	4d^{8}4f	3/2	689190	$4d^4_4 \bar{f}_{5/2}$	85.2771	85.4487	85.4144	85.6617
33	4d^{8}5p	5/2	690757	$(4\bar{d}^3_{3/2}4d^5_{5/2})_4 5p_{3/2}$	85.6074	85.6430	85.6177	84.9183
34	4d^{8}5p	5/2	694056	$(4\bar{d}^3_{3/2}4d^5_{5/2})_1 5p_{3/2}$	86.2761	86.0520	86.0376	85.5415
35	4d^{8}5p	1/2	695239	$(4\bar{d}^3_{3/2}4d^5_{5/2})_1 5p_{3/2}$	86.5389	86.1987	86.4222	85.8222
36	4d^{8}4f	3/2	697440	$4d^4_4 f_{7/2}$	86.3697	86.4716	86.5023	86.7867
37	4d^{8}4f	5/2	698751	$(4\bar{d}^3_{3/2}4d^5_{5/2})_2 4\bar{f}_{5/2}$	86.8275	86.6341	86.6812	86.9352
38	4d^{8}4f	5/2	701155	$(4\bar{d}^3_{3/2}4d^5_{5/2})_3 4f_{7/2}$	86.5695	86.9322	86.9251	87.1944
39	4d^{8}5p	5/2	701735	$4d^2_2 5p_{3/2}$	87.1092	87.0041	87.0408	86.3731
40	4d^{8}4f	1/2	702652	$(4\bar{d}^3_{3/2}4d^5_{5/2})_3 4f_{7/2}$	86.9067	87.1178	87.1082	87.2971
41	4d^{8}5p	7/2	703997	$(4\bar{d}^3_{3/2}4d^5_{5/2})_4 5p_{3/2}$	87.5382*	87.2845	87.2566	86.8773
42	4d^{8}5p	1/2	705669	$(4\bar{d}^3_{3/2}4d^5_{5/2})_2 5p_{3/2}$	87.7952	87.4918	87.4907	87.0046
43	4d^{8}4f	7/2	708748	$4d^4_2 4\bar{f}_{5/2}$	87.8852	87.8736	87.8309	88.2534
44	4d^{8}4f	5/2	711392	$(4\bar{d}^3_{3/2}4d^5_{5/2})_4 f_{7/2}$	88.2139	88.2014	88.1999	88.5561
45	4d^{8}4f	5/2	713643	$(4\bar{d}^3_{3/2}4d^5_{5/2})_3 4\bar{f}_{5/2}$	88.4606	88.4805	88.4592	88.9055
46	4d^{8}4f	5/2	721870	$4d^4_2 4f_{7/2}$	89.6583	89.5005	89.5035	89.9423
47	4d^{8}5p	1/2	723216	$4d^2_0 5\bar{p}_{1/2}$	90.7099	89.6674	89.7097	89.5125
48	4d^{8}4f	1/2	725785	$4d^2_2 4\bar{f}_{5/2}$	90.0249	89.9971	90.0379	90.3918
49	4d^{8}4f	1/2	737104	$4d^2_2 4\bar{f}_{5/2}$	91.8734	91.3893	91.4296	91.9682

Table 4. Cont.

Index	Configuration	J	Level†	State	Present	Exp [5]	HFR [15]	MCDHF [15]
50	$4d^85p$	3/2	745212	$4\bar{d}_0^25p_{3/2}$	92.9879	92.3946	92.3705	92.0573
51	$4d^84f$	3/2	749681	$(4\bar{d}_{3/2}^3 4d_{5/2}^5)_2 4\bar{f}_{5/2}$	90.9563 *	92.9486	92.8513	93.7464
52	$4d^84f$	1/2	753489	$(4\bar{d}_{3/2}^3 4d_{5/2}^5)_2 4\bar{f}_{5/2}$	94.3872	93.4208	93.4519	94.4965
53	$4d^84f$	5/2	864592	$4\bar{d}_4^4 4f_{7/2}$	106.0721 *	107.1958	107.1838	109.8049
54	$4d^84f$	7/2	870470	$4\bar{d}_4^4 4f_{7/2}$	107.4877 *	107.9246	108.0401	110.2660
55	$4d^84f$	3/2	874794	$4\bar{d}_2^2 4\bar{f}_{5/2}$	107.6293 *	108.4607	108.4489	110.8660
56	$4d^84f$	5/2	887203	$4\bar{d}_2^2 4\bar{f}_{5/2}$	109.4709 *	109.9992	110.0328	112.3180
57	$4p^54d^{10}$	1/2	924721	$4\bar{p}_{1/2}$	116.2848 *	114.6508	114.6494	115.8723

† Energy levels (in cm^{-1}) as represented in Churilov and Joshi [5], * Values with $4d^64f^3$ configuration included.

Table 5. Same as Table 2 but for Xe^{10+}.

Index	Configuration	J	Level†	State	Present	Exp [6]	HFR [14]	RCI [14]
1	$4d^8$	4	0	$4d_4^4$	0.0000	0.0000	0.0000	0.0000
2	$4d^8$	2	13140	$4d_4^4$	1.7415	1.6292	1.6811	1.8015
3	$4d^8$	3	15205	$4\bar{d}_{3/2}^3 4d_{5/2}^5$	1.8204	1.8852	1.8617	1.8688
4	$4d^8$	2	26670	$4\bar{d}_{3/2}^3 4d_{5/2}^5$	3.4080	3.3067	3.3112	3.4620
5	$4d^8$	0	32210	$4d_0^4$	4.2453	3.9935	4.0264	2.5905
6	$4d^8$	1	34610	$4\bar{d}_{3/2}^3 4d_{5/2}^5$	4.5407	4.2911	4.3065	4.5968
7	$4d^8$	4	40835	$4\bar{d}_{3/2}^3 4d_{5/2}^5$	5.4872	5.0629	5.0460	5.3922
8	$4d^8$	2	42900	$4\bar{d}_2^2$	5.4003	5.3189	5.3556	5.5356
9	$4d^8$	0	88130	$4\bar{d}_0^2$	11.0871	10.9267	10.9460	9.7872
10	$4d^75p$	3	725825	$(4\bar{d}_{3/2}^3 4d_4^4)_{5/2} 5\bar{p}_{1/2}$	89.8310	89.9909	90.0196	89.8633
11	$4d^75p$	4	731458	$(4\bar{d}_{3/2}^3 4d_4^4)_{7/2} 5p_{3/2}$	90.4439	90.6893	90.7270	90.5293
12	$4d^75p$	3	733755	$4d_{9/2}^3 5p_{3/2}$	90.7887	90.9741	91.0248	90.8299
13	$4d^75p$	4	737388	$(4\bar{d}_{3/2}^3 4d_4^4)_{7/2} 5p_{3/2}$	91.1980	91.4245	91.4241	91.1814
14	$4d^75p$	4	739542	$(4\bar{d}_{3/2}^3 4d_2^4)_{7/2} 5\bar{p}_{1/2}$	91.5316	91.6916	91.7102	91.6168
15	$4d^75p$	5	740348	$(4\bar{d}_{3/2}^3 4d_4^4)_{11/2} 5\bar{p}_{1/2}$	91.7221	91.7915	91.7767	91.7197
16	$4d^75p$	3	741800	$(4\bar{d}_{3/2}^3 4d_4^4)_{7/2} 5p_{3/2}$	91.8900	91.9715	91.9751	91.8800
17	$4d^75p$	3	744955	$4d_{3/2}^3 5p_{3/2}$	92.3054	92.3627	92.3530	92.9385
18	$4d^75p$	1	745470	$(4\bar{d}_{3/2}^3 4d_4^4)_{3/2} 5\bar{p}_{1/2}$	92.3464	92.4265	92.4299	92.3399
19	$4d^75p$	3	749351	$(4\bar{d}_2^2 4d_{5/2}^5)_{5/2} 5\bar{p}_{1/2}$	92.9282	92.9077	92.9050	93.5021
20	$4d^75p$	2	750512	$(4\bar{d}_{3/2}^3 4d_4^4)_{7/2} 5p_{3/2}$	93.1118	93.0517	93.0693	93.4798
21	$4d^75p$	2	753795	$(4\bar{d}_{3/2}^3 4d_2^4)_{1/2} 5p_{3/2}$	93.4853	93.4587	93.4608	93.8036
22	$4d^75p$	1	754745	$4d_{3/2}^3 5p_{3/2}$	93.8957	93.5765	93.6211	93.7532
23	$4d^75p$	4	756016	$(4\bar{d}_2^2 4d_{5/2}^5)_{9/2} 5\bar{p}_{1/2}$	93.6887	93.7341	93.7260	93.7626
24	$4d^75p$	1	758337	$(4\bar{d}_{3/2}^3 4d_4^4)_{5/2} 5p_{3/2}$	94.4733	94.0218	94.0413	94.2022
25	$4d^75p$	3	761266	$(4\bar{d}_{3/2}^3 4d_4^4)_{5/2} 5p_{3/2}$	94.3337	94.3850	94.3938	95.3887
26	$4d^75p$	4	763070	$(4\bar{d}_{3/2}^3 4d_2^4)_{7/2} 5p_{3/2}$	94.5816	94.6087	94.6466	94.6785
27	$4d^75p$	1	765770	$(4\bar{d}_{3/2}^3 4d_2^4)_{1/2} 5p_{3/2}$	95.2934	94.9434	94.9681	95.4116
28	$4d^75p$	3	766860	$(4\bar{d}_{3/2}^3 4d_2^4)_{7/2} 5p_{3/2}$	95.0988	95.0786	95.0791	96.0978
29	$4d^75p$	1	767369	$(4\bar{d}_{3/2}^3 4d_2^4)_{3/2} 5p_{3/2}$	95.2028	95.1417	95.1611	95.1833
30	$4d^75p$	2	773315	$(4\bar{d}_2^2 4d_{5/2}^5)_{3/2} 5p_{3/2}$	96.1325	95.8789	95.9466	96.4209
31	$4d^75p$	3	773715	$(4\bar{d}_2^2 4d_{5/2}^5)_{7/2} 5p_{3/2}$	96.1320	95.9285	95.9088	96.9597

Table 5. Cont.

Index	Configuration	J	Level†	State	Present	Exp [6]	HFR [14]	RCI [14]
32	$4d^75p$	4	773968	$(4\bar{d}^3_{3/2}4d^4_4)_{11/2}5p_{3/2}$	96.3462	95.9598	95.9886	96.3065
33	$4d^75p$	1	775030	$(4\bar{d}^2_24d^5_{5/2})_{3/2}5p_{3/2}$	96.4126	96.0915	96.1071	96.2977
34	$4d^75p$	3	780503	$(4\bar{d}^2_24d^5_{5/2})_{9/2}5p_{3/2}$	97.1319	96.7701	96.8204	97.9562
35	$4d^75p$	1	784035	$(4\bar{d}^2_24d^5_{5/2})_{1/2}5p_{3/2}$	97.4966	97.2080	97.2402	97.4814
36	$4d^75p$	2	786580	$4\bar{d}^3_{3/2}5p_{3/2}$	97.6818	97.5235	97.5240	97.4868
37	$4d^75p$	5	789029	$(4\bar{d}^2_24d^5_{5/2})_{9/2}5p_{3/2}$	97.9360	97.8272	97.8676	97.9756
38	$4d^75p$	1	791805	$4\bar{d}^3_{3/2}5p_{3/2}$	98.5246	98.1714	98.1737	100.6760
39	$4d^75p$	3	795135	$4\bar{d}^3_{3/2}5p_{3/2}$	98.9541	98.5842	98.5785	99.8198
40	$4d^75p$	3	801225	$(4\bar{d}^2_04d^5_{5/2})_{5/2}5\bar{p}_{1/2}$	99.9998	99.3393	99.3609	100.7918
41	$4d^75p$	1	830260	$(4\bar{d}^2_04d^5_{5/2})_{5/2}5p_{3/2}$	103.9132	102.9392	103.0239	103.4795
42	$4d^74f$	4	892420	$4d^3_{9/2}4f_{7/2}$	110.8675	110.6460	110.6962	113.0177
43	$4d^74f$	3	894941	$(4\bar{d}^3_{3/2}4d^4_4)_{11/2}4\bar{f}_{5/2}$	111.3093	110.9586	111.0141	113.5215
44	$4d^74f$	5	897383	$4d^3_{9/2}4f_{7/2}$	110.9844	111.2614	111.2278	113.2369
45	$4d^74f$	3	908390	$4\bar{d}^3_{3/2}4f_{7/2}$	112.8340	112.6261	112.6093	114.9623
46	$4d^74f$	4	911082	$(4\bar{d}^2_24d^5_{5/2})_{5/2}4\bar{f}_{5/2}$	112.7247	112.9598	112.9980	115.0362
47	$4d^74f$	2	911665	$(4\bar{d}^2_24d^5_{5/2})_{9/2}4\bar{f}_{5/2}$	112.7447	113.0321	113.0446	115.4546
48	$4d^74f$	3	912600	$(4\bar{d}^3_{3/2}4d^4_4)_{7/2}4f_{7/2}$	113.3634	113.1480	113.1855	115.4796
49	$4d^74f$	1	913877	$(4\bar{d}^3_{3/2}4d^4_4)_{7/2}4f_{7/2}$	112.8179	113.3064	113.3154	116.2031
50	$4d^74f$	2	924500	$(4\bar{d}^3_{3/2}4d^4_4)_{5/2}4f_{7/2}$	113.9633	114.6234	114.6270	117.0618
51	$4d^74f$	4	925626	$(4\bar{d}^3_{3/2}4d^4_4)_{11/2}4f_{7/2}$	114.0579	114.7631	114.7761	117.6640
52	$4d^74f$	0	933343	$(4\bar{d}^2_24d^5_{5/2})_{5/2}4\bar{f}_{5/2}$	117.7646	115.7198	115.7151	118.1618
53	$4d^74f$	3	935035	$4\bar{d}^3_{3/2}4\bar{f}_{5/2}$	115.4998	115.9296	115.9595	118.3774
54	$4d^74f$	5	938628	$(4\bar{d}^2_24d^5_{5/2})_{9/2}4\bar{f}_{5/2}$	116.8915	116.3751	116.4192	118.7650
55	$4p^54d^9$	2	944705	$4\bar{p}_{1/2}4\bar{d}^3_{3/2}$	118.9159	117.1285	117.1295	119.3615
56	$4p^54d^9$	2	951795	$4\bar{p}_{1/2}4d^5_{5/2}$	120.5650	118.0076	118.0396	120.3551
57	$4p^54d^9$	3	957488	$4\bar{p}_{1/2}4d^5_{5/2}$	122.7719	118.7134	118.7241	121.5465

† Energy levels (in cm^{-1}) as represented in Churilov et al. [6].

Table 2 presents a comparison of our results for Xe^{7+} with the NIST values [23]. In addition to the $j-j$ coupling representation, we have also included the notations of the states used in the NIST database to make the comparison convenient between the two sets of the results. We find from Table 2 that our calculated energies show an average deviation of nearly 1.5% with the corresponding energies from the NIST database [23]. A maximum variation of nearly 3% is found for the 5s4f $^3P_{1/2,3/2}$ levels. We have listed only those levels in Table 2 that are reported to be involved in emitting intense lines in the EBIT measurements of Fahy et al. [8] and Ali and Nakamura [9].

For Xe^{8+}, in our calculations we got two levels with leading contribution from $4d^97p$ $^1P_1$, one at 138.7018 eV (53.65% $4d^5_{5/2}7p_{3/2}$ ^1P + 37.44% $4\bar{d}^3_{3/2}7\bar{p}_{1/2}$ ^3P + 8.79% $4\bar{d}^3_{3/2}7p_{3/2}$ ^3D) and another at 140.2617 eV (44.29% $4d^5_{5/2}7p_{3/2}$ ^1P + 30.70% $4\bar{d}^3_{3/2}7\bar{p}_{1/2}$ ^3P + 24.90% $4\bar{d}^3_{3/2}7p_{3/2}$ ^3D). Considering the maximum contribution, we have classified the level at 138.7018 eV as $4d^97p$ $^1P_1$, and 140.2617 eV as $4d^97p$ $^3P_1$. This changed the energy order of $^1P_1$ and $^3P_1$ in our calculations with respect to those reported by Churilov and Joshi [5]. As can be seen from Table 3, the agreement between the measurements [5] and our results is within 0.8% for most of the cases. The maximum difference of nearly 3 eV is found for the $4d^94f$ $^1P_1$ level.

The energy levels of Xe^{9+} are listed in Table 4 and are compared with the measurements [5] as well as HFR and MCDHF calculations of Motoumba et al. [15]. The open-shell structure of Xe^{9+} leads to the formation of a large number of closely spaced fine-structure levels for its ground and excited state configurations. Consequently, it becomes extremely difficult to correctly identify these states as well as to label them uniquely in LS coupling notations. Churilov and Joshi [5] reported Xe^{9+} levels with the wavenumbers (in cm^{-1}) which are also included in Table 4 to guide us in right recognition of the states. From our calculations, we found that the inclusion of the triple excitation 4d^{6}4f^3 improves the match between the present energies and measurements for the higher 4d^{8}4f levels, while it deteriorates the agreement for other levels. Thus we have considered two sets of calculations for Xe^{9+}, one with and the other without including the CSF 4d^{6}4f^3. The energies marked with * in Table 4 indicate the inclusion of the CSF 4d^{6}4f^3. For 4p^{5}4d^{10} levels, our energy results overestimate the measurements [5] and theoretical results [15] by nearly 2 eV. Except for this transition, in most of the cases our energies show better agreements with the experimental results than the MCDHF calculations [15].

Table 5 presents a comparison of the present energies with the experimental energies from Churilov et al. [6] and RCI and HFR calculations of Motoumba et al. [14] for Xe^{10+}. Similar to Xe^{9+}, Xe^{10+} has an open shell structure and hence, we have included the wavenumbers reported in [6] so that the small spaced levels can be rightly identified. We learnt that adding the CSF 4p^{4}4d^{10} improves the energy of the 4d^8 levels, while including the CSF 4d^{5}4f^3 with triple excitation improves the energy of the higher 4d^{7}4f levels. The order of a few levels from 4d^8, 4d^{7}5p and 4d^{7}4f configurations are not as per the order reported in the measurements [6]. Similar cases are also observed in the RCI results [14]. Our reported energies show a deviation of nearly 2-4 eV for the 4p^{5}4d^9 levels, however, they are in good agreement with the RCI calculations by Motoumba et al. [14].

The comparison of our calculated wavelengths and transition rates with other theoretical and experimental results is shown through Tables 6–9. For Xe^{7+}, Table 6 includes the measurements from NIST EBIT and Cowan code calculations reported by Fahy et al. [8], compact EBIT results from Ali and Nakamura [9] as well as HFR calculations of Churilov and Joshi [5]. Though Table 6 shows a maximum deviation of 3.5 Å for levels of 4d^{9}5s4f configurations with indices 9 and 10, a good agreement is found between our reported transition rates and the calculated results from Cowan code [8].

Wavelengths and transition rates for Xe^{8+} from the present work are reported and compared in Table 7 with the measurements and other calculations [5,8–10,13]. Overall, our calculations are in good agreement with other results. However, a maximum deviation of 3.4 Å is found in the wavelength corresponding to 1 → 15 (4d^{10} ^{1}S$_0$ → 4d^{9}4f ^{1}P$_1$) transition. This is because from Table 3 our calculated energy of the 4d^{9}4f ^{1}P$_1$ level is overestimated by nearly 3 eV in comparison to the result reported by Churilov and Joshi [5]. It is further noticed for the above transition that our calculated wavelength shows a better match with that from Ivanova [13] and there is a good agreement among various values of the transition rate.

Table 6. Wavelengths and transition rates of Xe^{7+} for the transitions from 4d^{10}5s ^{2}S$_{1/2}$ state.

Index	J$_b$	Wavelength (nm)		Transition Rate (A) (10^{10}) (s^{-1})	
		Present	Other Reported	Present	Other Reported
10	3/2	11.9593	12.32 [a], 12.56 [b], 12.332 [c], 12.3243 [d]	128.093	140.75 [b], 211.225 [d]
9	1/2	11.9713	12.56 [b], 12.3265 [d]	122.349	141 [b], 210.8 [d]
8	1/2	16.5963	16.668 [c]	1.934	
7	3/2	17.0015	17.09 [a], 17.09 [b], 17.087 [c]	3.131	4 [b]
6	1/2	17.8218	17.6 [a], 17.61 [b], 17.603 [c]	0.399	0.35 [b]
5	1/2	17.9319	17.73 [a], 17.76 [b], 17.726 [c]	4.740	5 [b]
4	3/2	18.1815	17.98 [a], 17.92 [b], 17.958 [c]	0.766	0.5 [b]
3	3/2	18.4659	18.15 [a], 18.07 [b]	0.050	0.125 [b]
2	3/2	18.7259	18.44 [a], 18.31 [b], 18.4322 [c]	0.165	0.25 [b]

Experimental results: a—Fahy et al. [8], c—Ali and Nakamura [9], d—Churilov and Joshi [5]. Theoretical results: b—Fahy et al. [8].

Table 7. Wavelengths and transition rates of Xe^{8+} for the transitions from 4d^{10} $^1S_0$ state.

Index	J_b	Wavelength (nm)		Transition Rate (A) (10^{10}) (s^{-1})	
		Present	Other Reported	Present	Other Reported
43	1	8.5973	8.5420 ^{a}, 8.54 ^{b}, 8.54 ^{c}	13.099	12.333 ^{a}, 11.333 ^{c}
41	1	8.7491	8.6718 ^{a*}	3.246	3.167 ^{a}
38	1	8.8106	8.7294 ^{a*}	0.012	0.033 ^{a}
35	1	8.8073	8.7190 ^{a*}	0.110	0.033 ^{a}
33	1	8.9389	8.7517 ^{a}	1.783	1.333 ^{a}
31	1	8.8395	8.8444 ^{a}, 8.85 ^{b}, 8.85 ^{c}	1.686	1.933 ^{a}, 2.333 ^{c}
29	1	9.5763	9.6449 ^{a}, 9.63 ^{b}, 9.61 ^{c}, 9.639 ^{d}, 9.6218 ^{f}	57.797	51.267 ^{a}, 46.667 ^{c}
26	1	9.9908	9.9553 ^{a}, 9.963 ^{f}	2.201	2.2 ^{a}
24	1	10.1195	10.0732 ^{a*}, 10.0731 ^{f}	0.114	0.1 ^{a}
21	1	10.2993	10.2116 ^{a*}	0.205	0.267 ^{a}
19	1	10.3791	10.2815 ^{a}, 10.28 ^{b}, 10.29 ^{c},	4.599	3.7 ^{a}, 4 ^{c}
17	1	10.4826	10.3808 ^{a}, 10.38 ^{b}, 10.39 ^{c},	2.878	2.967 ^{a}, 3 ^{c}
15	1	11.6265	12.0133 ^{a}, 12.02 ^{b}, 12.00 ^{c}, 12.019 ^{d}, 11.5787 ^{f}	157.520	151.8 ^{a}, 152 ^{c}
13	1	14.3835	14.3614 ^{a}, 14.36 ^{b}, 14.31 ^{c}, 14.3127 ^{f}	0.207	0.2 ^{a}, 0.2 ^{c}
10	1	15.1469	15.0274 ^{a}, 15.1155 ^{f}	0.031	0.033 ^{a}
7	1	16.2010	16.1742 ^{a}, 16.18 ^{b}, 16.15 ^{c}, 16.177 ^{e}, 16.1343 ^{f}	1.700	1.5 ^{a}, 8.333 ^{c}
5	1	16.5223	16.5323 ^{a}, 16.53 ^{b}, 16.50 ^{c}, 16.536 ^{e}, 16.511 ^{f}	7.129	8.033 ^{a}, 1.333 ^{c}
3	1	16.8906	16.8202 ^{a}, 16.7548 ^{f}	0.001	0.007 ^{a}

Experimental results: a—Churilov and Joshi [5], a*—calculated wavelengths from the energy levels [5], b—Fahy et al. [8], d—Ali and Nakamura [10], e—Ali and Nakamura [9]. Theoretical results: c—Fahy et al. [8], f—Ivanova [13].

Table 8. Wavelengths and transition rates of Xe^{9+}. a and b denote the indices of initial and final levels, respectively.

a	J_a	b	J_b	Wavelength (nm)				Transition Rate (A) (10^{10}) (s^{-1})			
				Present	Exp [5]	HFR [15]	MCDHF [15]	Present	HFR [5]	HFR [15]	MCDHF [15]
2	3/2	57	1/2	10.8507	11.0133	11.0134	10.8926	182.421	189.800	192.000	155.000
1	5/2	56	5/2	11.3258	11.2714	11.2679	11.0387	2.746	1.617	1.717	0.613
1	5/2	55	3/2	11.5196	11.4312	11.4325	11.1833	30.098	123.550	125.500	137.000
2	3/2	56	5/2	11.5388	11.4879	11.4844	11.2437	170.353	177.667	180.000	154.000
1	5/2	54	7/2	11.5347	11.4880	11.4758	11.2441	174.181	180.000	183.750	155.000
1	5/2	53	5/2	11.6887	11.5661	11.5674	11.2913	154.107	163.267	166.333	146.000
2	3/2	55	3/2	11.7400	11.6541	11.6554	11.3938	126.264	47.375	48.250	13.300
1	5/2	51	3/2	13.6312	13.3390	13.3530	13.2255	0.177	0.300	0.199	0.118
1	5/2	50	5/2	13.3334	13.4189	13.4225	13.4682	0.210	0.325	0.393	0.448
2	3/2	52	1/2	13.4232	13.5729	13.5682	13.4112	3.761	3.100	3.390	2.600
2	3/2	50	3/2	13.6297	13.7272	13.7307	13.7747	0.358	0.450	0.365	0.172
1	5/2	46	5/2	13.8285	13.8529	13.8524	13.7849	0.072	0.067	0.082	0.062
2	3/2	49	1/2	13.7987	13.8816	13.8753	13.7883	0.764	1.050	1.210	0.585
1	5/2	45	5/2	14.0158	14.0126	14.0160	13.9456	0.043	0.050	0.041	0.039
2	3/2	48	1/2	14.0885	14.1032	14.0948	14.0344	0.448	0.150	0.019	0.023
1	5/2	43	7/2	14.1075	14.1094	14.1162	14.0487	0.096	0.125	0.166	0.100
2	3/2	47	1/2	13.9797	14.1545	14.1476	14.1754	0.450	0.550	0.635	0.880
1	5/2	41	7/2	14.1635	14.2046	14.2091	14.2712	0.512	0.525	0.514	0.565
1	5/2	39	5/2	14.2332	14.2505	14.2444	14.3545	0.079	0.067	0.059	0.109
1	5/2	36	3/2	14.3551	14.3382	14.3331	14.2861	0.031	0.225	0.104	0.050
2	3/2	45	5/2	14.3435	14.3488	14.3524	14.2745	0.123	0.100	0.127	0.095
2	3/2	44	5/2	14.3846	14.3954	14.3956	14.3322	0.072	0.050	0.026	0.026
1	5/2	34	5/2	14.3706	14.4079	14.4105	14.4941	0.080	0.083	0.073	0.068
1	5/2	33	5/2	14.4829	14.4771	14.4811	14.6004	0.433	0.233	0.230	0.412

Table 8. Cont.

a	J_a	b	J_b	Wavelength (nm)				Transition Rate (A) (10^{10}) (s^{-1})			
				Present	Exp [5]	HFR [15]	MCDHF [15]	Present	HFR [5]	HFR [15]	MCDHF [15]
1	5/2	32	3/2	14.5390	14.5096	14.5156	14.4737	0.093	0.475	0.455	0.029
2	3/2	42	1/2	14.4548	14.5150	14.5152	14.5939	7.686	10.050	10.350	10.000
1	5/2	31	3/2	14.4990	14.5325	14.5324	14.6292	2.850	2.350	2.338	2.550
1	5/2	30	7/2	14.5675	14.5397	14.5411	14.5202	0.146	0.038	0.049	0.013
2	3/2	40	1/2	14.6061	14.5788	14.5804	14.5438	0.220	0.100	0.065	0.164
2	3/2	39	5/2	14.5713	14.5983	14.5920	14.7032	3.675	3.017	3.150	4.417
2	3/2	38	5/2	14.6643	14.6107	14.6119	14.5614	0.055	0.267	0.380	0.028
1	5/2	28	7/2	14.6159	14.6148	14.6154	14.7224	0.241	0.125	0.141	0.353
1	5/2	27	3/2	14.6186	14.6413	14.6421	14.7388	0.728	0.600	1.003	0.973
1	5/2	26	5/2	14.6359	14.6448	14.6400	14.7605	0.011	0.217	0.243	0.084
1	5/2	25	3/2	14.6728	14.6532	14.6310	14.6145	0.331	0.400	0.181	0.005
2	3/2	37	5/2	14.6197	14.6622	14.6540	14.6059	0.001	0.183	0.207	0.021
2	3/2	35	1/2	14.6696	14.7381	14.7381	14.8026	0.750	0.950	0.910	0.990
1	5/2	23	5/2	14.7713	14.7418	14.7479	14.7139	0.356	0.100	0.105	0.001
1	5/2	21	3/2	14.7334	14.7618	14.7658	14.8638	5.566	5.650	5.925	6.700
2	3/2	34	5/2	14.7154	14.7640	14.7664	14.8497	1.073	1.100	1.093	0.930
1	5/2	20	7/2	14.8033	14.7734	14.7711	14.7386	0.141	0.163	0.155	0.022
1	5/2	19	5/2	14.8043	14.7956	14.8006	14.9278	3.264	5.350	5.750	6.983
1	5/2	18	3/2	14.8358	14.8333	14.8376	14.9588	0.014	1.300	1.238	0.190
2	3/2	33	5/2	14.8331	14.8359	14.8406	14.9613	1.752	2.150	2.183	1.933
2	3/2	32	3/2	14.8920	14.8709	14.8768	14.8283	0.025	1.200	1.163	4.98E−5
2	3/2	31	3/2	14.8500	14.8942	14.8944	14.9915	2.532	3.325	3.675	3.525
1	5/2	16	5/2	14.8871	14.9020	14.8957	15.0272	2.046	2.217	2.450	3.033
1	5/2	15	7/2	14.9443	14.9358	14.9330	15.0673	1.215	2.438	2.413	1.413
1	5/2	14	5/2	14.9971	14.9583	14.9569	15.1121	0.727	1.100	1.145	0.733
2	3/2	29	1/2	14.9798	14.9682	14.9592	14.9520	0.239	0.450	0.250	0.002
2	3/2	27	3/2	14.9755	15.0089	15.0097	15.1067	6.018	6.050	6.775	6.775
2	3/2	26	5/2	14.9937	15.0124	15.0075	15.1295	0.849	0.933	0.990	0.805
2	3/2	25	3/2	15.0324	15.0216	15.0206	14.9761	0.095	0.650	0.081	0.021
2	3/2	24	1/2	15.0536	15.0444	15.0216	15.1750	0.524	0.700	0.880	1.070
1	5/2	13	5/2	15.0447	15.0544	15.0495	15.1753	3.238	3.967	4.067	3.383
1	5/2	12	3/2	15.1143	15.1020	15.1011	15.2491	0.136	0.325	0.323	0.172
2	3/2	23	5/2	15.1358	15.1141	15.1219	15.0805	0.099	0.117	0.074	0.003
2	3/2	22	1/2	15.0778	15.1291	15.1336	15.2218	0.333	0.400	0.414	0.277
2	3/2	21	3/2	15.0960	15.1356	15.1397	15.2380	0.714	0.175	0.158	0.615
1	5/2	11	7/2	15.2049	15.1747	15.1702	15.3278	0.931	1.075	1.118	1.070
2	3/2	19	5/2	15.1705	15.1762	15.1763	15.3053	0.385	0.667	0.743	0.643
1	5/2	10	5/2	15.2245	15.2058	15.2055	15.3540	1.691	1.833	1.867	1.640
2	3/2	16	5/2	15.2574	15.2832	15.2763	15.4098	0.470	0.217	0.228	0.333
1	5/2	8	3/2	15.3249	15.2849	15.2825	15.4489	0.035	0.100	0.098	0.017
2	3/2	13	5/2	15.4230	15.4433	15.4381	15.5656	0.225	0.200	0.218	0.253
1	5/2	7	7/2	15.5108	15.4588	15.4604	15.6294	0.018	0.038	0.038	0.023
1	5/2	6	5/2	15.5055	15.4680	15.4682	15.6368	0.252	0.317	0.342	0.275
2	3/2	12	3/2	15.4962	15.4935	15.4924	15.6432	0.344	0.325	0.353	0.305
1	5/2	5	3/2	15.5325	15.5248	15.5287	15.4661	0.043	0.050	0.039	0.495
2	3/2	9	1/2	15.6492	15.6300	15.6327	15.7993	0.004	0.050	0.036	0.013
2	3/2	8	3/2	15.7176	15.6857	15.6833	15.8536	0.009	0.050	0.045	0.037
1	5/2	4	3/2	15.4108	15.8924	15.8973	15.6936	0.253	0.300	0.535	0.041
1	5/2	3	7/2	15.9560	15.8972	15.8947	16.0914	0.012	0.025	0.020	0.015
2	3/2	5	3/2	15.9361	15.9388	15.9428	15.8717	0.182	0.125	0.155	0.008
2	3/2	4	3/2	15.8079	16.3262	16.3316	16.1114	0.004	0.050	0.061	0.148

Table 9. Wavelengths and transition rates of Xe^{10+}. a and b refer to the indices of initial and final levels, respectively.

a	J_a	b	J_b	Wavelength (nm)				Transition Rate (A) (10^{10}) (s^{-1})			
				Present	Exp [6]	HFR [14]	RCI [14]	Present	HFR [6]	HFR [14]	RCI [14]
3	3	57	3	10.2507	10.6125	10.6094	10.3598	9.089	14.486	14.286	10.286
6	1	56	2	10.6861	10.9027	10.9013	10.7106	83.644	60.560	61.000	52.200
7	4	57	3	10.5712	10.9093	10.9066	10.6741	173.558	151.143	152.857	128.000
8	2	57	3	10.5634	10.9339	10.9364	10.6873	13.424	19.071	19.429	16.714
8	2	56	2	10.7658	11.0026	11.0028	10.7982	40.687	94.460	95.800	78.400
8	2	55	2	10.9222	11.0889	11.0924	10.8925	141.509	87.940	87.600	74.400
2	2	48	3	11.1075	11.1179	11.1192	10.9066	14.753	28.657	28.143	14.571
6	1	52	0	10.9504	11.1268	11.1288	10.9175	191.711	189.600	191.000	158.000
7	4	54	5	11.1292	11.1384	11.1323	10.9360	191.990	194.364	196.364	165.455
1	4	44	5	11.1713	11.1435	11.1469	10.9491	186.179	189.364	191.818	162.727
3	3	47	2	11.1774	11.1552	11.1514	10.9155	78.606	78.420	84.200	98.000
3	3	46	4	11.1794	11.1622	11.1561	10.9551	182.634	185.556	187.778	161.111
2	2	45	3	11.1605	11.1706	11.1770	10.9565	107.137	147.571	150.000	139.714
1	4	43	3	11.1387	11.1739	11.1684	10.9217	87.638	160.143	161.429	140.571
7	4	53	3	11.2700	11.1834	11.1785	10.9735	0.118	12.786	12.957	11.343
3	3	45	3	11.1684	11.1954	11.1952	10.9630	26.167	22.714	22.286	11.257
1	4	42	4	11.1831	11.2055	11.2004	10.9703	172.910	174.444	176.667	152.222
8	2	53	3	11.2611	11.2089	11.2098	10.9874	92.121	162.857	164.286	142.000
6	1	50	2	11.3308	11.2373	11.2385	11.0243	28.806	41.460	41.800	43.400
7	4	51	4	11.4197	11.3021	11.2990	11.0432	155.527	162.444	16.556	14.778
6	1	49	1	11.4506	11.3731	11.3738	11.1091	66.408	50.433	52.000	38.333
6	1	47	2	11.4584	11.4020	11.4021	11.1841	54.737	27.100	28.800	22.200
7	4	40	3	13.1183	13.1515	13.1458	13.0111	7.707	5.029	5.171	0.054
8	2	40	3	13.1062	13.1865	13.1891	13.0307	1.540	1.771	1.829	0.102
7	4	39	3	13.2651	13.2573	13.2557	13.1301	3.479	7.029	6.886	7.100
4	2	34	3	13.2287	13.2658	13.2590	13.1208	2.749	1.857	1.900	0.002
6	1	36	2	13.3114	13.2983	13.3005	13.3474	2.258	3.380	3.440	1.422
8	2	38	1	13.3138	13.3529	13.0699	12.7538	2.321	4.700	4.700	0.023
7	4	37	5	13.4111	13.3655	13.3573	13.3916	2.955	2.482	2.564	2.864
4	2	30	2	13.3713	13.3934	13.3841	13.3375	4.881	3.920	4.040	0.045
3	3	25	3	13.4018	13.4037	13.3991	13.2575	0.283	4.257	4.300	0.667
1	4	17	3	13.4320	13.4238	13.4250	13.3405	4.862	5.457	5.714	0.071
9	0	41	1	13.3566	13.4750	13.4651	13.2331	6.771	6.733	6.867	5.867
2	2	22	1	13.4540	13.4844	13.4853	13.4836	6.748	4.800	4.867	3.733
8	2	35	1	13.4625	13.4927	13.4935	13.4845	3.525	5.467	5.567	6.767
3	3	23	4	13.4959	13.4987	13.4965	13.4921	5.388	6.456	6.233	3.178
1	4	15	5	13.5174	13.5072	13.5093	13.5177	3.961	5.718	5.736	3.064
4	2	28	3	13.5220	13.5100	13.5106	13.3840	2.332	4.043	3.943	0.281
1	4	14	4	13.5455	13.5219	13.5191	13.5329	1.240	1.178	1.267	0.680
4	2	27	1	13.4934	13.5298	13.5270	13.4839	4.786	4.967	5.133	0.134
3	3	21	2	13.5258	13.5393	13.5355	13.4861	1.369	4.120	4.300	0.980
8	2	34	3	13.5160	13.5571	13.5554	13.4152	1.427	1.614	1.629	1.413
1	4	13	4	13.5951	13.5614	13.5614	13.5975	4.420	3.500	3.556	5.289
3	3	20	2	13.5812	13.5997	13.5936	13.5338	1.859	1.820	1.908	2.380
5	0	29	1	13.6310	13.6025	13.6045	13.3903	2.424	2.500	2.573	1.057
3	3	19	3	13.6085	13.6213	13.6182	13.5305	2.642	3.829	3.986	1.024
1	4	12	3	13.6564	13.6290	13.6209	13.6502	1.642	1.686	1.729	0.766
7	4	32	4	13.6458	13.6401	13.6332	13.6375	6.981	4.122	5.633	1.533
7	4	31	3	13.6780	13.6451	13.6452	13.5402	2.142	2.229	2.371	0.001
2	2	18	1	13.6840	13.6547	13.6624	13.6941	2.273	3.367	3.467	2.187
8	2	33	1	13.6228	13.6584	13.6619	13.6604	1.970	2.867	3.010	2.347
4	2	24	1	13.6149	13.6670	13.6652	13.6636	2.825	3.300	3.137	1.877
1	4	11	4	13.7084	13.6713	13.6656	13.6955	1.087	4.689	4.778	1.756
8	2	31	3	13.6649	13.6829	13.6919	13.5615	2.588	1.914	2.014	1.087
2	2	16	3	13.7533	13.7238	13.7312	13.7640	1.030	2.122	2.200	1.154
1	4	10	3	13.8019	13.7778	13.7730	13.7970	1.203	1.871	1.900	1.186
7	4	26	4	13.9161	13.8459	13.8374	13.8862	0.999	2.214	2.122	1.311

218

For Xe^{9+}, our wavelengths and transition rates are compared with the measurements [5] and HFR and MCDHF results [15] in Table 8. Our reported wavelengths show a good match with the experimental results [5] with an average difference of 0.5 Å. The two transitions $1 \to 4$ and $2 \to 4$, where 1, 2 and 4 refer to the indices assigned to the states of Xe^{9+}, show a maximum difference of nearly 5 Å. However, their transition rates are in good agreement with the reported results from Churilov and Joshi [5].

In Table 9, measurements and theoretical results from Churilov et al. [6] as well as HFR and RCI results of Motoumba [14] are included for Xe^{10+} along with our calculated wavelengths and transition rates. Previous studies [6,24] showed that there are two possible strong transition arrays of Xe^{10+} in 11.1 nm–11.3 nm and 13 nm–14 nm regions with possible applications in EUV Lithography [1]. Thus, we have reported results only for the transitions that fall in these ranges for Xe^{10+}. The HFR and RCI wavelengths are calculated from the energy levels provided in [14]. Our results show a maximum deviation of nearly 3.5 Å from measurements and HFR calculations. This discrepancy is found for the transitions from the 3rd, 7th and 8th states to the 57th state. Overall, a better match is seen between the present results and the RCI calculations. Our calculated transition rates agree well with the corresponding values from Churilov et al. [6] except for a few cases, that is, $3 \to 25$, $3 \to 21$ and $1 \to 11$ transitions. However, the present transition rates are in reasonable agreement with the RCI calculations for these transitions.

3.2. Cross Sections and Rate Coefficients

The atomic wavefunctions of the four ions are used in our RDW program to calculate the electron impact excitation cross sections for the E1 transitions in Xe^{7+}–Xe^{10+} ions. In the previous subsection, we have given a detailed comparison of our calculated results for energy levels, wavelengths and transition rates with other experimental and theoretical results and found an overall satisfactory agreement. This ensures the quality of the target ion's wavefunctions that are crucial in determining the accuracy of the scattering parameters. Moreover, the RDW method has been successfully implemented in the previous work on a variety of targets from closed to open-shell systems and neutral atoms to multiply or highly charged ions atoms/ions [25–30]. It has also been found that using RDW cross sections in a collisional radiative (CR) model provides plasma parameters that are in better agreement with the measurements [31–34]. Therefore, the success of a CR model depends heavily on the accuracy of the collision cross sections being fed to the model. In this connection, we have calculated cross sections for 9, 18, 75 and 57 transitions, respectively, for Xe^{7+}, Xe^{8+}, Xe^{9+} and Xe^{10+}. Their excitation energies, as discussed earlier, lie in the EUV region. For the sake of simplicity in presenting our results, we have shown only a few transitions graphically through Figure 1 for Xe^{8+}. However, cross sections for all the transitions considered in the four ions are provided in the supplementary file through Tables S1–S4 in the incident electron energy range 200–3000 eV. We notice the usual behaviour of the cross sections from Figure 1, that is, they decrease with increasing electron energies and their magnitudes follow the increasing order of the transition rates. Transitions which involve the change of the spin of the state have lesser cross sections as compared to those with the same spin.

Further, to make available our cross sections in a convenient manner, we have performed the fitting of our cross sections Equation (4) with two analytical forms. The first form is a rational fit and suitable for low energy, given by:

$$\sigma_{a \to b} = \frac{\sum_{i=0}^{n} x_i E^i}{1 + y_1 E + y_2 E^2}, \tag{5}$$

where $\sigma_{a \to b}$ is the excitation cross section from the initial level a to final level b and E is the energy of the incident electron. Both the cross section and the energy are considered in atomic units. x_is and y_is are fitting coefficients. The second fitting, appropriate for high energy, is performed using the Bethe–Born formula, that is,

$$\sigma_{a\to b} = \frac{1}{E}(d_0 + d_1 \ln(E)). \tag{6}$$

The Bethe–Born fitting is valid for energy above 2000 eV in the present case. The fitting parameters are provided in Tables 10–13 for Xe^{7+}, Xe^{8+}, Xe^{9+} and Xe^{10+} ions, respectively. The fitted and calculated cross sections agree within 5%.

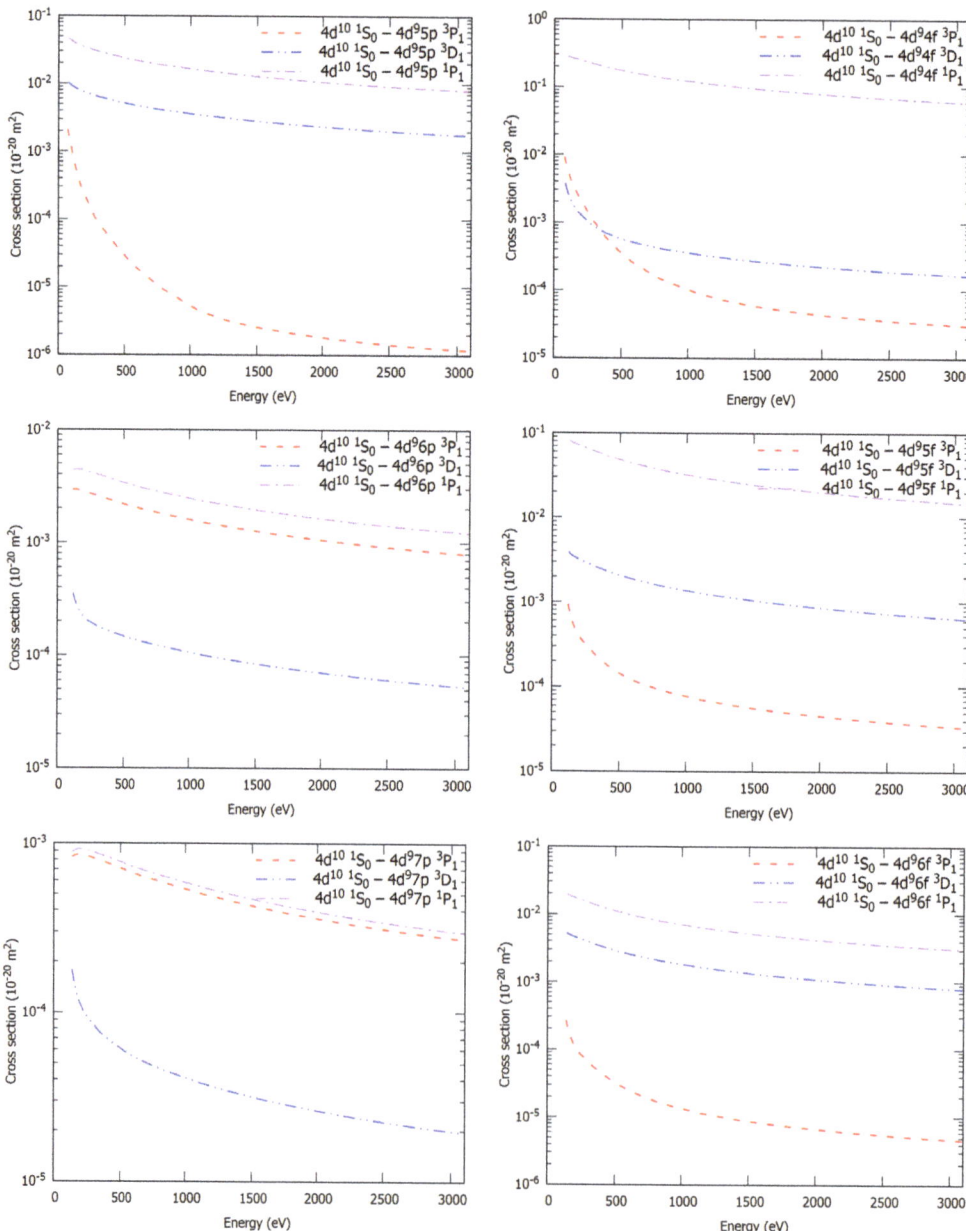

Figure 1. Integrated cross sections of Xe^{8+} as a function of incident electron energy.

We have also obtained the rate coefficient $k_{a \to b}$ at an electron temperature T for a transition from initial level a to final level b. For this purpose, our calculated excitation cross sections are used in the following expression:

$$k_{a \to b} = 2 \left(\frac{2}{\pi m_e}\right)^{1/2} (k_B T)^{-3/2} \int_{E_{ab}}^{\infty} E \, \sigma_{a \to b}(E) \exp\left(-\frac{E}{k_B T}\right) dE, \quad (7)$$

where m_e represents the mass of electron, k_B is the Boltzmann constant, E_{ab} denotes the excitation threshold energy for the transition from a to b and $\sigma_{a \to b}(E)$ is the calculated cross section at the incident electron energy E. The rate coefficients are provided through Tables 14–17 for Xe^{7+}–Xe^{10+} ions in the electron temperature range 5–100 eV. The values of rate coefficients rise rapidly at first and then there is a slower logarithmic increase. In order to clearly demonstrate this trend, Figure 2 displays rate coefficients for the transitions reported in Table 7 for Xe^{8+}. The same behaviour has been noticed in our previous work on excitation of highly charged xenon ions [25].

Table 10. Cross section fitting parameters of Xe^{7+} for the transitions from $4d^{10}5s\ ^2S_{1/2}$ state.

f	J_f	x_0	x_1	x_2	x_3	y_1	y_2	d_0	d_1
10	3/2	5.576E−01	1.286E−02	5.801E−04	−2.658E−06	3.022E−02	3.335E−03	−7.154E+00	4.556E+00
9	1/2	2.882E−01	−3.583E−02	1.310E−05	–	−8.965E−02	−4.299E−03	−3.466E+00	2.192E+00
8	1/2	2.390E−02	3.721E−03	−1.498E−05	1.072E−07	4.181E−01	7.597E−03	−1.399E−01	9.347E−02
7	3/2	6.595E−02	2.499E−03	−2.743E−05	1.472E−07	1.469E−01	1.871E−04	−6.290E−01	3.595E−01
6	1/2	−1.778E−03	−3.447E−03	2.617E−06	−5.192E−08	−1.066E+00	−3.835E−02	−3.549E−02	2.399E−02
5	1/2	6.352E−02	2.428E−03	3.769E−08	–	1.411E−01	1.820E−03	−4.145E−01	2.920E−01
4	3/2	5.399E−02	1.287E−02	−3.358E−05	2.916E−07	1.143E+00	2.860E−02	−1.234E−01	9.544E−02
3	3/2	−4.022E−03	−1.981E−04	1.350E−06	–	−7.126E−01	1.596E−03	−9.671E−03	6.795E−03
2	3/2	−7.036E−03	−1.887E−03	1.368E−05	−8.193E−08	−8.662E−01	−9.805E−03	−1.633E−02	1.929E−02

Table 11. Cross section fitting parameters for Xe^{8+} for the transitions from $4d^{10}\ ^1S_0$ state.

f	J_f	x_0	x_1	x_2	x_3	y_1	y_2	d_0	d_1
43	1	1.044E−01	−7.849E−03	−1.655E−05	–	1.709E−02	−7.292E−03	−3.341E−02	7.487E−02
41	1	2.816E−02	−2.014E−03	−4.603E−06	–	2.605E−02	−7.363E−03	−3.341E−02	7.487E−02
38	1	−4.591E−04	2.936E−05	−4.303E−08	6.919E−10	−3.475E−01	1.789E−02	6.634E−04	2.572E−04
35	1	1.021E−04	−9.405E−05	−3.567E−07	8.948E−10	−2.412E−01	−1.337E−02	−3.167E−03	2.348E−03
33	1	6.951E−03	−2.716E−03	−9.772E−06	3.338E−08	−5.202E−01	−2.366E−02	−6.374E−02	3.891E−02
31	1	4.165E−03	−1.042E−03	1.409E−06	−1.362E−08	−2.356E−01	−7.107E−03	−5.827E−02	3.553E−02
29	1	3.780E−01	−2.712E−02	−4.510E−05	–	−6.424E−03	−4.922E−03	−1.935E+00	1.679E+00
26	1	1.775E−02	−4.449E−03	−1.445E−05	–	−1.671E−01	−2.114E−02	−8.387E−02	7.213E−02
24	1	−2.540E−03	2.083E−04	3.607E−06	−1.109E−08	−4.955E−01	3.809E−02	−3.575E−03	3.621E−03
21	1	4.408E−04	−2.197E−04	4.829E−07	−3.464E−09	−2.846E−01	−6.943E−03	−1.061E−02	6.779E−03
19	1	2.079E−02	−5.369E−03	−8.215E−06	–	−2.274E−01	−1.032E−02	−2.413E−01	1.562E−01
17	1	1.443E−02	−5.786E−03	−9.969E−06	–	−3.936E−01	−1.756E−02	−1.552E−01	1.008E−01
15	1	1.214E+00	−4.966E−02	−1.393E−04	–	1.188E−02	−2.411E−03	−1.232E+01	7.758E+00
13	1	−1.350E−02	−6.530E−04	4.946E−06	−1.905E−08	−6.725E−01	−7.720E−04	−2.388E−02	1.930E−02
10	1	−5.999E−02	2.896E−03	−5.797E−05	3.560E−07	−8.149E−01	−1.112E−02	3.911E−03	1.751E−03
7	1	6.010E−02	9.396E−03	−4.047E−05	2.538E−07	4.611E−01	7.450E−03	−3.543E−01	2.263E−01
5	1	2.421E−01	2.923E−02	−5.968E−05	4.494E−07	3.173E−01	6.359E−03	−1.526E+00	1.009E+00
3	1	1.897E−03	1.477E−04	−4.298E−06	3.734E−08	−6.075E−01	1.325E−01	4.609E−04	2.199E−06

Table 12. Cross section fitting parameters for Xe^{9+}. a and b refer to the indices of the initial and final levels, respectively.

a	J_a	b	J_b	x_0	x_1	x_2	x_3	y_1	y_2	d_0	d_1
2	3/2	57	1/2	3.056E−01	1.176E−02	−1.971E−05	1.321E−07	1.698E−01	1.873E−03	−1.717E+00	1.207E+00
1	5/2	56	5/2	1.374E−02	1.759E−03	2.290E−06	2.758E−09	4.156E−01	1.212E−02	−5.725E−02	4.089E−02
1	5/2	55	3/2	8.823E−02	6.827E−03	1.098E−05	−5.737E−09	2.423E−01	6.028E−03	−4.267E−01	3.146E−01
2	3/2	56	5/2	1.035E+00	6.391E−02	6.011E−05	1.005E−07	2.016E−01	4.138E−03	−5.513E+00	4.014E+00
1	5/2	54	7/2	9.348E−01	5.812E−02	5.689E−05	8.184E−08	2.015E−01	4.163E−03	−5.017E+00	3.643E+00
1	5/2	53	5/2	6.786E−01	5.081E−02	8.792E−05	−7.732E−08	2.280E−01	5.637E−03	−3.405E+00	2.515E+00
2	3/2	55	3/2	5.657E−01	4.438E−02	8.448E−05	−9.669E−08	2.339E−01	6.025E−03	−2.817E+00	2.086E+00
1	5/2	51	3/2	1.483E−03	−2.150E−03	−6.311E−06	2.082E−08	−4.478E−01	−9.066E−02	7.413E−03	4.252E−03

Table 12. Cont.

a	J_a	b	J_b	x_0	x_1	x_2	x_3	y_1	y_2	d_0	d_1
1	5/2	50	3/2	−1.633E−03	−6.857E−04	−1.676E−06	3.357E−09	−8.329E−01	−5.028E−02	−1.824E−03	3.502E−03
2	3/2	52	1/2	−9.315E−03	−1.618E−02	−7.248E−05	1.933E−07	−2.187E+00	−1.254E−01	−6.090E−02	4.506E−02
2	3/2	50	3/2	−8.411E−03	−1.331E−03	−7.320E−07	−3.433E−09	−1.015E+00	−3.252E−02	−6.624E−03	9.189E−03
1	5/2	46	5/2	−9.020E−03	−6.737E−05	−6.880E−08	–	−8.231E−01	−9.125E−02	−1.445E−03	1.805E−03
2	3/2	49	1/2	−6.386E−03	−1.075E−03	−8.103E−06	3.510E−08	−9.694E−01	−4.186E−02	−1.319E−02	9.703E−03
1	5/2	45	5/2	−8.198E−03	2.644E−04	−9.617E−06	6.500E−08	−9.794E−01	−3.430E−02	−5.128E−04	1.133E−03
2	3/2	48	1/2	−4.603E−03	−2.201E−03	4.850E−06	−1.938E−08	−9.938E−01	1.151E−02	−9.463E−03	6.154E−03
1	5/2	43	7/2	−5.336E−03	−3.585E−04	−2.002E−05	1.056E−07	−9.708E−01	−3.847E−01	−1.592E−03	1.153E−03
2	3/2	47	1/2	−7.349E−04	−4.381E−04	−1.050E−07	−1.474E−09	−6.940E−01	−1.885E−02	−9.577E−03	6.063E−03
1	5/2	41	7/2	−2.347E−04	−1.700E−03	−2.480E−06	3.769E−10	−7.088E−01	−2.624E−02	−2.996E−02	1.924E−02
1	5/2	39	5/2	−3.032E−04	−1.082E−04	3.069E−07	−2.097E−09	−5.188E−01	−9.640E−03	−3.506E−03	2.239E−03
1	5/2	36	3/2	−9.068E−03	3.793E−04	−9.565E−06	6.537E−08	−1.031E+00	−1.342E−02	1.092E−03	5.686E−04
2	3/2	45	5/2	−1.961E−02	−6.052E−04	−1.407E−05	–	−1.028E+00	−8.287E−02	−4.095E−03	5.313E−03
2	3/2	44	5/2	4.846E−03	6.598E−04	5.100E−06	–	−3.904E−01	9.545E−02	2.191E−04	2.778E−03
1	5/2	34	5/2	−1.394E−03	−3.671E−04	−3.059E−07	−1.188E−09	−6.339E−01	−3.262E−02	1.056E−05	2.350E−03
1	5/2	33	5/2	−1.103E−03	−1.120E−03	−9.484E−07	−2.286E−09	−7.425E−01	−2.403E−02	−2.029E−02	1.306E−02
1	5/2	32	3/2	−8.471E−03	2.335E−04	−1.088E−05	8.284E−08	−1.071E+00	−2.748E−02	−1.700E−03	1.823E−03
2	3/2	42	1/2	4.540E−02	1.850E−02	−1.009E−05	2.004E−07	1.437E+00	4.170E−02	−1.740E−01	1.142E−01
1	5/2	31	3/2	1.616E−02	−1.804E−03	−2.207E−04	1.562E−06	1.606E−01	−6.303E−02	−8.327E−02	5.704E−02
1	5/2	30	7/2	−3.222E−02	1.096E−03	−3.375E−05	2.293E−07	−1.239E+00	−1.772E−02	−5.527E−03	5.304E−03
2	3/2	40	1/2	−6.778E−03	5.727E−05	−2.581E−06	2.117E−08	−1.105E+00	3.250E−03	−4.217E−03	3.194E−03
2	3/2	39	5/2	1.929E−02	−1.219E−02	−2.534E−05	–	−4.571E−01	−2.306E−02	−2.481E−01	1.680E−01
2	3/2	38	5/2	−1.191E−02	6.834E−05	−5.442E−06	–	−1.034E+00	−3.971E−02	−1.653E−03	2.362E−03
1	5/2	28	7/2	−9.910E−03	−3.222E−04	2.103E−06	–	−1.018E+00	2.659E−03	−1.408E−02	9.679E−03
1	5/2	27	3/2	7.091E−04	−1.521E−03	−4.489E−06	1.017E−08	−7.348E−01	−3.350E−02	−2.288E−02	1.492E−02
1	5/2	26	5/2	−7.491E−04	−2.049E−04	−1.806E−07	–	−5.123E−01	−6.014E−02	1.927E−03	3.460E−04
1	5/2	25	3/2	−1.649E−02	−7.656E−04	−1.481E−05	–	−1.169E+00	−8.421E−02	−9.228E−03	6.756E−03
2	3/2	37	5/2	1.347E−02	−1.652E−04	1.441E−06	–	−1.463E−01	1.037E−01	3.325E−03	−4.932E−04
2	3/2	35	1/2	−6.915E−03	−2.359E−03	−1.747E−05	−3.947E−09	−1.913E−01	−5.451E−02	−1.792E−02	1.170E−02
1	5/2	23	5/2	−2.843E−02	1.988E−04	−1.981E−05	1.415E−07	−1.255E+00	−1.060E−02	−1.509E−02	1.099E−02
1	5/2	21	3/2	3.088E−02	5.424E−03	3.431E−06	–	4.729E−01	1.200E−02	−1.802E−01	1.181E−01
2	3/2	34	5/2	−3.461E−02	−2.093E−02	4.367E−05	−4.088E−07	−3.517E+00	−9.442E−02	−7.586E−02	5.100E−02
2	3/2	20	7/2	1.357E−03	9.443E−04	7.988E−06	–	−4.844E−01	9.045E−02	−4.634E−03	5.359E−03
1	5/2	19	5/2	−7.530E+24	−4.281E+24	−3.989E+21	–	−3.507E+26	−1.152E+25	−1.611E−01	1.053E−01
1	5/2	18	3/2	−4.844E−04	−3.854E−03	−5.814E−09	–	−6.284E−01	−1.850E−02	3.802E−04	3.062E−04
2	3/2	33	5/2	4.114E−04	−1.002E−02	−3.286E−05	8.621E−08	−8.233E−01	−3.897E−02	−1.274E−01	8.530E−02
2	3/2	32	3/2	6.895E−03	8.497E−05	1.816E−06	–	−2.211E−01	1.019E−01	1.099E−03	4.752E−04
2	3/2	31	3/2	8.890E−03	−6.060E−03	−1.281E−05	–	−4.683E−01	−2.365E−02	−1.242E−01	8.251E−02
1	5/2	16	5/2	1.358E−03	−7.669E−03	−2.180E−05	4.608E−08	−8.152E−01	−3.729E−02	−1.020E−01	6.715E−02
1	5/2	15	7/2	−1.196E−03	−7.781E−03	−3.165E−06	9.722E−08	−8.377E−01	−4.796E−02	−6.951E−02	5.389E−02
1	5/2	14	5/2	−1.384E−03	−2.995E−03	−7.747E−06	1.481E−08	−8.195E−01	−3.810E−02	−3.340E−02	2.437E−02
2	3/2	29	1/2	−8.195E−04	−3.932E−04	−6.083E−07	–	−7.390E−01	−2.853E−02	−5.428E−03	3.977E−03
2	3/2	27	3/2	5.091E−02	4.394E−03	−3.825E−05	1.917E−07	3.152E−01	1.431E−03	−3.033E−01	2.013E−01
2	3/2	26	5/2	−1.883E−03	−5.228E−03	−1.323E−05	2.773E−08	−9.040E−01	−3.855E−02	−6.374E−02	4.271E−02
2	3/2	25	3/2	−1.608E−02	4.219E−04	−1.286E−05	8.943E−08	−1.603E+00	−6.194E−03	−3.532E−03	3.001E−03
2	3/2	24	1/2	−2.617E−03	−8.798E−04	1.155E−06	−1.013E−08	−1.011E+00	−2.273E−02	−1.343E−02	8.797E−03
1	5/2	13	5/2	4.754E−03	−1.234E−02	−2.252E−05	–	−7.931E−01	−3.492E−02	−1.657E−01	1.097E−01
1	5/2	12	3/2	−1.464E−03	−5.047E−05	3.431E−06	−1.568E−08	−6.706E−01	1.973E−02	−4.436E−03	3.120E−03
2	3/2	23	5/2	−8.887E−03	3.393E−04	1.236E−05	−4.550E−08	−1.347E+00	7.738E−02	−6.560E−03	4.980E−03
2	3/2	22	1/2	−7.425E−04	−8.053E−04	−2.337E−06	5.950E−09	−1.032E+00	−4.496E−02	−8.145E−03	5.670E−03
2	3/2	21	3/2	−3.277E−03	−3.982E−03	−1.117E−05	2.534E−08	−1.107E+00	−5.097E−02	−3.367E−02	2.447E−02
1	5/2	11	7/2	−2.037E−03	−5.243E−03	−1.403E−05	2.794E−08	−8.092E−01	−3.785E−02	−6.029E−03	4.342E−02
2	3/2	19	5/2	−5.526E−03	−2.375E−03	−8.007E−07	−9.625E−09	−9.796E−01	−3.047E−02	−2.758E−02	2.007E−02
2	3/2	10	5/2	−5.526E−03	−2.375E−03	−8.007E−07	−9.625E−09	−9.796E−01	−3.047E−02	−8.592E−02	5.951E−02
2	3/2	16	5/2	4.399E−04	−3.478E−03	−1.542E−05	4.863E−08	−8.465E−01	−4.849E−02	−3.464E−02	2.494E−02
1	5/2	8	3/2	−6.707E−04	6.903E−05	1.874E−06	−7.268E−09	−6.758E−01	7.029E−02	−1.007E−03	8.332E−04
2	3/2	13	5/2	−7.900E−04	−1.675E−03	−4.275E−06	8.673E−09	−9.697E−01	−4.261E−02	−1.788E−02	1.233E−02
1	5/2	7	7/2	−2.075E−04	1.583E−04	3.899E−06	−1.582E−08	−6.766E−01	1.330E−01	−7.710E−04	8.472E−04
1	5/2	6	5/2	−3.073E−03	−1.153E−03	−7.322E−07	−3.743E−09	−8.339E−01	−3.073E−02	−9.964E−03	9.362E−03
2	3/2	12	3/2	−3.205E−03	−2.176E−03	−5.431E−06	1.109E−08	−1.065E+00	−5.010E−02	−1.519E−02	1.277E−02
1	5/2	5	5/2	−2.835E−03	3.474E−04	4.194E−06	−1.756E−08	−8.477E−01	9.561E−02	1.555E−03	1.078E−03
2	3/2	9	1/2	4.353E−04	2.770E−05	2.759E−07	–	−6.872E−01	2.183E−01	−2.835E−02	6.334E−05
2	3/2	8	3/2	−1.293E−03	4.224E−05	−6.818E−07	3.227E−09	−5.073E−01	1.955E−04	1.282E−05	2.775E−04
1	5/2	4	3/2	−6.739E−02	1.116E−03	−1.703E−05	9.089E−08	−1.792E+00	7.802E−03	2.555E−03	7.192E−03
1	5/2	3	7/2	3.370E−04	3.605E−04	1.689E−06	–	−6.613E−01	1.489E−01	9.439E−04	5.927E−04
2	3/2	5	3/2	−5.758E−04	−1.325E−03	−6.612E−06	2.215E−08	−1.067E+00	−6.396E−02	−9.803E−03	7.328E−03
2	3/2	4	3/2	−3.864E−02	1.479E−03	−2.660E−05	1.627E−07	−1.324E+00	7.284E−03	8.685E−03	6.476E−04

Table 13. Cross section fitting parameters for Xe^{10+}. a and b refer to the indices of the initial and final levels, respectively.

a	J_a	b	J_b	x_0	x_1	x_2	x_3	y_1	y_2	d_0	d_1
3	3	57	3	3.856E−02	3.924E−03	7.081E−06	−6.509E−09	4.070E−01	1.123E−02	−1.383E−01	9.985E−02
6	1	56	2	6.774E−01	7.074E−02	1.372E−04	−1.478E−07	4.034E−01	1.167E−02	−2.190E+00	1.707E+00
7	4	57	3	6.893E−01	6.159E−02	9.215E−05	−3.809E−08	3.926E−01	1.023E−02	−1.975E+00	1.605E+00
8	2	57	3	8.608E−02	8.873E−03	1.555E−05	−1.118E−08	3.964E−01	1.111E−02	−2.862E−01	2.217E−01
8	2	56	2	2.070E−01	2.263E−02	4.735E−05	−6.084E−08	4.225E−01	1.266E−02	−6.544E−01	5.100E−01
8	2	55	2	7.935E−01	9.191E−02	2.120E−04	−3.230E−07	4.528E−01	1.434E−02	−2.329E+00	1.853E+00
2	2	48	3	1.169E−01	1.671E−02	4.725E−05	−9.097E−08	5.033E−01	1.795E−02	−3.641E−01	2.829E−01
6	1	52	0	3.670E−01	4.161E−02	9.169E−05	−1.278E−07	4.516E−01	1.411E−02	−1.045E+00	8.425E−01
7	4	54	5	1.342E+00	1.887E−01	5.396E−04	−1.066E−06	4.967E−01	1.772E−02	−4.146E+00	3.237E+00
1	4	44	5	1.340E+00	1.922E−01	5.601E−04	−1.131E−06	5.109E−01	1.846E−02	−4.056E+00	3.175E+00
3	3	47	2	3.669E−01	4.715E−02	1.266E−04	−2.403E−07	5.117E−01	1.771E−02	−9.723E−01	7.893E−01
3	3	46	4	1.397E+00	1.998E−01	5.833E−04	−1.179E−06	5.124E−01	1.855E−02	−4.192E+00	3.286E+00
2	2	45	3	8.901E−01	1.243E−01	3.531E−04	−6.938E−07	5.056E−01	1.803E−02	−2.655E+00	2.088E+00
1	4	43	5	4.440E−01	5.528E−02	1.411E−04	−2.504E−07	5.055E−01	1.708E−02	−1.162E+00	9.482E−01
7	4	53	3	−7.137E−04	−1.310E−04	−2.108E−07	4.500E−10	−8.434E−01	−2.446E−02	−2.417E−03	1.560E−03
3	3	45	3	1.678E−01	2.262E−02	6.238E−05	−1.203E−07	5.242E−01	1.848E−02	−4.570E−01	3.664E−01
1	4	42	4	1.091E+00	1.469E−01	4.094E−04	−8.016E−07	5.137E−01	1.814E−02	−3.034E+00	2.429E+00
8	2	53	3	8.118E−01	1.212E−01	3.721E−04	−7.946E−07	5.407E−01	2.022E−02	−2.344E+00	1.847E+00
6	1	50	2	3.221E−01	4.756E−02	1.453E−04	−3.097E−07	5.539E−01	2.078E−02	−8.763E−01	7.014E−01
7	4	51	4	1.079E+00	1.696E−01	5.509E−04	−1.248E−06	5.823E−01	2.269E−02	−2.918E+00	2.326E+00
6	1	49	1	4.580E−01	7.460E−02	2.517E−04	−5.931E−07	5.912E−01	2.345E−02	−1.269E+00	1.001E+00
6	1	47	2	6.249E−01	1.035E−01	3.485E−04	−8.087E−07	5.947E−01	2.369E−02	−1.746E+00	1.376E+00
7	4	40	3	−6.599E−02	−6.468E−02	−1.212E−04	8.066E−08	−4.000E+00	−1.507E−01	−2.142E−01	1.338E−01
8	2	40	3	−6.633E−03	−1.035E−02	−1.276E−05	−1.813E−08	−1.862E+00	−6.513E−02	−7.919E−02	4.795E−02
7	4	39	3	−4.284E−02	−3.422E−02	−7.159E−05	8.431E−08	−4.292E+00	−1.691E−01	−9.679E−02	6.300E−02
4	2	34	3	−2.599E−02	−3.106E−02	−5.495E−05	4.580E−08	−3.017E+00	−1.093E−01	−1.452E−01	8.824E−02
6	1	36	2	−7.498E−02	−5.240E−02	−1.229E−04	2.234E−07	−4.902E+00	−1.883E−01	−1.384E−01	8.802E−02
8	2	38	1	−4.106E−03	−5.230E−03	2.451E−06	−5.463E−08	−1.424E+00	−4.290E−02	−5.329E−02	3.259E−02
7	4	37	5	−1.177E−02	−1.583E−02	−1.377E−05	−7.590E−08	−1.439E+00	−5.348E−02	−1.325E−01	8.631E−02
4	2	30	2	−3.874E−02	−4.511E−02	−1.002E−04	1.610E−07	−3.260E+00	−1.246E−01	−1.880E−01	1.155E−01
3	3	25	3	−2.119E−03	−8.258E−04	2.084E−06	−1.516E−08	−1.192E+00	−2.525E−02	−1.124E−02	7.022E−03
1	4	17	3	1.777E+45	1.063E+45	2.215E+42	–	1.010E+47	3.643E+45	−1.483E−01	9.076E−02
9	0	41	1	−1.387E−01	−1.824E−01	−3.238E−04	2.822E−07	−3.300E+00	−1.189E−01	−7.989E−01	4.791E−01
2	2	22	1	−2.337E−02	−3.028E−02	−6.264E−05	8.367E−08	−2.559E+00	−9.786E−02	−1.581E−01	9.771E−02
8	2	35	1	−7.682E−03	−1.075E−02	−1.771E−05	1.329E−08	−1.830E+00	−6.477E−02	−8.502E−02	5.116E−02
3	3	23	4	1.788E+58	1.091E+58	2.091E+55	–	5.632E+59	1.994E+58	−2.775E−01	1.688E−01
1	4	15	5	−2.640E−02	−2.772E−02	−2.200E−05	−9.703E−08	−2.014E+00	−6.763E−02	−1.927E−01	1.188E−01
4	2	28	3	−2.220E−02	−2.563E−02	−4.240E−05	2.213E−08	−2.721E+00	−9.858E−02	−1.307E−01	8.002E−02
1	4	14	4	−5.409E−03	−6.585E−03	−1.025E−05	2.949E−09	−1.821E+00	−6.558E−02	−4.963E−02	3.060E−02
4	2	27	1	−1.486E−02	−1.840E−02	−3.223E−05	1.495E−08	−2.129E+00	−8.117E−02	−1.111E−01	6.996E−02
3	3	21	2	−1.110E−02	−5.965E−03	9.139E−06	−8.721E−08	−2.402E+00	−5.948E−02	−3.898E−02	2.400E−02
8	2	34	3	−6.230E−03	−8.586E−03	−8.745E−06	−2.580E−08	−1.466E+00	−5.191E−02	−7.861E−02	4.892E−02
1	4	13	4	−3.719E−02	−3.551E−02	−7.262E−05	9.392E−08	−2.661E+00	−1.010E−01	−1.755E−01	1.101E−01
3	3	20	2	−4.863E−03	−6.681E−03	−8.585E−06	−7.385E−09	−1.738E+00	−6.104E−02	−5.406E−02	3.297E−02
5	0	29	1	3.633E−02	7.715E−04	−6.337E−06	–	1.444E−01	−5.032E−04	−2.978E−01	1.827E−01
3	3	19	3	−2.710E−02	−2.308E−02	−2.867E−05	−2.763E−08	−3.004E+00	−1.040E−01	−1.065E−01	6.603E−02
1	4	12	5	1.856E−03	−3.206E−03	−1.852E−05	6.647E−08	−6.132E−01	−3.804E−02	−4.826E−01	3.226E−01
7	4	32	4	−4.462E−02	−5.445E−02	−1.052E−04	1.327E−07	−2.618E+00	−9.698E−02	−2.883E−01	1.760E−01
7	4	31	3	−2.038E−02	−1.556E−02	−2.229E−05	−1.144E−08	−3.069E+00	−1.105E−01	−6.650E−02	4.226E−02
2	2	18	1	−8.687E−03	−9.822E−03	−1.700E−05	1.232E−08	−2.372E+00	−8.731E−02	−5.611E−02	3.469E−02
8	2	33	1	−8.895E−03	−7.900E−03	−1.006E−05	−1.118E−08	−2.212E+00	−7.918E−02	−4.668E−02	2.964E−02
4	2	24	1	−1.114E−02	−1.292E−02	−2.677E−05	3.928E−08	−2.530E+00	−9.591E−02	−6.866E−02	4.244E−02
1	4	11	4	−4.827E−03	−4.479E−03	2.534E−07	−4.019E−08	−1.354E+00	−4.395E−02	−4.338E−02	2.779E−02
8	2	31	3	−1.813E−02	−2.261E−02	−2.995E−05	−1.856E−08	−2.118E+00	−7.447E−02	−1.504E−01	9.168E−02
2	2	16	3	−5.591E−03	−5.854E−03	1.359E−06	−5.623E−08	−1.363E+00	−4.263E−02	−5.966E−02	3.723E−02
1	4	10	3	−5.785E−03	−2.121E−03	8.237E−06	−5.687E−08	−1.435E+00	−2.622E−02	−2.446E−02	1.538E−02
7	4	26	4	−4.329E−03	−3.606E−03	5.849E−06	−6.065E−08	−1.192E+00	−3.268E−02	−4.228E−02	2.680E−02

Table 14. Rate coefficients for Xe^{7+} for the transitions from the state $4d^{10}5s\ ^2S_{1/2}$ at electron temperatures 5, 10, 20, 30, 50, 70, 100 eV.

Index	J_f	5	10	15	20	30	50	70	100
10	3/2	4.754E−23	1.111E−18	2.983E−17	1.507E−16	7.403E−16	2.561E−15	4.301E−15	6.296E−15
9	1/2	2.326E−23	5.378E−19	1.439E−17	7.259E−17	3.560E−16	1.230E−15	2.064E−15	3.020E−15
8	1/2	3.282E−22	4.250E−19	4.351E−18	1.356E−17	4.104E−17	9.603E−17	1.362E−16	1.756E−16
7	3/2	1.548E−21	1.689E−18	1.638E−17	4.981E−17	1.474E−16	3.401E−16	4.805E−16	6.186E−16
6	1/2	2.863E−22	2.176E−19	1.848E−18	5.218E−18	1.419E−17	3.013E−17	4.076E−17	5.054E−17
5	1/2	3.073E−21	2.303E−18	1.974E−17	5.645E−17	1.572E−16	3.456E−16	4.780E−16	6.049E−16
4	3/2	1.513E−21	1.015E−18	8.318E−18	2.315E−17	6.232E−17	1.320E−16	1.787E−16	2.217E−16
3	3/2	4.540E−22	2.561E−19	1.906E−18	4.933E−18	1.184E−17	2.120E−17	2.540E−17	2.758E−17
2	3/2	9.381E−22	4.936E−19	3.642E−18	9.475E−18	2.329E−17	4.412E−17	5.565E−17	6.444E−17

Table 15. Rate coefficients for Xe^{8+} for the transitions from the state $4d^{10}\ ^1S_0$ at electron temperatures 5, 10, 20, 30, 50, 70, 100 eV.

Index	J_b	5	10	15	20	30	50	70	100
43	1	2.593E−27	3.429E−21	3.495E−19	3.414E−18	3.198E−17	1.807E−16	3.674E−16	6.093E−16
41	1	1.123E−27	1.154E−21	1.082E−19	1.012E−18	9.086E−18	4.956E−17	9.922E−17	1.626E−16
38	1	6.405E−29	5.562E−23	4.740E−21	4.131E−20	3.321E−19	1.547E−18	2.759E−18	3.962E−18
35	1	4.422E−29	3.994E−23	3.516E−21	3.154E−20	2.664E−19	1.345E−18	2.562E−18	4.002E−18
33	1	3.437E−28	2.673E−22	2.309E−20	2.091E−19	1.839E−18	1.011E−17	2.070E−17	3.518E−17
31	1	2.381E−28	2.160E−22	1.962E−20	1.821E−19	1.639E−18	9.172E−18	1.889E−17	3.223E−17
29	1	1.835E−25	5.586E−20	3.501E−18	2.688E−17	1.987E−16	9.355E−16	1.769E−15	2.796E−15
26	1	2.470E−26	4.364E−21	2.275E−19	1.589E−18	1.067E−17	4.629E−17	8.436E−17	1.294E−16
24	1	7.512E−27	1.070E−21	5.033E−20	3.277E−19	1.985E−18	7.497E−18	1.236E−17	1.692E−17
21	1	4.471E−27	5.306E−22	2.387E−20	1.536E−19	9.361E−19	3.693E−18	6.413E−18	9.485E−18
19	1	6.855E−26	7.798E−21	3.552E−19	2.337E−18	1.494E−17	6.366E−17	1.168E−16	1.826E−16
17	1	5.769E−26	5.811E−21	2.537E−19	1.632E−18	1.019E−17	4.252E−17	7.724E−17	1.199E−16
15	1	5.115E−23	1.601E−18	4.726E−17	2.497E−16	1.278E−15	4.531E−15	7.652E−15	1.120E−14
13	1	3.100E−23	1.180E−19	1.668E−18	5.972E−18	1.999E−17	4.738E−17	6.447E−17	7.717E−17
10	1	1.695E−22	4.140E−19	5.012E−18	1.651E−17	5.025E−17	1.071E−16	1.351E−16	1.472E−16
7	1	5.544E−22	8.580E−19	9.307E−18	2.984E−17	9.275E−17	2.215E−16	3.166E−16	4.104E−16
5	1	3.354E−21	4.494E−18	4.655E−17	1.460E−16	4.447E−16	1.046E−15	1.487E−15	1.918E−15
3	1	1.862E−22	1.917E−19	1.715E−18	4.803E−18	1.219E−17	2.161E−17	2.459E−17	2.429E−17

Table 16. Rate coefficients for Xe^{9+} at electron temperatures 5, 10, 20, 30, 50, 70, 100 eV. a and b denote the indices of the initial and final levels, respectively.

a	J_a	b	J_b	5	10	15	20	30	50	70	100
2	3/2	57	1/2	2.383E−24	1.587E−19	5.989E−18	3.566E−17	2.043E−16	7.829E−16	1.355E−15	2.002E−15
1	5/2	56	5/2	2.130E−25	8.764E−21	2.815E−19	1.545E−18	8.152E−18	2.922E−17	4.910E−17	7.100E−17
1	5/2	55	3/2	2.345E−24	8.050E−20	2.438E−18	1.301E−17	6.680E−17	2.349E−16	3.918E−16	5.639E−16
2	3/2	56	5/2	2.992E−23	1.010E−18	3.043E−17	1.620E−16	8.309E−16	2.921E−15	4.879E−15	7.033E−15
1	5/2	54	7/2	2.686E−23	9.102E−19	2.746E−17	1.463E−16	7.508E−16	2.642E−15	4.413E−15	6.363E−15
1	5/2	53	5/2	2.498E−23	7.347E−19	2.115E−17	1.100E−16	5.514E−16	1.903E−15	3.152E−15	4.516E−15
2	3/2	55	3/2	2.270E−23	6.375E−19	1.807E−17	9.330E−17	4.640E−16	1.592E−15	2.630E−15	3.762E−15
1	5/2	51	3/2	3.640E−24	2.313E−20	3.949E−19	1.570E−18	5.934E−18	1.595E−17	2.333E−17	2.996E−17
1	5/2	50	3/2	1.068E−24	8.286E−21	1.508E−19	6.185E−19	2.407E−18	6.610E−18	9.761E−18	1.265E−17
2	3/2	52	1/2	6.258E−24	4.673E−20	8.517E−19	3.528E−18	1.409E−17	4.068E−17	6.262E−17	8.526E−17
2	3/2	50	3/2	4.433E−24	2.793E−20	4.728E−19	1.866E−18	6.962E−18	1.836E−17	2.652E−17	3.363E−17
1	5/2	46	5/2	4.080E−24	2.194E−20	3.467E−19	1.308E−18	4.574E−18	1.099E−17	1.473E−17	1.701E−17
2	3/2	49	1/2	4.423E−24	2.486E−20	4.047E−19	1.566E−18	5.731E−18	1.489E−17	2.139E−17	2.703E−17
1	5/2	45	5/2	4.347E−24	2.078E−20	3.161E−19	1.170E−18	4.018E−18	9.509E−18	1.265E−17	1.450E−17
2	3/2	48	1/2	4.152E−24	1.929E−20	2.938E−19	1.097E−18	3.860E−18	9.644E−18	1.354E−17	1.676E−17
1	5/2	43	7/2	2.148E−24	8.938E−21	1.300E−19	4.711E−19	1.588E−18	3.733E−18	4.999E−18	5.834E−18
2	3/2	47	1/2	2.157E−24	1.088E−20	1.717E−19	6.560E−19	2.384E−18	6.244E−18	9.103E−18	1.179E−17
1	5/2	41	7/2	6.800E−24	3.097E−20	4.759E−19	1.803E−18	6.552E−18	1.742E−17	2.581E−17	3.413E−17
1	5/2	39	5/2	1.605E−24	6.755E−21	9.910E−20	3.623E−19	1.244E−18	3.050E−18	4.267E−18	5.303E−18
1	5/2	36	3/2	7.305E−24	2.834E−20	4.022E−19	1.439E−18	4.775E−18	1.099E−17	1.444E−17	1.635E−17
2	3/2	45	5/2	1.533E−23	6.025E−20	8.618E−19	3.103E−18	1.042E−17	2.450E−17	3.286E−17	3.836E−17
2	3/2	44	5/2	2.408E−23	9.221E−20	1.306E−18	4.673E−18	1.555E−17	3.598E−17	4.744E−17	5.394E−17
1	5/2	34	5/2	4.306E−24	1.681E−20	2.411E−19	8.731E−19	2.973E−18	7.226E−18	1.003E−17	1.230E−17

Table 16. *Cont.*

a	J_a	b	J_b	5	10	15	20	30	50	70	100
1	5/2	33	5/2	7.734E−24	2.884E−20	4.129E−19	1.506E−18	5.247E−18	1.338E−17	1.938E−17	2.508E−17
1	5/2	32	3/2	8.124E−24	2.833E−20	3.885E−19	1.368E−18	4.475E−18	1.024E−17	1.350E−17	1.546E−17
2	3/2	42	1/2	4.613E−23	1.794E−19	2.640E−18	9.847E−18	3.555E−17	9.538E−17	1.431E−16	1.921E−16
1	5/2	31	3/2	2.637E−23	9.957E−20	1.449E−18	5.368E−18	1.922E−17	5.112E−17	7.628E−17	1.018E−16
1	5/2	30	7/2	2.690E−23	9.245E−20	1.263E−18	4.442E−18	1.453E−17	3.327E−17	4.382E−17	5.005E−17
2	3/2	40	1/2	8.092E−24	2.731E−20	3.721E−19	1.310E−18	4.313E−18	1.006E−17	1.351E−17	1.587E−17
2	3/2	39	5/2	8.348E−23	3.020E−19	4.332E−18	1.594E−17	5.666E−17	1.498E−16	2.231E−16	2.973E−16
2	3/2	38	5/2	1.412E−23	4.577E−20	6.131E−19	2.134E−18	6.910E−18	1.571E−17	2.066E−17	2.361E−17
1	5/2	28	7/2	1.513E−23	5.111E−20	6.990E−19	2.471E−18	8.200E−18	1.942E−17	2.651E−17	3.191E−17
1	5/2	27	3/2	7.840E−24	2.748E−20	3.892E−19	1.421E−18	5.004E−18	1.310E−17	1.940E−17	2.575E−17
1	5/2	26	5/2	3.487E−24	1.151E−20	1.551E−19	5.417E−19	1.765E−18	4.079E−18	5.473E−18	6.466E−18
1	5/2	25	3/2	1.754E−23	5.701E−20	7.676E−19	2.686E−18	8.794E−18	2.041E−17	2.736E−17	3.212E−17
2	3/2	37	5/2	2.612E−23	8.661E−20	1.166E−18	4.058E−18	1.308E−17	2.922E−17	3.762E−17	4.153E−17
2	3/2	35	1/2	8.531E−24	2.871E−20	3.986E−19	1.435E−18	4.941E−18	1.252E−17	1.808E−17	2.334E−17
1	5/2	23	5/2	3.329E−23	1.023E−19	1.352E−18	4.686E−18	1.519E−17	3.496E−17	4.667E−17	5.457E−17
1	5/2	21	3/2	6.701E−23	2.214E−19	3.085E−18	1.120E−17	3.930E−17	1.031E−16	1.531E−16	2.039E−16
2	3/2	34	5/2	3.199E−23	1.060E−19	1.473E−18	5.324E−18	1.855E−17	4.807E−17	7.077E−17	9.338E−17
1	5/2	20	7/2	4.990E−23	1.496E−19	1.952E−18	6.705E−18	2.141E−17	4.792E−17	6.233E−17	7.021E−17
1	5/2	19	5/2	6.960E−23	2.199E−19	3.011E−18	1.082E−17	3.750E−17	9.691E−17	1.426E−16	1.882E−16
1	5/2	18	3/2	2.000E−24	5.880E−21	7.619E−20	2.608E−19	8.315E−19	1.883E−18	2.500E−18	2.927E−18
2	3/2	33	5/2	6.316E−23	1.953E−19	2.647E−18	9.443E−18	3.243E−17	8.286E−17	1.211E−16	1.588E−16
2	3/2	32	3/2	2.371E−23	6.748E−20	8.645E−19	2.939E−18	9.270E−18	2.045E−17	2.630E−17	2.916E−17
2	3/2	31	3/2	5.716E−23	1.761E−19	2.392E−18	8.560E−18	2.958E−17	7.634E−17	1.124E−16	1.484E−16
1	5/2	16	5/2	5.005E−23	1.504E−19	2.023E−18	7.194E−18	2.466E−17	6.305E−17	9.231E−17	1.213E−16
1	5/2	15	7/2	5.519E−23	1.598E−19	2.115E−18	7.445E−18	2.517E−17	6.324E−17	9.144E−17	1.185E−16
1	5/2	14	5/2	2.637E−23	7.384E−20	9.644E−19	3.368E−18	1.128E−17	2.803E−17	4.028E−17	5.194E−17
2	3/2	29	1/2	5.911E−24	1.642E−20	2.119E−19	7.313E−19	2.397E−18	5.766E−18	8.082E−18	1.012E−17
2	3/2	27	3/2	1.516E−22	4.372E−19	5.824E−18	2.066E−17	7.093E−17	1.827E−16	2.692E−16	3.564E−16
2	3/2	26	5/2	3.923E−23	1.106E−19	1.452E−18	5.093E−18	1.717E−17	4.313E−17	6.249E−17	8.130E−17
2	3/2	25	3/2	1.773E−23	4.711E−20	5.928E−19	2.005E−18	6.334E−18	1.422E−17	1.869E−17	2.147E−17
2	3/2	24	1/2	1.122E−23	3.018E−20	3.867E−19	1.333E−18	4.372E−18	1.056E−17	1.488E−17	1.878E−17
1	5/2	13	5/2	9.271E−23	2.564E−19	3.361E−18	1.182E−17	4.012E−17	1.022E−16	1.496E−16	1.970E−16
1	5/2	12	5/2	9.180E−24	2.314E−20	2.848E−19	9.505E−19	2.958E−18	6.595E−18	8.745E−18	1.032E−17
2	3/2	23	5/2	1.708E−23	4.313E−20	5.355E−19	1.804E−18	5.711E−18	1.302E−17	1.745E−17	2.065E−17
2	3/2	22	1/2	6.343E−24	1.703E−20	2.196E−19	7.625E−19	2.539E−18	6.291E−18	9.032E−18	1.164E−17
2	3/2	21	3/2	2.815E−23	7.500E−20	9.657E−19	3.354E−18	1.118E−17	2.778E−17	3.997E−17	5.162E−17
1	5/2	11	7/2	5.762E−23	1.441E−19	1.813E−18	6.215E−18	2.043E−17	5.007E−17	7.158E−17	9.197E−17
2	3/2	19	3/2	3.113E−23	7.863E−20	9.875E−19	3.371E−18	1.097E−17	2.635E−17	3.707E−17	4.675E−17
1	5/2	10	5/2	6.855E−23	1.713E−19	2.166E−18	7.467E−18	2.480E−17	6.178E−17	8.934E−17	1.162E−16
2	3/2	16	5/2	3.111E−23	7.636E−20	9.594E−19	3.297E−18	1.091E−17	2.709E−17	3.910E−17	5.074E−17
1	5/2	8	3/2	6.708E−24	1.494E−20	1.753E−19	5.679E−19	1.698E−18	3.579E−18	4.538E−18	5.060E−18
2	3/2	13	5/2	1.836E−23	4.113E−20	5.002E−19	1.689E−18	5.481E−18	1.336E−17	1.910E−17	2.461E−17
1	5/2	7	7/2	1.445E−23	2.902E−20	3.275E−19	1.038E−18	3.015E−18	6.128E−18	7.566E−18	8.171E−18
1	5/2	6	5/2	2.825E−23	5.938E−20	6.983E−19	2.301E−18	7.188E−18	1.659E−17	2.279E−17	2.810E−17
2	3/2	12	3/2	2.849E−23	6.095E−20	7.265E−19	2.421E−18	7.711E−18	1.832E−17	2.573E−17	3.246E−17
1	5/2	5	3/2	1.985E−23	3.999E−20	4.555E−19	1.459E−18	4.336E−18	9.195E−18	1.178E−17	1.333E−17
2	3/2	9	1/2	5.039E−24	9.325E−21	1.017E−19	3.152E−19	8.889E−19	1.736E−18	2.079E−18	2.160E−18
2	3/2	8	3/2	1.994E−23	3.579E−20	3.874E−19	1.199E−18	3.385E−18	6.657E−18	8.035E−18	8.436E−18
1	5/2	4	3/2	1.038E−22	2.259E−19	2.666E−18	8.742E−18	2.687E−17	5.941E−17	7.797E−17	8.977E−17
1	5/2	3	7/2	4.994E−23	7.990E−20	8.335E−19	2.534E−18	7.045E−18	1.374E−17	1.659E−17	1.750E−17
2	3/2	5	3/2	1.982E−23	3.436E−20	3.840E−19	1.244E−18	3.873E−18	9.131E−18	1.286E−17	1.635E−17
2	3/2	4	3/2	1.237E−22	2.181E−19	2.388E−18	7.519E−18	2.207E−17	4.647E−17	5.915E−17	6.580E−17

Table 17. Rate coefficients for Xe^{10+} at electron temperatures 5, 10, 20, 30, 50, 70, 100 eV. a and b denote the indices of the initial and final levels, respectively.

a	J_a	b	J_b	5	10	15	20	30	50	70	100
3	3	57	3	6.000E−26	7.754E−21	3.640E−19	2.411E−18	1.531E−17	6.323E−17	1.124E−16	1.689E−16
6	1	56	2	2.790E−24	2.205E−19	8.794E−18	5.371E−17	3.146E−16	1.220E−15	2.113E−15	3.114E−15
7	4	57	3	2.171E−24	1.945E−19	8.079E−18	5.035E−17	3.006E−16	1.182E−15	2.056E−15	3.037E−15
8	2	57	3	2.751E−25	2.488E−20	1.038E−18	6.481E−18	3.882E−17	1.532E−16	2.674E−16	3.965E−16
8	2	56	2	9.893E−25	7.177E−20	2.781E−18	1.675E−17	9.668E−17	3.707E−16	6.388E−16	9.381E−16
8	2	55	2	5.066E−24	3.116E−19	1.143E−17	6.695E−17	3.761E−16	1.410E−15	2.407E−15	3.510E−15
2	2	48	3	1.071E−24	5.457E−20	1.881E−18	1.069E−17	5.826E−17	2.137E−16	3.617E−16	5.247E−16
6	1	52	0	2.469E−24	1.475E−19	5.359E−18	3.124E−17	1.746E−16	6.520E−16	1.111E−15	1.617E−15
7	4	54	5	1.287E−23	6.416E−19	2.195E−17	1.243E−16	6.750E−16	2.468E−15	4.173E−15	6.047E−15
1	4	44	5	1.376E−23	6.577E−19	2.219E−17	1.247E−16	6.727E−16	2.446E−15	4.125E−15	5.966E−15
3	3	47	2	3.669E−24	1.742E−19	5.860E−18	3.288E−17	1.769E−16	6.407E−16	1.077E−15	1.553E−15
3	3	46	4	1.452E−23	6.885E−19	2.317E−17	1.300E−16	7.004E−16	2.543E−15	4.287E−15	6.197E−15
2	2	45	3	8.931E−24	4.316E−19	1.461E−17	8.227E−17	4.444E−16	1.617E−15	2.728E−15	3.946E−15
1	4	43	5	4.116E−24	2.030E−19	6.917E−18	3.905E−17	2.114E−16	7.693E−16	1.296E−15	1.871E−15
7	4	53	3	1.136E−26	4.820E−22	1.543E−20	8.382E−20	4.312E−19	1.475E−18	2.386E−18	3.302E−18
3	3	45	3	1.646E−24	7.888E−20	2.662E−18	1.496E−17	8.062E−17	2.926E−16	4.926E−16	7.109E−16
1	4	42	4	1.116E−24	5.272E−19	1.771E−17	9.930E−17	5.340E−16	1.935E−15	3.256E−15	4.699E−15
8	2	53	3	9.624E−24	4.211E−19	1.380E−17	7.640E−17	4.060E−16	1.458E−15	2.447E−15	3.525E−15
6	1	50	2	4.261E−24	1.742E−19	5.579E−18	3.054E−17	1.604E−16	5.707E−16	9.531E−16	1.368E−15
7	4	51	4	1.660E−23	6.233E−19	1.940E−17	1.048E−16	5.426E−16	1.910E−15	3.176E−15	4.544E−15
6	1	49	1	7.470E−24	2.725E−19	8.402E−18	4.515E−17	2.328E−16	8.167E−16	1.357E−15	1.940E−15
6	1	47	2	1.036E−23	3.753E−19	1.155E−17	6.197E−17	3.192E−16	1.119E−15	1.859E−15	2.659E−15
7	4	40	3	1.002E−23	9.276E−20	1.818E−18	7.811E−18	3.238E−17	9.658E−17	1.511E−16	2.088E−16
8	2	40	3	3.387E−24	3.162E−20	6.211E−19	2.672E−18	1.109E−17	3.311E−17	5.187E−17	7.179E−17
7	4	39	3	6.289E−24	5.238E−20	9.900E−19	4.175E−18	1.697E−17	4.969E−17	7.704E−17	1.055E−16
4	2	34	3	7.327E−24	6.276E−20	1.199E−18	5.088E−18	2.085E−17	6.167E−17	9.628E−17	1.330E−16
6	1	36	2	9.279E−24	7.476E−20	1.397E−18	5.855E−18	2.365E−17	6.886E−17	1.065E−16	1.455E−16
8	2	38	1	3.278E−24	2.632E−20	4.907E−19	2.054E−18	8.282E−18	2.409E−17	3.726E−17	5.100E−17
7	4	37	5	1.082E−23	8.116E−20	1.479E−18	6.121E−18	2.439E−17	7.020E−17	1.080E−16	1.470E−16
4	2	30	2	1.187E−23	9.201E−20	1.701E−18	7.097E−18	2.860E−17	8.351E−17	1.296E−16	1.782E−16
3	3	25	3	1.059E−24	7.892E−21	1.425E−19	5.845E−19	2.290E−18	6.415E−18	9.664E−18	1.286E−17
1	4	17	3	1.007E−23	7.484E−20	1.364E−18	5.654E−18	2.263E−17	6.571E−17	1.018E−16	1.397E−16
9	0	41	1	4.570E−23	3.583E−19	6.650E−18	2.783E−17	1.126E−16	3.301E−16	5.139E−16	7.089E−16
2	2	22	1	1.136E−23	8.316E−20	1.508E−18	6.231E−18	2.486E−17	7.200E−17	1.114E−16	1.526E−16
8	2	35	1	5.936E−24	4.313E−20	7.792E−19	3.214E−18	1.279E−17	3.691E−17	5.698E−17	7.800E−17
3	3	23	4	2.014E−23	1.433E−19	2.576E−18	1.060E−17	4.215E−17	1.218E−16	1.883E−16	2.582E−16
1	4	15	5	1.563E−23	1.092E−19	1.947E−18	7.973E−18	3.147E−17	9.015E−17	1.386E−16	1.889E−16
4	2	28	3	1.011E−23	7.061E−20	1.260E−18	5.168E−18	2.046E−17	5.887E−17	9.080E−17	1.242E−16
1	4	14	4	4.171E−24	2.861E−20	5.068E−19	2.069E−18	8.143E−18	2.327E−17	3.573E−17	4.867E−17
4	2	27	1	9.004E−24	6.406E−20	1.149E−18	4.723E−18	1.872E−17	5.384E−17	8.293E−17	1.132E−16
3	3	21	2	3.436E−24	2.378E−20	4.215E−19	1.718E−18	6.736E−18	1.909E−17	2.912E−17	3.937E−17
8	2	34	3	6.615E−24	4.622E−20	8.232E−19	3.368E−18	1.328E−17	3.793E−17	5.821E−17	7.920E−17
1	4	13	4	1.636E−23	1.086E−19	1.903E−18	7.730E−18	3.027E−17	8.615E−17	1.320E−16	1.795E−16
3	3	20	2	4.594E−24	3.078E−20	5.411E−19	2.201E−18	8.637E−18	2.464E−17	3.783E−17	5.156E−17
5	0	29	1	2.657E−23	1.727E−19	3.009E−18	1.220E−17	4.774E−17	1.362E−16	2.093E−16	2.856E−16
3	3	19	3	9.822E−24	6.462E−20	1.129E−18	4.580E−18	1.791E−17	5.092E−17	7.803E−17	1.061E−16
1	4	12	5	6.170E−24	3.904E−20	6.709E−19	2.692E−18	1.037E−17	2.897E−17	4.387E−17	5.890E−17
7	4	32	4	2.599E−23	1.671E−19	2.902E−18	1.174E−17	4.586E−17	1.306E−16	2.006E−16	2.737E−16
7	4	31	3	7.252E−24	4.551E−20	7.824E−19	3.146E−18	1.219E−17	3.434E−17	5.237E−17	7.088E−17
2	2	18	1	5.581E−24	3.495E−20	6.011E−19	2.419E−18	9.395E−18	2.660E−17	4.071E−17	5.536E−17
8	2	33	1	4.742E−24	3.085E−20	5.366E−19	2.170E−18	8.453E−18	2.392E−17	3.654E−17	4.952E−17
4	2	24	1	6.198E−24	4.066E−20	7.104E−19	2.882E−18	1.128E−17	3.216E−17	4.938E−17	6.731E−17
1	4	11	4	5.338E−24	3.267E−20	5.556E−19	2.218E−18	8.514E−18	2.372E−17	3.593E−17	4.829E−17
8	2	31	1	1.404E−23	8.905E−20	1.538E−18	6.204E−18	2.415E−17	6.854E−17	1.051E−16	1.431E−16
2	2	16	3	7.166E−24	4.264E−20	7.187E−19	2.858E−18	1.094E−17	3.046E−17	4.617E−17	6.218E−17
1	4	10	3	3.794E−24	2.168E−20	3.586E−19	1.408E−18	5.291E−18	1.437E−17	2.139E−17	2.826E−17
7	4	26	4	6.860E−24	3.659E−20	5.936E−19	2.313E−18	8.653E−18	2.359E−17	3.535E−17	4.712E−17

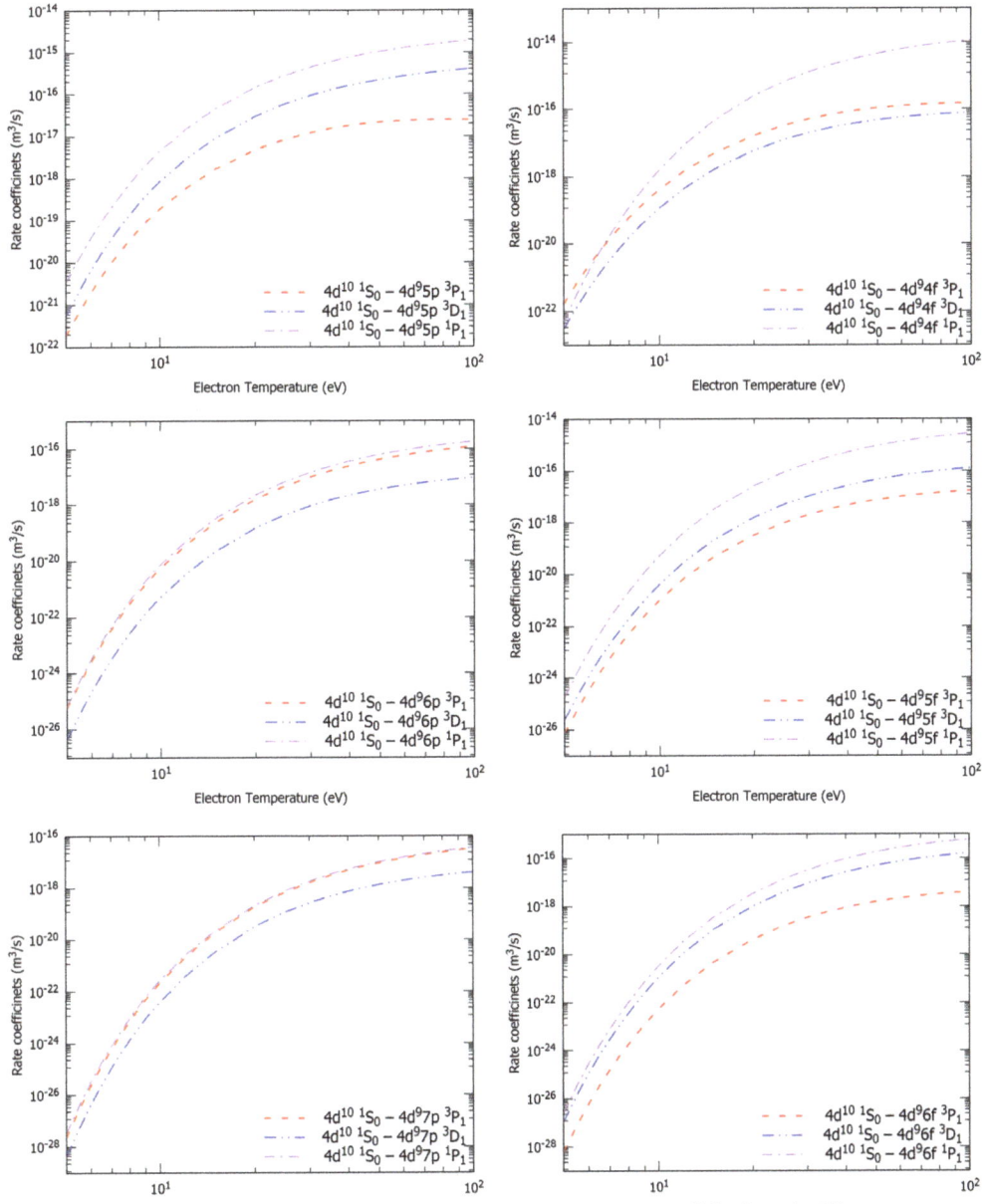

Figure 2. Excitation rate coefficients of Xe^{8+} as a function of electron temperature.

4. Conclusions

We employed the MCDF approach within the framework of the Dirac–Coulomb Hamiltonian, including the Breit and QED corrections using the GRASP2K program [21] and calculated the energy levels, wavelengths and transition rates for the electric dipole allowed transitions of Xe^{7+}, Xe^{8+}, Xe^{9+} and Xe^{10+} ions in the EUV range of 8–19 nm. These results are compared with other reported experimental and theoretical results and, overall, a good agreement is found. After confirming the reliability of our ionic wavefunctions, we used them in the RDW method to calculate the excitation cross sections for a total of 159 transitions in the four ions. To make our cross sections conveniently available for plasma modelling, we obtained the fitting parameters for these cross sections for both low and high incident electron energies. The maximum error in fitted cross sections is found to be well within 5% for most of the cases. Further, these cross sections are used to calculate the excitation rate coefficients for several electron temperatures ranging from 5 to 100 eV, assuming a Maxwellian electron energy distribution. Our cross sections and rate coefficients are reported for the first time, as no other experimental or theoretical results are available. We hope our results will be useful for the successful interpretation of EUV emissions from various sources.

Supplementary Materials: The following are available online at https://www.mdpi.com/2218-2004/9/4/76/s1, Table S1: Cross sections (10^{-20} m^2) for Xe^{7+} for the transitions from $4d^{10}5s\ ^2S_{1/2}$ state at incident electron energies 200, 300, 400, 500, 700, 1000, 1200, 1500, 2000, 2500, 3000 eV. Table S2: Cross sections (10^{-20} m^2) for Xe^{8+} for the transitions from $4d^{10}\ ^1S_0$ state at incident electron energies 200, 300, 400, 500, 700, 1000, 1200, 1500, 2000, 2500, 3000 eV. Table S3: Cross sections (10^{-20} m^2) for Xe^{9+} at incident electron energies 200, 300, 400, 500, 700, 1000, 1200, 1500, 2000, 2500, 3000 eV. a and b refer to the indices of the initial and final levels, respectively. Table S4: Cross sections (10^{-20} m^2) for Xe^{10+} at incident electron energies 200, 300, 400, 500, 700, 1000, 1200, 1500, 2000, 2500, 3000 eV. a and b refer to the indices of the initial and final levels, respectively.

Author Contributions: Both the authors have contributed equally in performing calculations and preparing the manuscript. All authors have read and agreed to the published version of the manuscript.

Funding: This research received no external funding.

Institutional Review Board Statement: Not applicable.

Informed Consent Statement: Not applicable.

Data Availability Statement: The data presented in this study are available in the article or supplementary material here.

Acknowledgments: Aloka Kumar Sahoo would like to acknowledge the Ministry of Human Resources and Development (MHRD) India for the award of a research fellowship.

Conflicts of Interest: The funders had no role in the design of the study; in the collection, analyses, or interpretation of data; in the writing of the manuscript, or in the decision to publish the results.

References

1. Abramov, I.S.; Gospodchikov, E.D.; Shalashov, A.G. Extreme-Ultraviolet Light Source for Lithography Based on an Expanding Jet of Dense Xenon Plasma Supported by Microwaves. *Phys. Rev. Appl.* **2018**, *10*, 1. [CrossRef]
2. Werner, K.; Rauch, T.; Ringat, E.; Kruk, J.W. First detection of krypton and xenon in a white dwarf. *Astrophys. J.* **2012**, *753*, L7. [CrossRef]
3. Otsuka, M.; Tajitsu, A. Chemical abundances in the extremely carbon-rich and xenon-rich halo planetary nebula H4-1. *Astrophys. J.* **2013**, *778*, 146. [CrossRef]
4. Beattie, J.R.; Matossian, J.N. Xenon ion sources for space applications (invited). *Rev. Sci. Instruments* **1990**, *61*, 348–353. [CrossRef]
5. Churilov, S.S.; Joshi, Y.N. Analysis of the $4p^64d^84f$ and $4p^54d^{10}$ Configurations of Xe X and Some Highly Excited Levels of Xe VIII and Xe IX Ions. *Phys. Scr.* **2002**, *65*, 40–45. [CrossRef]
6. Churilov, S.S.; Joshi, Y.N.; Reader, J.; Kildiyarova, R.R. $4p^64d^8$–($4d^75p + 4d^74f + 4p^54d^9$) Transitions in Xe XI. *Phys. Scr.* **2004**, *70*, 126–138. [CrossRef]
7. Cowan, R.D. *The Theory of Atomic Structure and Spectra*; Number 3; University of California Press: Berkeley, CA, USA, 1981.
8. Fahy, K.; Sokell, E.; O'Sullivan, G.; Aguilar, A.; Pomeroy, J.M.; Tan, J.N.; Gillaspy, J.D. Extreme-ultraviolet spectroscopy of highly charged xenon ions created using an electron-beam ion trap. *Phys. Rev. A–At. Mol. Opt. Phys.* **2007**, *75*, 1–12. [CrossRef]
9. Ali, S.; Nakamura, N. High resolution EUV spectroscopy of xenon ions with a compact electron beam ion trap. *J. Quant. Spectrosc. Radiat. Transf.* **2017**, *198*, 112–116. [CrossRef]
10. Ali, S.; Nakamura, N. Extreme ultraviolet spectroscopy of highly charged xenon and barium with a compact electron beam ion trap. *Nucl. Instruments Methods Phys. Res. Sect. B Beam Interact. Mater. Atoms* **2017**, *408*, 122–124. [CrossRef]
11. Merabet, H.; Kondagari, S.; Bruch, R.; Fülling, S.; Hahto, S.; Leung, K.L.; Reijonen, J.; Godunov, A.L.; Schipakov, V.A. EUV emission from xenon in the 10-80 nm wavelength range using a compact ECR ion source. *Nucl. Instruments Methods Phys. Res. Sect. B Beam Interact. Mater. Atoms* **2005**, *241*, 23–29. [CrossRef]

12. Safronova, U.I.; Bista, R.; Bruch, R.; Merabet, H. Relativistic many-body calculations of atomic properties in Pd-like ions. *Can. J. Phys.* **2008**, *86*, 131–149. [CrossRef]
13. Ivanova, E.P. Energy levels in Ag-like ($4d^{10}4f$, $4d^{10}5l$ (l = 0-3)), Pd-like ($4d^94f$ [J = 1], $4d^95p$ [J = 1], $4d^95f$ [J = 1]), and Rh-like ($4d^9$ [J = 5/2, 3/2]) ions with $Z \leq 86$. *At. Data Nucl. Data Tables* **2009**, *95*, 786–804. [CrossRef]
14. Bokamba Motoumba, E.; Enzonga Yoca, S.; Quinet, P.; Palmeri, P. Ab initio MCDHF/RCI and semi-empirical HFR calculations of transition probabilities and oscillator strengths in Xe XI. *J. Quant. Spectrosc. Radiat. Transf.* **2019**, *235*, 217–231. [CrossRef]
15. Motoumba, E.B.; Yoca, S.E.; Palmeri, P.; Quinet, P. Relativistic Hartree–Fock and Dirac–Fock atomic structure and radiative parameter calculations in nine-times ionized xenon (Xe X). *J. Quant. Spectrosc. Radiat. Transf.* **2019**, *227*, 130–135. [CrossRef]
16. Shen, Y.; Gao, C.; Zeng, J. Electron impact collision strengths and transition rates for extreme ultraviolet emission from Xe10+. *At. Data Nucl. Data Tables* **2009**, *95*, 1–53. [CrossRef]
17. Dressler, R.A.; hui Chiu, Y.; Zatsarinny, O.; Bartschat, K.; Srivastava, R.; Sharma, L. Near-infrared collisional radiative model for Xe plasma electrostatic thrusters: the role of metastable atoms. *J. Phys. D Appl. Phys.* **2009**, *42*, 185203. [CrossRef]
18. Gangwar, R.K.; Dipti; Srivastava, R.; Stafford, L. Spectroscopic diagnostics of low-pressure inductively coupled Kr plasma using a collisional–radiative model with fully relativistic cross sections. *Plasma Sources Sci. Technol.* **2016**, *25*, 035025. [CrossRef]
19. Gupta, S.; Gangwar, R.K.; Srivastava, R. Diagnostics of Ar/N2 mixture plasma with detailed electron-impact argon fine-structure excitation cross sections. *Spectrochim. Acta Part B At. Spectrosc.* **2018**, *149*, 203–213. [CrossRef]
20. Baghel, S.S.; Gupta, S.; Gangwar, R.K.; Srivastava, R. Diagnostics of low-temperature neon plasma through a fine-structure resolved collisional–radiative model. *Plasma Sources Sci. Technol.* **2019**, *28*, 115010. [CrossRef]
21. Jönsson, P.; Gaigalas, G.; Bieroń, J.; Fischer, C.F.; Grant, I. New version: Grasp2K relativistic atomic structure package. *Comput. Phys. Commun.* **2013**, *184*, 2197–2203. [CrossRef]
22. Sharma, L.; Surzhykov, A.; Srivastava, R.; Fritzsche, S. Electron-impact excitation of singly charged metal ions. *Phys. Rev. A* **2011**, *83*, 062701. [CrossRef]
23. Kramida, A.; Ralchenko, Y.; Reader, J.; NIST ASD Team. *NIST Atomic Spectra Database (ver. 5.8)*; National Institute of Standards and Technology: Gaithersburg, MD, USA, 2020. Available online: https://physics.nist.gov/asd (accessed on 21 August 2021)
24. Churilov, S.; Joshi, Y.N.; Reader, J. High-resolution spectrum of xenon ions at 13.4 nm. *Opt. Lett.* **2003**, *28*, 1478–1480. [CrossRef] [PubMed]
25. Bharti, S.; Sharma, L.; Srivastava, R. Electron impact excitation of Ge-like to Cu-like xenon ions in the extreme ultraviolet. *J. Phys. B At. Mol. Opt. Phys.* **2020**, *53*, 165001. [CrossRef]
26. Shukla, N.; Priti; Sharma, L.; Srivastava, R. Electron-impact excitations of highly charged tungsten ions and polarization study of their successive photon decay. *Eur. Phys. J. D* **2019**, *73*, 109. [CrossRef]
27. Priti.; Sharma, L.; Srivastava, R. Study of electron excitation of Rb-like to Br-like tungsten ions and polarization of their photon emission. *Eur. Phys. J. D* **2017**, *71*, 100. [CrossRef]
28. Das, T.; Sharma, L.; Srivastava, R. Electron impact excitation of the M-shell electrons from Zn-like through Co-like tungsten ions. *Phys. Scr.* **2012**, *86*, 035301. [CrossRef]
29. Dipti.; Das, T.; Sharma, L.; Srivastava, R. L-shell electron excitations of Mg- through O-like tungsten ions. *Phys. Scr.* **2014**, *89*, 085403. [CrossRef]
30. Dipti.; Das, T.; Sharma, L.; Srivastava, R. Electron impact excitation and polarization studies of Fe-like W48+ to Al-like W61+ ions. *Can. J. Phys.* **2015**, *93*, 888–897. [CrossRef]
31. Gangwar, R.K.; Sharma, L.; Srivastava, R.; Stauffer, A.D. C-R Model for Ar plasmas using reliable excitation cross-sections. *J. Physics: Conf. Ser.* **2012**, *388*, 042013. [CrossRef]
32. Dipti.; Gangwar, R.K.; Srivastava, R.; Stauffer, A.D. Collisional-radiative model for non-Maxwellian inductively coupled argon plasmas using detailed fine-structure relativistic distorted-wave cross sections. *Eur. Phys. J. D* **2013**, *67*, 203. [CrossRef]
33. Priti.; Dipti.; Gangwar, R.; Srivastava, R. Calculation of fully relativistic cross sections for electron excitation of cesium atom and its application to the diagnostics of hydrogen-cesium plasma. *J. Quant. Spectrosc. Radiat. Transf.* **2017**, *187*, 426–442. [CrossRef]
34. Priti.; Gangwar, R.K.; Srivastava, R. Collisional-radiative model of xenon plasma with calculated electron-impact fine-structure excitation cross-sections. *Plasma Sources Sci. Technol.* **2019**, *28*, 025003. [CrossRef]

Article

Elastic Scattering of Slow Electrons by Noble Gases—The Effective Range Theory and the Rigid Sphere Model

Kamil Fedus

Institute of Physics, Faculty of Physics, Astronomy and Informatics, Nicolaus Copernicus University, Grudziadzka 5/7, 87-100 Torun, Poland; kamil@fizyka.umk.pl

Citation: Fedus, K. Elastic Scattering of Slow Electrons by Noble Gases—The Effective Range Theory and the Rigid Sphere Model. *Atoms* **2021**, *9*, 91. https://doi.org/10.3390/atoms9040091

Academic Editors: Michael Brunger and David D. Reid

Received: 17 August 2021
Accepted: 27 October 2021
Published: 29 October 2021

Publisher's Note: MDPI stays neutral with regard to jurisdictional claims in published maps and institutional affiliations.

Copyright: © 2021 by the authors. Licensee MDPI, Basel, Switzerland. This article is an open access article distributed under the terms and conditions of the Creative Commons Attribution (CC BY) license (https://creativecommons.org/licenses/by/4.0/).

Abstract: We report on an extensive semi-empirical analysis of scattering cross-sections for electron elastic collision with noble gases via the Markov Chain Monte Carlo-Modified Effective Range Theory (MCMC−MERT). In this approach, the contribution of the long-range polarization potential ($\sim r^{-4}$) to the scattering phase shifts is precisely expressed, while the effect of the complex short-range interaction is modeled by simple quadratic expression (the so-called effective range expansion with several adjustable parameters). Additionally, we test a simple potential model of a rigid sphere combined with r^{-4} interaction. Both models, the MERT and the rigid sphere are based on the analytical properties of Mathieu functions, i.e., the solutions of radial Schrödinger equation with pure polarization potential. However, in contrast to MERT, the rigid sphere model depends entirely upon one adjustable parameter—the radius of a hard-core. The model's validity is assessed by a comparative study against numerous experimental cross-sections and theoretical phase shifts. We show that this simple approach can successfully describe the electron elastic collisions with helium and neon for energies below 1 eV. The purpose of the present analysis is to give insight into the relations between the parameters of both models (that translate into the cross-sections in the very low energy range) and some "macroscopic" features of atoms such as the polarizability and atomic "radii".

Keywords: electron elastic scattering; noble gases; scattering cross-sections

1. Introduction

Although great attention was devoted to electron collisions with atoms of noble gases over the years [1], scattering in a very low-energy range is still challenging both experimentally and theoretically. On the one hand, experiments at very low energies are scarce and burdened with high uncertainties since hard-to-reach energy and angular resolutions are required to carry out trustworthy measurements [2]. On the other hand, the theoretical description of complex (many-body) short-range effects in the electron–atom collision reached a high level of fidelity (see for example [3,4]), but numerical calculations become more and more computationally expensive and time-consuming with lowering electron energy. The most advanced contemporary theories involve such large basis sets and complicated equations that they are not easily applied to each specific target for which data are needed urgently. Therefore, a great value in understanding angular and energy variations of low-energy collisions can be brought by semi-empirical models, which give some insight into the relations between cross-sections and some "macroscopic" (i.e., measurable in other phenomena) features of the targets, like their polarizability and/or atomic "radii". Surprisingly, the very low-energy range is important for plasma modeling: say, in argon, which is the main component of "gas-discharge lamps", the mean temperature of electrons is 0.3 eV, i.e., the energy of the Ramsauer–Townsend minimum [5]. Noble gases are used also as additives in swarm experiments, to derive the very-low energy cross sections for molecules with other possible processes, like the vibrational excitations (CH_4, C_2H_2 [6,7]).

The effective range theory (ERT) is one of the most popular semi-empirical ways to describe slow-electron collisions with atoms. Originally, ERT has been introduced as a tool in the analysis and interpretation of low-energy neutron–proton scattering [8,9]. The theory expresses the s-wave scattering phase shift as a series of the projectile (neutron) momentum k. The series contains two adjustable parameters: A_0—the scattering length and R_0—the effective range of the interaction. O'Malley et al. [10] modified the ERT to show that a similar expression could be used to describe the scattering of a charged particle (such as electron and positron) by neutral atoms and simple non-polar molecules, i.e., in the presence of the long-range polarization potential ($\sim r^{-4}$). Later similar energy series expansions to that for s-wave phase-shift were introduced for higher partial waves (p and d waves) [11]. Due to its simplicity, the Modified Effective Range Theory (MERT) has gained considerable popularity. It has been frequently used to extrapolate measured cross-sections to the zero-energy [12–17]. Moreover, it is also used a support for complex multi-body calculations to determine the scattering length, see, for example [18,19].

Buckman and Mitroy [20] showed that the applicability of the original MERT is limited to very low energies (<1 eV) for noble gases. At such low energies, the experimental data to be extrapolated are scarce and characterized by relatively large uncertainties. The variety of experimental technique reflects in different possible systematic uncertainties. In case of integral (total) cross sections (ICS) these may be errors in pressure determination (due to the gas outflow from the scattering cell), angular resolution errors (due to the finite dimensions of detectors) and shift in energy determination (due to extremely fast timing of the signal in time-of-flight experiments). In the case of differential cross sections (DCS)—additionally, the impossibility of measuring small (below 10°) and large (above some 130°) scattering angles plays an important role. The contribution of all these errors to experimental data makes the MERT analysis less reliable. Idziaszek and Karwasz [21] proposed an alternative approach to the MERT series: phase shifts were obtained solving the Schrödinger equation with long-range polarization potential analytically using Mathieu functions, and the effective-range expansion was introduced only for the short-range part of the interaction potential. We showed [22–25] that such an approach allows expanding MERT applicability to much higher energies, where more accurate data are available. It is true for both positrons and electrons. The most significant advantage of the method is its simplicity—just a few parameters are used to describe the effect of complex, many-body interaction during the electron/positron collisions with atoms and molecules. Moreover, a new approach to MERT can be used to correct ex posteriori the experimental errors, as shown in [16]. Furthermore, understanding the physics behind the MERT parameters can help to provide more valuable data for an inverse scattering theory approach [26]. This approach aims to reconstruct the scattering potential from the experimental cross-sections, and MERT can potentially be a part of the inversion procedure.

In [27], we showed that an even simpler semi-empirical model than MERT could describe very low-energy positron (antielectron) interaction with noble gases, namely the rigid sphere approach. In this model, the interaction is described as a combination of an infinitive wall (hard-sphere) and the long-range polarization potential ($\sim r^{-4}$). Consequently, one needs just one parameter ("the atomic radii") to describe cross-sections at energies much below 1 eV. So far, this simple model has not been tested thoroughly for electron scattering by single atoms.

The goal of the present work is twofold. Firstly, we carry out an extensive (statistical) MERT analysis of a vast amount of datasets for electron collision with noble gases to study the systematics of parameters appearing in the effective-range expansion of the short-range potential. Using Monte Carlo methods, we provide confidence ranges for MERT parameters that are crucial for accurate predictions of cross-sections at low energies. At the same time, we examine the convergence of various available experimental data within the applied model. Secondly, we verify the applicability of the rigid sphere model to the low-energy electron scattering by noble gases. The paper is organized as follows: in Section 2, the principles of MERT and the rigid sphere model are briefly described.

In Section 3, the results of both models are presented and discussed. The paper concludes with a summary in Section 4.

2. Theoretical Models

2.1. Modified Effective Range Theory

The relative motion of a light electrically charged point particle and closed-shell atom is described by the following radial Schrödinger equation (within a partial-wave formalism in atomic units):

$$\left[\frac{d^2}{dr^2} - \frac{l(l+1)}{r^2} + \left(\frac{e^2\mu}{\hbar^2}\right)\frac{\alpha}{r^4} + V_s(r) + k^2\right]\Psi_l(r) = 0, \quad (1)$$

where l is the angular momentum quantum number, k is the wavenumber, α is the dipole polarizability, and $V_s(r)$ is the short-range potential. Note that the atomic units are employed throughout this paper. In particular, the electron mass (m_e), the Planck constant ($\hbar$) and the elementary charge (e) are equal to unity. Consequently, the reduced mass of the electron–atom system (μ) can be also approximated to one.

Since $V_s(r)$ can be neglected at large r, O'Malley et al. [10] proposed to include its contribution in appropriate boundary conditions subjected to analytical solutions of the Schrödinger equation with pure long-range polarization potential ($\sim r^{-4}$):

$$\left[\frac{d^2}{dr^2} - \frac{l(l+1)}{r^2} + \left(\frac{e^2\mu}{\hbar^2}\right)\frac{\alpha}{r^4} + k^2\right]\Phi_l(r) = 0. \quad (2)$$

The latter equation is identical with Mathieu's modified differential equation; hence $\Phi_l(r)$ can be expressed in terms of Mathieu functions, whose behavior at small and large distances r is determined by the standard boundary conditions (according to the quantum scattering theory) imposed on the scattering wavefunction:

$$\Phi_l(r) \stackrel{r\to 0}{\sim} r\sin\left(\frac{\sqrt{\alpha}}{r} + \gamma_l\right) \text{ and } \Phi_l(r) \stackrel{r\to\infty}{\sim} \sin\left(kr - l\frac{\pi}{2} + \eta_l\right) \quad (3)$$

where γ_l is a parameter determined by the short-range part of the interaction potential, while η_l is the scattering phase shift.

The boundary conditions provide the following expression for the scattering phase shift:

$$\tan\eta_l = \frac{m_l^2 - \tan^2\delta_l + B_l \tan\delta_l(m_l^2 - 1)}{\tan\delta_l(1 - m_l^2) + B_l(1 - m_l^2\tan^2\delta_l)}, \quad (4)$$

where $B_l = \tan(\gamma_l + l\pi/2)$ and $\delta_l = \frac{\pi}{2}(\nu_l - l - \frac{1}{2})$. Here m_l and ν_l denote the energy-dependent parameters which can be determined numerically from properties of the Mathieu functions (see the numerical procedures described in [21,22]).

Integral elastic (σ_{IE}), momentum transfer (σ_{MT}), and differential elastic ($d\sigma/d\omega$) cross-sections (all measured experimentally) are calculated using the standard partial wave expansions:

$$\sigma_{IE} = \frac{4\pi}{k^2}\sum_{l=0}^{\infty}(2l+1)\sin^2\eta_l(k) \quad (5)$$

$$\sigma_{MT} = \frac{4\pi}{k^2}\sum_{l=0}^{\infty}(l+1)\sin^2[\eta_l(k) - \eta_{l+1}(k)] \quad (6)$$

$$\frac{d\sigma}{d\omega} = \frac{1}{k^2}\left|\sum_{l=0}^{\infty}(2l+1)\exp\eta_l \sin\eta_l(k) P_l(\cos\theta)\right|^2 \quad (7)$$

where θ is the scattering angle and $P_l(x)$ are the Legendre polynomials.

O'Malley et al. [10] showed that energy dependence of parameter $B_l(k)$, related to the unknown short-range potential, has the following general form:

$$B_l(k) = b_l(0) + \frac{1}{2}\sqrt{\alpha e^2 \mu/\hbar^2}\rho_l(0,k)k^2. \tag{8}$$

where $b_l(0)$ is the zero-energy contribution and

$$\rho_l(0,k) = \int_0^\infty \Phi_l(0,r)\Phi_l(k,r) - \Psi_l(0,r)\Psi_l(k,r)dr. \tag{9}$$

Thus far all equations are exact. O'Malley et al. [10] proposed to approximate the latter parameter by the energy-independent value at zero-energy. Then $B_l(k)$ takes a form:

$$B_l(k) \approx b_l(0) + \frac{1}{2}\sqrt{\alpha e^2 \mu/\hbar^2}R_l k^2, \tag{10}$$

where $R_l = \rho_l(0,0)$. Equation (10) is similar to the effective range expansion of the scattering phase-shift in absence of the long-range potentials used to describe neutron–proton collisions [8,9]. Hence, in analogy to the original effective-range theory, we can call R_l as the "effective-range", though the physical meaning of this parameter is rather different. Since the error is of the order k^4, it is expected that the approximation is valid at low energies. We have already shown [21,22] that $\rho_l(0,k)$ changes rather slowly with increasing energy since MERT (using approximation (10)) is able to describe the scattering cross-sections almost up to the energy thresholds for the first inelastic processes.

In the zero energy limit both integral elastic (Equation (5)) and momentum transfer cross-sections (Equation (6)) can be expressed by the s-wave scattering length (A_0):

$$\sigma_{IE}(k) \approx \sigma_{MT}(k) = 4\pi A_0^2, \text{ for } k \to 0. \tag{11}$$

The s-wave scattering length can be expressed in terms of b_0 as $A_0 = -\sqrt{\alpha e^2 \mu/\hbar^2}/b_0$.

At low energies, the leading contributions come mainly from the first two or three partial waves ($l = 0, 1, 2$) while the contributions of higher partial waves are small and they are not modified by the short-range forces due to very high centrifugal barriers associated with large l numbers. Therefore the scattering phase-shifts experienced by higher partial waves can be described by the relations provided by Ali and Fraser [28]:

$$\tan \eta_l(k) = \alpha a_l k^2 + (\alpha^2 b_l + \beta c_l)k^4, \text{ for large } l, \tag{12}$$

where

$$a_l = \frac{\pi}{(2l+3)(2l+1)(2l-1)}, \tag{13}$$

$$b_l = \frac{\pi[15(2l+1)^4 - 140(2l+1)^2 + 128]}{[(2l+3)(2l+1)(2l-1)]^3(2l+5)(2l-3)}, \tag{14}$$

$$c_l = \frac{3\pi}{(2l+5)(2l+3)(2l+1)(2l-1)(2l-3)}. \tag{15}$$

Here β is the effective quadrupole polarizability of the target atom. The effective quadrupole polarizability comprises two terms: the adiabatic quadrupole interaction and the non-adiabatic dipole interaction, which in general are opposite in sign and of almost the same magnitude.

Substituting Equations (4) and (10) for two or three first partial waves (and Equation (12) for higher partial waves) into Equations (5)–(7) one gets relations which can be fitted to experimental data in order to determine the unknown parameters (b_l and R_l) of the effective range expansion of $B_l(k)$.

2.2. Rigid Sphere Approach

In the rigid sphere model, the interaction potential between the charged particle and the neutral polarizable atom has the following form:

$$V(r) = \begin{cases} \infty, & r < r_0 \\ -\alpha e^2/2r^4, & r > r_0 \end{cases} \qquad (16)$$

where r_0 is the radius of rigid sphere.

Since the radial Schrödinger equation for the potential $V(r)$ can be solved exactly using Mathieu functions, we showed in reference [27] that the expression for the scattering phase-shift of lth partial wave takes a following form:

$$\tan \eta_l = \frac{\sin \delta_l - [C_l m_l^2 + \cot(\pi \nu_l)(m_l^2 - 1)] \cos \delta_l}{\cos \delta_l + [C_l m_l^2 + \cot(\pi \nu_l)(m_l^2 - 1)] \sin \delta_l}, \qquad (17)$$

where m_l, ν_l and δ_l are the same parameters as in Equation (4). Energy-dependent parameter $C_l(k)$ can be determined from the continuity conditions imposed on the Mathieu functions at $r = r_0$ (see [27] for more details). The only adjustable parameter is r_0, the radius of the rigid sphere.

For a potential in Equation (16) the s-wave scattering length can be described analytically as a function of dipole polarizability (α) and the radius of the hard-sphere (r_0) as [29]:

$$A_0 = \sqrt{\alpha} \cot \left(\frac{\sqrt{\alpha}}{r_0} \right). \qquad (18)$$

Integral elastic (σ_{IE}), momentum transfer (σ_{MT}), and differential elastic ($d\sigma/d\omega$) cross-sections can be calculated using Equations (5)–(7).

3. Results

3.1. MERT

One can use nonlinear least-square regression procedures to fit MERT to chosen cross-section datasets and determine unknown parameters in the effective range approximation given by Equation (10). However, due to the multiparameter nature of the model, it seems to be more appropriate to use a Bayesian statistical inference for parameter estimation [30]. In contrast to the classical fitting, the Bayesian inference does not provide single point estimation in parameter space but rather the probability density functions (PDFs) of model parameters whose final form is shaped by (experimental or theoretical) observational data. Once posterior PDFs for each parameter are known, it is useful to provide a point estimation representing "best-fit" values together with an estimate of its errors. It can be done using either the mode or the mean value of PDF with the variance of distribution representing its uncertainty [30]. Generally, the larger the standard deviation of the parameter, the less sensitive model is to the changes of this parameter. Alternatively, one can give a credible region representing the predictive probability limit of the model due to parameters uncertainties (see [30] or [31] for a definition of this quantity).

Bayesian parameter estimation requires the computation of multi-dimensional integrals; a good solution for this computational problem consists of implementing Markov Chain Monte Carlo (MCMC) methods [30]. MCMC algorithms using prior PDF and likelihood functions generate a sequence of model parameters from a Markov Chain whose final stationary distribution is a desired posterior distribution. Here we adapt the MCMC Matlab toolbox by M. Laine [32] containing the Delayed Rejection and Adaptive Metropolis (DRAM) sampling algorithm with multivariate Gaussian proposal distributions introduced by Haario and co-workers [33]. We assume a Gaussian likelihood and (uninformative) prior PDF functions.

We choose available experimental total cross-sections (TCS) and momentum transfer cross-sections (MTCS) below the ionization threshold as the observational data. TCS are measured usually in the most accurate (and absolute) way using electron beam techniques (where electron collisions with single atoms are studied), while MTCS are derived indirectly from the measurements of swarm transport parameters (where a cloud of electrons drifting in an external electric field through dense atomic gas is investigated). Below the ionization energy, TCS correspond to integral elastic cross-sections described by Equation (5), while MTCS are given by Equation (6). To check the predictive capabilities of the present model, the mean values of MERT parameters are used to calculate differential cross-sections (DCS, Equation (7)) and compare with experiments. DCS are more sensitive than TCS and MTCS to the correct values of the scattering phase-shift, so the comparison with the experimental DCS is a good test for the correctness of the model.

3.1.1. Helium

In Figure 1a,b we show an example of Markov Chains (10^6 steps) for MERT parameters and corresponding posterior PDFs obtained by fitting the model to experimental TCS for electron–helium scattering by Buckman and Lohmann [34]. It was verified that below the ionization threshold (24 eV) only two first partials waves ($l = 0$ and $l = 1$) are distorted by the short-range interaction. Consequently, only four MERT coefficients (b_0, R_0, b_1, and R_1) were used as the fitting parameters. The solid line in Figure 1c shows the MERT model using mean values of determined PDFs, while the darkened gray area represents a 99% prediction interval.

Similar MCMC fits were done to other data including TCS by Szmytkowski et al. [35] and Shigemura et al. [36], as well as MTCS data available in the LXCat database: https://nl.lxcat.net/home/ (accessed on 1 August 2021). The latter data source includes calculations from S.F. Biagi's FORTRAN code Magboltz 8.97 [37], the IST Lisbon dataset, [38], and the Morgan dataset [39]. The mean values and standard deviations of MERT parameters are given in Table 1. In all studied cases, both PDFs for b_0 and R_0 parameters are characterized by relatively narrow standard deviations, however only b_0 mean values are comparable with each other. Although mean R_0 differs between fits, its values are relatively small, not far from zero. It suggests that the short-range interaction is rather weakly dependent on incident electron energy below the ionization threshold and the scattering is strongly governed by the scattering length alone (A_0). Large standard deviations for b_1 and R_1 demonstrate that model is weakly sensitive to both parameters. It reflects a small contribution of p-wave to the scattering process in almost the entire considered energy range. Although the p-wave phase shift increases slowly with electron energy, its contribution to cross-sections reaches of only about 20% at 20 eV i.e., the maximum energy considered. Consequently, it is difficult to determine b_1 and R_1 more precisely.

Table 1. Mean values and standard deviations of MERT parameters (appearing in the effective range approximation, Equation (10)) for e^-+He elastic scattering. The results were calculated using the dipole polarizability $\alpha = 1.407\ a_0^3$ [40] and the effective quadrupole polarizability $\beta = 0.0\ a_0^5$.

Data	$A_0(a_0)$		$R_0(a_0)$		b_1		$R_1(a_0)$	
	Mean	Std	Mean	Std	Mean	Std	Mean	Std
TCS (1×10^{-1}–20 eV) [34]	1.177	0.002	−0.058	0.015	−139	520	6	501
TCS (5×10^{-1}–20 eV) [35]	1.174	0.003	0.085	0.017	−86	519	−95	511
TCS (6×10^{-3}–20 eV) [36]	1.189	0.002	0.006	0.020	−90	528	−98	511
MTCS (1×10^{-4}–20 eV) [37]	1.180	0.003	0.132	0.034	−42	488	−91	475
MTCS (2×10^{-1}–20 eV) [38]	1.183	0.005	0.088	0.037	17	26	−10	34
MTCS (1×10^{-2}–20 eV) [39]	1.186	0.002	0.146	0.020	34	359	−87	440

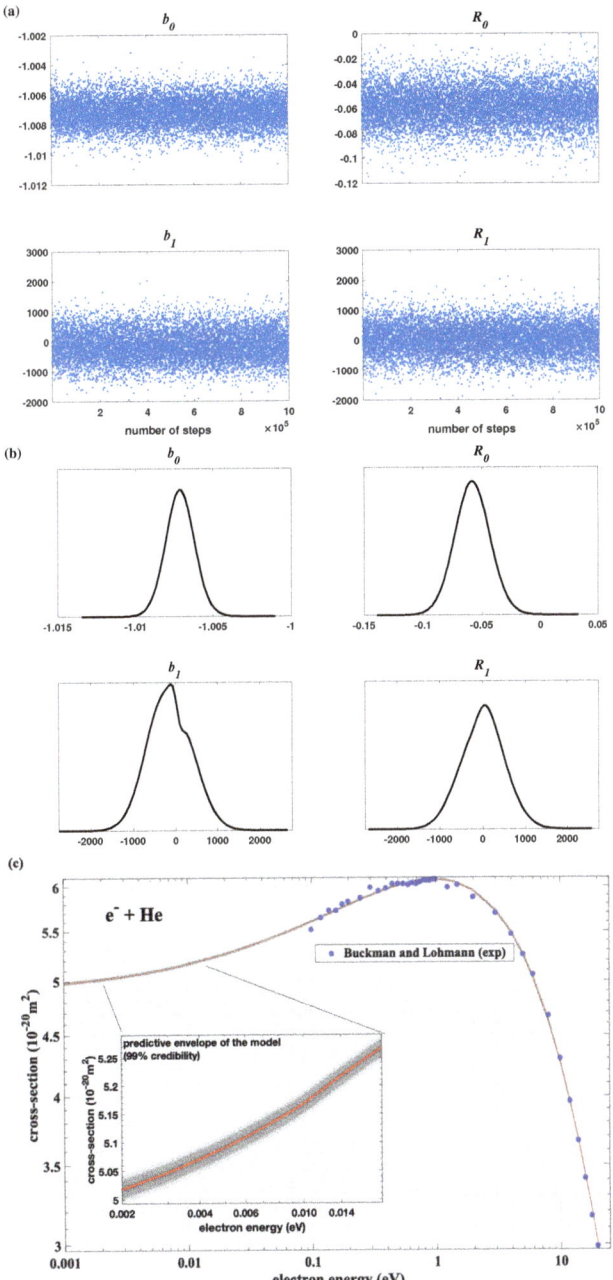

Figure 1. MCMC−MERT fit to experimental total cross−sections for electron−helium scattering by Buckman and Lohmann [34]: (**a**) Markov Chains for MERT parameters (b_0, R_0, b_1, R_1) determined during the fitting procedure. (**b**) Posterior probability density functions (PDFs) for MERT parameters estimated from Markov Chains. (**c**) MERT calculations using mean values of PDFs (solid line) and a 99% credible region (darkened gray area).

Interestingly, b_0 is very close to -1 in all fits (see Markov chains and PDFs in Figure 1a,b), it implies that the s-wave scattering length for He is numerically equal (within the error of the analysis) to the square root of dipole polarizability in atomic units: $A_0 \approx \sqrt{\alpha e^2 \mu/\hbar^2}$. Note however that this also corresponds to the position of the maximum value of the p-wave centrifugal barrier, see Figure 2. In other words, the position of the maximum of the repulsive long-range potential for p-wave determines effective spatial boundaries of the target seen by low-energy electrons when colliding with the He atom.

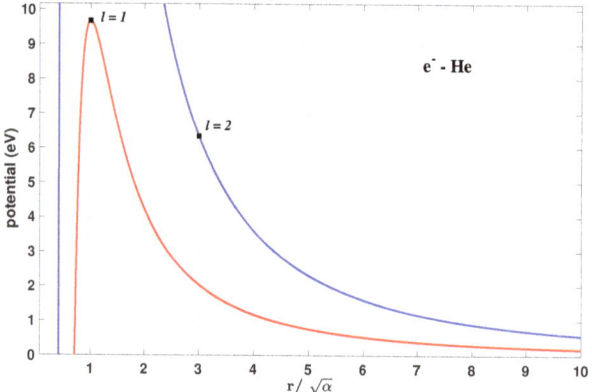

Figure 2. The positive (repulsive) part of the long-range electron−helium effective potentials for the p and d partial waves. The distance between interacting elements is scaled by the square root of dipole polarizability (in atomic units).

The MERT results are compared with experimental DCS in Figure 3. It is clear that the agreement is good. It proves that e^-−He elastic scattering below the ionization threshold is governed mainly by the s-wave scattering length. The latter quantity is equal approximately to the square root of dipole polarizability of the He atom (in atomic units).

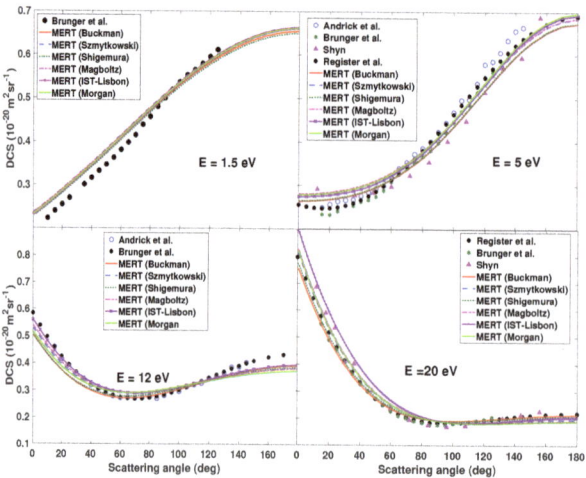

Figure 3. Angular dependencies of MERT−derived differential cross−sections at 1.5, 5, 12, and 20 eV for e^-−He scattering. The present results are compared with experimental data of Brunger et al. [41], Andrick et al. [42], Register et al. [43], and Shyn [44].

3.1.2. Neon

Similar MCMC−MERT analysis as for He has been done for other noble gases. For neon (Ne), TCS have been measured by many research groups below the threshold (16 eV) for the first Feshbach resonance (see references in [1,35]). Generally, good quality MERT fits can be achieved for many data. However, we found that only TCS by Szmytkowski et al. [35] and Shigemura et al. [36] covers enough wide energy range with sufficient resolution to determine MERT parameters confidently for both s and p partial waves. Both partial waves provide major contributions to the scattering cross-sections in the considered energy range. In the present analysis we take into account also swarm-derived MTCS from the LXCat database. This includes data by Puech [45], Morgan [39], Siglo [46], Robertson [47], and Magboltz 8.9 [37]. The results of MCMC−MERT fits are given in Table 2. For comparison, we also present the results of simultaneous MERT fit (using nonlinear least-squares regression) to the large collection of TCS datasets reported in [24].

This time, unlike for He, fitting the model to different datasets provide similar spreads of A_0 and b_1 mean values. Moreover, the R_0 parameter is positive in all cases, and it is much larger than for helium. On the other hand, the R_1 coefficient is small (it varies close to zero for different datasets). Hence the contribution of short-range interaction to the p-wave scattering is rather weakly dependent on the incident electron energy. Large standard deviations for b_2 and R_2 demonstrate that the model is weakly sensitive to both parameters since the contribution of d-wave to the scattering process is relatively small in almost the entire considered energy range (though not negligible at the upper part of the energy range).

In Figure 4 we compare MERT DCS with experimental data. In general, the agreement is good except for calculations using MERT parameters obtained from MTCS of Puech [45]. The discrepancy increases with the energy. This suggests that the interplay between the MERT parameter for p and d partial waves in this particular case is not correct.

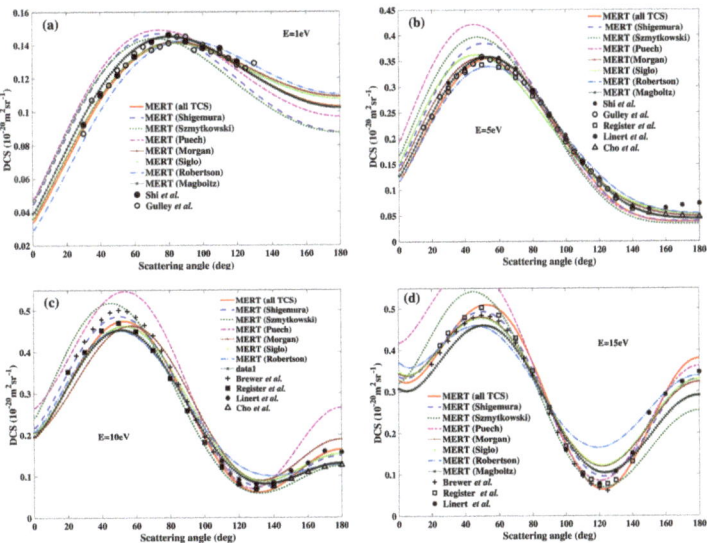

Figure 4. Angular dependencies of MERT−derived differential cross−sections at (**a**) 1, (**b**) 5, (**c**) 10, and (**d**) 15 eV for e^-−Ne scattering. The present results are compared with experimental data of Shi and Burrow [48], Linert et al. [49], Cho et al. [50], Register and Trajmar [43], Gulley et al. [51], and Szmytkowski et al. [35].

Table 2. Mean values and standard deviations of MERT parameters (appearing in the effective range approximation, Equation (10)) for e^-+Ne elastic scattering. The results were calculated using the dipole polarizability $\alpha = 2.571\ a_0^3$ [40] and the effective quadrupole polarizability $\beta = 0.0\ a_0^5$ [20].

Data	$A_0(a_0)$ Mean	Std	$R_0(a_0)$ Mean	Std	b_1 Mean	Std	$R_1(a_0)$ Mean	Std	b_2 Mean	Std	$R_2(a_0)$ Mean	Std
TCS (7×10^{-3}–16 eV) [36]	0.228	0.004	3.710	1.970	−0.192	0.014	−0.080	0.054	−1	50	1	50
TCS (5×10^{-1}–16 eV) [35]	0.225	0.007	1.955	4.18	−0.192	0.013	−0.042	0.030	0.228	501	6	501
all TCS (7×10^{-3}–16 eV) [24]	0.227	-	3.697	-	−0.231	-	−0.028	-	0.001	-	0.361	-
MTCS (1×10^{-4}–16 eV) [45]	0.241	0.002	3.652	0.180	−0.201	0.004	0.001	0.016	−0.472	40	1	50
MTCS (1×10^{-2}–16 eV) [39]	0.228	0.003	4.674	0.162	−0.225	0.007	−0.063	0.023	−0.455	48	1	49
MTCS (3×10^{-2}–20 eV) [46]	0.226	0.002	4.779	0.160	−0.223	0.005	−0.067	0.022	−0.235	46	0.722	48
MTCS (3×10^{-2}–7 eV) [47]	0.222	0.001	5.93	0.220	−0.239	0.004	0.074	0.026	−0.101	47	2	50
MTCS (1×10^{-4}–16 eV) [37]	0.224	0.001	3.596	0.366	−0.212	0.005	−0.090	0.014	0.008	0.055	0.436	0.25

3.1.3. Argon

In the case of argon (Ar), we found that the trustworthy MERT parameters can be obtained from the fits to TCS by Buckman and Lohmann [34], Ferch et al. [15], and Kurokawa et al. [52]. All of these datasets cover almost a full region of Ramsauer–Townsend minimum. In addition we verified that the following swarm-derived MTCS (from the LXCat database) can be analyzed confidently with MERT: Puech [45], Morgan [39], IST-Lisbon [38], Hayashi [53], and Magboltz 8.9 [37]. The results of MCMC−MERT fits are given in Table 3. Similar to Ne, both A_0 and b_1 are comparable for different datasets. However, the mean values of other MERT parameters (R_0, R_1, R_2, and b_2) are characterized by some spread, which prevents the determination of a confidence interval for these parameters. Nevertheless, most of the MERT parameters provide DCS that are in excellent agreement with experimental data, as shown in Figure 5. The exception is the fit to Puech dataset [45], where too much uncertainty for the d wave parameters is obtained and, consequently, the compliance with the measurements is lower.

Table 3. Mean values and standard deviations of MERT parameters (appearing in the effective range approximation, Equation (10)) for e^-+Ar elastic scattering. The results were calculated using the dipole polarizability $\alpha = 11.23\ a_0^3$ [40] and the effective quadrupole polarizability $\beta = 0.0\ a_0^5$ [20].

Data	$A_0(a_0)$ Mean	Std	$R_0(a_0)$ Mean	Std	b_1 Mean	Std	$R_1(a_0)$ Mean	Std	$b_2(a_0)$ Mean	Std	$R_2(a_0)$ Mean	Std
TCS (1.2×10^{-1}–10 eV) [34]	−1.500	0.010	−0.427	0.153	−0.448	0.011	0.072	0.037	0.206	0.001	0.315	0.014
TCS (8×10^{-2}–10 eV) [15]	−1.490	0.010	−0.142	0.010	−0.496	0.010	0.188	0.025	1.075	0.238	−0.272	0.175
all TCS (7×10^{-3}–10 eV) [52]	−1.400	0.010	−0.661	0.150	−0.463	0.016	0.130	0.046	0.339	0.092	0.213	0.065
MTCS (1×10^{-3}–10 eV) [37]	−1.460	0.010	0.101	0.167	−0.437	0.005	−0.198	0.054	0.069	0.022	0.425	0.012
MTCS (1×10^{-2}–10 eV) [53]	−1.490	0.010	0.845	0.472	−0.456	0.009	−0.017	0.163	0.206	0.136	0.317	0.104
MTCS (1×10^{-3}–10 eV) [38]	−1.560	0.010	1.557	0.198	−0.471	0.036	0.074	0.143	1.043	0.484	−0.305	0.394
MTCS (3×10^{-3}–10 eV) [39]	−1.490	0.010	1.189	0.044	−0.451	0.007	0.077	0.028	0.699	0.065	−0.063	0.054
MTCS (1×10^{-4}–10 eV) [45]	−1.570	0.020	1.742	0.396	−0.510	0.058	0.322	0.164	7.55	19.56	−5.53	15.92

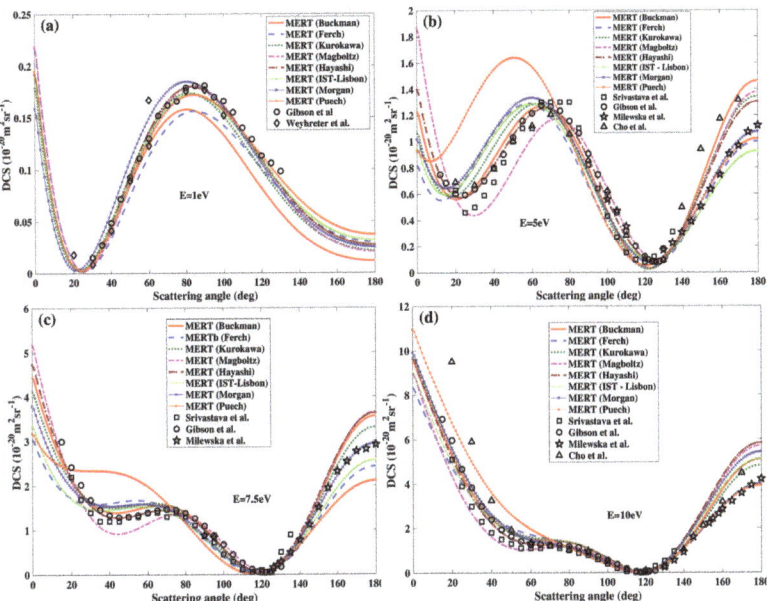

Figure 5. Angular dependencies of MERT−derived differential cross−sections at (**a**) 1, (**b**) 5, (**c**) 7.5, and (**d**) 10 eV for e^-−Ar scattering. The present results are compared with experimental data of Gibson et al. [54], Weyhreter et al. [55], Cho and Park [56], Srivastava et al. [57], and Milewska et al. [58].

3.1.4. Krypton

We analyzed a huge amount of available experimental TCS [35,52,59–61] and MTCS [37,39,46,62–67] for krypton (Kr) at low energies. We found that the fits to only three datasets (Buckman [59], Jost [61] and Hunter [64]) provide trustworthy MERT parameters that allow reconstructing experimental DCS below 10 eV. The results of fits are given in Table 4. For comparison, we also show the results of MERT fit (see [23]) to DCS measured with the magnetic-field angle analyzer, as reported by Zatsarinny et al. [68]. This experimental technique allows DCS measurements in full angular range (from 0° to 180°). Moreover, the data of Zatsarinny et al. [68] were obtained in a vast energy range with incredibly high resolution (15 meV). Consequently, as we showed in [23], the MERT parameters can be extracted quite accurately.

Similar to Ne and Ar, both A_0 and b_1 are comparable for all four datasets. Other MERT parameters are determined with much lower accuracy but still provide relatively good agreement with experimental DCS (see Figure 6).

Table 4. Mean values and standard deviations of MERT parameters (appearing in the effective range approximation, Equation (10)) for e^-+Kr elastic scattering. The results were calculated using the dipole polarizability $\alpha = 16.86\, a_0^3$ [40] and the effective quadrupole polarizability $\beta = 8.0\, a_0^5$ [20].

Data	$A_0(a_0)$		$R_0(a_0)$		b_1		$R_1(a_0)$		$b_2(a_0)$		$R_2(a_0)$	
	Mean	Std	Mean	Std	Mean	Std	Mean	Std	Mean	Std	Mean	Std
TCS (0.175–10 eV) [59]	−3.280	0.010	−0.509	0.068	−0.552	0.010	0.054	0.026	0.267	0.011	0.466	0.118
TCS (0.3–10 eV) [61]	−3.380	0.030	0.929	0.077	−0.664	0.012	0.121	0.027	0.249	0.019	0.503	0.026
DCS (<10 eV) [23]	−3.480	-	0.533	-	−0.599	-	0.125	-	0.039	-	0.720	-
MTCS (0.1–8 eV) [64]	−3.380	0.020	0.340	0.128	−0.527	0.030	−0.389	0.111	0.099	0.041	0.608	0.022

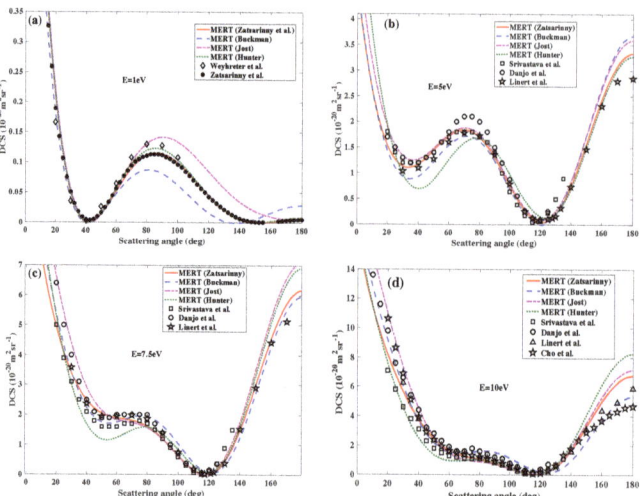

Figure 6. Angular dependencies of MERT−derived differential cross−sections at (**a**) 1, (**b**) 5, (**c**) 7.5, and (**d**) 10 eV for e^-−Kr scattering. The present results are compared with experimental data of Srivastava et al. [57], Danjo [69], Linert et al. [70], Cho et al. [71], Weyhreter et al. [55], and Zatsarinny et al. [68].

3.1.5. Xenon

The MCMC−MERT analysis of experimental TCS data for Xenon (Xe) has already been reported in [25]. In Table 5 we give only those MERT parameters that allow reconstructing experimental DCS below 10 eV. The most recent experimental TCS of Kurokawa et al. [52], and older measurements by Alle et al. [72] and Guskov et al. [73] are not included in the present analysis because the fits to these cross-sections do not provide correct DCS. Additionally, in the present work, we analyzed different MTCS [37,45,62,64,66,74], however only the fit to data by Hayashi [75] is consistent with DCS. For comparison, we also present in Table 5 the results of simultaneous robust MERT fit to all available TCS (using MATLAB routine for nonlinear least-square regression of multiple data sets) done in reference [25].

Since the d-wave plays an important role in e^-+Xe elastic scattering below 10 eV, it is much easier to determine MERT coefficients associated with this partial wave than for other noble gases. Consequently, this time all three parameters A_0, b_1, and b_2 are comparable between different sets given in Table 5. Moreover, even R_2 values are also of the same order. However, the spreads of R_0 and R_1 are too large to estimate the confidence intervals for both of them. Nevertheless, such uncertainties in both parameters do not have an important influence on DCS calculations, which are in good agreement with experiments (see Figure 7).

Table 5. Mean values and standard deviations of MERT parameters (appearing in the effective range approximation, Equation (10)) for e^-+Xe elastic scattering. The results were calculated using the dipole polarizability $\alpha = 27.04\ a_0^3$ [40] and the effective quadrupole polarizability $\beta = 16.8\ a_0^5$ [17].

Data	$A_0(a_0)$ Mean	Std	$R_0(a_0)$ Mean	Std	b_1 Mean	Std	$R_1(a_0)$ Mean	Std	$b_2(a_0)$ Mean	Std	$R_2(a_0)$ Mean	Std
TCS (0.125–10 eV) [60]	−6.510	0.050	−0.136	0.163	−0.690	0.048	0.023	0.040	0.220	0.035	0.593	0.040
TCS (0.2–10 eV) [61]	−6.870	0.011	−0.484	0.376	−0.670	0.082	0.232	0.057	0.170	0.083	0.663	0.071
TCS (0.5–10 eV) [35]	−6.750	0.500	0.462	0.526	−0.630	0.127	0.023	0.074	0.290	0.100	0.644	0.095
all TCS (0.5–10 eV) [25]	−6.490	-	0.097	-	−0.680	-	−0.019	-	0.200	-	0.668	-
MTCS (0.001–10 eV) [53]	−6.210	0.010	−0.043	0.181	−0.775	0.097	0.163	0.051	0.184	0.135	0.810	0.113

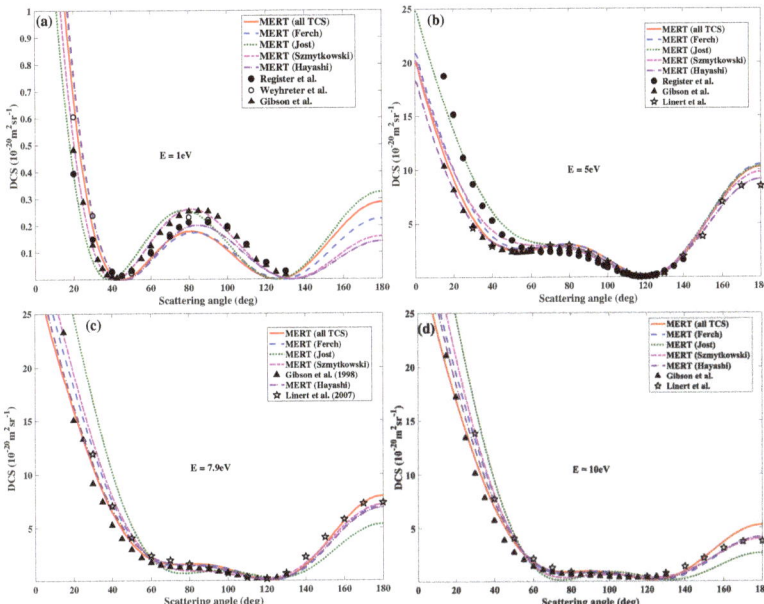

Figure 7. Angular dependencies of MERT−derived differential cross−sections at (**a**) 1, (**b**) 5, (**c**) 7.9, and (**d**) 10 eV for e^-−Xe scattering. The present results are compared with experimental data of Register et al. [76], Gibson et al. [77], Linert et al. [78], and Weyhreter et al. [55].

3.1.6. MERT Parameters

In Figure 8a, we show MERT-derived scattering length versus the dipole polarizability. We use values averaged over coefficients determined in MCMC−MERT analysis of different datasets (Tables 1–5). The standard deviations of the mean values are used to indicate the uncertainties in the determination of coefficients. For Ar, Kr, and Xe, the attractive polarization potential overcomes the repulsive exchange interaction due to relatively large dipole polarizabilities. Consequently, the scattering length is negative, and it changes linearly with polarizability (as shown by the dashed line). On the other hand, for He and Ne, the repulsive interaction with electrons is slightly dominant, making the scattering length positive, and a small deviation from the linear dependency $A_0(\alpha)$ is observed.

In Figure 8b, we plot the zero-energy contribution (b_1) of the short-range potential to the p-wave scattering phase-shift versus dipole polarizability. A clear regular tendency is observed, b_1 becomes more negative with increasing polarizability. We do not give a b_1 for helium due to the high uncertainties in MCMC−MERT analysis (see Table 1). However, the observed tendency suggests that this parameter is small (close to zero) for He.

Unfortunately, we can not make a similar plot for the b_2 parameter (i.e., the zero-energy contribution of short-range potential to the d-wave phase shift) due to too high uncertainty related to this coefficient. Nevertheless, a careful inspection of data from Tables 3–5 (Ar, Kr, and Xe) shows that, unlike b_1, the b_2 parameter is always positive.

Similarly to the b_2 parameter, the "effective ranges" (R_0, R_1, and R_2) can not be estimated accurately and they vary depending on the dataset used for analysis. Clearly, the effective-range corrections are relatively small in the low-energy regime in comparison to the leading contributions due to the s-wave scattering length, the p-wave, and the d-wave zero-energy contributions. Consequently, the effective-range parameters are strongly affected by measurement uncertainties in the experimental data in the low-energy domain. Extending the energy range to higher energies in MERT analysis does not work since the effective-range approximation (Equation (10)) becomes less accurate with increasing electron energy. Nevertheless, the present results show that the effective-range corrections may be comparable with leading contributions in the case of s-wave for Ne and d-wave for Xe, where the corresponding R_l values, obtained from different fits, are of the same order of magnitude.

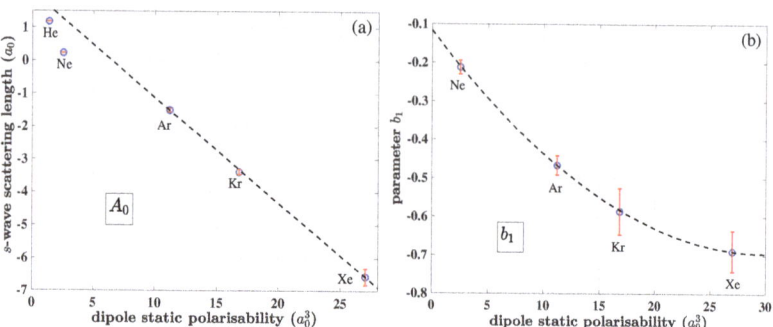

Figure 8. (a) MERT−derived s−wave scattering lengths and (b) parameter b_1 for rare gases plotted versus static dipole polarisability. The presented results are the mean values of MCMC−MERT analysis of different experimental cross−section datasets. The standard deviations of mean values are given to demonstrate the uncertainties in the determination of coefficients. The dashed lines are sketched as the guide to eyes to show general tendencies in $A_0(\alpha)$ and $b_1(\alpha)$ dependencies.

3.2. Rigid Sphere Model

The rigid sphere model requires the proper choice of the hard-core radius r_0. We found [27] that for positron scattering on noble gases, the r_0 corresponds to the positions of the principal maxima in the radial distributions of outermost atomic orbitals. It reflects the fact that the positron does not penetrate far inside the atom due to the strong repulsive static potential (that can be modeled as the hard core). The first attempt to apply a similar model for electron scattering was done by Reisfeld and Asaf [79] who proposed to use the atomic radii calculated from the van der Waals equations of state as the hard-core radii. They aimed to describe the scattering length for electron interaction with noble gases as a function of atomic dipole polarizability. However, such a choice of radii was criticized by R. Szmytkowski [80] who proved its incorrectness. If the rigid sphere model applies, we can benefit from Equation (18) relating r_0 with the scattering length. In our calculations we use mean values of the scattering length ($\langle A_0 \rangle$) determined in the present MERT analysis. Such a choice of r_0 determination gives negative radii for Ar, Kr, and Xe. This is obviously an unphysical outcome, limiting our analysis only to He and Ne, where r_0 is positive. Interestingly, a similar discrepancy between negative- and positive-scattering-length gases was noticed in multiple-scattering theories [81] describing electron interaction with dense gases. To solve this problem, Borghesani et al. [81–83] developed a hard-sphere-like model for electron multiple-scattering.

All parameters used in the present model are given in Table 6. The r_0 for electrons is much higher than the corresponding values for positrons [27]. It may be due to the different nature of the repulsive potential for both particles: positrons are repelled by static interactions while electrons are repulsed by the exchange potential.

Table 6. Parameters used in the rigid sphere model: the dipole polarizability (α), the mean value of the scattering length determined in the present MERT analysis ($\langle A_0 \rangle$), and the rigid sphere radius (r_0) determined from Equation (18).

Atom	$\alpha\,(a_0^3)$	$\langle A_0 \rangle\,(a_0)$	$r_0\,(a_0)$
He	1.407	1.181	1.50
Ne	2.671	0.228	1.14

In Figures 9 and 10 we show the scattering phase-shifts of s, p, and d-waves as well as the integral elastic cross-sections calculated using the rigid sphere model. Present results are compared with other theoretical and experimental determinations. For both gases, the model provides the s-wave and d-wave phase shifts that are in excellent agreement with other works to as high energy as 1 eV (for neon even up to 6 eV for s-wave). For p-wave, the agreement is worse; nonetheless, since its contribution is small compared to s-wave at low energies, the model can reconstruct experimental total cross-sections almost up to 1 eV for both atoms. This result suggests the in the case of He and Ne, the repulsive exchange potential felt by an incoming slow electron is sufficiently strong to be modeled by the infinitive barrier, while the attractive part of the potential (static and polarization) can be described effectively by the long-range r^{-4} interaction.

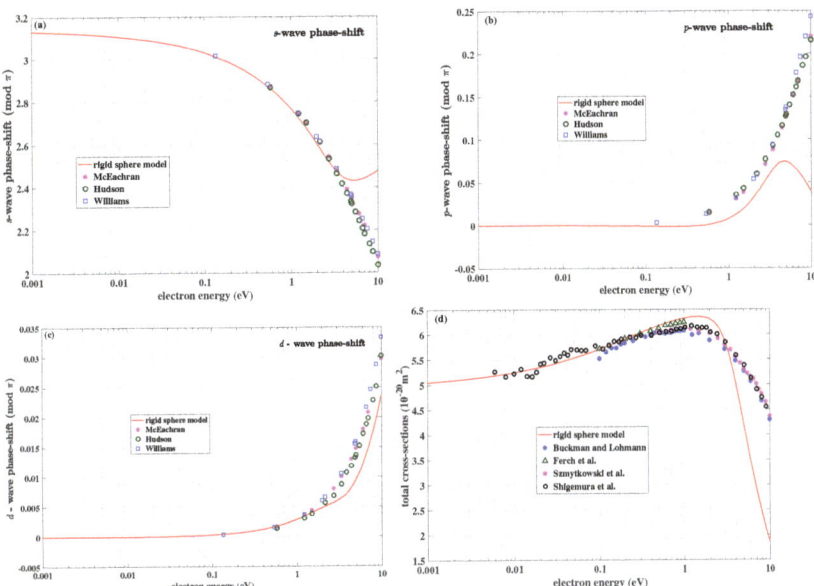

Figure 9. The rigid sphere model (solid lines) for low-energy e^-–He scattering: (**a**) s–wave phase–shift, (**b**) p–wave phase–shift, (**c**) d–wave phase–shift, and (**d**) integral elastic cross–sections. The model is compared with other works: phase–shifts by McEachran and Stauffer [84], Hudson et al. [85], and Williams [86]; total cross–sections by Buckman and Lohmann [34], Ferch et al. [87], Szmytkowski et al. [35], and Shigemura et al. [36].

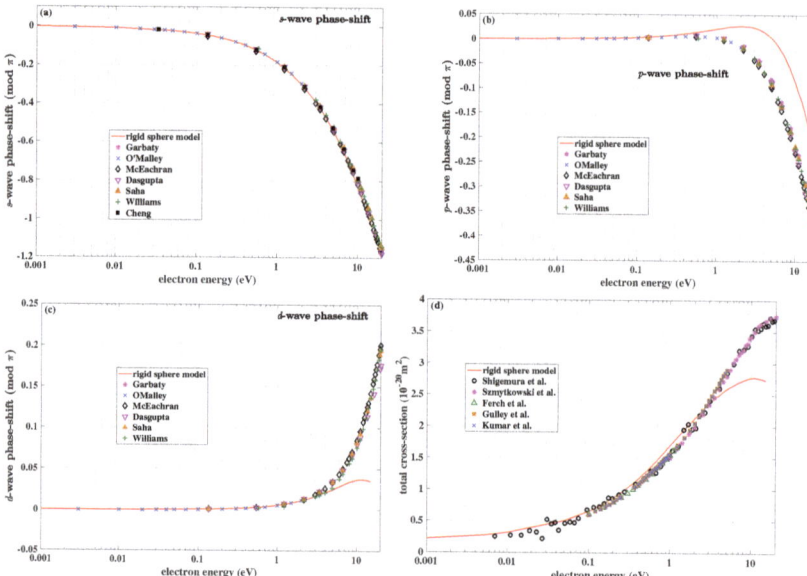

Figure 10. The rigid sphere model (solid lines) for low−energy e^-−Ne scattering: (**a**) s−wave phase−shift, (**b**) p−wave phase−shift, (**c**) d−wave phase−shift and (**d**) integral elastic cross−sections. The model is compared with other works: phase−shifts by Garbaty and LaBahn [88], O'Malley and Crompton [89], McEachran and Stauffer [90], Dasgupta and Bhatia [91], Saha [92], Williams [86], and Cheng et al. [18]; total cross−sections by Shigemura et al. [36], Szmytkowski et al. [35], Ferch et al. [93], Gulley et al. [51], and Kumar et al. [94].

4. Summary

We performed an extensive MCMC−MERT analysis of cross-sections for electron scattering from noble gases in the present work. We analyzed many experimental datasets of integral cross-sections, including total and momentum transfer cross-sections (TCS and MTCS). We selected those experimental data that comply with the differential cross-sections (DCS) within the current model. This statistical analysis was done to determine the confidence ranges for the MERT parameters appearing in the effective-range expansion of the short-range potential. We found that both the s-wave scattering length and the p-wave leading contribution can be determined confidently from available data. We showed that both parameters change in a regular manner with the dipole polarizability of atomic targets. On the other hand, other MERT parameters, including the "effective ranges", can not be determined with the same confidence. Nevertheless, some interesting tendencies can be spotted from the present study. In particular, the d-wave leading term seems to be positive for Ar, Kr, and Xe, where the d-wave contribution is not negligible below the threshold for the first inelastic process.

In the particular case of e^-–He scattering, we noticed that the s-wave scattering length is numerically equal to the square root of dipole polarizability of helium when expressed in atomic units. Interestingly, this also corresponds to the position of the maximum of the centrifugal potential barrier for the p partial wave. In other words, the repulsive part of p-wave interaction potential determines effective spatial boundaries of the helium atom "seen" by slow electrons. Similar correspondence is not observed for other noble gases.

We also verified the applicability of the rigid sphere model for low-energy electron interaction with noble gases. As could be expected, the hard-sphere model is roughly applicable for He and Ne only (which do not show the Ramsauer–Townsend minimum) since their integral cross-section changes slowly in the limit of zero energy (note also a similar approach for He by Borghesani in this issue [83]). The model can not be applied for argon, krypton, and xenon, where the repulsive exchange interaction is not strong enough with respect to the attractive part of the interaction potential. Consequently, the repulsive part can not be modeled effectively by the infinitive wall.

Finally, we showed in this paper that MERT could describe cross-sections at low energies for such highly polarizable systems as Kr and Xe. The question remains if our model is also applicable for other atomic targets, for example, tungsten (W) and beryllium (Be). Knowledge of cross-sections of atoms (including metals) is decisive in modeling plasmas, particularly in thermonuclear reactors. In tokamak-like reactors, the temperature and plasma density in the case of carbon-lining of the walls are well predicted by the theoretical simulations. However, in the case of a W-lined reactor, the discrepancy between the measured and modeled densities is by a factor of three [95]. It is due to the lack of reliable cross-sections. The study of MERT applicability for other atoms is in progress.

Funding: This research received no external funding.

Data Availability Statement: Not applicable.

Acknowledgments: The author would like to thank Grzegorz Karwasz (Nicolaus Copernicus University in Torun, Poland) for helpful suggestions and discussions.

Conflicts of Interest: The author declares no conflict of interest. The funders had no role in the design of the study; in the collection, analyses, or interpretation of data; in the writing of the manuscript, or in the decision to publish the results.

Abbreviations

The following abbreviations are used in this manuscript:

MCMC–MERT	Markov Chain Monte Carlo–Modified Effective Range Analysis
TCS	Total Cross–Sections
MTCS	Momentum Transfer Cross–Sections
DCS	Differential Cross–Sections
PDF	Probability Density Function
He	Helium
Ne	Neon
Ar	Argon
Kr	Krypton
Xe	Xenon

References

1. Zecca, A.; Karwasz, G.P.; Brusa, R.S. One century of experiments on electron-atom and molecule scattering: A critical review of integral cross-sections. *Rev. Nuovo Cim.* **1996**, *19*, 3. [CrossRef]
2. Szmytkowski, C.; Możejko, P. Recent total cross section measurements in electron scattering from molecules *Eur. Phys. J. D* **2020**, *74* 90.
3. Zatsarinny, O.; Bartschat, K. B-spline Breit–Pauli R-matrix calculations for electron collisions with neon atoms. *J. Phys. B* **2004**, *37*, 2173. [CrossRef]
4. Zatsarinny, O.; Bartschat, K. B-spline Breit–Pauli R-matrix calculations for electron collisions with argon atoms. *J. Phys. B* **2004**, *37*, 4693. [CrossRef]
5. Godyak, A.; Piejak, R.B. Abnormally low electron energy and heating-mode transition in a low-pressure argon rf discharge at 13.56 MHz. *Phys. Rev. Lett.* **1990**, *65*, 996. [CrossRef]
6. Song, M.-Y.; Yoon, J.-S.; Cho, H.; Itikawa, Y.; Karwasz, G.P.; Kokoouline, V.; Nakamura, Y.; Tennyson, J. Cross Sections for Electron Collisions with Methane. *J. Phys. Chem. Ref. Data* **2017**, *44*, 023101. [CrossRef]
7. Song, M.-Y.; Yoon, J.-S.; Cho, H.; Itikawa, Y.; Karwasz, G.P.; Kokoouline, V.; Nakamura, Y.; Tennyson, J. Cross Sections for Electron Collisions with Acetylene. *J. Phys. Chem. Ref. Data* **2017**, *46*, 013106. [CrossRef]
8. Bethe, H.A. Theory of the Effective Range in Nuclear Scattering. *Phys. Rev.* **1949**, *76*, 38. [CrossRef]
9. Blatt, J.M.; Jackson, J.D. On the interpretation of neutron-proton scattering data by the Schwinger Variational Method. *Phys. Rev.* **1949**, *26*, 18. [CrossRef]
10. O'Malley, T.F.; Spruch, L.; Rosenberg, L. Modification of EffectiveRange Theory in the Presence of a Long-Range (r^{-4}) Potential. *J. Math. Phys.* **1961**, *2*, 491. [CrossRef]

11. Malley, T.F.O.; Spruch, L.; Rosenberg, L. Low-Energy Scattering of a Charged Particle by a Neutral Polarizable System. *Phys. Rev.* **1962**, *125*, 1300. [CrossRef]
12. O'Malley, T.F. Extrapolation of Electron—Rare Gas Atom Cross Sections to Zero Energy. *Phys. Rev.* **1963**, *130*, 1020. [CrossRef]
13. Mann, A.; Linder, F. Low-energy electron scattering from halomethanes. I. Elastic differential cross section for e-CF4 scattering. *J. Phys. B At. Mol. Opt. Phys.* **1992**, *25*, 533. [CrossRef]
14. Lunt, S.L.; Randell, J.; Ziesel, J.-P.; Mrotzek, G.; Field, D. Very low energy electron scattering in some hydrocarbons and perfluorocarbons. *J. Phys. B At. Mol. Opt. Phys.* **1998**, *31*, 4225. [CrossRef]
15. Ferch, J.; Granitza, B.; Masche, C.; Raith, W. Electron-argon total cross section measurements at low energies by time-of-flight spectroscopy. *J. Phys. B* **1985**, *18*, 967. [CrossRef]
16. Karwasz, G.P.; Karbowski, A.; Idziaszek, Z.; Brusa, R.S. Total cross sections for positron scattering on benzene—Angular resolution corrections. *Nucl. Instrum. Methods Phys. Res. Sect. B* **2008**, *266*, 471. [CrossRef]
17. Kitajima, M.; Kurokawa, M.; Kishino, T.; Toyoshima, K.; Odagiri, T.; Kato, H.; Anzai, K.; Hoshino, M.; Tanaka, H.; Ito, K. Ultra-low-energy electron scattering cross section measurements of Ar, Kr and Xe employing the threshold photoelectron source. *Eur. Phys. J. D* **2012**, *66*, 130. [CrossRef]
18. Cheng, Y.; Tang, L.Y.; Mitroy, J.; Safronova, M.S. All-order relativistic many-body theory of low-energy electron-atom scattering. *Phys. Rev. A* **2014**, *89*, 012701. [CrossRef]
19. Green, D.; Ludlow, J.A.; Gribakin, G.A. Positron scattering and annihilation on noble-gas atoms. *Phys. Rev. A* **2014**, *90*, 032712. [CrossRef]
20. Buckman, S.J.; Mitroy, J. Analysis of low-energy electron scattering cross sections via effective-range theory. *J. Phys. B At. Mol. Phys.* **1989**, *22*, 1365. [CrossRef]
21. Idziaszek, Z.; Karwasz, G.P. Applicability of modified effective-range theory to positron-atom and positron-molecule scattering. *Phys. Rev. A* **2006**, *73*, 064701. [CrossRef]
22. Fedus, K.; Karwasz, G.P.; Idziaszek, Z. An analytic approach to modified effective range theory for electron and positron elastic scattering. *Phys. Rev. A* **2013**, *88*, 012704. [CrossRef]
23. Fedus, K. Modified effective range analysis of electron scattering from krypton. *Phys. Scr.* **2014**, *89*, 105401. [CrossRef]
24. Fedus, K. Electron Scattering from Neon Via Effective Range Theory. *Braz. J. Phys.* **2014**, *44*, 622. [CrossRef]
25. Fedus, K. Markov Chain Monte Carlo Effective Range Analysis of Low-Energy Electron Elastic Scattering from Xenon. *Braz. J. Phys.* **2016**, *46*, 1. [CrossRef]
26. Lun, D.R.; Amos, K.; Allen, L.J. Inversion of total and differential cross-section data for electron-methane scattering. *Phys. Rev. A* **1996**, *53*, 831. [CrossRef]
27. Fedus, K. A rigid sphere approach to positron elastic scattering by noble gases, molecular hydrogen, nitrogen and methane. *Eur. Phys. J. D* **2016**, *70*, 261. [CrossRef]
28. Ali, M.K.; Fraser, P.A. The contribution of long-range forces to low-energy phaseshifts. *J. Phys. B At. Mol. Phys.* **1977**, *10*, 3091. [CrossRef]
29. Szmytkowski, R. Analytical calculations of scattering lengths in atomic physics. *J. Phys. A: Math. Gen.* **1995**, *28*, 7333. [CrossRef]
30. Gregory, P. *Bayesian Logical Data Analysis for the Physical Sciences*; Cambridge University Press: New York, NY, USA, 2005.
31. Fedus, K.; Franz, J.; Karwasz, G.P. Positron scattering on molecular hydrogen: Analysis of experimental and theoretical uncertainties. *Phys. Rev. A* **2015**, *91*, 062701. [CrossRef]
32. Laine, M. MCMC toolbox for Matlab, available online: https://mjlaine.github.io/mcmcstat/ (accessed on 15 June 2021).
33. Haario, H.; Laine, M.; Mira, A.; Saksman, E. DRAM: Efficient adaptive MCMC. *Stat. Comput.* **2006**, *16*, 339. [CrossRef]
34. Buckman, S.J.; Lohmann, B. Low-energy total cross section measurements for electron scattering from helium and argon. *J. Phys. B At. Mol. Phys.* **1986**, *19*, 2547. [CrossRef]
35. Szmytkowski, C.; Maciag, K.; Karwasz, G. Absolute electron-scattering total cross section measurements for noble gas atoms and diatomic molecules. *Phys. Scipta* **1996**, *54*, 271. [CrossRef]
36. Shigemura, K.; Kitajima, M.; Kurokawa, M.; Toyoshima, K.; Odagiri, T.; Suga, A.; Kato, H.; Hoshino, M.; Tanaka, H.; Ito, K. Total cross sections for electron scattering from He and Ne at very low energies. *Phys. Rev. A* **2014**, *89*, 022709. [CrossRef]
37. Fortran Program, MAGBOLTZ 8.9, S.F. Biagi, Sept 2011 (from LXcat database). Available online: https://nl.lxcat.net/home/ (accessed on 1 August 2021).
38. Alves, L.L. The IST-Lisbon database on LXCat. *J. Phys. Conf. Ser.* **2014**, *565*, 1. [CrossRef]
39. Cross-Sections Assembled over the Course of 30 Years by WL Morgan—Suitable for Use with 2-Term Boltzmann Solvers. Available online: www.lxcat.net/Morgan (accessed on 1 August 2021).
40. Olney, T.N.; Cann, N.M.; Cooper, G.; Brion, C.E. Absolute scale determination for photoabsorption spectra and the calculation of molecular properties using dipole sum-rules. *Chem. Phys.* **1997**, *223*, 59. [CrossRef]
41. Brunger, M.J.; Buckman, S.J.; Allen, L.J.; McCarthy, I.E.; Ratnavelu, K. Elastic electron scattering from helium: Absolute experimental cross sections, theory and derived interaction potentials. *J. Phys. B* **1992**, *25*, 1823. [CrossRef]
42. Andrick, D.; Bitsch, A. Experimental investigation and phase shift analysis of low-energy electron-helium scattering. *J. Phys. B* **1975**, *8*, 393. [CrossRef]
43. Register, D.F.; Trajmar, S.; Srivastava, S.K. Absolute elastic differential electron scattering cross sections for He: A proposed calibration standard from 5 to 200 eV. *Phys. Rev. A* **1980**, *21*, 1134. [CrossRef]

44. Shyn, T.W. Angular distribution of electrons elastically scattered from gases: 2–400 eV on He. *Phys. Rev. A* **1980**, *22*, 916. [CrossRef]
45. Puech, V.; Mizzi, S. Collision cross sections and transport parameters in neon and xenon. *J. Phys. D: Appl. Phys.* **1991**, *24*, 1974. [CrossRef]
46. Meunier, J.; Belenguer, P.; Boeuf, J.P. Numerical model of an ac plasma display panel cell in neon-xenon mixtures. *J. Appl. Phys.* **1995**, *78*, 1995. [CrossRef]
47. Robertson, A.G. The momentum transfer cross section for low energy electrons in neon. *J. Phys. B Atom. Mol. Phys.* **1972**, *5*, 648. [CrossRef]
48. Shi, X.; Burrow, P.D. Differential scattering cross sections of neon at low electron energies. *J. Phys. B At. Mol. Phys.* **1992**, *25*, 4273. [CrossRef]
49. Linert, I.; Mielewska, B.; King, G.C.; Zubek, M. Elastic electron scattering in neon in the 110°–180° scattering angle range. *Phys. Rev. A* **2006**, *74*, 042701. [CrossRef]
50. Cho, H.; McEachran, R.P.; Buckman, S.J.; Tanaka, H. Elastic electron scattering from neon at backward angles. *Phys. Rev. A* **2008**, *78*, 034702. [CrossRef]
51. Gulley, R.J.; Alle, D.T.; Brennan, M.J.; Brunger, M.J.; Buckman, S.J. Differential and total electron scattering from neon at low incident energies. *J. Phys. B At. Mol. Phys. 1994*, **1994**, *27*, 2593. [CrossRef]
52. Kurokawa, M.; Kitajima, M.; Toyoshima, K.; Kishino, T.; Odagiri, T.; Kato, H.; Hoshino, M.; Tanaka, H.; Ito, K. High-resolution total-cross-section measurements for electron scattering from Ar, Kr, and Xe employing a threshold-photoelectron source. *Phys. Rev. A* **2011**, *84*, 062717. [CrossRef]
53. Hayashi, M. Bibliography of Electron and Photon Cross Sections with Atoms and Molecules Published in the 20th Century—Argon, Report. NIFS-DAT-72 of the National Institute for Fusion Science of Japan, *Report NIFS-DATA-79*; Japan National Institute for Fusion Science, Oroshicho, Toki, Gifu, Japan, 2003. Available online: http://www.nifs.ac.jp/report/nifs-data072.html (accessed on 1 August 2021).
54. Gibson, J.C.; Gulley, R.J.; Sullivan, J.P.; Buckman, S.J.; Chan, V.; Burrow, P.D. Elastic electron scattering from argon at low incident energies. *J. Phys. B* **1996**, *29*, 3177. [CrossRef]
55. Weyhreter, M.; Barzick, B.; Mann, A.; Linder, F. Measurements of differential cross sections for e–Ar, Kr, Xe scattering at $E = 0.05 - 2$ eV. *Z. Phys. D* **1988**, *7*, 333. [CrossRef]
56. Cho, H.; Park, Y.S. Low-energy Electron Scattering from Argon. *J. Korean Phys. Soc.* **2009**, *55*, 459. [CrossRef]
57. Srivastava, S.K.; Tanaka, H.; Chutjian, A.; Trajmar, S. Elastic scattering of intermediate-energy electrons by Ar and Kr. *Phys. Rev. A* **1981**, *23*, 2156. [CrossRef]
58. Mielewska, B.; Linert, I.; King, G.C.; Zubek, M. Differential cross sections for elastic electron scattering in argon over the angular range 130°–180°. *Phys. Rev. A* **2004**, *69*, 062716. [CrossRef]
59. Buckman, S.J.; Lohmann, B. The total cross section for low-energy electron scattering from krypton. *J. Phys. B* **1987**, *20*, 5807. [CrossRef]
60. Ferch, J.; Simon, F.; Strakeljahn, G. Abstracts of Contributed Papers. In Proceedings of the 15th International Conference on the Physics of Electronic and Atomic Collisions, Brighton, UK, 22–28 July 1987; Geddes, J., Gilbody, H.B., Kingston, A.E., Latimer, C.J., Walters, H.J.R., Eds.; North-Holland: Amsterdam, The Netherlands, 1987; p. 132.
61. Jost, K.; Bisling, P.G.F.; Eschen, F.; Felsmann, M.; Walther, L. Abstracts of Contributed Papers. In Proceedings of the 13th International Conference on the Physics of Electronic and Atomic Collisions, Berlin, Germany, 27 July– 2 August 1983; Geddes, J., Gilbody, H.B., Kingston, A.E., Latimer, C.J., Walters, H.J.R., Eds.; North-Holland: Amsterdam, The Netherlands, 1983; p. 91.
62. Koizumi, T.; Shirakawa, E.; Ogawa, I. Momentum transfer cross sections for low-energy electrons in krypton and xenon from characteristic energies. *J. Phys. B* **1986**, *19*, 2331. [CrossRef]
63. England, J.P.; Elford, M.T. Momentum Transfer Cross Section for Electrons in Krypton Derived from Measurements of the Drift Velocity in H_2-Kr Mixtures. *Aust. J. Phys.* **1988**, *41*, 701. [CrossRef]
64. Hunter, S.R.; Carter, J.G.; Christophorou, L.G. Low-energy electron drift and scattering in krypton and xenon. *Phys. Rev. A* **1988**, *38*, 5539. [CrossRef]
65. Mitroy, J. The Momentum Transfer Cross Section for Krypton. *Aust. J. Phys.* **1990**, *43*, 19. [CrossRef]
66. Pack, J.L.; Voshall, R.E.; Phelps, A.V.; Kline, L.E. Longitudinal electron diffusion coefficients in gases: Noble gases. *J. Appl. Phys.* **1992**, *71*, 5363. [CrossRef]
67. Brennan, M.J.; Ness, K.F. Momentum Transfer Cross Section for e-Kr Scattering. *Austr. J. Phys.* **1993**, *46*, 249. [CrossRef]
68. Zatsarinny, O.; Bartschat, K.; Allan, M. High-resolution experiments and B-spline R-matrix calculations for elastic electron scattering from krypton. *Phys. Rev. A* **2011**, *83*, 032713. [CrossRef]
69. Danjo, A. Electron scattering from Kr. I. Differential cross section for elastic scattering. *J. Phys. B* **1988**, *21*, 3759. [CrossRef]
70. Linert, I.; Mielewska, B.; King, G.C.; Zubek, M. Elastic electron scattering in krypton in the energy range from 5 to 10 eV. *Phys. Rev. A* **2010**, *81*, 012706. [CrossRef]
71. Cho, H.; Gulley, R.J.; Buckman, S.J. Elastic Electron Scattering from Krypton at Backward Angles. *J. Korean Phys. Soc.* **2003**, *42*, 71.
72. Alle, D.T.; Brennan, M.J.; Buckman, S.J. Abstract. In Proceedings of the 18th International Conference on Physics of Electronic and Atomic Collisions, Aarhus, Denmark, 21–27 July 1993; Andersen, T., Fastrup, B., Folkmann, F., Knudsen, H., Andersen, N., Eds.; American Institute of Physics: New York, NY, USA, 1993; p. 127.

73. Guskov, Y.; Savvov, R.V.; Slobodyanyuk, V.A. Time-of-flight measurements of the total cross-section for elastic scattering of low-energy electrons (E = 0.025–1.0 eV) by He, Ne, Ar, Kr and Xe. *Sov. Phys. Tech. Phys.* **1978**, *23*, 167.
74. Schmidt, B.; Berkhan, K.; Götz, B.; Müller, M. New experimental techniques in the study of electron swarms in gases and their impact on the determination of low energy electron scattering cross sections. *Phys. Scr.* **1994**, *53*, 30. [CrossRef]
75. Hayashi, M. Bibliography of Electron and Photon Cross Sections with Atoms and Molecules Published in the 20th Century—Xenon. In *Research Report NIFS-DATA Series*; Report NIFS-DATA-79; Japan National Institute for Fusion Science: Toki, Japan, 2003.
76. Register, D.F.; Vuskovic, L.; Trajmar, S. Elastic electron scattering cross sections for Xe in the 1–100 eV impact energy region. *J. Phys. B At. Mol. Phys.* **1986**, *19*, 1685. [CrossRef]
77. Gibson, J.C.; Lun, D.R.; Allen, L.J.; McEachran, R.P.; Parcell, L.A.; Buckman, S.J. Low-energy electron scattering from xenon. *J. Phys. B At. Mol. Phys.* **1998**, *31*, 3949. [CrossRef]
78. Linert, I.; Mielewska, B.; King, G.C.; Zubek, M. Differential cross sections for elastic electron scattering in xenon in the energy range from 5 eV to 10 eV. *Phys. Rev. A* **2007**, *76*, 032715. [CrossRef]
79. Reisfeld, G.; Asaf, U. Relation between the electron scattering length and the van der Waals approximation to the equation of state. *Phys. Rev. A* **1994**, *49*, 348. [CrossRef]
80. Szmytkowski, R. Calculation of the electron-scattering lengths for rare-gas atoms. *Phys. Rev. A* **1995**, *51*, 853. [CrossRef]
81. Borghesani, A.F.; Santini, M.; Lamp, P. Excess electron mobility in high-density gas. *Phys. Rev. A* **1992**, *46*, 7902. [CrossRef]
82. Borghesani, A.F.; Santini, M. Electron localization-delocalization transition in high-density neon gas. *Phys. Rev. A* **1992**, *45*, 8803. [CrossRef]
83. Borghesani, A.F. Accurate Electron Drift Mobility Measurements in Moderately Dense Helium Gas at Several Temperatures. *Atoms* **2021**, *9*, 52. [CrossRef]
84. McEachran, R.P.; Stauffer, A.D. Polarisation and exchange effects on elastic scattering of electrons from helium. *J. Phys. B At. Mol. Phys.* **1983**, *16*, 255. [CrossRef]
85. Hudson, E.T.; Bartschat, K.; Scott, M.P.; Burke, P.G.; Burke, V.M. Electron scattering from helium atoms. Phase shifts, resonance parameters and total cross sections. *J. Phys. B At. Mol. Phys.* **1996**, *29*, 5513. [CrossRef]
86. Williams, J.F. A phaseshift analysis of experimental angular distributions of electrons elastically scattered from He, Ne and Ar over the range 0.5 to 20 eV. *J. Phys. B At. Mol. Phys.* **1979**, *12*, 265. [CrossRef]
87. Ferch, J.; Raith, W.; Schröoder, K. Total cross section measurements for electron scattering from molecular hydrogen at very low energies. *J. Phys. B At. Mol. Phys.* **1980**, *13*, 1481. [CrossRef]
88. Garbaty, E.A.; LaBahn, R.W. Scattering of Slow Electrons by Neon and Argon. *Phys. Rev. A* **1971**, *4*, 1425. [CrossRef]
89. O'Malley, T.F.; Crompton, R.W. Electron-neon scattering length and S-wave phaseshifts from drift velocities. *J. Phys. B Atom. Mol. Phys.* **1980**, *13*, 3451. [CrossRef]
90. McEachran, R.P.; Stauffer, A.D. Elastic scattering of electrons from neon and argon. *J. Phys. B At. Mol. Phys.* **1983**, *16*, 4023. [CrossRef]
91. Dasgupta, A.; Bhatia, A.K. Scattering of electrons from neon atoms. *Phys. Rev. A* **1984**, *30*, 1241. [CrossRef]
92. Saha, H.P. Low-energy elastic scattering of electrons from neon atoms. *Phys. Rev. A* **1989**, *39*, 5048. [CrossRef] [PubMed]
93. Ferch, J.; Raith, W. University of Bielefeld, Germany, Unpublished work, 1985
94. Kumar, V.; Krishnakumar, E.; Subramanian, K.P. Electron-helium and electron-neon scattering cross sections at low electron energies using a photoelectron source. *J. Phys. B At. Mol. Phys.* **1987**, *20*, 2899. [CrossRef]
95. Guillemaut, C.; Pitts, R.A.; Kukushkin, A.S.; Gunn, J.P.; Bucalossi, J.; Arnoux, G.; Belo, P.; Brezinsek, S.; Brix, M.; Corrigan, G.; et al. Influence of atomic physics on EDGE2D-EIRENE simulations of JET divertor detachment with carbon and beryllium/tungsten plasma-facing components. *Nucl. Fusion* **2014**, *54* 093012. [CrossRef]

Article

Analytical Cross Section Approximation for Electron Impact Ionization of Alkali and Other Metals, Inert Gases and Hydrogen Atoms

Rusudan I. Golyatina [1] and Sergey A. Maiorov [1,2,*]

[1] Prokhorov General Physics Institute of the Russian Academy of Sciences, 38, Vavilov Str., 119991 Moscow, Russia; rusudan@intemodino.com
[2] Joint Institute for High Temperatures of the Russian Academy of Sciences, 13, Izhorskaya Str., Bd. 2, 125412 Moscow, Russia
* Correspondence: mayorov_sa@mail.ru

Abstract: The paper presents an analysis of data on the cross sections of electron impact ionization of atoms of alkali metals, hydrogen, noble gases, some transition metals and Al, Fe, Ni, W, Au, Hg, U. For the selected sets of experimental and theoretical data, an optimal analytical formula is found and approximation coefficients are calculated. The obtained semi-empirical formula reproduces the values of the ionization cross sections in a wide range of energies with an accuracy of the order of error of the available theoretical and experimental data.

Keywords: electron atomic collisions; ionization cross section; approximation of cross sections; alkali metals; noble gases

PACS: 34.80.Bm; 34.80.Dp; 51.50.+v, 51.10.+y, 52.80.Dy, 52.25.Fi, 34.80.Bm; 34.80.Dp

1. Introduction

The values of electron-atomic collision cross sections are used in various applications of gas-discharge plasma. The bibliography on cross sections of electron-atomic collisions has thousands of works, and probably an exhaustive review and selection of data is contained in the works [1–6]. However, it should be borne in mind that a critical analysis of the results of experimental data in the review work is very difficult due to the fact that the errors given in the original works of the order of 1–3% differ from each other sometimes by 50%. Therefore, in the review work, only a comparative analysis of the results obtained is really possible, which shows that at best, the relative errors of measuring cross sections are of the order of 5–10%, and more often 20–50%, sometimes reaching 100%.

The most convenient form of presenting experimental and computational-theoretical data is the selection of analytical approximations for them. Analytical approximation is the most convenient and simple for computer modeling, for obtaining values at intermediate points. In addition, it allows you to analyze the accuracy of the asymptotic approximation. We started a critical analysis and evaluation of the cross sections for electron scattering by noble gas atoms in a wide energy range in [7–10], where we found approximations for the cross sections of elastic and inelastic collisions of electrons with rare gas atoms. From a large number of experimental and calculated data on ionization cross-sections, by comparative analysis, we selected the data for approximation by our analytical dependence. Ionization by electron impact from the ground state of the atom is, perhaps, the most frequent method for the formation and maintenance of a gas-discharge plasma. With a large excess of the electron energy above the ionization threshold, both experimental methods and theory provide good accuracy in measuring cross sections. However, there are practically no experimental data for low energies, and therefore, it is difficult to speak about the accuracy of theoretical calculations in this energy range.

As before, when choosing data for approximating ionization cross sections, we limited ourselves to considering ionization from the ground state, which is sufficient for modeling applied problems of gas-discharge plasma.

2. Approximation of the Ionization Cross Section

The formulation of the problem of finding an analytical approximation of the ionization cross section of an atom by an electron impact is based on the use of known analytical estimates, the results of experimental measurements and numerical quantum mechanical calculations. In 1912, Thomson proposed the dependence of the ionization cross-section on the electron energy of the following form [11]:

$$\sigma_{ionization}(\varepsilon) = \frac{\pi e^4}{\varepsilon}\left(\frac{1}{I} - \frac{1}{\varepsilon}\right) \equiv 4\pi a_0^2 \frac{Ry^2(\varepsilon - I)}{\varepsilon^2 I} \qquad (1)$$

which is obtained for the case of a stationary valence electron at the energy of the incident electron $\varepsilon > I$. It gives a linear increase in the ionization cross section with a small excess of the collision energy over the ionization potential and reaches the maximum value $\sigma_{max} = \pi e^4/4I^2$ at the energy of the incident electron $\varepsilon = 2I$. Here, e—elementary charge, a_0—Bohr radius, Ry—ionization energy of a hydrogen atom. A more precise expression for the ionization cross section, which takes into account the spherically symmetric motion of the valence electron in the Coulomb field of the atomic residue, has the form [12]:

$$\sigma_{ionization}(\varepsilon) = \frac{\pi e^4}{\varepsilon}\left(\frac{5}{3I} - \frac{1}{\varepsilon} - \frac{2I}{3\varepsilon^2}\right) \qquad (2)$$

In this case, the maximum value $\sigma_{max} \approx \pi e^4/2I^2$ at the energy of the incident electron $\varepsilon = 1.85I$.

For the first time, a semi-empirical formula for approximating the initial section $I < \varepsilon < 2I$ of the dependence of the ionization cross section on the energy of the incident electron was proposed by Compton and Van Voorhees in 1925 [13] $\sigma_{ionization}(\varepsilon) = C_i(\varepsilon - I)$. Wannier proposed a power dependence with the exponent equal to 1.127 to approximate the initial section: $\sigma_{ionization}(\varepsilon) = C_i(\varepsilon - I)^{1.127}$, $\varepsilon > I$, which takes into account the interaction of the free and bound electrons [14].

Lotz in [15,16] analyzed the experimental and theoretical data available at that time and proposed a formula based on the Bethe–Born approximation, which has the form

$$\sigma_{ionization}(x) = [A \ln x + \sum_{k=1}^{N} B_k (\Delta x/x)^k]/xI^2, \quad x = \varepsilon/I, \ \Delta x = x - 1, \ x > 1 \qquad (3)$$

Since the first ionization potential I can serve as a natural scale of energy in the collision of electron with atom, it is therefore convenient to introduce the dimensionless energy: $x = \varepsilon/I$, $\Delta x = x - 1$, $x > 1$, A, B_k—fitting constants. The Lotz Formula (3) takes into account the universal dependence of the cross section on the ionization potential and is consistent with the asymptotic behavior of the Bethe formula $\sigma_{ionization}(\varepsilon) = (B + A\ln\varepsilon)/\varepsilon I$ [17].

There are also a number of other approaches to calculating ionization cross sections. For example, in [18], the paper presents semi-classical formula which allows the satisfactory evaluation of ionization cross-section for ionization of atoms. Their formula consists of the classical binary encounter approximation and the Born–Bethe approximation. This approach is applied to the rare gases, atomic nitrogen, and fluorine. Their approach leads to a better agreement with experimental results than the previous classical and semi-classical methods.

A theoretical binary dipole (BED) model which does not contain adjustable parameters is considered in [19]. There is also considered a simplified version, the so-called binary-encounter-Bethe (BEB) model. Both types of cross sections approximations have three basic components: the electron exchange term, the hard collision term, and the dipole interaction term. The ratios between these components were determined by requiring the asymptotic total ionization cross section to agree with the asymptotic form given by the Bethe theory.

In [20], the cross sections are computed using a combination of spherical complex optical potential formalism and complex scattering potential method. The results obtained for thirteen elements are presented in the form of tabular values and are in good agreement with available measurements and theoretical data. However, it should be noted that this good agreement again has an error of the order of 10–30%, which corresponds to the scatter of values from different sources. In addition, in the model used, it is necessary to know the cross sections for elastic collisions, and to calculate the ionization cross sections, a relation is introduced between the ionization and excitation cross sections with three adjustable parameters for each type of atom. According to the authors of the work, the error in determining the maximum value of the ionization cross section and the position of this peak is of the order of 10%. We took their data for manganese, for which the approximation we obtained is in much better agreement with the dependence of the maximum of the ionization cross section on the polarizability and ionization potential given there.

In [21], the calculated cross sections are obtained for electron–atom scattering processes represented by a complex potential. For tungsten, ionization cross sections are discussed in the electron energy region from threshold up to 5000 eV against the available data from the Deutsch–Märk formalism [18] and a semi-empirical complex scattering potential. Papers [20,21] contain a rather detailed analysis of various approaches to calculating the cross sections for electron–atom collisions (elastic and inelastic), and data are also given on the most reliable (according to the authors) experimental data.

Since for the numerical simulation of many problems in plasma physics, the most convenient form of representing the dependence of the ionization cross sections on energy is the analytical dependence, then, we made an attempt to approximate the dependence of the ionization cross section on energy by the following new formula:

$$\sigma_{ionization}(\Delta x) = \frac{\alpha \Delta x}{(1 + \beta \Delta x)^\gamma} \tag{4}$$

where α, β, γ—fitting constants. For $\alpha = 4\pi a_0^2 R_y^2 / I^2$, $\beta = 1$, $\gamma = 2$, it coincides with Thomson's Formula (1). Usually, when approximating by the Lotz Formula (3), 2–3 terms are used, whereas in our Formula (4) there is only 1 term with 3 fitting factors. In addition, our formula does not use a logarithmic dependence, and the power dependence makes it much more convenient to use both for theoretical analysis and for computer simulation.

To determine the coefficients α, β, γ, the problem of minimizing the root-mean-square deviation of the cross sections from their experimental values was solved by the standard method of coordinate descent:

$$\Delta^2 = \frac{1}{N} \sum_{i=1}^{N} \left[\frac{\sigma_{fit}(x_i) - \sigma_{exp}(x_i)}{\sigma_{exp}(x_i)} \right]^2 \tag{5}$$

where Δ—standard deviation, $\sigma_{exp}(x_i)$—experimental values, $\sigma_{fit}(x_i)$—calculated values in points x_i: $i = 1, \ldots, N$. Minimizing the relative deviation $[\sigma_{fit}(x_i) - \sigma_{exp}(x_i)]/\sigma_{exp}(x_i)$ instead of minimizing the simple deviation $\sigma_{fit}(x_i) - \sigma_{exp}(x_i)$ has the advantage of giving the correct statistical weight to cross sections at low and high impact electron energy. The tables show the value of the standard deviation in a percentage.

3. Results

The characteristics of atoms and experimental data, the error and parameters of the approximation of the ionization cross sections, as well as the general characteristics of the ionization cross sections for the found approximations are collected in twelve columns of Tables 1–4. The first column contains the name of the element and atom number, then the static dipole polarizability and ionization potential, which characterize the properties of the outer electron shell of atoms. In the fourth and fifth columns are the energy range and the number of points of the experimental data used, then the standard deviation of the approximation and the values of the approximation coefficients of the ionization cross sections. In the tenth and eleventh columns are the position of the maximum cross-section and the maximum cross-section according to the approximating formula; in the twelfth is the constant of the linear approximation of the initial section $C_{ion} = \alpha/I$ obtained from Formula (4). The data in all the tables for α, β, γ, ε_m and $\sigma(\varepsilon_m)$ are received by us and are new.

Table 1. Characteristics of hydrogen atoms and alkali metals, error and parameters of approximation, general characteristics of cross sections according to the found approximations.

Atom			Experiment			Approximation			Cross Section Value		
No, Symbol	K_0, a^3_0	I, eV	$\varepsilon_1 \div \varepsilon_N$, eV	N	Δ, %	α, Å²	β	γ	ε_m, eV	$\sigma(\varepsilon_m)$, Å²	C_i, Å²/eV
1, H	4.5	13.595	14.6 ÷ 3998	10	2%	0.827	0.351	1.91	56.2	0.628	0.061
3, Li	162	5.392	50 ÷ 500	6	1%	5.72	0.500	1.67	21.5	3.71	1.06
11, Na	162	5.139	6 ÷ 50	21	3%	9.56	0.521	1.90	16.1	4.93	1.86
19, K	287	4.339	50 ÷ 500	6	2%	6.54	0.362	1.57	25.3	6.47	1.51
37, Rb	310	4.176	50 ÷ 500	6	7%	4.83	0.206	1.82	28.9	6.69	1.16
55, Cs	385	3.893	50 ÷ 500	6	3%	3.87	0.127	1.81	41.7	8.76	0.994

Table 2. Characteristics of noble gas atoms, error and parameters of approximation, general characteristics of cross sections according to the found approximations.

Atom			Experiment			Approximation			Cross Section Value		
No, Symbol	K_0, a^3_0	I, eV	$\varepsilon_1 \div \varepsilon_N$, eV	N	Δ, %	α, Å²	β	γ	ε_m, eV	$\sigma(\varepsilon_m)$, Å²	C_i, Å²/eV
2, He	1.383	24.587	30 ÷ 4000	21	3%	0.365	0.287	1.91	119	0.34	0.015
10, Ne	2.68	21.564	30 ÷ 4000	21	6%	0.373	0.136	2.00	180	0.68	0.017
18, Ar	11.08	15.759	20 ÷ 4000	23	3%	2.92	0.285	1.86	80	2.83	0.185
36, Kr	16.74	13.996	20 ÷ 4000	22	3%	3.51	0.269	1.80	79	3.80	0.251
54, Xe	27.06	12.127	15 ÷ 4000	23	6%	4.30	0.259	1.76	74	4.99	0.355

Table 3. Characteristics of atoms of transition metals, error and parameters of approximation, general characteristics of cross sections according to the found approximations.

Atom			Experiment			Approximation			Cross Section Value		
No, Symbol	K_0, a^3_0	I, eV	$\varepsilon_1 \div \varepsilon_N$, eV	N	Δ, %	α, Å²	β	γ	ε_m, eV	$\sigma(\varepsilon_m)$, Å²	C_i, Å²/eV
22, Ti	148	6.83	10 ÷ 10,000	18	4%	19.1	0.654	1.85	19.1	8.17	2.80
25, Mn	101	7.432	8.0 ÷ 2000	29	8%	8.39	0.413	1.62	36.4	6.9	1.13
26, Fe	88	7.90	9.0 ÷ 200	59	5%	14.8	1.15	1.44	23.5	5.3	1.87
28, Ni	67	7.663	10 ÷ 10,000	17	6%	6.04	0.405	1.86	29.7	4.12	0.787
29, Cu	40	7.724	9.0 ÷ 200	59	2%	6.86	0.645	1.52	31.0	4.0	0.891
46, Pd	-	8.33	10 ÷ 10,000	17	3%	3.09	0.146	1.89	72.3	5.7	0.371
47, Ag	67	7.574	8.0 ÷ 200	60	8%	7.65	0.565	1.46	36.7	5.45	1.01
74, W	115	7.98	15 ÷ 5000	17	6%	7.12	0.379	1.62	42.0	6.39	0.891
79, Au	-	9.223	16 ÷ 21,800	15	8%	16.5	0.265	1.86	49.7	17.2	1.79

Table 4. Characteristics of atoms of some metals, error and parameters of approximation, general characteristics of cross sections according to the found approximations.

Atom			Experiment				Approximation			Cross Section Value		
No, Symbol	K_0, a_0^3	I, eV	$\varepsilon_1 \div \varepsilon_N$, eV	N	Δ, %	α, Å^2	β	γ	ε_m, eV	$\sigma(\varepsilon_m)$, Å^2	C_i, Å^2/eV
4, Be	37.8	9.323	9.4 ÷ 112	28	13%	3.22	0.338	2.20	32.3	2.1	0.346
12, Mg	72	7.646	8.0 ÷ 200	60	3%	13.7	0.714	1.87	19.9	5.3	1.79
13, Al	162	5.986	6.0 ÷ 200	60	5%	11.6	0.337	1.80	28.2	9.97	1.93
14, Si	37	8.157	9.0 ÷ 200	59	4%	9.97	0.503	1.61	34.8	6.82	1.22
80, Hg	34.4	10.434	10.9 ÷ 29.2	36	20%	1.00	0.222	1.74	73.9	1.37	0.096
82, Pb	-	7.415	8.0 ÷ 200	60	7%	12.8	0.592	1.52	31.5	8.20	1.74
92, U	-	5.65	7.5 ÷ 500	30	19%	5.04	0.329	1.73	29.2	4.72	0.89

Table 1 shows the results for the alkali metals and hydrogen atoms, because the hydrogen atom has one electron on the outer shell, as well as alkali atoms. The standard deviation of the found approximations is of the order of 2–7%, which corresponds in order of magnitude to the error of the initial data.

As a reference in Table 2 shows, similar data for noble gases were obtained in our previous work [22].

Table 3 shows the results for atoms of some transition metals. The experimental and theoretical data for Ti, Ni, and Pd were taken from [23]; Mn—from [20]; Fe, Cu, Ag—from [24]; W—from [21]; Au—from [25].

Table 4 shows the results for atoms of some metals, which are often used in various technological processes as working materials (for example, in the processes of etching or sputtering in microelectronics). Metal vapors often appear in the plasma as impurities due to sputtering of structural elements of installations (walls, cathodes, etc.). Experimental and theoretical data for beryllium are taken from [26]; Mg, Al, Si, Pb—from [24]; Hg—[27]; U—[28].

The results shown in Tables 1–4 allow for a critical analysis of both experimental and theoretical-computational data. Moreover, by interpolation or extrapolation, they can be used to obtain an estimate of the ionization cross sections for metal vapors for which data are not available. In particular, for platinum, experiments with which are carried out in a gyrotron discharge [29], the following values of the coefficients for approximating the cross sections can be recommended: $\alpha = 12$, $\beta = 0.32$, $\gamma = 1.72$.

4. Discussion

The experimental data and the approximating curves are shown in Figures 1–6 for H, Li, Na, K, Rb and Cs, respectively. In all plots, the experimental and theoretical values of the cross sections are shown by markers, and the solid curve is the found approximations. In addition, all figures show the values of the errors of the corresponding approximations. Solid curves in all the figures are original and obtained in this work.

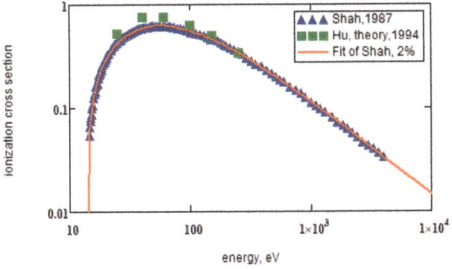

Figure 1. Electron impact ionization cross sections of hydrogen in Å^2.

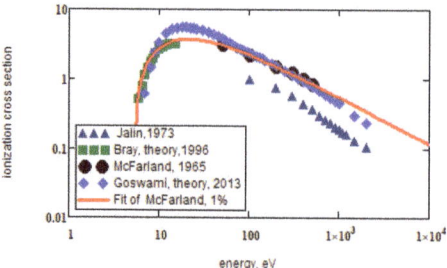

Figure 2. Electron impact ionization cross sections of lithium in $Å^2$.

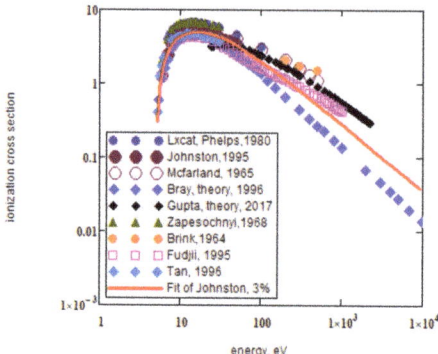

Figure 3. Electron impact ionization cross sections of sodium in $Å^2$.

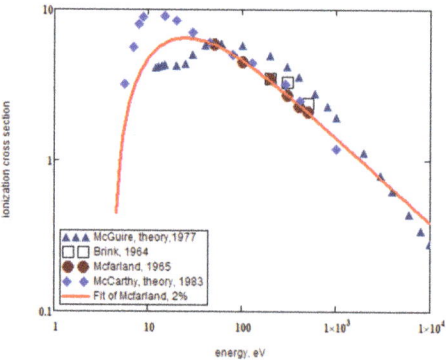

Figure 4. Electron impact ionization of potassium in $Å^2$.

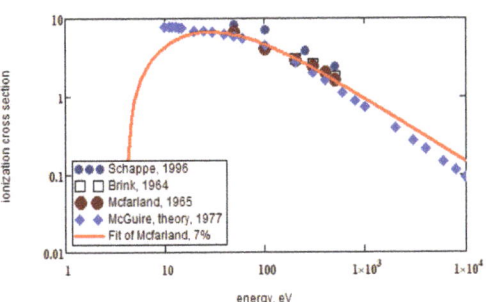

Figure 5. Electron impact ionization cross sections of rubidium in Å^2.

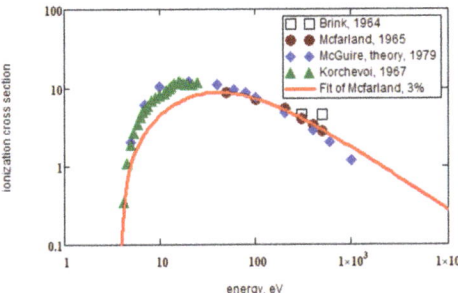

Figure 6. Electron impact ionization cross sections of cesium in Å^2.

Hydrogen. For hydrogen, there are many data, both theoretical and experimental, obtained with good accuracy. Figure 1 shows the data from the works [30,31]. The approximation coefficients for the values of the ionization cross sections from [30] are in Table 1.

Lithium. The data for lithium ionization cross sections are taken from [32–35] and are shown in Figure 2. The approximation is made for the values of the cross sections from [32]. In this work, there are only 6 experimental values, but the obtained approximation is in very good agreement with the data from [34] for low (<15 eV) energies. Therefore, we have chosen these data to determine the coefficients of analytical approximation of the ionization cross section.

Sodium. For sodium, there are many data [32,34,36–42]. They are shown in Figure 3. A large scatter is observed for energies above 100 eV. For the approximation, the ionization cross sections were taken from [38]. The obtained approximation is in good agreement with the majority of other authors even at $\varepsilon > 100$ eV.

Potassium. Data from the works [32,36,37,43] were analyzed for potassium; they are shown in Figure 4. The approximation is made for the values of the cross sections from [32].

Rubidium. The data for the ionization cross sections of rubidium were taken from the works [32,36,37,44]. The approximation is made for the data from [32]; see Figure 5.

Cesium. The data for the ionization cross sections of cesium were taken from the works [32,36,45,46]. The approximation is made for the data from [32]. This approximation is in good agreement with the theory [45] in the range 40 eV < ε < 150 eV; see Figure 6.

Thus, in this work, based on a review and critical analysis of the available experimental and theoretical data on the cross sections of electron impact ionization of alkali metal and hydrogen atoms, we have suggested new analytical approximation formula that have an error of the same order of magnitude as the experimental data. As preliminary results, similar analytical approximations were obtained for the ionization cross sections of atoms of some transition metals, and for atoms of some other metals, which are often used in various technological processes as working materials.

Author Contributions: R.I.G. performed fitting calculations, S.A.M. performed modeling. All authors equally contributed to preparation of the manuscript. All authors have read and agreed to the published version of the manuscript.

Funding: This work was funded by the State Assignment GZ BV10-2021 "Study of Innovative Synthesis of Micro- and Nanoparticles with a Controllable Composition and Structure Based on Microwave Discharge in Gyrotron Radiation".

Institutional Review Board Statement: Not applicable.

Informed Consent Statement: Not applicable.

Data Availability Statement: Numerical data for cross sections can be obtained from the authors upon request.

Conflicts of Interest: The authors declare no conflict of interest.

References

1. Huxley, G.H.; Crompton, R.W. *The Diffusion and Drift of Electrons in Gases*; Wiley: New York, NY, USA, 1974.
2. Petrović, Z.; Dujko, S.; Marić, D.; Malović, G.; Nikitović, Z.; Šašić, O.; Jovanović, J.; Stojanović, V.; Radmilović-Radenović, M.J. Measurement and interpretation of swarm parameters and their application in plasma modelling. *Phys. D Appl. Phys.* **2009**, *42*, 194002. [CrossRef]
3. Carbone, E.; Graef, W.; Hagelaar, G.; Boer, D.; Hopkins, M.; Stephens, J.; Yee, B.; Pancheshnyi, S.; van Dijk, J.; Pitchford, L.; et al. Data Needs for Modeling Low-Temperature Non-Equilibrium Plasmas: The LXCat Project, History, Perspectives and a Tutorial. *Atoms* **2021**, *9*, 16. [CrossRef]
4. Dutton, J. A survey of electron swarm data. *J. Phys. Chem. Ref. Data* **1975**, *4*, 577–856. [CrossRef]
5. Zecca, A.; Karwasz, G.P.; Brusa, R.S. One century of experiments on electron-atom and molecule scattering: A critical review of integral cross-sections. *Riv. Nuovo* **1996**, *19*, 1–146. [CrossRef]
6. Brusa, R.S.; Karwasz, G.P.; Zecca, A. Analytical partitioning of total cross sections for scattaring on noble gases. *Z. Für Phys. D At. Mol. Clust.* **1996**, *38*, 279287. [CrossRef]
7. Mayorov, S.A. Calculation of characterisctics of electron drift in neon under a dc electric field. *Bull. Lebedev Phys. Inst.* **2009**, *36*, 299–304. [CrossRef]
8. Kodanova, S.K.; Bastikova, N.K.; Ramazanov, T.S.; Maiorov, S.A. Drift of electrons in gas in spatially inhomogeneous periodic electric field. *Ukr. J. Phys.* **2014**, *59*, 371. [CrossRef]
9. Mayorov, S.A. Electron transport coefficients in a helium–xenon mixture. *Bull. Lebedev Phys. Inst.* **2014**, *41*, 285–291. [CrossRef]
10. Golyatina, R.I.; Maiorov, S.A. Characteristics of electron drift in an Ar–Hg Mixture. *Plasma Phys. Rep.* **2018**, *44*, 453–457. [CrossRef]
11. Thomson, J.J. XLII. Ionization by moving electrified particles. *Lond. Edinb. Dublin Pilos. Mag. Philos. J. Sci.* **1912**, *23*, 449–457. [CrossRef]
12. Gryziński, M. Two-Particle Collisions. I. General Relations for Collisions in the Laboratory System. *Phys. Rev.* **1965**, *138*, A305–A321. [CrossRef]
13. Compton, K.T.; Van Voorhis, C.C. Probability of Ionization of Gas Molecules by Electron Impacts. II Critique. *Phys. Rev.* **1926**, *27*, 724–731. [CrossRef]
14. Wannier, G.H. The Threshold Law for Single Ionization of Atoms or Ions by Electrons. *Phys. Rev.* **1953**, *90*, 817–825. [CrossRef]
15. Lotz, W.Z. An Empirical Formula for the Electron-Impact Ionization Cross-Section. *Physik* **1967**, *206*, 205–211. [CrossRef]
16. Lotz, W.Z. Electron-Impact Ionization Cross-Sections for Atoms up to Z = 108. *Physik* **1970**, *232*, 101–107. [CrossRef]
17. Sobel'man, I.I.; Vainshtein, L.A.; Yukov, E.A. *Excitation of Atoms and Broadening of Spectral Lines*; Springer Series on Atomic Optical and Plasma Physics; Springer: Berlin/Heidelberg, Germany, 1995; Volume 15. [CrossRef]
18. Deutsch, H.; Mark, T.D. Calculation of absolute electron impact ionization cross-section functions for single ionization of He, Ne, Ar, Kr, Xe, N and F. *Int. J. Mass Spectrom. Ion Process.* **1987**, *79*, Rl–R8. [CrossRef]
19. Yong-Ki, K.; Rudd, M. Eugene Binary-encounter-dipole model for electron-impact ionization. *Phys. Rev. A* **1994**, *50*, 3954–3967.
20. Kaur, J.; Gupta, D.; Naghma, R.; Ghoshal, D.; Antony, B. Electron impact ionization cross sections of atoms. *Can. J. Phys.* **2015**, *93*, 617–625. [CrossRef]
21. Blanco, F.; da Silva, F.F.; Limão-Vieira, P.; García, G. Electron scattering cross section data for tungsten and beryllium atoms from 0.1 to 5000 eV. *Plasma Sources Sci. Technol.* **2017**, *26*, 085004. [CrossRef]
22. Golyatina, R.I.; Maiorov, S.A. Analytical approximation of cross sections of collisions of electrons with atoms of inert gases. *Phys. Sci. Technol.* **2021**, *8*, 4–13. [CrossRef]
23. McGuire, E.J. Electron ionization cross sections in the Born approximation. *Phys. Rev. A* **1977**, *16*, 62–72. [CrossRef]
24. Freund, R.S.; Wetzel, R.C.; Shul, R.J.; Hayes, T.R. Cross-section measurements for electron-impact ionization of atoms. *Phys. Rev. A* **1990**, *41*, 3575–3595. [CrossRef]

25. Povyshev, V.M.; Sadovoy, A.A.; Shevelko, V.P.; Shirkov, G.D.; Vasina, E.G.; Vatulin, V.V. Electron-Impact Ionization Cross Sections of H, He, N, O, AR, XE, AU, PB Atoms and Their Ions in the Electron Energy Range from the Threshold up to 200 kev. JINR Preprint E9-2001-148. 2001, pp. 1–48. Available online: http://www1.jinr.ru/Preprints/2001/e9-2001-148.pdf (accessed on 1 August 2020).
26. Database BSR (Quantum-Mechanical Calculations by O. Zatsarinny and K. Bartschat). Available online: www.lxcat.net/BSR (accessed on 1 August 2020).
27. Database Siglo. Available online: www.lxcat.net/SIGLO (accessed on 1 August 2020).
28. Halle, J.C.; Lo, H.H.; Fite, W.L. Ionization of uranium atoms by electron impact. *Phys. Rev. A* **1981**, *23*, 1708–1716. [CrossRef]
29. Skvortsova, N.N.; Maiorov, S.A.; Malakhov, D.V.; Stepakhin, V.D.; Obraztsova, E.A.; Kenzhebekova, A.I.; Shishilov, O.N. On the dust structures and chain reactions induced over the regolith by gyrotron radiation. *JETP Lett.* **2019**, *109*, 441–448. [CrossRef]
30. Shah, M.B.; Elliott, D.S.; Gilbody, H.B. Pulsed crossed-beam study of the ionisation of atomic hydrogen by electron impact. *J. Phys. B At. Mol. Phys* **1987**, *20*, 3501–3514. [CrossRef]
31. Hu, W.; Fang, D.; Wang, Y.; Yang, F. Electron-impact-ionization cross section for the hydrogen atom. *Phys. Rev. A* **1994**, *49*, 989–991. [CrossRef]
32. McFarland, R.H.; Kinney, J.D. Absolute cross sections of lithium and other alkali metal atoms for ionization by electrons. *Phys. Rev.* **1965**, *137*, 1058–1061.
33. Jalin, R.; Hagemann, R.; Botter, R. Absolute electron impact ionization cross sections of Li in the energy range from 100 to 2000 eV. *J. Chem. Phys.* **1973**, *59*, 952–959. [CrossRef]
34. Bray, I.; Fursa, D.V. Calculation of ionization within the close-coupling formalism. *Phys. Rev. A* **1996**, *54*, 2991–3004. [CrossRef] [PubMed]
35. Goswami, B.; Saikia, U.; Naghma, R.; Antony, B. Electron impact total ionization cross sections for plasma wall coating elements. *Chin. J. Phys.* **2013**, *51*, 1172–1183.
36. Brink, G.O. Absolute ionization cross sections of the alkali metals. *Phys. Rev.* **1964**, *134*, 345–346. [CrossRef]
37. Database Phelps, A.V. Available online: www.lxcat.net/PHELPS (accessed on 1 August 2020).
38. Johnston, A.R.; Burrow, F.D. Electron-impact ionization of Na. *Phys. Rev. A* **1995**, *51*, R1735–R1737. [CrossRef]
39. Bhatt, P.; Gupta, S.P. Scattering ionization cross section of Sodium atom by electron impact etching. *IRJMST* **2017**, *8*, 248–255.
40. Zapesochnyi, I.P.; Aleksakhin, I.S. Ionization of alkali-metal atoms by slow electrons. *Zh. Eksp. Teor. Fiz.* **1968**, *55*, 76–85. Available online: http://www.jetp.ras.ru/cgi-bin/dn/e_028_01_0041.pdf (accessed on 1 August 2020).
41. Fujii, K.; Srivastava, S.K. A measurement of the electron-impact ionization cross section of sodium. *J. Phys. B At. Mol. Opt. Phys.* **1995**, *28*, L559–L563. [CrossRef]
42. Tan, W.S.; Shi, Z.; Ying, C.H.; Vuskovic´, L. Electron-impact ionization of laser-excited sodium atom. *Phyz. Rev. A* **1996**, *54*, R3710–R3713. [CrossRef]
43. McCarthy, I.E.; Stelbovlcs, A.T. Ionization: Test of a continuum optical model for electron scattering. *Phys. Rev. A* **1983**, *28*, 1328. [CrossRef]
44. Schappe, R.S.; Walker, T.; Anderson, L.W.; Lin, C.C. Absolute Electron-Impact Ionization Cross Section Measurements Using a Magneto-Optical Trap. *Phys. Rev. Lett.* **1996**, *76*, 4328–4331. [CrossRef] [PubMed]
45. McGuire, E.J. Scaled electron ionization cross sections in the Born approximation for atoms with $55 \leq Z \leq 102$. *Phys. Rev. A* **1979**, *20*, 445–456. [CrossRef]
46. Korchevoi, Y.P.; Przhonskii, A.M. Effective Electron Impact Excitation and Ionization Cross Sections for Cesium, Rubidium, and Potassium Atoms in the Pre-threshold Region. *Sov. Phys. JETP* **1967**, *24*, 1089. Available online: http://www.jetp.ras.ru/cgi-bin/dn/e_024_06_1089.pdf (accessed on 1 August 2020).

Article

Binary-Encounter Model for Direct Ionization of Molecules by Positron-Impact

Małgorzata Franz [1,*,†], Katarzyna Wiciak-Pawłowska [1,*,†] and Jan Franz [1,2,*,†]

1. Faculty of Applied Physics and Mathematics, Gdańsk University of Technology, 80-233 Gdańsk, Poland
2. Advanced Materials Center, Gdańsk University of Technology, 80-233 Gdańsk, Poland
* Correspondence: malobaro@pg.edu.pl (M.F.); katarzyna.pawlowska@pg.edu.pl (K.W.-P.); janfranz@pg.edu.pl (J.F.)
† These authors contributed equally to this work.

Abstract: We introduce two models for the computation of direct ionization cross sections by positron impact over a wide range of collision energies. The models are based on the binary-encounter-Bethe model and take into account an extension of the Wannier theory. The cross sections computed with these models show good agreement with experimental data. The extensions improve the agreement between theory and experiment for collision energies between the first ionization threshold and the peak of the cross section. The models are based on a small set of parameters, which can be computed with standard quantum chemistry program packages.

Keywords: positron impact ionization; positron-molecule scattering; binary-encounter-Bethe

Citation: Franz, M.; Wiciak-Pawłowska, K.; Franz, J. Binary-Encounter Model for Direct Ionization of Molecules by Positron-Impact. *Atoms* **2021**, *9*, 99. https://doi.org/10.3390/atoms9040099

Academic Editor: Grzegorz Piotr Karwasz

Received: 24 October 2021
Accepted: 20 November 2021
Published: 24 November 2021

Publisher's Note: MDPI stays neutral with regard to jurisdictional claims in published maps and institutional affiliations.

Copyright: © 2021 by the authors. Licensee MDPI, Basel, Switzerland. This article is an open access article distributed under the terms and conditions of the Creative Commons Attribution (CC BY) license (https://creativecommons.org/licenses/by/4.0/).

1. Introduction

We present two new models for the computation of cross sections for direct ionization of atoms and molecules by positron-impact. Positrons can ionize atoms and molecules by direct annihilation, positronium (Ps) formation and direct ionization. It is difficult to distinguish these channels in scattering experiments. As a consequence, the recent review articles by Brunger et al. [1] and Ratnavelu et al. [2] show only the sum of the cross sections for Ps-formation and direct ionization for the majority of targets. This shows the need for the development of an accurate theoretical model for the computation of the cross sections for direct ionization. Such a model can be used to deduct the cross section for Ps-formation from cross sections that cannot distinguish between different ionization channels.

For electron-impact ionization, Kim and Rudd [3,4] developed the binary-encounter-Bethe (BEB) model. In this model, the binary-encounter version of the Mott cross section for hard collisions at low collision energies is joined with the Bethe model for soft collisions at high collisions energies. The model gives ionization cross sections for molecules that contain light atoms with an accuracy of 10 percent over an energy range from the ionization threshold up to a few thousand electron volts. Another advantage of the BEB model is that it requires only quantities, which can be computed with standard quantum chemistry computer program packages. An attractive feature of this model is that it is free of any fitting parameters.

In order to formulate a BEB model for positron impact ionization, the similarities and differences between electron and positron impact have to be taken into account. For high collision energies—above a few hundred eV—the cross sections for both projectiles are similar. For positron-impact ionization, there is no exchange interaction between the projectile and the target. For energies close to the ionization threshold, the cross sections for electron and positron impact ionization are expected to be different because of the different charges of the projectiles. In the case of electron impact ionization, two electrons are ejected in opposite directions because of electron–electron repulsion. In contrast, after ionization by positron impact, an electron and a positron move in the same direction because of the mutual attraction (see, e.g., Chapter 5 in Charlton and Humberston [5]). Klar [6] showed, using Wannier theory [7], that, just above the ionization threshold, the cross sections for electron-impact and positron impact follow a power law of the type

$$\sigma(E) \propto (E-B)^{-\alpha}. \tag{1}$$

Here, E is the energy of the incoming projectile and B is the binding energy of the ejected electron. The exponent α has the value 1.127 if the projectile is an electron and 2.651 if the projectile is a positron. Recently Fedus and Karwasz [8] derived a binary-encounter-Bethe (BEB) model for positron-impact ionization. Their model is very similar to the BEB model of Kim and Rudd [3] for electron-impact ionization, but without the term describing the electron-exchange interaction. Furthermore Fedus and Karwasz [8] take the Wannier threshold law into account to correct the cross section for collision energies close to the ionization threshold. This is discussed in more detail in Section 2.

Rost and Heller [9] derived a similar threshold law with the help of semi-classical Feynman path integrals and predicted that the Wannier-type threshold law for positron impact is valid for energies up to about 3 eV above the ionization threshold. In order to increase the validity of the Wannier theory towards higher energies, Ihra et al. [10] extended it with unharmonic corrections. They derived a threshold law of the form

$$\sigma(E) \propto (E-B)^{-\alpha} e^{-\beta\sqrt{(E-B)}}, \tag{2}$$

with the values $\alpha = 2.640$ and $\beta = 0.73$. This equation agrees very well for energies up to 10 eV above threshold with the experimental data of Ashley et al. [11] for the cross section for positron-impact ionization of helium. More recently, Jansen et al. [12] extended this approach by including the contribution from higher partial waves, whereas Ihra et al. [10] considered only the lowest partial wave ($L = 0$), Jansen et al. [12] included the first 4 partial waves and found a large contribution from the D-wave. Their final expression for the threshold law is similar to the expression from Ihra et al. [10] but with the parameters $\alpha = 2.640$ and $\beta = 0.489$.

The purpose of this paper is to generalize the BEB-model for positrons [8] to follow the threshold law derived by Ihra et al. [10] with the parameters given in Jansen et al. [12]. In Section 2, we present the two theoretical models of Fedus and Karwasz [8], and two new models, which fulfill the threshold law of Jansen et al. [12]. In Section 3, we show comparisons between the theory and all recommended direct ionization cross section listed in the review by Brunger et al. [1]. In Section 4, the paper ends with conclusions.

2. Theoretical Model

The total cross section for direct ionization by positron impact can be written as the sum of the partial ionization cross sections for the n_{occ} occupied orbitals

$$\sigma(E) = \sum_i^{n_{occ}} \sigma_i(E). \tag{3}$$

Here, $\sigma_i(E)$ is the partial ionization cross section for ionization from orbital i. Each of them will be computed with the BEB models described below.

2.1. BEB-0 Model

Following the BEB model of Fedus and Karwasz [8], the partial ionization cross section is given by

$$\sigma_i^{BEB}(E) = \frac{S_i}{E + U_i + B_i} \frac{B_i}{E} \left[(E - B_i) + \frac{1}{2E}(E - B_i)(E + B_i) \ln \frac{E}{B_i} \right]. \tag{4}$$

Here, E is the kinetic energy of the incoming positron, B_i is the electron binding energy in orbital i and U_i is the expectation value of the kinetic energy of the bound electron in orbital i. Here, all energies are given in eV. The energy-independent prefactor is given by

$$S_i = 4\pi a_0^2 N_i \left(\frac{R}{B_i}\right)^2, \tag{5}$$

where $a_0 = 0.529 \times 10^{-10}$ m is the Bohr radius, N_i is the occupation number of the orbital and $R = 13.6$ eV is the Rydberg constant.

With the introduction of the reduced variables

$$t_i = \frac{E}{B_i} \quad \text{and} \quad u_i = \frac{U_i}{B_i} \tag{6}$$

the cross section can be written in the compact form, which we will refer to as BEB-0 model

$$\sigma_i^{\text{BEB-0}} = \frac{S_i}{t_i + u_i + 1}\left[\frac{\ln t_i}{2}\left(1 - \frac{1}{t_i^2}\right) + 1 - \frac{1}{t_i}\right]. \tag{7}$$

2.2. BEB-W Model

Fedus and Karwasz [8] introduced a scaling function in the denominator of the term in front of the brackets on the right hand side of Equation (7). This term regulates the behavior of the cross section at energies closely above the ionization threshold and ensures that the cross section follows the Wannier law. In the following, we call this the BEB-W model. The partial cross section is given by

$$\sigma_i^{\text{BEB-W}} = \frac{S_i}{t_i + u_i + 1 + f_i^{\text{W}}}\left[\frac{\ln t_i}{2}\left(1 - \frac{1}{t_i^2}\right) + 1 - \frac{1}{t_i}\right]. \tag{8}$$

Here, the scaling function is given by

$$f_i^{\text{W}} = \frac{C}{(t_i - 1)^{1.65}}. \tag{9}$$

Here, the exponent 1.65 follows from the exponent in the Wannier theory of Klar [6]. The exact value of the constant C is not known, and the Wannier law gives only the proportionality of the cross section. In practical application, a value of $C = 1$ is chosen [8].

2.3. BEB-A Model

In a similar way, we can modify the BEB-0 model so that it fulfills the threshold law derived by Jansen et al. [12]. We define the following expression as the BEB-A model

$$\sigma_i^{\text{BEB-A}} = \frac{S_i}{t_i + u_i + 1 + f_i^{\text{A}}}\left[\frac{\ln t_i}{2}\left(1 - \frac{1}{t_i^2}\right) + 1 - \frac{1}{t_i}\right]. \tag{10}$$

Here, we introduced the scaling function

$$f_i^{\text{A}} = \frac{C'}{(t_i - 1)^{\alpha - 1} e^{-\beta_i \sqrt{t_i - 1}}}, \tag{11}$$

where $\alpha = 2.640$. We choose the constant $C' = 1$; its value is not specified by the threshold law by Jansen et al. [12]. Here, we introduced the value

$$\beta_i = 0.489\sqrt{\frac{B_i}{2R}}, \tag{12}$$

which depends on the orbital i. This follows from the use of the reduced kinetic energy t_i in the expression for the cross section, instead of the excess kinetic energy $\Delta E = E - B_i$ as in the formulation of the threshold law.

2.4. BEB-B Model

The BEB-0 model can be modified in different ways to fulfill the threshold law of Jansen et al. [12]. An alternative is the introduction of an additional term in the brackets on the right hand side of Equation (7). We suggest the following expression for the partial ionization cross section, which we will call BEB-B model.

$$\sigma_i^{\text{BEB-B}} = \frac{S_i}{t_i + u_i + 1} \left[\frac{\ln t_i}{2} \left(1 - \frac{1}{t_i^2}\right) + h_i(t_i)\left(1 - \frac{1}{t_i}\right) + g_i(t_i)\left(1 - \frac{1}{t_i}\right)^\alpha \right]. \quad (13)$$

Here, the prefactor in the additional term is given by

$$g_i(t_i) = C_i e^{-\beta_i \sqrt{t_i - 1}}, \quad (14)$$

where the coefficients C_i are not specified by the threshold law, and we set them equal to 1. The product of the two terms is exactly the threshold law of Jansen et al. [12]. The exponential factor decreases for increasing energies and switches this term off for high energies. The function

$$h_i(t_i) = 1 - g_i(t_i) \quad (15)$$

switches on the second term in the brackets at collision energies, for which the cross section reaches its maximum value.

3. Results and Discussion

In the review by Brunger et al. [1], cross sections for direct ionization are recommended only for the four molecules: hydrogen (H_2), nitrogen (N_2), oxygen (O_2) and carbon monoxide (CO). In the following, we present results for all four molecules.

3.1. Molecular Hydrogen

The review by Brunger et al. [1] recommends for the direct ionization of molecular hydrogen by positron impact the experimental cross section data from Fromme et al. [13]. In these experiments the authors did not distinguish between the channels for direct ionization and Ps-formation. More recent experiments by Jacobsen et al. [14] took great care to distinguish between these different channels. For energies up to 100 eV, their cross section is about 30 percent lower than the values from Fromme et al. [13]. Recent calculations by Utamuratov et al. [15] with the convergent close-coupling (CCC) method are closer to the data from Jacobsen et al. [14] than to the data from Fromme et al. [13]. Therefore, we compare the results from the various BEB models with the data from Jacobsen et al. [14].

In Figure 1, we compare the cross sections for direct ionization from hydrogen molecules. The figure shows the computed cross section, which we obtained with the four BEB models, the experimental data from Jacobsen et al. [14] and the calculations by Utamuratov et al. [15] with the CCC method. In our calculations, we used the molecular parameters listed in the Hwang et al. [4], which are the same as those used by Fedus and Karwasz [8]. Therefore curves for BEB-0 and BEB-W are identical to those by Fedus and Karwasz [8]. The BEB-0 model gives the largest cross sections. The second largest cross sections are computed by the BEB-W model, followed by the BEB-B and BEB-A models. Close to the threshold, the BEB-B model gives slightly larger cross sections than the BEB-W model. For collision energies above 200 eV, all four BEB models give nearly identical cross sections. All of them are slightly larger than the experimental cross sections. For collision energies below 100 eV, the BEB-0 and BEB-W models overestimate the cross section, whereas the BEB-A and BEB-B models are very close to the experimental points. The cross sections computed with the CCC method overestimate the experimental cross sections for collision energies up to 100 eV. Here, results from the CCC method are very close to those obtained with the BEB-0 model. Between 100 eV and 500 eV, the CCC-results are close to the experimental data. Above 500 eV, they are close to the results from the four BEB models and are higher than the experimental values.

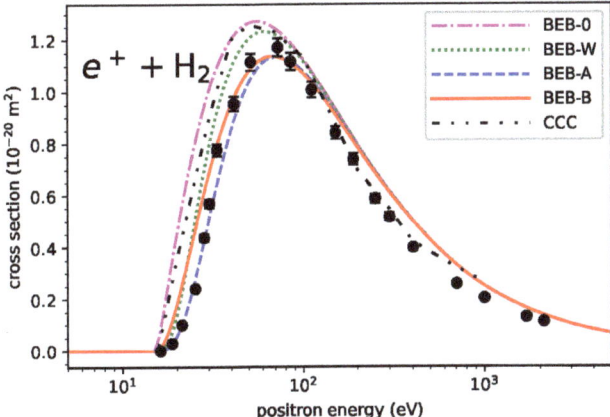

Figure 1. Direct ionization cross sections from H_2 molecules by positron impact. The results from calculations with the four different BEB models are shown by the magenta dash-dotted line (BEB-0 model), the green dotted line (BEB-W model), the blue dashed line (BEB-A model) and the solid red line (BEB-B model). The data from the calculations by Utamuratov et al. [15] with the CCC method are shown by the black dash-dotted-dotted line. Also shown are the experimental data (solid black circles with error-bars) from Jacobsen et al. [14]. The error-bars correspond to the experimental uncertainties of 3 per cent given by Jacobsen et al. [14].

3.2. Molecular Nitrogen

In Figure 2, we show the cross sections for direct ionization of molecular nitrogen by positron impact computed with the four BEB models. Also shown is the experimental data set from Marler and Surko [16], which is recommended in the review by Brunger et al. [1]. In the calculations with the BEB models, we used the molecular parameters listed in the Hwang et al. [4], which are also used by Fedus and Karwasz [8]. The BEB-0 model gives the largest cross sections, followed by the BEB-W model. The BEB-A and BEB-B model give nearly the same cross sections over the whole energy range. For collision energies above 200 eV, all four BEB-models give very similar cross sections. For collision energies below 100 eV, the BEB-0 and BEB-W models overestimate the cross section, whereas the BEB-A and BEB-B models are very close to the experimental values.

3.3. Molecular Oxygen

In Figure 3, we show the cross sections for direct ionization of molecular oxygen by positron impact computed with the various BEB models. As for molecular nitrogen, we show in the same figure the experimental data set from Marler and Surko [16], which is recommended in the review by Brunger et al. [1]. In the calculations with the BEB models, we used the molecular parameters given in the Hwang et al. [4]. These same values for these parameters are used by Fedus and Karwasz [8]. As observed for hydrogen and nitrogen, the BEB-0 model gives the largest cross sections, followed by the BEB-W model, followed by the BEB-A and BEB-B models, which give very similar results. For collision energies above 200 eV, the cross sections obtained with the four BEB-models are nearly identical. For collision energies below 100 eV, all four models are close to the experimental values and within the experimental uncertainties.

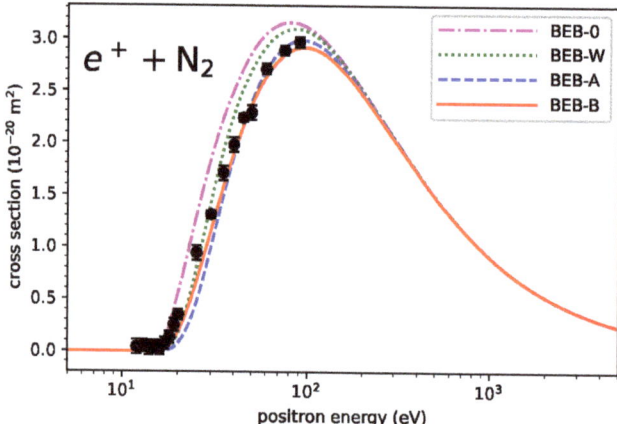

Figure 2. Direct ionization cross sections from N_2 molecules by positron impact. The results from calculations with the four different BEB models are shown by the magenta dash-dotted line (BEB-0 model), the green dotted line (BEB-W model), the blue dashed line (BEB-A model) and the solid red line (BEB-B model). Also shown are the experimental data (solid black circles with error-bars) from Marler and Surko [16]. The values of the error-bars show the experimental uncertainties are taken from the Table 12 in the review by Brunger et al. [1].

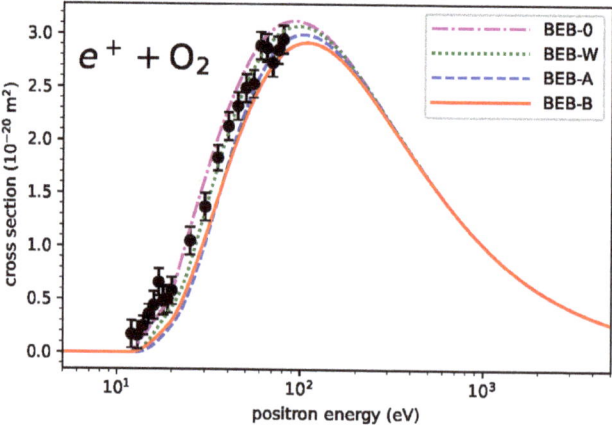

Figure 3. Direct ionization cross sections from O_2 molecules by positron impact. The results from calculations with the four different BEB models are shown by the magenta dash-dotted line (BEB-0 model), the green dotted line (BEB-W model), the blue dashed line (BEB-A model) and the solid red line (BEB-B model). Also shown are the experimental data (solid black circles with error-bars) from Marler and Surko [16]. The values of the error-bars show the experimental uncertainties are taken from the Table 15 in the review by Brunger et al. [1].

3.4. Carbon Monoxide

In Figure 4, we show the cross sections for direct ionization of carbon monoxide by positron impact. The results from calculations with the four different BEB models are shown together with the experimental data set from Marler and Surko [16], which is again the recommended data set in the review by Brunger et al. [1]. As already observed for the other targets, the BEB-0 model gives the largest cross section, followed by the BEB-W model. The cross sections computed with the BEB-A and BEB-B models are the smallest ones in this set and are very similar to each other. Above 200 eV, all four models give nearly identical results. The experimental data from Marler and Surko [16] are only available from the ionization threshold up to about 100 eV. For this target, the BEB-0 model agrees best with the available experimental data. The reason for the inferior performance of the BEB-A and BEB-B models might be due to the dipole moment of the carbon monoxide molecule. The threshold laws of Jansen et al. [12] have been derived for the ionization of atoms that are non-polar species. However, one should also keep in mind that there is a larger spread among the experimental data points than the other targets, and no experimental uncertainties are available for this set of data in Marler and Surko [16] or in the review by Brunger et al. [1].

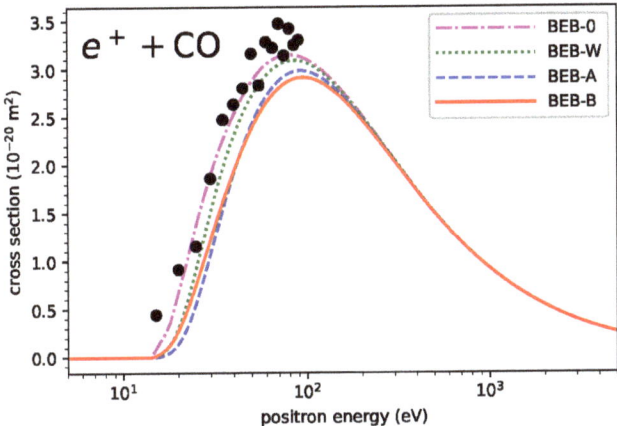

Figure 4. Direct ionization cross sections from CO molecules by positron impact. The results from calculations with the four different BEB models are shown by the magenta dash-dotted line (BEB-0 model), the green dotted line (BEB-W model), the blue dashed line (BEB-A model) and the solid red line (BEB-B model). Also shown are the experimental data (solid black circles) from Marler and Surko [16].

4. Conclusions

We introduced two binary-encounter Bethe models (BEB-A and BEB-B) for the calculation of cross sections for direct ionization of molecules by positron impact. Both models fulfill the threshold laws, derived by Jansen et al. [12]. We compared these models with the BEB-0 and BEB-W models from Fedus and Karwasz [8]. In the energy range from ionization threshold up to the maximum of the cross section around 100 eV, the BEB-A and BEB-B models show better agreement with the available experimental data for molecular hydrogen and nitrogen. For molecular oxygen, the cross sections computed with all four BEB models are within the experimental uncertainties. Carbon monoxide is the only polar molecule in the test set. Here, the BEB-0 model performs best, followed by the BEB-W model. This suggests that the influence of the dipole moment on the ionization cross section is important for energies from the ionization threshold up to the peak of the cross section.

Only a very limited number of cross sections for direct ionization by positron impact have been measured [1,2]. Furthermore, ab initio calculations are only available for the hydrogen molecule [15]. It is not expected that this situation will change in the next few years, because of the difficulty to distinguish direct ionization and Ps-formation channels experimentally. Taking into account the limitations, our present conclusions are: the BEB-A and BEB-B models are the best models for the calculation of cross sections for direct ionization by positron impact from non-polar molecules, and for polar molecules, the BEB-0 model seems to be the most reliable method.

There are more experimental data available for total ionization cross sections, which are the sums of cross sections for direct ionization and Ps-formation [1]. The BEB models discussed in this paper can be useful to extract the cross section for Ps-formation from this data.

Recently we suggested [17] to build up a database with cross sections for positron collision with molecules of biological interest. In the past few years, we computed elastic cross sections for various biomolecules [18–21]. The BEB model from this paper will enable us to fill the database with more data.

In two other recent publications [22,23], we computed elastic cross sections with the R-matrix method [24] and substracted them from the experimental total cross sections [1]. With this procedure, we obtained the sum of the cross sections for Ps-formation, direct ionization and other inelastic processes (e.g., electronic excitation). The BEB-model from this paper can help to disentangle the data further. Such cross section data are important for simulations of the effects of ion-beams on biological materials that are currently limited to secondary electrons (see, e.g., Taioli et al. [25]).

Author Contributions: Conceptualization, M.F. and J.F.; methodology, M.F., K.W.-P. and J.F.; software, M.F., K.W.-P. and J.F.; validation, M.F., K.W.-P. and J.F.; formal analysis, M.F., K.W.-P. and J.F.; investigation, M.F., K.W.-P. and J.F.; resources, M.F.; data curation, J.F.; writing—original draft preparation, M.F., K.W.-P. and J.F.; writing—review and editing, M.F.; visualization, M.F., K.W.-P. and J.F.; supervision, J.F.; project administration, J.F.; funding acquisition, J.F. All authors have read and agreed to the published version of the manuscript.

Funding: The research has been supported by the computer centres WCSS (Wroclawskie Centrum Sieciowo-Superkomputerowe, Politechnika Wroclawska) through grant number KDM-408 and CI TASK (Centrum Informatyczne Trójmiejskiej Akademickiej Sieci Komputerowej, Politechnika Gdańska).

Institutional Review Board Statement: Not applicable.

Informed Consent Statement: Not applicable.

Data Availability Statement: The data that support the findings of this study will be soon openly available in the MOST Wiedzy repository (https://mostwiedzy.pl/en/open-research-data/catalog, accessed on 22 November 2021).

Conflicts of Interest: The authors declare no conflict of interest.

Abbreviations

The following abbreviations are used in this manuscript:

BEB	binary-encounter-Bethe
BEB-0	binary-encounter-Bethe for positrons
BEB-W	binary-encounter-Bethe for positrons with Wannier-type threshold law
BEB-A	binary-encounter-Bethe for positrons with Jansen-type threshold law, version A
BEB-B	binary-encounter-Bethe for positrons with Jansen-type threshold law, version B
CCC	convergent close-coupling
eV	electron volt
Ps	Positronium

References

1. Brunger, M.; Buckman, S.J.; Ratnavelu, K. Recommended Positron Scattering Cross Sections for Atomic Systems. Positron Scattering from Molecules: An Experimental Cross Section Compilation for Positron Transport Studies and Benchmarking Theory. *J. Phys. Chem. Ref. Data* **2017**, *46*, 023102. [CrossRef]
2. Ratnavelu, K.; Brunger, M.J.; Buckman, S.J. Recommended Positron Scattering Cross Sections for Atomic Systems. *J. Phys. Chem. Ref. Data* **2019**, *48*, 023102. [CrossRef]
3. Kim, Y.-K.; Rudd, M.E. Binary-encounter-dipole model for electron-impact ionization. *Phys. Rev. A* **1994**, *50*, 3954–3967. [CrossRef] [PubMed]
4. Hwang, W.; Kim, Y.-K.; Rudd, M.E. New model for electron-impact ionization cross sections of molecules. *J. Phys. Chem.* **1995**, *104*, 2956–2966. [CrossRef]
5. Charlton, M.; Humberston, J.W. *Positron Physics*; Cambridge University Press: Cambridge, UK, 2001.
6. Klar, H. Threshold ionisation of atoms by positrons. *J. Phys. B At. Mol. Opt. Phys.* **1981** *14*, 4165–4170. [CrossRef]

7. Wannier, G.H. The Threshold Law for Single Ionization of Atoms or Ions by Electrons. *Phys. Rev.* **1953**, *90*, 817–825. [CrossRef]
8. Fedus, K.; Karwasz, G.P. Binary-encounter dipole model for positron-impact direct ionization. *Phys. Rev. A* **2019**, *100*, 062702. [CrossRef]
9. Rost, J.M.; Heller, E.J. Ionization of hydrogen by positron impact near the fragmentation threshold. *Phys. Rev. A* **1994**, *49*, R4289–R4292. [CrossRef]
10. Ihra, W.; Macek, J.H.; Mota-Furtado, F.; O'Mahony, P.F. Threshold Law For Positron Impact Ionization of Atoms. *Phys. Rev. Lett.* **1997**, *78*, 4027–4030. [CrossRef]
11. Ashley, P.; Moxom, J.; Laricchia, G. Near-Threshold Ionization of He and H_2 by Positron Impact. *Phys. Rev. Lett.* **1996**, *77*, 1250–1253. [CrossRef]
12. Jansen, K.; Ward, S.J.; Shertzer, J.; Macek, J.H. Absolute cross sections for positron impact ionization of hydrogen near threshold. *Phys. Rev. A* **2009**, *79*, 022704. [CrossRef]
13. Fromme, D.; Kruse, G.; Raith, W.; Sinapius, G. Ionisation of molecular hydrogen by positrons. *J. Phys. B At. Mol. Opt. Phys.* **1988**, *21*, L261. [CrossRef]
14. Jacobsen, F.M.; Frandsen, N.P.; Knudsen, H.; Mikkelsen, U. Non-dissociative single ionization of molecular hydrogen by electron and positron impact. *J. Phys. B At. Mol. Opt. Phys.* **1995**, *28*, 4675–4689. [CrossRef]
15. Utamuratov, R.; Kadyrov, A.S.; Fursa, D.V.; Zammit, M.C.; Bray, I. Two-center close-coupling calculations of positron–molecular-hydrogen scattering. *Phys. Rev. A* **2015**, *92*, 032707. [CrossRef]
16. Marler, J.P.; Surko, C.M. Positron-impact ionization, positronium formation, and electronic excitation cross sections for diatomic molecules. *Phys. Rev. A* **2005**, *72*, 062713. [CrossRef]
17. Franz, J. The POCOBIO Database for Computed Scattering Cross-Sections for Positron Collisions with Biomolecular Systems. *Acta Phys. Pol. A* **2017**, *132*, 1478–1481. [CrossRef]
18. Franz, J.; Gianturco, F.A. Low-energy positron scattering from gas-phase tetrahydrofuran: A quantum treatment of the dynamics and a comparison with experiments. *J. Chem. Phys.* **2013**, *139*, 204309. [CrossRef] [PubMed]
19. Franz, J.; Gianturco, F.A. Low-energy positron scattering from gas-phase pyrimidine: A quantum treatment of the dynamics and a comparison with experiments. *Phys. Rev. A* **2013**, *88*, 042711. [CrossRef]
20. Franz, J.; Gianturco, F.A.; Baccarelli, I. Low-energy positron scattering from gas-phase uracil. *Eur. Phys. J. D* **2014**, *68*, 183. [CrossRef]
21. Franz, J.; Gianturco, F.A. Low-energy positron scattering from DNA nucleobases: The effects from permanent dipoles. *Eur. Phys. J. D* **2014**, *68*, 279. [CrossRef]
22. Franz, J.; Franz, M. Low-energy positron scattering from gas-phase benzene. *Eur. Phys. J. D* **2019**, *73*, 192. [CrossRef]
23. Karbowski, A.; Karwasz, G.P.; Franz, M.; Franz, J. Positron Scattering and Annihilation in Organic Molecules. *Acta Phys. Pol. B* **2020**, *51*, 207–212. [CrossRef]
24. Baluja, K.; Zhang, R.; Franz, J.; Tennyson, J. Low-energy positron collisions with water: Elastic and rotationally inelastic scattering. *J. Phys. B At. Mol. Opt. Phys.* **2007**, *40*, 3515–3524. [CrossRef]
25. Taioli, S.; Trevisanutto, P.E.; de Vera, P.; Simonucci, S.; Abril, I.; Garcia-Molina, R.; Dapor, M. Relative Role of Physical Mechanisms on Complex Biodamage Induced by Carbon Irradiation. *J. Phys. Chem. Lett.* **2021**, *12*, 487–493. [CrossRef] [PubMed]

Article

Electron Impact Ionization of Metastable States of Diatomic Molecules

Annarita Laricchiuta [1,*], Roberto Celiberto [1,2] and Gianpiero Colonna [1]

[1] CNR ISTP (Istituto per la Scienza e Tecnologia dei Plasmi) Bari Section, 70126 Bari, Italy; roberto.celiberto@poliba.it (R.C.); gianpiero.colonna@cnr.it (G.C.)
[2] Dipartimento di Ingegneria Civile, Ambientale, del Territorio, Edile e di Chimica (DICATECh), Politecnico di Bari, 70125 Bari, Italy
* Correspondence: annarita.laricchiuta@cnr.it

Abstract: The Binary-Encounter Bethe approach was applied to the estimation of total ionization induced by electron impact in metastable states of diatomic molecules. The cross sections recently obtained for N_2 and CO are reviewed and the new results for H_2 are presented, discussing their reliability through the comparison with other theoretical methods.

Keywords: metastable states; electron-impact ionization; BEB approach; elementary processes in plasmas

1. Introduction

The kinetics of nonequilibrium, low-temperature plasmas is driven by the presence of radicals and excited species that can be regarded as reactivity enhancers, activating channels otherwise inaccessible and modifying the route to products. Mechanisms activated by excited species can significantly affect the efficiency of plasma technologies impacting different fields of applications, i.e., CO_2 plasma reduction for environment [1], plasma-assisted combustion [2], plasma medicine, and agriculture [3,4].

The assessed theoretical framework for the description of transient and stationary conditions of such plasmas is the state-to-state approach [5,6], where the quantum states of chemical species are treated independently in the master equations for the time evolution and characterized dynamically with state-specific cross sections and rate coefficients. The chemistry is coupled to the kinetics of free electrons and the internal and electron energy distributions are mutually affected. In this complex scenario, the metastable states, due to their considerably longer lifetimes with respect to radiating excited states, can play a role, acting also as a energy reservoir in the post-discharge relaxation phase and thus sustaining the plasma through the secondary collisions. This is the case of $N_2(A^3\Sigma_u^+)$ state in the nitrogen afterglow [7,8] and also in high-enthalpy hypersonic flows [9], of $CO(a^3\Pi)$ in CO_2 discharges [10] and the *odd* oxygen, i.e., $O_2(a^1\Delta_g)$, O^1S excited states, key in the control of ignition delay time in combustion [11]. The metastable $c^3\Pi_u$ and quasi-metastable $a^3\Sigma_g^+$ states of H_2 are relevant to the collisional radiative models for the simulation of negative ion sources for fusion [12].

Despite efforts to compile complete databases for state-resolved cross sections [13], the knowledge of data for electron scattering processes of metastables is still very scarce, thus requiring novel efforts of the quantum chemistry community. From the experimental point of view it poses difficulties entailing the preparation of the molecule in the excited state.

Focussing on the ionization process, the role of vibrational excitation of the molecular target in enhancing the ionization was investigated in the framework of classical approaches, i.e., the Gryzinski [14–19] and the universal function method [20–22], finding in general a small dependence on the vibrational quantum number. On the contrary a significant impact in the chemistry is expected for processes initiated from metastable excited states, characterized by a considerable reduction of the ionization threshold. The total ionization cross section of N_2 metastable was obtained within the formalism of Complex Scattering Potential [23] and also partial ionization cross sections for $N_2(A^3\Sigma_u^+)$ and $O_2(a^1\Delta_g)$ and $O_2(b^1\Sigma_g^+)$ to specific final molecular ion states were estimated in Refs. [20–22]. The H_2 ionization from metastable and excited states was comprehensively investigated with the Gryzinski approach [14] and with the quantum convergent close-coupling calculations (MCCC) [24], demonstrating the predictive character of the classical approach that well reproduces the most accurate theoretical results.

In this paper, the total ionization cross sections for metastable states of diatomic molecules derived in the framework of the Binary-Encounter Bethe (BEB) approach developed by Kim&Rudd [25,26] are discussed. The method, attractively combining simplicity and accuracy, was successfully and extensively applied to many atomic and molecular systems in the ground state, including fusion-relevant species containing heavy elements as beryllium/tungsten oxides, hydrides and nitrides [27], and also to the ionization of low-lying excited states of carbon, nitrogen and oxygen atoms [28]. Here, the results recently obtained for to the metastable states of N_2^* and CO^* [29] are reviewed and new results for H_2 molecule are presented, discussing the comparison with other theoretical methods.

2. BEB Approach

The BEB approach [25,26,30] is a derivation of the binary-encounter dipole model for electron-impact ionization of atoms and molecules, allowing the cross section estimation in those cases where the continuum dipole oscillator strength is not available.

The total ionization cross section is expressed as the sum of contributions from the electron shells

$$\sigma_{BEB}^{ion}(E) = \sum_i \frac{4\pi a_0^2 N R y^2}{B^2(t+u+1)} \left[\frac{\ln t}{2} \left(1 - \frac{1}{t^2}\right) + \left(1 - \frac{1}{t} - \frac{\ln t}{t+1}\right) \right] \quad (1)$$

with Ry the Rydberg constant, B the electron binding energy in the i-th orbital participating in the ionization process, N its occupation number. $t = E/B$ and $u = U/B$, $U = \langle p^2/2m \rangle$ being the average kinetic energy in the orbital.

Equation (1) is obtained assuming for the the continuum dipole oscillator strength, $\frac{df(w)}{dw}$, an analytical inverse power form

$$\frac{df(w)}{dw} = \frac{N}{(w+1)^2} \quad (2)$$

where $w = W/B$, with $W = E - B$ the energy of the ejected electron.

3. Results and Discussion

The BEB cross sections requires the estimation of orbital parameters entering Equation (1). Electronic structure calculations were performed with the GAMESS package [31,32].

In Ref. [29] ab initio unrestricted Hartree Fock (UHF) calculations were performed, with the aug-cc-pVTZ basis set, in the D2h symmetry point group at the equilibrium geometry of the metastable $N_2(A^3\Sigma_u^+)$ (R_{eq} = 1.2866 Å). The dominant configuration at R_{eq} is $(1\sigma_g^2 1\sigma_u^2 2\sigma_g^2 2\sigma_u^2 1\pi_u^3 3\sigma_g^2 1\pi_g^1)$. Following the procedure recommended in Ref. [26] the α and β orbital values for the binding energy and the kinetic energy were averaged. The threshold in the BEB approach depends on the B value for the highest occupied molecular orbital (HOMO) $1\pi_g$, and was obtained subtracting the values for the corresponding orbital in the α and β sets. This is the most critical aspect and determines the accuracy of the results. The UHF value of 8.47 eV [29] is in fact lower than the expected value of 10.47 eV, which corresponds to the first allowed, one-electron process of ionization connecting the metastable state of the N_2 molecule to the first excited state of the molecular ion, i.e., $N_2(A^3\Sigma_u^+(1\pi_u^3 3\sigma_g^2 1\pi_g^1)) - e(1\pi_g) \to N_2^+(A^2\Pi_u(1\pi_u^3 3\sigma_g^2))$. This process is highly favored with respect to the transition to the ground state of $N_2^+(X^2\Sigma_g^+(1\pi_u^4 3\sigma_g^1))$, with a threshold of 9.41 eV, that would require a two electron transition.

The total ionization cross section is displayed in Figure 1, also plotting the results obtained artificially modifying the binding energy of the $1\pi_g$ orbital, B^{HOMO}, to reproduce the experimental ionization threshold, as suggested in Ref. [26], the cross section being shifted in energy and slightly lowered in its maximum value. It is interesting to compare the BEB cross sections with the results obtained in the framework of the Complex Scattering Potential-ionization contribution (CSP-ic) formalism [23]. Actually, in this theoretical treatment the ionization threshold is an external parameter and two model were proposed, model A based on the theoretical value for the formation of the $N_2^+(X^2\Sigma_g^+)$ state, 9.41 eV, and model B where the value 10.1 eV, corresponding to the appearance potential in Ref. [33], is chosen. The two methods agree quite well and both predict an ionization cross section that, regardless the threshold, is greater than the experiments, also reported in Figure 1. In fact, the $N_2(A^3\Sigma_u^+)$ state is the only molecular metastable state investigated experimentally [33,34], the molecular beam prepared by quasi-resonant asymmetric charge transfer neutralization and with subsequent ionization by electron beam. The two measures were done with a different charge-transfer gas and the existence of the metastable in the neutralized beam was postulated on the basis of the observed lowering of the ionization threshold with respect to the ground state. As mentioned the apparent threshold in Ref. [33] is lower than the theoretical value predicted for the $N_2(A) \rightarrow N_2^+(A)$ process and it was attributed to presence of vibrationally excited $N_2(A)$ molecules in the beam. The reasons for discrepancies between theory and experiments, could be attributed to the fact that all channels are accounted for in the total ionization cross section, while experiments focus on the nondissociative ionization process. Furthermore, the procedure for the separation of ground and metastable contributions to the ion signal is critical and could be a source of uncertainty in the measure.

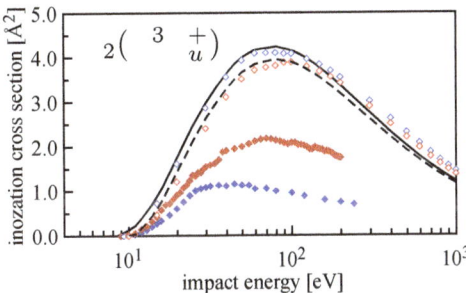

Figure 1. BEB cross sections for total ionization (solid lines) of $N_2(A^3\Sigma_u^+)$ metastable [29], (dashed line) BEB cross section with B^{HOMO} = 10.47 eV. CSP-ic results [23] for model A (blue open diamonds) and model B (red open diamonds). Experiments: (close blue diamonds) [33], (close red diamonds) [34].

The total ionization for the metastable state of CO molecule (Figure 2) was derived in the BEB approach [29], performing multiconfiguration self-consistent field (MCSCF) calculations not only at R_{eq} = 1.20574 Å , but also varying the molecular geometry, confirming the dominant role of the configuration $(3\sigma^2 4\sigma^2 5\sigma 1\pi^4 2\pi)$. The orbital parameters were again obtained with unrestricted Hartree Fock approach, finding the ionization threshold at 9.50 eV. This value is greater than the one estimated from the energy spectrum, 7.97 eV, corresponding to the one-electron ionization $CO(a^3\Pi) - e(2\pi) \rightarrow CO^+(^2\Sigma^+)$ as lowest-threshold channel.

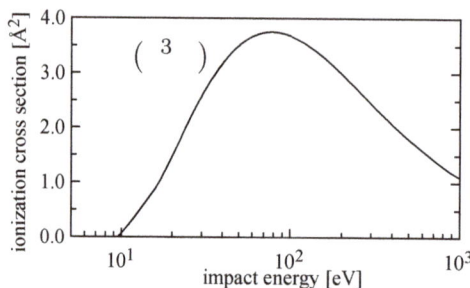

Figure 2. BEB cross sections for total ionization of CO($a^3\Pi$) metastable [29].

In the case of H_2, the ionization cross sections of the metastable $c^3\Pi_u$, of the other bound triplet $a^3\Sigma_g^+$ and of the three lowest singlet excited states were calculated firstly with the classical Gryzinski approach [35], deriving vibrationally-resolved datasets relevant to collisional-radiative models, and recently re-evaluated with the accurate MCCC approach [24] for the fundamental vibrational level $v = 0$ of the excited states. The total ionization for the c state was also estimated within the complex potential (CSP-ic) formalism [36], considering two models based on a different choice of the lowest threshold energy for the ionization. In model A, the energy limit was set to 2.82 eV, derived from the theoretical energy of the excited $c^3\Pi_u$ state estimated within the R-matrix approach [37], while in model B, the ionization was fixed at the experimental value 3.66 eV [38]. The significance of this choice is evident in the threshold behavior of the cross section, affecting the low-temperature rate of the process, however at high collision energies the two models converge.

Here, the two triplets $c^3\Pi_u$ and $a^3\Sigma_g^+$ are considered. In the ab initio step, MCSCF electronic structure calculations were preliminary performed, with the aug-cc-pV5Z basis set, at the equilibrium internuclear distance of each electronic state, confirming that a single determinant representation is accurate, being the configuration coefficient close to unity for both states. The excited configurations, $(1\sigma_g\, 1\pi_u)$ for $(c^3\Pi_u)$ and $(1\sigma_g\, 2\sigma_g)$ for $a^3\Sigma_g^+$, were then treated in the EKT (extended Koopmans' theorem) method [39], available in the GAMESS code, obtaining a quite accurate estimation of the ionization potential values. In fact, in the case of the a state the binding energy of the excited orbital, 3.6245 eV, is very close to the experimental threshold value 3.639 eV, while for the c state the EKT value, 3.31702 eV, is lower than the accurate threshold at 3.66 eV. The orbital parameters for the two states are reported in Table 1.

Table 1. Orbital binding energy, occupation number, orbital symmetry, and kinetic energy for $H_2(c^3\Pi_u)$ $(1\sigma_g\, 1\pi_u)$ and $H_2(a^3\Sigma_g^+)$ $(1\sigma_g\, 2\sigma_g)$ states at the corresponding equilibrium internuclear distance, i.e., $R_{eq}^c = 1.0376$ Å and $R_{eq}^a = 0.98879$ Å.

	B [eV]	N		U [eV]
$c^3\Pi_u$	22.59329	1	Ag	15.53490
	3.31702	1	B2u	5.66877
$a^3\Sigma_g^+$	25.5348	1	Ag	17.2390
	3.6245	1	Ag	2.7310

In Figure 3, the total ionization cross sections for the $c^3\Pi_u$ and $a^3\Sigma_g^+$ states of H_2 are displayed as a function of collision energy and compared with the other theoretical results. For the metastable, the Gryzinski and CSP-ic approaches both give values in good agreement with the quantum MCCC cross section, this last representing the reference, while the BEB model is about 10% lower at the maximum, the error reducing at higher energies. Differently, for the a state the BEB cross section compares significantly better with the accurate MCCC values, where the Gryzinski approach overestimates the maximum.

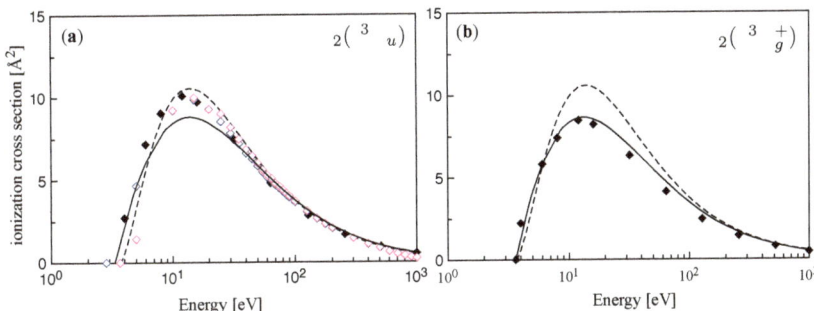

Figure 3. Total ionization cross section of H_2 (**a**) $c^3\Pi_u$ metastable and (**b**) $a^3\Sigma_g^+$ states. (solid line) BEB model; (dashed line) classical Gryzinski approach [14]; (close diamonds) MCCC method [24,40]; CSP-ic method [36] models A (blue open diamonds) and B (red open diamonds).

The ionization from excited states is characterized not only by the lowering of the energy threshold for the process, but also by a significant enhancement of the absolute value of the cross section with respect to the ground state. In fact, the peak value increases of a factor from 1.5 for N_2 and 1.7 for CO to 10 for H_2. In the hydrogen case, the enhancement factor is that large because of the significant difference in the binding energy of the ejected electron in the excited configurations with respect to the ground closed-shell configuration, that, in turn, favors the ionization process. The BEB model accuracy is acceptable also in the case of excited metastable states and related to the accuracy of the ab initio biding energy of the highest occupied orbital.

4. Conclusions

The derivation of cross sections for electron-impact-induced processes in metastable states of molecular species is a requirement for the creation of a complete kinetic scheme of nonequilibrium technological plasmas. Among electron-scattering processes, the ionization is key in the onset of electron density and the reduction of the threshold energy, when initiated from excited states, largely enhances the effect. The BEB model for ionization was widely used in the literature to estimate the cross sections for atoms and molecules in their ground states, due to the noticeable accuracy of results despite the simplicity of the formulation, free of external parameters, being the orbital values entering the working equation obtainable by standard electronic structure calculations. In this paper, the total ionization cross sections for metastables of diatomic molecules estimated within the framework of the BEB approach are discussed, comparing the results with those obtained with other more sophisticated theoretical methods, confirming discrepancies within 10% also characterizing the ground state calculations.

Author Contributions: Conceptualization and software, A.L.; analysis and discussion, A.L., R.C. and G.C.; writing—original draft preparation, A.L.; writing—review, A.L., R.C. and G.C. All authors have read and agreed to the published version of the manuscript.

Funding: This research received no external funding.

Conflicts of Interest: The authors declare no conflict of interest.

References

1. Pietanza, L.D.; Guaitella, O.; Aquilanti, V.; Armenise, I Bogaerts, A.; Capitelli, M.; Colonna, G.; Guerra, V.; Engeln, R.; Kustova, E.; Lombardi, A.; et al. Advances in non-equilibrium CO_2 plasma kinetics: A theoretical and experimental review. *Eur. Phys. J. D* **2021**, *75*, 237. [CrossRef]
2. Starikovskaia, S.; Lacoste, D.A.; Colonna, G. Non-equilibrium plasma for ignition and combustion enhancement. *Eur. Phys. J. D* **2021**, *75*, 231. [CrossRef]
3. Šimek, M.; Homola, T. Plasma-assisted agriculture: history, presence, and prospects—A review. *Eur. Phys. J. D* **2021**, *75*, 210. [CrossRef]

4. Fridman, A.A.; Friedman, G.G. *Plasma Medicine*; John Wiley & Sons: Chichester, UK, 2013.
5. Colonna, G.; Pintassilgo, C.D.; Pegoraro, F.; Cristofolini, A.; Popoli, A.; Neretti, G.; Gicquel, A.; Duigou, O.; Bieber, T.; Hassouni, K.; et al. Theoretical and experimental aspects of non-equilibrium plasmas in different regimes: Fundamentals and selected applications. *Eur. Phys. J. D* **2021**, *75*, 183. [CrossRef]
6. Capitelli, M.; Celiberto, R.; Colonna, G.; Esposito, F.; Gorse, C.; Hassouni, K.; Laricchiuta, A.; Longo, S. *Fundamental Aspects of Plasma Chemical Physics: Kinetics*; Springer Series on Atomic, Optical, and Plasma Physics; Springer: New York, NY, USA, 2016; Volume 85.
7. Colonna, G. On the relevance of superelastic collisions in argon and nitrogen discharges. *Plasma Sources Sci. Technol.* **2020**, *29*, 065008. [CrossRef]
8. Ricard, A.; Oh, S.G.; Guerra, V. Line-ratio determination of atomic oxygen and $N_2(A^3\Sigma_u^+)$ metastable absolute densities in an RF nitrogen late afterglow. *Plasma Sources Sci. Technol.* **2013**, *22*, 035009. [CrossRef]
9. Colonna, G.; Capitelli, M. The influence of atomic and molecular metastable states in high-enthalpy nozzle expansion nitrogen flows. *J. Phys. D Appl. Phys.* **2001**, *34*, 1812. [CrossRef]
10. Pietanza, L.D.; Colonna, G.; Capitelli, M. Non-equilibrium plasma kinetics of reacting CO: An improved state to state approach. *Plasma Sources Sci. Technol.* **2017**, *26*, 125007. [CrossRef]
11. Starik, A.M.; Kozlov, V.E.; Titova, N.S. On the influence of singlet oxygen molecules on the speed of flame propagation in methane-air mixture. *Combust. Flame* **2010**, *157*, 313–327. [CrossRef]
12. Wünderlich, D.; Scarlett, L.H.; Briefi, S.; Fantz, U.; Zammit, M.C.; Fursa, D.V.; Bray, I. Application of molecular convergent close-coupling cross sections in a collisional radiative model for the triplet system of molecular hydrogen. *J. Phys. D Appl. Phys.* **2021**, *54*, 115201. [CrossRef]
13. Celiberto, R.; Armenise, I.; Cacciatore, M.; Capitelli, M.; Esposito, F.; Gamallo, P.; Janev, R.; Laganà, A.; Laporta, V.; Laricchiuta, A.; et al. Atomic and molecular data for spacecraft re-entry plasmas. *Plasma Sources Sci. Technol.* **2016**, *25*, 033004. [CrossRef]
14. Wünderlich, D. Vibrationally resolved ionization cross sections for the ground state and electronically excited states of the hydrogen molecule and its isotopomeres. *At. Data Nucl. Data Tables* **2021**, *140*, 101424. [CrossRef]
15. Celiberto, R.; Janev, R.K.; Laricchiuta, A.; Capitelli, M.; Wadehra, J.M.; Atems, D.E. Cross section data for electron-impact inelastic processes of vibrationally excited molecules of hydrogen and its isotopes. *At. Data Nucl. Data Tables* **2001**, *77*, 161–213. [CrossRef]
16. Celiberto, R.; Capitelli, M.; Cacciatore, M. Electron impact direct dissociative-ionization cross sections from vibrationally excited H_2 molecules and translational energy distribution functions of protons. *Chem. Phys.* **1990**, *140*, 209–215. [CrossRef]
17. Cacciatore, M.; Capitelli, M.; Gorse, C. Non-equilibrium dissociation and ionization of nitrogen in electrical discharges: the role of electronic collisions from vibrationally excited molecules. *Chem. Phys.* **1982**, *66*, 141–151. [CrossRef]
18. Bauer, E.; Bartky, C.D. Calculation of inelastic electron-molecule collision cross sections by classical methods. *J. Chem. Phys.* **1965**, *43*, 2466–2476. [CrossRef]
19. Gryziński, M. Classical Theory of Atomic Collisions. I. Theory of Inelastic Collisions. *Phys. Rev.* **1965**, *138*, A336–A358, doi:10.1103/PhysRev.138.A336. [CrossRef]
20. Kosarim, A.V.; Smirnov, B.M.; Capitelli, M.; Celiberto, R.; Petrella, G.; Laricchiuta, A. Ionization of excited nitrogen molecules by electron impact. *Chem. Phys. Lett.* **2005**, *414*, 215–221. doi:10.1016/j.cplett.2005.08.012. [CrossRef]
21. Kosarim, A.V.; Smirnov, B.M.; Capitelli, M.; Laricchiuta, A.; Paniccia, F. Electron impact ionization cross sections of vibrationally and electronically excited oxygen molecules. *Chem. Phys. Lett.* **2006**, *422*, 513–517. [CrossRef]
22. Laricchiuta, A.; Capitelli, M.; Celiberto, R.; Colonna, G. *Dissociation and Ionization cross Sections and Rate Coefficients of Air Molecules by Electron Impact: The Role of Vibrational Energy*; AIAA Paper 2006-2898; American Institute of Aeronautics and Astronautics: Reston, VA, USA, 2006.
23. Joshipura, K.N.; Gangopadhyay, S.S.; Kothari, H.N.; Shelat, F.A. Total electron scattering and ionization of N, N_2 and metastable excited N_2^* $(A^3\Sigma_u^+)$: Theoretical cross sections. *Phys. Lett. A* **2009**, *373*, 2876–2881. [CrossRef]
24. Scarlett, L.H.; Savage, J.S.; Fursa, D.V.; Bray, I.; Zammit, M.C.; Schneider, B.I. Convergent close-coupling calculations of electrons scattering on electronically excited molecular hydrogen. *Phys. Rev. A* **2021**, *103*, 032802. [CrossRef]
25. Kim, Y.K.; Rudd, M.E. Binary-encounter-dipole model for electron-impact ionization. *Phys. Rev. A* **1994**, *50*, 3954. [CrossRef] [PubMed]
26. Hwang, W.; Kim, Y.K.; Rudd, M.E. New model for electron-impact ionization cross sections of molecules. *J. Chem. Phys.* **1996**, *104*, 2956–2966. [CrossRef]
27. Huber, S.E.; Mauracher, A.; Süß, D.; Sukuba, I.; Urban, J.; Borodin, D.; Probst, M. Total and partial electron impact ionization cross sections of fusion-relevant diatomic molecules. *J. Chem. Phys.* **2019**, *150*, 024306. [CrossRef] [PubMed]
28. Kim, Y.K.; Desclaux, J.P. Ionization of carbon, nitrogen, and oxygen by electron impact. *Phys. Rev. A* **2002**, *66*, 012708. [CrossRef]
29. Laricchiuta, A.; Pietanza, L.D.; Capitelli, M.; Colonna, G. Electron-CO excitation and ionization cross sections for plasma modeling. *Plasma Phys. Control. Fusion* **2018**, *61*, 014009. [CrossRef]
30. Tanaka, H.; Brunger, M.J.; Campbell, L.; Kato, H.; Hoshino, M.; Rau, A.R.P. Scaled plane-wave Born cross sections for atoms and molecules. *Rev. Mod. Phys.* **2016**, *88*, 025004. [CrossRef]
31. Schmidt, M.W.; Baldridge, K.K.; Boatz, J.A.; Elbert, S.T.; Gordon, M.S.; Jensen, J.H.; Koseki, S.; Matsunaga, N.; Nguyen, K.A.; Su, S.; et al. General atomic and molecular electronic structure system. *J. Comput. Chem.* **1993**, *14*, 1347–1363. [CrossRef]
32. Gordon, M.S.; Schmidt, M.W. *Theory and Applications of Computational Chemistry: The First Forty Years*; Dykstra, C.E., Frenking, G., Kim, K.S., Scuseria, G.E., Eds.; Elsevier: Amsterdam, The Netherlands, 2011; pp. 1167–1189.

33. Armentrout, P.B.; Tarr, S.M.; Dori, A.; Freund, R.S. Electron impact ionization cross section of metastable $N_2(A^3\Sigma_u^+)$. *J. Chem. Phys.* **1981**, *75*, 2786–2794. [CrossRef]
34. Freund, R.S.; Wetzel, R.C.; Shul, R.J. Measurements of electron-impact-ionization cross sections of N_2, CO, CO_2, CS, S_2, CS_2, and metastable N_2. *Phys. Rev. A* **1990**, *41*, 5861. [CrossRef] [PubMed]
35. Wünderlich, D. Vibrationally resolved ionization cross sections for the ground state and electronically excited states of the hydrogen molecule. *Chem. Phys.* **2011**, *390*, 75–82. [CrossRef]
36. Joshipura, K.N.; Kothari, H.N.; Shelat, F.A.; Bhowmik, P.; Mason, N.J. Electron scattering with metastable $H_2^*(c^3\Pi_u)$ molecules: ionization and other total cross sections. *J. Phys. At. Mol. Opt. Phys.* **2010**, *43*, 135207. [CrossRef]
37. Branchett, S.E.; Tennyson, J.; Morgan, L.A. Electronic excitation of molecular hydrogen using the r-matrix method. *J. Phys. B At. Mol. Opt. Phys.* **1990**, *23*, 4625. [CrossRef]
38. Herzberg, G. *Molecular Spectra and Molecular Structure. 1. Spectra of Diatomic Molecules*; Van Nostrand: New York, NY, USA, 1950.
39. Morrison, R.C. The extended Koopmans' theorem and its exactness. *J. Chem. Phys.* **1992**, *96*, 3718–3722. [CrossRef]
40. MCCC. Molecular Convergent Close-Coupling Database. 2021. Available Online: https://www.mccc-db.org/ (accessed on 19 December 2021).

Article

Total Cross Sections for Electron and Positron Scattering on Molecules: In Search of the Dispersion Relation

Fabio Carelli [1], Kamil Fedus [2,*] and Grzegorz Karwasz [2]

[1] Center of Excellence Astrochemistry & Astrophysics, Faculty of Physics, Astronomy and Informatics, Nicolaus Copernicus University, Grudziądzka 5/7, 87-100 Toruń, Poland; fabiocarelli79@gmail.com
[2] Institute of Physics, Faculty of Physics, Astronomy and Informatics, Nicolaus Copernicus University, Grudziądzka 5/7, 87-100 Toruń, Poland; karwasz@fizyka.umk.pl
* Correspondence: kamil@fizyka.umk.pl

Abstract: More than one hundred years of experimental and theoretical investigations of electron scattering in gases delivered cross-sections in a wide energy range, from few meV to keV. An analogy in optics, characterizing different materials, comes under the name of the dispersion relation, i.e., of the dependence of the refraction index on the light wavelength. The dispersion relation for electron (and positron) scattering was hypothesized in the 1970s, but without clear results. Here, we review experimental, theoretical, and semi-empirical cross-sections for N_2, CO_2, CH_4, and CF_4 in search of any hint for such a relation—unfortunately, without satisfactory conclusions.

Keywords: electron scattering; positron scattering; total cross-sections; dispersion relation

1. The Need for Cross Sections

Cross sections for electron scattering are the input data in modeling and diagnostics of industrial plasma, gas discharge [1], thermonuclear plasma [2,3], biological media [4,5], and atmospheric processes, including extra-solar planets [6]. Such modeling requires the knowledge of the total and partial (elastic, ionization, dissociation, and electronic, vibrational, rotational excitation) cross sections in a broad energy range. Out of the gases considered in this paper, CF_4 is used for etching SiO_2, in spite of the disadvantages resulting from the presence of hot radicals (with the energy of few eV) in $Ar/O_2/CF_4$ plasmas. CH_4 acts as an intrinsic cooler in carbon-lined tokamaks like JET, thanks to its high cross sections for the vibrational excitations in the region of a few eV, see reference [7]. Resonant processes in electron scattering in N_2 and CO_2 at a few eV (2.1 and 3.9 eV, respectively), enhancing the vibrational and rotational transitions, are the basis of high-power IR lasers [8]. For thermonuclear plasmas, the energy range up to 1 keV is of interest [9].

Experimental determinations are relatively easy for total cross section (TCS) in the energy range 1–100 eV, using beam methods [10]. In some gases, like N_2 and CH_4 [7], the uncertainty on the TCS is as low as 5%. At very low energies, swarm measurements, especially in gas mixtures, obtain self-consistent sets of partial cross sections, also for rotational and vibrational excitations [11]. However, as discussed for H_2O (e.g., reference [12]), such sets may not be unique. Good agreements (e.g., within few per cent) exist for ionization cross sections [13]. Scarce data are available for electronic excitations; however, their contribution to the TCS are usually only a few per cent. Measurements of vibrational excitations are difficult; similar to electronic excitations, they require a good energy resolution of analyzers and integrating differential cross sections (DCS) in the whole 0–180° angular range (see [14]). A "missing channel" in the measurements of partial cross sections in molecules is, frequently, the dissociation into neutral fragments (see [15]). All these partial cross sections should sum-up to the TCS. Our question is: may we deduce some more information from (pretty precise) measurements of total cross sections to derive partial ones? Are there any schemes of partitioning and/or semi-empirical indications?

The knowledge of positron-scattering cross sections is rather fragmentary. Positrons may be considered as complementary to electron scattering [16–18]; no exchange effects occur for positrons and the overall interaction is weaker, as the attractive polarization potential (of the electronic cloud) subtracts from the repulsive static potential of the nuclear core. Modeling is needed in studies of positron annihilation for the defectoscopy of the solid state [19] and for medical applications (positron emission tomography—PET). Experiments, theory, and semi-empirical models are the input data for further modeling, yielding improved sets of data (see [20]).

2. Semi-Empirical Models

Semi-empirical models have been developed to estimate partial cross sections. The models try to relate electron (and positron) scattering cross sections in different energy ranges to some molecular features, like the "radii" [21], total atomic number Z, dipole polarizability, electron binding energies in the target, etc. At the very low energy range, in particular for noble gases, the modified effective range theory (MERT) [22,23] extrapolates the elastic (integral and differential) cross section down to zero energy. The input data for MERT are the dipole polarizability and the integral and/or differential cross sections in the range of sub-eV, see the detailed discussion for CH_4 in reference [24]. MERT has also been applied to positron scattering, say in Ar and N_2, up to the energies of a few eV [25].

The relation to the dipole polarizability appears again in the intermediate (about 100 eV) energy range. Several authors [26,27] have indicated that the maxima of the ionization cross sections rise with the rise of dipole polarizability. As the ionization at these energies constitutes a significant part of the TCS, other works [28,29] suggested that the TCS in its maximum also depends on the polarizability. Thus, the question arises: why are the same molecular feature governed/reflected in the cross sections in two distant energy ranges?

For ionization cross sections, the most widely used is the Born-Bethe binary encounter model (BEB) [30]. It requires as input, data on the binding and kinetic energies of electrons on given electronic orbitals. However, as far as the BEB model is successful in calculating the total ionization cross section, i.e., the sum of ionization from single orbitals, it hardly predicts these partial ionization cross sections, see, for example, reference [31].

A modified version of BEB is also used to predict electronic excitation cross sections [32]. The input for this model is the optical oscillator strength that can be deduced from experimental zero-angle DCS for electronic excitations [33] at high (i.e., "Born", see reference [34]) energies.

Born approximation is also used for vibrational excitations in the region above the threshold. For infrared-active modes it is quite successful both for electron and positron [35] scattering. It is not useful in predicting the vibrational excitation in resonances. Note, in this issue, two papers going beyond Born approximation: by Ayouz et al. [36] for electron scattering on H_2O and by Poveda, do N. Varella and Mohallem [37] for positron scattering on H_2.

The region of few eV is the domain of resonant states in electron-molecule scattering. These states are usually classified as: (1) Feshbach resonances, resulting from the capturing of the incoming electron to a free electronic orbital of the target, and showing up as narrow structures in the elastic and TCS; and (2) shape resonances, due to temporary trapping of the incoming electron inside the effective (i.e., comprising the centrifugal barrier) potential well of the target, and showing-up as relatively broad maxima in TCS, frequently with a vibrational-like structure superimposed, see Figure 1 for N_2, and compare the highlighted figure of reference [38] showing the two types of resonances in TCS in N_2.

The contribution of Feshbach resonances to TCS is insignificant, but the shape resonances, say in N_2 (Figure 1) and CO_2 (Figure 2) give the maxima of TCS even by few folds higher than the potential-scattering "background" [39–41]. The contribution of the vibrational excitations in these maxima is high, roughly 1/6 of TCS in molecules like N_2

and CO and as much as 1/3 of TCS in $^2\Pi$ resonances in CO_2, N_2O, OCS, see Figure 2 for CO_2.

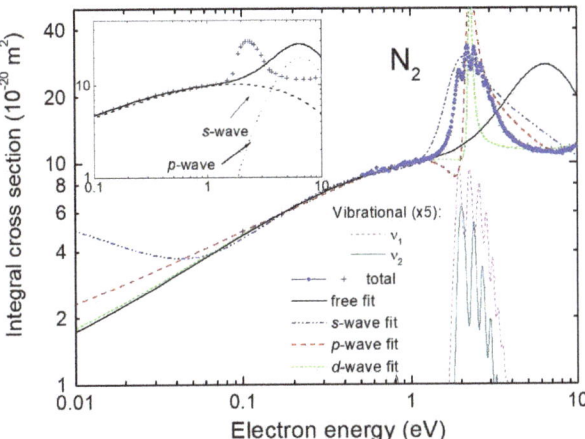

Figure 1. Integral (elastic, vibrational, total) cross sections for electron—N_2 scattering in the low energy range. MERT analysis [39] predicts a shape resonance: its position and width depend on the choice of the low-energy data used as the input for the analysis. Elastic cross sections re-edited from reference [39], vibrational excitation by Michael Allan [42], elaborated in reference [43]. TCS values are taken from reference [10].

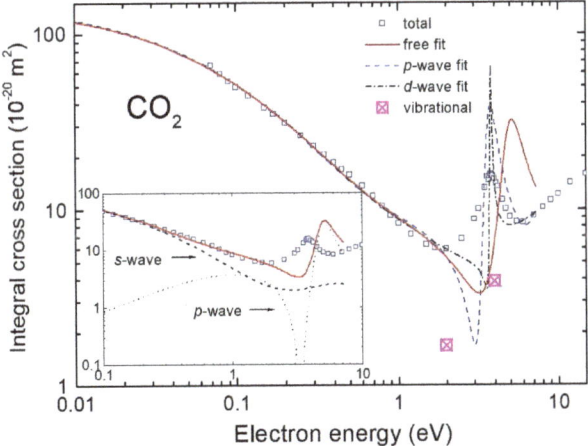

Figure 2. Integral (elastic and vibrational) cross sections for electron—CO_2 scattering in the low energy range. As for N_2, the MERT analysis [40] predicts a shape resonance. Elastic cross sections re-edited from reference [40], vibrational—measurements from the Kaiserslautern group [44], TCS—recommended values from reference [45].

Advanced theories, like complex Kohn [46], Schwinger multi-channel [47], Schwinger multi-channel with pseudo-potentials [48], close-coupling [49], and R-matrix [50] are needed to reproduce the existence of resonances, especially shape ones. However, extending the MERT analysis [25] to energies of a few eV (as compared to ca. 1 eV in previous works [23]) produced a rather unexpected result, namely resonant-like maxima in the integral elastic cross sections [24,39–41], see Figures 1–4 for N_2, CO_2, CH_4, and CF_4, respectively. These maxima appear from a fast change of single (s, p, d) phase shifts at energies of a few eV, see the insets in Figures 1 and 2. The positions, amplitudes, and widths of maxima depend on the partial-wave channel in which the resonance appears as small variations within the experimental uncertainties; the low-energy experimental data used for the MERT lead to the resonances in different channels (Figures 1 and 2). In CH_4 and CF_4 the resonances are broad and result from the contribution of more than one partial wave [24,41].

Obviously, semi-empirical analyses can not substitute more rigorous theories, but the lesson from such "MERT resonances [24,39–41]" is that the same potential may govern elastic cross sections in the few meV and few eV energy ranges (this is not the case of some ab-intio methods, using three different potentials in different energy ranges [51]).

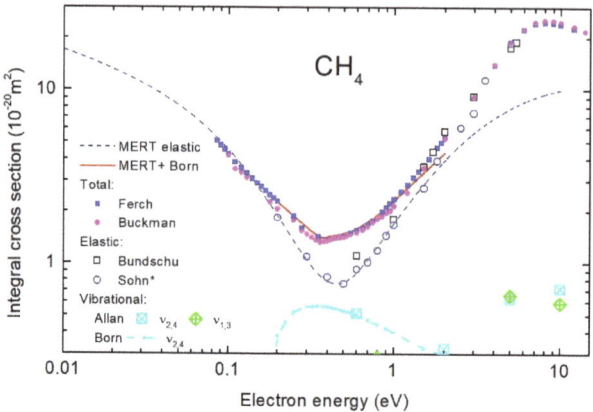

Figure 3. Integral (elastic, vibrational, total) cross sections for electron—CH_4 scattering in the low energy range. For references see reference [24].

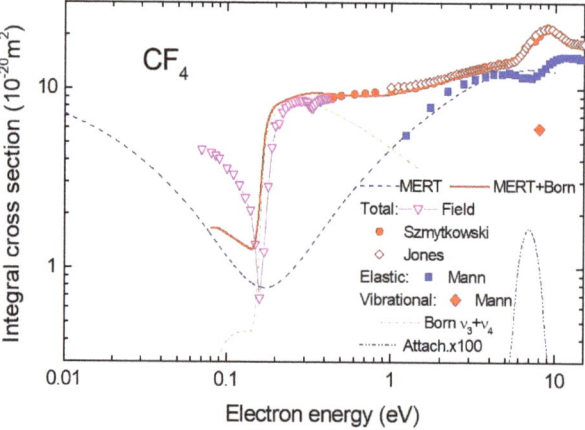

Figure 4. Integral (elastic, vibrational, total, dissociative electron attachment) cross sections for electron—CF_4 scattering in the low energy range. For references see reference [41].

3. Is Total Cross Section Merely a Sum of Partials?

Conceptually, TCS is considered as a sum of partial cross sections, that are usually regarded as independent quantities: this is a hidden hypothesis in many of the semi-empirical approaches. Furthermore, theories usually treat the elastic and inelastic channels independently. The approaches most successful recently, like the R-matrix [50] and Schwinger multi-channels [48] stop before the thresholds for electronic excitations and/or ionization.

In the intermediate energy range, a so-called optical potential [52] is commonly used in calculations of the summed inelastic cross sections (i.e., all electronic excitations and the ionization, also called "absorption" cross section), see, for example, [53]. Then, via some assuptions on the partitioning scheme, the ionization cross sections were derived [5]. However, relations between these schemes and the parameters used in BEB models for ionizations are not clear.

These approaches would suggest that scattering channels are independent. However, other theories indicate that including additional channels influences results. This is well seen in calculations of electronic excitations, say in H_2O [54] and also in calculations that go beyond the Born approximation of the near-threshold vibrational excitation for the same molecule, see reference [36] in this volume.

Generally, experimental hints for channel coupling are faint. Figure 4 for CF_4 would suggest that the vibrational excitation in CF_4 in the threshold region is simply summed to the elastic (MERT) part. However, in the resonant regions, the two channels are clearly coupled. The maximum in the vibrational channels anticipates the one in the elastic scattering; moreover, in the elastic channel, a kind of shoulder is seen, instead. A similar picture holds for NF_3 [31]. Does this phenomenon reflect a high value of the transition dipole moment (0.122a_0e in CF_4 as compared to 0.021 a_0e in CH_4 [55]) for the asymmetric stretching vibrational modes?

In some molecules, like N_2 and CO (see Figure 19 in reference [43]), a progression of high (up to $\nu = 11$) vibrational overtones in shape resonances was observed, but excitations of these modes are shifted in energy, see Figure 1 for N_2. This behavior has been recently reproduced in N_2 (and NO) shape resonances by the local optical potential model [56,57] that assumes coupling between the discrete and continuum states of the colliding system. The superposition of the elastic scattering and vibrational modes makes the whole resonance peak much broader (but lower), resulting from the MERT model.

For positron scattering, it seems rather clear that inelastic channels, like positronium-formation, sum-up with elastic channels, see Figure 5 for N_2. In the case of Ar, the theory that included absorption [58] indicated a step of the integral elastic cross section at the opening of the absorption channels, but the effect is too small to be proved experimentally at present. Another application of the optical potential for positron scattering at 100–300 eV in argon [59] showed that "absorption" effects reduce the DCS at intermediate (30–120°) angles but raise it by a factor of a few folds in the zero-angle limit.

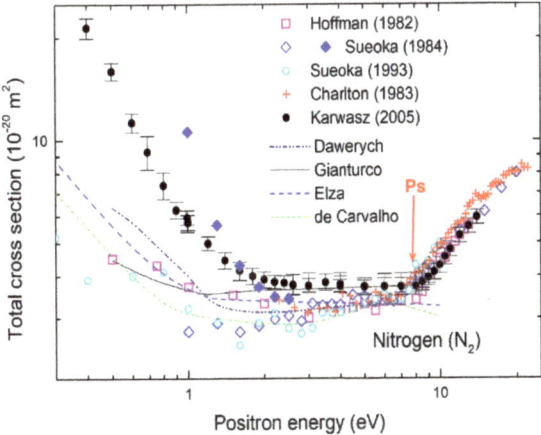

Figure 5. Total cross section for positron scattering on N_2. All experiments (in spite of their methodological uncertainties) indicate the rise of TCS towards zero energy (MERT domain), a flat, hard sphere-like region up to the threshold for the positronium formation (Ps—indicated by vertical arrow), and the rapid (a Wannier-like) rise of TCS above this threshold. For references see [60].

Figure 5 shows another interesting feature of the low-energy positron-scattering cross sections: a constant value of TCS in range up to the threshold for positronium formation. This feature is present in many targets, including H_2, CO_2, SF_6. Taking a geometrical cross section, one derives hard-sphere "dimensions" of the molecules, see reference [16]. Detailed models [21,61] explain that this feature comes from an inter-play between the short-range repulsive (i.e., of the nuclear core) and long-range attractive (due to the polarization) interactions. Note also that a hard-sphere model applied successfully by Borghesani [62] to electron-helium scattering (this issue).

Apart from He, TCS for electron scattering hardly relates to any "hard-sphere" radii. In N_2, the TCS at 5 eV (i.e., outside the resonance and still below the thresholds for electronic excitations) is lower by a factor of three for positrons than for electrons. Does it reflect a mere difference in the interaction potential or exchange effects? As the exchange effects should be less significant at high energies, it is worth exploiting the TCS in a broad energy range. This will be done via the dispersion relation that considers the high and very low energy ranges together.

4. Dispersion Relation

In optics, the dispersion relation, i.e., the dependence of the complex refraction index on the wavelength (Kronig-Kramers relations [52]) gives complete information on the optical properties of the material. The dispersion relation for electron (and positron) scattering has been formulated by Gerjuoy and Krall [63]. It relates the real part of the scattering amplitude $f(E,0)$ at a given energy E and zero scattering angle with the Born amplitude for direct (f_B) and exchange (g_B) scattering [64].

$$\Re f(E,0) = f_B(E,0) - g_B(E,0) + \frac{P}{4\pi^2} \int_0^\infty \frac{k'\sigma(E')}{E' - E} dE' \qquad (1)$$

Kauppila et al. [65], already in the 1980s, performed measurements of TCS up to 700 eV and checked the validity of the dispersion relation for electron and positron scattering on He, Ne, Ar. Their conclusion for electron scattering was negative (the relation does not hold) and the relation seemed valid for positron scattering on these three atoms, within the experimental uncertainties. Note, however, that in that time positron measurements at low energies were subject to big uncertainties, see Figure 5; similarly, in the high energy part, no Born region was reached, see Figure 6 (and compare with a similar Figure 7 for CO_2).

An extra term for electrons, as compared to positron scattering, comes from the exchange part of the scattering amplitude (g_B), that is non-analytic for negative energies [52]. However, the very idea of a dispersion relation led to the method of optical potential [6,59,66] widely used in calculations of absorption (i.e., electronic excitation and ionization) cross sections adding the elastic part and TCS.

The dispersion relation should hold for any arbitrarily chosen lower limit of integration, i.e., for any energy, like it was checked by de Heer and collaborators for H and He [67]. Choosing the low limit of integration at $E = 0$ simplifies the analysis: for non-polar molecules (like the four considered here) the scattering at zero energy is isotropic and the scattering amplitude $f(0,0)$ equals the minus scattering length. Consequently, the dispersion relation simplifies to:

$$-A_0 = f_B - g_B + \frac{1}{2\pi^2} \int_0^\infty \sigma(k') dk' \qquad (2)$$

The Born amplitude f_B is the Fourier transform of the scattering potential $U(r)$ corresponding to the wave vector transferred $K = k_i - k_f$ (k_i and k_f being the initial and final scattering vector).

$$f_B = -\frac{1}{4\pi} \int \exp(iKr) U(r) dr \qquad (3)$$

In principle, for an energy-independent potential (as should be the case of the static interaction), the Born amplitude for the zero-momentum transferred (i.e., for scattering into the forward direction) should also be energy independent. Further, DCS is the square of the scattering amplitude—in the Born approximation, it remains unchanged when the sign of the interaction potential changes. This should be the case of electron and positron scattering at "sufficiently" high energies, where the polarization potential may be disregarded. A series of works [68–70] started in the 1970s to verify the Born conditions in elastic scattering on molecules, see Figure 8 for CO_2.

For positron scattering, we are not aware of similar DCSs extending to zero angles as those shown in Figure 8. Kauppila et al. [71] measured DCS in Ar for electron and positron scattering at 300 eV; the experimental points at 30–90° coincide within experimental uncertainties, but the ab inito optical model [72] predicts the DCS at the zero angle by a factor of two lower for positrons than for electrons.

One could expect that the information on the opposite-sign of the short-range scattering potentials for positrons and electrons is "hidden" in the MERT parameters, in particular the "effective range". However, as one of us shows (KF) in this issue [73] it is not so straightforward. Nevertheless, in the next section we resume experimental data that can be useful in evaluation of the dispersion relation.

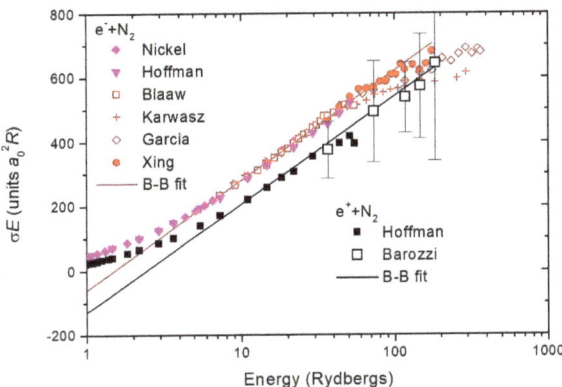

Figure 6. High-energy total cross sections for electron and positron scattering on N_2. The lines are the Bethe-Born fit, Equation (4). For references for electron scattering see the review [43]; for positrons Detroit [74] and Trento data [75] are used.

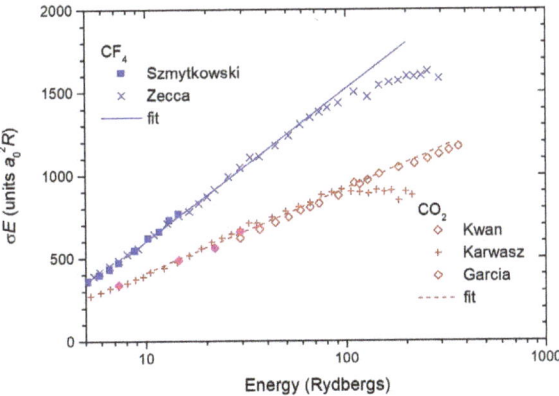

Figure 7. High-energy total cross sections for electron—CO_2 and CF_4 scattering. The line is the Bethe-Born fit, Equation (4). Experimental data are from Madrid laboratory [76], Trento [77,78], Detroit [79] and Gdańsk [80].

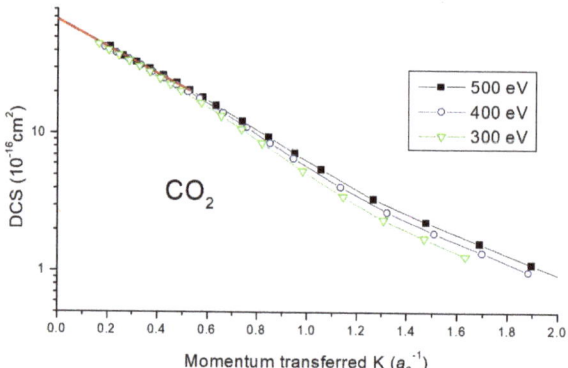

Figure 8. In search of the forward Born amplitude. Do DCSs at high energies tend to a constant value? Data for CO_2 are by Bromberg [69]; a single point for 10° at 400 eV by Iga et al. [81] coincides with Bromberg's data.

5. Experimental Input

Lack of experimental data was one of the obstacles in verifying the dispersion relation and its modifications in the past [64]. Here, we propose an "experimental" dispersion relation that requires, apart from total cross sections in a wide energy range (asymptotically from 0 to ∞), scattering length, i.e., the integral cross sections at zero energy and the elastic DCS at zero momentum transferred (i.e., asymptotically at zero angle) and high ("Born" [34]) energy.

In the zero-energy limit, the already mentioned new approach to MERT [24,39] consisted of fitting the phase shifts and cross sections directly, to increase the fidelity in the zero-energy limit and extend its applicability above 1 eV.

At high energies, two groups—from Trento [82–84] and Madrid University [76,85]— extended TCS measurements on molecules up to 3–5 keV. Trento measurements [83] above 1 keV were subject to the angular resolution error (mainly in the inelastic channel) underestimating the TCS at their highest energies by some 20–30% [7]. The Madrid group [76] used the energy analyzer at the exit of the scattering channel (therefore excluding electron scattered inelastically into forward angles), so their TCS are reliable up to their highest energies. They also promptly applied the Bethe-Born formula, extrapolating TCS into very high (up to relativistic) energies. This formula contains a logarithmic term that reflects the infinite range of the Coulomb interaction between target electrons and the incoming electron/positron [86].

$$\sigma(E) = A/E + B\log(E)/E. \tag{4}$$

The scattering length A_0 was adopted from the MERT-free fit in reference [39,40] for N_2 and CO_2, respectively, and from MERT fits in references [24,41] for CH_4 and CF_4, respectively.

Born forward scattering amplitude has been deduced from low-angle elastic differential cross sections at high energies. For N_2, numerous elastic DCS measurements were completed [68,70,87]; Zhang et al. [70] extrapolated them to the zero-angle, obtaining the value of 17.4×10^{-16} cm^2/sr (and declaring 1% error bar). For CO_2, the DCS measured [69] down to 2° already at 300–500 eV indicates a constant zero-angle value, of about 67×10^{-16} cm^2 (with an uncertainty of ±10%), see Figure 8.

For CH_4 and CF_4 we used the data of Sakae et al. [88], extending up to 700 eV, but the uncertainty of these values is high (some 20%). The lowest angle measured was 5°, the extrapolation was done via a polynomial fit (no details given), and the experimental data agree in shape with the model of Jain [51] but are a factor of three lower at the zero angle, agreeing with much earlier theory of Szabo and Ostlund [89].

Parameters A and B of the Born-Bethe fit to the electron TCS (Equation (4), Figures 6 and 7) are: −60, 310; −100, 510; 52, 232; and 317, 923, for N_2, CO_2, CH_4 (see ref. [7]), and CF_4, respectively. Note that the parameter B scales with the total number n of electrons in the target (the ratio B/n amounting to about 22 in units) — a similar conclusion in the high energy limit was drawn by García and Manero [90]. On the other hand, the TCS in its maximum (but outside resonance) correlates well [29] with the polarizability, see TCS values at 30 eV (around the maximum) in Table 1.

Table 1. In search for dispersion relation in electron-molecule scattering.

Molecule	$A_0\ (a_0)$	$f_B(\infty, 0)$ †	$(-A_0 - f_B)(a_0)$	$\int \text{TCS}\ (a_0)$ ‡	$\alpha\ (a_0^3)$ §	TCS@30 eV ¶	B ∥
N_2	+0.404 [39] +0.75 * [38]	7.89 [70]	−8.29 −8.64	16.5	11.5	12.8 [91]	310
CO_2	−6.65 [40]	15.4 [69]	−8.75	23.9	16.9	16.2 [77]	510
CH_4	−2.00 [24]	6.5 * [88]	−4.50	16.1	16.5	16.5 [92]	232
CF_4	−2.80 [41]	19 * [88]	−16.20	35.7	19.1	20.4 [80]	923

* data read from the figure. † The Born direct scattering amplitude $f_B(E = \infty, \theta = 0)$ is taken as the square root of the differential cross sections at zero angle and at sufficiently high energies (see Figure 8). ‡ The integral over TCS in the dispersion relation, Equation (2), is taken within limits 10^{-6} eV to 10^6 eV (this range assures the independence of the result from the limits of the integration); the uncertainty of the integral is some 10%. § For dipole polarizabilities we give experimental values (see NIST database [93]). ¶ TCS in column 7 are in 10^{-16} cm² units. ∥ B stays for the high-energy term in Bethe-Born TCS approximation, Equation (4) (in $a_0 R$ units, R being the Rydberg constant); the uncertainty is about 10%, see Figures 6 and 7.

The integral over the TCS in Formula (2) was completed in the energy range from 10^{-6} eV to 10^6 eV: such a choice assures that the value of the integral does not depend significantly (less than 1%) on the integration limits. The integral was performed in three sub-sets: (i) MERT region from 10^{-6} eV to 1 eV, see the discussion in Figures 1–4, (ii) the low and intermediate energy range 1–1000 eV, using the recommended TCS from reference [45], (iii) high energy range—using the extrapolations via Bethe-Born fit, see Figures 6 and 7. Results for electrons are given in Table 1.

The check of the dispersion relation for positrons is given in Table 2. The scattering length A_0 for N_2, CO_2, and CH_4 were taken from our previous papers [25,94]. We are not aware of the experimental TCS for CF_4 positron-scattering in the very low energy range. In the high energy limit it was noted [75] that TCS (for N_2, Ar, Kr) merge in the range of a few keV. As shown in Figure 6, for N_2, the coefficient B of the high-energy Bethe-Born fit is, within experimental uncertainties, equal for positrons and electrons. This result is also supported by the optical-model calculations by Khander et al. [95] (this issue) for electron and positron scattering on such a heavy atoms as radon. Parameters A and B of the Born-Bethe fit to positron TCS, Equation (4), are: −130, 310, −240, 510, 0, 232, 317, and 923, for N_2, CO_2, CH_4, and CF_4, respectively.

Table 2. In search for dispersion relation in positron-molecule scattering.

Molecule	$A_0(a_0)$	$f_B(\infty, 0)$ †	$(-A_0 - f_B)(a_0)$	$\int \text{TCS}\ (a_0)$	$\alpha\ (a_0^3)$	TCS@30 eV ‡
N_2	−9.27 [25]	−7.89 [70]	17.16	13.8	11.5	8.2 [74]
CO_2	−4.61 [40]	−15.4 [69]	20.01	18.7	16.9	10.2 [74]
CH_4	−5.60 to −8.50 * [24]	−6.5 [88]	12.10 15.00	13.8	16.5	10.6 [96] 11.1 [97]

* depending on low-energy experimental data used for MERT fit. † The absolute values of the Born direct scattering amplitude $f_B(E = \infty, \theta = 0)$ for positrons are taken equal to those for electrons even if we do not have "exact" theoretical either experimental evidence; the optical model by Jochain and Potvliege [59] for Ar predicts at 100–300 eV and zero-angle the DCSs lower by a factor of two for positrons than for electrons; the sign of the Born amplitude is negative as the (static) interaction is repulsive. ‡ TCS in column 7 are in 10^{-16} cm² units.

Let us review the main points from the present comparisons (see columns 4 and 5 in Tables 1 and 2). The dispersion relation, as proposed originally, seems to be quite reasonable in the case of positron scattering. The optical model [72] tells us that the Born amplitude for the real (static + polarization + absorption) potential may be lower for positrons than for electrons. In fact, for CH_4, where the DCS for electrons are probably underestimated (we are not aware of the data similar to these in Figure 8), the values in column four (the difference of terms) and column five (the integral) in Table 2 are equal within uncertainties. This would confirm the conclusion of Kauppila et al. that the dispersion relation holds for positron scattering on noble gases, and also on noble-like CH_4. To resolve the answer for N_2 and CO_2, the ab initio (i.e., not semi-empirical) Born amplitude for positrons is needed.

For electrons, the situation is more unclear; the very sign of the terms disagree. Moreover, the results suggest that the contribution of the Born exchange scattering amplitude (g_B) should be significantly greater than the Born direct scattering amplitude (f_B) to hold the dispersion relation. What remains is the question of resonances, does the dispersion relation holds when the projectile and the target molecule do not form bound states [98]? Out of the four discussed molecules none showed stable negative ions, only temporary negative states [99] decaying into radicals/atoms are formed via resonances (see example for CF_4 on Figure 4). In turn, detailed searches for resonances in positron scattering gave a negative result [100].

We are not able to draw clear conclusions from the present comparisons. Still, many of the experiment-deduced components of the dispersion relation lay within high uncertainty limits. For sure, different quantities in the dispersion relation are interlinked. The input from the theory is necessary.

Author Contributions: Conceptualization, supervision and original draft preparation, G.K.; formal analysis and investigation, F.C. and K.F. All authors have read and agreed to the published version of the manuscript.

Funding: This research received no external funding.

Institutional Review Board Statement: Not applicable.

Informed Consent Statement: Not applicable.

Data Availability Statement: Not applicable.

Acknowledgments: One of us recalls his very fruitful conceptual stay in Detroit (AD 1991), and especially the extraordinary hospitality of Walter Kauppila and Talbert S. Stein. F.C. thanks J. Franz for the hospitality in Poland in September 2021.

Conflicts of Interest: The authors declare no conflict of interest.

References

1. Dodt, D.; Dinklage, A.; Bartschat, K.; Zatsarinny, O. Validation of atomic data using a plasma discharge. *New J. Phys.* **2010**, *12*, 073018. [CrossRef]
2. Nakano, T.; Higashijima, S.; Kubo, H.; Asakura, N.; Fukumoto, M. The emission rates of CH, CD and C_2 spectral bands and a re-evaluation of the chemical sputtering yield of the JT-60U carbon divertor plates. *Nucl. Fusion* **2014**, *54*, 043004. [CrossRef]
3. Sahoo, A.K.; Sharma, L. Electron Impact Excitation of Extreme Ultra-Violet Transitions in Xe^7 – Xe^{10} Ions. *Atoms* **2021**, *9*, 76. [CrossRef]
4. Munoz, A.; Blanco, F.; García, G.; Thorne, P.A.; Brunger, M.J.; Sullivan, J.P.; Buckman, S.J. Single electron tracks in water vapour for energies below 100 eV. *Int. J. Mass Spectrom.* **2008**, *277*, 175. [CrossRef]
5. Sinha, N.; Antony, B. Mean Free Paths and Cross Sections for Electron Scattering from Liquid Water *J. Phys. Chem. B* **2021**, *125*, 5479. [CrossRef] [PubMed]
6. Modak, P.; Antony, B. Electron scattering from HNCO. *Eur. Phys. J. D* **2021**, *75*, 54. [CrossRef]
7. Song, M.Y.; Yoon, J.S.; Cho, H.; Itikawa, Y.; Karwasz, G.P.; Kokoouline, V.; Nakamura, Y.; Tennyson, J. Cross Sections for Electron Collisions with Methane. *J. Phys. Chem. Ref. Data* **2015**, *44*, 023101. [CrossRef]
8. Pietanza, L.D.; Guaitella, O.; Aquilanti, V.; Armenise, I.; Bogaerts, A.; Capitelli, M.; Colonna, G.; Guerra, V.; Engeln, R.; Kustova, E.; et al. Advances in non-equilibrium CO_2 plasma kinetics: A theoretical and experimental review. *Eur. Phys. J. D* **2021**, *75*, 237. [CrossRef]

9. Yoon, J.S.; Song, M.Y.; Han, J.M.; Hwang, S.H.; Chang, W.S.; Lee, B.; Itikawa, Y. Cross Sections for Electron Collisions with Hydrogen Molecules. *J. Phys. Chem. Ref. Data* **2008**, *37*, 913. [CrossRef]
10. Szmytkowski, C.; Możejko, P. Recent total cross section measurements in electron scattering from molecules. *Eur. Phys. J. D* **2020**, *74*, 90. [CrossRef]
11. Kawaguchi, S.; Takahashi, K.; Satoh, K. Electron collision cross section set for N_2 and electron transport in N_2, N_2/He, and N_2/Ar. *Plasma Sources Sci. Technol.* **2021**, *30*, 035010. [CrossRef]
12. Song, M.Y.; Yoon, J.S.; Cho, H.; Karwasz, G.P.; Kokoouline, V.; Nakamura, Y.; Tennyson, J. "Recommended" cross sections for electron collisions with molecules. *Eur. Phys. J. D* **2020**, *74*, 60. [CrossRef]
13. Lindsay, B.G.; Mangan, M.A. 5.1 Ionization: Datasheet from Landolt-Börnstein—Group I Elementary Particles, Nuclei and Atoms. In *Interactions of Photons and Electrons with Molecules*; Springer Materials; Springer: Berlin/Heidelberg, Germany, 2003; Volume 17C. [CrossRef]
14. Kłosowski, Ł.; Piwiński, M. Magnetic Angle Changer for Studies of Electronically Excited Long-Living Atomic States. *Atoms* **2021**, *9*, 71. [CrossRef]
15. Ptasińska, S. A Missing Puzzle in Dissociative Electron Attachment to Biomolecules: The Detection of Radicals. *Atoms* **2021**, *9*, 77. [CrossRef]
16. Karwasz, G.P. Positrons—An alternative probe to electron scattering. *Eur. Phys. J. D* **2005**, *35*, 267, [CrossRef]
17. Campeanu, R.I.; Whelan, C.T. Few Body Effects in the Electron and Positron Impact Ionization of Atoms. *Atoms* **2021**, *9*, 33. [CrossRef]
18. Carelli, F.; Gianturco, F.A.; Franz, J.; Satta, M. A dipole-driven path for electron and positron attachments to gas-phase uracil and pyrimidine molecules: a quantum scattering analysis. *Eur. Phys. J. D* **2015**, *69*, 143. [CrossRef]
19. Karwasz, G.P.; Zecca, A.; Brusa, R.S.; Pliszka, D. Application of positron annihilation techniques for semiconductor studies. *Alloy. Compd.* **2004**, *382*, 244. [CrossRef]
20. García-Abenza, A.; Lozano, A.I.; Oller, J.C.; Blanco, F.; Gorfinkiel, J.D.; Limao-Vieira, P.; García, G. Evaluation of Recommended Cross Sections for the simulation of Electron Tracks in Water. *Atoms* **2021**, *9*, 98.
21. Franz, J.; Fedus, K.; Karwasz, G.P. Do positrons measure atomic and molecular diameters? *Eur. Phys. J. D* **2016**, *70*, 155. [CrossRef]
22. O'Malley, T.F.; Spruch, L.; Rosenberg, L. Modification of Effective-Range Theory in the Presence of a Long—Range r^{-4} Potential. *J. Math. Phys.* **1961**, *2*, 491. [CrossRef]
23. Buckman, S.J.; Mitroy, J. Analysis of low-energy electron scattering cross sections via effective-range theory. *J. Phys. B.* **1989**, *22*, 1365. [CrossRef]
24. Fedus, K.; Karwasz, G.P. Ramsauer-Townsend minimum in methane—Modified effective range analysis. *Eur. Phys. J. D* **2014**, *68*, 93. [CrossRef]
25. Idziaszek, Z.; Karwasz, G. Applicability of modified effective-range theory to positron-atom and positron-molecule scattering. *Phys. Rev. A* **2006**, *73*. [CrossRef]
26. Harland, P.W.; Vallance, C. Ionization cross-sections and ionization efficiency curves from polarizability volumes and ionization potentials. *Int. J. Mass Spectr. Ion Proc.* **1997**, *171*, 173–181. [CrossRef]
27. Karwasz, G.P.; Możejko, P.; Song, M.Y. Electron-impact ionization of fluoromethanes—Review of experiments and binary-encounter models. *Int. J. Mass Spectrom.* **2014**, *365–366*, 232–237. [CrossRef]
28. Szmytkowski, C. On trends in total cross sections for electron (positron) scattering on atoms and molecules at intermediate energies. *Z. Phys. D* **1989**, *13*, 69–73. [CrossRef]
29. Karwasz, G.P.; Brusa, R.S.; Piazza, A.; Zecca, A. Total cross sections for electron scattering on chloromethanes: Formulation of the additivity rule. *Phys. Rev. A* **1999**, *59*, 1341. [CrossRef]
30. Kim, Y.K.; Rudd, M.E. Binary-encounter-dipole model for electron-impact ionization. *Phys. Rev. A* **1994**, *50*, 3954. [CrossRef]
31. Song, M.; Yoon, J.; Cho, H.; Karwasz, G.P.; Kokoouline, V.; Nakamura, Y.; Hamilton, J.R.; Tennyson, J. Cross Sections for Electron Collisions with NF_3. *J. Phys. Chem. Ref. Data* **2017**, *46*, 043104. [CrossRef]
32. Kawahara, H.; Suzuki, D.; Kato, H.; Hoshino, M.; Tanaka, H.; Ingolfsson, O.; Campbell, L.; Brunger, M.J. Cross sections for electron impact excitation of the $C^1\Pi$ and $D^1\Sigma^+$ electronic states in N_2O. *J. Chem. Phys.* **2009**, *131*, 114307. [CrossRef] [PubMed]
33. Xu, W.Q.; Ma, Z.R.; Peng, Y.G.; Du, X.J.; Xu, Y.C.; Wang, L.H.; Li, B.; Zhang, H.R.; Zhang, B.Y.; Zhu, J.H.; et al. Cross sections for the electron-impact excitations $\tilde{A}^1B_1$ and $\tilde{B}^1A_1$ of H_2O determined by high-energy electron scattering. *Phys. Rev. A* **2021**, *103*, 032808. [CrossRef]
34. Kang, X.; Xu, L.Q.; Liu, Y.W.; Wang, S.X.; Yang, K.; Peng, Y.G.; Ni, D.D.; Hiraoka, N.; Tsuei, K.D.; Zhu, L.F. A study on the validity of the first Born approximation for high-energy electron scattering with nitrogen molecules. *J. Phys. B At. Mol. Opt. Phys.* **2019**, *52*, 245202. [CrossRef]
35. Marler, J.P.; Surko, C.M. Systematic comparison of positron—And electron-impact excitation of the ν_3 vibrational mode of CF_4. *Phys. Rev. A* **2005**, *72*, 062702. [CrossRef]
36. Ayouz, M.; Faure, A.; Tennyson, J.; Kokoouline, V.; Tudorovskaya, M. Cross Sections and Rate Coefficients for Vibrational Excitation of H_2O by Electron Impact. *Atoms* **2021**, *9*, 62. [CrossRef]
37. Poveda, L.A.; Varella, M.T.d.N.; Mohallem, J.R. Vibrational Excitation Cross-Section by Positron Impact: A Wave-Packet Dynamics Study. *Atoms* **2021**, *9*, 64. [CrossRef]

38. Kitajima, M.; Kishino, T.; Okumura, T.; Kobayashi, N.; Sayama, A.; Mori, Y.; Kosaka, K.; Odigiri, F.; Hoshino, M.; Tanaka, H. Low-energy and very-low energy total cross sections for electron collisions with N_2. *Eur. Phys. J. D* **2017**, *71*, 139. [CrossRef]
39. Idziaszek, Z.; Karwasz, G.P. Modified effective-range theory for low energy e -N_2 scattering. *Eur. Phys. J. D* **2009**, *51*, 347–355. [CrossRef]
40. Idziaszek, Z.; Karwasz, G.P.; Brusa, R.S. Modified effective range analysis of low energy electron and positron scattering on CO_2. *J. Phys. Conf. Ser.* **2008**, *115*, 012002. [CrossRef]
41. Fedus, K.; Karwasz, G. Ramsauer–Townsend minimum in electron scattering from CF_4: Modified effective range analysis. *Eur. Phys. J. D* **2021**, *75*, 76. [CrossRef]
42. Allan, M. Excitation of vibrational levels up to $v = 17$ in N_2 by electron impact in 0–5 eV region. *J. Phys. B* **1986**, *18*, 4511. [CrossRef]
43. Zecca, A.; Karwasz, G.P.; Brusa, R.S. One century of experiments on electron-atom and molecule scattering: A critical review of integral cross-sections. *La Riv. del Nuovo C.* **1996**, *19*, 1–146. [CrossRef]
44. Antoni, T.; Jung, K.; Ehrhardt, H.; Chang, E.S. Rotational branch analysis of the excitation of the fundamental vibrational modes of CO_2 by slow electron collisions. *J. Phys. B* **1986**, *19*, 1377. [CrossRef]
45. Karwasz, G.P.; Brusa, R.S.; Zecca, A. 6.1 Total scattering cross sections: Datasheet from Landolt-Börnstein—Group I Elementary Particles, Nuclei and Atoms. In *Interactions of Photons and Electrons with Molecules*; Springer Materials; Springer: Berlin/Heidelberg, Germany, 2003; Volume 17C. [CrossRef]
46. Isaacs, W.A.; McCurdy, C.W.; Rescigno, T.N. Theoretical support for a Ramsauer-Townsend minimum in electron-CF_4 scattering. *Phys. Rev. A* **1998**, *58*, 309. [CrossRef]
47. Winstead, C.; McKoy, V.; Sun, Q. Low-energy elastic electron scattering by tetrafluoromethane (CF_4). *J. Chem. Phys.* **1993**, *98*, 1105–1109. [CrossRef]
48. Costa, R.F.d.; Varella, M.T.D.N.; Bettega, M.H.F.; Lima, M.A.P. Recent advances in the application of the Schwinger multichannel method with pseudopotentials to electron-molecule collisions. *Eur. Phys. J. D* **2015**, *69*, 159. [CrossRef]
49. Gianturco, F.A.; Lucchese, R.R. The elastic scattering of electrons from molecules: II. Molecular features and spatial symmetries of some resonant states. *J. Phys. B.* **1996**, *29*, 3955. [CrossRef]
50. Hamilton, J.R.; Tennyson, J.; Huang, S.; Kushner, M.J. Calculated cross sections for electron collisions with NF_3, NF_2 and NF with applications to remote plasma sources. *Plasma Sources Sci. Technol.* **2017**, *26*, 065010. [CrossRef]
51. Jain, A. Total (elastic+absorption) cross sections for e-CH_4 collisions in a spherical model at 0.10–500 eV. *Phys. Rev. A* **1986**, *34*, 3707. [CrossRef] [PubMed]
52. Thirumalai, D.; Staszewska, G.; Truhlar, D.G. Dispersion Relation Techniques for Approximating the Optical Model Potential for Electron Scattering. *Comments At. Mol. Phys.* **1987**, *20*, 217–243.
53. Goswami, B.; Naghma, R.; Antony, B. Calculation of electron impact total ionization cross sections for tungsten, uranium and their oxide radicals. *Int. J. Mass Spectr.* **2014**, *372*, 8. [CrossRef]
54. Gorfinkiel, J.D.; Morgan, L.A.; Tennyson, J. Electron impact dissociative excitation of water within the adiabatic nuclei approximation. *J. Phys. B* **2002**, *35*, 543. [CrossRef]
55. Bishop, D.M.; Cheung, L.M. Vibrational Contributions to Molecular Dipole Polarizabilities. *J. Phys. Chem. Ref. Data* **1982**, *11*, 119. [CrossRef]
56. Laporta, V.; Celiberto, R.; Vadehra, J.M. Theoretical vibrational-excitation cross sections and rate coefficients for electron-impact resonant collisions involving rovibrationally excited N_2 and NO molecules. *Plasma Sources Sci. Technol.* **2012**, *21*, 055018. [CrossRef]
57. Trevisan, C.S.; Houfek, K.; Shang, Z.; Orel, A.E.; McCurdy, C.W.; Rescigno, T.N. Nonlocal model of dissociative electron attachment and vibrational excitation of NO. *Phys. Rev. A* **2005**, *71*, 052714. [CrossRef]
58. Bartschat, K.; McEachran, R.P.; Stauffer, A.D. Optical potential approach to electron and positron scattering from noble gases. I. Argon. *J. Phys. B.* **1988**, *21*, 2789. [CrossRef]
59. Joachain, C.J.; Potvliege, R.M. Importance of absorption effects on fast positron-argon differential cross sections. *Phys. Rev. A* **1987**, *35*, 4873. [CrossRef]
60. Karwasz, G.P.; Pliszka, D.; Brusa, R.S. Total cross sections for positron scattering in argon, nitrogen and hydrogen below 20 eV. *Nucl. Instr. Meth. B* **2006**, *247*, 68. [CrossRef]
61. Fedus, K. A rigid sphere approach to positron elastic scattering by noble gases, molecular hydrogen, nitrogen and methane. *Eur. Phys. J. D* **2016**, *70*, 261. [CrossRef]
62. Borghesani, F.A. Accurate Electron Drift Mobility Measurements in Moderately Dense Helium Gas at Several Temperatures. *Atoms* **2021**, *9*, 52. [CrossRef]
63. Gerjuoy, E.; Krall, N.A. Dispersion Relations in Atomic Scattering Problems. *Phys. Rev.* **1960**, *119*, 705. [CrossRef]
64. Temkin, A.; Bhatia, A.K.; Kim, Y.S. A new dispersion relation for electron-atom scattering. *J. Phys. B* **1986**, *19*, L701. [CrossRef]
65. Kauppila, W.E.; Stein, T.S.; Smart, J.H.; Dababneh, M.S.; Ho, Y.K.; Downing, J.P.; Pol, V. Measurements of total scattering cross sections for intermediate-energy positrons and electrons colliding with helium, neon, and argon. *Phys. Rev. A* **1982**, *24*, 725. [CrossRef]
66. Salvat, F. Optical-model potential for electron and positron elastic scattering by atoms. *Phys. Rev. A* **2003**, *68*, 012708. [CrossRef]

67. Heer, F.J.d.; McDowell, M.R.C.; Wagenaar, R.W. Numerical study of the dispersion relation for e–H scattering. *J. Phys. B.* **1977**, *10*, 1945. [CrossRef]
68. Jansen, R.H.J.; Heer, F.J.d.; Luyken, H.J.; Wingerden, B.v.; Blaauw, H.J. Absolute differential cross sections for elastic scattering of electrons by helium, neon, argon and molecular nitrogen. *J. Phys. B.* **1975**, *9*, 185. [CrossRef]
69. Bromberg, J.P. Absolute differential cross sections of elastically scattered electrons. V. O_2 and CO_2 at 500, 400, and 300 eV. *J. Chem. Phys.* **1974**, *60*, 1717. [CrossRef]
70. Zhang, Y.; Ross, A.W.; Fink, M. Electron correlation and charge density study of N_2 and O_2 by high energy electron scattering. *Z. Phys. D* **1991**, *18*, 163–169. [CrossRef]
71. Hyder, M.A.; Dababneh, M.S.; Hsieh, Y.F.; Kauppila, W.E.; Kwan, C.K.; Mahdavi-Hezaveh, M.; Stein, T.S. Positron Differential Elastic-Scattering Cross-Section Measurements for Argon. *Phys. Rev. Lett.* **1986**, *57*, 2252. [CrossRef]
72. Joachain, C.J.; Vanderpoorten, R.; Winters, K.H.; Byron, F.W., Jr. Optical model theory of elastic electron- and positron-argon scattering at intermediate energies. *J. Phys. B* **1977**, *10*, 227. [CrossRef]
73. Fedus, K. Elastic Scattering of Slow Electrons by Noble Gases—The Effective Range Theory and the Rigid Sphere Model. *Atoms* **2021**, *9*, 91. [CrossRef]
74. Hoffman, K.R.; Dababneh, M.S.; Hsieh, Y.F.; Kauppila, W.E.; Pol, V.; Smart, J.H.; Stein, T.S. Total-cross-section measurements for positrons and electrons colliding with H_2, N_2, and CO_2. *Phys. Rev. A* **1982**, *25*, 1393. [CrossRef]
75. Barozzi, M. Misure di Sezione d'Urto Positrone-Molecola: Realizzazione dell'Apparato Sperimentale e Prime Misure. Master's Thesis, Universita' degli Studi di Trento, Trento, Italy, 1997.
76. Garcia, G.; Manero, F. Total cross sections for electron scattering by CO_2 molecules in the energy range 400–5000 eV. *Phys. Rev. A* **1996**, *53*, 250. [CrossRef]
77. Szmytkowski, C.; Zecca, A.; Karwasz, G.; Oss, S.; Maciąg, K.; Marinković, B.; Brusa, R.S.; Grisenti, R. Absolute total cross sections for electron-CO_2 scattering at energies form 0.5 to 3000 eV. *J. Phys. B* **1987**, *20*, 5817. [CrossRef]
78. Zecca, A.; Karwasz, G.P.; Brusa, R.S. Total-cross-section measurements for electron scattering by NH_3, SiH_4, and H_2S in the intermediate-energy range. *Phys. Rev. A* **1992**, *45*, 2777. [CrossRef]
79. Kwan, C.K.; Hsieh, Y.F.; Kauppila, W.E.; Smith, S.J.; Stein, T.S.; Uddin, M.N.; Dababneh, M.S. $e^{\pm}$—CO and $e^{\pm}$—CO_2 total cross-section measurements. *Phys. Rev. A* **1983**, *27*, 1328. [CrossRef]
80. Szmytkowski, C.; Krzysztofowicz, A.; Janicki, P.; Rosenthal, L. Electron scattering from CF_4 and CCl_4. Total cross section measurements. *Chem. Phys. Lett.* **1992**, *199*, 191. [CrossRef]
81. Iga, I.; Homem, M.G.P.; Mazon, K.T.; Lee, M.T. Elastic and total cross sections for electron-carbon dioxide collisions in the intermediate energy range. *J. Phys. B* **1999**, *32*. [CrossRef]
82. Karwasz, G.P. Intermediate-energy total cross sections for electron scattering on GeH_4. *J. Phys. B* **1995**, *28*, 1301. [CrossRef]
83. Zecca, A.; Szmytkowski, C.; Karwasz, G.; Brusa, R.S. Absolute total cross sections for electron scattering on CH_4 molecules in the 1-4000 eV energy range. *J. Phys. B* **1991**, *24*, 2747–54. [CrossRef]
84. Karwasz, G.; Brusa, R.S.; Gasparoli, A.; Zecca, A. Total cross-section measurements for e^-—CO scattering: 80–4000 eV. *Chem. Phys. Lett.* **1993**, *211*, 529–533. [CrossRef]
85. García, G.; Manero, F. Electron scattering by CH_4 molecules at intermediate energies (400–5000 eV). *Phys. Rev. A* **1998**, *57*, 1069. [CrossRef]
86. Bransden, B.H.; Joachain, C.J. *Physics of Atoms and Molecules*, 2nd ed.; Prentice-Hall: Hoboken, NJ, USA, 2003.
87. Dubois, R.D.; Rudd, M.E. Differential cross sections for elastic scattering of electrons from argon, neon, nitrogen and carbon monoxide. *J. Phys. B* **1976**, *9*, 2657. [CrossRef]
88. Sakae, T.; Sumiyoshi, S.; Murakami, E.; Matsumoto, Y.; Ishibashi, K.; Katase, A. Scattering of electrons by CH_4, CF_4 and SF_6 in the 75–700 eV range. *J. Phys. B.* **1989**, *22*, 1385. [CrossRef]
89. Szabo, A.; Ostlund, N.S. Calculation of high energy elastic electron-molecule scattering cross sections with CNDO wavefunctions. *J. Chem. Phys.* **1974**, *60*, 946–950. [CrossRef]
90. Garcia, G.; Manero, F. Correlation of the total cross section for electron scattering by molecules with 10–22 electrons, and some molecular parameters at intermediate energies. *Chem. Phys. Lett.* **1997**, *280*, 4373. [CrossRef]
91. Nickel, J.C.; Kanik, I.; Trajmar, S.; Imre, K. Total cross section measurements for electron scattering on H_2 and N_2 from 4 to 300 eV. *J. Phys. B* **2017**, *25*, 2427–2431. [CrossRef]
92. Kanik, I.; Trajmar, S.; Nickel, J.C. Total cross section measurements for electron scattering on CH_4 from 4 to 300 eV. *Chem. Phys. Lett.* **1992**, *193*, 281–286. [CrossRef]
93. Experimental values of Polarizability. Available online: https://cccbdb.nist.gov/xp1x.asp?prop=9 (accessed on 1 September 2021).
94. Fedus, K.; Karwasz, G.P.; Idziaszek, Z. Analytic approach to modified effective-range theory for electron and positron elastic scattering. *Phys. Rev. A* **2013**, *88*, 012704. [CrossRef]
95. Khandker, M.H.; Haque, A.K.F.; Haque, M.M.; Billah, M.M.; Watabe, H.; Uddin, M.A. Relativistic Study on the Scattering of $e^{\pm}$ from Atoms and Ions of the Rn Isonuclear Series. *Atoms* **2021**, *9*, 59. [CrossRef]
96. Dababneh, M.S.; Hsieh, Y.F.; Kauppila, W.E.; Kwan, C.K.; Smith, S.J.; Stein, T.S.; Uddin, M.N. Total-cross-section measurements for positron and electron scattering by O_2, CH_4, and SF_6. *Phys. Rev. A* **1988**, *38*, 1207. [CrossRef] [PubMed]

97. Sueoka, O.; Mori, S. Total cross sections for low and intermediate energy positrons and electrons colliding with CH_4, C_2H_4 and C_2H_6 molecules. *J. Phys. B* **1986**, *19*, 4035. [CrossRef]
98. Vrinceanu, D.; Msezane, A.Z.; Bessis, D.; Temkin, A. Exchange Forces in Dispersion Relations Investigated Using Circuit Relations. *Phys. Rev. Lett.* **2001**, *86*, 3256. [CrossRef] [PubMed]
99. Coat, Y.L.; Ziesel, J.P.; Guillotin, J.P. Negative ion resonances in CF_4 probed by dissociative electron attachment. *J. Phys. B.* **1994**, *27*, 965. [CrossRef]
100. Sullivan, J.P.; Gilbert, S.J.; Buckman, S.; Surko, C. Search for resonances in the scattering of low-energy positrons from atoms and molecules. *J. Phys. B* **2001**, *34*, L467. [CrossRef]

MDPI
St. Alban-Anlage 66
4052 Basel
Switzerland
Tel. +41 61 683 77 34
Fax +41 61 302 89 18
www.mdpi.com

Atoms Editorial Office
E-mail: atoms@mdpi.com
www.mdpi.com/journal/atoms

www.ingramcontent.com/pod-product-compliance
Lightning Source LLC
LaVergne TN
LVHW070156100526
838202LV00015B/1954